Modern Brazil

Recent Titles in Understanding Modern Nations

Modern China
Xiaobing Li

Modern Spain
Enrique Ávila López

Modern Mexico
James D. Huck Jr.

Modern India
John McLeod

Modern Saudi Arabia
Valerie Anishchenkova

MODERN BRAZIL

Javier A. Galván

Understanding Modern Nations

BLOOMSBURY ACADEMIC
NEW YORK • LONDON • OXFORD • NEW DELHI • SYDNEY

BLOOMSBURY ACADEMIC
Bloomsbury Publishing Inc
1385 Broadway, New York, NY 10018, USA
50 Bedford Square, London, WC1B 3DP, UK
29 Earlsfort Terrace, Dublin 2, Ireland

BLOOMSBURY, BLOOMSBURY ACADEMIC and the Diana logo
are trademarks of Bloomsbury Publishing Plc

First published in the United States of America by ABC-CLIO 2020
Paperback edition published by Bloomsbury Academic 2024

Copyright © Bloomsbury Publishing Inc, 2024

Cover photos: Amazon rain forest, Brazil. (Ulf Huebner/Dreamstime); Rio de Janeiro, Brazil. (Brendan Duffy/Alamy); Statue of Christ the Redeemer, Corcovado Mountain, Rio de Janeiro, Brazil. (David Davis Photoproductions/Alamy); Palace of Arts Rodin, Salvador, Brazil. (Galinasavina/Dreamstime)

All rights reserved. No part of this publication may be reproduced or
transmitted in any form or by any means, electronic or mechanical,
including photocopying, recording, or any information storage or retrieval
system, without prior permission in writing from the publishers.

Bloomsbury Publishing Inc does not have any control over, or responsibility for,
any third-party websites referred to or in this book. All internet addresses given
in this book were correct at the time of going to press. The author and publisher
regret any inconvenience caused if addresses have changed or sites have
ceased to exist, but can accept no responsibility for any such changes.

Library of Congress Cataloging-in-Publication Data
Names: Galván, Javier A., 1965– author.
Title: Modern Brazil / Javier A. Galván.
Description: Santa Barbara : ABC-CLIO, An Imprint of ABC-CLIO, LLC [2020] | Series: Understanding modern nations | Includes bibliographical references and index.
Identifiers: LCCN 2019056367 (print) | LCCN 2019056368 (ebook) | ISBN 9781440860317 (cloth) | ISBN 9781440860324 (ebook)
Subjects: LCSH: Brazil—Encyclopedias.
Classification: LCC F2504 .G35 2020 (print) | LCC F2504 (ebook) | DDC 981.003—dc23
LC record available at https://lccn.loc.gov/2019056367
LC ebook record available at https://lccn.loc.gov/2019056368

ISBN: HB: 978-1-4408-6031-7
PB: 979-8-7651-2698-1
ePDF: 978-1-4408-6032-4
eBook: 979-8-2161-1841-1

Series: Understanding Modern Nations

To find out more about our authors and books visit www.bloomsbury.com
and sign up for our newsletters.

The publisher has done its best to make sure the instructions and/or recipes in this book
are correct. However, users should apply judgment and experience when preparing
recipes, especially parents and teachers working with young people. The publisher accepts
no responsibility for the outcome of any recipe included in this volume and assumes no
liability for, and is released by readers from, any injury or damage resulting from the strict
adherence to, or deviation from, the directions and/or recipes herein. The publisher is not
responsible for any reader's specific health or allergy needs that may require medical
supervision, nor for any adverse reactions to the recipes contained in this book.
All yields are approximations.

Contents

Series Foreword	xiii
Preface	xv
Introduction	xxi

Chapter 1: Geography — 1
Overview — 1
   Amazon Basin and Rain Forest — 6
   Brasília and the Federal District — 9
   Climate — 10
   Deforestation — 11
   Earth Summit, Rio 2012 — 13
   Environment — 14
   Infrastructure: Roads, Airports, Ports, and Railways — 16
   Interoceanic Highway — 17
   Islands and Archipelagos — 18
   Itaipú Hydroelectric Power Plant — 20
   Main Cities and Urban Regions — 21
   Major Rivers — 23
   Mendes, Chico (1944–1988) — 24
   Offshore Oil and Natural Gas — 25
   The *Sertão* and Devastating Droughts — 27
   World Heritage Sites in the UNESCO — 28

Chapter 2: History — 31
Overview — 31
Timeline — 36
   Álvares Cabral, Pedro (1467 or 1468–1520) — 47
   Bandeirantes — 48
   Brazilian Empire: Pedro I (1798–1834) and Pedro II (1825–1891) — 49
   Captaincy Colonial System — 51
   Gold Rush and Minas Gerais — 54
   Isabel, Princess Regent of Brazil (1846–1921) — 56

Kubitschek de Oliveira, Juscelino (1902–1976) — 58
Operation Condor and Military Rule — 59
Paraguayan War (1864–1870) — 61
Silva, Benedita da (1942–) — 62
Slavery, Abolition, and African Heritage — 63
Tiradentes (1746–1792) and the Inconfidência Mineira — 65
Vargas, Getúlio (1882–1954) — 66

Chapter 3: Government and Politics — 69
Overview — 69
Constitutions — 73
Corruption and Political Scandals — 76
Electoral System — 79
Foreign Policy — 81
Human Rights — 83
Law Enforcement — 84
Lula da Silva, Luiz Inácio (1945–) — 86
Political Parties — 87
Political Patronage — 90
Rousseff, Dilma (1947–) — 91
Temer, Michel (1940–) — 93
United Nations and Brazil — 95
Women's Rights — 96
Workers' Party (PT) in Power — 98

Chapter 4: Economy — 100
Overview — 100
Agrarian Reform — 103
Austerity Measures of 2016 — 104
Automobile Industry — 106
BRICS Economic Group — 107
Cardoso, Fernando Henrique (1931–) — 108
Coffee Exports — 109
Embraer, Empresa Brasileira de Aeronáutica — 111
Energy Industry: Electricity, Oil, Ethanol, and Renewable Sources — 112
Favelas (Slums) — 114
Foreign Investment — 115
Labor Migration — 117
Major Exports — 118
Manufacturing — 119
Mercosul/Mercosur — 121
Mineral Wealth — 122
Petrobras, the National Oil Company — 123
Stock Exchanges: Bovespa, BM&F, and B3 — 125
Tourism — 126

Trading Partners	128
World Trade Organization (WTO)	129

Chapter 5: Religion and Thought — 131
Overview — 131

Candomblé and Macumba	134
Catholicism	135
De Souza Chaui, Marilena (1941–)	137
Freire, Paulo (1921–1997)	138
Freyre, Gilberto (1900–1987)	139
Liberation Theology	141
Messianism and Miracle Workers	142
Nossa Senhora Aparecida, Brazil's Patron Saint	143
Orixás, African Gods	145
Protestant Religions	146
Spiritism	148
Universal Church of the Kingdom of God	149

Chapter 6: Social Classes and Ethnicity — 152
Overview — 152

African Ancestry and Influence	154
Distribution of Wealth and Income Disparity	156
Education and Upward Mobility	157
Favelas, Mocambos, and *Alagados* (Slums)	158
Indigenous Populations	160
Landless Rural Workers Movement (MST)	162
Mixed Ethnicities: *Caboclo, Cafuso, Mameluco,* and *Mulatto*	163
Modern Immigration	164
Parentela	165
Poverty, Social Conflict, and Protests	166
Racism and Discrimination	168
Urban Crime	169

Chapter 7: Gender, Marriage, and Sexuality — 172
Overview — 172

Abortion Laws	174
Dating and Courting	176
Desquite and Divorce	177
Domestic Violence	178
Feminism	180
Gender and Parenting Roles	181
Gender Equality	182
LGBTQ Community and Rights	184
Maternity and Paternity Leave	186
Raising Children	187

Representation in Government	189
Representation in the Workforce	190
Suffrage	192
Wedding Traditions and Celebrations	193

Chapter 8: Education — 195
Overview — 195

Affirmative Action Policies	198
Ávila, Artur (1979–)	199
Bolsa Família: Welfare Program with Education Incentives	200
Education Reforms of 2016	201
Higher Education and Major Universities	203
INEP, National Institute for Educational Studies and Research	205
Literacy Rates	206
Private, International, and Religious Schools	207
Public Education: Elementary and Secondary Schooling	208
Scientific and Technical Research	210
Unipalmares, University for Afro-Descendent Students	212
Vestibular Testing for College Admission	213

Chapter 9: Language — 215
Overview — 215

Formality Levels	218
Hand Gestures	220
Indigenous Languages	221
Nicknames	222
Sign Language (LIBRAS)	224
Spelling Reform	225
Tupi-Guarani Influence	227

Chapter 10: Etiquette — 229
Overview — 229

Bargaining	231
Clothing and Dressing Appropriately	232
Formal Business Meetings	234
Intermediaries: *Colonels* and *Despachantes*	235
Jeitinho, Finding a Way	236
Machismo	238
Personal Space and Privacy	239
Punctuality and Concepts of Time	241
Table Manners	242

Chapter 11: Literature and Drama — 244
Overview — 244

Amado, Jorge (1912–2001)	247
Bandeira, Manuel (1886–1968)	248

Contemporary Writers	250
Da Cunha, Euclides (1866–1909)	251
De Andrade, Oswald (1890–1954)	253
Guimarães Rosa, João (1908–1967)	254
Lima Barreto, Alfonso (1881–1922)	255
Literary Canon	256
Literary Censorship by the Military	258
Machado de Assis, Joaquim Maria (1839–1908)	260
Modern Theater and Playwrights	262
Modernism in Brazil	263
Postindependence Literature	264

Chapter 12: Art and Architecture — 267
Overview — 267

Aleijadinho (1730 or 1738–1814)	270
Baroque Art and Architecture in Minas Gerais	272
Cinto, Sandra (1968–)	274
Costa, Lúcio (1902–1998): Brasília's Urban Planner	276
French Artistic Mission	277
Mendes da Rocha, Paulo (1928–)	278
Modern Art Week, São Paulo, 1922	279
Niemeyer, Oscar (1907–2012)	281
Ouro Preto	282
Popular Arts and Crafts	283
Portinari, Cândido (1903–1962)	285

Chapter 13: Music and Dance — 287
Overview — 287

Bossa Nova	290
Carnival	291
"Girl from Ipanema" Song	292
Jobim, Antônio Carlos (1927–1994)	293
Música Popular Brasileira (MPB)	294
Música Sertaneja	296
Musical Instruments	297
Regional Music and Dance	299
Samba Music and Dance	300
Tropicália	301
Villa-Lobos, Heitor (1887–1959)	303

Chapter 14: Food — 305
Overview — 305

Cafezinho, a Small Shot of Strong Coffee	307
Caipirinha, a National Cocktail	308
Carne de Sol, Dried Salted Meat	309

Churrasco, Brazilian Barbecue	310
Contemporary Brazilian Chefs	312
Feijoada, Brazil's National Dish	313
Mealtimes and Eating Habits	315
Minas Gerais Gastronomy	316
Regional Sweets	317
Zero Hunger Strategy in Brazil	319

Chapter 15: Leisure and Sports — 321
Overview — 321

Basketball	323
Beach and Sand	324
Brazilian Jiu-Jitsu	325
Capoeira	327
Family Outings and Vacations	328
Futebol (Soccer)	329
Mega Sena, Brazilian Lottery	332
Motor Sports: Formula 1 and Grand Prix	333
Olympic Games, Rio de Janeiro 2016	334
Paralympic Games 2016	336
Pelé (1940–), Ronaldinho (1980–), and Neymar (1992–)	337
Soccer FIFA World Cup 2014	339
Telenovelas	340

Chapter 16: Media and Popular Culture — 343
Overview — 343

Cinema and Film Festivals	345
Cultural Icons	347
Folia de Reis, Three Wise Men Celebration	348
Major Newspapers	349
Meirelles, Fernando (1955–)	351
Reality Television Shows	352
Rede Globo and Other Television Networks	353
Salles, Walter, Jr. (1956–)	355
Social Media and Internet Use	356
Sports Icons	357
Xuxa (1963–)	359

Appendix A: A Day in the Life — 361

A Day in the Life of a University Student	361
A Day in the Life of an Office Worker	362
A Day in the Life of a Housewife	363
A Day in the Life of an Agricultural Working Family	364

Appendix B: Glossary of Key Terms	365
Appendix C: Facts and Figures	373
Appendix D: Holidays	381
Selected Bibliography	385
Index	397

Series Foreword

We live in an evolving world, a world that is becoming increasingly globalized by the minute. Cultures collide and blend, leading to new customs and practices that exist alongside long-standing traditions. Advancing technologies connect lives across the globe, affecting those from densely populated urban areas to those who dwell in the most remote locations in the world. Governments are changing, leading to war and violence but also to new opportunities for those who have been oppressed. The *Understanding Modern Nations* series seeks to answer questions about cultures, societies, and customs in various countries around the world.

Understanding Modern Nations is geared toward readers wanting to expand their knowledge of the world, ideal for high school students researching specific countries, undergraduates preparing for studies abroad, and general readers interested in learning more about the world around them. Each volume in the series focuses on a single country, with coverage on Africa, the Americas, Asia and the Pacific, and Europe.

Each country volume contains sixteen chapters focusing on various aspects of culture and society in each country. The chapters begin with an overview, which is followed by short entries on key topics, concepts, ideas, and biographies pertaining to the chapter's theme. In a way, these volumes serve as "thematic encyclopedias," with entries organized for the reader's benefit. Following a general preface and introduction, each volume contains chapters on the following themes:

- Geography;
- History;
- Government and Politics;
- Economy;
- Religion and Thought;
- Social Classes and Ethnicity;
- Gender, Marriage, and Sexuality;
- Education;
- Language;
- Etiquette;
- Literature and Drama;
- Art and Architecture;

- Music and Dance;
- Food;
- Leisure and Sports; and
- Media and Popular Culture.

Each entry concludes with a list of cross-references and further readings, pointing readers to additional print and electronic resources that might prove useful.

Following the chapters are appendices, including the "A Day in the Life" feature, which depicts "typical" days in the lives of people living in that country, from students to farmers to factory workers to stay-at-home and working mothers. A glossary, facts and figures section, and holidays chart round out the appendices. Volumes include a select bibliography, as well as sidebars that are scattered throughout the text.

The volumes in the *Understanding Modern Nations* series are not intended to be comprehensive compendiums about every nation of the world, but instead are meant to serve as introductory texts for readers, examining key topics from major countries studied in the high school curriculum as well as important transitioning countries that make headlines daily. It is our hope that readers will gain an understanding and appreciation for cultures and histories outside of their own.

PREFACE

Brazil is one of the most visited countries in Latin America. Its musical rhythms, cultural traditions, rich history, religious festivals, carnival celebrations, mouthwatering cuisine, and environmental beauty continue to attract travelers from around the world. The goal of this book is to offer an updated view of contemporary Brazil that provides a general background for all the topics discussed but also incorporates the latest information available from modern reliable sources. It also seeks to include groups of people frequently left out of a national narrative, including women, street performers, racial-minority groups, folk artisans, and average citizens. This book highlights their role in contemporary Brazil.

Modern Brazil is written as a reference source with entries following an encyclopedia format. The major components are organized into sixteen chapters. The end of the book also includes a list of Brazilian holidays, a select bibliography, a glossary of key terms, an alphabetical index, and a useful set of updated practical facts and figures (a list of presidents, as well as geographical, economic, and demographic data). At the end, the book also includes a section titled "A Day in the Life" intended to illustrate a typical daily routine of four average people living in Brazil. Each of the sixteen chapters includes a brief introduction and a list of carefully selected entries to illustrate the main people, concepts, organizations, and important events related to that topic, but always making sure to cover iconic figures as well as contemporary issues. Each individual entry includes suggestions for further readings of reliable sources to guide readers toward additional information.

Chapters 1 and 2 cover the vast geography and unique history of Brazil. Chapter 1 deals with physical geography (rivers, the Atlantic coastline, the Amazon rainforest, islands, natural resources, and major cities) as well as population distribution. It also illustrates more contemporary concerns related to accelerated deforestation, urbanization problems, climate issues, and devastating droughts in the northern regions. In addition, it highlights some of the modern challenges of building an adequate infrastructure in a country of continental proportions, including railways, airports, roads, commercial ports, hydroelectric power plants, and even a highway capable of reaching both the Atlantic and Pacific oceans to facilitate exports. Chapter 2 offers a broad foundation of the unique historical experience in Brazil, which is different than the rest of Latin America. When the Portuguese arrived in 1500, they found over a thousand tribes of indigenous groups (mostly Tupi and Guaraní), but they initially neglected the new territories and eventually settled along the Atlantic coast, a population pattern that still exists in modern Brazil. The importation of large numbers of African slaves in the middle of the sixteenth century was based on the need for labor for the sugar industry. Then a unique event occurred when Napoleon Bonaparte conquered Portugal in 1808; he offered the Portuguese kings the option to leave the country. They came to settle in Brazil, and they ran their global empire from Rio de Janeiro. The eventual Brazilian independence in 1822 was less bloody than the wars of independence fought by its Latin American neighbors against Spain. Chapter 2 highlights important individuals related to the colonial period (1500–1822), insurrection attempts, the Brazilian Empire period (1825–1891), the formation of a democratic Brazil, ruthless dictators, regional wars, and the construction of a modern nation. It also includes a helpful timeline that covers important historical events that extends all the way up to modern times and recent events. For over five hundred years, the three major ethnic groups in Brazil (European, indigenous, and African) have engaged in large-scale miscegenation, which created the highly racially mixed population that exists in Brazil nowadays, but it also helped shape cultural traditions related to language, religion, music, art, and social structure. Chapters 1 and 2 serve as a general foundation to understand the next few chapters dealing with more contemporary topics, such as government, politics, and the economy.

Chapter 3 focuses on the existing system of government and politics, and Chapter 4 discusses how the current economy affects most Brazilians. The existing democratic constitution dates from 1988; it was approved after a devastating military rule that lasted from 1964 until 1985. It provides the legal foundation for the role of all three branches of government (executive, legislative, and judicial) and a complex electoral system that currently has representatives from thirty-five registered political parties. At the beginning of the twenty-first century, the Workers' Party (Partido dos Trabalhadores, PT) was in charge of the Brazilian presidency from 2002 to 2016. Presidents Luiz Inácio Lula da Silva (1945–) and Dilma Rousseff (1947–) implemented social and economic policies that lifted millions of people out of poverty. However, they were also involved in major investigations regarding some of the largest irregularities and corruption schemes in Brazilian history. President Lula was imprisoned from April 2018 to November 2019, and President Rousseff was removed from office in 2016 (even though she was not found criminally guilty of any charges). Her replacement was Michel Temer (1940-), who was also detained and interrogated in 2019 regarding corruption schemes. All these scandals sparked massive street protests because politicians were stealing millions of dollars while they were implementing budget cuts from public programs that include an already-inadequate education system, a failing health care program, and basic social protections. As a result, most Brazilians nowadays are either rather apathetic or extremely angry about their political leaders. Nevertheless, most average citizens are usually willing to discuss how the economy affects them on a daily basis. Chapter 4 explores the thriving modern Brazilian economy, which is based on a large-scale export model. There are five major components that drive large sectors of the national economy: the state-owned enterprises that include Petrobras and the production of energy, high-level manufacturing in aeronautics and the car industry, tremendous mineral wealth, tourism services, and the massive agrobusiness industry that has turned Brazil recently into a major global exporter of vegetables, beef, and coffee. The government has signed a multitude of recent international agreements that keep its economy humming, and its bureaucrats routinely present positive numbers at international economic forums. This book, however, also discusses how millions of Brazilians are still living in *favelas* (urban slums) in unsanitary conditions, as well as the contradiction of Brazil being a major food exporter, but it cannot manage to feed millions of its own people living in abject poverty.

Chapters 5 through 10 focus on social issues related to social classes, ethnicity, religion, gender, education, language, and etiquette. Chapter 5 explains how Catholicism is the largest religion in Brazil, but it coexists with the veneration of multiple gods (*orixás*) from African religions, such as Candomblé and Macumba. However, in the last thirty years, protestant religions have experienced tremendous growth in Brazil, especially among the poorest marginalized sectors of society. Chapter 6 delves into the thorny subject of ethnicity and social classes within the context of a highly stratified society where the vast majority of the poor are black and the wealthy class is mostly white. Most Brazilians nowadays no longer accept the outdated notion of Brazil as a racial democracy where all the races get along just fine. In fact, most Brazilians of mixed ethnicity (*caboclo, cafuso, mameluco, mulatto,* and *pardos*) confirm that racism is alive and thriving in Brazil, and that the disadvantaged groups in society routinely experience discrimination. In addition, this chapter covers the immense income disparities that have turned Brazil into one of the most inequitable countries in the world. Consequently, in the last twenty years, Brazilians have frequently taken to the streets to protest untenable social conditions that include extreme poverty, high crime rates, a stalled land-reform promise, and a sense of helplessness that truncates the possibility for upper mobility. Chapter 7 turns the discussion to gender roles in society, including the representation of men and women in both government and the workforce. It covers cultural traditions related to dating, weddings, raising children, parenting roles, abortion laws, *desquite* (legal separation), and divorce. In addition, this chapter deals with contemporary social concerns, including gender equality, LGBTQ rights, and the regrettable high levels of domestic abuse that now rank Brazil as having the seventh-highest rate of violence against women in the world. Chapter 8 explains the structure, merits, and deficiencies of both public and private education systems in Brazil from preschool to high school levels. It also illustrates the apparent contradiction that the public education system is failing while the system of public federal universities is essentially free, though these universities are ranked far more highly than their expensive private counterparts. Finally, it covers successful government programs that have increased literacy rates and the affirmative-action laws implemented to provide access to higher education, discourage racism, and promote economic equality. Chapter 9 focuses on language as a form of expression, including the influence of Tupi-Guarani in modern Brazilian Portuguese, the spelling reforms to facilitate literacy, and the development of the Portuguese sign language (LIBRAS). Chapter 10 illustrates how Brazilians interact with each other in society. People constantly need to navigate a set of social rules to function properly in a society that appears to be friendly but also includes an extremely bureaucratic system. Sometimes, Brazilians have to follow social etiquette, such as dressing formally for a meeting, arriving on time for an interview, following appropriate table manners, and respecting personal space in conversations. However, many social interaction norms are somewhat negotiable. Brazilians even have a name for this: *jeitinho*, or finding a way. For example, bargaining for lower prices is an expected tradition. The use of *despachantes* (intermediaries) is common to help people navigate routine but cumbersome tasks such as renewing a driver's license. Finally, Brazilians place a high value on personal relationships; therefore, they are more flexible with the concept of time for casual interactions. Consequently, they constantly try to control time to fit their own needs instead of the other way around.

The next few chapters (11 through 14) explore the tangible cultural components produced by Brazilians, including literature, arts and architecture, music and dance, and delicious food. Chapter 11 covers multiple literary movements that have continuously attempted to define what it means to be Brazilian. It includes writers from the national literary canon, such as Jorge Amado (1912–2001) and Joaquim Machado (1839–1908), but also emerging contemporary novelists. Chapter 12 illustrates how Brazilians are very creative, and their talent is reflected in colorful art, detailed crafts, and striking architecture, all of which have been influenced by historical events. During the 1700s, the artistic style called *Barrocco Mineiro* emerged as a local artistic expression that was uniquely Brazilian, especially in the town of Ouro Preto. Then the French Artistic Mission in 1816 officially changed the way art was taught and produced in the country by establishing an Academy of Fine Arts with a preference for neoclassical art. During the twentieth century, the Week of Modern Art Festival in 1922 officially solidified the modernism movement in Brazil that would inspire future generations. It was a radical call to abandon European traditions and develop new forms of artistic expression that reflected Brazilian themes but also included an intrinsic agenda to institute social change. An overall theme in Brazilian art is the continuous search for a national identity. The ultimate display of modernism came in the 1950s when Oscar Niemeyer (architect), Lúcio Costa (urban planner), and Roberto Burle Marx (landscape designer) designed a brand-new capital city from scratch to be called Brasília. The entire city was built in only four years and inaugurated in 1960. At the time, it was the largest experiment in modernist architecture, and it continues to impress people even today. Present-day artists have been enriched by previous Brazilian talent, but they usually have a wider international reach. For example, Sandra Cinto is a Brazilian contemporary artist who works with multiple platforms, including pen drawings, paintings, sculptures, and performance installations. From 2010 to 2018, she has had exhibits in five different countries. Following the trend of Brazilian creativity, Chapter 13 deals with the rich national heritage of music and dance. At an international level, people are often familiar with the soothing sounds of the bossa nova musical style reflected in the famous song "The Girl from Ipanema," the fast-paced rhythm and dance choreography of samba, and the exotic display of Carnival at Rio de Janeiro. This book, however, also explores the current trends in Brazilian music that dominate the airwaves, including *música popular brasileira* (MPB) and *música sertaneja* (Brazilian country music). Finally, chapter 14 turns the book's attention to mouthwatering Brazilian food. Contemporary Brazilian cuisine is actually a collection of regional dishes that reflect local traditions and styles of cooking. If there is such a thing as a national dish or drink, it would be *feijoada* (a stew with black beans and different cuts of meat cooked in a clay pot) and *caipirinha* (an alcoholic cocktail prepared with sugar, lime, and *cachaça* liquor). While this chapter highlights the merits of multiple contemporary chefs running trendy (and exclusive) restaurants, it also discusses the uncomfortable reality that Brazil still struggles with significant problems of poverty, hunger, and malnutrition. The existing income inequalities mean that poor people still suffer from basic food insecurities. To address the problem, President Luiz Inácio Lula da Silva (1945–) implemented the Fome Zero program (Zero Hunger Strategy) in 2003 with the explicit purpose of reducing extreme poverty and hunger nationwide. Thus far, the results are impressive, and Brazil is now a model for other developing nations regarding effective strategies to combat extreme hunger.

Brazilians certainly like to have fun. Chapters 15 and 16 explore multiple forms of personal leisure and entertainment, including sports, media, cinema, and contemporary popular culture. Without a doubt, *futebol* (soccer) is the king of sports in Brazil, but basketball, Brazilian jiu-jitsu, and Formula 1 racing are extremely popular. Brazil received global attention recently when it played host to three major international sporting events: the 2014 FIFA Soccer World Cup, the 2016 Olympic Games, and the 2016 Paralympic Games. In addition to sports, families enjoy weekend gatherings, as well as beach and nature outings. The power of television entertainment cannot be understated in Brazilian media; it has produced numerous famous telenovelas that usually capture national audiences and are exported to multiple countries. In the last ten years, however, reality television shows have dominated prime-time programming in all the major television networks. Chapter 16 also explores the resurgence of a vibrant Brazilian cinema industry supported by multiple film festivals and contemporary talented directors. In the twenty-first century, however, the expansion of the Internet, social networks, and mobile phones has changed how Brazilians communicate with one another, watch entertainment, stay informed, and listen to music.

This book would not have been published without a team of people who supported the project. First of all, I thank Kaitlin Ciarmiello, the acquisitions editor at ABC-CLIO. She offered constant suggestions, corrections, and encouraging comments to keep the project on track. Her patience, knowledge, and professionalism were incredible assets to complete this manuscript. Finally, I want to dedicate this book to my wife, Maya E. Alvarez-Galván, and my son, Marco A. Galván; they both provided support during the time I was writing this book.

INTRODUCTION

Brazil is a complex country with a fascinating history and rich cultural traditions. It is often described in superlatives. It is by far the largest country in Latin America, and it has physical land borders with ten neighboring nations. It has also been blessed with an abundance of natural resources. The Amazon region has the largest rain forest on the planet and the world's most voluminous river, but their existence is in constant peril due to deforestation practices. In addition, the 2006 oil discovery of the Tupi field on the Atlantic coast is estimated to be one of the largest oil fields in the Americas, and it has recently made Brazil not only energy independent but also a net exporter of oil and natural gas. Moreover, in 2018, Brazil became both the largest producer and exporter of coffee in the world. Such projects, together with an export-based economic approach, have sparked a tremendous growth of the national economy in the last twenty years, which is now considered to be the eighth largest in the world. From a demographic perspective, the Instituto Brasileiro de Geografia e Estatística (IBGE) reported 185,712,213 inhabitants on the 2010 census, which makes Brazil the country with the fifth-largest population in the world (after China, India, the United States, and Indonesia). The official IBGE estimated population for 2019 is already beyond 210 million people. In addition, Brazil actually has the largest concentration of black population in the world, even larger than any country in Africa, and it also accounts for the largest number of Catholics in the world. Brazilians like to have fun, and they are passionate about *futebol* (soccer); they are tremendously proud that their country has won the FIFA World Cup five times; no other country has accomplished such an achievement. Sometimes, however, Brazil is defined by foreigners who often compare it to its Latin American neighbors. Brazil is unique in the sense that its national language is Portuguese while the rest of Latin America speaks Spanish. The Portuguese heritage also made Brazil the only country to ever have a monarch living in Latin America when Napoleon Bonaparte forced the Portuguese kings into exile; they moved to Brazil in 1807 and ruled their global empire from Rio de Janeiro.

My goal in writing this book is to provide an updated and critical view of contemporary Brazil that is accessible to undergraduate and high school students but could also be used as a general reference source. Most tourists who visit this popular South American country usually limit themselves to the popular sights that include fun beaches, intriguing tropical rain forests, and spectacular waterfalls. While such natural beauty is important, it only offers a superficial view of Brazil. When people are willing to step away from the main sights, another Brazil quickly reveals itself. The real Brazil is a blend of multiple elements that coexist sometimes seamlessly and other times in direct contrast. For example, Brazilian art, music, literature, and religion are a wonderful blend of its European past, indigenous roots, and African heritage. They have all contributed to what are today truly Brazilian forms of expression. Simple walks also reveal a stark contrast of extreme wealth right next to abject poverty. While Brazilian politicians highlight the prosperous economy in international economic forums, there is also a blunt modern reality of millions of people living below the poverty line in unsanitary conditions in urban *favelas* (slums). Brazil continues on its path of aggressive urbanization, which makes the rural parts of the country vulnerable to political neglect in terms of economic investment and an adequate agricultural reform that serves the needs of small farmers. The most vivid example is the extreme poverty experienced in the semiarid northeast region of the *sertão* where devastating droughts continue to punish regional crops and people's livelihood. Local residents lack political clout; consequently, their needs are not top priority in the capital city of Brasília. It is also ironic that part of the recent economic success is based on exporting food (especially beef and soybeans), but the country cannot manage to feed millions of Brazilians who live in pervasive poverty.

Brazil faces tremendous contemporary challenges. The public education system is inefficient, chronically underfunded, and extremely overcrowded. It does not adequately prepare students for modern jobs, which truncates their opportunities for social mobility. For example, the country has a thriving manufacturing sector in advanced products such as aviation and automobile industries, but the large majority of Brazilians lack enough education and training for such jobs, which creates even larger economic disparities in the nation. From a social perspective, violent crime is on the rise to unprecedented levels in Brazil, and since 2018, the government has resorted to using the military to police a civilian population—a strategy that has resulted in constant reports of police brutality. Spousal abuse has increased dramatically in the last twenty years, and Brazilian women suffer incredibly high levels of domestic abuse in spite of the implementation of federal laws to combat such violence; even the Human Rights Watch Organization forcefully condemned such chronic use of violence in 2017. Children are supposed to represent the future, but Brazil suffers from a persistent problem of homelessness, and hundreds of thousands of those affected are children who are routinely exposed to exploitation, abuse, drugs, and underpaid labor practices. Racism is prevalent in Brazil despite the outdated concept of the country defined as a racial democracy. General observations show that wealthier Brazilians tend to be white, and the poor populations are almost always black or *pardo* (racially mixed). The environment continues to deteriorate throughout the nation, especially as recent government administrations pursue more aggressive policies of agribusiness for export, which has resulted in corporate interests converting vast plots of protected land in the Amazon region to agriculture and beef pasture lands. For example, President Bolsonaro took office in January 2019, and he immediately issued a controversial executive order to transfer the responsibility of certifying indigenous territories as protected lands from the National

Indian Foundation (FUNAI) to the Ministry of Agriculture, which has been actively advocating for years on behalf of cattle ranchers and farmers to have greater access to protected lands to expand economic development. Overall, Brazil continues to be one of the most inequitable societies in the world, even as millions of people are struggling to move out of extreme poverty. The correlation between socioeconomic class and racial categories is much more complex than it appears on the surface. Faced with multiple apparent social injustices, Brazilians have organized massive street protests during the last ten years to express their discontent regarding a failing public education system, the inadequacy of the national health-care program, excessive government spending to subsidize international events (such as the 2014 Soccer World Cup and the 2016 Olympics), and a recent wave of legal cases involving high-level politicians in massive government corruption.

While modern Brazil certainly faces serious deficiencies and persistent problems, most Brazilians seem cautiously hopeful about the future of their country. Part of the optimism is based on the fact that federal and state governments have actually been effective agents of change by implementing specific policies that aim to reduce poverty rates, increase school participation, and prepare more Brazilians of all backgrounds for professional jobs. In fact, a few social policies have been extremely effective. For example, Brazil embarked on a massive literacy campaign during the late 1990s, and the IBGE 2010 census data shows that literacy rates have reached 92 percent, which is a tremendous achievement. In addition, social welfare programs, such as Bolsa Família and Brasil Sem Miséria, successfully lifted millions of people out of extreme poverty from 2013 to 2018. The Bolsa Família is a conditional cash-transfer program that offers payments to low-income families with the condition that children must attend school consistently. Since education provides a possible path for upper mobility, the government approved a controversial affirmative action policy in 2012 that sets racial quotas for admission at public federal universities. The goal is to reduce racial exclusion and to provide a path for economic improvement. Congress went even further in 2014 by passing another law that extended affirmative action quotas for government jobs. In fact, 20 percent of all federal jobs in public service are supposed to be filled by blacks or mixed-race underprivileged applicants by 2020. The overarching goal of the federal government to expand access to higher education and well-paying jobs is to discourage racial discrimination, provide access to more employment opportunities, and therefore promote economic equality.

Brazilian cultural traditions offer an incredible view into one of the most fascinating countries in the Western Hemisphere. They represent the immense creative talent that exists in the country. For example, the traditional soothing sounds of bossa nova and energetic samba rhythms provide unique representations of Brazilian music. In the last ten years, however, *música sertaneja* (Brazilian country music) has become one of the most popular contemporary genres on national radio. Brazil also has a long history of creative people that includes literary canon masterpieces by Machado de Assis (1839–1908), the unmistakable baroque art of Aleijadinho (1738–1814), the famous "Girl from Ipanema" song, and the television icon Xuxa (1963–). More recently, modern literature, art, architecture, and cinema have captured the attention of the world, including the futuristic architectural style of Oscar Niemeyer (1907–2012), the catchy songs released by pop icon Anitta (1993–), the thought-provoking paintings and sculptures of Adriana Varejão (1964–), and films directed by Fernando Meirelles (1955–). For sports fans, Brazil became the epicenter of international sporting events when it hosted both the 2014 FIFA World Soccer Cup and the 2016 Summer Olympics in Rio de Janeiro.

My hope is that this book provides readers with the desire to find out more about Brazil and hopefully visit this wonderful South American country to discover its natural beauty, rich history, and fascinating cultural traditions.

Brazil

CHAPTER 1

GEOGRAPHY

OVERVIEW

Brazil is a country of continental proportions, and its geographical features are often described using superlatives. The Federative Republic of Brazil (República Federativa do Brasil) covers a total area of 3,286,426 square miles (8,511,804 square kilometers). It is the largest country in South America and the fifth-largest country in the world (after Russia, Canada, China, and the United States). It borders every country in South America except Chile and Ecuador. While the Amazon River is the largest waterway in the country (4,007 miles or 6,449 kilometers), it is also the second-largest river in the world, after the Nile River (4,145 miles or 6,671 kilometers). On the east side, the entire coastline faces the Atlantic Ocean with a length of 4,654 miles (7,491 kilometers). Brazil's numerous beaches attract foreign tourists and local visitors to a plethora of outdoor activities. The Portuguese established settlements along the coast in the 1500s, and today, the majority of Brazilians still live along the coastline. Due to its unique colonial heritage, Brazil is the only Portuguese-speaking country in Latin America. The country got its name from the brazilwood trees (*pau brasil*) harvested by the Portuguese colonizers because they had a strong red dye color inside, which looked similar to a glowing amber (*brasa*).

Over 90 percent of Brazil is technically in a tropical zone. However, the northeast region regularly experiences devastating droughts, and floods are common in sections of the Amazon during heavy precipitation periods. Most of the country has a year-round tropical climate, with the exception of the southern region, which offers four distinct seasons. Brazil does not have earthquakes, hurricanes, tornadoes, or extreme cold weather.

While there are plenty of natural attractions in Brazil, what makes it a unique country with a vibrant culture is its people. From a demographic point of view, Brazil is incredibly and wonderfully complex. Based on the 2010 census, the Instituto Brasileiro de Geografia e Estatística (IBGE) reported 185,712,213 inhabitants, which makes Brazil the country with the fifth-largest population in the world (after China, India, the United States, and Indonesia). Since that census, the official IBGE estimated population for 2019 is expected to reach 211 million people. The national census data also reveals that Brazil is the largest Roman Catholic country in the world. The IBGE 2019 regional population estimates also show an increase in urbanization since the two most

The Five Regions of Brazil

populated cities in the country are São Paulo (12 million inhabitants) and Rio de Janeiro (6.5 million people). Most of the demographic and geographic statistics used in this section are the official numbers reported by the IBGE.

From an administrative perspective, Brazil has twenty-six states and a Federal District, where the capital of Brasília is located. Due to its large territory, Brazil was divided into five regions during the 1940s. This decision was based on practicality in order to gather, manage, and disseminate data. These five regions do not have any political representation, receive dedicated funding, or serve a specific administrative function. However, the demographic information collected is used to develop public policy at both federal and state levels. The geographic, environmental, and demographic highlights of each region are described in the following.

THE NORTH REGION

The largest region of the country, commonly known as Amazônia, actually includes six states: Acre, Amapá, Amazonas, Pará, Rondônia, and Roraima. Despite its large area of 1,494,976 square miles (almost 4 million square kilometers), roughly 42 percent of the national territory, this is the least populated region of Brazil. The IBGE estimates for 2019 show over 18 million people in the region. As a size comparison, the Amazon basin is larger than Argentina and twice the size of Mexico. Major cities in the region include Manaus (in Amazonas), as well as Belém and Santarém (in Pará). The Amazon River and its tributaries form the fluvial system that dominates the geography of the region, which has international borders with Colombia, Venezuela, Peru, Bolivia, Guyana, Suriname, and French Guiana.

The Brazilian Ministry of the Environment (Ministério do Meío Ambiente, or MMA) manages data and preservation programs on the rich diversity of flora and wildlife, but they also face a constant struggle to reduce deforestation and environmental degradation. The MMA estimates that almost 10,000 square miles (16,193 square kilometers) of rain forest are destroyed every year due to deforestation, which is the equivalent of losing an area the size of two football fields every single minute.

THE NORTHEAST REGION

The northeast region includes nine states: Alagoas, Bahia, Ceará, Maranhão, Paraíba, Pernambuco, Piauí, Rio Grande do Norte, and Sergipe. It covers an area of 602,774 square miles (1,561,178 square kilometers), which is almost 18 percent of the national territory. All these states have access to the ocean. This is the region where Pedro Álvares Cabral landed in 1500, and where the Portuguese established early colonial settlements, such as Pernambuco. The first capital of Brazil was also established here in the city of Salvador. This area was the center of African slavery and sugar production during the Portuguese colonial period (1500 to 1822); currently, Bahia reflects the heritage of a vibrant Afro-Brazilian population.

According to the 2019 IBGE population estimates, this is the second most populated region of the country (after the southeast region), and it includes almost 60 million Brazilians (27 percent of the national population). However, this region has the lowest living standards in the nation. Despite its small size, it actually has four separate climate regions that offer a stark contrast from the Atlantic coast to the desertlike interior. Historically, the large arid region of the *sertão* has suffered drastic droughts. The *sertão* is by far the least developed part of the country, a pervasive condition that has limited attempts to thrive on agriculture and light ranching.

THE CENTRAL-WEST REGION

The central-west region includes the Federal District (Brasília) and four states: Goiás, Tocantins, Mato Grosso, and Mato Grosso do Sul. It covers 622,426 square miles (1,612,077 square kilometers). Comparatively, the region is larger than Peru or South

The Pantanal marshlands are the largest of their type in the world, and almost two-thirds of them are located in the central-west region of Brazil. Recently, the area has become well known for ecotourism opportunities. (iStockPhoto)

Africa, and three times the size of Spain. The area covers roughly 22 percent of the national territory, but it includes slightly over 16 million inhabitants, or 7 percent of the national population. This is the only region without access to the ocean. However, it includes two significant river systems: the Paraguay and Paraná rivers both start in Brazil, and they flow south toward Argentina. The area also includes two important ecosystems of Pantanal and Cerrado. Pantanal is well known for ecotourism, and Cerrado includes significant portions of fertile agricultural land that has experienced tremendous growth in the last twenty years. This region is the home of the current federal capital city of Brasília, which was built from scratch in the 1950s as an attempt to resettle people away from the coast and the southern areas of the country. Architect Oscar Niemeyer created a modern and futuristic city that continues to attract people to marvel at his contemporary architectural style.

THE SOUTHEAST REGION

The southeast region includes four states: Espírito Santo, Minas Gerais, Rio de Janeiro, and São Paulo. Its territory covers 358,027 square miles (576,188 square kilometers), which makes it only about 10 percent of the national landmass. However, the IBGE 2019 estimates show that 42 percent of the national population lives here (over 87 million people). The topography is known as mountain territory, including the Serra do Mar Mountain Range and the iconic geographical features of Rio de Janeiro, such as Corcovado and Sugar Loaf Mountains.

The southeast region has the highest national living standards since it is the most industrialized region in the country. Actually, over 55 percent of the gross domestic product (GDP) is produced in these four states. For example, Minas Gerais became an important mining center since gold was discovered during the colonial period, and it has remained an important center of mineral exploration and production. In modern times, the state of Espírito Santo continues to thrive with large-scale coffee production contributing toward making Brazil the number one exporter of coffee in the world. The state of São Paulo is the financial and manufacturing center of the nation. It also contributes significantly to coffee exports. Rio de Janeiro and its beaches continue to be the top tourism destination for foreigners, and it recently hosted major international events, including the 2014 FIFA Soccer World Cup and the Olympic Games in 2016. Most economic indicators show that major cities in the region are thriving; ironically, they also include sections of extreme poverty, especially people who migrated from rural regions in search of a better life.

THE SOUTH REGION

This is the smallest of all five regions in Brazil. It includes the states of Paraná, Rio Grande do Sul, and Santa Catarina. It has international southern borders with Argentina, Uruguay, and Paraguay. Its area of 358,000 square miles (576,145 square kilometers) is only about 7 percent of the national territory. The IBGE estimates for 2019 show a population of almost 30 million people, making it the third most populated region in Brazil.

The Paraná river system provides irrigation for the region, but it also includes significant attractions. At the location where Argentina, Paraguay, and Brazil meet, the Paraná River feeds the iconic Iguaçu Falls, a natural wonder and a UNESCO World Heritage site. In addition, the Itaipú Dam (located at the southern Paraguayan border) is the largest hydroelectric plant in the world in terms of how much energy it produces. Since irrigation is widely available in the area, it makes the wide Pampas grasslands ideal for large cattle ranching operations, agriculture based on grain production, and increasingly, growing soybeans for export to China. Since the entire region is located below the Tropic of Capricorn, it is different from the rest of Brazil because it experiences four distinct seasons and even occasional snow in the wintertime. The climate and agricultural prospects enticed a significant number of immigrants from Germany and Italy to settle in the region, and they have made important contributions to Brazilian economy and culture.

Further Reading
Brazil Government Official Portal. http://brazil.gov.br
Crocitti, John J., and Monique Vallance (eds.). 2011. *Brazil Today: An Encyclopedia of Life in the Republic* (2 volumes). Santa Barbara, CA: ABC-CLIO.

Instituto Brasileiro de Geografia e Estatística—Brazilian Institute of Geography and Statistics (IBGE). "Censo 2010." Accessed June 15, 2019. http://ibge.gov.br

Meade, Teresa A. 2010. *A Brief History of Brazil*. New York: Checkmark Books.

Ministry of the Environment. Ministério do Meio Ambiente (MMA). http://mma.gov.br

Philander, George S. 2012. *Encyclopedia of Global Warming and Climate Change*, Second Edition. Princeton, NJ: Princeton University Press.

Tosta, Antonio Luciano de Andrade, and Eduardo F. Coutinho (eds.). 2016. *Brazil*. Santa Barbara, CA: ABC-CLIO.

Amazon Basin and Rain Forest

The Amazon basin is the region in South America that is drained by the main Amazon River and over 1,100 of its tributaries. The description of the area is often a collection of superlatives. While most of the Amazon basin is located within Brazil, its enormous territory actually extends into another seven countries: Colombia, Ecuador, Peru, Bolivia, Venezuela, Guyana, and Suriname. The large drainage basin covers almost 40 percent of the entire southern continent, measuring 2.9 million square miles (7.5 million square kilometers). From a comparative perspective, the entire Amazon basin is ten times larger than France, larger than Argentina, and almost three times the size of Mexico. Terminology can be confusing, and it is important to clarify it. The Amazon basin expands over multiple countries; however, within Brazil, the IBGE officially labels this region as "Amazônia Legal" for the purpose of collecting and managing data and resources related to it. Moreover, there is also a state called Amazonas located in northern Brazil. In addition, most of the Amazon basin territory is classified as the Amazon rain forest—generally called Amazônia—and it is considered the largest rain forest on the planet, occupying over 2 million square miles (5.5 million square kilometers). This region represents over 50 percent of the rain forests left in the world.

The dominant geographical feature of the Amazon basin is the Amazon River; it starts in the Andes Mountains, and it flows from west to east before emptying into the Atlantic Ocean near the city of Belém. Its length of 4,345 miles (6,992 kilometers) makes it the second-longest river in the world after the Nile River in northeastern Africa. Recent studies published in 2010 and 2014 claim to have found a more distant origin of the Amazon River about 49 miles (80 kilometers) farther than previously thought, which would make it the longest river in the world (Contos and Tripcevich, 2014). While geographers have not yet reached a consensus on the issue, an indisputable fact is that the Amazon River drains more water into the ocean than any other river on Earth, at a rate of 7.5 million cubic feet per second (209,000 cubic meters per second), which is five times more than the mighty Congo River in Africa and almost twelve times more than the Mississippi River in the United States. The amount of water released by the Amazon River represents over 20 percent of the fresh water drained into the world's oceans. For the purpose of collecting and tracking information, geographers generally

The Amazon forest along the Rio Negro. The Amazon Basin includes over 1,100 tributaries that drain into the Amazon River as it flows toward the Atlantic Ocean. (3000ad/Dreamstime.com)

divide the Amazon River into two parts. The Upper Amazon is the collection of river systems from Peru, Colombia, Ecuador, Venezuela, and Brazil that drain into the Salimões River and its tributaries. The Lower Amazon starts at the junction where the Salimões River meets the Rio Negro near the large city of Manaus. For almost 4 miles (6 kilometers), these two rivers run parallel to each other without mixing. This popular region is known as the "Meeting of the Waters," or Encontro das Águas. The Amazon River sustains a rich ecosystem that includes large mammals, abundant species of fish, and large reptiles that include anaconda snakes and caimans.

The Amazon rain forest supports an incredible biodiversity of flora and fauna. As a wet tropical forest, the region offers the largest collection of living animals and plants in the world. It includes over 2.5 million types of insects, over 2,000 species of birds and mammals, at least 40,000 cataloged plant species, over 350 reptiles, more than 400 amphibians, and over 2,200 types of freshwater fish. However, the large array of dense coniferous forest and vegetation is constantly threatened by deforestation. Recent studies have revealed that Brazil loses roughly 4.246 square miles (11,000 square kilometers) every year, an area equivalent to two football fields every minute (Reuters, 2016). The main reasons for converting forested areas to other purposes include cattle ranching, aggressive agricultural expansion, and infrastructure projects, such as highways, dams, and power plants. When land is lost to deforestation, it also increases the loss of multiple animal and plant species.

While the loss of Amazon rain forest territory is alarming, there is hope for its protection in the near future. Rain forest environmentalists are actively engaged in conservation projects in conjunction with both official agencies and nongovernmental organizations (NGOs) in order to establish a sustainable balance among economic development, addressing the needs of crucial infrastructure projects, as well as fighting for the protection and regeneration of forested areas. For example, since the year 2000, the World Wildlife Fund (WWF) has cooperated with the Brazilian government for the creation of a large-scale conservation project called the Amazon Region Protected Areas Program (ARPA); they have already set aside over 128 million acres (over 200,000 square miles) as protected areas of territory to fight against deforestation and safeguard the fragile ecosystem. The project has been so successful that it received additional funding by the World Bank in order to expand the conservation efforts of this crucial habitat as part of a national park system. In addition to such programs, the Brazilian National Institute of Amazonian Research (INPA) has also implemented the use of satellite devices and remote sensors to improve the government's reaction to devastating fires caused by severe droughts that have affected the Amazon area in the last few years.

See also: Chapter 1: Overview; Earth Summit, Rio 2012; Climate; Deforestation; Environment; Infrastructure: Roads, Airports, Ports, and Railways; Interoceanic Highway; Major Rivers.

Further Reading

Brazilian National Institute of Amazonian Research—Instituto Nacional de Pesquisas da Amazônia (INPA). http://portal.inpa.gov.br

Contos, James, and Nicholas Tripcevich. 2014. "Correct Placement of the Most Distant Source of the Amazon River in the Mantaro River Drainage." *Area* 46, no.1 (March): 27–39. Accessed May 29, 2019. https://www.researchgate.net/publication/260335001_Correct_placement_of_the_most_distant_source_of_the_Amazon_River_in_the_Mantaro_River_drainage

IBGE. "Legal Amazon." Instituto Brasileiro de Geografia e Estatística (IBGE). Accessed June 1, 2019. http://ibge.gov.br/english/geociencias/geografia/amazonialegal.shtm?c=2

Lewinsohn, Thomas M., and Paulo Inácio Prado. 2005. "How Many Species Are There in Brazil?" *Conservation Biology* 19, no. 3 (June): 619–624. Accessed June 29, 2019. https://www.researchgate.net/publication/229719401_How_Many_Species_Are_There_in_Brazil

Penn, James R. 2001. *Rivers of the World: A Social, Geographical, and Environmental Sourcebook*. Santa Barbara, CA: ABC-CLIO.

Reuters. 2016. "Brazil Losing Forest the Size of Two Football Fields a Minute." NDTV.com, April 29. Accessed July 7, 2019. http://www.ndtv.com/world-news/brazil-losing-forest-the-size-of-two-football-fields-per-minute-1400934

Vidal, John. 2005. "Rainforest Loss Shocks Brazil." *Guardian*, May 20. Accessed July 28, 2019. https://www.theguardian.com/news/2005/may/20/brazil.environment

World Wildlife Fund. "Amazon." http://worldwildlife.org/places/amazon

World Wildlife Fund. "Deforestation and Threats." World Wildlife Fund. Accessed June 1, 2019. http://www.worldwildlife.org/threats/deforestation

Brasília and the Federal District

The federal capital of Brazil is Brasília. The city was designed from scratch, and it was officially inaugurated on April 21, 1960, by President Juscelino Kubitschek (1902–1976). The general goal was to create a new capital located away from the most densely populated southeast region of Brazil. Brasília is actually the third national capital city. Salvador was the original capital from 1549 to 1763. Then Rio de Janeiro became the second capital from 1763 until 1960.

President Kubitschek (served 1956 to 1961) had a vision to industrialize Brazil by investing heavily in economic development and make "fifty years of progress in just five years." He set aside almost 20,000 square miles (50,000 square kilometers) to create the Federal District. A national competition to develop a new city was quickly under way. Brasília became a national symbol of social change and modernization; consequently, it became known as the "City of Hope." The three winners of the design competition worked together to convert the dream into a reality. Urban planner Lúcio Costa (1902–1998) crafted a city based on two main avenues (axes): The Monumental Axis concentrates all the political and administrative functions of government in a section of the city; the Residential Axis was conceived to include housing along with schools, commerce, churches, and recreation to create cohesive, self-sufficient neighborhoods. Oscar Niemeyer (1907–2012) was the chief architect for the main government and official buildings, including the National Congress, the Supreme Court building, the Presidential Palace, the Presidential Residence, and the Cathedral of Brasilia. Niemeyer incorporated a consistent modernism style by combining simplicity and modernity focused on simple lines and columns. Roberto Burle Marx (1909–1994) was selected as landscape designer. He planned gardens for open spaces throughout the city, especially the Esplanada dos Ministérios—a large lawn area surrounded by wide avenues and multiple government buildings and iconic memorials.

The Praça dos Três Poderes (Three Powers Square) is a central location that includes buildings for the three branches of federal government. The Palácio do Planalto houses the presidential offices. The Congresso Nacional contains the meeting places for both the Senate and Chamber of Deputies. The Supremo Tribunal Federal includes the highest federal court. Near the area, there are multiple government administrative buildings also designed by Oscar Niemeyer. The Palácio da Alvorada (the Presidential Palace), where the first family resides, is located away from the Three Powers Square on a special peninsula along Lake Paranoá.

Due to its modernist architectural style and unique design, Brasília was designated as a UNESCO World Heritage site in 1987. Aside from its primary role as political and administrative center, Brasília has also become an important hub for higher education, film festivals, sports, and transportation. It has now surpassed its projected population of 500,000 people, and the 2010 census revealed that it has already reached almost 2.5 million people. Such demographic growth, however, has generated contemporary social problems of housing, traffic, unemployment, and the growth of *favelas* (slums) along the outskirts of the City of Hope.

See also: Chapter 1: Overview. Chapter 2: Kubitscheck de Oliveira, Juscelino (1902–1976). Chapter 3: Overview. Chapter 11: Overview; Modernism in Brazil; Chapter 12: Niemeyer, Oscar (1907–2012).

Further Reading

Decker, Thomas. 2016. *Brasilia: Life beyond Utopia*. New Haven, CT: Yale University Press.

Governo de Brasília Official Website. http://www.brasilia.df.gov.br

Instituto Brasileiro de Geografia e Estatística (IBGE). "Census 2010." http://ibge.gov.br

Climate

Brazil has a large territory that covers most of South America, and its climate varies according to both its latitude and altitude. It is the only country in the world through which the equator and the Tropic of Capricorn traverse, and they both have an effect on the national climate. The equator line goes right through the mouth of the Amazon River in the tropical northern region of the country. The Tropic of Capricorn (located at 23°26' south latitude) creates more temperate zones in the southern part of Brazil. While almost 90 percent of the country is technically located in a tropical zone, the majority of Brazilians actually live in regions that are cooled by ocean winds, mountain altitude, and even polar fronts.

Most people imagine the Amazon region to be extremely hot; however, it hardly ever reaches temperatures over 90° F (32° C). The Amazon region in the north is humid most of the time since it gets almost 80 inches (2,000 mm) of rain a year. However, the Amazon also has a dry season that lasts three to four months.

The other climate extreme in Brazil is located in the most southern regions south of the Tropic of Capricorn. The winters here occur between June and September, and it is common to see snow and frost in the mountains of three states: Paraná, Santa Catarina, and Rio Grande do Sul. Other cities such as Porto Alegre, São Paulo, and Curitiba occasionally experience below-freezing temperatures in the winter as well.

Mild temperatures are common in cities and regions located at low elevations. While Brazil does not have really high mountains, cities such as Belo Horizonte and the capital city of Brasília enjoy moderate temperatures between 50 and 86° F (15 and 30° C) because they are located at roughly over 3,000 feet high (1,000 meters). Another reason for mild temperatures is the ocean breeze and winds that cool cities located along the Atlantic coast that include Salvador, Rio de Janeiro, and Recife.

The *sertão* is the driest (and the poorest) region of Brazil. This semiarid area is located in the interior of the northeast region of the country. Its semi-desert vegetation is useful to sustain low-commercial-rate ranching. While this territory does get some rain, it is very sporadic and unpredictable. Actually, since 2010, this region has experienced devastating droughts. During the regular dry season, the area experiences hot temperatures that routinely reach over 100°F (39°C).

Climate change is a serious concern in Brazil since it has already affected agricultural production, rainfall patterns in the Amazon basin, and the potential desertification of areas in the northeast region. Consequently, President Michel Temer of Brazil expressed the country's commitment to the Paris Agreement on Climate Change in 2016 by offering to drastically reduce greenhouse gas emissions in the future.

See also: Chapter 1: Overview; Amazon Basin and Rain Forest; Climate; Deforestation; Environment; Major Rivers; The *Sertão* and Devastating Droughts.

Further Reading

Edwards, Todd L. 2008. *Brazil: A Global Studies Handbook*. Santa Barbara, CA: ABC-CLIO.

Meade, Teresa A. 2010. *A Brief History of Brazil*. New York: Checkmark Books.

Prengaman, Peter. 2016. "Brazil Ratifies Paris Agreement with Pledge to Sharply Reduce Emissions." *Guardian,* September 13. Accessed August 1, 2019. https://www.theguardian.com/environment/2016/sep/13/brazil-ratifies-paris-agreement-with-pledge-to-sharply-reduce-emissions

Deforestation

Deforestation can be defined as the permanent destruction of a forest in order to convert the land for another purpose. On a yearly basis, Brazil is the country that loses the largest amount of rain forest in the world. Recent studies have revealed that it loses roughly 4,246 square miles (11,000 square kilometers) every year, an area equivalent to two football fields every minute (Reuters, 2016). Since rain forests soak harmful carbon dioxide, they can help to reduce the acceleration of global climate change. Consequently, these alarming figures have prompted official ministries and nongovernmental organizations (NGOs) to make drastic decisions about managing and saving as much of the Amazon forest as possible.

The main reasons for Amazon deforestation include cattle ranching, illegal logging, fires, soybean farming, and new infrastructure projects. During the 1990s, the Brazilian government actively promoted the conversion of forest land for cattle ranching in the Amazon region to foster economic growth. By 2003, over 80 percent of Brazilian beef exports came from the Amazon region (CIFR, 2007). In the state of Mato Grosso, a significant area has replaced trees with soybean cultivation mainly as exports to Europe and China, a practice that has created serious concerns among environmentalists. In addition, both legal and illegal logging operations in the Amazon use very aggressive methods that also destroy collateral trees not intended for the timber

The Amazon region suffers from deforestation, which is primarily created by illegal logging, devastating fires, infrastructure projects, and the expansion of agribusiness into soybean farming and cattle ranching. (iStockphoto.com)

market. Moreover, the development of infrastructure projects has increased to provide access to previously remote areas of the Amazon to accommodate the needs of ranching operations, booming agribusiness, and population growth. For example, when the Trans Amazonian Highway (route BR-320) was inaugurated in 1972, it destroyed large sections of forest along its path while also displacing thousands of indigenous people from their natural habitat. Other building projects of multiple dams to generate hydroelectric power also flooded large areas of the Amazon forest.

While most of the information regarding Amazon deforestation is discouraging, there is hope for improvements. International summits have mostly agreed that losing the Amazon rain forest has global consequences since it accelerates climate change and reduces the habitat of flora and wildlife that could potentially benefit humanity in the future. Consequently, Brazil's government is currently working with NGOs—such as Greenpeace and World Wildlife Fund—to establish protocols that fight illegal logging, restrict the expansion of land designated for soybean cultivation, and work with cattle ranchers to balance their needs with a more sustainable development and management of the Amazon forest.

See also: Chapter 1: Overview; Amazon Basin and Rain Forest; Climate; Earth Summit, Rio 2012; Environment; Infrastructure: Roads, Airports, Ports, and Railways; Interoceanic Highway.

Further Reading

Center for International Forestry Research (CIFR). 2007. "Beef Exports Fuel Loss of Amazonia Forest." Center for International Forestry Research. Accessed August 1, 2019. https://web.archive.org/web/20071209222459/http://www.cifor.cgiar.org:80/Publications/Corporate/NewsOnline/NewsOnline36/beef_exports.htm

Reuters. 2016. "Brazil Losing Forest the Size of Two Football Fields a Minute." NDTV.com. April 29. Accessed July 12, 2019. http://www.ndtv.com/world-news/brazil-losing-forest-the-size-of-two-football-fields-per-minute-1400934

Richard, Christopher, and Leslie Jermyn. 2002. *Cultures of the World: Brazil.* New York: Marshall Cavendish.

Vidal, John. 2005. "Rainforest Loss Shocks Brazil." *Guardian,* May 20. Accessed August 1, 2019. https://www.theguardian.com/news/2005/may/20/brazil.environment

World Wildlife Fund. "Deforestation and Threats." *World Wildlife Fund.* Accessed August 2, 2019. http://www.worldwildlife.org/threats/deforestation

Earth Summit, Rio 2012

The Earth Summit, Rio 2012 was held in Rio de Janeiro in 2012. This conference was organized with the purpose of galvanizing international organizations and governments into committing to sustainable development while taking into account both economic and environmental goals. The meeting has multiple names and acronyms. Its official name is the United Nations Conference on Sustainable Development. The international event was originally held in Rio de Janeiro in 1992 (called the Rio Conference). Consequently, the 2012 meeting is also known as Rio+20, since it was held twenty years after its inception.

The summit provided two main themes for presentations and discussions. The first theme was to search for consensus on how to build a green economy with sustainable development that lifts people out of poverty. In order to achieve such an ambitious goal, multiple nations and agencies requested financial support for developing countries. The second theme was to find specific pathways that could improve international coordination to protect the environment and consider the rights of indigenous populations. Overall, the topics discussed in the conference presentations included a more efficient use of water supplies, the consequences of climate change, alternative sources of energy to replace fossil fuels, the use of public transportation that reduces gas emissions, reviews of manufacturing practices to reduce toxic waste, and the balance of achieving economic growth without further destroying the environment.

The summit was the biggest event ever organized by the United Nations. A total of 192 nations participated in the summit, including 130 heads of state. In addition, more than 2,300 representatives of non-governmental organizations (NGOs) were also active participants at the international forum. There was a notable absence of key government leaders from Germany (Angela Merkel), the United States (Barack Obama), and the

United Kingdom (David Cameron), which was commonly interpreted as industrialized nations not giving the environment an urgent priority.

The summit also drew a large number of environmental protesters and activists advocating for the rights of indigenous populations. Since the event was held in Brazil, well-organized protests focused on issues of deforestation and development projects that threaten the Amazon environment as well as the displacement of indigenous groups in the region.

The result of the conference was a document titled "The Future We Want," which aims to protect the oceans, improve food security, strengthen global environmental management, and promote a green economy. While the specific written outcomes provide global agreements among governments, it was wholeheartedly criticized by environmentalists and the defenders of low-income populations. From an anti-poverty point of view, the agreements are too vague, and they do not provide specific commitments to protect the environment nor to fight increasing financial inequalities worldwide.

See also: Chapter 1: Overview; Climate; Deforestation; Environment; Infrastructure: Roads, Airports, Ports, and Railways; Mendes, Chico (1944–1988).

Further Reading

United Nations. 2012a. "Implementation of Agenda 21 and the Outcomes of the World Summit on Sustainable Development." United Nations. Accessed July 30, 2019. http://www.un.org/ga/search/view_doc.asp?symbol=A/C.2/67/L.45&referer=/english/&Lang=E

United Nations. 2012b. "United Nations Conference on Sustainable Development, Rio+20." United Nations, June 22. Accessed July 30, 2019. http://sustainabledevelopment.un.org/rio20

Watts, Jonathan, and Liz Ford. 2012. "Rio+20 Earth Summit: Campaigners Decry Final Document." *Guardian,* June 6. Accessed July 30, 2019. https://www.theguardian.com/environment/2012/jun/23/rio-20-earth-summit-document

Environment

The environment in Brazil is under constant threat from deforestation, soil erosion, urban air pollution, desertification, and even economic development. Since the 1980s, deforestation of the Amazon region has received international attention. The main culprits were illegal logging and the expansion of cattle ranching operations. In addition, during the 1990s, the central region of Brazil experienced a dramatic increase in soybean cultivation developed mainly for exports. The consequence of these practices was considerable soil erosion that also affected rivers due to the use of pesticides. Another alarming concern is that in urban areas such as São Paulo and Belo Horizonte, air pollution increased due to higher population and higher carbon emissions released by automobiles and factories. While larger cities have more resources to deal with basic sanitation and medical consequences related to air pollution, midsize cities have struggled due to the lack of funds. In the *sertão* interior section of the northeast region, droughts have become increasingly more common and more devastating. As a result, the local vegetation of this semiarid region is disappearing, and the main concern is the prospect of desertification affecting the area. Finally, Brazil has to manage environmental concerns while simultaneously supporting economic development. The government has created multiple infrastructure projects that make isolated areas more accessible. For example, the creation of the Interoceanic Highway to link the Atlantic and Pacific Oceans created opportunities for farmers in the landlocked states of Rondônia, Mato Grosso, and Acre to export their produce via Peru to the Pacific Ocean and on to Asian markets. However, the same project was decried by conservationists and environmental activists because the highway destroyed areas of the Amazon basin and also relocated large numbers of indigenous populations who did not benefit from such infrastructure projects.

Brazil takes environmental issues very seriously. Under the precepts of the current constitution established in 1988, President Michel Temer appointed Sarney Filho in 2016 as his minister of the environment, which is a federal-level cabinet position in charge of running the Ministério de Meio Ambiente (MMA) and the Brazilian Institute for the Environment and Renewable Resources, or Instituto Brasileiro do Meio Ambiente e Dos Recursos Naturais Renováveis (IBAMA). There are also multiple nongovernmental organizations (NGOs) operating in Brazil in close cooperation with both federal and regional government representatives. They include the World Wildlife Fund (WWF), SOS Atlantic Forest, and the Pro-Nature Foundation. Furthermore, in order to address the urgency of environmental action at a global scale, Brazil organized the Earth Summit 2012 in Rio de Janeiro. In addition, President Temer in 2016 ratified the Paris Agreement on Climate Change by offering to drastically reduce greenhouse gas emissions and hence improve the quality of life for Brazilians.

See also: Chapter 1: Overview; Amazon Basin and Rain Forest; Climate; Deforestation; Earth Summit, Rio 2012; Interoceanic Highway; Mendes, Chico (1944–1988); The *Sertão* and Devastating Droughts. Chapter 3: Temer, Michel (1940–).

Further Reading

Brazilian Institute for the Environment and Renewable Resources. Instituto Brasileiro do Meio Ambiente e Dos Recursos Naturais Renováveis (IBAMA). http://www.ibama.gov.br

Meade, Teresa A. 2010. *A Brief History of Brazil*. New York: Checkmark Books.

Ministry of the Environment. Ministério do Meio Ambiente (MMA). http://mma.gov.br

Philander, George S. 2012. *Encyclopedia of Global Warming and Climate Change*, Second Edition. Princeton, NJ: Princeton University Press.

World Wildlife Fund. "Deforestation and Threats." *World Wildlife Fund*. Accessed July 14, 2017. http://www.worldwildlife.org/threats/deforestation

Infrastructure: Roads, Airports, Ports, and Railways

According to the CIA World Factbook 2019 statistical data, Brazil has 4,093 airports, 1,242,700 miles (2 million kilometers) of roads, 7 major commercial ports, and 18,527 miles (29,817 kilometers) of railways. However, these transportation networks do not necessarily connect to each other very effectively.

Brazil is keenly aware that its infrastructure is a significant impediment to improving its national economy and productivity. Most roads are in constant need of repair; the largest deepwater seaport of Santos is a bottleneck for hundreds of ships waiting to unload their cargo; and railways are very limited. As a result, President Dilma Rousseff launched a massive infrastructure plan in 2015 to attract $64 billion U.S. ($198 billion *reais*) in private investment over the next five years. The general goal was to bring both national and international firms to bid on specific concessions to build, operate, or improve roads, airports, railways, and seaports. In addition, regional governments have also developed plans for a bidding process of private-public partnerships to invest in local sanitation projects. The plan was to award all the concessions by 2016 and for projects to start by 2018. The government's vision is that these projects will generate construction jobs in the short term, but they will also help industries to increase productivity.

In order to attract foreign investors, the federal government of Brazil had to make significant reforms to its financing regulations, its cumbersome bureaucracy, and the legal framework to subsidize funding for public works. The underlying concept was to make capital investments more market-friendly and less controlled by government agencies, which often have led to allegations of corruption.

The Brazilian plans to improve infrastructure already show tangible results. The Industrial Bank of China started an infrastructure fund of $50 billion U.S. to finance multiple infrastructure projects, including the development of a single rail line to reach the Pacific coast of Peru to export iron ore to China. In addition, the China Development Bank provided a line of credit worth $3.5 billion U.S. for the state-controlled oil company Petrobras to undertake oil exploration projects. In a separate auction, the airports in São Paulo, Brasilia, and Campinas were awarded to private investment firms in 2012 as part of an auction to upgrade and renovate them before the 2014 FIFA Soccer World Cup. In Rio de Janeiro, the Porto Maravilha development project created a public-private alliance to revitalize part of Rio's waterfront real estate. The project also built 43 miles (70 kilometers) of new roads, three sewage treatment plants, and over 430 miles (700 kilometers) of sewage and waterworks.

The magnitude of such ambitious infrastructure projects soon revealed immense over-budget costs, especially for sports stadiums needed for the 2016 Olympics. The government's response to finance such overruns was to cut social services and increase transportation prices, which sparked social activism and massive street protests.

See also: Chapter 1: Interoceanic Highway; Main Cities and Urban Regions. Chapter 3: Rousseff, Dilma (1947–). Chapter 4: Foreign Investment; Petrobras, the National

Oil Company. Chapter 6: Poverty, Social Conflict, and Protests. Chapter 15: Overview; Olympic Games, Rio de Janeiro 2016; Soccer FIFA World Cup 2014.

Further Reading

DeFotis, Dimitra. 2017. "China to Invest $50 Billion in Brazil Infrastructure." *Barron's*, May 15. Accessed August 1, 2019. http://www.barrons.com/articles/china-to-invest-50-billion-in-brazil-infrastructure-1431699917

Genasci, Lisa. 2012. "Infrastructure in Brazil, the World Cup, and Olympics." *Americas Quarterly*, Fall. Accessed August 1, 2019. http://www.americasquarterly.org/Brazil-the-World-Cup-and-Olympics

Reuters. 2015. "Brazil Launches Massive Infrastructure Plan." *Maritime Executive*, June 9. Accessed August 1, 2019. http://maritime-executive.com/article/brazil-launches-massive-infrastructure-plan

Trevisani, Paulo. 2015. "Brazil to Fight Economic Woes with Infrastructure Plan." *Wall Street Journal*, June 9, 2015. Accessed August 1, 2019. https://www.wsj.com/articles/brazil-plans-to-reduce-government-role-in-new-infrastructure-projects-1433855132

Interoceanic Highway

The Interoceanic Highway, inaugurated in 2011, was designed to link Peru and Brazil. More specifically, it connects two Brazilian ports (Santos and Rio de Janeiro) on the Atlantic coast with three Peruvian ports (Ilo, San Juan de Marcona, and Port of Matarani) along the Pacific Ocean. The highway stretches for 3,400 miles (5,471 kilometers) from the breezy beaches of Rio de Janeiro, slowly climbing its way through the vast pasture lands of Mato Grosso and the thick-forest Amazon state of Rondônia, upward to the Andes Mountains cloud environment, past snow-covered glaciers at 16,000 feet of altitude, and then back down toward the Pacific Ocean in southern Peru. Overall, the project was a remarkable engineering accomplishment that sometimes conquered incredibly difficult terrain. The completion of the highway accommodated the renovation of multiple bridges and existing roads plus the task of clearing jungle areas and rocky Andean mountain territory to create new roads.

The Brazilian part of the highway (Estrada do Pacifico) is mostly flat from metropolitan São Paulo all the way to Rio Branco, the capital of the isolated interior state of Acre. This large section was accomplished mainly by updating and extending Brazil's Highway BR-317. Then three Brazilian roads (BR-364, BR-317, and Rio Branco do Sul) join together as they reach the border town of Assis, cross the Binational Bridge over the Acre River, and arrive at the town of Iñapari, Peru. This area also includes a border with Bolpebra, Bolivia. Once the Interoceanic Highway crosses into Peru, it becomes Highway 30 (Carretera Interoceánica) for almost seven hours of driving passing near the ancient city of Cusco (providing better access to Machu Picchu ruins) before it splits into three separate highway routes to reach the Pacific Ocean.

The possibility of creating a highway in South America that links the Atlantic and Pacific Oceans was planned for decades. For Peru, it provides access to an isolated area of the country that was previously not integrated into the national economy. For Brazil, the goal of reaching the Pacific Ocean was largely intended to provide easier transportation of export goods to the Asian markets, especially since China overtook the United States as Brazil's largest trading partner in 2009.

While the creation of a superhighway intended to bring progress and economic prosperity to both countries, it also generated great concern among environmentalists who want to protect the Amazon region. Conservationists argue that new construction has accelerated soil erosion, deforestation, and illegal logging operations in territories parallel to the new highway. In addition, the construction of two new hydroelectric power stations also created two new dams (San Antonio and Jirau) without consulting the needs of the indigenous populations in the region. From the economic, social, and environmental perspectives, it will take at least a decade to evaluate the benefits of building such a super highway. As with many other projects affecting the Amazon region, only time will tell.

See also: Chapter 1: Amazon Basin and Rain Forest; Deforestation; Environment; Infrastructure: Roads, Airports, Ports, and Railways; Major Rivers; Mendes, Chico (1944–1988).

Further Reading

Garcia-Navarro, Lulu. 2009. "The Amazon Road: Paving Paradise for Progress?" National Public Radio, September 14. Accessed July 31, 2019. http://www.npr.org/2009/09/14/112535943/the-amazon-road-paving-paradise-for-progress

Reel, Monte. 2014. "Traveling from Ocean to Ocean across South America." *New York Times Magazine,* February 19. Accessed July 31, 2019. https://www.nytimes.com/2014/02/23/magazine/south-america-road-trip.html?_r=0

Robinson Chavez, Michael, and Patrick J. McDonnell. 2010. "Peruvians Brace as Superhighway Unfolds." *Los Angeles Times,* October 31, 2010. Accessed July 31, 2019. http://articles.latimes.com/2010/oct/31/world/la-fg-peru-road-20101031

Islands and Archipelagos

Brazil is mostly famous for the Amazon rain forest, Carnival, samba music, a Portuguese colonial past, and the beaches of Rio de Janeiro. One geographical secret that is not well known at an international level is that Brazil also has amazingly beautiful islands and archipelagos off the Atlantic coast and even right in the middle of its mighty rivers.

Perhaps the most famous of all Atlantic islands is the Archipelago of Fernando de Noronha. It is located 224 miles (360 kilometers) off the eastern coast. It is technically part of the state of Pernambuco, and it includes the main island, twenty-one small islands, and multiple rocks; they all form part of the Noronha Chain of Volcanic Mountains that are mostly under water in the Atlantic Ocean. The main island of Fernando de Noronha is 5 miles long and 1.86 miles wide (8 kilometers by 3 kilometers). The island was used as a prison from the late 1700s all the way to the 1950s. In order to deter jail mates from building rudimentary rafts, the government ordered all the trees to be cut down. The deforestation project had a devastating effect on the island's ecosystem. Consequently, the Noronha Marine National Park was created in 1988 to allow the marine ecosystem to recover. Since the 1980s, interest in the island has increased. Visitors are attracted to its sandy beaches, numerous waterfalls, snorkeling, and deepwater diving. However, in order to protect these islands, only 460 people are allowed to visit per day, after paying an environmental tax. Most visitors agree that the fee is worth it.

Not all Brazilian islands are actually on the ocean. The Ilha do Marajó (Marajo Island) is located right at the mouth of the Amazon River as it empties out into the Atlantic Ocean. While it has a unique location, this is not a small landmass; it is actually the largest river island in the world. It is 133 miles long (295 kilometers) and 120 miles wide (200 kilometers), which is slightly over 19,000 square miles (50,000 square kilometers). It is larger than the entire state of Maryland or Massachusetts, or even Switzerland. It is surrounded by both the Amazon and Paraná rivers, and it faces the Atlantic Ocean. Administratively, it is located within the state of Pará, which has promoted the island based on ecotourism and the ancient crafts produced by the Marajoara indigenous people.

Other islands located on the Atlantic Ocean that are also highly ranked for their vegetation and natural beauty include Ilha de Cardoso, Atol da Rocas, Ilha do Mel, Ilhabela Archipelago, Ilha de Santa Catarina, Ilha Grande, Ilha do Campeche, and Vitória Archipelago. Other river islands along the Amazon River include Ilha Tupinambarana and Bananal Island. The Brazilian Institute for the Environment and Renewable Resources (IBAMA) constantly monitors the ecological impact of human activity on these islands in order to preserve them and simultaneously promote sustainable development.

See also: Chapter 1: Overview; Amazon Basin and Rain Forest; Climate; Earth Summit, Rio 2012; Environment; Major Rivers.

Further Reading

Brazilian Institute for the Environment and Renewable Resources. Instituto Brasileiro do Meio Ambiente e Dos Recursos Naturais Renováveis (IBAMA). http://www.ibama.gov.br

Meyer, Amelia. 2010. *Islands of Brazil*. Accessed August 1, 2019. https://www.brazil.org.za/islands-of-brazil.html

World Wildlife Fund. "Island Atoll off the Atlantic Coast of Brazil: Fernando de Noronha." World Wildlife Fund. Accessed August 1, 2019. https://www.worldwildlife.org/ecoregions/nt0123

Itaipú Hydroelectric Power Plant

The Barragem de Itaipu (in Portuguese) or the Represa de Itaipú (in Spanish) is the world's largest generator of renewable clean energy. "Itaipu" is the name of a river island that already existed at the location where the dam was to be built; in the Guarani language, it means "the sounding stone." The dam is located along the Paraná River, which forms a natural border between Brazil and Paraguay. It is the second-largest river in Brazil (after the Amazon River) and the eighth-largest river in the world, but its course had to be rerouted in order to build the power plant. The structure was built with reinforced concrete in order to control the flow of the Paraná River and create a reservoir for the power plant. The dam itself is 643 feet high (196 meters), equivalent to the height of a 65-story building. The massive engineering project was originally conceived by the two nations as part of a binational agreement during the 1960s. The Ata do Iguaçu (Iguaçu Act) was signed on July 22, 1966, and construction started in 1971. The electric power plant was completed in 1984.

The Itaipú Hydroelectric Plant includes twenty generating units (turbines and generators) to produce energy for both Paraguay and Brazil (ten units each) with a capacity of 700 megawatts each. In 2016, the hydroelectric plant reached a new world record of producing 103,098,366 megawatts per hour (MWh), surpassing the production of the Three Gorges Dam in China. However, Paraguay does not use all the energy

The Itaipú Hydroelectric Plant is located at the Paraná River at the border with Paraguay. It is the largest dam in the world dedicated to the production of renewable clean energy. (Itaipú Binacional)

produced; as a result, the excess energy is exported to Brazil to be used in far-flung cities such as São Paulo and Rio de Janeiro located about 500 miles (800 kilometers) away. The binational Ata de Iguaçu Treaty expires in 2023, and Paraguay has expressed serious concerns about the terms to which it originally agreed, especially regarding the price of electricity it receives from Brazil. The threat of reopening negotiations analyzing the specific details of the agreement has recently created diplomatic tension between the two nations.

The construction of the Itaipú power plant generated controversial social and environmental problems. In order to start the project, over 10,000 families had to be relocated because they lived close to the Paraná River. In addition, the government had to destroy the Guaíra Falls in order to make the flow of the river available for navigation. These falls served as a natural barrier used to separate multiple species of fish found in two different ecosystems. The result was that species of fish invaded another ecosystem, and there was a substantial reduction on the number of fish able to survive in the region.

See also: Chapter 1: Overview; Climate; Environment; Infrastructure: Roads, Airports, Ports, and Railways; Major Rivers; World Heritage Sites in the UNESCO.

Further Reading

Itaipu Dam Official Government Site. http://www.itaipu.gov.br

Júnior, Júlio et al. 2009. "A Massive Invasion of Fish Species after Eliminating a Natural Barrier in the Upper Paraná Basin." *Neotropical Ichthyology* 7, no. 4: 709–718.

Terminski, Bogumil. 2015. *Development-Induced Displacement and Resettlement: Theoretical Frameworks and Current Challenges.* Hannover, Germany: Ibidem Press.

Main Cities and Urban Regions

According to the Instituto Brasileiro de Geografia e Estatística (IBGE), almost 90 percent of Brazil's population lives in large metropolitan areas. The top ten most populated cities in the country also happen to be state capitals. As part of its methodology, the IBGE's official population estimates for 2018 include the municipality numbers rather than the metropolitan area by itself (see Table 1.1).

São Paulo is the largest city in both Brazil and all of South America. As an industrial powerhouse, it constitutes the largest economy in the nation, and it includes the main financial and business centers of the country. It is also the hub of the national textile industry.

Rio de Janeiro is the most visited city by foreign tourists. Its iconic beaches, harbor, natural geographical beauty, monuments, and nightlife are recognized worldwide. It is also the second-largest economy in the country. Cariocas (local inhabitants) call the city by its nickname of Cidade Maravilhosa, or Marvelous City. Rio de Janeiro served as the second national capital from 1763 until 1960.

Table 1.1: TEN MOST POPULATED CITIES

Rank	City	State	Population
1	São Paulo	São Paulo	12,176,866
2	Rio de Janeiro	Rio de Janeiro	6,688,927
4	Brasília	Distrito Federal	2,974,703
4	Salvador	Bahia	2,857,329
5	Fortaleza	Ceará	2,643,247
6	Belo Horizonte	Minas Gerais	2,501,576
7	Manaus	Amazonas	2,145,444
8	Curitiba	Paraná	1,917,185
9	Recife	Pernambuco	1,637,834
10	Goiânia	Goiás	1,495,705

Portuguese colonizers established the city of Salvador as the first official national capital in 1549; it served such administrative purpose until 1763. Today, it still retains its colonial past reflected in its baroque architecture and cultural traditions based on African heritage, dance festivals, musical legacy, religious celebrations, and regional food.

Brasília is the current administrative federal capital, established in 1960. It was created from scratch with the vision to relocate part of the population to the interior of the country away from the populous southern region. It was built in a modernist style that became representative of Brazil's ambitions of industrialization and progress during the 1960s. Consequently, it became known as the City of Hope. Based on its unique architecture, UNESCO declared the entire city as a World Heritage Site in 1987.

Fortaleza is a thriving commercial center located right on the beach in the northeast region of Brazil. Its position on the Atlantic Ocean gives it a vibrant feel that is in sharp contrast to the nearby *sertão* arid interior region that suffers from devastating droughts and harsh living conditions. Fortaleza's beaches and waterparks attract both Brazilian and international tourists.

The five largest cities in Brazil mentioned here (based on population) are mostly described in superlatives that highlight their unique features. It is true that these metropolitan centers offer jobs in the industrial and financial sectors. However, not everyone benefits equally from the wealth created in these cities. The quick pace of Brazilian urbanization also brought with it other social consequences that include poor living conditions in *favelas* (slums), violent crime, and air pollution. Consequently, recent massive street protests started in 2013, and they have revealed the widespread discontent among the lower-income population that demands better medical care, lower transportation costs, and an end to persistent corruption at all levels of government.

See also: Chapter 1: Overview; Brasília and Federal District; The *Sertão* and Devastating Droughts. Chapter 4: *Favelas* (Slums). Chapter 6: Overview; Poverty, Social Conflict and Protests; Urban Crime; Chapter 11: Modernism in Brazil.

Further Reading

Crocitti, John J., and Monique Vallance (eds.). 2012. *Brazil Today: An Encyclopedia of Life in the Republic* (2 volumes). Santa Barbara, CA: ABC-CLIO.

Instituto Brasileiro de Geografia e Estatística (IBGE). "Official Population Estimate for Brazil, June 2018. https://agenciadenoticias.ibge.gov.br/agencia-sala-de-imprensa/2013-agencia-de-noticias/releases/22374-ibge-divulga-as-estimativas-de-populacao-dos-municipios-para-2018

Major Rivers

A simple look at a hydrographic map of Brazil quickly reveals a complex system of rivers and tributaries; they all drain into the Atlantic Ocean. While the Amazon and Paraná Rivers receive most of the attention, other river systems also provide important means of transportation, irrigation, and clean production of energy. These rivers support the lives of millions of people, flora, and wildlife along their banks.

The Amazon River is the second-longest river in the world at 4,000 miles (6,437 kilometers), slightly after the Nile River, but it is the largest river in terms of water volume. As a comparison, it carries more than ten times more water than the Mississippi River. Its high water volume is created by dozens of tributaries, including the Rio Negro and the Madeira-Mamoré-Grande River, which are themselves two of the largest rivers in the world. Moreover, due to its unique position near the equator, the Amazon River has two separate flood seasons a year (Vincent, 2003, p. 3)

The Araguaia River runs northeast for a length of 1,632 miles (2,627 kilometers) before it meets the Tocantins River, which also runs for an additional 1,522 miles (2,450 kilometers). The Tocantins River empties into the Atlantic Ocean right next to the mouth of the Amazon River. Some of the largest threatened species of aquatic mammals actually manage to thrive on this river, including tucuxi (freshwater dolphins) and Amazon manatees. In addition, the Ihla do Bananal in the Araguaia River is the largest fluvial island in the world without an ocean coastline. It is 220 miles long (350 kilometers) and 34 miles wide (55 kilometers).

The Paraná River runs a length of 3,032 miles (4,880 kilometers) through Brazil, Argentina, and Paraguay. It covers most of southern Brazil. It connects with both the Uruguay and Paraguay rivers and then to the larger Río de La Plata before reaching the Atlantic Ocean. One of its prominent features is the Iguazu Falls, a popular tourist attraction with a collection of 275 waterfalls spreading over a two-mile area. Near the border with Paraguay, the Paraná River also feeds the Itaipú hydroelectric power plant, the largest of its kind in the world.

The São Francisco River is one of the few limited sources of water in the otherwise semiarid northeast region of Brazil. The river runs for 1,800 miles (2,897 kilometers), and it supports light agriculture and cattle ranching along its banks. The water flow is controlled by dams in order to provide drinking water and the generation of electricity from the Paulo Alonso hydroelectric power plant.

See also: Chapter 1: Overview; Amazon Basin and Rain Forest; Earth Summit, Rio 2012; Islands and Archipelagos; Itaipú Hydroelectric Power Plant; World Heritage Sites in the UNESCO.

Further Reading

Instituto Brasileiro de Geografia e Estatística (IBGE). 2010. "Water Resources." Accessed August 1, 2019. http://ibge.gov.br/english/geociencias/recursosnaturais/hidrogeo/hidrogeo_int.shtm

Monteiro-Neto, Cassiano, Tarcísio Teixeira Alves-Junior, and Francisco J. Capibaribe Ávila. 2000. "Impact of Fisheries on the Tucuxi and Rough-Toothed Dolphin Populations off Ceará State, Northeastern Brazil." *Aquatic Mammals* 26, no. 1: 49–56. Accessed August 1, 2019. http://www.aquaticmammalsjournal.org/share/AquaticMammalsIssueArchives/2000/AquaticMammals_26-01/26-01_Monteiro-Neto.pdf

National Water Agency of Brazil. Agência Nacional de Águas (ANA). https://www.ana.gov.br

Vincent, Jon S. 2003. *Culture and Customs of Brazil*. Westport, CT: Greenwood Press.

World Wildlife Fund. "Amazon." World Wildlife Fund. Accessed August 1, 2019. https://www.worldwildlife.org/places/amazon

Mendes, Chico (1944–1988)

Chico Mendes, born Francisco Alves Mendes Filho, was a Brazilian rubber trapper in the Amazon region. He was also a union activist who defended the rights and living conditions of peasants and indigenous populations in the region. He was born in the small town of Xapuri, located in the state of Acre. Like his father, Mendes started working as a rubber trapper when he was only nine years old since schooling was not available in the region. In 1975, he became the secretary of the Rubber Trappers Union. Ten years later, he was the union leader highlighting the threats to the trappers' way of life, which included deforestation, the expansion of cattle ranching, and the construction of new roads in the Amazon region. Trappers often used *empates* (human barricades) as a strategy to block heavy machinery attempting to tear down large forested areas of trees. In an effort to offer an alternative solution to the destruction of the Amazon forest, Mendes addressed the federal government in Brasília, where he proposed the creation of "extracted reserves," or regions set aside to be managed by local communities allowed to harvest the products naturally produced by the Amazon forest, such as rubber, nuts, fruits, and plant oils. His proposal for conservation had cogency; as a result, the United Nations gave him the Global 500 Award in 1987 acknowledging his environmental struggle to protect the rain forest.

While Mendes developed a strong international reputation as an environmentalist, he also acquired numerous enemies. His main adversaries were cattle ranchers in the region who had formed the Rural Democratic Union (UDR) in 1985 to protect their economic interests. At a national level, they mounted a legal strategy to overturn land reform laws. At the local level in the isolated Amazon region, however, UDR members participated in intimidation, beatings, and even the assassination of multiple environmental activists (Rocha, 2013). Mendes received police protection because he was the target of numerous death threats.

Francisco "Chico" Mendes was assassinated on December 22, 1988, by Darcy Alves da Silva, the son of a powerful ranch owner. He used a .22 caliber rifle to kill Mendes with a single shot while he was in his own backyard. The two policemen assigned to protect Mendes were busy playing dominoes inside the house. In December 1990, three men were sentenced to nineteen years in prison for Mendes's murder: Darcy Alves da Silva (the shooter), Darly Alves da Silva (Darcy's father), and Jerdir Pereira (ranch assistant).

Mendes left a legacy as a passionate environmentalist who defended the rights of rubber trappers and vehemently opposed the destruction of the Amazon rain forest. Since his death, over sixty extractive reserves have been officially created in the Amazon area as tools to reduce deforestation in Brazil. In 2007, the Ministry of the Environment (MMA) established the Chico Mendes Institute for Conservation of Biodiversity (ICMBio) with the mission to promote sustainable environmental development.

See also: Chapter 1: Overview; Amazon Basin and Rain Forest; Deforestation; Environment; Earth Summit, Rio 2012; Major Rivers.

Further Reading:

Ministry of the Environment. Ministério do Meio Ambiente (MMA). http://mma.gov.br

Revkin, Andrew. 2004. *The Burning Season: The Murder of Chico Mendes and the Fight for the Amazon Rain Forest*. Washington, DC. Island Press.

Rocha, Jan, and Jonathan Watts. 2013. "Brazil Salutes Chico Mendes 25 Years after His Murder." *Guardian,* December 20. Accessed July 15, 2019. https://www.theguardian.com/world/2013/dec/20/brazil-salutes-chico-mendes-25-years-after-murder

Offshore Oil and Natural Gas

In October 2006, the Tupi oil field was discovered. It turned out to be the largest oil discovery in the Americas in more than thirty years. It is located in the Santos Basin about 160 miles (250 kilometers) off the coast of Rio de Janeiro. The finding was the result of deepwater exploration projects undertaken by the Brazilian national oil company Petrobras. This oil field was found 6,600 feet (2,000 meters) underwater and then under another 16,000 feet (5,000 meters) of sand, salt, and rocks. This type of formation is known as the pre-salt layer. The field is expected to provide between 5 and 8 billion barrels of recoverable oil, which will increase Brazil's general oil reserves by almost 62 percent. Production officially started in 2009. In 2010, the Tupi field was renamed the Lula Oil Field. For the purposes of ownership, the government set up a

> **EXPORTING NATURAL RESOURCES**
>
> Brazil has a wealth of natural resources that have made it a powerful economy based on exports to global markets. These include iron ore, nickel, bauxite, gold, and precious gems. At the beginning of the twenty-first century, Brazil invested heavily in its mining sector, which has already paid dividends based on significant exports. By 2010, Brazil reached the production of industrial minerals (manganese, lead, bauxite, tin, and copper) worth $35 billion U.S. By 2015, extractive industries of minerals, oil, and gas represented 30 percent of total annual exports. As a result, Brazil became the second-largest global producer of iron ore and the thirteenth-largest exporter of gold. Consequently, Brazil has become more attractive for foreign capital investments.
>
> **Sources:** Natural Resource Governance Institute. https://resourcegovernance.org/our-work/country/brazil
>
> Soutter, Will. 2012. "Brazil: Mining, Minerals, and Fuel Resources." *AZO Mining*, July. Accessed June 29, 2019. http://www.azomining.com/article.aspx?ArticleID=51

block labeled BM-S-11 that includes the Lula Field as well as other three oil and gas fields (Tupi Sul, Iracema, and Iara). Petrobras owns the 65 percent majority while the company Gala Energia owns 10 percent, and the BG Group owns the other 25 percent. The combined value of the oil found within the block is estimated between $45 and $60 billion U.S. The large amount of newly discovered oil has turned Brazil into a major oil exporter.

The discovery of offshore oil fields also yielded large amounts of natural gas, enough to make Brazil an exporter to nearby countries such as Argentina and Bolivia. In addition, the national energy needs have also increased. As of 2010, most of the electricity in Brazil is generated using hydropower from river dams. However, recent devastating droughts have made water levels unpredictable. Consequently, there is considerable transformation at play to use hydrothermal systems to produce more energy by using natural gas, which is now in large supply. Actually, offshore fields now produce over 90 percent of the oil and almost 75 percent of the natural gas in Brazil.

By 2010, Brazil was extremely optimistic about its future regarding its reserves of oil and natural gas. However, a surge of corruption investigations in 2014 created chaos in political and economic circles in Brazil. It led to the resignation—and sometimes imprisonment—of multiple high-level politicians with links to Petrobras contractors. The result was that Brazil's congress created significant legislative reform regarding the monopoly of Petrobras in order to make the energy industry more transparent, stable, competitive, and accountable. Now, foreign companies are allowed to bid for concessions in oil exploration and production, infrastructure development, and oil refinery share agreements. Brazil's oil boom turned the country into a major exporter, but its new energy policies and regulations made it more attractive for foreign capital investments.

See also: Chapter 1: Overview. Sidebar: Exporting Natural Resources. Chapter 3: Corruption and Political Scandals; Lula da Silva, Luiz Inácio (1945–). Chapter 4: Foreign Investment; Major Exports; Petrobras, the National Oil Company. Chapter 6: Poverty, Social Conflict, and Protests.

Further Reading

Clemente, Jude. 2016. "Brazil's Oil Production Expected to Continually Increase." *Forbes*, July 12. Accessed July 1, 2019. https://www.forbes.com/sites/judeclemente/2016/07/12/brazils-oil-production-expected-to-continually-increase/#1906ff8d2678

National Agency of Petroleum, Natural Gas, and Biofuels Official Website (ANP). www.anp.gov.br

Oddone, Décio. 2016. "Oil & Gas in Brazil: A New Silver Lining?" *Atlantic Council*, July. Accessed July 1, 2019. http://www.atlanticcouncil.org/publications/reports/oil-gas-in-brazil-a-new-silver-lining

Petrobras National Oil Company Official Website. http://www.petrobras.com.br/pt

The *Sertão* and Devastating Droughts

The *sertão* is a semiarid terrain located in the interior of the northern region of Brazil. The word makes reference to a remote and isolated place, similar to the term "backcountry" or "outback." Since the vast majority of Brazilians lives along the coast, the national stereotype views the *sertão* as extremely poor and constantly struck by catastrophic droughts. The *sertanejos* (people from the *sertão*) live in the harsh conditions of an area that expands to multiple states, including parts of Bahia, Pernambuco, Ceará, Rio Grande do Norte, and especially Piauí.

The climate is mostly determined by the erratic rainfall patterns of the region. Sometimes, sudden storms create flash floods; mostly, however, minimal amounts of rain cause extreme droughts. For several decades now, the inconsistent levels of rain have cleared land for cattle ranching instead of farming. Consequently, the local vegetation has been degraded, and the government does not provide much support for agricultural operations. The result is that subsistence farmers suffer from reoccurring famines.

The local cowboys (*vaqueiros*) are often represented as rugged individuals working with goats and cows while dressed completely in leather outfits despite the suffocating heat. The reason for their specialized gear is that the local vegetation consists mostly of *caatinga*, spiny plants that can severely pierce the skin; even the horses wear protective leather plates. The constant struggle of life in the *sertão* has been represented in both Brazilian literature and cinema. The captivating novel *Vidas Secas* (Barren Lives) illustrates the stoic attitude toward life typical of the *sertanejos*. The 1998 film *Central do Brasil* (Central Station) guides viewers through a visual representation of the harsh living conditions of the region. However, these narratives offer mostly a nostalgic version of the *sertão*. The current reality is that most cowboys in northern Brazil are simply poor agricultural workers who cannot afford to own any land.

Since 2010, the intensity of droughts in the *sertão* has increased significantly. According to Brazil's Agência Nacional de Águas (ANA)—National Agency of Water—the region has experienced the worst drought in decades: the meager rivers are dry, and cattle are dying. Since 2012, more than 12 million people have been impacted, and more than 1,000 municipalities have asked for federal assistance. However, this is the poorest region of the country, and it still suffers from the lowest allocation of government resources (Nobrega, 2014). The government's response was the creation of an assistance program called Garantia Safra that provides money to small farmers who have lost their crops. By 2019, it had already helped over 70,000 families. While helpful, the program is only a short-term solution. Recognizing that water is a vital resource in high demand, the Brazilian government hosted the 8th World Water Forum in Brasília in 2018. The goal was to find creative solutions to existing water problems.

See also: Chapter 1: Overview; Climate; Deforestation; Environment. Chapter 6: Poverty, Social Conflict, and Protests. Chapter 10: Overview. Chapter 16: Overview; Cinema and Film Festivals.

Further Reading

Arons, Nicholas G. 2004. *Waiting for Rain: The Politics and Poetry of Drought in Northeast Brazil.* Tucson: University of Arizona Press.

Mance, Henry, and Serra Talhada. 2010. "Brazil's Backlands Cowboys Struggle to Survive." *BBC News,* April 25. Accessed August 1, 2019. http://news.bbc.co.uk/2/hi/americas/8575075.stm

National Water Agency of Brazil. Agência Nacional de Águas (ANA). https://www.ana.gov.br

Nobrega, Camila. 2014. "Desperately Seeking Solutions for Worst Drought in Decades in Brazil." *Guardian*. March 24. Accessed August 1, 2019. https://www.theguardian.com/global-development-professionals-network/2014/mar/24/brazil-desperate-for-drought-solutions

World Heritage Sites in the UNESCO

Brazil has twenty locations that have been designated as World Heritage Sites by the United Nations Educational, Scientific, and Cultural Organization (UNESCO). Thirteen of these sites are cultural, and the other seven are natural sites. They include colonial towns, architectural ruins, and natural reserves with significant biodiversity of plant and animal life. The variety of these sites reflects the rich cultural traditions of Brazil as well as the beauty of its natural habitats and landscapes. These heritage sites attract millions of tourists to Brazil every year.

The following list includes the thirteen properties that have been designated as cultural sites (and the year in which they were approved):

- Brasilia (1987)
- Historic Centre of Salvador de Bahia (1985)
- Historic Centre of São Luís (1997)
- Historic Centre of the Town of Diamantina (1999)
- Historic Centre of the Town of Goiás (2001)
- Historic Centre of the Town of Olinda (1982)
- Historic Town of Ouro Preto (1980)
- Jesuit Missions of the Guaranis: San Ignacio Mini, Santa Ana, Nuestra Señora de Loreto and Santa Maria Mayor (Argentina), Ruins of Sao Miguel das Missoes (Brazil) (1983)
- Pampulha Modern Ensemble (2016)
- Rio de Janeiro: Carioca Landscapes between the Mountain and the Sea (2012)
- Sanctuary of Bom Jesus do Congonhas (1985)
- São Francisco Square in the Town of São Cristóvão (2010)
- Serra da Capivara National Park (1991)

Another seven locations in Brazil have been officially inscribed as natural sites:

- Atlantic Forest South-East Reserves (1999)
- Brazilian Atlantic Islands: Fernando de Noronha and Atol das Rocas Reserves (2001)
- Central Amazon Conservation Complex (2000)
- Cerrado Protected Areas: Chapada dos Veadeiros and Emas National Parks (2001)
- Discovery Coast Atlantic Forest Reserves (1999)
- Iguaçu National Park (1986)
- Pantanal Conservation Area (2000)

As of 2019, Brazil has submitted another twenty-three properties to be considered by the UNESCO World Heritage Committee. The list below is arranged in chronological order by the year in which they were submitted.

- Eglise et Monastère de Sao Bento, Rio de Janeiro (1996)
- Palais de la Culture, ancien siège du Ministère de l'Education et de la Santé, Rio de Janeiro (1996)
- Parc national du Pico da Neblina (Amazonas) (1996)
- Parc national de la Serra da Bocaina (São Paulo—Rio de Janeiro) (1996)
- Réserve biologique d'Atol das Rocas (Rio Grande do Norte) (1996)
- Station écologique de Taim (Rio Grande do Sul) (1996)
- Station écologique du Raso da Catarina (Bahia) (1996)
- Canyon du Rio Peruaçu, Minas Gerais (1998)
- Anavilhanas Ecological Station (1998)
- Serra do Divisor National Park (1998) More . . .
- Serra da Canastra National Park (1998)
- Cavernas do Peruaçu Federal Environmental Protection Area (APA)/Veredas Do Peruaçu State Park (1998)

- Serra da Capivara National Park and Permanent Preservation Areas (1998)
- Gold Route in Parati and its landscape (2004)
- Valongo Wharf Archaeological Site (2014)
- Cultural Landscape of Paranapiacaba: Village and railway systems in the Serra do Mar Mountain Range, São Paulo (2014)
- Ver-o-Peso (2014)
- Amazonia Theaters (2015)
- Brazilian Fortresses Ensemble (2015)
- Cedro Dam in the Quixadá Monoliths (2015)
- Geoglyphs of Acre (2015)
- Itacoatiaras of Ingá River (2015)
- Sítio Roberto Burle Marx (2015)

See also: Chapter 1: Overview; Amazon Basin and Rain Forest; Brasília and the Federal District; Environment; Main Cities and Urban Regions; Islands and Archipelagos; Major Rivers. Chapter 5: Overview. Chapter 6: Overview; African Ancestry and Influence. Chapter 11: Overview. Chapter 12: Baroque Art and Architecture in Minas Gerais; Niemeyer, Oscar (1907–2012); Ouro Preto. Chapter 13: Overview; Carnival.

Further Reading
UNESCO. World Heritage List. http://whc.unesco.org/en/etateparties/br
UNESCO. World Heritage Sites: Tentative List. http://whc.unesco.org/en/tentativelists

CHAPTER 2

HISTORY

OVERVIEW

Before the Europeans

Before the Portuguese arrived in 1500, historians estimate that between 2 and 6 million indigenous people lived on the Brazilian coast divided in over 1,000 tribes. They belonged to three main coastal groups: the Guaraní, the Tapuia, and the Tupi. However, there are few specific details of their accomplishments because they never developed highly advanced civilizations, such as the Mayas, Aztecs, or Incas, who left clear evidence of their advancements. Unknown to the indigenous people in the Americas, their world was being divided by the Europeans in the late 1400s. The Treaty of Tordesillas of 1494 was a papal decree that divided all the non-European territories around the world between Spain and Portugal. The agreement determined that all the lands located 370 leagues east of Cape Verde Islands belonged to Portugal, including the yet-to-be-discovered Brazil.

The Colonial Period (1500–1822)

On April 22, 1500, Pedro Álvares Cabral was the first European to arrive at the Atlantic coast of what is now Brazil. At that time, however, the Portuguese were more interested in other profitable markets in Asia, India, and Africa; therefore, they left Brazil unattended for over thirty years. It was not until 1534 that King João III of Portugal decided to settle the colony in South America, but not at the crown's expense. He divided Brazil into fifteen hereditary captaincies handed out to twelve individuals. They were supposed to encourage European migration, develop their region, and spark economic activity. The captaincy system was a failure, and the Portuguese Kingdom finally decided in 1549 to take over most of the territories. The first step was to set up the capital city of Salvador in the territory of Bahia.

The Portuguese crown decided to take control of Brazil to convert it into a viable commercial center. The economic history of Brazil has gone through multiple one-product export cycles. However, the need for labor had to be resolved with each period. During the early 1500s, the Portuguese used Indian labor to harvest and export brazilwood, which was highly coveted in Europe for its red dye. The indigenous people died in large numbers due to exposure to deadly diseases brought by the Europeans and by being worked to death. The second export product was sugar; it started in the middle of the 1500s when the Portuguese established large sugar plantations in the northeast region of Brazil. This time, Portugal imported large numbers of African slaves to Brazil to make this venture profitable. In fact, Brazil imported over 4 million slaves during the colonial period, more than any other country in the Western Hemisphere. The sugar industry was lucrative for over one hundred years.

The third economic cycle occurred in the interior province of Minas Gerais when *bandeirantes* (private expeditions of slave hunters) discovered gold, emeralds, and diamonds in the late 1600s. The gold rush created a demographic movement not previously experienced in Brazil, bringing people from around the world to try their fortune, including owners of former sugar plantations who brought all their African slaves. The first half of the 1700s represented an economic impetus for the southern regions of Brazil, while reducing sugar production in the northeast territories. Consequently, in 1763, the capital city was moved to Rio de Janeiro for both political and economic reasons since the southern region had obtained a more prominent role in international trade.

Napoleon Bonaparte took over Portugal in 1808, and it had a profound effect on Brazil. The Portuguese King, Dom João VI, and his court actually moved to South America and settled in Rio de Janeiro. He quickly transformed the country by establishing universities, banks, an educational system, and multiple infrastructure projects. However, when Napoleon was defeated in Europe, King João returned to Portugal, leaving his son Pedro I in charge of Brazil, who in turn declared Brazil's independence on September 7, 1822.

The Brazilian Empire (1822–1889)

Immediately after gaining independence from Portugal in 1822, Pedro I declared himself the first ruler of the new Brazilian Empire. He governed for nine years and returned to Europe, leaving his young son Pedro II (only five years old) in charge of Brazil. The country was under the tutelage of multiple regents until 1840 when the Brazilian parliament declared Pedro II to be old enough to rule a nation at fourteen years old. During his period, Brazil expanded its territory considerably after winning the devastating Paraguayan War (1865–1870). While slavery continued to flourish in Brazil, multiple abolitionist movements also gained strength in the 1800s. Isabel, Princess Regent of Brazil, signed the Golden Law (Lei Áurea) to abolish slavery in 1888, which made Brazil the last country in the Americas to completely abolish the institution. However, former slave owners were not compensated for their freed slaves, and they supported a coalition of landed elite and the military to carry out a coup d'état that removed the Brazilian Empire rulers in 1889. Brazilians were then free to select their own leaders without a monarchy.

The First Republic (1889–1930)

The constitution of 1891 changed Brazil's government in profound ways, especially because it moved away from a centralized structure and provided more autonomy to individual states. While the military still played a significant role in politics, an

On September 7, 1822, Pedro I declared Brazilian independence from Portugal with his famous proclamation of "independence or death" along the banks of the Ipiranga River in the state of São Paulo. He then declared himself the first ruler of the new Brazilian Empire. (National Library of Brazil/Library of Congress)

alliance developed between the two most economically powerful states of São Paulo and Minas Gerais. The former produced immense quantities of coffee, and the latter dominated the cattle industry in Brazil. The agreement known as *café com leite* (coffee with milk) essentially allowed the two states to alternate running the presidential office. The country had a period of economic prosperity based on exporting cotton, coffee, and rubber. Then, during and after World War I, large numbers of immigrants from Europe and Japan flocked to Brazil, which changed the demographic composition of the nation once again. While progress seemed apparent in Brazil, most of the economy was actually dominated by landed elite and political barons; the working classes did not benefit from the economic improvements of the nation, especially the poor states located in the northeast region.

The Era of Getúlio Vargas (1930–1945)

Getúlio Vargas served in multiple elected positions in his state of Rio Grande do Sul and at federal levels. He did not have a military background. He was not likely to become a dictator, but he still ended up ruling with an iron fist. The 1930 election was clouded by accusations of electoral fraud. Vargas was defeated, but massive protests erupted. In the ensuing political chaos, the military intervened to install Vargas as an interim president, but he ruled initially from 1930 until 1945. During this period, he followed a practical ideology without serving a specific political party. He was clearly anticommunist. He advocated for the working classes, and he even received the nickname "father of the poor," but he was simultaneously anti-union. After facing a potential defeat in the 1938 elections, Vargas himself engineered a coup d'état that dissolved the national congress and placed him in complete control of the government by making allegations of a fictional communist conspiracy. The new government labelled Estado Novo (New State) essentially became a military dictatorship that oppressed Brazilians even further. The military stepped in once again and gave Vargas an ultimatum to resign or be deposed. He opted to give up his presidential role in 1945; this marked the end of what has become known as the Old Republic.

The Second Republic (1945–1963)

The new democratic government of 1945 provided more opportunities for universal suffrage. The federal government also took a central role in developing employment opportunities for Brazilians by managing large industries in a centralized management style. Brazil seemed to be on a path to progress and industrial development.

In 1950, Getúlio Vargas managed to reinvented himself and returned to power after being overwhelmingly and democratically elected as president once again. He proposed a comprehensive economic plan to industrialize the nation. During this period, he created two of the most powerful government industries that are still functioning today: Petrobrás and Electrobrás. However, he faced massive social protests, and this time, he could not rule with his old authoritarian style. When the military threatened to remove him from office again, he committed suicide in 1954.

The next ten years were dominated by democratic leaders with ambitious plans for Brazil. President Juscelino Kubitschek was elected under the motto "Fifty Years of Progress in Five." His administration developed massive infrastructure projects that provided employment to large number of Brazilians but also improved the sluggish economy. His most notable achievement was the inauguration of Brazil's brand-new capital city of Brasília in 1960. It was designed and built in a modernist style that is still considered contemporary today. Kubitschek managed to complete his entire term as president (1956–1961) by working with groups from the labor sector, urban leaders, and rural elite. His successor, João Goulart, was a former labor minister who tried to rule with a populist approach that was unpopular with employers, conservative politicians, and the military. During the 1960s, Brazil experienced extreme economic difficulties, but Goulart also had to fight the top military generals for political control of multiple government agencies. Eventually, a group of military leaders deposed President João Goulart to establish a military dictatorship in Brazil.

Military Dictatorship (1964–1985)

It is important to highlight that this particular military dictatorship was not the work of a single person, but rather a sequence of military rulers who were expected to serve their time and then hand power over to their successor as part of the military institution. During this period, thousands of Brazilians were arrested, tortured, disappeared, and killed, sometimes as part of Operation Condor, which coordinated intelligence-sharing agreements among multiple dictators in Argentina, Brazil, Paraguay, Uruguay, Chile, and Bolivia. For more than twenty years, the armed forces imposed censorship, torture, and death in Brazil. While the economy had improved drastically during the 1970s, social and economic conditions turned negative by the early 1980s, and the generals allowed democratic elections again. Tancredo Neves (a civilian) won the presidential election of 1985, but he died of an illness before taking office. His vice president, José Sarney, became the first civilian president in more than twenty years. He faced overwhelming social, economic, and political challenges.

Return to Democracy (1985–Present) and Contemporary Challenges

The process of political reconstruction in Brazil began with the new constitution of 1988. In order to prevent future centralized authoritarian regimes, it reduced the power of the executive office while simultaneously strengthening the legislative and judicial branches. Its progressive nature also provides specific mechanisms to give the individual states more fiscal autonomy. Brazil has managed to avoid another military intervention in its political process, and the 1988 constitution is still in force today.

The next two presidents, Fernando Collor de Mello (1990–1992) and Fernando Cardoso (1995–2003), had the unenviable task of creating economic stabilization while dealing with almost uncontrollable inflation rates. Collor de Mello took multiple unpopular steps to curb inflation. Moreover, he faced corruption charges and was overwhelmingly impeached by Congress in 1992. His vice president, Itamar Franco, finished the rest of the term. Franco appointed Fernando Cardoso as his finance minister in 1993. Cardoso managed to launch a successful program to control Brazil's runaway inflation; it was called the Plano Real (Plan Real). The positive reception of the economic plan made Cardoso extremely popular, which he converted into a successful campaign for the presidency. He managed to serve his full term (1995–1999) and was even reelected for a second term (1999–2003).

The labor movement had increased in strength and ambition since the 1970s. Luiz Inácio Lula da Silva founded the Partido dos Trabalhadores (Workers' Party, or PT) as an opposition force to the existing political structure. In 2002, "Lula" was elected president, ushering in a period aiming to protect the poor and the working people of Brazil. He quickly introduced policies to increase the minimum wage, improve education, and implement new social-welfare programs. He was then reelected president in 2006. His most iconic program was the Bolsa Familia (Family Fund), which still provides aid to almost 11 million of the poorest families in the nation. His successor was Dilma Rousseff, elected in 2011 as the first female president of the country; she was reelected in 2014. She also followed the PT ideology and continued advocating for the disadvantaged people in the country.

Brazil became highly visible on the global stage when it hosted multiple international events: the Miss Universe Pageant in 2011, the 2014 Soccer World Cup, and the 2016 Summer Olympics. However, these events also provided a prominent platform for massive and relentless social protests for Brazilians to express their frustration and distrust of government leaders. As a result, serious allegations of corruption and administrative mismanagement have rocked Brazil's political world recently. President Rousseff was impeached in 2016 and former President Lula was convicted of corruption in 2017.

Michel Temer, the vice president who replaced Rousseff, was also accused of corruption in federal court in 2017, and he was banned from seeking reelection in 2018. Then Jair Bolsonaro (1955–), an ultraconservative politician, was elected president in 2018. When he took over in January 2019, he quickly unveiled policies that were clearly beneficial to large businesses and detrimental to lower-income Brazilians and ethnic minority populations. Brazil still faces seemingly insurmountable challenges and opportunities for the near future that include the unequal distribution of wealth, a lingering economic recession, a dramatic increase in violent crime, an increasingly powerful industrial sector, and the need for more improvements in education.

Further Reading

Brazil Government Official Portal. http://brazil.gov.br

Crocitti, John J., and Monique Vallance (eds.). 2011. *Brazil Today: An Encyclopedia of Life in the Republic* (2 volumes). Santa Barbara, CA: ABC-CLIO.

De Andrade Tosta, Antonio Luciano, and Eduardo F. Coutinho (eds.). 2016. *Brazil*. Santa Barbara, CA: ABC-CLIO.

Edwards, Todd L. 2008. *Brazil: A Global Studies Handbook*. Santa Barbara, CA: ABC-CLIO.

Meade, Teresa A. 2010. *A Brief History of Brazil*. New York: Checkmark Books.

Sachs, Ignacy, Jorge Wilheim, and Paulo Sérgio Pinheiro. 2009. *Brazil: A Century of Change*. Chapel Hill: University of North Carolina Press.

Skidmore, Thomas E. 2010. *Brazil: Five Centuries of Change*. New York: Oxford University Press.

Vincent, Jon S. 2003. *Culture and Customs of Brazil*. Westport, CT: Greenwood Press.

TIMELINE

Year	Events
Before Common Era (BCE)	
9000	The remains of a female body (labeled Luzia Woman) found in Minas Gerais, Brazil, offer evidence of the earliest human habitation in the Western Hemisphere.
6000	Pottery found in the Amazon basin is dated using radiocarbon methods, revealing the presence of an ancient culture in the Americas.
2000	The Amazon basin includes indigenous groups such as the Waika, Shirishana, Yanomami, and Guarajibo.
Common Era (CE)	
1300s–1400s ACE	The indigenous ethnic groups who lived in the Brazilian territory before the arrival of the Europeans included Tupis, Guaranis, and Arawaks.

1494	The Treaty of Tordesillas, named after a small town in northern Spain, divides the non-European lands between the Spanish and Portuguese kingdoms following an imaginary line established 370 leagues west of Cape Verde Islands. The Portuguese received the territory that is now the Brazilian coastal region.
1500	A Portuguese expedition of thirteen ships led by Pedro Álvares Cabral arrives in Porto Seguro; he names the area Ilha da Vera Cruz (Land of the Holy Cross). Brazilwood is the only product harvested by the Portuguese as a valuable export for the next thirty years.
1530	Martim Alfonso de Soussa is placed in charge of creating recognition of Brazil for the Portuguese crown by expelling French invaders, surveying the Atlantic coast, and planting sugar cane as a potential crop for export.
1534	King Dom João III of Portugal orders the division of the newly discovered territory of Brazil into fifteen private, autonomous, and hereditary captaincies. Each captaincy is given to a *donatário*, who had complete political, judicial, and administrative powers.
1539–1543	Francisco de Orellana leads an expedition to explore the Amazon region.
1549	Tomé de Souza establishes the city of Salvador da Bahia, which becomes the first capital of the Governor General of Brazil as a centralized Portuguese colony. The first group of Jesuit priests arrives in Brazil.
1565	The Portuguese establish the city of Rio de Janeiro.
1570s	The Portuguese start a wide campaign to capture Indian slaves from the interior territories. Groups of warriors, who were usually of mixed race (Indian and Portuguese) called *bandeirantes*, are provided with weapons to head to the interior in search of gold and Indians. They would eventually extend the occupied boundaries of Brazil.
1580	King Phillip II of Spain takes over the throne of Portugal, effectively ruling both empires until 1640. In Brazil, Jesuit priests begin the operation of *aldeias* (villages) to convert and educate Indians into the Christian faith.
1590s	By this time, sugar has become Brazil's most significant export to the European markets. Its profitable gains are based on the labor of African slaves.
1624	The Dutch invasion of the northeast region of Brazil (using the West India Company as a vessel) establishes Recife as its capital city. Within twenty years, the Dutch are producing more sugar in their tiny territory than all of Brazil and its vast (but inefficient) Portuguese resources.

1640	Portuguese King João IV establishes the Bragança dynasty and declares independence from Spain. The Portuguese begin to explore and settle the Amazon region, and they establish the city of Santarém.
1649	The Portuguese defeat and expel the Dutch from Recife; the Dutch would eventually leave all Brazilian territories by 1654.
1660	The city and port of Manaus are established along the Amazon River. This post would eventually become the largest and most opulent city in the Amazon region.
1693	Gold is discovered in Minas Gerais, creating a new gold rush that attracts thousands of potential new inhabitants to the interior region. The subsequent discovery of diamonds in the regional mines further increases the interest of outsiders both from Brazil and abroad.
1695	The Portuguese attack and completely destroy Palmares, the largest community of runaway slaves in Brazil, which had over 80,000 inhabitants at the time.
1727	Coffee is first introduced to Brazil. Coffee plantations spread quickly in the Paraíba Valley (Rio de Janeiro area) to plant, grow, cultivate, and export coffee worldwide. At the time, nobody knew that Brazil would eventually become the number one exporter of coffee in the world by the beginning of the twenty-first century.
1750	The Treaty of Madrid offers an agreement of new boundaries between Portugal and Spain providing Brazil with a larger territory.
1755	Marquis of Pombal makes Indian slavery illegal in Brazil.
1759	The Marquis of Pombal expels all Jesuits from the Portuguese Empire and its territories.
1763	The colonial capital city of Brazil is moved from Salvador to Rio de Janeiro. Part of the decision is to obtain larger control of the mining areas nearby and a reflection of the political clout of the southern region.
1788–1789	The Inconfidência Mineira (Minas Gerais Conspiracy) had the goal to declare the independence of Minas Gerais; it was swiftly squashed by the Portuguese. This plot is considered the most daring attempt at independence in Brazil during the colonial period. While there were another five organizers in the insurgency, only Tiradentes was condemned to death because all the others were local oligarchs.
1792	Joaquim José da Silva Xavier (known as Tiradentes, or tooth puller) is hanged for his role in the Inconfidência Mineira. To make an example out of him, his body was decapitated, his head was prominently displayed in his town of Ouro Preto. The rest of the

body was savagely cut into quarters and the parts displayed around town; his house was demolished; and the ground was salted so that nothing else would ever grow on that site again. Today, April 21 is a national holiday in Brazil to remember this iconic martyr.

1807–1808	In November 1807, after Napoleon Bonaparte invaded the Iberian Peninsula, the Portuguese royal family and its entire court of almost 10,000 people move to Brazil. This is the only time a European king actually visits the Americas and eventually runs his entire empire from a colony. They initially arrive at the city of Salvador in January 1808, but move to Rio de Janeiro a month later.
1810	Since the British had provided protection to the Portuguese king and secured his passage across the Atlantic, King João of Brazil signs a treaty providing the British with complete control over Brazilian trade.
1810–1812	King João orders the creation of specific schools of medicine, agriculture, economics, as well as a military academy in Brazil. The printing press arrives in Brazil for the first time, and scholars begin writing a national history.
1815	Brazil is officially declared a kingdom, and João becomes effective king one year later.
1821	King João returns to Portugal, leaving his son Pedro in charge of Brazil.
1822	On September 7, Prince Pedro declares Brazilian independence from Portugal. Then, on December 1, he becomes Pedro I by declaring himself Emperor of Brazil. In modern times, September 7 is a national holiday to celebrate Brazilian independence.
1824	New constitution sets up three branches of government, but it gives the emperor a special feature called "moderating power" providing him with the authority to dissolve an entire parliament, as well as the freedom to appoint regional governors and national senators.
1831	Pedro I abdicates his throne after multiple threats of popular rebellion. He leaves his son as the heir to the throne, even though he was only five years old.
1831–1840	The Brazilian throne is placed in a regency provisionary government until Pedro II can come of age. During this period, provinces obtain partial autonomy from the centralized government.
1841	Pedro II is crowned as Emperor of Brazil when he is fifteen years old. For Brazilians, he was an important symbol because he was born in Brazil.
1850	Slave trade formally ends in Brazil (but not slavery itself) after pressure from Great Britain.
1858	Coffee emerges as Brazil's major export to international markets.

1864–1870	War of Paraguay against the Triple Alliance made up of Brazil, Uruguay, and Argentina. The end of the war proves extremely destructive for Paraguay, but the Brazilian Empire emerges with a military force that had gained strategic experience.
1870	The Freedom of the Womb Law frees children born of slave mothers from this year forward. However, these children had to remain as slaves until they reached the age of twenty-one.
1885	The Sexagenarian Law provides freedom for slaves over sixty-five without any compensation for their owners.
1888	Isabel, Princess Regent of Brazil, signs the Golden Law that abolishes slavery in all its forms. Brazil is the last country in the Americas to abolish the institution.
1889	The military forces Emperor Pedro II out of power and officially declares the first republic.
1890	Author Joaquim Maria Machado de Assis publishes his novel *Dom Casmurro* and establishes himself as one of the most respected writers and playwrights of Latin America.
1890s-1910s	Immigrants arrive in Brazil in large numbers from Japan, Europe, and the Middle East.
1890–1930	The states of São Paulo and Minas Gerais create an alliance to alternate control of the federal government. The alternation of presidents from these two states became known as *café com leite* (coffee with milk) since Minas Gerais had a powerful economy based on cattle ranching and São Paulo was an economic powerhouse based on coffee production.
1891	The first democratic constitution of Brazil is approved.
1894	José de Morais Barros becomes the first civilian president in Brazil.
1895	The first official soccer game is played in Brazil at a competitive level.
1879	Massacre at Canudos (state of Bahia) represents one of the deadliest insurrections Brazil ever experienced when the military kill almost 30,000 inhabitants refusing to give up their plans to develop an independent community in the northeast territory.
1922	The Semana de Arte Moderna (Week of Modern Art) event held in São Paulo initiates a cultural movement that would revolutionize how Brazilians express themselves in art, literature, architecture, theater, and music with national pride. The Brazilian Federation for Feminine Progress is established. The Communist Party is founded.
1930	Getúlio Vargas is placed in office as part of a provisional government after a successful coup d'etat.
1931	The right to vote is approved for literate women over twenty-one.

1933	Sociologist and historian Gilberto Freyre publishes his seminal book *Casa Grande & Senzala* (Masters and Slaves) as a detailed study of races and cultures in Brazil.
1934	A new constitution is promulgated in Brazil, and Getúlio Vargas is elected president of Brazil under the new constitution.
1937	Facing strong opposition, Vargas orchestrates a coup d'état against his own government in order to dismantle congress; he then becomes an authoritarian ruler supported by the military. He introduces the Estado Novo (New State), a euphemism for a repressive dictatorship.
1942	Brazil declares war on the Axis powers as part of World War II. Over 25,000 Brazilian soldiers participated in infantry battles in Italy. It was the only Latin American country to send troops to the war.
1945	A contradiction becomes apparent in Brazil as soldiers are sent to fight for freedom and democracy in Europe, but they live under a brutal dictatorship at home. Consequently, Vargas is deposed by the military on October 29. A new constitution provides states with more autonomy from the federal government.
1950	In one of the most inexplicable chapters in Brazilian politics, ex-dictator Getúlio Vargas reinvents himself, and he is democratically and freely reelected as a civilian president of Brazil.
1953	Two of the largest state-owned industries are created: Petrobrás (the national oil company) and Electrobrás (the national electrical company).
1954	Under the threat of being removed by the military once again, Getúlio Vargas commits suicide by shooting himself in the chest.
1955	Juscelino Kubitschek is elected president. The next few years generate economic growth in Brazil.
1960	President Kubitschek inaugurates Brasília as the new capital of Brazil. With its modernist style, the "City of Hope" becomes a symbol of progress on a path of industrialization. Janio Quadros is elected president, but he has to resign after a few months; his vice president, João Goulart, takes over amid a widespread economic and political crisis.
1962	Antônio Carlos Jobim and Vinicius de Moraes write the famous song "Garota de Ipanema" ("Girl from Ipanema"). The iconic lyrics and sensual melody made Brazilian bossa nova jazz-style of music known worldwide.
1964	The military deposes the civilian government to take over the country; over the next twenty-one years, five generals function as presidents with extremely authoritarian regimes.

1968	The military approves Institutional Act #5, which closes universities, censors the media, and bans labor unions.
1972	Trans-Amazonian Highway is completed.
1979	Congress approves an amnesty law to forgive all political crimes during the dictatorship.
1982	Brazil stops making payments on its foreign debt, which is one of the largest on a global scale.
1985	The military steps down from power, and democracy returns to Brazil. Brazilians vote on the first direct and democratic presidential election since 1960. Civilian government is restored in Brazil.
1988	Environmentalist Francisco "Chico" Mendes is assassinated for defending the rights of unionized rubber trappers and proposing alternatives to the deforestation of the Amazon. A new constitution is approved; it restricts the power of the president. The 1988 constitution is still vital today. Illiterate people are finally allowed to vote under the new law of universal suffrage.
1989	Fernando Collor de Mello is the first directly elected president of Brazil. This is the first time television coverage had a significant effect on the outcome of a national election.
1992	Amid an environment of out-of-control inflation, President Collor de Mello is impeached for corruption and embezzlement; he is replaced by his vice president, Itamar Franco. Earth Summit in Rio de Janeiro brings attention to environmental and climate concerns on a global stage.
1993	Fernando Enrique Cardoso is confirmed as the finance minister.
1994	Inflation reaches a rate of 2,500 percent. Cardoso's program called the "Real Plan" is implemented with the aim to reduce inflation rates and provide a stable economy; his plan proves to be successful. The country establishes the Agência Espacial Brasileira, Brazilian Space Agency (AEB), under civilian control
1995	Fernando H. Cardoso becomes president of Brazil after reducing inflation. He authorizes a controversial distribution of land among the poorest peasants in Brazil.
1997	The 1988 constitution is amended to allow presidents to run for reelection.
1998	Fernando Cardoso finishes his presidential term and is reelected for another term at the executive office.
2000	The celebration of Brazil's 500th anniversary includes multiple protests by indigenous groups claiming racial genocide and poor living conditions.
2002	Brazil wins its fifth Soccer World Cup in Japan. Members of the Movimento dos Trabalhadores Sem Terra, Landless Workers Movement (MST), stage protests and demand land reform at the federal level.

2003	After his fourth attempt, Luiz Inácio Lula da Silva takes office as the thirty-fifth president of Brazil with José Alencar as his vice president representing the Partido dos Trabalhadores, or Workers' Party (PT). He approves the new program of social welfare (Bolsa Família) for poor families as long as their children stay in school and are vaccinated.
2004	In an attempt to increase its global profile, Brazil applies for a permanent seat at the United Nations Security Council. It also successfully launches its first space rocket as part of an ambitious agenda by the Agência Espacial Brasileira, Brazilian Space Agency (AEB).
2005	President Lula da Silva offers a public apology on national television due to multiple allegations of corruption that forced the resignation of high-ranking politicians from the Workers' Party (PT).
2006	With a high rate of approval (especially among the poor), President Lula da Silva is reelected as president.
2007	The Tupi Oil Field is discovered deep underwater in the Santos Basin roughly 160 miles (250 km) off the coast of Rio de Janeiro. As one of the largest oil discoveries in the Western Hemisphere, it would make Brazil not only energy self-sufficient, but also an oil and natural gas exporter. The Brazilian Anti-Slavery Taskforce discovers and frees over 1,000 people working as slaves in sugar plantations in the Amazon region.
2008	A specialized commission in the Brazilian Congress strikes down a proposal to legalize abortion. Brazil became a major oil exporter, but it rejects an invitation to join the OPEC organization.
2009	China surpasses the United States as Brazil's largest partner in trade.
2011	Dilma Rousseff is elected as the first female president of Brazil; she represents the Partido dos Trabalhadores, or Workers' Party (PT). The Interoceanic Highway is inaugurated connecting Brazilian ports on the Atlantic Ocean to multiple Peruvian coastal towns along the Pacific Ocean. The federal government implements a new welfare program (Sem Miseria) with the aim of helping millions of people living in extreme poverty.
2012	Congress approves new affirmative action laws that require universities to increase the percentage of spaces allocated to racial minority students.
2013	Street protests intensify around the country decrying the high cost of infrastructure projects to host the 2014 Soccer World Cup while citizens face higher transportation costs and reductions in health care and other public services.
2014	President Dilma Rousseff is reelected, but allegations of corruption force multiple members of her cabinet to resign from office.

	Brazil hosts the 2014 FIFA World Soccer Cup, but the national pride is bruised when Germany won the cup and not the home team. Street protests continue their momentum, but they evolve to express their discontent regarding endemic corruption and inefficient government bureaucracy.
2016	President Dilma Rousseff is impeached and removed from office on August 31. Vice President Michel Temer takes over the presidency.
2017	February. Brazil and Bolivia sign an agreement for the construction of a massive binational hydroelectric project along the Madeira River at the Guajará-Mirim border. It is expected to cost $4.6 billion U.S., and it will provide electricity to both countries.
2017	July 12. Former president Luiz Inácio Lula da Silva (2003–2010) is convicted of corruption and money laundering. He is sentenced to nine years in prison, but he appeals the verdict.
2017	August. Brazilian attorney general files formal federal charges of corruption against President Michel Temer. He is the first incumbent president to face criminal charges in Brazil.
2017	August. A coalition of Brazilian Army, Navy, and local law enforcement forces conducts a massive security operation in four *favelas* (slums) in Rio de Janeiro in order to control the rampant cases of hijacking and drug trafficking.
2017	August. According to the Economic Commission for Latin America and the Caribbean (ECLAC), Brazil is the leader in receiving foreign investment funds in Latin America. It receives over 47 percent of total direct investment into the region.
2017	President Michel Temer overturns the protected status of the Renca Amazonian Reserve in order to attract foreign investment in mining operations. At 46,000 square kilometers (18,000 square miles), it is almost the size of Denmark. The region is supposed to include rich deposits of copper, iron ore, nickel, manganese, and gold. Politicians from opposing parties have declared this action as the biggest environmental attack on the Amazon of the last fifty years only to benefit private interests. The measure is quickly overturned by a federal court to provide protection to over 10,000 indigenous people living in the area.
2017	In September, the foreign ministers of the G4 Group (Brazil, Germany, India, and Japan) present a formal request to restructure the membership of the United Nations Security Council, and they petition for a permanent seat in the Security Council with veto power.
2017	October. The police arrest the chair of the Brazilian Olympic Committee and the director of operations for the Rio 2016 Olympic Games to investigate allegations of fraud and their participation in a sophisticated scheme to pay judges who eventually selected Rio de Janeiro as the official site for the 2016 Summer Olympics.

2018	February. President Temer signed a decree that places the military in charge of security in Rio de Janeiro to combat extreme increases in street crime and gang violence. He also created a new Ministry of Public Security, a federal cabinet position to fight crime nationwide.
2018	March 18–23. Brasília hosts the eighth World Water Forum organized by the World Water Council. Their mission is "to facilitate water conservation, protection, development, and management on an environmentally sustainable basis for the benefit of all life."
2018	March. In an effort to highlight the importance of women at the technical levels of cinema, the National Agency of Cinema (Ancine) together with the Ministry of Culture (MinC) present throughout March a series of Brazilian films directed by female filmmakers at the Museu de Arte Moderna (MAM) in Rio de Janeiro.
2018	March. The Brazilian Congress approves rules to regulate the use of mobile transportation apps such as Uber and Cabify nationwide while also providing flexibility for local governments to monitor their business practices.
2018	April. After multiple unsuccessful appeals, ex-president Luiz Inácio Lula da Silva is incarcerated to serve a twelve-year sentence on charges of corruption and money laundering at a federal prison in Curitiba.
2018	May. The Open Sky Agreement between the United States and Brazil goes into effect allowing the expansion of air service between the two countries, which encourages price competition and a potential benefit for customers.
2018	September. A massive fire completely destroys Brazil's National Museum, the largest national history museum in Latin America. The 200-year-old museum housed a valuable collection of over 20 million scientific and historical items.
2019	January. Newly elected President Jair Bolsonaro transfers the responsibility from certifying indigenous territories as protected lands from the National Indian Foundation (FUNAI) to the minister of agriculture, which has been actively advocating for years on behalf of cattle ranchers and farmers to have greater access to protected lands to expand economic development. This executive action is a devastating blow to indigenous rights.
2019	January. The Bolsonaro administration makes significant changes to the Freedom of Information Act after a contentious relationship with the press during his campaign. The executive order allows a wide network of federal officials to label more documents as "secret" for fifteen years.
2019	July. The Mercosur commercial bloc (Brazil, Argentina, Uruguay, and Paraguay) finalizes the negotiations for a free trade agreement with

2019	the European Free Trade Commission (EFTA); it is the largest commercial agreement ever reached by the South American bloc.
2019	September. A wave of widespread devastating fires burns at an alarming rate throughout the Amazon region. President Bolsonaro is furiously criticized for initially letting the fires burn following an approach with a misguided euphemism of "environmental management." Brazilian critics have loudly opposed his policies that clearly favor the conversion of protected Amazon lands for cattle raising, mining, and hydropower plants.
2019	November. Former president Luiz Inácio Lula da Silva is released from prison.

Further Reading

Brazilian Government Official Portal. http://brasil.gov.br

Del Priore, Mary, and Renato Pinto Venâncio. 2001. *O livro de ouro da história do Brasil*. Rio de Janeiro: Ediouro.

Galván, Javier A. 2013. "Getulio Dornelles Vargas, Brazil (1930–1945) and (1951–1954)" in *Latin American Dictators of the 20th Century: The Lives and Regimes of 15 Rulers*. Jefferson, NC: McFarland: 40–48.

Globo News Network in Brazil. http://redeglobo.globo.com/Portal/institucional/folder eletronico/ingles/g_globo_brasil.html

Governo de Brasília Official Website. http://www.brasilia.df.gov.br

Instituto Brasileiro de Geografia e Estatística—Brazilian Institute of Geography and Statistics (IBGE). 2010. "Census 2010." Brasilia. Accessed May 15, 2019. http://ibge.gov.br

Mann, Richard. 2019. "Mercosur to Finalize Trade Agreement with EFTA; Bolsonaro Targets the US." *Rio Times*, July 17. Accessed July 22, 2019. https://riotimesonline.com/brazil-news/brazil/mercosur-to-finalize-trade-agreement-with-wealthy-efta-bolsonaro-also-targets-u-s

Meade, Teresa A. 2010. *A Brief History of Brazil*. New York: Checkmark Books.

Ministry of the Environment. *Ministério do Meio Ambiente* (MMA). http://mma.gov.br

National Agency of Petroleum, Natural Gas, and Biofuels Official Website (ANP). www.anp.gov.br

Petrobras National Oil Company Official Website. http://www.petrobras.com.br/pt

Ribeiro, Darcy, and Gregory Rabassa. 2000. *The Brazilian People: The Formation and Meaning of Brazil*. Gainesville: University Press of Florida.

The Rio Times Newspaper. http://riotimesonline.com

Skidmore, Thomas E. 2010. *Brazil: Five Centuries of Change*. New York: Oxford University Press.

Superior Electoral Court (TSE), Official Government Website. http://english.tse.jus.br

Tosta, Antonio Luciano de Andrade, and Eduardo F. Coutinho (eds.). 2016. *Brazil*. Santa Barbara, CA: ABC-CLIO.

United Nations Official Website. http://www.un.org

> **LUZIA WOMAN—THE OLDEST SKELETON IN THE AMERICAS**
>
> In 1975, archeologists discovered a skeleton in a cave near Lapa Vermelha in Minas Gerais, Brazil. The French-Brazilian expedition that discovered the skull and multiple bones in excellent condition tested the remains, and they determined that it was 11,500 years old, which makes it the oldest skeleton ever discovered in the Americas. They nicknamed it Luzia.
>
> Anthropologists determined that Luzia was approximately twenty years of age and almost five feet tall. The controversy arose when it was revealed that her features were Negroid and not Mongoloid. This claim implies that the Western Hemisphere might have been initially settled by African people and not by the North-Asian ancestors of modern-day South American Indians.
>
> **Sources:** Rohter, Larry. 1999. "An Ancient Skull Challenges Long-Held Theories." *New York Times*, October 26, 1999. Accessed June 29, 2019. http://www.nytimes.com/1999/10/26/science/an-ancient-skull-challenges-long-held-theories.html

Álvares Cabral, Pedro (1467 or 1468–1520)

Pedro Álvares Cabral was a Portuguese nobleman and navigator credited as the first European to reach Brazilian territory. He was born in Belmonte, Portugal, but records are not definitive as to what year he was actually born (1467 or 1468). He was appointed by King Manuel 1 of Portugal in 1500 as the captain to the second expedition to India following a newly traced maritime route that went around southern Africa. The two goals of this venture were to bring valuable spices to Europe and to create *feitorias* (permanent trading posts) in India that would break the monopoly of commerce controlled by Italian, Arab, and Turkish middlemen. On March 9, 1500, Álvares Cabral sailed from Lisbon with thirteen ships and over 1,000 men under his command.

Álvares Cabral was thrown off course as he traveled west. When he first found land, he named it Island of the True Cross. On April 22, 1500, he took possession of this territory on behalf of the King of Portugal. This apparent island was South America, and the territory would eventually become Brazil. He immediately sent one of his ships back to Portugal to notify the king of the new acquired territory. After making contact with some of the locals, he moved the fleet north to a large natural harbor he named Porto Seguro (Safe Port). Over the next ten days, the crew met more local people, obtained provisions, and prepared the ships to continue the voyage to India.

During the Atlantic crossing toward Africa, the expedition lost four ships, but it finally landed in Calicut, India, on September 13, 1500. The local rulers allowed Álvares Cabral to establish a trading post, but they were subsequently attacked by Muslim traders. He retaliated by bombarding the city from his ships. He then traveled to Cochin, a port in India where he obtained valuable spices. He loaded the remaining six ships with this important cargo before heading back to Portugal. He arrived back in Lisbon on July 21, 1501. From a financial point of view, the maritime expedition was an overwhelming success for the Portuguese Crown.

The Portuguese explorer Vasco de Gamma was the first European to reach India by traveling around Africa, but the expedition led by Álvares Cabral was the first naval operation to actually stop in four continents: Europe, the Americas, Asia, and Africa. After his return, he married Dona Isabel de Castro, a wealthy noblewoman, in 1503, and they had four children. He was never appointed to lead another major expedition, and he quietly retired to Santarém, Portugal, in 1509, where he died in 1520. In Brazil, his legacy is generally remembered as the first European to arrive to its shores, an action that changed the course of history for all Brazilians.

See also: Chapter 2: Overview; *Bandeirantes*; Timeline.

Further Reading

Greenlee, William Brooks. 1995. *The Voyage of Pedro Álvares Cabral to Brazil and India: From Contemporary Documents and Narratives*. New Delhi: J. Jetley.

Newitt, Malyn. 2005. *A History of Portuguese Overseas Expansion 1400–1668*. New York: Routledge.

Skidmore, Thomas. 2003. *Uma História do Brasil*, Fourth Edition. São Paulo: Paz e Terra.

Bandeirantes

Bandeirantes were the leaders and organizers of *bandeiras* (private expeditions) to explore the interior territory of Brazil throughout the seventeenth century. These expeditions got their name from the Portuguese word *bandeira* (flag), which they used to carry to identify them. After the discovery of the Brazilian territory by Pedro Álvares Cabral in 1500, the Portuguese Crown did not assign explorers to venture beyond the shores, and they were also limited by the boundaries determined by the 1494 Treaty of Tordesillas between Spain and Portugal. Consequently, the Portuguese mostly lived and traded along the Atlantic coast.

Bandeirantes, however, were private individuals in search of riches and not interested in conquering land for the king. Their goals were to capture Indians to sell them as slaves and to find minerals, especially silver and gold, and eventually also diamonds. Most of these fortune seekers came from the region of São Paulo, which was originally called the Captaincy of São Vicente. A large number of them were of mixed racial background (European and Indian) and often spoke both Portuguese and regional indigenous languages. Most *bandeiras* consisted of almost 200 men who were funded by wealthy individuals in São Paulo; their expeditions to the rugged interior often lasted for months and even years at a time. Since they were not agents of the government, they could ignore the political demarcations of the Treaty of Tordesillas. *Bandeirantes*, however, never took political or physical control over the territories they explored. By the end of the 1600s, large numbers of Indians died from disease, and *bandeirantes* focused more on finding minerals than capturing more Indian slaves for agriculture in the São Paulo region.

By the beginning of the eighteenth century, the Spanish did not have any significant settlements in the central part of South America, except for a few isolated Jesuit missions. Therefore, the ownership of unoccupied territories became a significant political issue. To address that problem, the Treaty of Madrid in 1750 declared that the land would belong to whoever had settled it and occupied it, and the villages originally settled by the *bandeirantes* became officially part of Brazil. As a result, their exploration efforts actually expanded Brazilian territory and its borders. This land became the current states of Mato Grosso, Pará, Tocantins, Mato Grosso do Sul, and part of Amazonas.

Bandeirantes are remembered in Brazil as leaders of private expeditions who contributed toward the national territorial expansion and the discovery of mineral wealth. Some of the most famous bandeirantes include Antonio Rodrigues Arzao, Raposo Talavares, Fernão Dias Pais, and Domingos Jorge Velho. They are especially recognized in the current state of São Paulo, where their memory is highlighted in multiple roads, schools, monuments, public squares, and roads. Even the state government palace in the city of São Paulo is called the Palacio dos Bandeirantes. At a national level, however, the legend of bandeirantes is not always completely positive since they did capture over 300,000 indigenous people to be used as slaves in agricultural and mining industries.

See also: Chapter 2: Overview; Gold Rush and Minas Gerais; Slavery, Abolition, and African Heritage. Chapter 3: Overview.

Further Reading

Carvalho Franco, Francisco de Assis. 1989. *Dicionário de bandeirantes e sertanistas do Brasil*. São Paulo: Editora da Universidade de São Paulo.

Hemming, John. 1978. *Red Gold: The Conquest of the Brazilian Indians, 1500–1760*. Cambridge, MA: Harvard University Press.

Meade, Teresa A. 2010. "Bandeirantes" in *A Brief History of Brazil*, 21–23. New York: Checkmark Books.

Brazilian Empire: Pedro I (1798–1834) and Pedro II (1825–1891)

Brazil went from being a Portuguese colony for over 300 years (1500–1815) to becoming a kingdom in 1815, obtaining independence in 1822, and then evolving into an independent empire. The Brazilian Empire lasted sixty-seven years from 1822 until 1889, and it only had two rulers from the Bragança dynasty: Dom Pedro I (1822–1831) and Dom Pedro II (1840–1889).

The presence of the monarchy in South America is a unique feature of Brazilian history. Brazil is also the only Portuguese-speaking country in Latin America. In addition, it managed to retain most of its territory unified after independence because it did not experience internal civil wars (as occurred in the Spanish Viceroyalties of New Spain and New Granada).

In 1808, Napoleon Bonaparte invaded the Iberian Peninsula, unleashing a chain of events that would be extremely crucial for Brazil. The first consequence was that the Portuguese monarchy was forced to go into exile. King João VI, who was ruling as a temporary regent, moved the entire royal family to the overseas colony of Brazil; they settled in Rio de Janeiro. The city became the headquarters for the entire Portuguese Empire. Only seven years later, King João VI elevated Brazil from a colonial status to be part of the new Kingdom of Portugal, Brazil, and the Algarves. In 1820, a successful revolution in Portugal expelled the French from Lisbon, and a new Constitutional Assembly demanded the return of its rightful king to Portugal. King João VI complied with their request, leaving his son Prince Dom Pedro in charge of Brazil to rule as a regent on his behalf. Urged by multiple groups, the young prince (twenty-four years old) declared Brazilian independence on September 7, 1822, and fought a few battles against the remaining Portuguese soldiers. Finally, on October 12, 1822, he was given the title of Dom Pedro I, Constitutional Emperor and Perpetual Defender of Brazil. A new empire was born, and he was officially crowned emperor on December 1 of the same year. The United States was the first nation to recognize Brazil as an independent nation in May 1825. Portugal finally recognized Brazilian sovereignty in August 1825.

Dom Pedro I ruled as the first emperor of Brazil (1822 to 1831) with a constitution that included four separate branches of government: legislative, executive, judicial, and moderating. While it was a liberal constitution, different groups were divided about what the role of the monarchy should be. At the end, it became a centralized government with elected deputies and senators, but with an emperor who served as the executive and also had moderating powers to dismiss the entire parliament if so desired.

The period from 1826 to 1831 proved to be challenging for Dom Pedro I. First, the Cisplatine Province in the southern part of the country launched a rebellion that drew Brazil into a futile war with Argentina in 1826, which ended with the territory becoming the independent nation of Uruguay in 1828. Meanwhile, the Brazilian emperor's father died in Lisbon, effectively making Don Pedro I the new king of Portugal, but he abdicated in favor of his oldest daughter in order to remain in Brazil. Three years later, in 1831, when the Portuguese throne was in jeopardy due to dubious claims by other royal family members, Dom Pedro I left his position as Brazilian emperor and returned to Portugal. He abdicated the Brazilian throne, and left his son Pedro II to be his successor. The problem was that his son was only five years old, and the laws of the time required emperors to be eighteen. Consequently, a custodial regency was created to run the government and to train the young heir until he came of age. The lack of a clear power figure created chaos in Brazil, and multiple minor civil wars broke out. The need for a central governing figure became increasingly important, and a constitutional amendment was approved to reduce the minimum age for an emperor to fourteen years old. On July 23, 1840, he was crowned Dom Pedro II, Emperor of Brazil.

The centralized government approach followed by Dom Pedro II was crucial for the survival of Brazil. He ruled for forty-seven years, from 1841 until 1889. In spite of the initial political uncertainty, the economy was actually robust and stable. The new emperor wanted to modernize Brazil, an approach that brought railroads, telephone service, sewer systems, steam navigation, multiple factories, public electric lighting, and large numbers of European immigrants. The country also increased its exports of coffee, cacao, rubber, and sugar. Dom Pedro also created a professional military that was tested in the successful overthrow of Argentine dictator Rosas in 1852, and emerged victorious from the brief Paraguayan War in 1865.

Dom Pedro, however, did not train a successor to the empire. The rightful heir was his daughter Isabel. She was constitutionally allowed to be emperor, but neither her father nor the ruling classes found her to be an appealing possibility. She was, nonetheless, extremely important for Brazilian history. When her father was out of the country, she functioned as a regent, and she signed the Lei Áurea (Golden Law) in 1888, which completely abolished slavery in Brazil. The outrage of the coffee plantation owners was channeled to support a coup d'état orchestrated by the military. On November 15, 1989, the emperor was deposed, and he returned to Europe with the entire royal family. The period of the Brazilian Empire (1822–1889) transformed Brazil in profound ways. Today, Brazil still celebrates the Day of Independence on September 7th as a national holiday.

See also: Chapter 2: Overview; Isabel, Princess Regent of Brazil (1846–1921); Paraguayan War (1864–1870); Slavery, Abolition, and African Heritage. Chapter 3: Overview.

Further Reading

Barman, Roderick J. 1998. *Brazil: The Forging of a Nation, 1798–1852*. Redwood City, CA: Stanford University Press.

Lustosa, Isabel. 2006. *D. Pedro I: Um herói sem nemhum caráter*. São Paulo: Companhia das Letras.

Meade, Teresa A. 2010. *A Brief History of Brazil*. New York: Checkmark Books.

Skidmore, Thomas. 1999. *Brazil: Five Centuries of Change*. New York: Oxford University Press.

Vianna, Hélio. 1994. *História do Brasil: Período colonial, monarquia, e república*, Fifteenth Edition. São Paulo: Melhoramentos.

Vincent, Jon S. 2003. *Culture and Customs of Brazil*. Westport, CT: Greenwood Press.

Captaincy Colonial System

The Treaty of Tordesillas created an imaginary line (located 370 leagues west of the Cape Verde Islands) that divided the New World in 1494; everything to the west belonged to Spain, and all the territories to the east were assigned to Portugal,

Table 2.1: FIFTEEN HEREDITARY CAPTAINCIES

Hereditary Captaincies	*Donatários*
Maranhão (section one)	Fernão Aires and João de Barros
Maranhão (section two)	Fernando Álvares de Andrade
Ceará	António Cardoso de Barros
Rio Grande	João de Barros and Aires da Cunha
Itamaracá	Pero Lopes de Sousa
Pernambuco	Duarte Coelho Pereira
Baía de Todos os Santos	Francisco Pereira Coutinho
Ilhéus	Jorge de Figueiredo Correia
Porto Seguro	Pero Campos de Tourinho
Espírito Santo	Vasco Fernandes Coutinho
São Tomé	Pero de Góis da Silveira
São Vicente (section one)	Martim Afonso de Sousa
Santo Amaro	Pero Lopes de Sousa
São Vicente (section two)	Martim Afonso de Sousa
Santana	Pero Lopes de Sousa

including the current Brazilian coastal region. After navigator Pedro Álvares Cabral landed in Brazil in 1500, Portugal essentially neglected it for thirty years. When other European nations started to explore South America, Portugal finally decided to occupy Brazil and launched an expedition led by Martim Afonso de Sousa in 1530.

In 1534, the surveyed land was divided into fifteen hereditary captaincies given to twelve private entrepreneurs (*donatários*). Each one of them would become the owner, developer, and administrator of their captaincy. The map of the captaincies was designed as strips that run parallel to the equator line; they began at the Atlantic Ocean and extended inland to the border demarcated according to the Treaty of Tordesillas. Table 2.1 above is organized geographically from north to south.

The captaincy system was mostly a failure, which triggered administrative colonial changes. Only two of the captaincies were successful. Pernambuco thrived by exporting sugar, and São Vicente also exported sugar but generated considerable income selling indigenous slaves. Then in 1549, the Portuguese Kingdom decided to take over all administrative functions of the colony, and it created the Governorate General of Brazil while still respecting the local captaincies as local provinces. Tomé de Sousa was the first governor, and he established the first national capital city of Salvador de Bahia. He also brought the first group of Jesuits, who would eventually develop Brazil's educational system. In 1572, the country was further split into two separate administrative units: Bahia in the north and Rio de Janeiro in the south. As the Brazilian economy developed over the next two centuries, administrative changes sparked a shuffle of captaincies based on multiple territorial mergers, annexation, and division. In 1815, Brazil became part of the United Kingdom of Brazil, Portugal and Algarves, and all the remaining captaincies were incorporated as provinces of the new administration.

Brazilian Captaincies

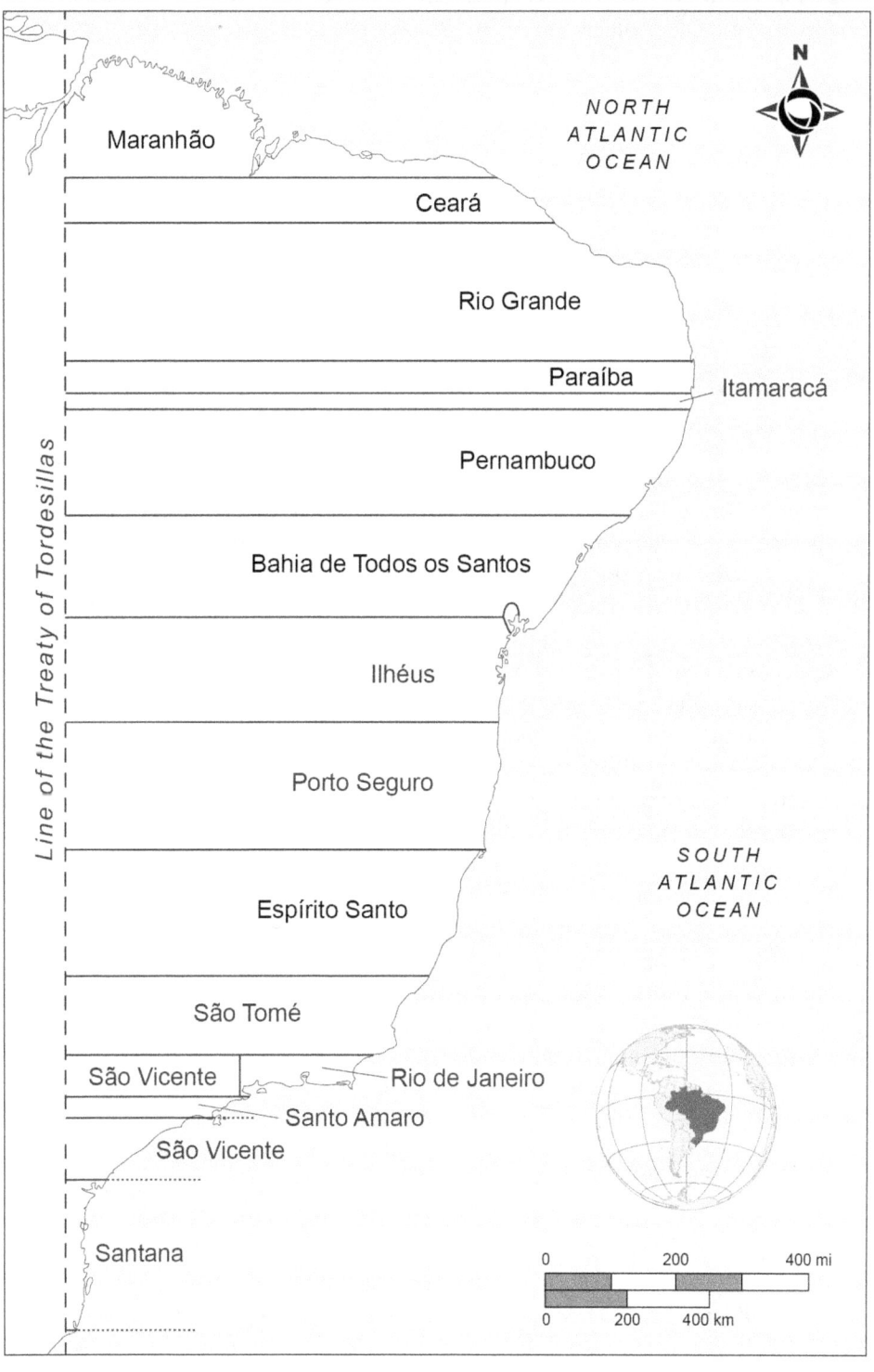

See also: Chapter 2: Overview; Álvares Cabral, Pedro (1467 or 1468–1520); Brazilian Empire: Pedro I (1798–1834) and Pedro II (1825–1891).

Further Reading

Bethell, Leslie. 1987. *Colonial Brazil.* New York: Cambridge University Press.

Lockhart, James, and Stuart B. Schwartz. 1983. *Early Latin America: A History of Colonial Spanish America and Brazil.* New York: Cambridge University Press.

Priore, Mary Del, and Renato Pinto Venâncio. 2001. *O livro de ouro da história do Brasil.* Rio de Janeiro: Ediouro.

Gold Rush and Minas Gerais

The Brazilian *bandeirantes* were leaders of private expeditions who explored the interior hinterlands of the country during the seventeenth century in search of fortunes based on capturing Indians to be sold for slavery. They ventured into inhospitable environments that were not always clearly demarcated for Portugal or Spain. Toward the 1690s, just as the sugar trade and exports were plummeting, these explorers from São Paulo discovered gold in the Mantiqueira Mountains of a territory that is now the current interior state of Minas Gerais. Their discovery sparked a massive demographic movement that deeply affected multiple aspects of Brazilian life and society. The towns of Ouro Preto (Black Gold) and Vila Rica (Rich Village) became the principal locations of gold production and exploitation. The mining process was a labor-intensive activity based mostly on alluvial panning on the local mountain rivers. At the dawn of the eighteenth century, the gold rush had started when thousands of Portuguese colonists from the northeast region, along with their slaves, moved in large numbers to Minas Gerais located north of Rio de Janeiro.

The gold rush prompted the Portuguese government to establish the first comprehensive colonization plan for the interior of Brazil. For over 200 years since the arrival of Pedro Álvares Cabral in 1500, the Portuguese crown had concentrated its activities mostly on the trade ports located along the Atlantic coast. The new gold prospectors and fortune seekers extended the population that settled further west into the interior of South America under the control of the Portuguese. Moreover, the discovery of diamonds in the 1720s brought even more people to the region, including plantation owners who abandoned their sugarcane fields in the northeast region to go south in search of gold, and they brought all their African slaves along with them. Historians in Brazil agree that almost 400,000 Portuguese colonists settled in the area, along with almost 500,000 African slaves who were forced to work in the gold mines. In fact, by 1725, the territory of Minas Gerais became the most populous state in the entire nation. Portugal's role in the mining operations was minimal since they did not have technological expertise in the industry; their role was mostly limited to making sure their bureaucrats collected the "royal fifth of all gold production (or 20 percent)" for the crown. Nevertheless, the massive migration led to a discussion among the two European powers in South America to revisit the terms of their territorial arrangement. The result was the Treaty of Madrid signed in 1750, which provided Brazil with an additional territory of over 6 million square kilometers (2.3 million square miles). The new demarcation created a new official border based on the territories occupied by both Spain and Portugal. The modern-day borders that Brazil shares with its multiple neighbors in South America were roughly the result of the territorial exploration sparked by the discovery of gold during the late 1600s and early 1700s.

Gold exports peaked by 1750, and they provided a strong stimulus to the transatlantic economy. It is estimated that over 75 percent of the gold being used in Europe at this time had been imported from Brazil. The economy had improved dramatically, and a new focus emerged in the southeast region of Brazil since most of the gold was shipped out using the ports of Rio de Janeiro. Gold exports also made the Portuguese crown extremely wealthy. In order to provide better access and flow of gold, slaves, and supplies to the interior region of Minas Gerais, the king moved the colonial capital city from Salvador to Rio de Janeiro, which prospered for almost twenty years. However, the gold boom did not last long. By the late 1780s, the gold supply was depleted rapidly in mines and rivers along the mountainous terrain of Minas Gerais. Neither the Portuguese crown nor individual entrepreneurs used their wealth from the gold rush to invest in creating new industries or an infrastructure foundation for the future. Gold was just another export product in the historical economic pattern of Brazil that went from one boom cycle to the next. By the end of the 1700s, most mining companies were bankrupt and left the region; the country transitioned quickly into a long period of economic stagnation.

The legacy of the gold rush left a physical imprint in the towns in Minas Gerais. During the mining boom, a few Brazilians used their wealth to fund multiple churches that were built and decorated using an ornate baroque style. The towns of Villa Rica, Diamantina, and São João del Rei have elaborate baroque architecture as well as multiple government buildings and private mansions that originated from the 1700s. The city of Ouro Preto was designated as a UNESCO World Heritage Site in 1980 due to its baroque architecture from the eighteenth century that includes ornate churches, elaborate fountains, numerous bridges, and picturesque public squares. The most salient art from the baroque period was created by the talented sculptor Aleijadinho. Today, multiple cities and towns in Minas Gerais continue to display their rich cultural heritage through education and conservation; moreover, it has recently been turned into a profitable tourism industry.

See also: Chapter 2: Overview; *Bandeirantes*; Isabel, Princess Regent of Brazil (1846–1921); Slavery, Abolition, and African Heritage. Chapter 3: Overview. Chapter 6: Overview; African Ancestry and Influence; Indigenous Populations. Chapter 11: Overview. Chapter 12: Overview; Aleijadinho (1730 or 1738–1814); Baroque Art and Architecture in Minas Gerais; Ouro Preto.

Further Reading

Boxer, Charles Ralph. 1969. "Brazilian Gold and British Traders in the First Half of the Eighteenth Century." *Hispanic American Historical Review* 49, no. 3 (August): 454–472. JSTOR, Accessed August 1, 2019. http://jstor.org/stable/2511780

Crocitti, John J., and Monique Vallance (eds.). 2012. *Brazil Today: An Encyclopedia of Life in the Republic* (2 volumes). Santa Barbara, CA: ABC-CLIO.

Meade, Teresa A. 2010. *A Brief History of Brazil*. New York: Checkmark Books.

Priore, Mary Del, and Renato Pinto Venâncio. 2001. *O livro de ouro da história do Brasil*. Rio de Janeiro: Ediouro.

Ribeiro, Darcy, and Gregory Rabassa. 2000. *The Brazilian People: The Formation and Meaning of Brazil*. Gainesville: University Press of Florida.

Skidmore, Thomas. 1999. *Brazil: Five Centuries of Change*. New York: Oxford University Press.

Vincent, Jon S. 2003. *Culture and Customs of Brazil*. Westport, CT: Greenwood Press.

Isabel, Princess Regent of Brazil (1846–1921)

Dona Isabel was born in Rio de Janeiro on July 29, 1846, at the Palace of Saint Christopher. She was the oldest daughter of Brazilian Emperor Dom Pedro II, and her mother was Empress Teresa Cristina. The Brazilian constitution allowed her to inherit the throne, and she was the first heir in the line of succession. Therefore, she carried the official title of Princess Imperial. When she was baptized on November 15, 1846, she received the full name of Isabel Cristina Leopoldina Augusta Micaela Gabriela Rafaela Gonzaga. She also belonged to the Brazilian side of the Bragança dynasty, which was her last name. Isabel married a French prince called Gaston, Count of Eu on October 15, 1864; it was an arranged marriage, and they had three sons.

Princess Isabel served as the regent of the Brazilian Empire three times when her father was out of the country. Each time, she made significant decisions that enhanced her support for abolitionist causes. During her first regency (May 1871 to March 1872), she signed the Freedom of the Womb Law on September 27, 1871, which provided freedom to children who were born after that date. Her second regency (March 1876 to September 1877) was not very popular due to personal reasons. She suffered a miscarriage and then experienced another difficult pregnancy that left her extremely vulnerable and secluded. Her absence from the public eye, even during times of natural disasters in the northern regions, created further social discussions about her suitability to be an effective ruler. Her third and last regency (June 1887 to August 1888), however, would mark her legacy in Brazil. Her highest accomplishment was signing Lei Áurea (Golden Law) on May 13, 1888, which declared the complete abolition of slavery. It was a clear and succinct text that left no room for ambiguity. All slaves were declared free without any conditions. It did not provide any compensation for slave owners or support for former slaves. Brazil was the last country in the Americas to abolish slavery. However, her bold actions had political

> **GOLDEN LAW OF ABOLITION—LEI ÁUREA**
>
> The Golden Law (Lei Áurea) completely abolished slavery in Brazil on May 13, 1888. It was signed by Isabel, Princess Regent of Brazil. The specific language of the law was very clear and succinct in order to avoid any ambiguities. It simply stated the following:
>
> > Article 1: From this date forward, slavery is declared abolished in Brazil.
> > Article 2: All dispositions to the contrary are revoked.
>
> The law did not offer any compensation to slave owners or any support for the freed slaves. Brazil was the last country in the Western Hemisphere to abolish slavery. However, it sparked an outrage from the upper classes, which resulted in toppling the Brazilian Empire rulers and the creation of a democratic nation in 1889.
>
> **Sources:** Candido, Mariana P. 2007. "Lei Áurea" in *Encyclopedia of Emancipation and Abolition in the Transatlantic World*, edited by Junius Rodríguez, p. 442. London: Routledge.

consequences. The royal family lost all support from the plantation owners, who held a lot of political power. They encouraged and supported the military in orchestrating a coup d'état. Consequently, the Brazilian Empire was officially deposed on November 15, 1889.

After being removed from power, the royal family returned to Europe. Princess Isabel spent the following thirty years in France, where she died on November 14, 1921. Her husband died in 1922. The remains of both Isabel and Gaston were returned to Brazil in 1951, and they were finally placed at the Petrópolis Cathedral in 1971. In Brazil, Princess Isabel is still popularly remembered nowadays with the nickname "A Redentora" (The Redemptress) based on her unwavering support for the complete abolition of slavery.

See also: Chapter 2: Overview; Brazilian Empire: Pedro I (1798–1834) and Pedro II (1825–1891); Slavery, Abolition, and African Heritage. Sidebar: Golden Law of Abolition—Lei Áurea.

Further Reading

Barman, Roderick J. 2002. *Princess Isabel of Brazil: Gender and Power in the Nineteenth Century*. Wilmington, DE: Wilmington Scholarly Resources.

Edwards, Todd L. 2008. *Brazil: A Global Studies Handbook*. Santa Barbara, CA: ABC-CLIO.

Longo, James McMurtry. 2008. *Isabel Orleans-Bragança: The Brazilian Princess Who Freed the Slaves*. Jefferson, NC: McFarland.

Skidmore, Thomas. 1999. *Brazil: Five Centuries of Change*. New York: Oxford University Press.

Kubitschek de Oliveira, Juscelino (1902–1976)

Juscelino Kubitschek de Oliveira, or JK as he was commonly known, was the twenty-first president of Brazil. He served his complete term in the executive office (quite an accomplishment at the time) from 1956 until 1961. He was born on September 12, 1902, in Diamantina, Minas Gerais. Before going into politics, he studied medicine and worked as a medic in the military. In Brazil, he is often remembered for providing political stability during a tumultuous period, promoting economic development, and most of all, for the construction of a brand-new capital city built from scratch: Brasília.

When Kubitschek transitioned into politics, he served at multiple levels of both legislative and executive branches of government. His first position was as the mayor of Belo Horizonte (1940–1945), where he worked tirelessly to improve the city's deficient infrastructure. Next, he was elected to Congress as a federal deputy (1946–1950). Afterwards, Kubitschek returned to the executive branch and served as governor of Minas Gerais (1951–1955), where he accomplished multiple public works in the fields of energy (hydroelectric plants and new regional energy company) and transportation (new roads and bridges) that improved the quality of life for his constituents. After dictator Vargas committed suicide in 1954, presidential elections became possible. Kubitschek campaigned for the highest executive office with the slogan "fifty years of progress in five," and he was elected in 1955. Throughout his presidential term (1956–1961), he demonstrated political savvy by working effectively with all the opposition parties. His aggressive agenda of development was focused on five key elements: industry, energy, food, education, and transportation. His administration provided a blueprint for the economy to improve, and it became successful with private investment and without the bureaucratic burden of maintaining state-owned companies.

Kubitschek is best remembered for the development of Brasília (the third capital of Brazil) as a symbol of progress and hope. The construction of this brand-new city started in February 1957, and it was inaugurated in 1960. While the city is widely recognized by the iconic modernist architectural style of Oscar Niemeyer, its strategic role was to develop the interior part of the country. Its new roads and airports connected regions that were isolated, and it opened possibilities for industrial and economic development not previously considered.

After the armed forces took over Brazil in 1964, Kubitschek went into exile to live in Europe and the United States. He returned to Brazil in 1967; however, he was killed in a car accident on August 22, 1976. His legacy is remembered with multiple locations that bear his name, including highways, airports, parks, plazas, libraries, and schools. His remains are buried in the Juscelino Kubitschek Memorial in Brasília.

See also: Chapter 1: Overview; Brasília and the Federal District. Chapter 2: Overview; Timeline; Vargas, Getúlio (1882–1954). Chapter 11: Overview; Niemeyer, Oscar (1907–2012).

Further Reading

Alexander, Robert. 1991. *Juscelino Kubitschek and the Development of Brazil*. Athens: Ohio University Center for International Studies.

Meade, Teresa A. 2010. *A Brief History of Brazil*. New York: Checkmark Books.

Sachs, Ignacy, Jorge Wilheim, and Paulo Sérgio Pinheiro. 2009. *Brazil: A Century of Change*. Chapel Hill: University of North Carolina Press.

Operation Condor and Military Rule

The armed forces of Brazil, including the powerful generals from São Paulo and Rio de Janeiro, carried out a coup d'état on April 1, 1964. They deposed the democratically elected president João Goulart, who fled into exile to neighboring Uruguay in the south. Multiple conservative groups backed the military because President Goulart sought to implement a massive land reform package and to coordinate the nationalization of large companies in order to improve the national economy. The landed elite and wealthy industrialists feared that such reforms were steps toward communism, and they found an ideological ally in the United States. During the 1960s, there was deep concern that the successful Cuban Revolution of 1959 would spread throughout Latin America. Consequently, the United States supported the armed forces coup in Brazil. When it was successful, Washington quickly recognized the military government as legitimate, and it hailed the Brazilian commitment to fight international communism.

The Brazilian military government lasted over twenty years from April 1, 1964, until March 15, 1985. During this period, the armed forces committed atrocities on its own population in order to further their economic agenda, social reforms, and political control. Unjustified arrests, torture, and killings became commonplace. Political parties were prohibited. The media and the arts were heavily censored. Large numbers of people were routinely "disappeared" without apparent reason or justification.

It is important to highlight, however, that the Brazilian military government was not a personal dictatorship. Instead, there were five separate rulers from the armed forces who were expected to serve an appropriate period of time and then coordinate a transition of power to the next military replacement. All five of them received the official title of President of Brazil. In sequential order, they were: Humberto de Alencar Castelo Branco (1964–1967), Artur da Costa e Silva (1967–1969), Emílio Garrastazu Médici (1969–1974), Ernesto Geisel (1974–1979), and João Figueiredo (1979–1985). President Figueiredo faced an increasing number of large-scale demonstrations and massive events of civil unrest. While he was a former general and head of the national Intelligence Service of Brazil, he actually proposed a gradual *abertura* (democratization of the political process) by allowing other political parties to organize. He even promoted the possibility that military power could be transferred to civilian rule via democratic elections in which the armed forces would not present a candidate. The process started by allowing the election of civilian governors in

1981. Finally, democratic presidential elections were held in 1985, and Tancredo Neves—a civilian—won the presidency. However, he fell gravely ill, and he died before taking office. Vice President José Sarney took over as the first civilian president after the military regime.

Multiple dictatorships emerged simultaneously in South America during the 1960s and 1970s. They all had opponents who actively resisted their ironfisted rule. In 1975, the rulers of six South American military dictatorships (Argentina, Bolivia, Brazil, Chile, Paraguay, and Uruguay) created a secret agreement to share intelligence to track and eliminate their opponents, even across borders. It was called Operation Condor, and it lasted until the early 1980s. During this period, military officers from these countries attended the School of the Americas in Panama where the Unites States taught them counterinsurgency techniques and trained them on counterintelligence operations. This was the worst era of political oppression in South America. Dozens of Brazilian officers also went to London to receive training on enhanced interrogation techniques and psychological warfare operations that they put to use in secret detention centers and concentration camps. During the time Operation Condor was in operation, it is estimated that over 60,000 people were killed, or "disappeared." Since the capture, torture, killings, and secret disposal of bodies were all clandestine activities, the exact numbers do not exist in official records.

Dilma Rousseff, a former president of Brazil from 2011 to 2016, was a victim herself of sadistic torture by the military dictatorship in the 1970s. When she was young, she was a member of the urban guerrilla group called Revolutionary Armed Vanguard Palmares (VAR Palmares). Her alias was Estela. After she was arrested on January 16, 1970, she was held for almost three years at the Tiradentes prison in São Paulo where she was severely beaten and tortured with electric shocks. After she obtained her freedom in late 1972, she went on to study economics. Once she entered politics and public service, Dilma Rousseff decided not to play the torture victim in public. Instead, she pushed for transparency and a serious review of the dictatorship and its human rights abuses. In 2014, while she was already president of Brazil, she revealed the results of the detailed investigation carried out by an impartial Truth Commission. The report offered extremely painful details on the systematic abuses carried out by the Brazilian military that included torture and murder of political opponents. The commission confirmed in its 2,000-page report that 191 people were killed in Brazil, thousands were imprisoned and tortured, and 243 people simply "disappeared" during the military dictatorship. The report also made it clear that the abuses were not the responsibility of an individual ruler but rather a cohesive and well-coordinated political plan to eliminate opponents to the regime. President Rousseff heard calls for strict punishment for the perpetrators, but she called for national unity rather than a personal drive to punish her own attackers.

See also: Chapter 2: Overview. Chapter 3: Overview; Human Rights; Rousseff, Dilma (1947–). Chapter 10: Overview. Chapter 11: Overview; Literary Censorship by the Military.

Further Reading

Dávila, Jerry. 2013. *Dictatorship in South America*. Hoboken, NJ: Wiley.

McSherry, J. Patrice. 2005. *Predatory States: Operation Condor and Covert War in Latin America*. Lanham, MD: Rowman & Littlefield.

Meade, Teresa A. 2010. *A Brief History of Brazil*. New York: Checkmark Books.

Nilson, Cezar Mariano. 1998. *Operación Cóndor: Terrorismo de estado en el Conosur*. Buenos Aires: Lholé-Lumen.

Priore, Mary Del, and Renato Pinto Venâncio. 2001. *O livro de ouro da história do Brasil*. Rio de Janeiro: Ediouro.

Rohter, Larry. 2000. "Brazil Opens Files on Region's Abuses in Age of Dictators." *New York Times,* June 9. Accessed July 21, 2019. http://www.nytimes.com/2000/06/09/world/brazil-opens-files-on-region-s-abuses-in-age-of-dictators.html

Rohter, Larry. 2014. "Exposing the Legacy of Operation Condor." *New York Times,* January 24. Accessed July 21, 2019. https://lens.blogs.nytimes.com/2014/01/24/exposing-the-legacy-of-operation-condor

Skidmore, Thomas. 1999. *Brazil: Five Centuries of Change*. New York: Oxford University Press.

Watts, Jonathan, and Jan Rocha. 2014. "Brazil President Weeps as She Unveils Report on Military Dictatorship's Abuses." *Guardian,* December 10. Accessed July 21, 2019. https://www.theguardian.com/world/2014/dec/10/brazil-president-weeps-report-military-dictatorship-abuses

Paraguayan War (1864–1870)

The Paraguayan War is also known as the War of the Triple Alliance. Between 1864 and 1870, Paraguay fought against the alliance of Uruguay, Argentina, and the Brazilian Empire. It was one of the bloodiest wars fought in South America and resulted in massive numbers of military and civilian deaths, although there is no agreement on the exact number of casualties.

After all the independence movements were completed by the 1830s in South America, the emerging countries had regional border disputes. Both Brazil and Argentina had a history of meddling in Uruguay's affairs. In addition, Brazil could only reach its interior province of Mato Grosso by using riverboats up the Paraguayan River, which traversed Paraguay's territory. The prelude to the Paraguayan War was an internal rebellion in Uruguay, which resulted in the death of a few Brazilian citizens living in that country. In order to show regional fortitude, Brazil invaded Uruguay in December 1864, and the dispute was resolved in three months. However, neighboring Paraguay was under the rule of dictator Francisco Solano López, who had aspirations of becoming an influential regional power. He had warned Brazil that Paraguay would defend Uruguay in case of a military intervention.

On December 14, 1864, Paraguay invaded the Brazilian province of Mato Grosso, which triggered the Paraguayan War. Dictator Solano subsequently also invaded the

Argentine border province of Corrientes, which forced Argentina's Congress to declare war on Paraguay in May 1865. In the same month, Argentina, Uruguay, and Brazil signed the Secret Treaty of the Triple Alliance in Buenos Aires. By the middle of 1866, the alliance was fighting on multiple fronts against Paraguay using infantry, naval, and cavalry units. During the following three years, there were massive battles where tens of thousands of people died. The Triple Alliance eventually defeated Paraguay when it took over the capital city of Asunción on January 1, 1869. Dictator Solano was quickly captured and killed. Finally, a provisional government was set up in Paraguay in March 1870.

The War of the Triple Alliance had catastrophic effects for Paraguay. Most estimates declare that it lost between 55 and 60 percent of its population and large sections of its national territory. Argentina took the Chaco area in the north, which is now essentially the Missiones Province. Brazil's gain allowed it to expand further west into parts of modern-day provinces of Mato Grosso do Sul, Santa Catarina, and Paraná.

Brazil emerged victorious from the Paraguayan War. It gained territory, but it also incurred significant foreign debt. In addition, the war forged a more cohesive and experienced military. In fact, at the end of the war, people hailed Brazilian commander Luís Laves de Lima e Silva, rather than the emperor, as a national hero. Brazilian society started to see the monarchy and the military as two disassociated parts of government. Brazilians also started to question the usefulness of an emperor in a country that was already becoming a significant powerhouse in South America.

See also: Chapter 2: Overview; Brazilian Empire: Pedro I (1798–1834) and Pedro II (1825–1891); Slavery, Abolition, and African Heritage.

Further Reading

Edwards, Todd L. 2008. *Brazil: A Global Studies Handbook*. Santa Barbara, CA: ABC-CLIO.

Hooker, Terry D. 2008. *The Paraguayan War*. Nottingham, UK: Foundry Books.

Leuchars, Chris. 2003. *To the Bitter End: Paraguay and the War of the Triple Alliance*. Westport, CT: Greenwood Press.

Silva, Benedita da (1942–)

Benedita Souza Da Silva Sampaio (Benedita da Silva), or simply "Bene" as she is commonly known, is an Afro-Brazilian politician and social activist who advocates for the rights of women, the poor, and all Afro-Brazilians, especially in a country that claims to be a racial democracy. Her humble beginnings make her relatable to the social problems that continue to affect the majority of the low-income population in Brazil.

Since childhood, Benedita da Silva faced incredible adversities and challenges. She grew up in extreme poverty in the Chapéu Mangueira favela (slum) near Rio de Janeiro. She started working as a young child in order to contribute to the household. She did not attend elementary school regularly, but she finally finished the equivalent of high school education when she was forty years old. She immediately attended university and eventually earned a college degree. On a personal level, she suffered several miscarriages and the death of two of her children at early ages. She has been married three times, but she is twice a widow since her first two husbands also died.

Her political career started in 1982 when she was elected to the city council of Rio de Janeiro; she was the first black woman ever elected to that position. She had started on a path that would break multiple political barriers for people of color and women in Brazil. Next, as a member of the Partido dos Trabalhadores, or Workers' Party (PT), she was elected in 1986 as a federal deputy in congress. Eight years later, she became the first female federal senator in 1994. After obtaining significant legislative experience at multiple levels, she decided to seek an executive position and was elected as vice-governor of the State of Rio de Janeiro in 1998. When the acting governor resigned his position to run for president, Benedita da Silva took over as governor. Again, she was the first black person and also the first woman to ever hold that executive office. Subsequently, she left the governor's office to join President Lula da Silva in 2003 as his minister of social development. When the same president decided to run for reelection in 2006, she was in charge of the general coordination of his presidential campaign, which he won. In 2007, she returned home to serve as the director of the Human Rights Office for the State of Rio de Janeiro.

Benedita da Silva continues to be a tireless social and political activist who advocates for the rights of women, the poor, and Afro-Brazilians. As a politician, she proposed and supported laws that would benefit racial minorities, including the approval of affirmative action policies in universities, combating human trafficking practices, promoting better heath in community clinics, and demanding an open discussion regarding racial discrimination and income inequality in Brazil.

See also: Chapter 3: Overview; Women's Rights. Chapter 6: Overview; African Ancestry and Influence; Poverty, Social Conflict, and Protests; Racism and Discrimination. Chapter 8: Affirmative Action Policies.

Further Reading

Applebaum, Nancy P., Anne Macpherson, and Karin A. Rosemblatt (eds.). 2003. *Race and Nation in Modern Latin America*. Chapel Hill: University of North Carolina Press.

Benjamin, Medea, and Maria Luisa Mendonça. 1997. "Benedita da Silva: Community Activist and Senator, Brazil." *NACLA Report on the Americas* 31, no. 1: 13.

Silva, Benedita da, Medea Benjamin, and Maisa Mendonça. 1997. *Benedita da Silva: An Afro-Brazilian Woman's Story of Politics and Love*. Oakland, CA: Institute for Food and Development Policy.

Slavery, Abolition, and African Heritage

During the early 1500s, the Portuguese relied on forced labor to make their overseas ventures profitable. Initially, they captured Brazilian Native Americans and forced them

An illustration from an early nineteenth-century French account of travels in Brazil shows slaves wearing iron collars as punishment. Brazil was the last country in the Western Hemisphere to abolish slavery with the Golden law of 1888. (Library of Congress)

into slavery, but they quickly died in large numbers. Consequently, the Portuguese decided to import African slaves to become the main labor force. Historians estimate that 10 to 12 million African slaves were forcefully transported from their homeland to the Americas. During the 350 years of slavery in Brazil, the country received over 4 million African slaves. From a comparative perspective, this is almost 900 percent more slaves than the number of Africans taken to North America. It is also a number similar to the total number of African slaves taken to the Caribbean and North America combined. In Brazil, African slaves became the main labor force during the Portuguese colonial period (1500–1822) and even after independence in 1822 during the Brazilian Empire era (1822–1888). They were forced to work in sugar plantations, gold mines, and coffee plantations. Throughout the centuries, African slaves in Brazil mixed in high numbers with both white settlers and indigenous populations.

The abolition of slavery in Brazil came about in a series of incremental steps and not as the result of a bloody conflict (as occurred in the United States). The abolitionist movement started soon after Brazil obtained its independence in 1822. José Bonifacio Andrada da Silva was a well-respected politician and abolitionist who had worked on the legal framework to achieve national independence. In 1825, he proposed the notion of gradual emancipation. During the 1840s and 1850s, there was an increase in cases of voluntary manumission in which slave owners simply released their own slaves. Then, as part of the recruitment efforts for the Paraguayan War (1864–1870), the federal government offered freedom to Brazilian slaves who enlisted in the military. Soon after, abolitionist Joaquim Nabuco formed the Anti-Slavery Society to increase political pressure toward complete emancipation. His efforts were influential since the legislative branch began to approve significant laws to address the problem. In 1871, Congress promulgated the Freedom of the Womb Law, which freed children (of slave parents) born after that year. In 1885, Congress also approved the Sexagenarian Law that freed slaves over sixty years of age. However, it was the Golden Law of 1888 that finally provided the complete abolition of slavery. Isabel, Princess Regent of Brazil, signed the Lei Aurea on May 13, 1888. This was an executive action that was ratified by the legislative branch as well, and it went into effect immediately. Brazil was the last country in the Western Hemisphere to abolish the institution of slavery. The African heritage of the slave population had a profound impact on Brazilian culture, including music, arts and crafts, dance, multiple religions, mixed ethnicities, literature, food, and sports.

> **QUILOMBOS AND LAND RIGHTS FOR DESCENDANTS OF RUNAWAY SLAVES**
>
> Article 68 of the 1988 Brazilian Constitution states "the definitive property rights of remnants of *quilombos* that have been occupying the same lands are hereby recognized, and the state should grant them the title to such lands." The government considered Article 68 largely symbolic, but multiple communities quickly filed legal claims demanding titles to their lands. As of 2014, already 2,400 communities of black farmers have been recognized as *quilombos* (former communities of runaway slaves), but only 217 have received land titles. Bureaucratic delays have become common in a program estimated to distribute 4.4 million acres of land. If all the legal challenges and barriers are won, this will be the world's largest slavery reparations program.
>
> **Sources:** Planas, Roque. 2014. "Brazil's 'Quilombo' Movement May Be the World's Largest Slavery Reparations Program." *Huffington Post*, August 26. Accessed June 29, 2019. http://www.huffingtonpost.com/2014/07/10/brazil-quilombos_n_5572236.html

See also: Chapter 2: Overview; Brazilian Empire: Pedro I (1798–1834) and Pedro II (1825–1891); Gold Rush and Minas Gerais; Isabel, Princess Regent of Brazil (1846–1921); Paraguayan War (1864–1870). Chapter 3: Overview. Chapter 6: Overview; African Ancestry and Influence; Mixed Ethnicities: *Caboclo, Cafuso, Mameluco, and Mulatto*.

Further Reading

Araujo, Ana Lucia. 2015. *African Heritage and Memories in Brazil and the South Atlantic World*. Amherst, NY: Cambria Press.

Meade, Teresa A. 2010. *A Brief History of Brazil*. New York: Checkmark Books.

Park, Michelle. 2013. "History of Slavery and Abolition in Brazil." Exoduscry.com. August 30. Accessed August 22, 2019. http://exoduscry.com/blog/general/history-of-slavery-and-abolition-in-brazil

Vincent, Jon S. 2003. *Culture and Customs of Brazil*. Westport, CT: Greenwood Press.

Tiradentes (1746–1792) and the Inconfidência Mineira

The Inconfidência Mineira was a regional Brazilian independence revolt in 1789 that proved to be unsuccessful. Its aim was to obtain regional autonomy from the Portuguese kingdom. By the middle of the eighteenth century, the production of gold in the state of Minas Gerais was declining, and the region could no longer sustain its tax obligation to the Portuguese crown. Lisbon responded by demanding an additional tax. The burdensome tax sparked local discontent and attracted multiple influential individuals to organize an insurrection precisely on the day the tax was supposed to be collected. That day was known as the *derrama*. The leaders of the rebellion were military officers, intellectuals, poets, philosophers, and amateur dentists. Most of the leaders were upper-class members of the oligarchy who were inspired by the success of previous revolutions in France and the United States. Their plan was to lead a rebellion by killing the governor and claiming regional independence on the *derrama* day when most Brazilians would be extremely resentful of the foreign occupiers. However, one of the organizers, Joaquim Silvério dos Reis, notified the Portuguese troops in advance; the insurrection plan was squashed, and the leaders were all arrested.

Queen Maria I of Portugal commuted the original sentences of death and life imprisonment to all the *inconfidêntes* (traitors through a breach of faith) except for one; instead, they were exiled to Angola for the rest of their lives. The remaining leader was Joaquim José da Silva Xavier, who was better known by the nickname Tiradentes (or "tooth puller") due to his occasional practice of amateur dentistry. He was the only leader of the conspiracy without a personal fortune or an aristocratic background. He was imprisoned in Rio de Janeiro during his three-year trial, and he was eventually hanged on April 21, 1792. The Portuguese authorities decided to make a visual example out of him in order to deter further insurrections. The Portuguese authorities accomplished their task in a very dramatic fashion. First, his body was decapitated, and his head was prominently displayed in his hometown of Ouro Preto. Then the rest of his body was savagely cut into quarters, and the limbs were posted around towns in the province of Minas Gerais where he had gathered support for his enlightened ideas. After that, his house was completely demolished, and the ground was salted so that nothing would ever grow again on that site. Tiradentes was the only leader of the Inconfidência Mineira to be executed. As a result, he became a national martyr and a symbol of foreign oppression. Today, April 21 is an official national holiday in Brazil to commemorate his death.

See also: Chapter 2: Overview; Timeline; Gold Rush and Minas Gerais.

Further Reading

Maxwell, Kenneth R. 1973. *Conflicts and Conspiracies: Brazil and Portugal 1750–1808.* New York: Cambridge University Press.

Meade, Teresa A. 2010. *A Brief History of Brazil.* New York: Checkmark Books.

Russell-Wood, A. J. R. (ed.). 1975. *From Colony to Nation: Essays on the Independence of Brazil.* Baltimore, MD: Johns Hopkins University Press.

Vargas, Getúlio (1882–1954)

Getúlio Dornelles Vargas had a profound impact on Brazilian politics and economy during the first half of the twentieth century. He was born on April 19, 1882, and raised in the southern state of Rio Grande do Sul as part of a wealthy family of ranchers. His public service began in 1909 when he was elected as a state deputy (representative). Then in 1922, he was elected as a federal deputy to the National House of Representatives.

Four years later, he led the Ministry of Finance, and then returned to Rio Grande do Sul to serve as its governor in 1928.

Brazil became independent from Portugal in 1822. What followed was a period as an empire that lasted until 1889. Brazil then became a democratic republic, and the constitution replaced the emperor with a president elected directly by the people. However, the presidency position was dominated by two states: Minas Gerais and São Paulo. The former was the largest producer of milk in the country, and the latter dominated the national production of coffee. These two states came to an agreement to alternate the presidency; the alliance became known as the coffee-with-milk (*café com leite*) political period that lasted until 1930. The political coalition benefitted mostly the wealthy regions, but it was detrimental to the poorest states in the country. The alliances of this Old Republic period were disrupted when multiple political parties entered the presidential election race in 1930. Allegations of corruption and electoral fraud were common. However, when Vargas's running mate, João Pessoa, was assassinated, it was widely viewed as a direct violation of the electoral process. His murder brought together a political coalition of coffee producers, multiple opposition leaders, and *tenentes* (young military officers). The result was that the military stepped in on October 24, 1930, to depose the alleged winner of the election, Júlio Prestes, and installed Getúlio Vargas as the interim president.

Vargas had four distinct periods as president of Brazil. First, he served as the temporary president from 1930 to 1934. During this period, he extended the right to vote to all women, appointed new governors throughout the nation, and kept the structure of the legislative system. Vargas took over as president as the world was suffering the consequences of the market collapse in the United States in 1929. Brazil's coffee and sugar industries were deeply affected. Nevertheless, he had plans to move Brazil from an agricultural country to a modern and industrialized nation. Toward the end of his interim period as president, he agreed to form a constitutional assembly, which was in charge of writing the new constitution of 1934. The new assembly elected Getúlio Vargas as president again from 1934 to 1937. During his second period, the country experienced massive protests, but Vargas quickly squashed them using a decree called "90 days of state emergency," which included the suspension of civil liberties and the arrest of political opponents. The national congress kept extending the decree for the last two years of his presidency in order to rule with a repressive style. In 1937, the last year of his presidency, Vargas's regime engineered and orchestrated a supposed threat by communist rebels to take over the country. The government staged a coup d'état in an attempt to "protect the nation." In order to legitimize Vargas's extension of power, a new constitution was created. The third period was named the Estado Novo (or New State) from 1937 to 1945, and this is the stage where Vargas became a dictator. He quickly dismissed the national congress, banned all political parties, and cancelled the scheduled elections of 1938. He censored the media and ordered the national education curriculum changed. This period was an unusual combination of ruling with an iron fist while simultaneously cultivating an image of benefitting the poor populations of Brazil. Vargas approved a large number of welfare programs intended to help the less fortunate, and he also financed popular activities such as soccer team matches, samba schools, and carnival celebrations. The irony is that while being a dictator, he also earned the nickname "father of the poor" in Brazil. Despite the populist message, the number of protests demanding democratic elections continued to increase, and he finally resigned in 1945. A new constitution was created the same year in order to avoid another dictatorship in the future. New democratic elections were held, and Eurico Dutra served as the next president, but he was not very popular. Getúlio Vargas sensed an opportunity, and he organized an alliance of urban workers, wealthy investors, and young professionals to create a political coalition. Following a political makeover, Vargas beat all political odds, and he was reelected as president once again in 1950 to serve from 1951 until 1954.

Vargas still had dreams to make Brazil an industrialized country. During his last period in office, he worked with all the branches of government to create two massive national industries that are still functioning today: Petrobrás (the national oil company) and Electrobrás (the national electricity company). These two companies created the foundation for a modern industry that generated jobs on a massive scale. They also prompted the creation of other industries, including the Vale Mining Corporation, the National Motors Company for car manufacturing, and the São Francisco Hydroelectric Company.

Vargas still faced multiple threats from political opponents, but he could no longer act as a dictator under the 1946 constitution. Nevertheless, he tried to imprison opponents and create false charges to censor the media and political organizations. The military eventually intervened and gave Vargas an ultimatum to resign from power. He decided to shoot himself in the chest on August 24, 1954. He was seventy-two years old. Getúlio Vargas left a mixed legacy in Brazilian life that included a destructive dictatorship, a path for national industrialization, and the creation of welfare programs for the poor.

See also: Chapter 2: Overview; Timeline. Chapter 3: Overview; Constitutions. Chapter 4: Energy Industry: Electricity, Oil, Ethanol, and Renewable Sources; Petrobras, the National Oil Company.

Further Reading

Foundation Getulio Vargas Official Website. http://portal.fgv.br/en

Galván, Javier A. 2013. "Getúlio Dornelles Vargas, Brazil (1930–1945) and (1951–1954)," in *Latin American Dictators of the 20th Century: The Lives and Regimes of 15 Rulers*, 40–48. Jefferson, NC: McFarland.

Hentschke, Jens R. (ed.). 2006. *Vargas and Brazil: New Perspectives*. New York: Palgrave Macmillan.

Levine, Robert M. 1998. *Father of the Poor? Vargas and His Era*. New York: Cambridge University Press.

Williams, Daryle. 2001. *Culture Wars in Brazil: The First Vargas Regime, 1930–1945*. Durham, NC: Duke University Press.

CHAPTER 3

GOVERNMENT AND POLITICS

OVERVIEW
Government Administration

Brazil has had seven constitutions. The current constitution of 1988 defines the República Federativa do Brazil as a federal presidential republic based on a representative democracy. It provides the electoral framework for a multiparty system where the president functions simultaneously as the head of state and the head of government.

For administrative purposes, Brazil is organized into four entities: the federal government, twenty-six states, a federal district (Brasília), and municipalities. Similar to the United States, the federal government functions as a central unit divided into three branches independent from each other: executive, legislative, and judicial. The elected president runs the executive office with the assistance of appointed cabinet members. The legislative branch is controlled by the National Congress, which includes two chambers: the Federal Senate and the Chamber of Deputies. The judicial branch includes the Supreme Federal Court, the Superior Court of Justice, the National Justice Council, and the network of Regional Federal Courts.

The 1988 constitution was designed to counter the national history of strong central military governments in Brazil by providing the states with a great sense of autonomy. The twenty-six states have control over their own administration (following guidelines from the national constitution), and they are largely financially independent from the federal government. The states hold elections every four years for a governor and members of the state assembly. The Assembléia Legislativa differs from the federal legislative branch in one specific aspect: the state assemblies are unicameral organizations with only deputies and no senators. The governor appoints the judiciary but only from a predetermined list of members of the State Law Court made up of attorneys who have passed state-level merit exams.

Municipalities are administrative units at the local level. The *município* is essentially an area with an urban core seat (*sede*) and the surrounding suburbs or rural regions called *distritos*. Municipalities take the name from the main town or city. They are also semiautonomous since they have their own constitution, collect local taxes from citizens and businesses, run their own regional police force, and approve local laws and ordinances, as long as their decisions do not contradict the constitutions at the state and federal levels. The actual administration of each municipality is done by a *prefeito* (mayor) directly elected to a four-year term and a single-branch of *câmara de vereadores* (council chamber), which is also elected for four years.

The Federal District is an unusual administrative unit in Brazil. It is certainly linked to the federal government, but it is not part of the federal administration, even though the Palácio do Planalto Presidential Palace, the official Alvorada Palace Presidential Residence, the Federal Congress, and the Supreme Federal Courts are all located within its boundaries. It does not have the same level of autonomy as the twenty-six states, and it is not organized as a municipality. The Federal District is administered by a governor, and it is officially defined as an indivisible entity comprised of the capital city Brasília and a few suburban cities.

The Electoral System

The administration of government at the federal, state, and municipal levels depends on the active participation of Brazilians in a complex electoral system. Under the 1988 constitution, it is mandatory for all people between eighteen and seventy years of age to register and vote. Only two groups of people can vote on a voluntary basis: teenagers over sixteen years of age and illiterate or disabled people.

The federal electoral system in Brazil is rather complicated because it offers a blend of two democratic approaches. First, Brazilians elect their executive leaders (president, state governors, as well as mayors of state capitals and large cities) following a presidential system using a potential two-round structure. If the initial results do not reveal one single candidate who obtains 50 percent of the vote, then the top two candidates participate in a second round of votes to select a winner. However, mayors of smaller towns and cities—along with federal senators—follow a slightly different system. They are elected by a simple majority following a single round of voting where the winner is defined as the individual with the most votes. Overall, general elections are held every two years. During a voting year, the first round of elections takes place on the first Sunday of October, and the second round (if necessary) is scheduled for the last Sunday of October. Since voting is a civil responsibility, the constitution defines general election days as official national public holidays. Any holiday that happens on a Sunday is taken on the following Monday. Consequently, Brazilians are not required to work so they can fulfill their civic duty.

The electoral system to select representatives to the Federal Chamber of Deputies (the lower house in Congress) follows a different configuration. Brazilians elect their federal deputies following a parliamentary system based on the number of votes their respective political party receives across the entire nation. This system of proportional representation also applies to all state deputies and city council members. In the absence of primary elections for these positions, the same party might potentially have several candidates running for a given district at the same time. All these candidates must campaign relentlessly in order to stand out among other candidates not only from their own political party but also from the other thirty-five parties registered in Brazil. As a result, candidates to the Chamber of Deputies often strategize to become part of a political coalition that is appealing to voters (labor, rural, religious conservative, etc.).

A tangible benefit of this approach is that such coalitions are more likely to attract corporate donations. In addition, they involve more volunteers from multiple social organizations, such as labor unions, farming advocates, student groups, and environmental activists.

The Superior Electoral Court (TSE) has jurisdiction over all election-related matters and disputes in Brazil. The national electoral law defines all the specific rules for candidates running for public office. For example, it requires that all the politicians who hold executive positions (such as governors), and are running for office, must resign six months before the election. Specific requirements also state that independent candidates are not allowed on the ballot; they all must belong to a registered political party. In addition, Congress passed legislation in 1994 that restricts campaign financing. More specifically, Law No. 8,713 requires all political candidates to present to the TSE an itemized list of all the contributors to their political campaigns along with a detailed account of all expenses.

The Brazilian Superior Electoral Court is certainly aware of the complexity of the voting system. It estimates that slightly over 20 percent of voters routinely make mistakes on the ballot, abstain from voting, or leave sections incomplete. Nevertheless, Brazil has a high rate of voter participation in elections that hovers around 85 percent. Sometimes, Brazilians even exercise their suffrage right as an act of protest by showing up to vote and simply checking one or two items on a long list of candidates, coalitions, and propositions. At the beginning of the twenty-first century, Brazilians have frequently expressed their displeasure with political corruption and fiscal mismanagement by using the electoral system. During the last two decades, however, hundreds of thousands of Brazilians have also taken to the streets to protest the unsustainable levels of corruption and impunity that are constantly reported in the media involving their political representatives.

Recent Political Scandals

For the last fifteen years, multiple scandals have revealed unprecedented levels of corruption, electoral fraud, political entitlement, and systematic graft as part of an intricate web of high-level elected officials, party leaders, corporate executives, and wealthy industrialists. For example, in the electoral arena, former president Lula da Silva and the Workers' Party (Partido dos Trabalhadores, PT) were involved in the *mensalão* scandal reported in 2004. The government gave construction contracts to preferred companies to build Brazil's infrastructure at inflated prices. These corporations would then channel the additional money to politicians in the form of cash, cars, homes, and vacations in order to buy their votes. When the *mensalão* scandal became public news, multiple PT politicians had to resign. President Lula was cleared of any wrongdoing, and nobody went to prison. Brazilians were becoming even more pessimistic about their political leaders.

When the economy worsened in 2008, the government could no longer finance the social programs that were the foundation of the PT popularity. In 2012, President Dilma Rousseff announced cuts to public spending and the implementation of severe austerity measures. Brazilians did not take the new policies well, especially in an environment of continuous political scandals. Consequently, massive demonstrations erupted throughout the country in 2013 protesting price increases in public transportation, a failing health-care program, and inadequate schools, especially when the government was lavishly spending money on new stadiums for the 2014 Soccer World Cup. While street protests became more frequent, even larger scandals were about to be revealed.

The federal police launched an undercover investigation in March 2014 into regional money laundering operations in Curitiba, Paraná. Its code name was Operação Lava Jato (Operation Car Wash). Federal agents stumbled into an unprecedented web of corruption that connected federal politicians, party leaders, appointed ministers, and wealthy business owners. The Car Wash investigation of widespread corruption and money laundering operations forced multiple elected officials to resign. Their testimony revealed that the corruption included leaders from most political parties and highly connected businessmen. When politicians urged President Rousseff to stop the Car Wash investigation, she refused. As a result, a few members of Congress accused her of illegal use of funds from the federal budget and swiftly called for her impeachment. In an environment politically charged against corruption, she was investigated and removed from office for six months. Subsequently, in March 2016, millions of people protested against the PT government and demanded the resignation of President Rousseff. After a detailed investigation, she was impeached in August 2016 for inappropriate use of public funds; however, she was never found guilty of corruption or personal appropriation of funds. Vice President Michel Temer took over as president of Brazil. However, he was also accused of corruption and electoral irregularities. On June 2016, he was convicted of violating multiple election laws but was allowed to remain as president. However, he was declared ineligible to run for reelection in 2018.

While Brazilians are increasingly becoming more despondent about politics and public administration, they are very proud of their cultural traditions, especially sports. Brazil captured the world's attention as the recent host of the 2014 Soccer World Cup and the 2016 Summer Olympics. However, even the beauty of sports was tainted by allegations of corruption and bribes. The head of the Brazilian Olympic Committee, Carlos Arthur Nuzman, was arrested in October 2017 as part of an international investigation alleging that he paid bribes to make sure Rio de Janeiro was selected as the host of the 2016 Olympic Games. The investigation uncovered information that the former governor of Rio de Janeiro, Sérgio Cabral, was also involved in the scheme. Cabral was convicted of money laundering and paying illegal bribes, receiving a prison sentence of fourteen years. The current wave of corruption cases against powerful politicians has shown Brazilians that justice can still prevail in a country where impunity was widely tolerated until very recently.

Further Reading

Ames, Barry. 2002. *The Deadlock of Democracy in Brazil*. Ann Arbor: University of Michigan Press.

Edwards, Todd L. 2008. "Politics and Government" in *Brazil: A Global Studies Handbook*, 137–195. Santa Barbara, CA: ABC-CLIO.

Georgetown University. "Constitution of the Federative Republic of Brazil." Political Database of the Americas. http://pdba.georgetown.edu/Constitutions/Brazil/brazil.html

Georgetown University. "Electoral Systems: Brazil." Political Database of the Americas. http://pdba.georgetown.edu/Elecdata/Brazil/brazil.html

Gómez Bruera, Hernán F. 2013. *Lula, the Workers' Party, and the Governability Dilemma in Brazil*. Florence, KY: Routledge.

Kingstone, Peter R., and Timothy J. Power (eds.). 2000. *Democratic Brazil: Actors, Institutions, and Processes*. Pittsburgh, PA: University of Pittsburgh Press.

Lloyd, Ryan, and Carlos Oliveira. 2017. "How Brazil's Electoral System Led the Country into Political Crisis." *Washington Post*, May 25. Accessed August 1, 2019. https://www.washingtonpost.com/news/monkey-cage/wp/2016/05/25/how-brazils-electoral-system-led-the-country-into-political-crisis/?utm_term=.9d492a9128b4

Power, Timothy, and Matthew Taylor (eds.). 2011. *Corruption and Democracy in Brazil: The Struggle for Accountability*. Notre Dame, IN: University of Notre Dame Press.

Superior Electoral Court (TSE), Official Government Website. http://english.tse.jus.br

Watts, Jonathan. 2017. "Operation Car Wash: Is This the Biggest Corruption Scandal in History?" *Guardian*, June 1. Accessed August 1, 2019. https://www.theguardian.com/world/2017/jun/01/brazil-operation-car-wash-is-this-the-biggest-corruption-scandal-in-history

Constitutions

Brazil has had seven different constitutions ever since it declared its independence from Portugal on September 7, 1822. Each one of them included unique features that addressed the needs of the country at that specific time in history.

The Imperial Constitution of 1824

The first ruler of independent Brazil was an emperor. Pedro I came to power in 1822, and he created a unique political system in South America. It resembled more of a presidential monarchy. In fact, he actually started the process to create a national constitution that was promulgated in 1824. It created a political system with four separate powers: the legislative branch with senators and deputies, the judiciary branch ruling the court system, the executive state council that advised the emperor, and a "moderator" that was vested in the emperor himself. The *moderator* position gave the emperor the power to dissolve Congress and appoint federal judges. This constitution also touched on multiple civil matters, such as defining Catholicism as the official religion and excluding all slaves from receiving Brazilian citizenship.

The Old Republic Constitution of 1891

The Brazilian monarchy was terminated when Emperor Pedro II was removed from power on November 15, 1889. A new constitution was created following the model of the United States placing emphasis on individual rights and freedom. By removing the position of a moderator, it created a structure of three branches of government (executive, legislative, and judicial). It also established a federalist system in which states received more autonomy. On the civilian side, it provided universal male suffrage, abolished the death penalty, and created the separation of Church and State.

The Short-Lived Constitution of 1934

Brazil was in economic and political chaos during the 1930s. Getúlio Vargas came to power in 1930 as an interim president. The country was in the process of developing a new constitution, which was promulgated in 1934, and Vargas accepted it in order to legitimize his official position in power. It strengthened the democratic system by creating an electoral court to supervise elections. It also codified important social benefits for Brazilians, including a national minimum wage, paid vacations, and monetary compensation for unjustified firing from a job. This constitution was very progressive in terms of labor protections, but it only lasted three years.

Constitution of the Estado Novo in 1937

On November 10, 1937, Getúlio Vargas announced that he was taking drastic steps to protect the country from a fictional communist coup. His plan included a new constitution that provided unprecedented powers to the president while dramatically reducing the influence of Congress and the judiciary. All political parties were forbidden; state governors were appointed by the president; and mayors were in turn appointed by the new governors. The dictatorship instituted capital punishment for a vague category of enemies and traitors of the state.

The Post-Vargas Constitution of 1946

The military removed Vargas from office in 1945, and a Constitutional Congress wrote a new constitution approved in 1946. Its main goal was to restore individual liberties and to reduce the powers of the executive branch. It expanded the political and economic powers of individual states. It also protected Brazilians from censorship and defined the rights of legal privacy at home. From an electoral perspective, it allowed voters to select different candidates for all positions, including the possibility of selecting a president and a vice president from different political parties.

Military Constitution of 1967

The armed forces took over the country on April 1, 1964, and they installed a series of five military presidents that lasted until 1985. From a legal point of view, they pretended to be a democracy by initially accepting the existing constitution. However, they soon declared that it was obsolete and no longer served the needs of the country. The new 1967 constitution made judicial decisions subject to presidential control, disbanded all political parties, and drastically reduced the autonomy of individual states. Elections were only allowed at the local level but not for federal positions or in cities considered crucial for national security (over 500 of them). All civilian gatherings (such as concerts, theater plays, literary discussions, and art exhibits) of people were considered a threat to public security, and they had to be previously authorized and supervised by the military.

The Current Constitution of 1988–Present

The military allowed democratic elections in 1985, and they lost the majority of elected positions. Consequently, Brazil returned to civilian rule. The process of creating and promulgating a new constitution was completed in 1988; its principal tenants were a reaction to the previous twenty-one years of military dictatorship. This is still the current constitution in Brazil. Its format follows a preamble and nine titles, which are divided into separate chapters and then subsequent articles; the articles themselves are organized into short and succinct clauses listed by using roman numerals.

The 1988 constitution aimed to protect individual freedoms by creating a new Civil Code, a Children's and Youth Code, and a Consumer's Defense Code. It also approved laws prohibiting discrimination against minority and ethnic groups. It was also designed to increase direct participation of citizens in the political process, such as allowing individuals to propose new laws. As the needs of the country change, multiple amendments have already been made to delete contradictory language and to improve the efficiency of government.

During recent years (starting in 2010), Brazilians have engaged in massive street protests regarding the never-ending scandals of corruption and allegations of financial mismanagement that have plagued the federal government. The 1988 constitution protects their civil right to engage in public gatherings and nonviolent protests. While their frustration is aimed at the executive and legislative branches, there is a high respect for the judicial institutions in Brazil. In fact, the Supreme Court has shown the citizenry that it is truly independent since it has conducted trials of corruption against prominent politicians that include former presidents (such as Luiz Inácio Lula da Silva), multiple ministers (including Alfredo Nascimiento, minister of transportation under Dilma Rousseff), and a long list of senators and federal deputies who have been forced to resign. As of 2017, even the former president Michel Temer is fighting legal and legislative battles regarding financial investigations and corruption charges.

See also: Chapter 3: Overview; Constitutions; Corruption and Political Scandals; Lula da Silva, Luiz Inácio (1945–); Political Parties; Rousseff, Dilma (1947–); Temer, Michel (1940–). Chapter 6: Overview; Racism and Discrimination.

Further Reading

Edwards, Todd L. 2008. "Politics and Government," in *Brazil: A Global Studies Handbook*, 137–195. Santa Barbara, CA: ABC-CLIO.

Georgetown University. "Constitutions of Brazil." Political Database of the Americas: Constitutions of the Federative Republic of Brazil (in English). http://pdba.georgetown.edu/Constitutions/Brazil/brazil.html

Kingstone, Peter R., and Timothy J. Power (eds.). 2000. *Democratic Brazil: Actors, Institutions, and Processes*. Pittsburgh, PA: University of Pittsburgh Press.

Superior Electoral Court (TSE), Official Government Website. http://english.tse.jus.br

Corruption and Political Scandals

The Workers' Party (Partido dos Trabalhadores, PT) was in charge of the Brazilian presidency from 2002 to 2016. Their social and economic policies lifted millions of people out of poverty while simultaneously increasing domestic production and negotiating new export agreements. Presidents Lula da Silva (1945–) and Dilma Rousseff (1947–) enjoyed tremendous popularity during periods of their respective terms in office. However, beginning in 2004, multiple scandals became public that revealed unprecedented levels of corruption, electoral fraud, and systematic graft as part of an intricate web of high-level elected officials, party leaders, corporate executives, and wealthy industrialists. In efforts to improve transparency, the PT in power implemented significant reforms to the legal system, which gave federal prosecutors stronger tools to fight corruption.

President Lula da Silva was elected in 2002; it was the first time the PT held the highest office in Brazil. However, the PT only obtained a minority in Congress, which forced party leaders to make coalitions with other minor parties in order to advance the PT's legislative agenda of increasing social welfare, improving education, and protecting the environment. PT party leaders arranged monthly payments to politicians of other parties as bribes for their votes in Congress. Their scheme was discovered in 2004 and labeled *mensalão* (monthly payments). The government would give construction contracts to a few specific companies to build Brazil's public works at inflated prices. These corporations would then channel the additional money to politicians in other forms such as cash, cars, homes, and vacations. When the *mensalão* scandal became public news, multiple PT politicians had to resign. President Lula was cleared of any wrongdoing, and nobody went to prison.

President Lula was reelected in 2006, but an electoral scandal quickly emerged. Lula's campaign manager had paid for a dossier of private information with the intent to discredit political opponents, which is illegal. Again, the scandal was all over the news, a few key PT politicians resigned, but again nobody faced criminal charges. Brazilians were continuously shocked by political scandals, but they were used to a culture of impunity. When the number of reported corruption cases became common, people started protesting on the street. At first, there were no coordinated groups or well-articulated protests; people were simply expressing their anger and frustration.

The PT managed to calm the public discontent when its candidate Dilma Rousseff was elected in 2010 as the first female president in the history of Brazil. Her economic policies created more jobs and improved exports to unexpected levels. She also implemented social policies to help the less affluent population of Brazil. However, she also

Luiz Inácio Lula da Silva (commonly known as "Lula") served as president of Brazil from 2003 to 2011, leading the Workers' Party (Partido dos Trabalhadores, PT). He is recognized for improving the lives of average workers and low-income Brazilians. (Marcelo33158/Dreamstime.com)

cut public spending and recommended severe austerity measures. Brazilians did not take the new policies well, especially in an environment of continuous political scandals. Consequently, massive demonstrations erupted throughout the country in 2013 protesting price increases in public transportation, a failing health-care program, and inadequate schools, especially when the government was lavishly spending money on new stadiums for the 2014 Soccer World Cup. While street protests became larger and more frequent, things were about to get even worse.

In March 2014, the federal police launched an investigation into money laundering operations of small businesses in Curitiba, the capital of the southern state of Paraná. Its codename was Operação Lava Jato (Operation Car Wash). Federal agents discovered that small-time operators were actually working on behalf of large corporations and government agencies. They stumbled into an unprecedented web of corruption that connected federal politicians, party leaders, appointed ministers, and wealthy business owners. The arrest of Nestor Cerveró (a former director of the national oil company Petrobras) provided evidence the company knowingly overpaid construction companies by hundreds of millions of dollars to build refineries, oil rigs, drilling stations, and office buildings. These companies would then channel the extra money into special accounts used to fund the political parties of the same politicians who had originally appointed them to run Petrobras.

The Car Wash investigation revealed widespread corruption and money laundering operations that forced several elected officials to resign. The public (and most politicians) did not expect serious consequences. This time, however, Judge Sérgio Moro took an unusual step in Brazil; he denied bail to all the wealthy politicians and corporate leaders. When he kept them in prison while going to trial, they started to share details, hoping for a plea agreement. They revealed that the corruption included politicians from most political parties and specific wealthy businessmen. The owner of Odebrecht (the largest construction company in Latin America) was detained and sentenced to prison for his role in the construction scheme with Petrobras. The two brothers who owned JBS (one of the largest meat-packing firms in the world) accepted a plea bargain in exchange for testimony and details regarding their illegal donations to political parties. In addition, multiple ministers, senators, and federal deputies were arrested and sent to prison.

Politicians from different branches urged President Rousseff to order the federal government to stop the Car Wash investigation, but she strongly refused. In the middle of this political chaos, a few members of Congress accused President Rousseff of illegal use of funds from the federal budget and swiftly called for her impeachment. In an environment politically charged against corruption, she was investigated and temporarily removed from office for six months. Subsequently, in March 2016, millions of people protested against the PT government. This time, they were vociferously demanding

Dilma Rousseff in Rio de Janeiro. Rousseff was the first woman elected as president in Brazil. She served from 2010 until 2016, when she was impeached and removed from office. (Celso Pupo Rodrigues/Dreamstime.com)

President Rousseff's resignation. After a detailed investigation, she was impeached and removed from office in August 2016 due to inappropriate use of public funds; however, she was never found guilty of corruption or personal appropriation of funds. Vice President Michel Temer took over as president of Brazil, but he represented the rival party, the Brazilian Democratic Party Movement, PMDB. President Temer, however, was immediately involved in legal controversies. On June 2016, he was convicted of violating multiple election laws. He was allowed to remain as president, but he was declared ineligible to run for reelection in 2018.

In April 2018, after multiple unsuccessful appeals, former president Luiz Inácio Lula da Silva was incarcerated to serve a twelve-year sentence for charges of corruption and money laundering at a federal prison in Curitiba. In the meantime, Brazil's economy has contracted, unemployment is increasing, and foreign investment has slowed down. It appears that all Brazilians will end up paying the price for all the recent political scandals of corruption.

See also: Chapter 3: Overview; Lula da Silva, Luiz Inácio (1945–); Political Parties; Rousseff, Dilma (1947–); Temer, Michel (1940–); Workers' Party (PT) in Power. Chapter 6: Poverty, Social Conflict, and Protests.

Further Reading

Connors, Will. 2016. "5 Things to Know about Brazil's Corruption Scandal." *Wall Street Journal,* March 4. Accessed July 1, 2019. https://blogs.wsj.com/briefly/2016/03/04/5-things-to-know-about-brazils-corruption-scandal

Gómez Bruera, Hernán F. 2013. *Lula, the Workers' Party, and the Governability Dilemma in Brazil.* Florence, KY: Routledge.

Kiernan, Paul. 2015. "Brazil's Petrobras Reports Nearly $17 Billion in Asset and Corruption Charges." *Wall Street Journal,* April 22. Accessed July 1, 2019. https://www.wsj.com/articles/brazils-petrobras-reports-nearly-17-billion-impairment-on-assets-corruption-1429744336

Motta Ferraz, Octavio Luiz. 2017. "As Corruption Scandals Spread, Brazil Struggles to Uphold Rule of Law." *Econotimes,* September 11. Accessed July 1, 2019. https://www.econotimes.com/As-corruption-scandals-spread-Brazil-struggles-to-uphold-the-rule-of-law-892137

Watts, Jonathan. 2017. "Operation Car Wash: Is this the Biggest Corruption Scandal in History?" *Guardian,* June 1. Accessed July 1, 2019. https://www.theguardian.com/world/2017/jun/01/brazil-operation-car-wash-is-this-the-biggest-corruption-scandal-in-history

Electoral System

According to the present-day constitution approved in 1988, voting is both a right and a responsibility. Consequently, it is mandatory for all people between eighteen and seventy years of age to register and vote. Teenagers can vote on a voluntary basis beginning at sixteen years old. It is also voluntary for all people who are illiterate or disabled.

Brazil's electoral system is very complex because it combines sections of two democratic approaches. First, Brazilians elect their executive leaders (president, state governors, as well as mayors of state capitals and large cities) following a presidential system using a potential two-round configuration. If there is no single candidate who obtains 50 percent of the vote, then the top two candidates participate in a second round of votes. However, mayors of smaller towns and cities—along with federal senators—are elected by a simple majority following a single round of voting where the winner is defined as the individual with the most votes. The first round of elections takes place on the first Sunday of October, and the second round (if necessary) is scheduled for the last Sunday of October. Overall, general election days are defined as official national public holidays in the constitution. Any holiday that happens on a Sunday is taken on the following Monday.

In addition, the House of Deputies (the lower house in Congress) elects its members following a parliamentary system based on the number of votes their respective political party receives across the entire nation. This system of proportional representation also applies to all state deputies and city council members. All these candidates must campaign relentlessly in order to stand out among other candidates not only from their own political party but also from the other thirty-five parties registered in Brazil. One effective strategy for candidates to the House of Deputies to stand out is to become part of a political coalition that resonates with voters (labor, rural, religious conservative, etc.). Such coalitions are more likely to attract corporate donations. They also involve more volunteers from multiple social organizations, such as labor unions, farming advocates, and student groups.

Brazilian electoral law also provides detailed rules for all candidates running for public office. For example, it requires that all the politicians who hold executive positions (such as governors), and are running for office, must resign six months before the election. Independent candidates are not allowed on the ballot; they all must belong to a registered political party. Moreover, Congress passed legislation in 1994 that restricts campaign financing. More specifically, Law No. 8,713 requires all political candidates to present a detailed list of all the contributors to their political campaigns along with a detailed account of all expenses to the Superior Electoral Court (TSE).

Given the complexity of the voting system in Brazil, the Superior Electoral Court estimates that slightly over 20 percent of voters routinely make mistakes on the ballot, abstain from voting, or leave sections incomplete. Nevertheless, Brazil has a high rate of voter participation in elections that hovers around 85 percent. Sometimes, Brazilians even exercise their suffrage right as an act of protest by showing up to vote and simply checking one or two items on a long list of candidates, coalitions, and propositions. At the beginning of the twenty-first century, Brazilians have frequently expressed their displeasure with political corruption and fiscal mismanagement by using the electoral system.

See also: Chapter 3: Overview; Constitutions; Political Parties. Chapter 6: Overview. Chapter 10: Intermediaries: *Colonels* and *Despachantes*.

Further Reading

Edwards, Todd L. 2008. "Politics and Government," in *Brazil: A Global Studies Handbook*, 137–195. Santa Barbara, CA: ABC-CLIO.

Georgetown University. "Political Database of the Americas: Electoral Systems, Brazil." http://pdba.georgetown.edu/Elecdata/Brazil/brazil.html

Kingstone, Peter R., and Timothy J. Power (eds.). 2000. *Democratic Brazil: Actors, Institutions, and Processes*. Pittsburgh, PA: University of Pittsburgh Press.

Lloyd, Ryan, and Carlos Oliveira. 2016. "How Brazil's Electoral System Led the Country into Political Crisis." *Washington Post,* May 25. Accessed July 25, 2019. https://www.washingtonpost.com/news/monkey-cage/wp/2016/05/25/how-brazils-electoral-system-led-the-country-into-political-crisis/?utm_term=.9d492a9128b4

Superior Electoral Court (TSE), Official Government Website. http://english.tse.jus.br

Foreign Policy

The 1988 Brazilian constitution provides the president with the authority to set foreign policy priorities while Congress reviews international treaties, ratifies diplomatic appointments, and sets the legislative framework needed to carry out foreign policy. The Ministry of Foreign Affairs (known as Itamaraty) is the government agency that conducts foreign relations with other nations and international agencies. Diplomats follow a pragmatic approach to advance Brazilian priorities related to politics, economics, business, finances, culture, and consular relations. During the twenty-first century, Brazil has followed a parallel approach to strengthen its relations with its South American neighbors while simultaneously increasing its diplomatic stature at a global stage.

Brazil was one of the founding-member countries of the United Nations (UN) in 1945. It has been elected a member of the UN Security Council ten times, and it has provided troops for peacekeeping operations in the Middle East, Mozambique, Congo, Angola, Cypress, Haiti, and East Timor. To enhance its international presence, Brazil also maintains ambassadors in New York, Rome, Paris, and Geneva that serve as headquarters for multiple UN agencies, including the UN Children's Fund (UNICEF), the World Food Program (WFP), the UN High Commissioner for Refugees (UNHCR), and the World Health Organization (WHO). Since the 1980s, Brazil has been more assertive in seeking a permanent seat in the UN Security Council with veto power. To accomplish its goal, it joined the Group of Four (G4), which includes Brazil, Japan, India, and Germany. In 2017, the G4 formally requested a more definitive role in the Security Council. Their claim is that the expansion of members to the Security Council will make the body more legitimate, effective, and representative of the needs of all countries.

> **FOREIGN AID: FROM RECIPIENT TO DONOR**
>
> Brazil has recently discovered international aid as an important tool of its foreign policy. This is a crucial transition because Brazil used to receive foreign aid, and it is now a donor of international assistance. The Agência Brasileira de Cooperação (ABC) coordinates foreign aid by focusing on agricultural projects and education partnerships. The flagship program called South-to-South is designed to work with other developing countries in Latin America and Africa. For example, ABC coordinates Food Acquisition Programs in Ethiopia, Malawi, Niger, Senegal, and Mozambique where it purchases agricultural products from local small farmers and then distributes the food to vulnerable populations. These successful programs now work in coordination with the United Nations World Food Program (WFP).
>
> **Sources:** Troilo, Pete. 2012. "Setting Its Own Course, Brazil Foreign Aid Expands and Evolves." *Devex News*, July 9. Accessed June 29, 2019. https://www.devex.com/news/setting-its-own-course-brazil-foreign-aid-expands-and-evolves-78631

Brazil also views foreign aid as a crucial component of foreign policy. It offers approximately $1 billion U.S. every year; almost 60 percent goes to countries in Africa, 20 percent to Latin America, and smaller amounts to Asia. The main sectors supported with overseas aid are education and agricultural development. The aid is provided not only in monetary terms, but also in technical support, scientific expertise, and economic advice.

During the twenty-first century, Brazil has pursued multiple strategic alliances. President Dilma Rousseff increased Brazil's leadership role as a regional power in Mercosur (or Mercosul in Portuguese), a trade group that includes Brazil, Argentina, Venezuela, Uruguay, and Paraguay. President Lula da Silva (1945–) became a driving force representing Brazil as part of BRICS, a powerful group that includes Brazil, Russia, India, China, and South Africa. Their combined economic and political power has the potential to significantly influence world diplomacy.

See also: Chapter 3: Overview; Constitutions; Lula da Silva, Luiz Inácio (1945–); Rousseff, Dilma (1947–); United Nations and Brazil. Chapter 4: BRICS Economic Group; Mercosul/Mercosur.

Further Reading

Frayssinet, Fabiana. 2011. "Brazil: From Development Aid Recipient to Donor." *Inter Press Service (IPS) News Agency*, April 15. Accessed July 29, 2019. http://www.ipsnews.net/2011/04/brazil-from-development-aid-recipient-to-donor

General Assembly of the United Nations Official Website. http://www.un.org/en/ga

Kraul, Chris, and Patrick McDonnell. 2008. "Brazil's Lula Takes Center Stage in Latin America." *Los Angeles Times*, October 5. Accessed July 29, 2019. http://latimesblogs.latimes.com/laplaza/2008/10/brazils-lula-ta.html

Mercosur Mercado Común del Sur Official Website. http://www.mercosur.int

Ministry of Foreign Affairs of Brazil Official Website. http://www.itamaraty.gov.br/en

United Nations Official Website. http://www.un.org

Human Rights

Brazil ratified the American Convention of Human Rights when it was created in 1969. This organization assigned the Inter-American Commission of Human Rights to ensure that nation members complied with the articles of the agreement. Working in parallel fashion, Brazil upholds the right of its citizens to free speech, and it strongly condemns slavery and torture. The country has also passed specific laws against modern-day slavery, child abuse, and police brutality. However, the legal advances seem to exist mostly on paper since the reality is very different for Brazilians.

Human Rights Watch representatives in Brazil routinely report on excessive numbers of cases of domestic abuse, slavery, and violence against children. While multiple laws have been approved to protect women, most police officers are not trained to deal with these cases of violence, and actually present barriers for women who want to report their suffering. For example, documented cases show that attacks against women have increased 139 percent from 2010 to 2015 in the state of Roraima, the region with the highest statistics of such abuses. In the case of slavery, it is strictly forbidden in the Brazilian constitution. However, "debt slavery" is still a pervasive problem for workers in isolated Amazon cattle ranches who are forced to work to pay a never-ending debt. The government created a specialized force in 1995 to address the problem. Since its genesis, it has actually freed over 30,000 people from slavery, but the problem has not been eradicated. The constitution also provides specific protections for children, and Brazil works with the United Nations (UN) and UNICEF to guarantee children's rights. Nevertheless, the UN reports that over 500,000 children in Brazil are sexually exploited every year. It also corroborates that most sexual crimes committed against children are hardly ever investigated.

The violations of basic human rights in Brazil have recently sparked multiple riots and social protests. They are mostly related to the inhumane treatment of people in prisons, as well as generalized police brutality and torture of detainees. The National Penitentiary Department has reported that, for over a decade, the prison system has been operating over 35 percent beyond its designed capacity, which leads to excessive overcrowding, unsanitary conditions, and inadequate protection for prisoners. It is common for prisoners to be beaten, tortured, and even killed without official explanations. The 1988 constitution specifically forbids torture. However, the Brazilian National Human Rights Secretariat acknowledged in 2017 that torture existed within the penal system. Moreover, based on excessive numbers of police killings in Rio de Janeiro, Amnesty International declared in 2017 that the Brazilian government is not doing enough to stem the human rights crisis. Most cases of police brutality are not reported because Brazilians in general fear that officers operate in an environment of impunity and nothing will be done to resolve this social problem.

See also: Chapter 3: Overview; Constitutions; Law Enforcement; United Nations and Brazil; Women's Rights. Chapter 6: Overview; Poverty, Social Conflict, and Protests.

Further Reading

Amnesty International. http://amnesty.org

Bice, Arthur. 2009. "Government Fights Slave Labor in Brazil." *CNN World,* October 21. Accessed July 30, 2019. http://www.cnn.com/2009/WORLD/americas/01/09/brazil.slavery

Canineu, Mari Laura. 2017. "No, We Don't Like to Be Beaten Up." *Human Rights Watch,* July 11. Accessed July 30, 2019. https://www.hrw.org/print/306472

Darlington, Shasta, et al. 2017. "Slavery in the Amazon: Thousands Forced to Work on Brazil's Cattle Ranches." *CNN World,* May 11. Accessed July 30, 2019. http://www.cnn.com/2017/04/26/americas/brazil-amazon-slavery-freedom-project/index.html

Human Rights Watch—Brazil. https://www.hrw.org/americas/brazil

Lyons, Kate. 2017. "Killing by Brazilian Police Branded a Human Rights Crisis as Body Count Rises." *Guardian,* May 4. Accessed July 30, 2019. https://www.theguardian.com/global-development/2017/may/04/killings-brazilian-police-human-rights-crisis-un-review

United Nations Human Rights, Office of the High Commissioner for Human Rights. 2016. "Report of the Special Rapporteur on Torture, and other Cruel, Inhumane, or Degrading Treatment, or Punishment on His Mission to Brazil." *United Nations Human Rights Commission,* January 21. Accessed July 30, 2019. http://ap.ohchr.org/documents/dpage_e.aspx?si=A/HRC/31/57/Add.4

Law Enforcement

The Brazilian Constitution of 1988 stipulates that public security is a right of all Brazilians. Consequently, the functions of law enforcement and maintaining order are the responsibility of the government. To achieve these goals, Article 144 of the constitution defines the roles and jurisdictions of five police forces. They are divided into three federal institutions and two state-level forces. Their police activity to maintain public order varies according to their respective jurisdictions.

Federal Institutions

The Federal Police (Departamento de Polícia Federal, or PF) works with crimes against the federal government, including the legislative and judicial branches. The PF is also in charge of fighting international terrorism and drug trafficking. In addition, they issue passports to Brazilian citizens, control border security, and manage the immigration department. Another function of the PF is to offer security to all airports, maritime ports, and other ports of entry into the country.

The Federal Highway Police (Polícia Rodoviária Federal, or PRF) has the jurisdiction to maintain order in all federal highways and facilitate the flow of traffic. Its headquarters are in Brasília, but they also maintain specific patrol points in all states and municipalities around the country. While they work to maintain order, they do not have dedicated units to investigate crimes.

The Federal Railways Police (Polícia Ferroviária Federal, or PFF) maintains order by patrolling and preventing vandalism on the federal highway system. They also help with security of the Metropolitan Trains of the cities of São Paulo and Salvador. They do not investigate crimes.

State Institutions

The Civil Police (Polícia Civis) has the main task of investigating crimes at the state level under the command of a State Delegate. Furthermore, each police district is under the command of a local delegate, who in turn answers to the State Delegate. The Civil Police investigates crimes, and it also enforces the law at the local level. However, they usually do not patrol the local streets or use clearly marked uniforms.

The Military Police and Fire Brigade (Polícias Militares, or PM; Corpos de Bombeiros Militares, CBM) work together at the state level. The Military Police must clearly identify themselves to the public by using marked uniforms, vehicles, and badges. While they are military in nature, they are well trained to preserve public order and to protect the civilian population.

Other Security Forces (not officially recognized in the constitution)

Brazil also has Navy, Army, and Air Force Police, but they are not part of the State Military Police because they are strictly internal units to investigate issues related to their respective armed forces branch of the military. During times of national emergency, however, these soldiers have been used to maintain public order, especially in recent social clashes in Rio de Janeiro.

Since the beginning of the twenty-first century, reports of police brutality and excessive violence have increased in Brazil. Human Rights Watch (HRW) in Brazil has reported multiple cases of controversial massacres of civilians by military police, especially in poor and marginalized neighborhoods and *favelas*. HRW has reported on the common tactics of torture by local police, inhumane conditions in Brazilian prisons, and people detained for extremely excessive periods of time before going to court or even being charged with a crime. In addition, accusations of corruption and abuse have led to multiple prison riots and street protests.

See also: Chapter 3: Overview; Corruption and Political Scandals; Human Rights. Chapter 4: *Favelas* (Slums). Chapter 6: Overview; Poverty, Social Conflict, and Protests; Urban Crime.

Further Reading

Brazilian Federal Police Department Official Website, Ministério da Justiça e Segurança Pública. "Histórico de DPF." http://www.pf.gov.br/institucional/historico

Georgetown University. "Constitution of the Federative Republic of Brazil." Political Database of the Americas. http://pdba.georgetown.edu/Constitutions/Brazil/brazil.html

Kingstone, Peter R., and Timothy J. Power (eds.). 2000. *Democratic Brazil: Actors, Institutions, and Processes.* Pittsburgh, PA: University of Pittsburgh Press.

Kraul, Chris, and Marcelo Soares. 2009. "Brazil's Police Killings Condemned by Human Rights Watch." *Los Angeles Times,* December 9. Accessed July 6, 2019. http://articles.latimes.com/2009/dec/09/world/la-fg-brazil-cops9-2009dec09

Lula da Silva, Luiz Inácio (1945–)

Luiz Inácio Lula da Silva (most commonly known simply as "Lula") is one of the most recognizable Brazilian presidents. He was born on October 25, 1945, in Caetés, Pernambuco, located in the northeast region of the country. He came from a large family of humble means; the seventh of eight children, he worked during his childhood as a shoe shiner, street vendor, and at an automobile factory. As an adult, he became a relentless labor organizer. He worked his way up until he was elected president of the Metallurgical Workers' Union in the São Paulo region with a high concentration of car manufacturing plants.

For Lula da Silva, it was a natural progression to get involved in politics. He was one of the founding members of the Workers' Party (Partido dos Trabalhadores, PT) in 1980. It was designed as a leftist party to oppose the oppressive military regime in power at that time. Lula quickly evolved into a persistent politician with a moral compass seeking to improve the lives of average workers, the poor, and the undereducated people of Brazil. His first attempt at elected office occurred in 1982 when he ran for governor of São Paulo; he lost. He returned four years later to win a seat in the Federal Congress in 1986. As a leading member of the PT, he had an active role in writing a new democratic constitution after the military government lost in the 1985 elections.

After two unsuccessful campaigns, Lula was eventually elected and served two terms as president of Brazil (2003–2011). He quickly reaffirmed his commitment to help underprivileged people by working with Congress to pass legislation to reform the complicated tax code, improve retirement benefits, offer better labor protections, and revise the university educational system. He also introduced the popular welfare program Bolsa Escola (School Allowance) for families in extreme poverty, but it was conditional on school attendance for children in the home. The economy also improved dramatically during Lula's time in office. As an emerging economy in Latin America, Brazil's foreign debt complicated the government finances. At the start of the twenty-first century, Brazil diversified its export economy with agriculture, manufacturing, oil extraction, and the service industry. As a result, Brazil paid off all its foreign debt in 2008, and it actually became a lending nation for the first time in the global market.

Brazil has experienced multiple political scandals since 2010, and former president Lula da Silva was not exempt from accusations. Most of his political, economic, and social achievements have been compromised as allegations of criminal activity emerged against him. In fact, on July 12, 2017, he was convicted of corruption and money laundering in a federal court. He was subsequently sentenced to nine years in prison. However, in April 2018, after multiple unsuccessful appeals, ex-president Luiz Inácio Lula da Silva was incarcerated to serve a twelve-year sentence for charges of corruption and money laundering at a federal prison in Curitiba. His legacy as a defender of vulnerable people of Brazil is now mixed with a criminal record.

See also: Chapter 3: Overview; Constitutions; Corruption and Political Scandals; Political Parties. Chapter 4: Overview. Chapter 6: Overview. Chapter 8: Bolsa Família: Welfare Program with Education Incentives.

Further Reading

Crocitti, John J., and Monique Vallance (eds.). 2012. *Brazil Today: An Encyclopedia of Life in the Republic* (2 volumes). Santa Barbara, CA: ABC-CLIO.

Kingstone, Peter R., and Timothy J. Power (eds.). 2000. *Democratic Brazil: Actors, Institutions, and Processes*. Pittsburgh, PA: University of Pittsburgh Press.

Meade, Teresa A. 2010. *A Brief History of Brazil*. New York: Checkmark Books.

Political Parties

The 1988 constitution provided the framework for the current Brazilian multiparty political system. Dozens of parties quickly emerged with a stated ideology that was not always clear to the voters. In addition, multiple parties had similar names. In order to reduce potential confusion (and to help illiterate people), all the parties that registered with the Tribunal Superior Eleitoral (TSE, or Superior Electoral Court) received a two-digit number that served as the main identifier, even if the party somewhat modified its name. As of 2016, there are thirty-five registered political parties. Table 3.1 lists the parties registered in Brazil (in alphabetical order).

While the list of political parties is long, five parties tend to dominate most of the state and national political arenas. Most presidents, congressmen, senators, and governors come from the Workers' Party (PT), the Brazilian Social Democracy Party (PSDB), the Brazilian Democratic Movement Party (PMDB), the Progressive Party (PP), and the Democrats (DEM). Most of the smaller parties participate in a strategy best described as a coalition democracy by creating alliances in order to appeal to voters.

See also: Chapter 3: Overview; Constitutions; Electoral System; Workers' Party (PT) in Power.

Table 3.1: POLITICAL PARTIES REGISTERED IN BRAZIL (IN ALPHABETICAL ORDER)

Name (Portuguese) and Abbreviation	Name of Political Party (English)	Ideology	Electoral Number
Avante (AVANTE)	Avante	Labor, Nationalism, Populism	70
Democracia Cristã (DC)	Christian Democracy	Center-right, Christian democracy	27
Democratas (DEM)	Democrats	Christian democracy, Economic liberalism	25
Livres (LIVRES)	Free	Center-right, Libertarianism, Social liberalism	17
Partido Comunista Brasileiro (PCB)	Brazilian Communist Party	Communism, Marxism-Leninism	21
Partido Comunista do Brasil (PCdoB)	Communist Party of Brazil	Communism, Marxism-Leninism	65
Partido da Causa Operária (PCO)	Workers' Cause Party	Trotskyism	29
Partido da Mobilização Nacional (PMN)	Party of National Mobilization	Agrarianism, Leftist nationalism	33
Partido da Mulher Brasileira (PMB)	Party of the Brazilian Women	Center-left, Women's rights	35
Partido da República (PR)	Party of the Republic	Nationalism	22
Partido da Social Democracia Brasileira (PSDB)	Brazilian Social Democracy Party	Social democracy, Social liberalism	45
Partido Democrático Trabalhista (PDT)	Democratic Labor Party	Democratic socialism, Populism, Labor movement	12
Partido do Movimento Democrático Brasileiro (PMDB)	Brazilian Democratic Movement Party	Centrism, Populism	15
Partido dos Trabalhadores (PT)	Workers' Party	Democratic socialism	13
Partido Humanista da Soliedariedade (PHS)	Humanist Party of Solidarity	Christian democracy, Distributism	31
Partido Novo (NOVO)	New Party	Right-wing, Economic liberalism	30
Partido Popular Socialista (PPS)	Socialist People's Party	Social democracy, Social liberalism	23
Partido Progressista (PP)	Progressive Party	Populism	11
Partido Pátria Livre (PPL)	Free Homeland Party	Socialism, Left-wing nationalism	54

(continued)

Table 3.1: POLITICAL PARTIES REGISTERED IN BRAZIL (IN ALPHABETICAL ORDER) (CONTINUED)

Name (Portuguese) and Abbreviation	Name of Political Party (English)	Ideology	Electoral Number
Partido Renovador Trabalhista Brasileiro (PRTB)	Brazilian Labor Renewal Party	Populism, Nationalism, Conservatism	28
Partido Republicano Brasileiro (PRB)	Brazilian Republican Party	Christian democracy, Social conservatism	10
Partido Republicano da Ordem Social (PROS)	Republican Party of the Social Order	Economic liberalism, Social conservatism, Republicanism	90
Partido Republicano Progressista (PRP)	Progressive Republican Party	Populism, Conservatism	44
Partido Social Cristão (PSC)	Social Christian Party	Conservatism	20
Partido Social Democrático (PSD)	Social Democratic Party	Centrism, Economic liberalism	55
Partido Socialismo e Liberdade (PSOL)	Socialism and Liberty Party	Democratic socialism, Anti-capitalism	50
Partido Socialista Brasileiro (PSB)	Brazilian Socialist Party	Social democracy, Democratic socialism	40
Partido Socialista dos Trabalhadores Unificado (PSTU)	United Socialist Workers' Party	Far Left, Trotskyism	16
Partido Trabalhista Brasileiro (PTB)	Brazilian Labor Party	Centrism, Populism, Nationalism	14
Partido Trabalhista Cristão (PTC)	Christian Labor Party	Conservatism, Christian democracy	36
Partido Verde (PV)	Green Party	Green politics, Progressivism	43
Patriota (PATRI)	Patriot	Conservatism, Nationalism, Christian fundamentalism, Right-wing populism	51
Podemos (PODE)	Podemos	Populism, Labor	19
Rede Sustentabilidade (REDE)	Sustainability Network	Social democracy, Green movement	18
Solidariedade (SD)	Solidarity	Labor movement	77

Sources: Georgetown University. "Political Parties of Brazil." Political Database of the Americas. http://pdba.georgetown.edu/Parties/Brazil/desc.html

Superior Electoral Court (TSE), Official Government Website. http://english.tse.jus.br

Further Reading

Edwards, Todd L. 2008. "Politics and Government" in *Brazil: A Global Studies Handbook*, 137–196. Santa Barbara, CA: ABC-CLIO.

Font, Mauricio A. 2003. *Transforming Brazil: A Reform Era in Perspective*. Oxford, UK: Rowman and Littlefield.

Georgetown University. "Political Parties of Brazil." Political Database of the Americas. http://pdba.georgetown.edu/Parties/Brazil/desc.html

Superior Electoral Court (TSE), Official Government Website. http://english.tse.jus.br

Political Patronage

Similar to other countries around the world, the federal government in Brazil provides financial resources for roads, schools, water projects, hospitals, and so on. However, the Brazilian electoral system is mostly based on identity with a political party and coalitions created based on a targeted group of voters. In addition, the current constitution of 1988 set up a system in which political patronage is not only legal but extremely important. The current Brazilian legislative branch is split between the Senate and the Chamber of Deputies; the latter creates the national budget. The House of Deputies is an appropriate branch to analyze how patronage works in Brazil, starting at the federal level and trickling down to the state, municipalities, cities, and even small rural communities.

It is quite common for deputies to use the national budget to generate support for other candidates from their own political party. Therefore, the financial use of political patronage is utilized in Brazil within the existing structure of mayors, municipal leaders, governors, and public employee unions in order to influence local elections in a legal manner. The incumbent political party then controls large economic resources that can be used to perpetuate its position of electoral power.

The 1988 constitution was designed with a decentralized system of fiscal powers that is transferred to local, regional, and state governments. The constitution also allows each federal deputy at the Chamber of Deputies to submit up to twenty budgetary amendments to the national budget. The purpose of such amendments must be used to provide public works projects to the communities they represent. This type of pork-barrel politics is extremely common in Brazil. In fact, the effectiveness of federal politicians is often determined by the type of material benefits they can bring to their region, especially in poor agricultural communities. The main function of deputies is to get resources for the communities that elected them. The most important benefit that federal politicians can provide is local jobs, which is done by funding multiple public-works projects.

It is fairly clear that federal deputies reward municipalities based on the electoral support they provide, but analyzing the details is important. Federal politicians channel funds to the regions where they obtain high numbers of votes, which in turn determines the type of public works (hospitals, schools, roads, factories, etc.) and jobs that are funded in specific regions, especially around elections time. While federal politicians are supposed to represent all their constituents equally and fairly, the reality is very different. For example, municipalities with a high degree of electoral support might get a brand-new hospital (and all the construction jobs that go with the project), while other regions with less definitive political support for the party might only get a few pieces of medical equipment for an existing clinic.

Recent studies have shown that the allocation of federal money for municipal public works has actually generated a larger gap in local income distribution. Politicians at the municipal, state, and federal levels can certainly report and publicize the specific number of jobs and public services provided to the areas they represent. These public-works projects provide local short-term jobs. However, the large building contracts are usually assigned to individuals, families, and corporations that were wealthy already, thus increasing the regional income gap.

See also: Chapter 2: Overview; Timeline. Chapter 3: Overview; Constitutions; Electoral System; Political Parties. Chapter 4: Overview.

Further Reading

Cox, Gary W., and Mathew D. McCubbins. 1986. "Electoral Politics as a Redistributive Game." *Journal of Politics* 48, no. 2 (May): 370–389.

Edwards, Todd L. 2008. "Politics and Government" in *Brazil: A Global Studies Handbook*, 137–195. Santa Barbara, CA: ABC-CLIO.

Finan, Frederico S. 2004. *Political Patronage, Corruption, and Local Development*. PhD Dissertation, University of California, Berkeley.

Graham, Richard. 1990. *Patronage and Politics in Nineteenth-Century Brazil*. Stanford, CA: Stanford University Press.

Hagopian, Frances. 1987. *The Traditional Political Elite and the Transition to Democracy in Brazil*. Notre Dame, IN: Helen Kellogg Institute for International Studies: University of Notre Dame Press.

Rousseff, Dilma (1947–)

Dilma Vana Rousseff (commonly known as "Dilma") was the first female president of Brazil. She was born on December 14, 1947, in Belo Horizonte, which is the capital city of the interior state of Minas Gerais in the southeastern region of Brazil. Her father was a Bulgarian immigrant attorney named Pedro Rousseff, and her mother was a schoolteacher named Dilma Jane da Silva. Dilma had one surviving older brother named Igor.

During her twenties, Rousseff was attracted to a socialist/Marxist ideology. Her political views were shaped by the military dictatorship that ruled Brazil from 1964 to 1985. In 1967, she joined the Comando de Libertação Nacional (COLINA), a socialist group that advocated an armed struggle against the oppressive regime. She quickly became an activist. This is where she met her future husband, Carlos Galeno Linhares. They were both invited to take leadership roles in a more radical organization called the Revolutionary Armed Vanguard Palmares (VAR Palmares). After her alleged participation in multiple underground activities, she was arrested on August 12, 1970, as part of a sting operation. Dilma was tortured and severely beaten for twenty-two days. She was convicted to six years in prison, but she was released from jail in 1972.

Upon her release from prison, Rousseff registered at the Minas Gerais Federal University, and she finished her degree in economics in 1977. It was during her studies that she had her only daughter (Paula Rousseff Aráujo) in 1976. During the next seven years, her political views evolved and led her to participate within the political structure instead of trying to overthrow the system.

The Brazilian military government lost the elections in 1985, and Rousseff quickly noticed the possibilities for change. She worked on the successful political campaign of Alceu Collares for mayor of Porto Alegre, and he appointed Rousseff as municipal treasury secretary. This was her first political position in public service. Collares went on to become governor of Rio Grande do Sul, and he appointed Rousseff as state secretary of Mines, Energy, and Communications—a position she held twice (1993–1995 and 1998–2002). She proved to be extremely efficient by improving electric service capacity and coordinating massive infrastructure improvement projects.

In 2002, Brazil was swept by a wave of optimism when Luiz Inácio Lula da Silva (1945–) won the presidency representing the Workers' Party (PT). He appointed Rousseff as his minister of energy based on her extensive experience running a regional energy agency. In this role, she implemented policies to expand the services offered by Petrobras (the national oil company), which added tens of thousands of jobs. She also launched a popular program, Luz para Todos (Electricity for All), to subsidize electrical services to poor families and to develop infrastructure into remote and rural areas in the northeast region of Brazil. These programs made her increasingly popular. In 2005, President Lula appointed Rousseff as his chief of staff, a position she held until 2010 when she stepped down in order to run for president.

Dilma Rousseff became the first female president in Brazil in 2010 with an overwhelming majority, receiving almost 56 million votes. She had extremely positive ratings during her first term in office (2011–2014). She kept Brazil on a positive economic path that increased agricultural production, developed new export agreements, and improved advanced manufacturing of cars, cargo ships, and airplanes. She was a populist, and she always tried to help the less fortunate Brazilians. For example, she eliminated the federal tax on basic consumer products that included potatoes, tomatoes, bananas, rice, meat, beans, bread, butter, apples, and sugar. When she was reelected in 2014, she still had a wide margin of popularity against her political rivals, but her optimism would not last long.

Brazil experienced massive street protests at the beginning of 2015. Their rage was based on accusations of corruption against Rousseff during the time she was part of the board of directors of Petrobras from 2010 to 2013. While no evidence was offered for such accusations, multiple political groups quickly called for her impeachment. Public employee unions organized multiple strikes that paralyzed the nation a few days at a time. Social organizations gathered in large numbers to protest the exorbitant amounts of money being spent on preparations for the 2014 Soccer World Cup while the government was not adequately funding schools or social services. The international attention provided by the media was also used by labor organizers to show hundreds of thousands of people protesting the corruption tied to government contracts related to building facilities for the upcoming 2016 summer Olympics while the country still suffered from basic problems of poverty and hunger. By July 2015, her approval rating had dropped to only 9 percent, the lowest rate in modern political times.

Impeachment proceedings against President Rousseff started on December 3, 2015, in the Chamber of Deputies (lower house of Congress) based on allegations of budgetary mismanagement (not corruption or personal misappropriation of funds). After months of investigation, the Federal Senate suspended Rousseff from office on May 12, 2016, for a period of six months. Vice President Michel Temer (1940–) took over the government while her case was further evaluated. On August 31, 2016, the Senate voted 61–20 to impeach Rousseff; she was found guilty of breaking budgetary laws. She was then formally impeached and removed from her post as the thirty-sixth president of Brazil.

See also: Chapter 2: Operation Condor and Military Rule. Chapter 3: Overview; Constitutions; Corruption and Political Scandals; Law Enforcement; Political Parties; Temer, Michel (1940–); Worker's Party (PT) in Power. Chapter 4: Overview; Petrobras, the National Oil Company. Chapter 6: Poverty, Social Conflict, and Protests. Chapter 15: Soccer FIFA World Cup 2014; Olympic Games, Rio de Janeiro 2016.

Further Reading

Bennett, Allen. 2017. "Dilma Rousseff Biography." Jusbrasil.com.br. Accessed July 11, 2019. https://agencia-brasil.jusbrasil.com.br/noticias/2319394/news-in-english-dilma-rousseff-biography

Crocitti, John J., and Monique Vallance (eds.). 2012. *Brazil Today: An Encyclopedia of Life in the Republic* (2 volumes). Santa Barbara, CA: ABC-CLIO.

McKirdy, Euan. 2016. "Impeachment Proceedings against Brazil's Dilma Rousseff: What's Up?" CNN, May 12. Accessed July 11, 2019. http://www.cnn.com/2016/05/10/americas/brazil-rousseff-impeachment-explainer/index.html

Romero, Simon. 2016. "Dilma Rousseff Is Ousted as Brazil's President in Impeachment Vote." *New York Times,* August 21. Accessed July 11, 2019. https://www.nytimes.com/2016/09/01/world/americas/brazil-dilma-rousseff-impeached-removed-president.html

Temer, Michel (1940–)

Michel Miguel Elias Temer Lulia (1940–) was elected vice president of Brazil during the 2010 elections representing the Democratic Movement Party (PMDB), which follows a conservative ideology from the center-right. His position is somewhat difficult to navigate because the Brazilian electoral system allows voters to select a president and a vice president from different political parties. Temer served as vice president with President Dilma Rousseff, who represents the Workers' Party (Partido dos Trabalhadores, PT), which is ideologically liberal and to the left.

Michel Temer was born on September 23, 1940, in Tietê, São Paulo. His parents migrated from Lebanon to Brazil in 1925 fleeing the social and political chaos after World War I. Temer obtained his college degree at the Law School of the University of São Paulo in 1963. He also completed a doctorate degree in law from the Pontifical Catholic University in São Paulo. As an expert in constitutional law, he worked as a university professor and also published three seminal books on the subject.

Michel Temer has had a long political career, mostly at the federal level. He started as a politician in 1987 shortly after the military regime lost federal elections. He served in the Chamber of Deputies (the lower house of Congress), for six consecutive terms. During that period, he was selected to act as the president of the Chamber of Deputies on three separate occasions. In fact, he was part of the 1988 National Constituent Assembly in charge of designing and promulgating the current constitution of Brazil. He also served as chairman of the largest political party in Brazil, the Partido do Movimento Democrático Brasileiro (PMDB) from 2001 until 2016.

Brazil erupted into political turmoil when President Dilma Rousseff faced charges of financial mismanagement in 2015. When the Senate accepted the impeachment indictment against her, she was removed from office for a period of maximum 180 days. Michel Temer became acting president of Brazil starting on May 12, 2016. After an investigation, the Senate decided on August 31, 2016, that Rousseff was guilty of the charges against her and voted to impeach her. At this point, Michel Temer became the thirty-seventh president of Brazil; he was expected to finish Rousseff's term until December 31, 2018. At seventy-seven years of age, he is the oldest executive leader Brazil has ever had. He immediately changed his entire cabinet, and he was heavily criticized for appointing only white men to all the ministerial posts, even though Brazil is one of the most racially diverse countries in the Western Hemisphere.

Michel Temer came to the executive office amid multiple accusations of participating in Rousseff's impeachment only to cover up investigations of corruption against himself and his political allies. Once he was in office as the president, secret recordings emerged in which Temer was heard planning to obstruct the investigation of corruption cases. Even his anti-corruption minister had to resign only twenty days after he was appointed. This led to accusations of impeachment against Temer. Moreover, in December 2016, industrialist Marcelo Odebrecht confirmed that he paid bribes to President Temer in exchange for construction contracts. As Brazilians grew increasingly frustrated, they demanded Temer's resignation. In addition, multiple public-sector unions staged massive protests, and he had to call federal troops to remove the angry protesters. He continued facing political and legal challenges amid persistent accusations of corruption. On June 2, 2016, a regional Election Court in São Paulo formally convicted Temer of violating multiple election laws; his punishment was to be banned from running for any political office for eight years. Consequently, he was allowed to remain as president, but he became ineligible to run for reelection in 2018.

See also: Chapter 3: Overview; Constitutions; Corruption and Political Scandals; Electoral System; Political Parties; Rousseff, Dilma (1947–); Workers' Party (PT) in Power.

Further Reading

Crocitti, John J., and Monique Vallance (eds.). 2012. *Brazil Today: An Encyclopedia of Life in the Republic* (2 volumes). Santa Barbara, CA: ABC-CLIO.

Greenwald, Glenn. 2016. "Credibility of Brazil's Interim President Collapses as He Receives 8-Year Ban on Running from Office." *Intercept,* June 3. Accessed May 2, 2019. https://theintercept.com/2016/06/03/credibility-of-brazils-interim-president-collapses-receives-8-year-ban-on-running

President Michel Temer Official Government Website. http://micheltemer.com.br/

Romero, Simon. 2016. "Brazil's President, Michel Temer, Embroiled in New Corruption Scandal. *New York Times,* November 26. Accessed May 2, 2019. https://www.nytimes.com/2016/11/25/world/americas/brazil-president-temer-corruption.html

United Nations and Brazil

Brazil was one of the fifty-one founding-member countries of the United Nations (UN) since its inception on October 24, 1945. It is also an active participant in all the UN specialized agencies, including multiple peacekeeping operations on the global stage. Brazil has contributed military forces assigned to UN peacekeeping operations in the Middle East, Mozambique, Congo, Angola, and Cypress. In more recent times, Brazilian soldiers have served missions in Haiti and East Timor. In addition, Brazil has been elected a member of the UN Security Council ten times. To enhance its international presence, Brazil maintains permanent missions with ambassadors in four locations that serve as headquarters for multiple agencies organized by the United Nations, including the following:

a. **New York**: UN General Assembly, Security Council, Human Rights Council, Peacebuilding Commissions, UN Children's Fund (UNICEF), and the United Nations University (UNU).
b. **Rome**: Food and Agricultural Organization (FAO), World Food Program (WFP), and the International Fund for Agricultural Development (IFAD).
c. **Paris**: United Nations Educational, Scientific, and Cultural Organization (UNESCO), and the International Institute for Educational Planning.
d. **Geneva**: World Trade Organization (WTO), International Telecommunications Union (ITU), World Meteorological Organization (WMO), UN High Commissioner for Refugees (UNHCR), and the World Health Organization (WHO).

Since its inception in 1945, only five countries have veto power to derail any resolution in the UN's Security Council (China, France, Russia, United Kingdom, and the United States). However, since the 1980s, Brazil has been an active proponent of reforming the

Security Council. In recent times, during the presidencies of Luiz Inácio Lula da Silva (2003–2011) and Dilma Rousseff (2011–2016), Brazil has become more assertive in seeking a permanent seat on the UN Security Council with veto power. To accomplish its goal, it joined a coalition of countries that became known as the Group of four (G4) that includes Brazil, Japan, India, and Germany. They have grown in strength and resolve. In 2017, the G4 formally requested a more definitive role in the Security Council. Their claim is that the expansion of members to the Security Council will make the body more legitimate, effective, and representative of the needs of all countries. They stated that the number of members has grown from 51 countries in 1951 to 193 members in 2017, and that the existing list of countries in the Security Council no longer reflects the current global realities. The G4 Group also highlighted the recent process under which Secretary General António Guterres has launched a structural reform of the United Nations, and that it is imperative to reform the Security Council in order to face the complexities of modern-day challenges. In addition, they presented evidence of the financial, military, and emergency support that the G4 members currently provide to existing UN missions around the world. Finally, the ministers of the G4 countries have gained the overwhelming support of a large number of current UN member states to undertake the reform of the Security Council.

See also: Chapter 1: World Heritage Sites in the UNESCO. Chapter 3: Overview; Lula da Silva, Luiz Inácio (1945–); Rousseff, Dilma (1947–). Chapter 4: World Trade Organization (WTO).

Further Reading

Brazil's Permanent Missions to the United Nations. https://www.un.int/brazil

Edwards, Todd L. 2008. "Politics and Government" in *Brazil: A Global Studies Handbook*, 137–195. Santa Barbara, CA: ABC-CLIO.

General Assembly of the United Nations Official Website. http://www.un.org/en/ga

Ministry of Foreign Affairs of Brazil. 2017. "Meeting of the Foreign Ministers of the G4 Countries—Brazil, Germany, India, and Japan—on United Nations Security Council Reform." Ministry of Foreign Affairs of Brazil. Official Joint Press Statement. September 21. Accessed May 25, 2019. http://www.itamaraty.gov.br/en/press-releases/17475-g4 meeting-set17-jointstatement

Ministry of Foreign Affairs of Brazil Official Website. http://www.itamaraty.gov.br/en

United Nations Official Website. http://www.un.org

United Nations System of Agencies. https://web.archive.org/web/20080109184227/http:// www.un.org/aboutun/chart_en.pdf

Women's Rights

Brazil is a former Portuguese colony. Consequently, it inherited the patriarchal traditions of the Iberian Peninsula as well as a Catholic background, both of which affected the way women were viewed in Brazil. A male-dominant tradition imposed during the colonial period (1500–1822) placed women in a position of economic dependency. In addition, Brazil is now the largest Roman Catholic country in the world, and its doctrine continues to influence the reproductive rights of Brazilian women.

The Brazilian government has taken significant steps to improve the condition of women in all aspects of life. Women received suffrage in 1932. Under the current 1988 constitution, Article 5 grants all women and men the same legal rights and responsibilities. Under the umbrella of economic rights, all citizens (including women) can inherit and own property. Women have the same legal access to employment and education as men. In addition, following labor law, women are guaranteed 120 days of paid maternity leave, and men get 7 days. Under the code of civil and family law, the minimum age for marriage without parental consent is eighteen years old, and divorce became legal in 1977. Overall, Brazil has multiple social organizations that have fought arduously to protect the legal and political rights of women. At an international level, the Brazilian government is an active member of Human Rights Watch and the Convention on the Elimination of All Forms of Discrimination Against Women (CEDAW).

While women have certainly made tremendous advances in Brazil, they still suffer from gender inequality. They face significant struggles related to reproductive rights. Abortion is illegal in Brazil, except for cases of rape or when the mother's life is in danger. Consequently, do-it-yourself, unsafe abortions result in too many deaths. To combat such problems, the government made sterilization legal (and free) in 1996 for women over twenty-five years of age. Then, much under the strong opposition of the Catholic Church, contraception became more common in the 1980s under the program Bem-Estar Familiar do Brasil (BEMFAM). The government has taken an active role in subsidizing the cost of birth control pills and sterilization procedures by using public clinics and hospitals, and by 2011, Brazil had already experienced a significant reduction in family size.

Despite all the government's efforts, Brazil has not been able to eradicate or even reduce the worrisome levels of violence against women. Human Rights Watch representatives in Brazil routinely report on excessive numbers of cases of domestic abuse. The federal government is keenly aware of this endemic problem. Politicians have acted the way they know best, by creating new laws aimed at protecting women. The Maria da Penha Law was signed by President Lula da Silva in 2006 in order to prevent domestic abuse and to ensure justice is carried out when it happens. It strengthened the penal code and police procedures to handle such cases. Congress even created a new cabinet position at a ministerial level called the Secretariat of Women's Policy, which is appointed by the president. The person in that position is in charge of protecting the legal rights of Brazilian women. The problem is that the killing of women by their partners has continued to increase. While multiple laws have been approved to protect women, most police officers are not trained to deal with cases of violence against women, and actually present barriers for women who want to report their suffering. For example, documented cases show that attacks against women increased 139 percent from 2010 to 2015 in the state of Roraima, the region with the highest statistics of such abuses. As a result, President Dilma Rousseff signed another law against femicide in 2015 that imposes stricter penalties for killing young girls and women. The new law also provides the legal, financial, and institutional framework to take preventative measures that protect women.

See also: Chapter 3: Overview; Constitutions; Human Rights; Law Enforcement; United Nations and Brazil.

Further Reading

Amnesty International. http://amnesty.org

Caetano, André J., and Joseph E. Potter. 2004. "Politics and Female Sterilization in Northern Brazil." *Population and Development Review* 30, no. 1 (March): 79–108.

Canineu, Mari Laura. 2017. "No, We Don't Like to Be Beaten Up." *Human Rights Watch*, July 11. Accessed July 22, 2019. https://www.hrw.org/print/306472

Human Rights Watch—Brazil. https://www.hrw.org/americas/brazil

Tamkins, T. 2004. "In Brazil, Women Who Lack Knowledge about Fertility Control Are Those Most Likely to Become Sterilized." *International Family Planning Perspectives* 23, no. 2 (June): 102–103.

United Nations Women. "Maria da Penha Law." United Nations. http://www.unwomen.org/en/news/stories/2011/8/maria-da-penha-law-a-name-that-changed-society

Workers' Party (PT) in Power

The Workers' Party (Partido dos Trabalhadores, PT) was founded in 1980 by a leftist group opposed to the military dictatorship that ruled Brazil from 1964 to 1985. The coalition of intellectuals, artists, journalists, and union leaders created a political party with a central ideology best described as democratic socialism. The Supreme Electoral Court recognized the PT as an official party in 1982. After the military left power in 1985, the PT quickly started winning elections for mayors in large cities that included Porto Alegre, Fortaleza, and Belo Horizonte.

When the PT candidate Luiz Inácio, Lula da Silva (1945–) won the presidential elections in 2002, he sparked tremendous optimism in Brazil, and he became widely known as "Lula." He immediately expanded the Bolsa Família welfare program that lifted millions of Brazilians out of poverty. It provided basic food while expecting children to attend school as a condition to receive social assistance. Lula was easily reelected in 2006, and the PT party solidified its position by winning more seats in the Senate and House of Deputies. The stage was set for another PT candidate to continue the work following a democratic socialist model.

Dilma Rousseff became Lula's protégé. She had served as his secretary of energy and then his chief of staff. She represented the PT party in the 2010 elections, and she became the first woman to ever win a presidential election in Brazil, with an overwhelming majority of the votes. She immediately proposed an aggressive economic agenda that sparked advanced manufacturing in the airplane and automobile industries, developed new export partnerships, and provided incentives to accelerate agricultural production. Her commitment to addressing the needs of workers and the less fortunate populations helped her to be reelected in 2014. Her popularity, however, quickly suffered a dramatic change.

The government of Dilma Rousseff faced massive street protests in 2015. These were the culmination of multiple scandals that had rocked Brazilian politics since a decade before. For example, the *mensalão* scandal of 2005 provided evidence of a scheme of offering bribes for votes and the discovery of special slush accounts to promote illegal voting activities. Multiple PT politicians had to resign, but President Lula was cleared of any wrongdoing. Then the 2006 electoral scandal proved that Lula's campaign manager had purchased private information with the intent to discredit political opponents. Again, the scandal was all over the news, and key PT politicians resigned. As more scandals appeared routinely on the news, the public was become increasingly despondent and more skeptical about their local political leaders. In June 2013, massive protests erupted throughout the country protesting price increases in public transportation, a failing health-care program, and inadequate schools, especially when the federal government was spending excessive amounts of money on new stadiums for the 2014 World Cup. Then Operação Lava Jato (Operation Car Wash) exploded to unexpected proportions in 2014. The investigation regarding widespread corruption and money laundering operations forced several elected officials to resign. In addition, multiple ministers, senators, and federal deputies were arrested and sent to prison. In the middle of this political chaos, President Rousseff was accused of illegal use of funds, and she was removed from office for six months. She was then quickly impeached in August 2016 for inappropriate use of public funds; however, she was cleared of all charges related to corruption or personal appropriation of funds. The period of political control in the hands of the PT was over; Vice President Michel Temer (from the rival Brazilian Democratic Party Movement, PMDB) took over as president of Brazil.

See also: Chapter 3: Overview; Corruption and Political Scandals; Lula da Silva, Luiz Inácio (1945–); Political Parties; Rousseff, Dilma (1947–); Temer, Michael (1940–). Chapter 6: Poverty, Social Conflict, and Protests. Chapter 8: Bolsa Família: Welfare Program with Education Incentives.

Further Reading

Gómez Bruera, Hernán F. 2013. *Lula, the Workers' Party, and the Governability Dilemma in Brazil*. Florence, KY: Routledge.

Hunter, Wendy. 2010. *The Transformation of the Workers' Party in Brazil, 1989–2009*. Cambridge, UK: Cambridge University Press.

Kiernan, Paul. 2015. "Brazil's Petrobras Reports nearly $17 Billion in Asset and Corruption Charges." *Wall Street Journal,* April 22. Accessed May 23, 2019. https://www.wsj.com/articles/brazils-petrobras-reports-nearly-17-billion-impairment-on-assets-corruption-1429744336

CHAPTER 4

ECONOMY

OVERVIEW

The International Monetary Fund (IMF) ranked Brazil in 2018 as the eighth-largest economy in the world. With a nominal gross domestic product (GDP) of $2.08 trillion U.S., it is the largest modern economy in Latin America, and the second largest in the Western Hemisphere, after the United States. Its GDP for 2018 was largely dominated by the services sector with 76 percent, followed by light and advanced industry with 18 percent, and trailed by agriculture with almost 6 percent. To reach this position, Brazil entered multiple bilateral trade agreements as well as regional trade accords that include the BRICS group (Brazil, Russia, India, China, and South Africa) and Mercosur (with Argentina, Paraguay, Uruguay, and Bolivia). It has also established strategic steps for fiscal order, and it liberalized its economy to increase private and foreign investment. As a result, Brazil is an active member in other economic international organizations that include the World Trade Organization (WTO), the G20 group, and the Cairns Group. Since 2000, the Brazilian economy experienced a contraction from 2006 to 2013; it went through a recession lasting from 2014 to 2015, but it has shown significant improvements since 2016.

The Brazilian government has offered tremendous incentives to domestic producers to increase exports. In 2017, Brazil exported almost $218 billion U.S. worth of materials and products to its top five trading partners (in order of amounts of exports) that include China, the European Union, the United States, Argentina, and Japan. In turn, Brazil imported $150 billion of goods from its top five suppliers: the European Union, China, the United States, Argentina, and South Korea. In 2012, China became Brazil's number one trading partner, replacing the United States. The Ministry of Development and Foreign Trade (MDIC) continues to pursue international treaties to increase export markets for Brazilian products, especially to multiple countries in Africa and the Middle East.

Agriculture and cattle ranching are big business in Brazil. Collectively known as agribusiness, this sector of the economy contributes heavily to international exports. First of all, Brazil is the largest exporter of coffee in the world, and it also has the largest cattle herd on the planet with almost 200 million heads of cattle. In addition, it produces almost 80 percent of all orange juice consumed around the world, and it has become the largest exporter of soybeans, especially to China. Brazil is also number five in international exports of both sugarcane and refined sugar. On the surface, these numbers give a general appearance of wealth and prosperity for farmers. However, the reality is that Brazil has an extremely uneven pattern of land distribution. Most of the beneficiaries from agribusiness are large corporations that work together with the government to participate in trade and commerce on a large scale. Consequently, large protests have emerged since the 1970s with demands for land for small farmers. The Landless Rural Workers Movement (Movimento dos Trabalhadores Rurais Sem Terra, MST) was founded in 1984, and it quickly became the most vocal organization defending millions of rural families who demanded land reform and social change. The result was that the current Brazilian constitution of 1988 provided hope for a comprehensive agricultural reform. However, it also specifically prohibits expropriation of private land by government agencies. Currently, President Jair Bolsonaro (1955–) and his allies in Congress have expressed recent support for lobbyists working on behalf of agricultural corporations who use their political influence to stop and delay land redistribution programs.

Brazil has a prosperous manufacturing industry that aims to supply both its domestic needs and export markets. The main sectors include minerals (steel and mining), cement, appliances (refrigerators, computers, and television sets), paper products, as well as higher-end complex finished goods (aircraft, automobiles, cellular phones, electronics, machinery equipment, and petrochemicals). Almost every major car company has a production plant in Brazil. Most of the factories for production are located in the southern and southeast regions of the country; this is an enormous commercial region that generates almost 60 percent of all industrial production in Latin America. In addition, Brazil's mineral wealth is extensive, including large reserves of copper, nickel, tin, lead, gold, zinc, uranium, and bauxite. Since the country has provided economic stability since 2000, large amounts of foreign investment have been infused into the manufacturing industry. For example, the national aircraft manufacturer Embraer completed a joint venture with Boeing Company in 2018 to produce small jets for international markets.

The energy sector represents a significant component of the Brazilian economy. With the discovery of the largest oil reserves in the Western Hemisphere located off the coast of Rio de Janeiro, Brazil has generated enough oil for its national needs since 2006, and it became a net oil exporter in 2007. In terms of electricity, almost 90 percent of the national needs are produced by hydroelectric power plants. The Itaipu Dam—located on the Parana River at the border with Paraguay—is the second-largest hydroelectric plant in the world. Together with the Tucurui Dam in Northern Brazil, the country generates enough energy to export it to its regional neighbors in Paraguay and Argentina. The two largest energy companies in the country are government owned: the oil conglomerate Petrobras and the electrical giant Electrobras.

The official message from the Brazilian government in 2018 offers accounts of incredible economic improvements. However, the widespread social discontent in the country reflects an entirely different reality, especially for lower-income Brazilians. On the one hand, the value of the BM&F Bovespa stock market has increased over 60 percent since 2016. The amounts of materials and goods exported also increased in 2017 to 2018. *Forbes* magazine listed Brazil in 2016 as the fifth country with the most billionaires.

These macroeconomic numbers certainly reflect that things are improving for some people and large businesses, but a closer look also shows that for the majority of Brazilians, things are actually getting worse. The reason is that the Brazilian government has embarked since 2015 on a series of austerity measures that essentially cut government spending to balance yearly budgets. In 2015, President Dilma Rousseff approved a cut of $17 billion U.S. that dramatically reduced the budget for social programs, cut thousands of government jobs, lowered education expenditures, and froze salaries for public employees. Then in 2016, the Brazilian Senate approved an even more drastic austerity package introduced by President Michel Temer (1940–) that effectively froze federal spending for the next twenty years, regardless of future needs. The United Nations has labeled such policies as the most punitive in the world for lower-income populations. Still, President Temer claimed that even further changes were needed in order to restore confidence in the national economy. This time, the targets were active workers and retired pensioners. In April 2017, the lower house in the Brazilian Congress approved a proposal to restructure labor laws and overhaul the pension system. Meanwhile, in spite of major improvements to the economy announced by the federal government, the minimum wage has remained virtually unchanged at slightly less than $4,000 U.S. a year. It seems that the working class is suffering the consequences of multiple imposed austerity measures.

These contradictory reports regarding the economic outlook of Brazil have resulted in massive street protests because Brazilians are fed up with scores of federal politicians continuously mired in corruption scandals while they have neglected the needs of public education, general health care, and social programs for the most vulnerable populations. Ironically, as vigorous protests continue in Brazil, the value of the stock market and the levels of foreign investment keep improving. Apparently, investors and politicians seem to like the austerity measures imposed on the Brazilian population.

Further Reading

Baer, Werner. 2014. *The Brazilian Economy: Growth and Development*. Boulder, CO: Lynne Rienner.

Brainard, Lael, and Leonardo Martinez-Diaz. 2009. *Brazil as an Economic Superpower? Understanding Brazil's Changing Role in the Global Economy*. Washington, DC: Brookings Institution Press.

Branford, Sue, and Maurício Torres. 2017. "How Brazil's Temer Administration Is Provoking Violence against Agrarian Reform." *Pacific Standard*, June 2. Accessed July 2, 2019. https://psmag.com/social-justice/temer-administration-is-provoking-violence-against-agrarian-reform

Bray, Chad, and Stanley Reed. 2018. "Petrobras of Brazil to Pay $2.95 Billion over Corruption Scandal." *New York Times*, January 3. Accessed July 1, 2019. https://www.nytimes.com/2018/01/03/business/dealbook/brazil-petrobras-corruption-scandal.html

Brazilian Ministry of Development and Foreign Trade (MDIC) Official Website. http://www.mdic.gov.br

Brazilian Ministry of Mines and Energy (MME) Official Website. http://www.mme.gov.br

Brazilian National Bank for Economic and Social Development (BNDES), Official Website. https://www.bndes.gov.br/wps/portal/site/home

BRICS Official Website. http://www.infobrics.org

Oliveira, José Maria de, and Nidi Bueno. 2015. *Trade Liberalisation in Brazil: Market Structure, Economic Performance, and Manufacturing.* Rockville, MD: GlobalSouth Press.

Phillips, Dom. 2016. "Brazil Senate Approves Austerity Package to Freeze Social Spending for 20 Years." *Guardian.* December 13. Accessed July 2, 2019. https://www.theguardian.com/world/2016/dec/13/brazil-approves-social-spending-freeze-austerity-package

Watts, Jonathan. 2017. "Operation Car Wash: Is this the Biggest Corruption Scandal in History?" *Guardian.* June 1. Accessed July 2, 2019. https://www.theguardian.com/world/2017/jun/01/brazil-operation-car-wash-is-this-the-biggest-corruption-scandal-in-history

World Trade Organization (WTO) Official Website. https://www.wto.org

Agrarian Reform

Brazil has one of the most uneven patterns of land distribution in the world. It started in 1534 when the King of Portugal divided its new colony into fifteen hereditary captaincies, and conceded them to twelve private individuals (*donatários*). Most of the captaincies failed; the ones that succeeded (Pernambuco and São Vicente) either used slave labor or exploited their workers. Brazil became independent in 1822, but it had already established an agricultural system with large landowners who yielded considerable political power and a small group of farmers who struggled to make a living.

During the 1960s, Brazil experienced multiple protests demanding land reform. Groups of desperate peasants organized into a critical mass and requested tangible government action. The church-based Pastoral Land Commission (CPT) became a strong advocate of land reform to combat rural poverty. Then, the Landless Rural Workers Movement (Movimento dos Trabalhadores Rurais Sem Terra, MST) was founded in 1984, and it quickly became the most vocal organization defending millions of rural families who demanded land reform and social change. The MST advocated the occupation of idle land to force the government into making decisions regarding peasant families. The federal government avoided the expropriation of private land, and instead promoted the relocation of thousands of poor peasant families to the Amazon region.

The current Brazilian constitution of 1988 provided hope for a comprehensive agricultural reform. However, it also specifically prohibits expropriation of private land by government agencies. The result was that land occupations became more common during the 1990s. The decade coincides with the Brazilian government's plan to aggressively promote exports to improve its economy, and agricultural exports were a big part of the plan. The government tried to generate sufficient jobs for farmers, but it actually created even further inequality in land tenure by granting large corporations even more immense tracks of land aimed at commercial cattle ranching and agricultural exports. The new export-led agribusiness sponsored by the government became more technically efficient, included complex financial transactions, redirected irrigation systems, provided new access roads, and even included scientific support. Small farmers could simply not compete with large domestic and transnational companies in the new agricultural scheme, and most of them actually sold their land to corporations.

The goal of achieving agrarian reform in order to reduce poverty and income inequality in Brazil currently faces additional hurdles. The MST estimates that almost 5 million families are candidates for land redistribution, and the organization has taken a more aggressive public stand that places government officials on the defensive. However, peasant organizations claim that landowners were responsible for multiple attacks and assassinations of peasant leaders in 2017. In addition, former president Michel Temer (1940–) and current president Jair Bolsonaro (1955–) have expressed support for lobbyists working on behalf of agricultural corporations that use their political influence to stop and delay land redistribution programs. Conflict among the different groups is likely to increase.

See also: Chapter 3: Bolsonaro, Jair (1955–); Temer, Michel (1940–). Chapter 4: Overview; Major Exports. Chapter 6: Landless Rural Workers Movement (MST).

Further Reading

Branford, Sue, and Maurício Torres. 2017. "How Brazil's Temer Administration Is Provoking Violence against Agrarian Reform." *Pacific Standard,* June 2. Accessed July 12, 2019. https://psmag.com/social-justice/temer-administration-is-provoking-violence-against-agrarian-reform

Edwards, Todd L. 2008. *Brazil: A Global Studies Handbook.* Santa Barbara, CA: ABC-CLIO.

Gaspar, Lúcia. 2009. "Agrarian Reform in Brazil." Joaquim Nabuco Foundation, September 16. Accessed July 12, 2019. http://basilio.fundaj.gov.br/pesquisaescolar_en/index.php?option=com_content&id=909

Landless Rural Workers Movement (MST) Official Website. http://www.mst.org.br

Pastoral Land Commission Official Website. https://cptnacional.org.br

Austerity Measures of 2016

On August 2015, the Brazilian government declared that it was officially in one of its worst recessions in history. Consequently, President Dilma Rousseff (1947–) and her finance minister, Joaquim Levy, announced a drastic austerity package worth $17 billion U.S. that dramatically reduced the budget for social programs, cut thousands of government jobs, lowered education expenditures, and froze salaries for public employees. As a result, multiple massive street protests erupted as Brazilians were fed up with scores of politicians mired in corruption scandals while they lavishly spent billions of dollars on infrastructure projects for the 2016 Olympics, but they neglected public education, general health care, and social programs for the most vulnerable populations. It turns out, however, that the fiscal situation was about to get even worse.

The Brazilian Senate approved in 2016 an even more drastic austerity package introduced by President Michel Temer that effectively froze federal spending for the next twenty years. Officials at the United Nations have labeled such policies the most punitive in the world for lower-income populations. Such measures triggered another wave of street protests, but Temer claimed that he was trying to bring discipline to a runaway budget that previous administrations had allowed to soar out of control. By placing a rigid spending cap, it officially restricts any potential budgetary increases due to population growth or economic improvement. The law effectively froze the federal budget from 2016 until 2037 regardless of the potential future needs for education, health care, infrastructure, national defense, pensions, or natural disasters. Multiple economists suggest that Brazil is placing the burden of the financial crisis on the poor populations of Brazil instead of raising the generous corporate tax rate of only 27.5 percent currently enjoyed by corporations. Violent protests and crashes erupted throughout Brazil to oppose the reach of this two-decade constitutional amendment, but Temer was not done yet.

President Temer claimed that further changes were needed in order to restore confidence in the national economy. On April 2017, the lower house in the Brazilian Congress approved a proposal to restructure labor laws and overhaul the pension system. The new laws would reduce compensation for labor abuses, allow employers to increase workers' hours for the same salary, and drastically cut pensions for retired workers. While the working class seems to be suffering the consequences of multiple imposed austerity measures, the Brazilian stock market actually went up almost 20 percent in 2017. As more vigorous protests continue in Brazil, investors and politicians seem to like the austerity measures imposed on the Brazilian population.

See also: Chapter 3: Rousseff, Dilma (1947–); Temer, Michel (1940–). Chapter 4: Overview. Chapter 6: Poverty, Social Conflict, and Protests.

Further Reading

Phillips, Dom. 2016. "Brazil Senate Approves Austerity Package to Freeze Social Spending for 20 Years." *Guardian,* December 13. Accessed July 8, 2019. https://www.theguardian.com/world/2016/dec/13/brazil-approves-social-spending-freeze-austerity-package

Rivett-Carnac, Mark. 2015. "Brazil Unveils a $17 Billion Austerity Package as Recession Bites." *Time,* September 14. Accessed July 11, 2019. http://time.com/4034369/brazil-economy-austerity-crisis-oil

Romero, Simon. 2017. "Brazil Gripped by General Strike over Austerity Measures." *New York Times,* April 18. Accessed July 8, 2019. https://www.nytimes.com/2017/04/28/world/americas/brazil-general-strike.html

Automobile Industry

Brazil produces an average of 3 million cars a year. Most of the largest world brands have set up manufacturing plants to produce automobiles in the southern regions, including General Motors, Ford, Honda, Nissan, Toyota, Mitsubishi, BMW, Volkswagen, Mercedes-Benz, Renault, Hyundai, and Fiat. The massive automotive industry in Brazil is regulated by the Associação Nacional dos Fabricantes de Veículos Automotores (Anfavea). Since 1956, this agency has overseen manufacturing operations of cars and agricultural machinery. In turn, the Brazilian Anfavea agency is part of the global regulator Organisation Internationale des Contructeurs d'Áutomobiles (OICA), which is based in Paris, France. Brazil, however, does not have its own car brand.

A brief history of the automotive industry can illustrate how Brazil became one of the largest car manufacturers in Latin America. During the 1960s, multiple foreign car companies set up factories. Ford and Chevrolet produced trucks and cars for the local market. Mercedes-Benz built trucks and buses, and Fiat became a local powerhouse with large factories. At that time, Brazil delivered roughly 133,000 cars a year. During the 1970s and 1980s, however, it implemented an economy closed to the rest of the world; therefore, these brands dominated the Brazilian market with a significant increase of production nearing 1 million cars a year.

After the fall of military rule in 1985, the Brazilian economy experienced trade liberalization during the 1990s. Import tariffs were removed, and other companies, including Peugeot, Honda, Audi, Nissan, Renault, and Citroën, set up plants in Brazil to use them for distribution in South America,. By the year 2000, Brazil was producing 1.5 million cars a year and 2.5 million by 2005.

Brazil became the sixth-largest car manufacturer in the world in 2008 when it surpassed France by delivering more than 3 million cars. The euphoria of such an accomplishment, however, was short-lived due to a worldwide financial crisis. The level of car production was reduced in 2016 to slightly over 2 million cars a year. The financial crisis of 2008 has lingered in Brazil for more than ten years, and the purchase power for the middle class has not returned to previous levels. Consequently, Brazilians are still somewhat ambivalent about their financial future regarding employment and social security. Consequently, they postpone making large purchases, including cars.

The federal government continues to support the automotive industry because it generates thousands of well-paid jobs and much-needed taxes. In 2012, it offered special incentives to manufacturers to produce fuel-efficient cars. However, this was viewed as a subsidy, and the World Trade Organization declared in 2016 that the policy amounted to illegal trade practices and protectionism. Brazil complied with the WTO regulations, and it aims to remain as the leading car manufacturer in South America.

See also: Chapter 4: Overview; Foreign Investment; Major Exports; Trading Partners; World Trade Organization (WTO).

Further Reading

Associação Nacional dos Fabricantes de Veículos Automotores (Anfavea) Official Website. http://www.anfavea.com.br

Muller, Joanne. 2012. "Why the World's Automakers Love Brazil." *Forbes,* October 22. Accessed July 1, 2019. https://www.forbes.com/sites/joannmuller/2012/10/05/why-the-worlds-automakers-are-loving-brazil/#2cfd482e7826

Oliveira, José Maria de, and Nidi Bueno. 2015. *Trade Liberalisation in Brazil: Market Structure, Economic Performance, and Manufacturing.* Rockville, MD: GlobalSouth Press.

BRICS Economic Group

BRICS is an economic group of five industrialized nations that exercise significant regional influence in their respective areas of the world. The acronym stands for Brazil, Russia, India, China, and South Africa. They all have emerging economies, and they all belong to the G-20 group of wealthiest nations in the world. Since its inception in 2006, the purpose of the economic bloc has been to encourage commercial agreements, political cooperation, as well as educational and cultural exchanges among the five nation members. According to 2015 data, these nations include a combined population of over 3.5 billion. In monetary terms, BRICS members represent $16.6 trillion U.S. of combined gross domestic product (GDP), which equates to almost 22 percent of global GDP.

The term BRICS was first used in 2001 by Jim O'Neill, who was the chairman of Goldman Sachs Asset Management at the time. The first meeting of foreign ministers from Brazil, Russia, India, and China took place in September 2006 in New York City. However, the first diplomatic meeting and first annual summit took place in Russia on June 16, 2009. South Africa joined the group later on December 24, 2010. Since then, the annual meetings are held in alternating locations among the five nation members.

The BRICS nation members agreed to take specific steps to improve commercial ties, reduce import taxes and tariffs, generate local jobs, and fund infrastructure projects. For example, they created the BRICS New Development Bank in 2014 based in Shanghai with an initial investment of $50 billion U.S., with each country contributing $10 billion. The goal is to control their financing needs and not depend on the lending terms dictated by the International Monetary Fund (IMF) in Washington, D.C. In Brazil, the New Development Bank funded an infrastructure project worth $67 U.S. million in 2018 to build six wind farms to generate clean electricity. In addition, BRICS nations have been implementing an enhanced communication system since 2012 by installing a network of fiber-optic submarine cables. The favorable trade agreements have already produced tangible results. China became Brazil's number one exports partner in 2017, replacing the United States. China also replaced Europe in 2018 as the top importer of Russian oil. Looking toward the future, former president Temer of Brazil declared in May 2018 that he wants his country to be a leader in the effort to establish a reserve pool of global currencies to help BRICS nations to better navigate another potential economic crisis in the future.

See also: Chapter 1: Infrastructure: Roads, Airports, Ports, and Railways. Chapter 4: Overview; Trading Partners. Sidebar: Foreign Aid: From Recipient to Donor.

Further Reading

BRICS Official Website. http://www.infobrics.org

Carmody, Pádraig. 2013. *The Rise of BRICS in Africa: The Geopolitics of South-South Relations.* London: Zed Books.

Chun, Kwang. 2013. *The BRICS Superpower Challenge: Foreign and Security Policy Analysis.* Burlington, VT: Ashgate Publishing.

Paraskova, Tsvetana. 2018. "China Is Replacing Europe as Russia's Number One Oil Customer." *Business Insider,* May 2. Accessed July 16, 2019. http://www.businessinsider.com/china-is-replacing-europe-as-russias-no-1-oil-customer-2018-5?r=UK&IR=T

Cardoso, Fernando Henrique (1931–)

Fernando Henrique Cardoso was born in Rio de Janeiro on June 18, 1931. He has practiced three major professions: sociologist, university professor, and politician. His family heritage includes privileged immigrants from Portugal who were politicians during the years of the Brazilian Empire (1822–1889). It also includes grandparents of African descent. In Brazil, he is widely known mostly by his initials FHC, especially in São Paulo, where he spent most of his life. He attended the University of São Paulo, where he earned a doctorate degree in sociology.

Cardoso achieved a prosperous career as a sociologist and college professor of political science. While he was a professor at the University of São Paulo, he published a seminal book in 1979 titled *Dependency and Development in Latin America*, which became almost mandatory reading for most college students throughout Latin America. He also lectured at Cambridge University in England, as well as Stanford University and Brown University in the United States.

As a politician, Cardoso served in multiple elected positions. After the military dictatorship fell in 1985, the country was on a path to a democratic transition. Cardoso was elected a federal senator in 1986 to represent the state of São Paulo. In 1987, he participated in the creation of the new democratic constitution of 1988, which is still currently in place. Between 1992 and 1993, he worked as the Brazilian minister of foreign affairs. Then he was appointed to serve from 1993 to 1994 as the minister of finance at a time when Brazil was experiencing enormous economic challenges. Cardoso left his minister position in 1994 in order to run for the presidency, which he won with an overwhelming majority.

Cardoso was the first Brazilian president to be reelected to a consecutive term. In total, he served in the executive office from 1995 until 2002. He is widely credited for stabilizing the economy during difficult periods of runaway inflation. Part of his strategy was to implement a privatization program to sell off ineffective state enterprises, including the national phone company Telebras and the mining giant Companhia Vale do Rio Doce. These steps attracted foreign investment. He also initiated an aggressive social agenda to reduce poverty in the country. Social programs such as Auxílio Gas provided subsidized domestic gas for poor families, Bolsa Alimentaçao provided meals to disadvantaged populations, and Bolsa Escola provided monetary assistance to families who kept their children in school.

After his presidency, Cardoso returned to academia. He continued writing for influential Brazilian newspapers. He is also a visiting scholar at Brown University, where he lectures on political science and economic policy. Moreover, he joined the Club de Madrid, a group made up of former presidents working toward peace, democracy, and global prosperity.

See also: Chapter 4: Overview; Foreign Investment.

Further Reading

Cardoso, Fernando Enrique. 1979. *Dependency and Development in Latin America*. Oakland: University of California Press.

Edwards, Todd L. 2008. *Brazil: A Global Studies Handbook*. Santa Barbara, CA: ABC-CLIO.

Koifman, Fábio. 2002. *Presidentes do Brasil: De Deodoro a FHC*. Rio de Janeiro: Editora Rio.

Vidal Luna, Francisco. 2014. *The Economic and Social History of Brazil since 1889*. Cambridge, UK: Cambridge University Press.

Coffee Exports

Brazil is the largest coffee producer and exporter in the world. After crude oil, coffee is the second-largest traded commodity in the planet. In 2018, the total amount of coffee global exports was a combined $30.6 billion U.S.. According to the 2018 report by the *World's Top Exports*, the five major exporters of coffee (based on highest monetary value worth of coffee) were:

1. Brazil: $4.4 billion U.S. (14.3% of total global coffee exports)
2. Vietnam: $3.1 billion (10.2%)
3. Germany: $2.5 billion (8.3%)
4. Switzerland: $2.4 billion (8.3%)
5. Colombia: $2.3 billion (7.6%)

Francisco de Melo Palheta first planted coffee in 1727 in the state of Pará, and Brazil quickly became a massive commercial producer by the early 1840s. The

Men, women, and children pick coffee berries in a field in Brazil, around 1900. In 2018, Brazil was the largest coffee producer and exporter in the world. With over 30 percent of the world's production, the coffee industry employs over 10 million people in contemporary Brazil. (Library of Congress)

southeastern region of Brazil offered fertile land and appropriate weather to expand commercial coffee production. The end of slavery in 1888 almost threatened the end of an economic cycle based on coffee exports, but Brazil managed to transition to an economy based on paid wages. By the early 1930s, it had developed a large monopoly in the global coffee market. For the next five decades, Brazil dominated the exports of both ground and instant coffee, especially to the United States.

The Brazilian government actively supports the coffee industry in both domestic and global markets; federal policies offer backing because it generates both jobs and local taxes. The government also invests in infrastructure, including roads, rail, and ports to facilitate exports. The top three largest consumers of coffee in the world are the United States, Brazil, and Germany. In Brazilian culture, a *cafezinho* (small shot of strong coffee) is a daily common tradition enjoyed with friends, at the office, and in business meetings. Fortunately, Brazil can supply all the coffee it needs for its daily cultural ritual. The United States is the largest global consumer of coffee, but since it does not produce enough to satisfy its own domestic needs, it has the largest deficit in the context of international coffee trade. That is precisely where Brazil comes in because the United States is the largest market for Brazilian coffee exports, followed by the European Union and Japan.

As of 2018, Brazil remains the top coffee producer in the world. It generates more than 30 percent of international coffee production, and it represents almost 10 percent of the total Brazilian export commodities. The crop has spread to over twelve states, but it is dominated by the states of Rio de Janeiro, Minas Gerais, São Paulo, Paraná, Bahia, and Espírito Santo. Its network generates millions of jobs in thousands of coffee plantations, processing plants, and transportation operations. The Brazilian Coffee Exporters Council (Ce Cafe) projects that coffee production and exports will continue to rise annually for the next decade.

See also: Chapter 4: Overview; Major Exports; Trading Partners. Chapter 14: *Cafezinho*, a Small Shot of Strong Coffee.

Further Reading

Brazilian Coffee Exporters Council (Ce Café) Official Website. http://www.cecafe.com.br/en

King, Winfield Conwell. 2017. *Brazil's Coffee Industry*. London: Forgotten Books.

Mello, Juliana. 2012. "Brazilian Coffee Industry." *Brazil Business,* October 14. Accessed July 29, 2019. http://thebrazilbusiness.com/article/brazilian-coffee-industry

Workman, Daniel. 2018. "Coffee Exports by Country." *World's Top Exports,* May 29. Accessed July 29, 2019. http://www.worldstopexports.com/coffee-exports-country

Embraer, Empresa Brasileira de Aeronáutica

Embraer (Empresa Brasileira de Aeronáutica) is a Brazilian aircraft manufacturer that also provides aviation maintenance services. Its headquarters are located in São José dos Campos in São Paulo State. It started as a small company to provide airplanes for the domestic market, but it has grown into an international corporation with airplanes for multiple markets (military defense, executive jets, commercial airliners, cargo planes, and agricultural aircraft). In 2018, it delivered 90 commercial aircraft worth over $6 billion U.S. in revenue. Its main competitor is the Canadian aircraft manufacturer Bombardier.

The Brazilian government created Embraer in 1969 to develop a national aircraft industry. At first, it was completely owned by the federal government. It started producing a small turboprop-engine passenger airplane called the EMB 110 Bandeirante. During the 1970s, it focused on military fighter jets for the Brazilian Air Force with models AT-26 Xavante and EMB 312 Tucano. During the 1980s, Embraer developed its first successful commercial airliner called EMB 120 Brasilia, which was quickly purchased by regional airlines in South America. Afterwards, the government implemented a wave of privatizations, and Embraer was sold on December 7, 1994. Nowadays, Embraer trades as a public company in two separate stock exchanges: the Brazilian BM&F and the New York Stock Exchange (NYSE). However, the Brazilian government kept a significant number of golden shares that provides them with veto power.

After private ownership of Embraer took over management, it quickly developed an expansion plan. It continued to receive government contracts for military and small planes. The new plan was to develop small business jets and also other options for commercial airlines between seventy and one hundred seats. Consequently, Embraer developed models Legacy 600 in 2000, Phenom 100 in 2005, and Phenom 300 in 2008. The venture was extremely profitable, and Embraer delivered its 1,000th executive jet in 2016. For commercial aviation, Embraer created the EMB 190. Then it released its E2 jet in 2011, which received fifty orders in 2014 from Air Costa, a low-cost airline from India with a total transaction value of almost $3 billion U.S. In addition, the company expanded its military aircraft beyond fighting jets to compete in the military cargo sector. First, it developed the Embraer KC-390 exclusively for the Brazilian Air Force, but the Brazilian Postal Office quickly showed interest in the aircraft. Then Argentina and other MERCOSUR trade partners also placed orders for these planes. In 2016, overall, Embraer delivered 225 planes.

Embraer has grown into an international conglomerate in order to handle different aspects of its business model. While most of the manufacturing is still done in Brazil, it opened another production facility at the Orlando International Airport in Florida. In addition, it established two new facilities for Embraer Aircraft Maintenance Services in Nashville, Tennessee, and Ribatejo, Portugal. The company also maintains offices in Paris, Beijing, Singapore, Washington, D.C., and Florida. As of 2018, the future of Embraer looked extremely bright as it finalized the agreement to create a commercial jet venture with Boeing Company. It will provide a significant combined advantage for manufacturing, engineering, and marketing.

See also: Chapter 4: Overview; Automobile Industry; Embraer, Empresa Brasileira de Aeronáutica; Foreign Investment; Major Exports; Mercosul/Mercosur; Trading Partners.

Further Reading

Adghirni, Samy, and Julie Johnsson. 2018. "Embraer Jumps with Boeing Deal Talks in Final Stage." *Bloomberg News,* June 12. Accessed July 1, 2019. https://www.bloomberg.com /news/articles/2018-06-12/embraer-jumps-with-boeing-deal-talks-said-to-be-in-final -stage

Embraer (Empresa Brasileira de Aeronáutica) Official Website. https://embraer.com/br/pt

Rodengen, Jeffrey L. 2009. *The History of Embraer.* Fort Lauderdale, FL: Write Stuff Enterprises.

Energy Industry: Electricity, Oil, Ethanol, and Renewable Sources

Since 2015, Brazil has been self-sufficient in terms of its energy needs. While Brazil is the largest consumer of energy in South America, it actually exports energy to neighboring countries in the form of oil, natural gas, ethanol, and electricity. The federal government operates a network of agencies in charge of setting and implementing its energy policy, including the National Agency of Petroleum, National Gas and Biofuels (ANP), the Ministry of Mines and Energy (MME), and the National Council for Energy Policy (CNPE). In addition, the federal government owns the largest national oil company (Petrobras) and the largest electricity company (Electrobrás). In 2000, Brazil approved laws that broke the monopoly of state-owned companies and sparked a liberalization process to allow foreign investments to make the energy sector more efficient and competitive.

After the discovery of extremely large oil reserves at the Campos and Santos basins off the Atlantic coast, Brazil became completely self-sufficient in its oil needs. In 2015, it became a net exporter of both crude oil and finished oil products supported by a network of refineries and oil tankers owned by Petrobras. Since natural gas is often produced together with oil exploration, Petrobras also controls the production and distribution of almost 90 percent of all natural gas reserves. It is used mostly for domestic consumption at homes and light industries.

Brazil produces almost 80 percent of its electricity by using hydroelectric power plants. Since the country has large rivers, the use of their currents to generate electricity is an immense industry. In fact, the Itaipu Dam (built on the Parana River on the border with Paraguay) is the second-largest hydroelectric power plant in the world. This type of renewable energy generates so much wattage that Brazil actually sells electricity to neighboring Paraguay and Argentina. Brazil also draws energy from two existing nuclear power plants called Angra II and III. These plants have faced more recent social opposition due to their high operating costs, the relatively small production of electricity, and the potential environmental damage.

Since the 1970s, Brazil has been a leader of biomass fuels by using sugarcane to produce ethanol, which is blended into the gasoline used by cars and trucks. Today, most fuels used in car engines have a 25 percent blend of ethanol. In addition, Brazil is one of the leading exporters of ethanol to international markets.

The future is bright for the implementation of wind power to produce energy. The northeast region of the country is specifically poised to expand on this technology because the winds are particularly strong between May and December, precisely when severe droughts lower the water levels in regional rivers and hence reduce hydroelectric production. Since the government's approval of the Incentive Program for Alternative Sources of Electric Energy (most commonly known as Proinfa), wind turbines now generate enough energy to provide electricity to over 400,000 homes.

See also: Chapter 4: Overview; Petrobras, the National Oil Company.

Further Reading

Brazil Electricity Regulatory Agency (ANEEL) Official Website. http://www2.aneel.gov.br

Brazilian Ministry of Mines and Energy (MME) Official Website. http://www.mme.gov.br

Casey, Claire. 2013. "Is Brazil the Energy Power of the Future?" *Americas Quarterly,* Summer. Accessed July 10, 2019. http://www.americasquarterly.org/is-brazil-the-energy-power-of-the-future

Petrobras Official Website. http://www.petrobras.com.br/en

Pomela, Marina. 2015. "Energy Sources in Brazil." *Brazil Business,* May 13. Accessed July 10, 2019. http://thebrazilbusiness.com/article/energy-sources-in-brazil

Favelas (Slums)

Brazil has one of the highest levels of economic inequality in the world. While *Forbes* magazine published in 2012 that the number of Brazil billionaires was on the rise, the country also has crushing levels of poverty. Most Brazilian cities and urban centers now include *favelas* (slums or shantytowns) that house low-income dwellers who are unable to afford housing in the city. Based on 2010 census data provided by the Brazilian Institute of Geography and Statistics (IBSE), 6 percent of the national population lives in *favelas*. That means that almost 11.5 million people survive in housing conditions without appropriate electricity, water, sanitation, and sewer services throughout the country. Those numbers, however, are likely to be much higher since the data related to such populations are not always reported truthfully.

The first *favelas* were established in Rio de Janeiro in the late 1800s as soldiers returned from the Canudo War, but they did not have a place to live. They started to occupy small pieces of land and building small shacks that quickly grew into a community. During the 1950s and 1960s, thousands of people migrated from the countryside looking for jobs. However, unable to find employment, most people ended up living in such urban slums. These shantytowns quickly became associated with crime and poverty. Consequently, the military rule during the 1970s attempted to eradicate *favelas* by relocating people. The program essentially failed because people could not find affordable housing alternatives. During the 1980s and 1990s, *favelas* became associated with extreme violence ruled by gangs involved in the drug trade. In attempts to take control of crime and violence in *favelas* throughout the country, Brazil created the Pacifying Police Units (UPPs) in 2008 as a combination of law enforcement and social services. The general goal was to provide protection to favela residents and to reclaim control of the slums from drug dealers. However, when the UPP units became militarized, the residents of *favelas* constantly complained of human rights abuses and torture by the Pacifying Police that was supposed to protect them.

The 2014 World Soccer Cup and the 2016 Summer Olympics provided unprecedented levels of international attention on Brazil, especially on Rio de Janeiro. The Brazilian government was concerned about the media coverage regarding *favelas*, and President Michel Temer (1940–) proposed a plan to be tough on crime. Consequently, Rio de Janeiro implemented aggressive policies to control local violence starting in 2013. The result was an increase in military patrol of Rio's slums. When the residents complained about forced relocation from *favelas* to make way for infrastructure projects for the Olympics, the response was an even stronger military intervention that escalated to brutal arrests, torture, intimidation, and even weekly cases of residents being killed in altercations with the Pacifying Police.

See also: Chapter 3: Temer, Michel (1940–). Chapter 4: Overview. Chapter 6: Poverty, Social Conflict, and Protests.

Further Reading

Cuadros, Alex. 2016. "Brazil's Olympics Meet Its Favelas." *New Yorker,* August 8. Accessed August 1, 2019. https://www.newyorker.com/news/news-desk/brazils-olympics-meet-its-favelas

Instituto Brasileiro de Geografia e Estatística—Brazilian Institute of Geography and Statistics (IBGE). 2010. "Census 2010." Brasilia. Accessed July 15, 2019. http://ibge.gov.br

Londoño, Ernesto, and Shasta Darlington. 2018. "Brazil's Military Is Put in Charge of Security in Rio de Janeiro." *New York Times,* February 16. Accessed July 15, 2019. https://www.nytimes.com/2018/02/16/world/americas/brazil-rio-military-security.html

Penglase, R. Ben. 2014. *Living with Insecurity in a Brazilian Favela: Urban Violence and Daily Life.* New Brunswick, NJ: Rutgers University Press.

Foreign Investment

Beginning on 2008, Brazil experienced almost a decade of a deep recession; however, foreign direct investment (FDI) improved significantly in 2017. In fact, Brazil now captures the largest percentage of FDI in Latin America. According to the United Nations Economic Commission for Latin America and the Caribbean (ECLAC), Brazil received 47 percent of all foreign investment in the region worth roughly $79 billion U.S. in 2018. Brazil is an attractive market for investment due to its large population of 211 million people, abundance of raw materials and natural resources, oil self-sufficiency, and a central geographical position that provides access to the rest of South America. In addition, Brazilian companies have become more competitive in the world. Actually, trade statistics provided by Santander Trade Office report that, in 2017, nine out of ten acquisitions by foreign companies in Latin America happened in Brazil. The top three countries to invest in Brazil are the United States, Spain, and the Netherlands.

In spite of all the policies aimed at increasing its role in global trade, Brazil still has significant restrictions for foreign direct investment. Moreover, large numbers of individual foreign investors and companies continue to see Brazil as a risky investment due to its handling of recent economic crises, massive social protests, a murky tax system, and inflexible labor laws. Foreigners are able to purchase land and real estate freely; the only restrictions are related to property located near international borders with other countries. In 2013, the land ownership legislation (Law 5709) was amended to limit the purchase of massive amounts of agricultural land by foreign companies to less than 25 percent of the overall area of any municipality in Brazil. Aspects of the national economy where foreign investment is more restricted include the insurance sector, aviation, television media, and other monopolies such as electricity plants and the production of energy.

> ### JORGE PAULO LEMANN (1939–), THE RICHEST MAN IN BRAZIL
>
> Jorge Paulo Lemann was born in Rio de Janeiro. In 2019, *Forbes* magazine estimated his wealth at $23 billion U.S., which ranked him as the thirty-sixth richest person in the world and the wealthiest person in Brazil. He made his initial fortune in investment banking with Banco Garantia, which he sold in 1998. Later, he founded the private equity firm 3G with partners Carlos Sicupira and Marecel Telles. They created the world's largest beer company, AB InBev, by acquiring Brazilian brewery Brahma, Belgian corporation Interbrew, and American company Anheuser-Busch/Budweiser. 3G also acquired other well-known American brands, such as Burger King and Kraft, which in turn includes Oscar Meyer and Kool-Aid. In addition, Warren Buffet partnered with 3G to acquire Heinz. Lemann now lives in Switzerland after his children were almost kidnapped in Brazil.

The Brazilian government takes an active role in promoting foreign direct investment by creating special economic free zones and offering initial tax exemptions in specific export industries. In addition, the Brazilian National Bank for Economic and Social Development (BNDES) actively encourages and finances projects that inject FDI into the Brazilian economy to improve infrastructure. In its recent ambitious plan titled *Vision 2035: Brazil Developed*, the BNDES envisions a robust Brazilian economy by 2035 by actively working with FDI to finance and complete strategic projects in the following fields: agriculture, metallurgy, health services, logistics, telecommunications, and green energy.

See also: Chapter 4: Overview; Major Exports; Trading Partners.

Further Reading

Alves, Lise. 2017. "Brazil Led Region's Direct Foreign Investment Inflows in 2016." *Rio Times*, August 11. Accessed July 25, 2019. http://riotimesonline.com/brazil-news/rio-business/brazil-led-regions-direct-foreign-investment-inflows-in-2016

Brazilian National Bank for Economic and Social Development (BNDES) Official Website. https://www.bndes.gov.br/wps/portal/site/home

Santander Trade. "Brazil: Foreign Investment." Santander Trade Portal. Accessed July 25, 2019. https://en.portal.santandertrade.com/establish-overseas/brazil/foreign-investment

United Nations Economic Commission for Latin America and the Caribbean (ECLAC) Official Website. https://www.cepal.org/en

Workman, Daniel. 2018. "Brazil's Top 15 Trading Partners." *World's Top Exports*, Feb 6. Accessed July 25, 2019. http://www.worldstopexports.com/brazils-top-import-partners

Labor Migration

Brazilian migration patterns have historically been tied to economic factors. First, the Portuguese forcibly brought African slaves to work in sugar plantations during the colonial period (1500–1888). After slavery was abolished in 1888, there were three distinct waves of immigrants who came to Brazil. From the 1880s to1890s, the government encouraged migrants from European countries who eventually settled in the southern part of the country to work in the emerging coffee industry. Almost 2 million Europeans came from Portugal, Italy, Spain, Germany, China, and Korea. The general goal was to encourage economic growth, but also to make Brazilian society a bit more "white and civilized." The second wave came from 1900 to the 1930s when another 2 million Europeans arrived after World War I from Russia, Romania, Poland, and Italy. The first large group of 189,000 Japanese also arrived during this period and established themselves near São Paulo. The third wave came from 1930 to 1960 to work mostly in agriculture. Over 100,000 Spaniards also came to work mostly in industrial jobs. Then more than 30,000 immigrants arrived from Lebanon and Syria; they were mostly entrepreneurs who opened small businesses. Then, when the military government took over Brazil in 1964, they stopped policies aimed at attracting immigrants.

Recent migration is also tied to economic factors. From 1990 to 2010, Brazil received large numbers of both legal and illegal immigrants, especially from Argentina, Colombia, South Korea, Peru, and Bolivia. In 1991, Brazil was a founding member of Mercosul/Mercosul, a strategic alliance to improve the flow of goods, currency, and people. The regional trading bloc includes Brazil, Argentina, Paraguay, Uruguay, and Bolivia. The agreement has produced tremendous commercial benefits, especially for Brazil since it is the largest economy in South America. However, the countries were supposed to coordinate immigration policies, but they have never been implemented.

Brazil has a large economy that requires both university-trained employees and low-skilled workers. Since 2010, the federal government has encouraged educated foreigners to come to Brazil, and the Labor Ministry offers work visas for engineers, entrepreneur investors, computer scientists, industrial managers, and infrastructure project managers. Between 2000 and 2004, almost 110,000 work visas were provided to people from the United States, France, Great Britain, and Germany. On the other hand, Brazil also offers millions of low-skill jobs in agriculture, ranching, tourism, and manufacturing. Consequently, it attracts tens of thousands of workers from both Central and South America. Since Brazil is a large territory that borders nine countries, it is extremely difficult to control all entry points, especially in remote unpopulated regions. The numbers of illegal immigrants are difficult to verify, but most recent government estimates are 200,000 Peruvians, 25,000 Bolivians, 25,000 Colombians, and 50,000 Koreans. The Brazilian government has not implemented strict policies to deport illegal immigrants; similarly, it has not made any effort to provide amnesty to legalize undocumented workers.

See also: Chapter 4: Overview; Manufacturing; Mercosul/Mercosur.

Further Reading

Amaral, Ernesto Friedrich, and Wilson Fusco. 2005. "Shaping Brazil: The Role of International Migration." Migration Policy Institute, June 1. Accessed July 1, 2019. https://www.migrationpolicy.org/article/shaping-brazil-role-international-migration

Martin, Phillip. 2006. *Managing Labor Migration in the Twenty-First Century.* New Haven, CT: Yale University Press.

Mercosur Official Website. http://www.mercosur.int

Roett, Riordan (ed.). 1999. *Mercosur: Regional Integration, World Markets.* Boulder, CO: Lynne Rienner.

Major Exports

Since 2014, Brazil has retained its position as the seventh-largest economy in the world. The Brazilian government has taken an active role in developing an export-oriented economy. In that capacity, it has negotiated dozens of bilateral trade agreements at the global stage. Brazil is also a member of two trading blocs that expand the reach of Brazilian exports: Mercosur is the South American trade group that includes Argentina, Brazil, Uruguay, Paraguay, and Bolivia; BRICS is an economic partnership that galvanizes the commercial interests of influential countries such as Brazil, Russia, India, China, and South Africa. While negotiating trade deals for Brazilian exports abroad, the government also invests heavily domestically to encourage an economy that facilitates exports. For example, it has funded massive infrastructure projects that include highways, railroads, ports, energy plants, electricity grids, and airports, all of which have the domestic advantage of generating thousands of regional jobs. The main Brazilian exports include primary goods such as coffee, cocoa, beef, poultry meat, orange juice, raw and refined sugar, iron ore, minerals, refined petroleum, as well as manufactured products that include airplanes, electronics, and cars. Overall, Brazil is the largest exporter of coffee and raw sugar in the world. In addition, it is the third-largest exporter of beef and cocoa to global markets.

According to *Trading Economics*, a repository of research data on international trade, Brazilian exports increased dramatically during 2017 and 2018 as global markets recuperated from a trade slump after the 2008 international financial crisis. During 2017, Brazilian exports reached U.S. $217.7 billion, boosted by a significant increase in agricultural exports including beef and soybeans, especially to China. In 2018, there was a slight increase on exports during the first six months, but the year eventually revealed a small decrease of 2.8 percent compared to 2107 reaching only $211.8 billion U.S. caused by a reduction of exporting manufactured goods (aircraft, cars, shoes, and electronics) and primary products (cocoa and orange juice). Overall, trade to China continued to increase, but exports to Mexico, the European Union, and the United States were reduced during this period.

According to the Brazilian Ministry of Development and Foreign Trade (MDIC), the top five trading partners for Brazilian goods in 2018 were China, the United States, Argentina, the Netherlands, and Japan. China became the number one trading partner for Brazil in 2012, surpassing the United States. In the near future, the MDIC will be actively pursuing treaties to expand Brazilian exports to the Middle East and African nations based on agricultural products, industrial minerals, auto parts, and light commercial aircraft. In addition, Brazil has recently pursued action against multiple countries using the World Trade Organization (WTO) as arbitration to defend a fair competition of Brazilian products in global markets.

See also: Chapter 1: Sidebar: Exporting Natural Resources. Chapter 4: Overview; BRICS Economic Group; Mercosul/Mercosur; Trading Partners; World Trade Organization (WTO).

Further Reading

Brazilian Ministry of Development and Foreign Trade (MDIC) Official Website. http://www.mdic.gov.br

Oliveira, José Maria de. 2015. *Trade Liberalisation in Brazil: Market Structure, Economic Performance, and Manufacturing.* Rockville, MD: GlobalSouth Press.

Trading Economics Research. https://tradingeconomics.com/brazil/exports

Verotti Farah, Ana Gabriela. 2013. "Largest Trading Partners of Brazil." *Brazil Business,* October 24. Accessed August 1, 2019. http://thebrazilbusiness.com/article/largest-trading-partners-of-brazil

Workman, Daniel. 2018. "Brazil's Top 15 Trading Partners." *World's Top Exports,* Feb 6. Accessed August 1, 2019. http://www.worldstopexports.com/brazils-top-import-partners

World Trade Organization Official Website. https://www.wto.org

Manufacturing

Brazil has a vibrant manufacturing industry aimed at both domestic and export markets. It includes commodities in agribusiness (agricultural products, fertilizers, and beef), minerals (steel and mining), cement, appliances (refrigerators and television sets), paper products, as well as higher-end complex goods (aviation, automobiles, cellular phones, electronics, and petrochemicals). Manufacturing accounts for roughly 25 percent of the annual gross domestic product (GDP). Most of the factories for production are located in the southern and southeast regions of the country; this is an enormous commercial region that generates almost 60 percent of all industrial production in Latin America.

The current environment of market-friendly policies is relatively recent in Brazil. During the 1970s and 1980s, the military regime essentially closed the country to foreign influences. After its demise in 1985, the new democratic Brazil implemented

> **ANNUAL CHRISTMAS BONUS SALARY**
>
> Brazilian labor law requires companies to provide an extra monthly salary payment to all registered employees who worked the entire year. This bonus payment is typically paid in December. If an employee only worked part of the year, then the bonus payment is calculated as 1 ½ of the respective monthly salary for each month actually worked. This is a concept that does not exist in the United States, but it is legally mandatory in Brazil. Since it is based on the salary for twelve months, it is also called *décimo terceiro salário* (thirteenth salary). This term has become more common in the last ten years since multiple large companies now split the bonus payment in two, one provided in June and the other one in December.

liberalization policies to encourage foreign trade and investment during the 1990s. The governments of presidents Fernando Henrique Cardoso (1995–2002) and Luiz Inácio Lula da Silva (2003–2011) agreed to open the Brazilian economy, which attracted foreign investment and created the conditions for Brazil to become a regional economic powerhouse. They both implemented a privatization program to sell ineffective government-owned industries (the telephone company Telebras and the mining conglomerate Vale do Rio Doce) to the private sector. This policy generated federal income while simultaneously making those industries more competitive. At the beginning of the twenty-first century, the government invested heavily in massive infrastructure projects (highways, airports, deep ports, and energy plants) to facilitate further industrialization, regional trade, and global exports.

The recent manufacturing growth is a result of both Brazilian companies and multinational corporations operating in Brazil. For example, the proudly Brazilian Embraer (Empresa Brasileira de Aeronáutica) is based in the state of São Paulo, but it has grown into an international conglomerate that produces airplanes for multiple markets (military defense, executive jets, commercial airliners, cargo planes, and agricultural aircraft). In 2017, it generated almost $6 billion U.S. in revenue based on sales and aircraft maintenance services. Meanwhile, southern Brazil also houses automobile manufacturing plants for most of the world's brands, including General Motors, Ford, Honda, Nissan, Toyota, Mitsubishi, BMW, Volkswagen, Mercedes-Benz, Renault, Hyundai, and Fiat. The massive automotive industry produces an average of 3 million cars a year.

The Brazilian government must become more competitive in order to maintain its economic position in a globalized economy. In 2011, it launched a program called Brasil Maior aiming to increase the competitiveness of domestic industries. The overall goal was to effectively link three crucial groups: industry, technology, and foreign trade policy. By 2015, this plan had already led to a reduction in corporate taxes, more energy savings, clarification of investment legal contracts, as well as Internet start-up businesses supported by venture capital (both foreign and domestic). One of the major hurdles to overcome, however, is the inadequate educational system. As Brazil becomes more technologically advanced, it must generate a more educated force with technical, scientific, and engineering skills.

See also: Chapter 4: Overview; Automobile Industry; Embraer, Empresa Brasileira de Aeronáutica; Cardoso, Fernando Enrique (1931–); Foreign Investment; Major Exports.

Further Reading

Embraer (Empresa Brasileira de Aeronáutica) Official Website. https://embraer.com/br/pt

Muller, Joanne. 2012. "Why the World's Automakers Love Brazil." *Forbes,* October 22. Accessed July 1, 2019. https://www.forbes.com/sites/joannmuller/2012/10/05/why-the-worlds-automakers-are-loving-brazil/#2cfd482e7826

Oliveira, José Maria de, and Nidi Bueno. 2015. *Trade Liberalisation in Brazil: Market Structure, Economic Performance, and Manufacturing.* Rockville, MD: GlobalSouth Press.

Trading Economics. "Brazil Manufacturing Production 2019." https://tradingeconomics.com/brazil/manufacturing-production

Mercosul/Mercorsur

In 1991, a group of South American countries created a strategic alliance to improve the flow of goods, currency, and people. The regional bloc was established by the Treaty of Asunción under the names Mercosul, Mercosul, and Ñemby Ñemuha, which stands for Mercado Comum do Sul in Portuguese, Mercado Común del Sur in Spanish, and Nemby Ñemuha (Southern Market) in Guarani. These are the three official languages of Mercosul. The original agreement to create the regional group was amended in 1994 at the Treaty of Ouro Preto signed in Brazil. Four of the original founding members are Brazil, Argentina, Paraguay, and Uruguay. Bolivia was accepted as a full member in 2015. Venezuela was one of the initial full members, but it was suspended in 2016 by unanimous decision due to its lack of compliance with human rights protections.

Mercosur/Mercosul created an infrastructure to oversee its trade policies, legal framework, jurisdiction disputes, educational exchanges, and monetary policy. First of all, the official headquarters of Mercosur are located in Montevideo, Uruguay. The highest court to oversee legal matters related to Mercosur disputes is based in Asunción, Paraguay. In December 2004, all countries agreed to establish the Mercosur Parliament with eighteen representatives from each nation regardless of the country's population, gross domestic product (GDP), amounts of exports, or political affiliations. The bloc proposed the use of the "gaucho" as a common currency for trade, but the plan was never implemented. Since these countries are connected by geography, the main issues defined by common policy include customs and border issues, sea and land transportation, agricultural policy, energy production and sharing, macroeconomic policies, tax and monetary trade definitions, commercial agreements, migration, technical standards, educational coordination, as well as issues related to labor and employment.

Mercosur agreements have already generated tangible benefits. In terms of commercial trade among nation members, it grew from $10 billion U.S. in 1991 to $88 billion in 2010, and it continues to increase. A significant part of the trade increase was based on agricultural, industrial, and energy exports. In the field of education, a subcommittee worked on creating certificates and university degrees that are accepted in all member nations. In addition, the curriculum of elementary and middle school is also now coordinated to be accepted in all Mercosur countries, except when it entails technical studies. The idea is to produce a labor force with similar skills across nations.

Mercosur/Mercosul recently embarked on a new strategy to negotiate as a Common Market with countries outside its members. In 2004, it negotiated a trade agreement with the Andean Community of Nations (CAN) regional bloc that includes Colombia, Ecuador, and Peru. It also signed commercial agreements with Israel in 2007, Egypt in 2010, and Lebanon in 2014. In addition, Mercosur finalized agreements with both New Zealand and Mexico to join Mercosul as observer countries. Brazil continues to be a leader in the Mercosul regional group, especially because it has the largest and most dynamic economy of all the member nations.

See also: Chapter 4: Overview; Foreign Investment; Major Exports; Trading Partners.

Further Reading

Margheritis, Ana (ed.). 2003. *Latin American Democracies in the New Global Economy.* Boulder, CO: Lynne Rienner.

Mercosur Official Website. http://www.mercosur.int

Rivera, Salvador. 2014. *Latin American Unification: A History of Political and Economic Integration Efforts.* Jefferson, NC: McFarland.

Roett, Riordan (ed.). 1999. *Mercosur: Regional Integration, World Markets.* Boulder, CO: Lynne Rienner.

Mineral Wealth

Brazil is one of the top twenty global economies, partly based on its wealth of natural resources. During the 2010s, the Brazilian government has worked in tandem with private industry to foster a series of international treaties that include export agreements of minerals either in raw form or finished products. Due to the large territory of the country, the mineral wealth is immense. An evaluation of natural resources in 2011 revealed that Brazil was sitting on an estimated $726 billion U.S. worth of metals and iron ore reserves with thirty-one years of production. In 2015, Brazil was established as a leading global mineral producer, and it actively traded eighty mineral commodities on international markets.

The mineral statistics reveal a series of superlatives. On the global stage, Brazil has the fifth-largest reserves of iron ore in the world, and it is the second-largest producer of iron ore. It is also the seventh-largest producer of tin and the thirteenth-largest gold producer. Brazil is also a significant producer of niobium, bauxite, and aluminum. International demand for minerals and metals has placed Brazil as a leading exporter of copper, lead, manganese, asbestos, gemstones, fertilizers, and phosphate rock. As a result, Brazil has become more attractive for foreign capital direct investments in both the mining and mineral industries, as well as infrastructure projects such as ports and roads to get those materials to export facilities.

In 2018, the United States imposed tariffs on aluminum (10 percent) and steel (25 percent) on multiple countries, which had a significant impact on Brazilian exports. Brazil is the sixth-largest aluminum producer in the world; in 2010, these exports were worth $1.7 billion U.S. In 2014, Brazil was the fifth-largest net exporter of steel in the world, which generated $1.5 billion U.S. on exports. In addition, Brazil supplies large quantities of both aluminum and steel to the thriving national automotive industry. The production of these two metals alone provides over 240,000 direct jobs. While Brazil exports minerals and metals to over seventy countries (especially to China, Japan, France, South Korea, and Germany), the U.S. tariffs still have had a negative impact on the national economy. A visit by U.S. vice president Mike Pence to Brazil in June 2018 specifically included this topic on the agenda, but it did not result in a revised agreement to exempt Brazil from such tariffs.

See also: Chapter 1: Sidebar: Exporting Natural Resources. Chapter 4: Automobile Industry; Foreign Investment; Major Exports.

Further Reading

Brazilian Ministry of Development and Foreign Trade (MDIC) Official Website. http://www.mdic.gov.br

Darlington, Shasta. 2018. "The U.S. Says It Has a Tariff Deal with Brazil; Brazil Disagrees." *New York Times,* May 2. Accessed July 29, 2019. https://www.nytimes.com/2018/05/02/business/us-brazil-tariffs.html

Lubin, Gus. 2011. "15 Countries Sitting on a Fortune of Metals and Minerals." *Business Insider,* September 1. Accessed July 29, 2019. http://www.businessinsider.com/countries-metal-mineral-wealth-2011-9

Natural Resource Governance Institute. https://resourcegovernance.org/our-work/country/brazil

Soutter, Will. 2012. "Brazil: Mining, Minerals, and Fuel Resources." *AZO Mining,* July. Accessed September 12, 2019. http://www.azomining.com/article.aspx?ArticleID=51

Trading Economics Research. https://tradingeconomics.com/brazil/exports

Petrobras, the National Oil Company

Petrobras (Petróleo Brasileiro S.A.) is a Brazilian petroleum international corporation founded in 1953 by President Getúlio Vargas (1882–1954). Its headquarters are in Rio de Janeiro. The federal government owns 54 percent of the company, while the Brazilian Sovereign Fund and the Brazilian Development Bank each own 5 percent, for a total of 64 percent government control. The rest is owned by private investors. In 2016, Petrobras generated $87 billion U.S.in revenue, and its shares are traded in stock exchanges in São Paulo, New York, and Madrid. Brazil produces enough oil to cover its own domestic needs and now exports oil products abroad. Petrobras also owns significant oil operations in Europe, Africa, North America, South America, and Asia. In 2019, it met its target of producing roughly 2.6 million barrels of oil daily.

Petrobras operates six different business sections in the production of energy. First, the most profitable operations include crude oil and oil products. Second, exploration operations go beyond oil to also include natural gas. Third, it operates a complex network of transportation and logistics for the distribution of biodiesel, ethanol, and oil products throughout Brazil. Fourth, it manages national delivery of natural gas and electric power. Fifth, it coordinates international exploration, refining, and production of oil products in overseas locations. Finally, it also manages an immense amount of sugar production to convert it into ethanol and electricity.

The future of Petrobras looks extremely positive based on exploration projects, proven oil reserves, and export agreements. It has proven developed reserves of over 8 billion barrels of oil equivalent and almost 6 billion barrels in undeveloped reserves. In 2000, it reached a world record for deepwater oil exploration with a depth of 6,158

A Petrobras gas station in Rio Grande do Sul State. Petróleo Brasileiro S.A. (simply known as Petrobras) is the Brazilian national oil company founded in 1953. It is involved in oil exploration, energy reserves management, and oil exports. (Alf Ribeiro/Dreamstime.com)

feet (1,877 meters). In 2007 and 2008, Petrobras announced one of the largest oil discoveries in the world located in the Santos Basin roughly 186 miles (300 kilometers) off the coast of Rio de Janeiro. This basin includes the Lula oil field, the Sugar Loaf Field, and the Jupiter Field. Based on the proven large oil reserves, China lent Brazil $10 billion U.S. in 2009 in exchange for a constant supply of 60,000 to 100,000 barrels of oil per day.

Petrobras has faced enormous scandals recently. In 2014, the largest corruption scandal in Brazilian history was discovered, and Petrobras was central to the special investigation called Operation Carwash. It unveiled a complex web of Petrobras bureaucrats working with politicians and corporations to overcharge Petrobras for construction and maintenance services in exchange for monetary political bribes worth $3 billion U.S. The unprecedented level of corruption led to the arrest of both Petrobras officials and federal politicians. Massive protests demanded criminal charges against President Dilma Rousseff (1947–) and former president Luiz Inácio Lula da Silva (1945–) because both had been members of Petrobras's board of directors.

See also: Chapter 3: Corruption and Political Scandals; Rousseff, Dilma (1947–); Lula da Silva, Luiz Inácio (1945–). Chapter 4: Overview; Energy Industry: Electricity, Oil, Ethanol, and Renewable Sources; Major Exports; Trading Partners.

Further Reading

Bray, Chad, and Stanley Reed. 2018. "Petrobras of Brazil to Pay $2.95 Billion over Corruption Scandal." *New York Times,* January 3. Accessed July 21, 2019. https://www.nytimes.com/2018/01/03/business/dealbook/brazil-petrobras-corruption-scandal.html

Novais, Andréa. 2011. "Understand Petrobras." *Brazil Business,* November 24. Accessed July 21, 2019. http://thebrazilbusiness.com/article/understand-petrobras

Petrobras National Oil Company Official Website. http://www.petrobras.com.br/en

Valle, Sabrina, and Denyse Godoy. 2016. "Brazil Gets $10 Billion Chinese Loan in Oil Supply Deal." *Bloomberg News,* February 26. Accessed July 21, 2019. https://www.bloomberg.com/news/articles/2016-02-26/petrobras-gets-10-billion-from-china-to-shore-up-finances

Stock Exchanges: Bovespa, BM&F, and B3

On August 23, 1890, Emilio Rangel Pestana founded the original stock exchange in Brazil under the name Bolsa de Valores de São Paulo (Bovespa). It has since provided multiple services to the stock market in Brazil and served as a barometer of the national economy. At the beginning, Bovespa was owned by the federal government, and up until the 1960s, it actually appointed all the brokers authorized to trade in the stock exchange. By 1966, the stock market became more independent and self-regulated; it is currently supervised by the Comissão de Valores Mobiliários (CVM), which functions in a similar manner as the Securities and Exchange Commission in the United States. During the 1970s, Bovespa introduced trading by phone and a computerized system of record keeping, which were revolutionary at the time. Then in 1997, Bovespa established a new system of electronic trading that became the standard in Brazil.

On May 8, 2008, Bovespa merged with the Brazilian Mercantile and Futures Exchange (BM&F), a transaction that created the second-largest stock exchange in the world at the time. The new company was called BM&F Bovespa, and it included 381 large companies that actively traded on the new stock exchange. Its highest record was reached on August 17, 2011, when it traded at a value of $14.8 billion U.S. (R$23.7 billion). While BM&F Bovespa is based in São Paulo, it also has offices in Shanghai, New York City, London, and Rio de Janeiro.

In December 2015, the BM&F Bovespa made its first attempt to acquire CETIP, which is the largest depository of private securities and derivatives in Latin America. Its headquarters are in Rio de Janeiro. As of June 2018, it had over $2 trillion U.S. in assets held in custody for its clients. Based on its solid reputation, CETIP has the responsibility to collect taxes on all stock trades on behalf of the Brazilian federal government. However, the bid was rejected based on its low valuation. Then, after rigorous negotiations, the two companies merged on March 30, 2017, creating the largest stock exchange in Brazil and the thirteenth-largest exchange in the world. The result was the current stock exchange located in São Paulo called the B3, which stands for Brasil Bolsa Balcão S.A. It is a public company that trades using the ticker symbol B3SA3. In Brazil, it also has representative offices in Alphaville and Rio de Janeiro. In addition, it keeps offices in Shanghai, London, and New York to assist its potential foreign investors, customers, and regulators. International strategists estimate that Brazilian stocks will increase in value between 15 and 38 percent in 2019 (Andrade, 2018).

See also: Chapter 4: Overview; Embraer, Empresa Brasileira de Aeronáutica; Petrobras, the National Oil Company.

Further Reading

Andrade, Vinicius. 2018. "Strategists Bet on a Long-Awaited Economic Rebound to Fuel Brazil's Stocks." *Bloomberg News*, December 17. Accessed May 15, 2019. https://www.bloomberg.com/news/articles/2018-12-17/strategists-bet-on-long-awaited-economic-rebound-to-fuel-brazil

B3: Brasil Bolsa Balcão S.A. Official Website. http://www.b3.com.br/pt_br

Baer, Werner. 2013. *The Brazilian Economy: Growth and Development*. Denver, CO: Lynne Rienner.

CETIP: OTC Private Securities and Derivatives Official Website. https://www.cetip.com.br

Ximenes, Ângela. 2016. *Eduardo da Rocha Azevedo: A Bovespa e a BM&F*. São Paulo: Contexto.

Tourism

Brazil is the most visited country in South America and the second most popular tourist destination in Latin America (after Mexico). From an economic point of view, tourism has become a major industry in Brazil and a significant component of the national economy. Brazil offers a wide array of options for tourists, including beaches, natural attractions, ecotourism that protects the environment, adventure destinations, as well as historic towns and cultural festivals. The most popular destinations are Rio de Janeiro for leisure, the Amazon jungle and river for adventure and ecotourism, the unique waterfalls of Foz do Iguaçu, São Paulo for business, Salvador de Bahia for its Afro-Brazilian culture, twenty UNESCO World Heritage Sites, and the state of Minas Gerais for its wealth of artistic, historical, and cultural sites. The World Heritage Sites are seventeen cultural sites and another seven natural sites. They include colonial towns, architectural ruins, and natural reserves with significant biodiversity of plant and animal life. The variety of these sites reflects the rich cultural traditions of Brazil as well as the beauty of its natural habitats and landscapes. They attract millions of tourists to Brazil every year.

Tourism is so important to the Brazilian economy that the federal government includes a secretary to run the Ministry of Tourism. In turn, the ministry has created Embratur (the Brazilian Institute of Tourism) to promote, market, and support tourism efforts throughout the country to both domestic and international visitors. Its 2008 National Strategic Tourism Plan highlighted the need to improve security and to prepare for a massive influx of tourists during the 2014 FIFA Soccer World Cup and the 2016 Olympics. Consequently, the federal budget provided significant funds to improve security at the most visited locations throughout the country. The efforts have seen significant results already. The World Tourism Organization (WTO) reported that international tourism to Brazil in increased significantly since 2000. While there was a brief decline from 2008 to 2010 due to the global financial downturn, the numbers picked up again in 2012. According to the national statistics provided by the Ministry of Tourism, during 2018, slightly over 11.6 million international visitors came to Brazil, while 95.5 million Brazilians vacationed throughout the vast national territory. The Ministry of Tourism invests in this sector of the economy because it generates revenue, but it also provides 1.87 million jobs directly related to tourism. Their statistics also show that the highest number of international visitors come from Argentina, the United States, France, and Germany followed by Mercosul neighboring countries (Uruguay, Paraguay, and Chile). Since tourism is a thriving industry in Brazil, it continues to attract direct foreign investment to expand infrastructure projects that include highways, airports, and port facilities.

See also: Chapter 1: Amazon Basin and Rain Forest; Environment; World Heritage Sites in the UNESCO. Chapter 4: Overview; Foreign Investment; Mercosul/Mercosur.

Further Reading

Brazilian Ministry of Development and Foreign Trade (MDIC) Official Website. http://www.mdic.gov.br

Embratur Brazilian Institute of Tourism Official Website. http://www.embratur.gov.br

Ministério do Turismo Official Website. http://www.turismo.gov.br

Smale, Will. 2011. "Brazil Prepares for Major Tourism Boom." BBC World, November 28. Accessed May 1, 2019. https://www.bbc.co.uk/news/business-15824562

UNESCO World Heritage List. http://whc.unesco.org/en/etateparties/br

Trading Partners

At the beginning of the twenty-first century, Brazil became an emerging economy. In that capacity, the federal government took a more active role with a carefully crafted plan to support exports to global markets by encouraging improvement in agribusiness, heavy manufacturing, and logistics. It negotiated multiple bilateral agreements for both imports and exports. In addition, it was a founding member of two crucial regional trading blocs. Mercosur includes agreements with Argentina, Brazil, Uruguay, Paraguay, and Bolivia; BRICS is an economic group that includes influential countries such as Brazil, Russia, India, China, and South Africa. In order to facilitate the logistics for export products, the Brazilian federal government has funded massive infrastructure projects that include highways, railroads, ports, energy plants, electricity grids, and airports, all of which generate thousands of regional jobs. Overall, Brazil shipped $239.9 billion U.S. worth of products around the world in 2018: roughly 44 percent was exported to Asian countries, 19.2 percent to the European Union, and 16.9 percent to other Latin American nations.

According to the *World's Top Exports* report for 2018, the top ten countries that imported Brazilian products (in terms of monetary value) are listed below. The parenthesis also shows the total percentage of total Brazilian exports. Together, these ten countries imported almost 60 percent of all Brazilian products.

1. China: $64.2 billion U.S. (26 percent of total Brazilian exports)
2. United States: $29.1 billion (12.1 percent)
3. Argentina: $15 billion (6.2 percent)
4. Netherlands: $13.1 billion (5.4 percent)
5. Chile: $6.4 billion (2.7 percent)
6. Germany: $5.2 billion (2.2 percent)
7. Spain: $5.2 billion (2.2 percent)
8. Mexico: $4.5 billion (1.9 percent)
9. Japan: $4.3 billion (1.8 percent)
10. India: $3.9 billion (1.6 percent)

The top three trading partners for Brazilian goods are China, the United States, and Argentina. According to the Brazilian Ministry of Development and Foreign Trade (MDIC), China became the number one trading partner for Brazil in 2012, surpassing the United States, which is now the second-largest destination for Brazilian products. For example, Brazil is the largest exporter of soybeans to China. Similarly, Brazil is also the main trading partner to import Chinese products (worth $33.7 billion U.S. in 2018). The two countries even worked together to build the massive infrastructure project of the Interoceanic Highway to get Brazilian products to the Pacific Ocean connecting with Peruvian ports to ship goods to China. Looking to the north, Brazil has increased its exports to the United States since 2017, especially by shipping oil, steel, mineral fuel, coffee, and beverages. Brazil imported high-end equipment from the

United States, especially large aircraft, precision medical instruments, heavy machinery, and electrical equipment. While Argentina and Brazil have been trade partners under the MERCOSUR bloc, they have had recent commerce disputes in which they both increased tariffs and trade barriers to protect local industries related to food, furniture, automobile parts, and textiles. In the near future, the MDIC is actively pursuing treaties to expand Brazilian exports to Africa and the Middle East based on industrial minerals, auto parts, light aircraft, and agribusiness.

See also: Chapter 1: Interoceanic Highway. Chapter 4: Overview; Major Exports.

Further Reading

Brazilian Ministry of Development and Foreign Trade (MDIC) Official Website. http://www.mdic.gov.br

Oliveira, José Maria de. 2015. *Trade Liberalisation in Brazil: Market Structure, Economic Performance, and Manufacturing.* Rockville, MD: GlobalSouth Press.

Verotti Farah, Ana Gabriela. 2013. "Largest Trading Partners of Brazil." *Brazil Business,* October 24. Accessed June 11, 2019. http://thebrazilbusiness.com/article/largest-trading-partners-of-brazil

Workman, Daniel. 2019. "Brazil's Top 15 Trading Partners." *World's Top Exports,* January 26. Accessed June 11, 2019. http://www.worldstopexports.com/brazils-top-import-partners

World Trade Organization (WTO)

Brazil has a long history of belonging to international regulatory trade organizations. It has been a member of the General Agreement on Tariffs and Trade (GATT) since 1948. This legal agreement works with signatory countries to reduce trade barriers and the elimination of special commerce preferences. Brazil also joined the World Trade Organization (WTO) on January 1, 1995; it is an intergovernmental organization that regulates international trade. In the last fifteen years, Brazil has been involved in three major WTO legal disputes with other countries over the issue of illegal government subsidies to local industries.

Australia, Brazil, and Thailand filed an official legal complaint in 2005 accusing the European Community of illegally subsidizing sugar exports, which placed these three countries at an economic disadvantage in global markets. The matter was satisfactorily resolved through arbitration on October 28, 2005, when the European Community agreed to remove the subsidies it was providing for sugar exports and consequently providing an equal competitive field in international sugar markets.

Since 2016, Brazil has tried to resolve a WTO dispute alleging that the Canadian government has unlawfully engaged in providing subsidies worth up to $3 billion U.S. to aircraft manufacturer Embradier, which directly competes with the Brazilian commercial jet maker Embraer. Brazil claims that the Canadian subsidies are against WTO rules because they negatively affect international competitiveness. Canada responded that the aerospace industry is commonly subsidized around the world, but Brazil contended that heavily discounted government loans in fact amount to illegal subsidies that allowed Embradier to sell aircraft at artificially low prices that distort international markets. The legal disagreement was moved to arbitration when the WTO ruled against Canadian subsidies, and the two countries agreed to participate in a dispute panel in 2017.

Also in 2017, Brazil was the target of a formal complaint in the WTO when Japan and the European Union declared unfair competition because Brazil provides subsidies to a wide group of economic groups including electronics, automobiles, and steel production. According to the accusers, Brazil has provided almost $8 billion U.S. in illegal subsidies to these industries since 2010. The WTO ruled against Brazil in April 2017, and it ordered the South American nation to remove those subsidies within ninety days. President Temer (1940–) worked with Congress to remove such subsidies and reiterated the need for a comprehensive tax reform in Brazil that relies more on innovation and less on subsidized incentives to improve international trade.

See also: Chapter 4: Overview; Embraer, Empresa Brasileira de Aeronáutica; Major Exports; Trading Partners.

Further Reading

Brainard, Lael, and Leonardo Martinez-Diaz. 2009. *Brazil as an Economic Superpower? Understanding Brazil's Changing Role in the Global Economy.* Washington, DC: Brookings Institution Press.

General Agreement on Tariffs and Trade Organization (GATT) Official Website. https://www.wto.org/english/tratop_e/gatt_e/gatt_e.htm

Haynes, Brad, and Alonso Soto. 2017. "Brazil Challenges Canada at WTO over Bombardier Funding." *Reuters,* February 8. Accessed July 20, 2019. https://www.reuters.com/article/us-bombardier-investment-wto-idUSKBN15N1XG

Paraguassu, Lisandra, and Silvio Cascione. 2017. "WTO Orders Brazil to Remove Subsidies, Government to Appeal." *Reuters,* August 29. Accessed July 20, 2019. https://www.reuters.com/article/us-brazil-wto/wto-orders-brazil-to-remove-subsidies-government-to-appeal-idUSKCN1B92QV

World Trade Organization (WTO) Official Website. https://www.wto.org

CHAPTER 5

RELIGION AND THOUGHT

OVERVIEW

The massive statue of *Cristo Redentor* (Christ the Redeemer) overlooking Rio de Janeiro is one of the most iconic monuments in Brazil. The statue of Jesus Christ is 98 feet tall (30 meters), and its open arms reach 92 feet (28 meters). It represents the importance of Christianity in Brazil, especially Catholicism. Jesuit missionaries introduced the religion to Brazil in the 1500s during the Portuguese colonial period, and it has remained a consistent component of Brazilian culture. According to the 2010 census, 123 million Brazilians define themselves as Catholics, which makes it the country with the largest number of Catholic followers in the world. However, a closer look at contemporary data reveals that the country's religious diversity is extremely complex, and it reflects a historical process that has blended European, African, and indigenous traditions—all of which contribute to a rich array of celebrations, holidays, customs, and festivals that make Brazil a unique country.

The composition of religious affiliation in Brazil has shifted dramatically during the last thirty years. All indicators provided by the census data gathered by the Brazilian Institute of Geography and Statistics (IBGE) show that the number of Catholics has declined significantly from 90 percent of all Brazilians in 1970 to only 65 percent of the national population in 2010. The growth of religious followers has occurred mostly in Protestant churches. By 2010, slightly over 22 percent of the population (42.3 million Brazilians) identified themselves as Protestant, including Methodists, Pentecostals, Baptists, Presbyterians, Mormons, Jehovah's Witnesses, and Adventists. This number represents a growth of 16 million converts in a ten-year period from 2000 to 2010. However, a more detailed analysis of the number of Protestant followers reveals that Pentecostal churches have experienced most of the significant growth in the last three decades. This group includes the Universal Church of the Kingdom of God (UCKG), Foursquare Church Gospel, Assemblies of God, and the Maranatha churches. The Pentecostal ministries followed a conversion strategy that targeted isolated and poor communities as well as low-income neighborhoods often ignored by the Catholic Church. The UCKG, founded by Edir Macedo in 1977, is the most prominent of all the Pentecostal Evangelical churches. It quickly expanded throughout Brazil as well as Europe, Africa, and the United States. For the 2010 census, it reported over 4,500 temples located throughout Brazil. Part of their successful expansion has been accomplished with effective use of social media and the wide appeal of television evangelists because the UCKG owns Rede Record, the second-largest television network in Brazil. Their explosive growth has generated unwanted negative publicity resulting in accusations against the UCKG ministries of fraud and exploitation of its followers for the purpose of enriching its religious leaders.

Afro-Brazilian religions, such as Candomblé and Macumba, have also become more visible in the last two decades, reaching an estimated 2 million worshippers, mostly in the state of Salvador da Bahia; and Rio de Janeiro. Candomblé is based on oral tradition, and it does not follow a holy book. It also does not have a binary distinction of good versus evil. Its followers believe that Oludumaré was the Supreme Creator of the world, including other intermediary gods called *orishas* (*orixás* in Portuguese), who serve as a link between worshippers and the spiritual world. The word *candomblé* means "dance in honor of the gods." Consequently, dance and music are crucial aspects of religious ceremonies where participants become possessed or entranced by orishas. When Portuguese colonizers tried to convert African slaves to Christianity, the slaves gave Christian names to their own African gods. Therefore, Iemanja (the goddess of rivers and water) became syncretized with the Virgin Mary as the Queen of the Heavens and Seas, and Oxala (the god of harvest and fertility) was represented by Jesus Christ. By following this practice, the slaves pretended to worship Christian figures to avoid prosecution while praying to their own African *orixás* all along. Today, the majority of worshippers following Candomblé and Macumba also consider themselves Catholic.

Another unique religious feature in Brazil is the growth of Spiritism founded by Hyppolyte Léon Denizard Rivail in France during the 1800s. He believed that humans can communicate with highly intelligent spirits using mediums to go between the physical and the spiritual world. Using the pseudonym Allan Kardec, he wrote five books (*The Spirits' Book, The Mediums' Book, The Gospel According to Spiritism, Heaven and Hell,* and *The Genesis According to Spiritism*), which became the foundation of what is best described as a hybrid belief system of religion, philosophy, and science. During the early 1900s, the Kardecian philosophy spread worldwide. It was particularly well accepted in Brazil, where Catholicism was not as strong as in the Spanish colonies in the Americas, and the government did not oppose it. The Kardecian movement became popular among the upper classes of Brazil, who quickly established Spiritist centers, hospitals, and charity institutions that created curiosity among the larger population. According to the IBGE, Brazil had over 4 million Spiritism followers in 2010, which makes it the country with the largest number of Spiritist believers in the world. Spiritism does not operate using the generally accepted perceptions of an established religion. It is more of a philosophy and a way of life. It has no religious leaders, and followers do not meet in traditional churches. Their locations are called Spiritist centers, associations, or societies. Believers gather at informal meetings without strict rituals to discuss doctrine based on Kardec's books, organize charity events, and apply spiritual healing to the sick. Other meetings are specifically held by mediums to communicate with spirits. Spiritists also believe in reincarnation.

Philosophy and Thought

Brazil has produced influential philosophers and social scientists who have made a global impact with their views and proposals. Three of them clearly stand out. First,

Gilberto Freyre was a Brazilian historian, anthropologist, journalist, congressman, and sociologist. He published a trilogy of books that analyzed Brazilian civilization through new perspectives. The first, and most notable, book, *Casa grande e senzala* (often translated as *The Masters and the Slaves: A Study in the Development of Brazilian Civilization*), was published in 1933. This seminal sociological study redefined the view of multiple races as a unifying heritage of Brazilian identity. Freyre placed black culture and traditions at the center of Brazilian history. He also advanced the concept of Brazil as a "racial democracy," which argues that it had less racial discrimination than other countries with black populations in the Americas. Second, in the field of education, another influential Brazilian was Paulo Freire, an educator and philosopher who argued that education is a mechanism for social change. Based on his own experiences with poverty, he made a commitment to work toward improving the lives of the poor people in Brazil. His 1970 book *Pedagogy of the Oppressed* was an instant success, and it became crucial reading material in most teacher training programs worldwide. Third, following the line of education but with a deep connection to the world of politics, one of the most recognized contemporary philosophers today is Marilena de Souza Chaui. An accomplished author, university professor, and political activist, she is a professor of political philosophy at the University of São Paulo. She has published several books that explore reflective philosophical topics, personal development, political issues, and cultural narratives.

Religion and Politics

The current Constitution of Brazil clearly separates church and state. However, the Catholic Church has had a strong influence on social matters such as the fact that abortion is still illegal in Brazil and divorce only became available in 1977. However, Protestant churches have recently started making significant inroads into shaping society based on their conservative values. For example, the UCKG has already ventured into the political arena by being a founding member of the Brazilian Republican Party as a platform to get Protestant candidates elected to government positions that shape social policies. Brazilian Protestants are following a well-crafted strategy of becoming elected representatives of conservative moral values. For example, Pentecostal bishop Marcello Crivella was elected mayor of Rio de Janeiro in 2017. As with so many aspects of Brazilian society, time will tell if they succeed at a national level. The religious diversity in Brazil has created a society that is simultaneously very religious but also spiritually fluid, impacting moral values, family traditions, holiday celebrations, education, and even politics. It all makes Brazil a cultural melting pot with multiple social layers that are discovered as people get to know Brazilians.

Further Reading

Bevins, Vincent. 2012. "Brazil's Evangelical Churches Rewrite the Rules of Politics." *Los Angeles Times*, October 21. Accessed May 1, 2019. http://articles.latimes.com/2012/oct/21/world/la-fg-brazil-evangelicals-20121022

Capone, Stefania. 2010. *Searching for Africa in Brazil: Power and Tradition in Candomblé*. Durham, NC: Duke University Press.

Instituto Brasileiro de Geografia e Estatística—Brazilian Institute of Geography and Statistics (IBGE). 2010. "Census 2010." Accessed May 1, 2019. http://ibge.gov.br

Mayo, Peter. 2008. *Liberating Praxis: Paulo Freire's Legacy for Radical Education and Politics*. Westport, CT: Praeger.

Pew Research Center. 2013. "Brazil's Changing Religious Landscape." July 18. Accessed May 1, 2019. http://www.pewforum.org/2013/07/18/brazils-changing-religious-landscape

Schmidt, Bettina E. 2016. *Contemporary Religions in Brazil*. Oxford, UK: Oxford University Press.

Smith, Christian. 1991. *The Emergence of Liberation Theology: Radical Religion and Social Movement Theory*. Chicago: University of Chicago Press.

Universal Church of the Kingdom of God, Official English Website. http://www.uckg.org

Candomblé and Macumba

The Portuguese brought more than 4 million African slaves to Brazil, and the slaves brought with them their religious beliefs from the Yoruba and Bantu regions of West Africa. During the slavery period in Brazil (1500 to 1888), their religious rituals evolved and incorporated elements of European Catholicism and local indigenous practices. Today, Candomblé and Macumba are two religions with African roots that are still practiced in Brazil. Most of the Candomblé followers are concentrated in the state of Salvador da Bahia; and Macumba is mostly practiced in the region of Rio de Janeiro.

Candomblé is based on oral tradition, and it does not follow a holy book. It also does not have a binary distinction of good versus evil. Its followers believe that Oludumaré was the Supreme Creator of the world, including other intermediary gods called *orishas* (*orixás* in Portuguese), who serve as a link between worshippers and the spiritual world. The word *candomblé* means "dance in honor of the gods." Consequently, dance and music are crucial aspects of religious ceremonies where participants become possessed or entranced by orishas. This religion was forbidden in Brazil for centuries, and its followers learned to function in clandestine locations. Candomblé even today has no centralized authority, and its religious ceremonies are still held in temples called *casas* (houses) or *terreiros* (yards) individually owned by the head priest (*pai de santo*) or head priestess (*mãe de santo*). The most traditional rituals are directed by a female priestess. One of the most historically recognized head priestesses from Salvador da Bahia, was Mãe Menininha do Gantois (1894–1986) from the House of the Mother of Waters who was a pivotal advocate to obtain the legal recognition of Candomblé as a formal religion in Brazil.

Macumba blends African religious beliefs with aspects of European spiritualism, which believes that living people can communicate with the souls of their deceased ancestors. Most of the religious rituals of Macumba are very similar to those practiced by Candomblé followers. The main difference is that in Macumba, worshippers and dancers can be possessed not only by orishas but also by the soul of an ancestor.

Worshippers believe that an ancestor's soul can speak to them using an entranced priest as a vehicle for communication. In addition, a possessed *pai do santo* (lead priest) sometimes performs specific healing ceremonies by placing animal feathers over an afflicted area and blowing cigar smoke all over the body of a specific follower.

Candomblé and Macumba sects have continued to expand in Brazil to a current estimate of 2 million worshippers. In addition, the rituals are practiced in several neighboring countries, such as Argentina, Venezuela, Uruguay, and Paraguay. However, it is important to highlight that the majority of worshippers following Candomblé and Macumba also considers themselves Catholic.

See also: Chapter 2: Overview; Brazilian Empire; Slavery, Abolition, and African Heritage. Chapter 3: Overview. Chapter 6: Overview; African Ancestry and Influence.

Further Reading

Bramley, Serge. 1994. *Macumba*. San Francisco: City Lights Books.

Capone, Stefania. 2010. *Searching for Africa in Brazil: Power and Tradition in Candomblé*. Durham, NC: Duke University Press.

Parés, Luis Nicolau. 2013. *The Formation of Candomblé: Vodun History and Ritual in Brazil*. Chapel Hill: University of North Carolina Press.

Schmidt, Bettina E. 2016. *Contemporary Religions in Brazil*. Oxford, UK: Oxford University Press.

Voeks, Robert A. 1997. *Secret Leaves of Candomble: African Magic, Medicine, and Religion in Brazil*. Austin: University of Texas Press.

Catholicism

In terms of numbers, Brazil is the largest Catholic country in the world. According to the official 2010 census taken by the IBGE, 64.6 percent of the population, or slightly over 130 million people, identified themselves as Catholic. However, the numbers seem to be declining mostly based on the increase of Evangelical Protestant churches that have proliferated in Brazil during the last thirty years.

Jesuit priests arrived in Brazil during the first royal mission in 1549, and they played a crucial role in establishing an educational system in the new colony. However, the Catholic Church never took a primary role in politics. From a comparative point of view, it never became a powerful institution as it did in the Spanish colonies. While the Portuguese arrived in the current Brazilian territory in 1500, the first Catholic diocese was established fifty years later in 1551. The diocese aimed to convert the American Indians and African slaves to Catholicism, but the church was relatively tolerant of their rituals. Consequently, the type of Catholicism practiced was influenced by local cultures. Brazil has always had problems filling the spirituals needs of all Brazilians due to a shortage of priests, especially in rural and less populated regions. In fact, the powerful National Conference of Brazilian Bishops (CNBB) has recently acknowledged

Ruins of São Miguel das Missões in Brazil, a Jesuit mission founded in the eighteenth century to convert the Guaraní Indian population to Catholicism. While they were initially allowed to expand in Brazil, the Portuguese government eventually expelled all the Jesuits in 1759. (Andre Tomasi)

that large numbers of Brazilians define themselves as Catholic, but do not attend services consistently. The CNBB's conservative estimate claims that only 20 percent of Brazilian Catholics actually attend Mass and participate regularly in other church programs. In addition, Afro-religions (Candomblé and Macumba) continue to be popular, and Evangelical churches have experienced tremendous growth in the country—all of which contribute to reduce the number of Catholics in Brazil.

The Catholic Church faces serious challenges. The majority of the Brazilian population follows a laissez-faire attitude that also extends to religious practices. The lack of enough priests has led rural and isolated communities to follow their own blend of folk Catholicism. While the Protestant religions started gaining territory in the mid-1950s, there has been a recent proliferation of Evangelical Pentecostal churches in Brazil. They target the Amazon region and the poor outskirts of large cities like Rio de Janeiro and São Paulo. In large urban areas, Pentecostals fill a void by preaching in regions where poverty, prostitution, alcoholism, and violence are common.

Despite the difficult times ahead, the Catholic Church still holds considerable influence in Brazil. During the late 1980s, it made a clear effort to obtain more political influence among conservative political candidates in order to shape social policy. For example, abortion is still illegal in Brazil. The Vatican has continued to demonstrate its support by scheduling papal visits to this crucial country. Pope Benedict XVI went to Brazil in 2007, and the current Pope Francis visited in 2013. In addition, the church's educational tradition has left a tangible imprint on the country. Catholic universities are consistently placed at the top levels of annual national rankings. Four private institutions are highly sought after in Brazil: the Pontifical Catholic Universities in Rio de Janeiro, Rio Grande do Sul, São Paulo, and Minas Gerais. Their graduates are likely to continue to shape the future of Brazil.

See also: Chapter 2: Overview. Chapter 5: Overview; Candomblé and Macumba; Liberation Theology; *Orixás*, African Gods.

Further Reading

BBC. 2005. "Factfile: Roman Catholics around the World." *BBC News,* April 1. Accessed June 7, 2019. http://news.bbc.co.uk/2/hi/4243727.stm

Crocitti, John J., and Monique Vallance (eds.). 2012. *Brazil Today: An Encyclopedia of Life in the Republic* (2 volumes). Santa Barbara, CA: ABC-CLIO.

Instituto Brasileiro de Geografia e Estatística—Brazilian Institute of Geography and Statistics (IBGE). 2010. "Census 2010." Accessed June 7, 2019. http://ibge.gov.br

Scalon, Maria Celi. 2003. "Catholics and Protestants in Brazil." *America Magazine,* August 18. Accessed June 7, 2019. https://www.americamagazine.org/issue/447/article/catholics-and-protestants-brazil

De Souza Chaui, Marilena (1941–)

Marilena de Souza Chaui is a Brazilian philosopher, accomplished author, university professor, and political activist. Born on September 4, 1941, in the metropolis of São Paulo, she is the daughter of a schoolteacher, Laura de Souza Chaui, and a journalist father, Nicholas Alberto Chaui. She obtained a master's degree in 1967 and a doctorate in 1971. Chaui also completed postgraduate work at the National Library of Paris. She had two children (Luciana and William Joseph) from her first marriage to José Augusto de Mattos Berlinck. She is now married to Michael Hall, a history professor at the State University of Campinas in the state of São Paulo.

Chaui is a professor of modern philosophy with a concentration in political philosophy at the University of São Paulo. Her main line of research is on the history of modern philosophy. She has published several books that explore reflective philosophical topics, personal development, political issues, and cultural narratives. Her bibliography includes the following books (English titles): *What Is Ideology?*; *Culture and Democracy: The Competent Speech and Other Speeches*; *Writings on University*; *Sexual Repression*; *Brazil: Founding Myth and Authoritarian Society*; *The Rib of the Real: Immanence and Freedom in Spinoza*; *Introduction to the History of Philosophy*; *Invitation to Philosophy*; *Cultural Citizenship*; *Simulacrum and Power*. While most of the books had moderate success, it was the bestseller *O que é ideologia?* (What Is Ideology?) that sold the most copies, over 100,000. The Ministry of Education and Culture of Brazil made it a mandatory textbook in public schools in the country.

Chaui has participated as a political activist linked to the Partido dos Trabalhadores, or Workers' Party (PT). In this capacity, she served as the municipal secretary of culture for the city of São Paulo from 1989 to 1992 during the term of Mayor Luiza Erundina. Chaui later expressed that her work as secretary of culture allowed her to link her work on political philosophy with the reality faced by average citizens and their view of political problems at the national level. However, she started expressing very strong political views in 2013, generating heated controversy when she openly criticized the middle class of Brazil. In her speeches, she uses extremely derogatory terms to describe middle-class Brazilians as ignorant, arrogant, and extremely conservative. As a militant for the PT, she often advocated for popular politicians that included former PT presidents Luiz Inácio Lula da Silva and Dilma Rousseff. The problem is that Lula was imprisoned for corruption from 2018 to 2019 and Rousseff was impeached.

See also: Chapter 2: Overview. Chapter 5: Overview.

Further Reading

De Souza Chaui, Marilena. 2002a. "Fundamentalismo religioso: La cuestión del poder teológico-político," in *Filosofia Política Contemporanea: Controversias sobre civilización, imperio y ciudadanía*, edited by Atílio A. Boran, 117–134. Buenos Aires: Clacso.

De Souza Chaui, Marilena. 2002b. *Introduction to the History of Philosophy: From Pre-Socrates to Aristotle*. São Paulo: Companhia das Letras.

De Souza Chaui, Marilena. 2003. *Culture and Democracy: The Competent Speech and Other Speeches*. São Paulo: Cortez Editora.

Freire, Paulo (1921–1997)

Paulo Reglus Neves Freire was a Brazilian educator and philosopher who argued that education is a mechanism for social change. He was born on September 19, 1921, in the city of Recife in the state of Pernambuco located in the northeast region of Brazil. While he was originally raised by a family with financial security, life changed dramatically during the depression of the 1930s. When his father died in 1934, the family lost almost everything, and Freire experienced hunger, poverty, and educational decline. His family eventually recovered financially, but his experiences with poverty shaped his point of view. He made a commitment to work toward improving the lives of the less fortunate populations of Brazil.

Paulo Freire became a lawyer by training at the University of Recife, but he never actually practiced his legal profession. Instead, he became a teacher at secondary schools, where he met his wife, Elza Maria Costa de Oliveira. He also became involved with adult literacy programs, which he quickly viewed as a political necessity since—at that time—literacy was a constitutional requirement to vote on presidential elections.

These experiences led Freire to view education as a crucial tool for social change and upward mobility. His theory of "critical pedagogy" argued that education should not be a simple transmission of facts from teachers to students, but rather aim to develop a social consciousness among poor and oppressed populations. His 1970 book *Pedagogy of the Oppressed* was an instant success, and it became crucial reading material in most teacher training programs worldwide. Freire published over twenty books on topics related to education, pedagogy, and social change, including *Pedagogy of the Oppressed*; *Education for Critical Consciousness*; *Education, the Practice of Freedom*; *The Politics of Education: Culture, Power, and Liberation*; *Literacy: Reading the Word & the World* (with D. P. Macedo); *Pedagogy of the City*; *Pedagogy of Freedom: Ethics, Democracy and Civic Courage*; and *Politics and Education*.

Paulo Freire and his work had a global impact in the field of education. His methodology advocates the development of curriculum that addresses social justice. In order to disseminate his work, the Paulo Freire Institute was established in 1991 in São Paulo. From its original location, it has expanded to multiple countries, and its archives are now managed from its headquarters at the University of California at Los Angeles (UCLA) Graduate School of Education. Freire received honorary doctorate degrees from multiple universities to recognize his work in educational pedagogy, and he was also awarded international prizes for his philosophy of education that addresses the needs of poor populations around the world.

See also: Chapter 5: Overview. Chapter 6: Overview; Distribution of Wealth and Income Disparity; Education and Upper Mobility; Poverty, Social Conflict, and Protests.

Further Reading

Darder, Antonia. 2017. *Reinventing Paulo Freire: A Pedagogy of Love*. New York: Routledge.

Freire Institute of Critical Pedagogy. http://www.freire.org/paulo-freire

Mayo, Peter. 2008. *Liberating Praxis: Paulo Freire's Legacy for Radical Education and Politics*. Westport, CT: Praeger.

McLaren, Peter. 2000. *Che Guevara, Paulo Freire, and the Pedagogy of Revolution*. Lanham, MD: Rowman & Littlefield.

Torres, Carlos A., and Pedro Noguera (eds.). 2008. *Social Justice Education for Teachers: Paulo Freire and the Possible Dream*. Rotterdam, Netherlands: Sense.

Freyre, Gilberto (1900–1987)

Gilberto de Mello Freyre was a Brazilian historian, anthropologist, journalist, congressman, and sociologist. He was born on March 15, 1900, in Recife in the state of Pernambuco located in the northeast region of the country. He finished most of his college education outside of Brazil: a bachelor's degree at Baylor University in Texas and a master's at Columbia University in New York.

Freyre published a trilogy of books that analyzed Brazilian civilization through new perspectives. The first book, *Casa grande e senzala* (often translated as *The Masters and the Slaves: A Study in the Development of Brazilian Civilization*), was published in 1933. This seminal sociological study redefined the view of multiple races as a unifying heritage of Brazilian identity. Freyre placed black culture and traditions at the center of Brazilian history. The second book, *Sobrados e mucambos* (*The Mansions and Shanties: The Making of Modern Brazil*), released in 1938, offered a historical analysis of the decline of power in rural regions and the rise of urban influence in all aspects of Brazilian life. The book also offers a sociological contrastive analysis of race relations among whites, blacks, Indians, and mixed races. The third book, *Order & Progress: Brazil from Monarchy to Republic*, was published in 1957. This is a historical account of Brazil going through multiple stages: a Portuguese colony, independence, empire, democratic republic, and dictatorships. It is based on historical data and documents, especially government records. It also offers a detailed analysis of the imprint that educational and religious institutions left on the country and that continue to shape modern Brazil.

Freyre obtained recognition both in Brazil and internationally based on his sociological, anthropological, and historical analysis of Brazilian society and cultures. He advanced the concept of Brazil as a "racial democracy," which argues that Brazil had less racial discrimination than other countries with black populations in the Americas. As a journalist, he worked as the editor of two important newspapers in Brazil: *Diario de Pernambuco* and *A Província*. Due to his seminal work on Brazilian history and society, Freyre received multiple honorary degrees from the Sorbonne University in Paris and Columbia University in New York. He was also honored with the awards of Gran-Cruz of the Ordem do Infante Dom Henrique in Portugal and Knight Commander of the Order of the British Empire in Great Britain. At a local level, the airport in his hometown of Recife was renamed in his honor as the Recife Gilberto Freyre International Airport. While his academic work has been highly praised, his role in the political arena was controversial. He was accused of being a Communist in the 1930s, and he responded by aligning himself with conservative right-wing parties. However, he lost a lot of followers in Brazil when he publicly supported the military dictatorship of President Humberto Castelo Branco during the 1960s.

See also: Chapter 5: Overview. Chapter 6: Overview; Racism and Discrimination; *Favelas, Mocambos,* and *Alagados* (Slums).

Further Reading

Braga-Pinto, César. 2005. "Sugar Daddy: Gilberto Freyre and the White Man's Love for Blacks," in *The Masters and the Slaves: Plantation Relations and Mestizaje in American Imaginaries*, edited by Alexandra Isfahani-Hammond, 19–33. London: Palgrave.

Buke, Peter, and Maria Lúcia G. Pallares-Burke. 2008. *Gilberto Freyre: Social Theory in the Tropics*. Oxford, UK: Peter Lang.

Isfahani-Hammond, Alexandra. 2005. *White Negritude: Race, Writing, and Brazilian Cultural Identity*. London: Palgrave Macmillan.

Liberation Theology

Liberation theology is based on Christian doctrine, but it focuses on the active participation of priests and church leaders to liberate the burdens of the poor and other oppressed groups in society. The term "liberation theology" was first used by Gustavo Gutiérrez in 1971. He is a Catholic priest from Peru who advocated for an ecclesiastical involvement to alleviate poverty and social injustices in Latin America. His book *A Theology of Liberation* became a crucial reference source when the movement took hold in the 1970s, and multiple priests challenged the traditional hierarchy of the Catholic Church for not defending the needs of the poor. Other priests supported the movement, including Jon Sobrino in Spain, Juan Luis Segundo in Uruguay, and Leonardo Boff in Brazil. All of them claimed that Catholic priests should be agents of social change and not only dispensers of spiritual relief.

The Vatican retaliated against the proponents of liberation theology by removing priests from their popular assignments, excommunicating some of them, and even issuing strict guidelines against the practice of liberation theology worldwide. In Brazil, the Vatican removed the powerful cardinal of São Paulo Dom Paulo Evaristo Arns in 1973 for adopting the concept of "preferential option for the poor." Theologian priest Leonardo Boff was accused of Marxism. In addition, the Vatican was particularly displeased when Brazilian archdioceses adopted a grassroots model of Ecclesiastical Base Communities (CEBs), which sent priests out into the community to celebrate Mass in public at low-income locations such as street corners, parks, and rural fields. This progressive move represented a break from the conservative Catholic tradition of ornate churches being the center of religion. The Vatican viewed these liberal approaches as secularization steps that challenged the church leadership. For example, when liberal priests saw the needs of the poor communities up close, they started to support challenges to the antiquated land tenure laws in Brazil, which resulted in political and legal action against a massive government bureaucracy. Moreover, when Brazil transitioned into a democracy in 1985, the Catholic ruling hierarchy in Rome was particularly concerned with such radical social movements being associated with their priests because it would potentially lose political influence in Brazil. Therefore, it directed Brazilian priests to focus on their religious role and to abandon their concern for social and political problems.

By the end of the 1900s, the impact of liberation theology had dissipated, but the Catholic Church still faces contemporary problems. A serious concern is the lack of enough priests to preach to a populous nation that claims to be mostly Catholic but does not even attend religious services on a regular basis. In addition, the expansion of Evangelical churches in Brazil has occurred extremely fast in the last thirty years, especially the Pentecostal denominations. In the meantime, Catholic leaders in the Vatican continue to bring Brazilian liberal priests to testify before interrogation panels to make sure they are under control and not spreading messages of liberation to peasants, workers, and community organizers. As for theologian priest Leonardo Boff, he continues to serve as an emeritus professor of religion and ethics at the State University of Rio de Janeiro.

See also: Chapter 5: Overview; Catholicism; Protestant Religions; Universal Church of the Kingdom of God.

Further Reading

De La Torre, Miguel A. 2004. *Handbook on U.S. Theologies of Liberation*. Atlanta, GA: Chalice Press.

Gutiérrez, Gustavo A. 1998. *A Theology of Liberation: History, Politics, and Salvation*. Maryknoll, NY: Orbis Books.

Riding, Alan. 1984. "Brazil Tests Limits of Liberation Theology." *New York Times,* September 9. Accessed June 12, 2019. http://www.nytimes.com/1984/09/09/weekinreview/brazil-tests-limits-of-liberation-theology.html

Smith, Christian. 1991. *The Emergence of Liberation Theology: Radical Religion and Social Movement Theory*. Chicago: University of Chicago Press.

Messianism and Miracle Workers

Based on the number of followers, Brazil is the largest Catholic country in the world. Historically, however, the Catholic Church has never had enough priests to tend to the spiritual needs of all Brazilians, and the current rural populations do not have regular access to a Catholic priest. Consequently, these isolated communities have adapted into a special form of informal folk Catholicism with unclear religious doctrine. During the late 1800s, in the harsh environment of the northeast region of Brazil, traveling preachers who announced the end of the world found a receptive audience because they were promoting the advantages of a new and fairer society. During their travels, they gained a reputation as miracle workers. The two most important ministers from the 1870s were Antônio Conselheiro (The Counselor) and Padre Cícero. Now, in contemporary Brazil, these rural ministers are still viewed as saints, and they have a following among the poorest populations of Brazil.

Antônio Maciel, more commonly known as Antônio Conselheiro, started to spread his message presaging the end of the world in the state of Bahia during the 1870s. More specifically, he claimed that the world was scheduled to end in 1899. Preaching to the poorest populations in Bahia, he developed a reputation as a miracle worker, and he soon had a large number of followers. He established his "New Jerusalem" in the town of Canudos, Bahia. However, Brazil became an independent republic in 1888, and the new civilian leaders viewed his anti-government and anti-tax message as a direct threat. After multiple warnings and failed attempts to defeat him, the government mounted a decisive attack in 1897 against the town controlled by this unique preacher. Most of the population was killed, including their controversial leader Antônio Conselheiro. However, a legend continues to keep his message alive, even today.

Cícero Romão Batista (more commonly known as Padre Cícero) was a priest during the 1870s who also worked with the poor peasant populations of the state of Ceará. This is a region continuously plagued with devastating droughts that make life extremely difficult for farmers. This inhospitable region of Brazil never received much attention from the Catholic Church. Consequently, Father Cícero developed a loyal following of worshippers. In 1890, one of his devoted followers received the host as part of the Holy Communion, and blood spilled from her mouth. The parishioners claimed that Father Cícero had performed the miracle of converting the woman into the flesh and blood of Jesus Christ. The Catholic Church investigated the incident and determined that there was no miracle. Subsequently, Padre Cícero was excommunicated and expelled from the church, but his followers continued to see him as a source of religious miracles. They believed that he could turn dry lands into fertile soil and hence combat poverty in the region. Father Cícero died in 1934. He is still extremely popular today. His hometown of Juazeiro de Norte in the state of Ceará built a statue that serves as a focal point for thousands of pilgrims who visit his grave every year.

See also: Chapter 2: Overview. Chapter 5: Overview; Catholicism.

Further Reading

Chacon, Vamireh. 1990. *Deus é Brasileiro: O imaginário do mesianismo político no Brasil* (in Portuguese). Rio de Janeiro: Civilização Brasileira.

Matta, Roberto da. 1996. *Understanding Messianism in Brazil: Notes from a Social Anthropologist.* Washington, DC: IDB Cultural Center.

Myscofski, Carole A. 1989. *When Men Walk Dry: Portuguese Messianism in Brazil.* Oxford, UK: Oxford University Press.

Nossa Senhora Aparecida, Brazil's Patron Saint

Our Lady of Aparecida is the national patron saint of Brazil. Locally, she is known by two names: Nossa Senhora Aparecida and Nossa Senhora da Conceição Aparecida. She is the Brazilian version of the Blessed Virgin Mary. The Annual Feast Day in her honor has been continuously celebrated on October 12 since 1822. Brazilians' veneration of her image is so important that in 1980 the National Congress declared October 12 an official national holiday, and the national festivities are now codified into the national constitution.

Based on the account of Catholic worshippers, three fishermen (Domingos Garcia, João Alves, and Filipe Pedroso) first discovered a headless statue of the Virgin Mary when they were fishing on the Paraíba River in October 1717. Then their nets found the head of the statue, which is slightly less than 3 feet tall (40 centimeters). Afterwards, they claim that a miracle allowed them to catch unusually large quantities of fish. They also noticed that the clay statue was a black version of Our Lady of the Immaculate Conception.

The devotion given to the image of Nossa Senhora Aparecida has grown continuously since its discovery, especially among Afro-Brazilians who viewed her as the first black image of the Virgin Mary. The number of people coming to see the image increased over time, and the family of Filipe Pedroso built a humble shelter for it. Decades later,

Basilica of the National Shrine of Our Lady of Aparecida in the town of Aparecida, Brazil. She is the Brazilian version of the Virgin Mary. The Brazilian Congress approved October 12 as a federal holiday to celebrate Brazil's patron saint. (Gilvan Oraggio/Dreamstime.com)

in 1834, the town built a church for the statue that is now known as the Old Basilica. Given the popularity of the statue and people's faith, Pope Pius IX declared it the official patron saint of Brazil in 1930. The location quickly became the focus of multiple pilgrimages by people seeking help from the saint. Its followers were devastated when a person stole the statue on May 16, 1978. While he was being chased by security guards, he dropped the clay figure, smashing into over 200 pieces. The statue was meticulously restored immediately by artist Maria Helena Chartuni from the Art Museum of São Paulo, and it was once again displayed for its Catholic followers in 1979.

The small figure is currently housed in the Basilica of the National Shrine of Our Lady of Aparecida, which is in the town of Aparecida in the state of São Paulo. The "New Basilica" building was designed in the shape of a Greek cross by architect Benedito Calxto. It can accommodate up to 45,000 worshippers, and it is the second-largest basilica in the world, surpassed only by St. Peter's Basilica in Vatican City. The basilica was officially consecrated by Pope John Paul II on July 4, 1980, during his first visit to Brazil. Since then, other popes have also held Mass there; the most recent celebration was held by Pope Francis in 2013.

The cultural and religious influence of Nossa Senhora Aparecida has spread throughout Brazil. There are many parks, churches, plazas, and religious schools named after her. It is also a common name for Brazilian women. In addition, her story has been portrayed in films and popular telenovelas (soap operas).

See also: Chapter 5: Overview; Catholicism.

Further Reading

BBC. 2005. "Factfile: Roman Catholics around the World." *BBC News,* April 1. Accessed July 7, 2019. http://news.bbc.co.uk/2/hi/4243727.stm

National Shrine of Our Lady of Aparecida Official Website (in Portuguese). http://www.a12.com/santuario

Our Lady Aparecida Profile. *Catholic Saints Index.* http://catholicsaints.info/our-lady-aparecida

Orixás, African Gods

During the colonial period in Brazil (1500 to early 1800s), the Portuguese imported more than 4 million African slaves to Brazil, mostly from the Yoruba and Bantu regions of West Africa. Their religious practices managed to survive, especially in the northeast region of Brazil. Nowadays, Candomblé and Macumba are two religions with African roots that are still practiced in Brazil. These polytheistic religions include more than 400 *orixás* (African gods) that guide individual worshipers through the perils and joys of life.

Candomblé followers believe that Oludumaré was the Supreme Creator of the world, including other intermediary gods called *orixás* in Portuguese. These deities serve as a link between worshippers and the spiritual world. When Portuguese colonizers tried to convert African slaves to Christianity, the slaves gave Christian names to their own African gods. By following this practice, the slaves pretended to worship Christian figures to avoid prosecution while praying to their own African *orixás* all along. Therefore, Iemanja (the goddess of rivers and water) became syncretized with the Virgin Mary as the Queen of the Heavens and Seas. Exu (the most evil spirit of all the gods) became associated with Satan. Oxala (the god of harvest and fertility) was represented by Jesus Christ. Since all *orixás* usually have specific symbolism, Candomblé followers also created parallelisms with multiple Catholic saints. For example, Xangô (the warrior) was paired with Saint Peter, and Ogun (the hunter god) was associated with Saint Anthony. The double identities associated with Catholic saints and African gods have become almost indistinguishable. In fact, most Afro-Brazilians who are Candomblé believers also consider themselves Catholic.

Candomblé practitioners believe that each person gets a unique *orixá* to protect them, guide them through life, and define their sense of morality. Each *orixá* is connected to a specific animal, musical rhythm, food, color, and day of the week. Worshippers also believe that each individual character is strongly influenced by their own deity. All the elements associated with *orixás* are displayed in religious rituals. The word *candomblé* means "dance in honor of the gods." Consequently, dance and music are crucial aspects of religious ceremonies where participants become possessed or entranced by *orixás*.

The number of Brazilians embracing Candomblé practices has increased in the last thirty years. However, Candomblé has also lost followers since the emergence of Evangelical religions in Brazil during the late 1980s. The tremendous growth of Pentecostal churches has been especially difficult since they have accused Candomblé followers of "devil worshipping" and participating in unnatural rituals. In the future, all attempts to define religious affiliation in Brazil will continue to be a complex endeavor since it is never a straightforward description.

See also: Chapter 2: Overview; Slavery, Abolition, and African Heritage. Chapter 3: Overview. Chapter 5: Overview; Catholicism; Protestant Religions. Chapter 6: Overview; African Ancestry and Influence.

Further Reading

Capone, Stefania. 2010. *Searching for Africa in Brazil: Power and Tradition in Candomblé.* Durham, NC: Duke University Press.

García-Navarro, Lulu. 2013. "Brazilian Believers of Hidden Religion Step Out of the Shadows." *National Public Radio,* September 16. Accessed June 18, 2019. https://www.npr.org/sections/parallels/2013/09/16/216890587/brazilian-believers-of-hidden-religion-step-out-of-shadows

Johnson, Paul Christopher. 2002. *Secrets, Gossip, and Gods: The Transformation of Brazilian Candomblé.* Oxford, UK: Oxford University Press.

Parés, Luis Nicolau. 2013. *The Formation of Candomblé: Vodun History and Ritual in Brazil.* Chapel Hill: University of North Carolina Press.

Schmidt, Bettina E. 2016. *Contemporary Religions in Brazil.* Oxford, UK: Oxford University Press.

Protestant Religions

Portugal introduced Catholicism to Brazil in the 1500s. After the 1822 independence, other European immigrants and American missionaries introduced Christian Protestant churches. Anglicans settled in Rio de Janeiro in 1822, and the Lutheran Church was established in 1827. Toward the end of the 1800s, Methodists, Baptists, Seventh-Day Adventists, and Presbyterians were all active in Brazil, mostly propagated by U.S. missionaries. By the 1960s, Protestants made up 5 percent of the national population, but they grew to 15.4 percent of all Brazilians by the year 2000.

Looking at contemporary numbers, the IBGE offers data that reveals a steady decline of Catholic followers and a significant rise in the number of Brazilians who identify as Protestant. The last three decades show a considerable shift of religious affiliation in Brazil. More specifically, the 2010 census indicates that 64 percent of the population was Catholic (or 123.2 million people), which represents a decline from 83 percent in 2000 and a remarkable reduction from 92 percent recorded in the 1970 census. By contrast, the recent 2010 census results reveal that 42.3 million Brazilians (or 22 percent of the national population) identify as Protestant, which represents a growth of 16 million converts in a period between from 2000 to 2010.

A closer analysis of the number of Protestant followers reveals another significant trend. Up until the 1970s and early 1980s, the traditional Protestant churches were made up of Adventists, Baptists, Presbyterians, Mormons, and Lutherans. However, the number of churches with Pentecostal affiliation started to grow tremendously in the late 1980s. The Pentecostal churches group includes the Universal Church of the Kingdom of God (UCKG), Foursquare Church Gospel, Assemblies of God, and the Maranatha churches. The Pentecostal ministries targeted isolated and poor communities as well as low-income neighborhoods often ignored by the Catholic Church. The UCKG, founded by Edir Macedo in 1977, is the most prominent of all the Pentecostal Evangelical churches. It quickly expanded throughout Brazil as well as Europe, Africa, and the United States. For the 2010 census, it reported over 4,500 temples located throughout Brazil. Part of their successful expansion has been accomplished with television evangelists because they own Rede Record, the second-largest television network in Brazil.

Protestant churches in Brazil are also looking to the future to make significant inroads into shaping society based on their conservative values. For example, the UCKG has already ventured into the political arena by being a founding member of the Brazilian Republican Party as a platform to get Protestant candidates elected to government positions who will then shape social policies. The Catholic Church usually works behind the scenes to influence politicians, but the Brazilian Protestants are following a well-crafted strategy of becoming elected representatives of conservative moral values. Pentecostal bishop Marcello Crivella was already elected mayor of Rio de Janeiro in 2017. As with so many aspects of Brazilian society, time will tell if they succeed at a national level.

CHILDREN AS HEALERS AND MIRACLE WORKERS

At the end of the 1990s, a wave of six- and eight-year-old children gained popularity in Brazil as preachers with self-claimed healing powers. The most famous of these child miracle workers is Alani Santos, who preaches at the Pentecostal Church of the Miracle near Rio de Janeiro. Long lines of people seek this young child to cure them of cancer, HIV, and arthritis. She was born in 2004 and started preaching in her father's church when she was three years old. These young pastors preach at small churches and sold-out stadiums. They also spread their message on radio shows, Internet channels, and social media. Critics claim that they simply offer false promises while raking in huge profits from vulnerable people.

Further Reading

Shapiro, Samantha M. 2015. "The Child Preachers of Brazil." *New York Times,* June 11. Accessed June 19, 2019. https://www.nytimes.com/2015/06/14/magazine/the-child-preachers-of-brazil.html?smid=pl-share

See also: Chapter 5: Overview; Catholicism; Universal Church of the Kingdom of God.

Further Reading

Bevins, Vincent. 2012. "Brazil's Evangelical Churches Rewrite the Rules of Politics." *Los Angeles Times,* October 21. Accessed July 15, 2019. http://articles.latimes.com/2012/oct/21/world/la-fg-brazil-evangelicals-20121022

Instituto Brasileiro de Geografia e Estatística (IBGE). "Census 2010." Brasilia. Accessed July 15, 2019. http://ibge.gov.br

Londono, Diana. 2012. "Evangelicals in Brazil." Council on Hemispheric Affairs, December 5. Accessed July 15, 2019. http://www.coha.org/evangelicals-in-brazil

Madambashi, Andrea. 2012. "Protestant Churches in Brazil Experience Mixed Growth, Decline; Huge Increase for Pentecostals." *Christian Post,* July 27. Accessed July 15, 2019. https://www.christianpost.com/news/protestant-churches-in-brazil-experience-mixed-growth-decline-huge-increase-for-pentecostals-78950

Spiritism

During the 1800s in France, Hyppolyte Léon Denizard Rivail claimed that he observed unique phenomena, which he attributed to incorporeal intelligence, or spirits. He began collecting information on the apparent communication with spirits. Using the pseudonym Allan Kardec, he wrote five books to explain how mediums function as go-betweens to connect the physical and the spirit world. These books (*The Spirits' Book, The Mediums' Book, The Gospel According to Spiritism, Heaven and Hell,* and *The Genesis According to Spiritism*) became the foundation of what is best described as a hybrid belief system of religion, philosophy, and science. During the early 1900s, the Kardecian philosophy spread worldwide. It was particularly well accepted in Brazil, where Catholicism was weak, and the government did not oppose it. The Kardecian movement became popular among the upper classes of Brazil, who quickly established Spiritist centers, hospitals, and charity institutions that created curiosity among the larger population. According to the IBGE, Brazil had over 4 million Spiritism followers in 2010, which makes it the country with the largest number of believers in the world.

Spiritism does not operate using the generally accepted perceptions of an established religion. It is more of a philosophy and a way of life. It has no ministers, priests, or religious leaders. Followers do not meet in traditional churches, temples, or cathedrals. Their locations are called Spiritist centers, associations, or societies. Believers gather at informal meetings without strict rituals to discuss doctrine based on Kardec's books, organize charity events, and apply spiritual healing to the sick. Other meetings are specifically held by mediums to communicate with spirits. Spiritists also believe on reincarnation. The doctrine claims that people have an internal moral compass that aims for intellectual improvement because it will increase their knowledge in future lives. It is this knowledge that allows advanced beings to provide healing to the sick, both physical and spiritual. However, science does not support Spiritist healing over the use of traditional medicine.

Brazil has had two of the most influential Spiritism leaders in the world. Xico Xavier (1910–2002) was one of the most popular Spiritist mediums in Brazil. He was a prolific writer who published over 400 books to enhance the understanding of Allan Kardec's doctrine. They sold millions of copies in Brazil, and they were translated to other languages. Xavier was an advocate of Spiritism in academic circles, public television, and radio programs. The other leader was Bezerra de Menezes (1831–1900). The most famous group of Spiritist centers in contemporary Brazil is named after him; the Centro Espírita Bezerra de Menezes (CEABEM) is headquartered in Fortaleza. It offers regular meetings, radio programming, spiritual sessions, children's education, and charity societies. Multiple CEABEM centers are located throughout Brazil, including Rio de Janeiro, Natal, and São Paulo. The Spiritism movement in Brazil has actively used mass media since the 1960s to spread a positive message via radio, television, Internet, and current social media. In fact, the topic of Kardecian doctrine is still popular in recent soap operas (*Escrito nas estrelas* in 2010 and *Além do tempo* in 2015) and contemporary films (*Nosso lar* in 2000 and *O Diario de um espirito* in 2008).

See also: Chapter 5: Overview; Catholicism.

Further Reading

Bragdon, Emma. 2004. *Kardec's Spiritism: A Home for Healing and Spiritual Evolution.* Lakeland, FL: Lightening Up Press.

Hess, David. 1991. *Spirits and Scientists: Ideology, Spiritism, and Brazilian Culture.* University Park: Pennsylvania State University Press.

Schofield, Alfred T. 2003. *Modern Spiritism: Its Science and Religion.* Philadelphia: Blakiston's & Son.

Universal Church of the Kingdom of God

The Igreja Universal do Reino de Deus is a Pentecostal Christian Church founded by Edir Macedo in 1977 in Rio de Janeiro. It quickly expanded in poor neighborhoods in Brazil, and began establishing ministries in Europe, Africa, and the United States. At an international level, it is known as the Universal Church of the Kingdom of God (UCKG). By 2010, it reported over 4,500 temples located in over 1,500 cities throughout Brazil. The UCKG now has more ministers than Catholic priests in the country. Their aggressive expansion has also brought unwanted attention and accusations of charlatanism, corruption, and money laundering.

The UCKG follows most doctrines preached by Pentecostal denominations. The organization believe their ministers are endowed with divine powers, which can be used for healing and exorcism. It also promotes the concept of prosperity theology, which provides success and spiritual happiness here on earth, as opposed to waiting until after death to reap the rewards of good behavior. In addition, the UCKG expects its followers to pay a tithe of 10 percent of all income directly to the church in order to maintain its operating expenses. Its ministers claim that there is a direct correlation between tithe contributions and eternal salvation.

The initial success of the UCKG was based on local ministries in poor neighborhoods and other areas neglected by the Catholic Church. However, in 1989, Edir Macedo and the church leaders made a strategic decision to compete for national space. As a result, the church purchased Rede Record to launch its television ministry, which was an incredible success. By 2015, it became the second-largest television network in the country after Rede Globo. In addition, UCKG leaders became founding members of the Brazilian Republican Party as a platform to launch political candidates with conservative points of view that were different from the Catholic Church. After a few unsuccessful campaigns, the party managed to elect Bishop Marcelo Crivella (Macedo's nephew) as the mayor of Rio de Janeiro; he took office in 2017.

The UCKG and its leaders have faced multiple social controversies and legal challenges. One of the most common accusations is that the UCKG collects incredible amounts of money in donations, but most of it goes to enrich founder Edir Macedo and other top church officials, while the church still benefits from government subsidies and its nonprofit status. With an estimated personal fortune of over $2 billion U.S., Macedo is considered the wealthiest bishop in the world. The UCKG financial practices generated a federal investigation and charges of money laundering in the United Kingdom. Related charges filed in multiple countries also accuse the church of fraud and charlatanism for offering false promises of healing while demanding money from the poorest populations they serve. Meanwhile in Africa, the UCKG has faced serious accusations of religious intolerance, which have resulted in the church being either suspended or banned completely from Angola, Madagascar, and Zambia. The United Nations even ordered a study into the lack of religious tolerance practiced by the UCKG, and the 2009 report revealed that this church consistently made derogatory remarks about Jews, Catholics, Muslims, other Protestants, and especially followers of Afro-Brazilian religions. While all these controversies have rocked the UCKG ministry, they continue to expand in the number of followers while also gaining political and economic power along the way.

See also: Chapter 5: Overview; Catholicism; Protestant Religions.

Further Reading

Macedo, Edir. 2012. *Nothing to Lose*. São Paulo: Planeta.

Phillips, Tom. 2010. "Brazil's Evangelical Revolution Sees Miracle Healers Take Centre Stage." *Guardian*, October 29. Accessed July 12, 2019. https://www.theguardian.com/world/2010/oct/29/brazil-evangelical-revolution-miracle-healers

Universal Church of the Kingdom of God, Official English Website. http://www.uckg.org

Van Wyk, Ilana. 2015. *The Universal Church of the Kingdom of God in South Africa*. Johannesburg: Wits University Press.

Watts, Jonathan. 2014. "Brazil's Evangelicals Become a Political Force to Be Reckoned with." *Guardian,* October 1. Accessed July 12, 2019. https://www.theguardian.com/world/2014/oct/01/brazil-evangelicals-politics-presidential-election

CHAPTER 6

SOCIAL CLASSES AND ETHNICITY

OVERVIEW

From a social point of view, Brazil is an extremely complex country. For the last five decades, however, it was quite common to describe the country as a "racial democracy" where different ethnicities essentially got along just fine. This outdated concept is still pervasive among certain groups nowadays, but simple conversations with Brazilians quickly reveal that racial discrimination is very much alive. It is only in the twenty-first century that Brazil has really engaged in meaningful open discussions regarding the rights of indigenous groups, the contributions of Afro-Brazilians to the national culture, how people with mixed ethnicities (*caboclo, cafuso, mameluco,* and *mulatto*) reflect historical interactions, and the pernicious effects of racism and discrimination on the disadvantaged groups in society.

Brazil is one of the most inequitable countries in the world. A few individuals have amassed unimaginable amounts of wealth while millions of Brazilian families still linger in extreme poverty. While this contrast is not a recent development, Brazilians have recently brought the topic to the forefront by engaging in massive national street protests that denounce the extreme inequalities in wealth distribution and income disparities in the country. Average activists have dispelled the notion of a racial democracy by openly stating that there is a direct correlation in Brazil between race and socioeconomic class. The racial disparities are visually tangible. The wealthy, well-educated, and professionals are overwhelmingly white, and the large majority of poor population groups are black and *pardo* (mixed race). The low-wage classes are at a disadvantage coming up in an inadequate public education system that severely underprepares students for university admission and handicaps them for future well-paying jobs.

Recently, Brazil has made significant national economic improvements, but the benefits have not necessarily trickled down to the most disadvantaged groups. The problem with such international economic progress is that it has sparked a tremendously high cost of living, which significantly impacts low-income populations. Consequently, Brazil now suffers from a multitude of contemporary problems that are mostly rooted in poverty. In fact, the 2010 census published by the Instituto Brasileiro de Geografia e Estatística (IBGE) shows that 26 percent of the population lives below the poverty line, and 16.2 million Brazilians barely survive on the equivalent of $1.30 U.S. a day (Croix, 2012). Moreover, over 12 million Brazilians live in *favelas, mocambos,* and *alagados* (slums or shantytowns) in unsanitary conditions. Moreover, the combination of stagnant wages and high levels of inflation between 2015 and 2018 disproportionately affected the poor populations who spend most of their income on food and basic necessities. The social frustration is very palpable throughout the country. For example, in rural settings, the Landless Rural Workers Movement (Movimento dos Trabalhadores Sem Terra, or MST) includes over 1.5 million members trying to obtain land for poor peasants. Their political activism has reached desperate tactics that include land occupation, which has in turn sparked a backlash from multiple conservative groups and media in Brazil. In metropolitan areas, urban crime has spiked in the last ten years, and the government has responded with overwhelming force by unleashing the military to patrol the violent streets of Rio de Janeiro, São Paulo, and Recife. As a result, social conflict has recently intensified as Brazilians routinely see politicians involved in corruption scandals and spending billions of dollars to subsidize international sports events while ignoring social problems that disproportionately affect the poor, such as endemic poverty, a deficient public education system, inadequate health-care programs, and high inflation rates that diminish the purchasing power of all Brazilians.

Despite the negative outlook regarding social conditions and race relations in Brazil, the country is making significant improvements to reduce economic inequality and income disparities. The government has been an effective agent of change by implementing policies that aim to reduce poverty rates, increase school participation, and prepare more Brazilians of all backgrounds for professional jobs. In fact, social welfare programs, such as Bolsa Família and Brasil Sem Miséria, successfully lifted millions of people out of extreme poverty from 2013 to 2018. The Bolsa Família is a conditional cash transfer program that offers payments to low-income families with the condition that children must attend school consistently. Since education provides a possible path for upward mobility, the government approved a controversial affirmative action policy in 2012 that sets racial quotas for admission at public federal universities. It addressed the disparity that while almost 50 percent of the national population is either black or *pardo* (mixed race), until recently they only represented 5 percent of the total number of university students. The goal is to reduce racial exclusion and to provide a path for economic improvement. Congress went even further in 2014 by passing another law that extended affirmative action quotas for government jobs. In fact, 20 percent of all federal jobs in public service were supposed to be filled by blacks or mixed-race underprivileged applicants by 2016. The overarching goal of the federal government to expand access to higher education and well-paying jobs is to discourage racial discrimination, provide access to more employment opportunities, and therefore promote economic equality.

Further Reading

Barbara, Vanessa. 2015. "In Denial over Racism in Brazil." *New York Times,* March 23. Accessed July 21, 2019. https://www.nytimes.com/2015/03/24/opinion/vanessa-barbara-in-denial-over-racism-in-brazil.html

Bohn, Simone. 2016. "Social Classes and Ethnicity," in *Brazil,* edited by Antonio Luciano de Andrade Tosta and Eduardo F. Coutinho, 120–140. Santa Barbara, CA: ABC-CLIO.

Bringel, Breno. 2016. "2013–2016: Polarization and Protests in Brazil." Open Democracy, February 18. Accessed July 21, 2019. https://www.opendemocracy.net/democraciaabierta/breno-bringel/2013-2016-polarization-and-protests-in-brazil

Chiesa Gonçalves, Aline. 2017. *The Influence of the Bolsa Família Program in Education.* Düsseldorf, Germany: Novas Edições Acadêmicas.

Corrigan, Gemma. 2015. "Is Brazil Making Progress on Inequality? World Economic Forum, September 7. Accessed July 21, 2019. https://www.weforum.org/agenda/2015/09/is-brazil-making-progress-on-inequality

Croix, Sarah de Sainte. 2012. "Brazil Strives for Economic Equality." *Rio Times,* February 7. Accessed July 21, 2019. https://riotimesonline.com/brazil-news/rio-business/brazil-strives-for-economic-equality

Instituto Brasileiro de Geografia e Estatística (IBGE). 2011. *Censo demográfico de 2010: Resultados do universo.* Rio de Janeiro: IBGE. http://ibge.gov.br

Ondetti, Gabriel A. 2008. *Land, Protest, and Politics: The Landless Movement and the Struggle for Agrarian Reform in Brazil.* University Park: Pennsylvania State University Press.

Simões, Soraya Silveira. 2012. *Favelas Cariocas.* Rio de Janeiro: Editora Garamond.

Vincent, Jon S. 2003. *Culture and Customs of Brazil.* Westport, CT: Greenwood Press.

African Ancestry and Influence

The influence of African heritage is prevalent throughout contemporary Brazilian culture. Over 4 million slaves left a tangible imprint on music, religion, literature, sports, food, dance, and art. Since the country was colonized from the north, the city of Salvador in the state of Bahia was the first national capital city and the main hub for the slave trade. Today, Salvador is considered the epicenter of Afro-Brazilian culture, which is displayed in regional celebrations, music, and religious rituals.

African influence is also visible in contemporary Brazilian cuisine. The general practice during the colonial period (1500 to 1800s) was to blend common Portuguese meals with local ingredients and either Amerindian or African cooking styles. For example, *feijoada* is a national dish rooted in a Portuguese recipe of beans and meat. The African slaves adapted the dish by adding manioc flour and replacing beef with less costly cuts of pork available to them, such as pig's feet, tail, and ears. *Feijoada* is now prepared throughout Brazil with multiple variations.

Brazil has a strong legacy of sports excellence, and some of its most legendary athletes are black, especially in *futebol* (soccer) and basketball. Perhaps the most iconic figure is the charismatic Edson Arantes do Nascimento, simply known as Pelé. The International Olympic Committee voted Pelé in 1999 as the Best World Athlete of the twentieth century. *Futebol* is the king of sports in Brazil, and this recognition produced immense national pride. In addition, the martial art of capoeira widely practiced in contemporary Brazil was developed by Africans and distinguished by its acrobatic choreography style.

Carnival reflects the ultimate influence of African heritage in Brazil. It incorporates fast-paced samba music, captivating dance choreographies, and an intoxicating energy unmatched by any other celebration in Brazil. Carnival is a major televised festivity that displays the beauty of the Brazilian people, and the marketing side of it usually highlights the sensuality of *mulatto* women. However, black and mixed-race Brazilians constitute roughly 52 percent of the national population, but they are vastly underrepresented in the media, including television, cinema, and fashion shows.

A samba dancer performs at the Carnival parade at the Sambódromo in Rio de Janeiro. The dance and rhythms are based on African religious traditions practiced during the slave period in Brazil (1500s to 1888). (David Davis/Dreamstime.com)

Spirituality is extremely important for Afro-Brazilians, and it reflects their ability to adapt to different social conditions. While they are predominately Catholic, the African religions of Candomblé, Macumba, and Umbanda also have large followings, especially in Brasília, Rio de Janeiro, and Porto Alegre. The large majority of them do not see any contradiction in believing in both Catholic saints and African gods called *orixás*. The dual belief system offers them a way to remain rooted in their African spiritual heritage and to embrace Catholicism as the dominant religion of Brazil.

See also: Chapter 2: Slavery, Abolition, and African Heritage. Chapter 5: Candomblé and Macumba; *Orixás*, African Gods. Chapter 6: Overview. Chapter 13: Carnival; Samba Music and Dance. Chapter 14: *Feijoada*, Brazil's National Dish. Chapter 15: *Futebol* (Soccer).

Further Reading

Darlington, Shasta. 2013. "From Samba to Carnival: Brazil's Thriving African Culture." CNN, July 24. Accessed July 10, 2019. https://www.cnn.com/2012/10/23/world/africa/african-culture-brazil/index.html

Kilkenny, Salome. 2011. "Brazil's African Heritage." *Network Journal,* June 22. Accessed January 10, 2020. https://tnj.com/us-brazil-cooperation/

Murphy, John P. 2006. *Music in Brazil.* Oxford, UK: Oxford University Press.

Phillips, Tom. 2011. "Brazil Census Shows African Brazilians in the Majority for the First Time." *Guardian,* November 17. Accessed July 10, 2019. https://www.theguardian.com/world/2011/nov/17/brazil-census-african-brazilians-majority

Sansone, Livio. 2003. *Blackness without Ethnicity: Constructing Race in Brazil.* New York: Palgrave Macmillan.

Distribution of Wealth and Income Disparity

Brazil has experienced tremendous economic growth during the last twenty years, but the country still suffers from extreme social and income inequities. The statistics regarding wealth disparities are sobering. The World Bank 2014 report on Brazil revealed that 20 percent of the richest Brazilians have an income that is thirty-three times the total combined income of the poorest 20 percent of the country. The Global Agenda Agency and the World Economic Forum declared in 2015 that in countries such as Brazil, the poorest 50 percent of the population controls less than 10 percent of the total national wealth (Mohammed, 2015). In addition, the 2010 census published by the Instituto Brasileiro de Geografia e Estatística (IBGE) shows that 26 percent of the population lives below the poverty line, and 16.2 million Brazilians barely survive on the equivalent of $1.30 U.S. a day (Croix, 2012). Moreover, the combination of stagnant wages and high levels of inflation between 2015 and 2018 disproportionately affected the poor populations who spend most of their income on food and basic necessities.

Based on the disheartening poverty statistics, the federal government implemented specific programs to reduce the income inequity gap. In fact, social welfare programs, such as Bolsa Família and Brasil Sem Miséria, successfully lifted millions of people out of extreme poverty from 2013 to 2018. However, the public education system is still a drastic failure. Most economists, sociologists, and education experts in Brazil agree that there is an axiomatic relationship between education success and a reduction of economic inequality. Lack of access to a good education limits future job opportunities. As a result, Brazil has become a dualist country tilted in favor of privileged groups; it is evident in the juxtaposition of private/public schools and formal versus informal employment.

The 2010 census also confirmed that there is a correlation in Brazil between race and income disparities. The majority of poor populations tend to be black or *pardo* (mixed-race heritage), and white Brazilians earn significantly more than their dark-skin counterparts. Similarly, wealthier white families can afford to send their children to private schools, and they facilitate acceptance to high-caliber universities, which then leads to professional jobs with higher incomes. Meanwhile, the poor linger in a deficient public education system that reduces future opportunities and labor options. In order to repair the discrepancies in access to higher education by dark-skin Brazilians, the federal government implemented a controversial racial university acceptance quota system in 2012 for its prestigious federal universities The Ministry of Education expects to see tangible results beginning in 2020; the expectation is that university graduation rates translate into professional jobs that will reduce income disparities in the country.

See also: Chapter 6: Overview; Education and Upward Mobility; Poverty, Social Conflict, and Protests. Chapter 8: Affirmative Action Policies; Higher Education and Major Universities; Public Education: Elementary and Secondary Schooling.

Further Reading

Corrigan, Gemma. 2015. "Is Brazil Making Progress on Inequality?" World Economic Forum, September 7. Accessed May 15, 2019. https://www.weforum.org/agenda/2015/09/is-brazil-making-progress-on-inequality

Croix, Sarah de Sainte. 2012. "Brazil Strives for Economic Equality." *Rio Times,* February 7. Accessed May 15, 2019. https://riotimesonline.com/brazil-news/rio-business/brazil-strives-for-economic-equality

Instituto Brasileiro de Geografia e Estatística (IBGE). 2011. *Censo demográfico de 2010: Resultados do universo.* Rio de Janeiro: IBGE. http://ibge.gov.br

Mohammed, Amina. 2015. "Deepening Income Inequality." The Global Agenda, World Economic Forum. Accessed May 15, 2019. http://reports.weforum.org/outlook-global-agenda-2015/top-10-trends-of-2015/1-deepening-income-inequality/?doing_wp_cron=1548960354.6721160411834716796875

Education and Upward Mobility

Education is a crucial factor that can significantly contribute to upward social mobility. Brazil is a country with alarming social and income inequalities, but politicians are keenly aware that education has a direct effect on the standard of living of all Brazilians. During the last twenty years, the government has implemented policies to remedy the immense education and income gaps throughout the nation. For example, the Bolsa Família is a conditional cash transfer program implemented in 2003 by President Lula da Silva (1945–); it offers payments to low-income families with the condition that children must attend school and be vaccinated. In addition, President Dilma Rousseff (1947–) signed into law the controversial affirmative action policy in 2012 to set racial quotas for admission at public federal universities. It addressed the disparity that almost 50 percent of the national population is either black or *pardo* (mixed race), but until recently, they only represented 5 percent of the total number of university students. The goal is to reduce racial exclusion and to provide a path for economic improvement. The Bolsa Família program has been recognized worldwide for its tremendous success, especially because it has contributed toward lifting millions of Brazilians out of extreme poverty in the last fifteen years. The racial quota system at public universities, however, has generated strong opinions by both advocates and opponents.

Brazilians constantly stage protests against the disappointingly low quality of the public education system, which results in future lack of opportunities for low-income families. Primary and secondary schools cannot even adequately house all their students. Consequently, classrooms are routinely overcrowded, and local schools offer education in shifts that include only four hours of instruction per day (morning, midday, and evening shifts). In addition, teachers generally lack basic classroom supplies and work for low pay. Ironically, some of the highest-performing universities in Brazil are public, which are completely funded by the government and free for students. They are usually better than most private universities. Therefore, the admission process into public federal universities is fiercely competitive, and most of the spots go to better-prepared students who usually came from private high schools.

Opponents of university affirmative action programs propose that the Ministry of Education needs to concentrate on fixing the underperforming elementary and secondary education systems instead of forcing unprepared students into higher education programs. Nevertheless, the government expects to see positive tangible results by 2020, and it is preparing for the next step that promotes access to professional jobs with better pay. To that end, Congress passed a law in 2014 that extended affirmative action quotas for government jobs. In fact, 20 percent of all federal jobs in public service were supposed to be filled by blacks or mixed-race underprivileged applicants by 2016. The overarching goal of the federal government to expand access to higher education is to discourage racial discrimination, provide access to more employment opportunities, and therefore promote economic equality.

See also: Chapter 3: Lula da Silva, Luiz Inácio (1945–); Rousseff, Dilma (1947–). Chapter 6: Overview. Chapter 8: Affirmative Action Policies; Education Reforms of 2016; Higher Education and Major Universities.

Further Reading

Ali, Raiesa. 2015. "Income Inequality and Poverty: A Comparison of Brazil and Honduras." Council of Hemispheric Affairs, July 1. Accessed July 15, 2019. http://www.coha.org/income-inequality-and-poverty-a-comparison-of-brazil-and-honduras

Carneiro, Julia. 2013. "Brazil's Universities Take Affirmative Action." *BBC News*, August 28. Accessed July 15, 2019. https://www.bbc.com/news/business-23862676

Chiesa Gonçalves, Aline. 2017. *The Influence of the Bolsa Família Program in Education*. Düsseldorf, Germany: Novas Edições Acadêmicas.

Favelas, Mocambos, and *Alagados* (Slums)

The hillside *favelas* (slums) of Rio de Janeiro are notorious. *Favelas* are poor communities usually built on occupied land that is not owned by the people who took it over as part of a speedy invasion practice. In general, these illegal, poorly built shacks are improvised buildings that lack basic sanitation services, electricity, trash pickup

Panoramic view of the Rocinha favela in Rio de Janeiro, Brazil, on August 22, 2015. In recent decades, the gap between rich and poor in Brazil's cities has widened. The 2010 census revealed that over 12 million Brazilians live in similar poor communities throughout Brazil that often lack electricity and basic sanitation services. (Mandritoiu/Dreamstime.com)

arrangements, or simple running water. Sometimes, the tenants manage to make an illegal connection to the city's electrical grid to power basic electronics at home. Occasionally, *favelas*, such as the Rocinha in Rio de Janeiro, grow so large that they resemble average neighborhoods with bus services and business establishments. However, *favelas* are not limited to Rio de Janeiro. Such tenements are present in most major Brazilian cities, but they are known by different names. In the state of Bahia, *alagados* are large slums built on stilts on top of the swampy waters of Baía de Todos os Santos. In the state of Rio Grande do Sul, they are called *vilas de malocas*. Their northern counterparts in Pernambuco are called *mocambos*. All these makeshift communities house millions of poor people in complete poverty and unsanitary conditions. The 2010 census published by the Instituto Brasileiro de Geografia e Estatística (IBGE) reveals that over 12 million Brazilians people live in *favelas*. The largest percentage of favela residents is concentrated in the northern region of the country, and they are predominantly black. For example, the city of Fortaleza (an area with 4 million people in the state of Caerá) recognizes more than 200 separate *favelas* that comprise over 25 percent of its urban population. As the pace of urbanization continues to accelerate in the twenty-first century, Brazilians keep migrating from rural regions to large cities in search of a better life. This marginalized group of uneducated migrants often ends up living in urban slums.

During the last five years, Brazil has experienced steep increases in urban violent crime, and much of it originates in favela communities. Homicides and violent crimes have recently soared throughout Brazil. Former president Michel Temer (1940–) made the controversial decision in 2018 to send the military to fight crime and drug trafficking in *favelas* of Rio de Janeiro controlled by gangs. Then President Jair Bolsonaro (1955–) was elected in 2018 with tough-on-crime campaign promises. More recently in January 2019, residents of Fortaleza experienced an intense wave of violence where gangs destroyed public property, committed gruesome murders, and boldly planted explosives in police stations. Bolsonaro also sent military reinforcements to control the unusual level of violence. However, such forces have been repeatedly accused of police brutality. They killed more than 5,000 people in 2017, which is an average of fourteen Brazilians per day. Favela residents end up suffering from local crime and then also at the hands of police forces who are supposed to protect them.

See also: Chapter 3: Temer, Michael (1940–); Chapter 6: Overview; Poverty, Social Conflict, and Protests.

Further Reading

Faiola, Anthony, and Anna Jean Kaiser. 2018. "A Once-Trendy Rio Slum Is Now at War: The Murders in a Popular Brazilian Favela Reflect Rising Violence in a Country in Crisis." *Washington Post,* January 5. Accessed June 9, 2019. https://www.washingtonpost.com/sf/world/2018/01/05/this-trendy-rio-favela-appeared-in-a-hollywood-kids-movie-now-the-bullets-are-back/?noredirect=on&utm_term=.22c662a5a3a9

Instituto Brasileiro de Geografia e Estatística (IBGE). 2011. *Censo demográfico de 2010: Resultados do universo.* Rio de Janeiro: IBGE. http://ibge.gov.br

Rapoza, Kenneth. 2016. "Brazil Is Murder Capital of the World, but Rio Is Safer than Compton, Detroit, St. Louis . . ." *Forbes,* January 29. Accessed June 6, 2019. https://www.forbes.com/sites/kenrapoza/2016/01/29/months-before-rio-olympics-murder-rate-rises-in-brazil

Simões, Soraya Silveira. 2012. *Favelas Cariocas.* Rio de Janeiro: Editora Garamond.

Vincent. Jon S. 2003. *Culture and Customs of Brazil.* Westport, CT: Greenwood Press.

Indigenous Populations

The number of the indigenous population in Brazil has been drastically reduced since the arrival of the Europeans in 1500. At the time, almost 2 million indigenous people were divided into two major groups: the Tupi who lived along coastal regions and the Tapuia who settled in the interior territories. In addition, the Carib and Nuaraque groups lived mostly in the Amazon region. Most groups were seminomadic tribes who survived by hunting, fishing, gathering food, and light agriculture.

According to the 2010 census published by the Instituto Brasileiro de Geografia e Estatística (IBGE), there are now about 250,000 Indians in Brazil, roughly 0.2 percent of the country's population of 140 million Brazilians. The dramatic reduction was caused by wars, European diseases, and miscegenation with other racial groups. The

European colonizers quickly started having children with Indian women, and the result was a generation of mixed-race children known as *caboclo* or *mameluko*. They quickly became the most numerous ethnic group in colonial Brazil. Today, there are over 200 small Indian tribes that live isolated mostly in the northern Amazon region. Others have left their local tribes and moved to urban areas in search of a better life.

Since the colonial period, different Brazilian governments have created policies aimed at dealing with Indian affairs, which means that indigenous people have rarely been in charge of making significant national decisions about themselves. During the 1960s, reservation lands (mostly in the Amazon regions and the southern border with Paraguay) were set aside for native populations. In addition, the Fundação Nacional do Índio (FUNAI) was established to protect their culture and rights. Furthermore, the current constitution of 1988 includes the so-called "Indian Chapter" that specifically provides protection for indigenous cultural practices, denounces policies of forced social integration, and provides specific rights to establish indigenous lands based on their usage, customs, and traditions.

One of the most alarming contemporary concerns for Brazilian indigenous populations is the constant struggle to have their constitutional rights enforced, especially dealing with land issues. For example, some tribal lands are rich in natural resources, which attract non-Indian squatters, but the government does not expel them. However, when tribal lands are not clearly demarcated, cattle ranchers routinely encroach into open pastoral lands. When Indian groups file legal protests, the courts routinely rule against them. In addition, the federal government has moved incredibly slowly in the process of legally recognizing official boundaries of indigenous lands.

The future does not seem very positive for Brazilian indigenous groups. President Jair Bolsonaro (1955–) took office in January 2019, and he immediately issued a controversial executive order to undermine indigenous rights. He officially took away the responsibility of certifying indigenous territories as protected lands from the National Indian Foundation (FUNAI) and transferred it to the Minister of Agriculture, which has been actively advocating for years on behalf of cattle ranchers and farmers to have greater access to protected lands to expand economic development. Moreover, the new conservative government is embarking on procedures to revise the constitution by 2020, and over one hundred amendment proposals specifically target the reduction of indigenous rights while simultaneously arguing for an economic strategy that reduces government regulations and environmental protections.

See also: Chapter 6: Overview.

Further Reading

Fundação Nacional do Índio (FUNAI). http://www.funai.gov.br

Instituto Brasileiro de Geografia e Estatística (IBGE). 2011. *Censo demográfico de 2010: Resultados do universo.* Rio de Janeiro: IBGE. http://ibge.gov.br

Londoño, Ernesto. 2019. "Jair Bolsonaro, on Day 1, Undermines Indigenous Brazilians' Rights." *New York Times.* January 2. Accessed July 20, 2019. https://www.nytimes.com/2019/01/02/world/americas/brazil-bolsonaro-president-indigenous-lands.html

Landless Rural Workers Movement (MST)

The Landless Rural Workers Movement is known in Brazil as the Movimento dos Trabalhadores Sem Terra, or simply by its initials MST. It was established in 1984 in the state of Paraná. Over the next thirty years, the social movement grew to include over 1.5 million members distributed among twenty-three of the twenty-six states in Brazil. In a country where land distribution is extremely unequal (3 percent of the people own over 68 percent of all commercially arable land), the MST's main goal is to obtain land for poor peasants. Through social and political activism, the main strategy used by MST members is to engage in massive land occupations based on their interpretation of Article 186 of the current 1988 constitution of Brazil, which states that land must serve a social function. The Brazilian constitution also mentions that the federal government should expropriate rural property for the purpose of agrarian reform if such land is not performing its social function. The MST organizes land occupations (squatting), and it then applies political pressure together with legal petitions to convert the occupied land into formal expropriation and eventually land ownership for small-farm workers. Consequently, farm owners started forming their own armed groups to defend their property from land invasions. The MST tactics have sparked a passionate backlash from multiple conservative groups and media in Brazil, and more than 1,700 MST activists have been killed since the movement was created in 1984. As a result, the MST functions with a decentralized organizational structure with roughly fifteen leaders who are hardly ever seen together in order to avoid potential arrests and deadly personal attacks.

The ultimate goal of the MST is to achieve a national comprehensive agrarian reform. They view it as a path toward social justice. Its members consider land ownership as a strategy to reduce social inequality, an opportunity to improve their income, and a way to increase their political influence. When rural workers achieve land ownership, they can become vested participants in the food production process, which allows them to reap the benefits of economic development. The MST became politically active during the 2000s by actively supporting Presidents Luiz Inácio Lula da Silva (1945–) and Dilma Rousseff (1947–). However, the MST became disillusioned when both leaders seemed to actually slow down the discussions regarding land reform. More recently, during the 2010s, the election of more conservative presidents (such as Michel Temer and Jair Bolsonaro) with connections to agribusiness corporate interests have turned the current prospect of a comprehensive agrarian reform into a distant possibility.

See also: Chapter 3: Lula da Silva, Luiz Inácio (1945–); Rousseff, Dilma (1947–). Chapter 6: Overview; Distribution of Wealth and Income Disparity.

Further Reading

Fernandes, Barnard Mancano. 2000. *The Formation of the MST in Brazil*. Petropolis, Brazil: Editora Vozes.

Meszaros, George. 2013. *Social Movements, Law, and the Politics of Land Reform: Lessons from Brazil*. London: Routledge.

Movimento Sem Terra (MST) Official Website. http://mstbrazil.org

Ondetti, Gabriel A. 2008. *Land, Protest, and Politics: The Landless Movement and the Struggle for Agrarian Reform in Brazil*. University Park: Pennsylvania State University Press.

Wolford, Wendy. 2010. *This Land Is Ours Now: Social Mobilization and the Meanings of Land in Brazil*. Durham, NC: Duke University Press.

Mixed Ethnicities: *Caboclo, Cafuso, Mameluco,* and *Mulatto*

Contemporary Brazil is one of the most diverse nations in the world in terms of race and ethnicity. The main groups include Indian, white, black, and Mongoloid Asian. These groups have mixed in Brazil for over 500 years; the miscegenation process was quite common since the arrival of the Europeans in 1500. Consequently, specific terminology is used to identify mixed-race groups that fit under the general umbrella term *pardo* (brown or mixed race). For example, a child of white and indigenous parents is called *caboclo* or *mameluko*. A person of mixed black and white heritage is a *mulatto*, and the children of black and Indian parents are called *cafusos*. Sometimes, a person with black, white, and indigenous ancestry is referred to as a *juçara*. In addition, hundreds of thousands of Japanese migrated to Brazil during the twentieth century, and they started to intermarry during the 1970s, especially to white Brazilians. Their children are known as *ainocô*. It is important to highlight that these mixed-race groups collectively self-identified as *pardos* (brown) are not small minority groups but rather a sizable population in Brazil.

The latest 2010 census revealed that, for the first time in Brazilian history, nonwhite people are the majority of the national population with 50.7 percent. This number includes respondents who labeled themselves either as black or *pardo*. Conversely, whites fell from 53.7 percent in the previous 2000 census to 47.7 percent in 2010. The Brazilian Institute of Geography and Statistics (IBGE) explains that the census categories (white, black, Indio, and *pardo*/mixed race) are usually based on skin color and not necessarily ruled by a strict or demonstrable definition of race and ancestry. A further analysis of the 2010 census data shows that the 50.7 percent of the nonwhite population equates to 97 million Brazilians. This number includes 15 million blacks (7.6 percent) and 82 million mixed-race people (43.1 percent of the national population). In addition, slightly over 2 million people identified themselves as Asian, and 817,000 labeled themselves as Indian or Native Brazilian.

The IBGE also highlighted important social indicators based on the 2010 census data. Among the positive trends, child illiteracy rates were reduced to a low 3.9 percent and school attendance rates are higher. It also revealed persistent income inequalities between northern and southern Brazil as well as between rural and urban regions. Moreover, the IBGE noted an acute income disparity showing that the wealthiest 10 percent of Brazilians earned 44.5 percent of all national income, while the poorest

10 percent of the population only earned 1.1 percent of the total income. Additional observations indicate that the poorest 10 percent of the population is made up of 76.3 percent blacks and mixed-race Brazilians with only 23.7 percent white. While discrimination is not always overt in Brazil, income disparities show that the higher social classes consist mostly of white people, and the poorest population includes an extremely high number of black Brazilians.

See also: Chapter 6: Overview.

Further Reading

Bohn, Simone. 2016. "Social Classes and Ethnicity," in *Brazil*, edited by Antonio Luciano de Andrade Tosta and Eduardo F. Coutinho, 120–140. Santa Barbara, CA: ABC-CLIO.

Instituto Brasileiro de Geografia e Estatística (IBGE). 2011. *Censo demográfico de 2010: Resultados do universo*. Rio de Janeiro: IBGE. http://ibge.gov.br

Phillips, Tom. 2011. "Brazil Census Shows African-Brazilians in the Majority for the First Time." *The Guardian*, November 17. Accessed June 25, 2019. https://www.theguardian.com/world/2011/nov/17/brazil-census-african-brazilians-majority

Vincent, Jon S. 2003. *Culture and Customs of Brazil*. Westport, CT: Greenwood Press.

Modern Immigration

Brazil welcomed millions of immigrants during the twentieth century, and they made significant contributions to the national culture. From 1900 to 1930, over 2 million Europeans arrived after World War I from Russia, Poland, Italy, and Romania. In addition, over 200,000 Japanese immigrants settled in São Paulo and Paraná. During the 1950s and early 1960s, Brazil embarked on a path of industrialization under President Getúlio Vargas, and it actively recruited nearly 200,000 immigrants from Syria, Lebanon, and Spain. However, the military dictatorship from 1964 to 1985 developed a nationalistic fervor that discouraged further immigration.

In 1980, the Brazilian government established for the first time the Conselho Nacional de Imigração as a federal agency to implement national policies regarding work permits, legal residency, and different types of visas (tourist, student, permanent, diplomatic). Then Congress approved the new immigrant law in 1981 that gave preference to immigrants who possessed university degrees. However, the 1980s and early 1990s resulted in failed economic policies that made Brazil less attractive to educated migrants. Therefore, those who came were less skilled workers, which generated complaints by national labor unions.

The period between the 1990s and early 2000s was a blend of both legal and illegal migration. During these decades, Brazil emerged as an economic powerhouse in South America. The most noticeable group to migrate legally were South Koreans who came to establish the new textile industry in Brazil, and they prospered tremendously. To make the industry profitable, they relied on hiring illegal immigrants (especially

Peruvians, Bolivians, and Central Americans who sneaked through the porous land borders) because they were willing to work for lower wages. The government needs workers in its new industrialized economy, and as of 2019, it has not established any formal policies to control illegal immigration.

The strong Brazilian economy of the twenty-first century is engaged in global alliances that often include migration cooperation agreements. Brazil has become a leader of the regional common market Mercosul with Argentina, Paraguay and Uruguay. It is also part of the BRICS economic alliance that includes Brazil, Russia, India, China, and South Africa. In addition, Brazil cooperates with the United Nations High Commission for Refugees, and it has accepted thousands of refugees from Afghanistan, Colombia, Angola, and Sierra Leone since 2000.

Two recent events have reshaped Brazilian immigration. In 2017, President Michel Temer (1940–) signed the new immigration law (Law 13.445) that provides exactly the same rights to foreign residents available to Brazilian citizens, including social security, owning property, and access to jobs. It also made provisions to its generous immigration policies regarding regulations to authorize legal residence for people who originally entered Brazil with a temporary visa. Then in 2018, Brazil was overwhelmed when over 50,000 Venezuelans crossed the northern border while running away from the economic and political crisis in their home country.

See also: Chapter 3: Temer, Michel (1940–). Chapter 4: BRICS Economic Group; Mercosul/Mercosur. Chapter 6: Overview.

Further Reading

Friedrich, Ernesto A., and Wilson Fusco. 2005. "Shaping Brazil. The Role of International Migration." Migration Policy Institute, June 1. Accessed May 24, 2019. https://www.migrationpolicy.org/article/shaping-brazil-role-international-migration

Londoño, Ernesto. 2018. "Their Country Is Being Invaded: Exodus of Venezuelans Overwhelms Northern Brazil." *New York Times,* April 28. Accessed May 24, 2019. https://www.nytimes.com/2018/04/28/world/americas/venezuela-brazil-migrants.html

Parentela

From childhood, most Brazilians grow up surrounded by a close network of people designed for social interaction, which is made up of relatives (*parentes*) and close family friends. The word *parentela* literally means "extended family" and includes people related by blood, relatives acquired through marriage, close family friends, connections through religious associations, and even the help who work in the house. As a result, most Brazilians actively participate in social interactions on a regular basis in a reciprocal process that encompasses both benefits and responsibilities. Children develop an identity within a close group that includes extended family members such as grandparents, uncles, aunts, godparents, cousins, and the cleaning ladies. These relationships usually carry into adult life.

From a comparative point of view, Americans value independence, self-reliance, and individual achievements. Brazilian culture, however, places a strong emphasis on cooperation and social relationships. This network will regularly gather for casual intergenerational meals at home, help its members with small financial troubles, provide suggestions to navigate complicated bureaucratic transactions, act as mediators in case of marital problems, and offer personal recommendations for potential jobs. As a general result, most adult Brazilians would not claim to be successful based on individual tenacity and hard work; instead, they are keenly aware that their *parentela* had an influential role in their development. These practices do exist in the United States, but they are usually provided by other social organizations that offer assistance and companionship, such as church groups, senior citizen centers, food pantries, job placement networks, and counseling services.

Foreigners are often surprised by how certain social concepts (such as nepotism, time, and close family ties) function in Brazil. However, these can all be reasonably explained by the practice of *parentela*. For example, nepotism is not necessarily viewed as a problem in companies and institutions because business owners often prefer to hire an applicant who is recommended by one of the existing trusted employees. When it comes to time, Brazilians deal with it in a more flexible way. If relatives or close family friends show up at home unannounced, it would be rude to not invite them in, even if that means arriving late for a meeting or appointment. Time and punctuality are more fluid social constructs in Brazil. On a personal level, Brazilian culture does not necessarily encourage independence and self-reliance; consequently, most young adults remain at home until their late twenties or even until marriage. When they do move out, they tend to settle near their parents' home in order to continue their family relationships. In fact, being lonely is likely perceived as an indication that something is socially wrong. This observation then triggers some type of action by concerned relatives that is often addressed during the next weekend gathering with food, drinks, and music.

See also: Chapter 6: Overview. Chapter 10: Punctuality and Concepts of Time.

Further Reading

Edwards, Todd L. 2008. *Brazil: A Global Studies Handbook.* Santa Barbara, CA: ABC-CLIO.

Vincent, Jon S. 2003. *Culture and Customs of Brazil.* Westport, CT: Greenwood Press.

Poverty, Social Conflict, and Protests

Brazil is one of the most inequitable countries in the world. While multiple government programs (e.g., Bolsa Família and Brasil Sem Miséria) have lifted millions of people out of extreme poverty, recent national economic improvements have sparked a tremendously high cost of living, which significantly impacts low-income groups. In fact, the 2010 census showed that over 12 million Brazilians live in *favelas* (slums). Consequently, social conflict has recently intensified as Brazilians routinely see politicians involved in corruption scandals and spending billions of dollars to subsidize international sports events while ignoring social problems that disproportionately affect the poor, such as endemic poverty, a deficient public education system, inadequate healthcare programs, and high inflation rates.

Since 2013, Brazilians have organized massive street protests to repudiate national policies that negatively impact the most vulnerable populations. In June 2013, poor Brazilians mobilized to take over public plazas and streets to air specific grievances against steep increases in bus fees, low-quality public education, and stagnant wages. The level of activism increased as demonstrations erupted in size due to social media notices. In 2014, protests intensified when the national teachers' union organized a massive strike followed by the street sweepers' strike in Rio de Janeiro. Then on March 15, 2015, over 3 million Brazilians protested unprecedented levels of corruption exposed by an undercover operation called Lava Jato (Car Wash) as evidence of collusion between politicians and business executives to steal billions of dollars from the national coffers while the government imposed austerity measures on public spending to fight an economic recession. These protests took place in over 200 cities in all twenty-six states nationwide. Several politicians and businessmen are now in prison (including former president Lula da Silva), but activists continue to decry excessive government subsidies for international events, such as the 2014 Soccer World Cup and the 2016 Summer Olympics. More recently, over 600,000 truck drivers staged protests over incredibly high surges in fuel prices in May 2018. Their anger is based on government actions to increase consumption prices to cover national budget deficiencies while even more graft scandals exposed federal politicians stealing billions of dollars from the national treasury. The truckers' strike paralyzed supermarkets, restaurants, and even airports. They view fuel policies as evidence that government leaders act like thieves, and the poor have to pay the bill. President Temer (1940–) sent the military and federal police to clear the blocked highways, and they arrested hundreds of truckers, but he ordered a slight reduction of fuel prices. President Bolsonaro (1955–) took over in 2019, and he has pursued an even stronger approach against protesters.

See also: Chapter 3: Corruption and Political Scandals; Lula da Silva, Luiz Inácio (1945 –); Temer, Michel (1940–). Chapter 4: *Favelas* (Slums); Chapter 6: Overview; Distribution of Wealth and Income Disparity; *Favelas*, *Mocambos*, and *Alagados* (Slums). Chapter 8: Bolsa Família.

Further Reading

Bringel, Breno. 2016. "2013–2016: Polarization and Protests in Brazil." Open Democracy, February 18. Accessed July 18, 2019. https://www.opendemocracy.net/democraciaabierta/breno-bringel/2013-2016-polarization-and-protests-in-brazil

Corrigan, Gemma. 2015. "Is Brazil Making Progress on Inequality? World Economic Forum, September 7, 2015. Accessed July 18, 2019. https://www.weforum.org/agenda/2015/09/is-brazil-making-progress-on-inequality

Hearst. Chesney. 2013. "Social Media Energizes the Brazil Protests." *Rio Times,* June 253. Accessed July 18, 2019. https://riotimesonline.com/brazil-news/rio-politics/social-media-energizes-the-brazil-protests

Phillips, Don, and Sam Cowie. 2018. "Brazilian President Sends in Army as Truck Protest Paralyzes Country." *Guardian,* May 25. Accessed July 18, 2019. https://www.theguardian.com/world/2018/may/25/brazil-protests-latest-temer-clears-trucks-highways-army

Racism and Discrimination

A large number of Brazilians seem to be in denial of the existence of racism and discrimination in the country. To justify that position, they usually offer four specific arguments and theories. First, the national constitution already has specific antidiscrimination laws. Second, the immense differences regarding income, education, and employment between blacks and whites is routinely explained away as issues related to socioeconomic classes and not necessarily based on race. Third, people still believe in the pervasive notion that Brazil is a "racial democracy" as proposed in 1933 by sociologist Gilberto Freyre, claiming that Brazilians are so racially mixed that they essentially do not have racial prejudices toward one another. Finally, unlike the United States and South Africa, Brazil has never had any racial segregation laws or prohibition of interracial marriages. While these notions certainly have cogency, they do not reflect the reality of contemporary daily life in Brazil, especially for blacks and *pardos* (brown or mixed race).

Sometimes, specific data can provide evidence to refute general opinions. The 2010 census data published by the IBGE showed that over 51 percent of Brazilians defined themselves as either black or *pardo*. Blacks are only 6.7 percent of the national population, but they are 70 percent of all Brazilians living in extreme poverty. In addition, blacks earn less than half of what whites earn. Blacks also have lower education levels than their white counterparts, and they are significantly less represented in professional fields where family connections and nepotism are common practice. Racial inequality also reveals that blacks are more likely to be incarcerated or killed by police than whites in similar circumstances. In fact, as of 2018, blacks make up over 55 percent of the people killed by military police forces, and they represent 62 percent of people in prison nationwide. Besides data, any visitor who pays attention to social interactions in Brazil will likely realize that there is a connection between race and social class. For example, over 55 percent of residents in the famous Rio de Janeiro *favelas* (slums) are black. A visit to a professional office building quickly reveals that the overwhelming majority of managers are white, and the custodians are typically black.

The problem with the outdated concept of racial democracy in Brazil is that by definition nobody is racist. Consequently, racial discrimination cannot be debated for possible solutions. The federal government, however, is aware of the legacy of injustice toward racial minorities, and it has enacted specific affirmative action policies to address such inequalities, especially by setting aside a specific number of spaces at federal public universities for racial minorities and a percentage of civil service jobs. The concept of racial democracy has been challenged since the 1970s when researcher Skidmore claimed that this notion has been perpetrated by the Brazilian elite to avoid discussing tangible forms of racial oppression. However, his arguments and government affirmative action programs have not been able to change a pervasive opinion that Brazilian blacks belong at the bottom of this highly stratified society that pretends to have no racial prejudices.

See also: Chapter. Chapter 6: Overview; Distribution of Wealth and Income Disparity; Poverty, Social Conflict, and Protests. Chapter 8: Affirmative Action Policies.

Further Reading

Barbara, Vanessa. 2015. "In Denial over Racism in Brazil." *New York Times,* March 23. Accessed June 12, 2019. https://www.nytimes.com/2015/03/24/opinion/vanessa-barbara-in-denial-over-racism-in-brazil.html

Freyre, Gilberto. 1987. *The Masters and Slaves: A Study in the Development of Brazilian Civilization.* Translated by Samuel Putnam. Berkeley: University of California Press.

Instituto Brasileiro de Geografia e Estatística (IBGE). 2011. *Censo demográfico de 2010: Resultados do universo.* Rio de Janeiro: IBGE. http://ibge.gov.br

Skidmore, Thomas E. 1974. *Black into White: Race and Nationality in Brazilian Thought.* New York: Oxford University Press.

Urban Crime

For the last ten years, Brazil has experienced a significant increase in violent crime throughout the country. The last five years, however, have been particularly difficult for average Brazilians, who have seen the emergence of a crime wave in urban settings, especially in murders, rapes, robberies, and violent assaults. Actually, quick muggings, home invasions, and kidnapping have become commonplace.

Recent crime statistics have identified Brazil as one of the most dangerous countries in the world. For example, the 2019 Crime Index Report lists Brazil as the third most dangerous country in the Western Hemisphere. In addition, the prestigious think tank Consejo Cuidadano para la Seguridad Pública y Justicia Penal (Center for Public Security and Criminal Justice) identified Brazil as the fourth most dangerous country in the Americas, after Venezuela, Honduras, and Trinidad and Tobago. The report lists the fifty most dangerous cities in the world for violent crime, and Brazil has seventeen cities on that list, which makes it the leader in mortal gunshot wounds. The numbers of homicides and rapes have risen so high in the last ten years that they have reached double the rates of what the World Health Organization considers average at ten homicides for 100,000 inhabitants. National statistics also reveal a local struggle to control violence in urban settings. Across Brazil, 61,000 people were murdered in 2016; in comparison, this number is higher than the yearly estimated deaths in Syria's civil war. In

> **MARIA DA PENHA LAW FOR VIOLENCE AGAINST WOMEN**
>
> On August 7, 2006, President Lula da Silva (1945–) signed federal law number 11.340. It was specifically designed to combat the endemic problem of domestic violence against women in Brazil. It honors Maria da Penha Maia Fernandes, a victim of domestic abuse whose husband tried to kill her twice in 1983. The law created stricter criminal sentences for domestic abuse, and it also funds shelters that protect battered women. The Brazilian National Council of Justice reported that as of August 2011, prosecutors have already pursued 331,000 cases and obtained 110,000 final judgments against abusers. However, critics argue that resources are mostly limited to urban areas, and rural women do not receive much help.
>
> **Sources:** "Law no. 11.340 of 7 August 2006." *Planalto Presidential Palace.* August 7, 2006. Accessed June 29, 2019. http://www.planalto.gov.br/ccivil_03/_ato2004-2006/2006/lei/l11340.htm

Rio de Janeiro, that number reached 6,590 deaths in 2017, including 120 police officers (Faiola and Kaiser, 2018). Local police forces seem unprepared to fight such increases in crime rates due to slashed budgets, inadequate training, lack of equipment, and high attrition rates of police officers.

In September 2018, President Temer (1940–) sent the military to fight drug trafficking and out-of-control gang violence in Rio de Janeiro's dangerous *favelas*. Military forces engaged in brutal practices to regain control of civilian spaces, which resulted in thousands of arrests throughout 2018. Their efforts seem to be working since Rio de Janeiro and São Paulo did not make the 2019 list of the most dangerous cities in Brazil. These numbers reflect the institutional capabilities to control local crime. However, civilian criticism argues that security forces are being too aggressive in their shoot-to-kill strategies that already killed over 5,000 civilians in 2017, an average of fourteen Brazilians a day (Kaiser, 2019). While such civilian complaints of excessive force are being investigated, crime has increased dramatically in the northern region of Brazil. In January 2019, the recently installed President Bolsonaro (1955–) authorized the deployment of military forces to fight outbreaks of gang violence in Fortaleza, which has become the city with the highest incidents of violent crime in the nation.

See also: Chapter 3: Temer, Michel (1940–). Chapter 6: Overview, *Favelas, Mocambos,* and *Alagados* (Slums).

Further Reading

Consejo Cuidadano para la Seguridad Pública y Justicia Penal. http://www.seguridadjusticiaypaz.org.mx/

Crime Index by Country 2019. www.numbeo.com/crime/rankings_by_country.jsp

Faiola, Anthony, and Anna Jean Kaiser. 2018. "The Murders in a Popular Brazilian Favela Reflect Rising Violence in a Country in Crisis." *Washington Post,* August 5. Accessed February 20, 2019. https://www.washingtonpost.com/sf/world/2018/01/05/this-trendy

-rio-favela-appeared-in-a-hollywood-kids-movie-now-the-bullets-are-back/?noredirect=on&utm_term=.10b016a9540b

Kaiser, Anna Jean. 2019. "It's Complete Chaos: Brazilian State Overwhelmed by Rush of Gang Violence." *Guardian,* January 9. Accessed February 20, 2019. https://www.theguardian.com/world/2019/jan/09/brazil-ceara-violence-fortaleza-gangs-bolsonaro

Rapoza, Kenneth. 2016. "Brazil Is Murder Capital of the World, but Rio Is Safer than Compton, Detroit, St. Louis . . ." *Forbes,* January 29. Accessed February 20, 2019. https://www.forbes.com/sites/kenrapoza/2016/01/29/months-before-rio-olympics-murder-rate-rises-in-brazil

CHAPTER 7

GENDER, MARRIAGE, AND SEXUALITY

OVERVIEW

During the last thirty years, Brazil has experienced tremendous social, economic, political, and cultural changes. During the 1980s and 1990s, women obtained more education, and they became part of the national workforce at an accelerated rate. They entered fields typically dominated by men, such as business administration, science, manufacturing, and government. The representation of women in the workforce has certainly increased since the late 1980s, and currently feminist organizations are the driving force to support women willing to venture into politics. Consequently, gender roles have had to adjust to a new modern society, especially when the 2010 census revealed that the traditional family structure with a working father and a stay-at-home mother is no longer the norm in Brazil.

From a demographic and social perspective, Brazil is certainly changing. According to the 2010 census, the number of single-mother households went from 19.5 percent in 2002 to 46.4 percent in 2010. In addition, there has been an increase in same-sex couples, divorced parents, *desquitados* (legally separated), and reconstituted families with children from previous marriages. While wealthy Brazilians may choose to have a husband as the financial provider and a mother at home who takes care of the children, the modern economic reality for most middle- and low-income families is that both parents have to work. Single mothers sometimes work two jobs, and they rely on extended family for assistance with household responsibilities. As a consequence, these changes have had an effect on how children are raised and how parents prepare them to be well-adjusted members of a new modern society that aims to eliminate gender inequalities.

The election of Dilma Rousseff (1947–) as the first female president of Brazil in 2010 sparked optimism among the general population, especially women. She promised to fight for the rights of women in a political arena that is still largely dominated by men. On the surface, her presidency can be viewed as a new phenomenon in Brazilian politics, but it is actually the culmination of a long struggle by feminist groups that actively advocated for women throughout the twentieth century. Based on political and social pressure, these groups succeeded in obtaining the women's right to vote in 1932. More recently, they supported legislation that approved gender political quotas in 1995 requiring 30 percent of all candidates listed on electoral ballots to be women. However, their efforts have not translated into a larger number of women elected to public office. The

2018 national elections were a disappointment because women represent 52 percent of the population, but they were only elected to 15 percent of the positions in Congress (77 out of 531 seats). The urgency of increasing the representation of women in government is crucial because the legislature drives social policy (and funding), and female voices need to be heard when political decisions are being made for all Brazilians.

For the last three decades, Brazil has implemented social policies to improve the lives of all Brazilians, including women, all racial groups, indigenous people, low-income families, workers, and members of the LGBTQ community. Some of these policies are intended to prevent discrimination and reduce gender inequalities, but there is always room for improvement. For example, the constitution of 1988 (and its amendments in 1996) legally establishes men and women as equals, and it also forbids any type of discrimination. When it comes to families trying to manage the daily basic tasks of raising children, parents welcomed a new policy approved in 2016 that generously expanded both maternity and paternity leave in order to take care of a newborn or a young child. Another positive policy occurred when Congress approved same-sex marriage nationwide in 2013, which now provides same-sex couples all the same legal rights as any other marriage. While lesbian, gay, bisexual, transgender, and queer (LGBTQ) organizations recognize the social gains they have made, they fiercely denounce the grim recent statistics published by the influential Grupo Gay da Bahia (GGB) showing that 130 brutal assassinations of LGBTQ members occur every year, and that hate crimes based on homophobia continue to increase in Brazil. In addition, a recent swing in the political pendulum toward a more conservative approach to government has threatened many social advances. The arrival of President Michel Temer (1940–) in 2016 ushered in a conservative wave of politicians that seems steadfast in overturning previously approved liberal policies. For example, abortion is still illegal in Brazil; it is only allowed when a woman is raped, when her life is at risk, and in cases of fetal anencephaly. Having an illegal abortion is technically a crime, but the Brazilian Ministry of Health estimates the yearly number of abortions at slightly over 1 million (Coutinho, 2016, 335). However, conservative politicians (supported by powerful religious lobbies) actually proposed a bill in 2018 that authorizes even further restrictions on abortion, even in cases of rape or cases of microcephaly caused by the Zika virus. This legislation is largely viewed as a group of extremely conservative men making decisions about the reproductive rights of women, all without hearing a single voice of an elected or appointed woman to any of the legislative committees or judicial proceedings. Moreover, compared to men, women continue to face lower wages, higher unemployment rates, political underrepresentation, and domestic abuse.

Street violence in Brazilian cities has reached alarming proportions since 2015. In fact, both Presidents Temer and Jair Bolsonaro (1955–) ordered the military to patrol sections of Rio de Janeiro because the local police were unable to curb the rising levels of violence. Within this unprecedented level of social unrest, the compounded problem for women is that some of the worst abusers are inside their own homes. Regrettably, machismo is not only alive but actually increasing. Brazilian women suffer incredibly high levels of domestic abuse. In fact, Brazil has the seventh-highest rate of violence against women in the world; a woman is assaulted every fifteen seconds, and one is murdered every two hours. Since 1985, more than 92,000 Brazilian women have been killed by a husband, partner, or family member (Hargreaves, 2015). To reduce spousal abuse, the government responded with the 2006 Maria da Penha Law that imposes stricter criminal penalties for domestic violence. Congress also approved a "femicide" law in 2016, and it also funded social awareness campaigns to eliminate discrimination, sexism, and violence against women. As with many other aspects of Brazilian life, time will tell if a cultural shift occurs to reduce the suffering of abused women.

Further Reading

Coutinho, Rodrigo R. 2016. "Abortion and Family Planning," in *Brazil,* edited by Antonio Luciano de Andrade Tosta and Eduardo F. Coutinho, 334–335. Santa Barbara, CA: ABC-CLIO.

Hargreaves, Melanie. 2015. "Brazil's 'Machismo': A Licence for Abuse." *New Internationalist*, May 13. Accessed May 3, 2019. https://newint.org/features/web-exclusive/2015/05/13/brazil-domestic-violence

Instituto Brasileiro de Geografia e Estatística—Brazilian Institute of Geography and Statistics (IBGE). 2011. *Census 2010.* Accessed August 3, 2019. http://ibge.gov.br

Mott, Luiz R. B. 2004. *Homofobia: Violação dos direitos humanos dos gays, lésbicas, travestis e transexuais no Brasil.* Salvador, Bahia, Brazil: Grupo Gay da Bahia (GGB) and Human Rights Commission.

Tosta, Antonio Luciano de Andrade, and Eduardo F. Coutinho (eds.). 2016. *Brazil.* Santa Barbara, CA: ABC-CLIO.

Uchoa, Pablo. 2016. "Maria da Penha: The Woman Who Changed Brazil's Domestic Violence Laws." *BBC News*, September 22. Accessed May 9, 2019. https://www.bbc.com/news/magazine-37429051

Vincent, Jon S. 2003. *Culture and Customs of Brazil.* Westport, CT: Greenwood Press.

Abortion Laws

Abortion is illegal in Brazil. The current constitution (dating from 1988) provides two specific exceptions when abortion is allowed: when a woman was raped and in cases when her life is in danger. In both cases, the abortion must be performed by a medical practitioner. The legal guidelines to terminate a pregnancy are specifically coded into the Brazilian Penal Code. It is mandatory to obtain the written consent of the pregnant woman before the procedure. If she is unconscious—or defined as legally incompetent—then her legal representative must sign on her behalf. When a woman seeks to have an abortion on her own, she (or anyone helping her) could face serious legal consequences. The Penal Code, which dates back to 1940, provides specific guidelines for legal punishment under Articles 123, 124, 125, and 126 for performing an illegal abortion. Article 124 declares that a self-performed abortion is legally sanctioned with one to three years in prison. Article 125 clearly indicates that performing an abortion without the consent of the pregnant woman is punishable by three to ten years imprisonment. Article 126 stipulates that additional incarceration can be added if an abortion was performed (with or without consent) on a minor under fourteen years of age, a mentally handicapped woman, or when consent was obtained under fraud or threat of violence.

While having an illegal abortion has serious legal consequences, the modern reality is that abortions are rather common in Brazil. Studies by the Brazilian Ministry of Health estimate the yearly number of abortions at slightly over 1 million (Tosta and Coutinho, 2016, 335). Roughly 20 percent of Brazilian women under forty years of age have had at least one abortion. The World Health Organization estimated that at least 100,000 women a year have unsafe, clandestine abortions in Brazil, which often result in serious medical consequences and even death. In 2005, Brazilian doctors reported that over 200,000 women were admitted to hospitals for complications related to an unsafe abortion (Downie, 2010). Consequently, they have become an expensive burden on the public health system. Moreover, abortion practices disproportionately affect poor women the most (especially black women), since wealthy women can travel to other countries to have an abortion.

On the surface, Brazil appears to be a very liberal country, but a closer look reveals a long history of conservative social policies that maintain old traditions in place. This contradiction is currently being debated on the topic of reproductive rights. On the one hand, multiple organizations advocating for women's rights demand that abortion be made legal. In fact, the Supreme Court heard arguments in August 2018 precisely to decriminalize abortion through twelve weeks of pregnancy. On the other side, the powerful lobbies of the Catholic Church and Evangelical leaders have had a recent influence in national politics. In fact, the Brazilian Congress now includes a large number of conservative leaders who are bitterly opposed to relaxing abortion laws. As a matter of fact, politicians actually drafted a bill in 2018 that proposed further restrictions on abortion, even in cases of rape or microcephaly caused by the Zika virus. The national elections of 2018 also had an impact on the future of potential abortions in Brazil, especially because large numbers of extremely conservative politicians took office in 2019.

See also: Chapter 3: Women's Rights. Chapter 7: Gender Equality.

Further Reading

Andreoni, Manuela, and Ernesto Londoño. 2018. "Brazil's Supreme Court Considers Decriminalizing Abortion." *New York Times*, August 3. Accessed July 11, 2019. https://www.nytimes.com/2018/08/03/world/americas/brazil-abortion-supreme-court.html

Brazilian Penal Code. http://www.oas.org/juridico/mla/pt/bra/pt_bra-int-text-cp.pdf

Coutinho, Rodrigo R. 2016. "Abortion and Family Planning," in *Brazil*, edited by Antonio Luciano de Andrade Tosta and Eduardo F. Coutinho, 334–335. Santa Barbara, CA: ABC-CLIO.

Downie, Andrew. 2010. "Abortions in Brazil, Though Illegal, Are Common." *Time*, June 2. Accessed July 11, 2019. http://content.time.com/time/world/article/0,8599,1993205,00.html

Dating and Courting

Family life is an essential element of Brazilian culture. However, Brazil is a large country, and it is not wise to make generalizations about family life and expectations. While traditional families with a working father and a stay-at-home mother are still common, recent demographic data from the 2010 census reveals that the family structure has expanded to include single-parent households (usually the mother), same-sex marriages, childless couples, and families with a mixture of children from previous marriages.

Families in this contemporary setting are the ones that establish the expectations for young Brazilian boys and girls who are ready to start dating. Boys are often encouraged to start dating early in life and to have several relationships before they settle down. On the other hand, young girls are usually advised to delay dating, focus on school, learn how to perform household chores, and remain "pure" until marriage. While young women have more freedom nowadays, boys are still given more latitude and freedom when it comes to dating and courting a potential partner.

Brazilian young boys and girls are very similar to couples in other countries. When they are dating, they enjoy dancing, shopping, hanging out with friends, going to the movies, playing at the beach, and participating in sports activities. Constant communication via their mobile devices is extremely popular. Since family households frequently include multiple generations living together, young couples have very little privacy. When they are sexually active, they often go to motels, which are usually rented by the hour in Brazil. The quality of the motel depends on the price, but there is always an inherent risk in these sexual adventures.

Brazil has high rates of single-parent families (especially from low-income populations), astronomical documented cases of AIDS, and some of the most shocking numbers of violence against women. Consequently, the reality of contemporary life in Brazil has changed how parents approach discussing sexual activity with their young sons and daughters. Each family has its own approach, all the way from simply telling kids to avoid sex to having open conversations about sexual protection. In order to protect their sons and daughters from the current increase in street violence, parents have even become more tolerant about letting them "date at home," which could be allowing the couple to simply watch a movie, letting them drink alcohol, or even not saying anything when the son spends private time with his girlfriend in his bedroom.

Since Brazilian families are usually a large network of extended family members, when a person introduces a new partner to the family, that person is then included in gatherings with the entire family. Gaining acceptance by a partner's family is important because family ties are very strong in Brazil. In fact, most grown children stay at home until they get married, even if they have the financial means to move out. When they eventually move out, they usually look for a place near their parents.

The concept of dating across different races is not often discussed in Brazilian culture. While Brazil is often known abroad as a "racial democracy," this is a fallacy; racism is alive and well. High-middle and upper classes (which tend to have light skin color) are not always accepting of the notion of daughters in the family dating a dark-skin man (Pimentel Siqueira, 2016, 201). Nevertheless, these are values usually fomented by a previous generation, and it is becoming more common to see mixed-race teenage couples, even when they might be hiding it from their parents.

See also: Chapter 7: Overview; Gender and Parenting Roles; Raising Children.

Further Reading

Debiaggi, Sylvia Dantas. 2003. "Famílias Brasileiras em um novo contexto cultural," in *Fronteiras cruzadas: Enticidade, gênero, e redes sociais*, edited by Ana Cristina Braga Martes and Soraya Fleischer, 174–197. São Paulo: Paz e Terra.

Pimentel Siqueira, Domingos Sávio. 2016. "Family and Etiquette," in *Brazil*, edited by Antonio Luciano de Andrade Tosta and Eduardo F. Coutinho, 187–203. Santa Barbara, CA: ABC-CLIO.

Richard, Christopher, and Leslie Jermyn. 2002. *Cultures of the World: Brazil*. New York: Marshall Cavendish.

Desquite and Divorce

Divorce was approved in Brazil in 1977. The powerful lobby of the Catholic Church used its influence to block multiple previous legislative efforts to legalize divorce in the country. The Church can exercise a lot of political pressure since Brazil is, after all, the largest Roman Catholic country in the world. Before 1977, Brazilians with financial means had to travel to neighboring Bolivia, Uruguay, or Mexico to obtain a legal divorce. It is important to highlight that the approval of divorce happened right in the middle of Brazil's brutal military dictatorship (1964–1985). Large groups of Brazilian women (from different races, economic levels, and political parties) were crucial to creating coalitions that defend women's rights based on concepts proposed by the United Nations International Year of the Woman in 1975. In addition, Brazilian women entered the workforce in large numbers during the 1970s, started obtaining more education than men, and began demanding gender equality. Without the possibility of divorce, women had to find another way to escape dysfunctional and often dangerous relationships.

Since divorce was not a legal option until 1977, Brazilians have had another legal procedure available to them called *desquite* (or legal separation). The application has to be filed with the family court in most major cities, but it used to take months because it originally required mutual consent by the two parties. However, legislative efforts reduced the bureaucracy, and currently one spouse can request a separation simply by claiming incompatibility, and a *desquite* can now be obtained within a few days. It provides a legal separation status for the two spouses, but it does not provide *desquitados* with the freedom to remarry. The most common causes to file for a *desquite* continue to be either spousal abuse or households where the husband does not allow the wife to work for a paycheck. The judicial process of applying for a *desquite* seems rather illogical, but it was used simply as a convenient way to get around the problem of obtaining a divorce. Large cities such as São Paulo, Brasilia, and Rio de Janeiro experienced a large increase of requests for a *desquite* during the early 1970s, but the numbers were reduced after divorce became legal in 1977. Perhaps it was a way to control a potential social problem by providing an intermediate solution to the practice of forcing people to remain in dysfunctional marriages.

At the beginning of the twenty-first century, the stereotype of a Brazilian family with a working father, a stay-at-home mother, and two children at school is no longer the norm. The latest data from the 2010 census provided by the Instituto Brasileiro de Geografia e Estadística (IBGE) reveals that there is considerable growth in the number of consensual unions (domestic partnerships), families headed by women, childless families, and reconstituted families whose parents were divorced and then remarried (Tosta and Coutinho, 2016, 150).

See also: Chapter 6: Sidebar on Maria da Penha Law for Violence against Women. Chapter 7: Overview; Domestic Violence; Gender and Parenting Roles; Gender Equality; Raising Children. Chapter 10: Machismo.

Further Reading

Howe, Marvine. 1974. "Divorce Is Out, but Brazilians Break Up Anyway." *New York Times*, December 3. Accessed July 13, 2019. https://www.nytimes.com/1974/12/03/archives/divorce-is-out-but-brazilians-break-up-anyway-elections-help.html

Instituto Brasileiro de Geografia e Estatística—Brazilian Institute of Geography and Statistics (IBGE). 2011. *Census 2010*. Accessed July 13, 2019. http://ibge.gov.br

Rocha-Coutinho, Maria Lúcia. 2016. "Gender, Marriage, and Sexuality," in *Brazil*, edited by Antonio Luciano de Andrade Tosta and Eduardo F. Coutinho, 140–155. Santa Barbara, CA: ABC-CLIO.

Domestic Violence

Brazil is increasingly becoming a more violent country, and for many women, the most dangerous space is inside their own homes. Multiple national and international organizations have published alarming statistics during the last ten years that reveal how pervasive domestic violence is against women. For example, the Brazilian government agency Departamento Intersindical de Estatística e Estudos Socioeconômicos (DIEESE) published the 2011 Annual Report on Women to offer reliable statistical data to local, state, and federal agencies; it showed that 40 percent of women suffer physical or psychological abuse by their male partners. In addition, the federal government via the Secretariat for Women's Policies published in 2015 another detailed study documenting that every seven minutes a Brazilian woman is a victim of domestic violence. According to the nongovernmental organization Marias, the main reasons for family abuse perpetrated by men against women include adultery, excessive jealousy, alcoholism, drug use, financial problems, and pervasive stubborn machismo. Regrettably, male abuse is not only alive but actually increasing in Brazil. In fact, Brazil has the seventh-highest rate of violence against women in the world; a woman is assaulted every fifteen seconds, and one is murdered every two hours. Since 1985, over 92,000 Brazilian women have been killed by a husband, partner, or family member (Hargreaves, 2015). The Human Rights Watch organization (HRW) condemned such rampant violence against women with a report in 2017 demonstrating that local law enforcement agencies often dismiss complaints filed by women, fail to investigate the accusations, and then do not even prosecute most cases of domestic violence.

The Brazilian federal government is keenly aware of the well-documented increase in domestic abuse cases in Brazil, and the legislature has approved specific laws to protect women. The Domestic Violence Law of 2006 under Article 5 legally defines domestic violence as "any action or omission motivated by gender that results in death, physical, sexual or psychological suffering, moral, or patrimonial hazard." In order to provide more law enforcement resources dedicated to protecting women, President Lula da Silva (1945–) signed the Maria da Penha Law for Violence against Women later in 2006 to punish perpetrators of domestic abuse. Then President Rousseff (1947–) signed a stricter law in March 2013 that changed the federal penal code to include 'femicide," which was defined as crimes that involve domestic violence, discrimination, or contempt for women that result in their death. These laws provide funds to train police agencies on how to handle reports of domestic abuse and to finance the creation of safe houses where women can seek refuge with their children. An ongoing national campaign using television, radio, and social media is also trying to develop social consciousness regarding the pernicious effects of domestic abuse. The goal is to create cultural awareness in Brazil and to eliminate discrimination, sexism, and violence against women.

See also: Chapter 3: Lula da Silva, Luiz Inácio (1945–); Rousseff, Dilma (1947–); Women's Rights. Chapter 7: Feminism; Gender and Parenting Roles; Maria da Penha Law for Violence against Women Sidebar. Chapter 10: Machismo.

Further Reading

Armand de Bonneval, Philippe. 2016. "Brazil's Stubborn Machismo." Council on Hemispheric Affairs, October 25. Accessed July 13, 2019. http://www.coha.org/brazils-stubborn-machismo

Departamento Intersindical de Estatística e Estudos Socioeconômicos (DIEESE). 2011. *Anuário das Mulheres Brasileiras 2011* (Annual Report on Women 2011). São Paulo: DIEESE. https://www.dieese.org.br/anuario/2011/anuarioMulheresBrasileiras2011.html

Hargreaves, Melanie. 2015. "Brazil's 'Machismo': A Licence for Abuse." *New Internationalist*, May 13. Accessed July 13, 2019. https://newint.org/features/web-exclusive/2015/05/13/brazil-domestic-violence

Uchoa, Pablo. 2016 "Maria da Penha: The Woman Who Changed Brazil's Domestic Violence Laws." *BBC News*, September 22. Accessed July 13, 2019. https://www.bbc.com/news/magazine-37429051

Vincent, Jon S. 2003. *Culture and Customs of Brazil*. Westport, CT: Greenwood Press.

Feminism

Brazil has a reputation for developing some of the most successful feminist movements in Latin America. Their efforts began toward the end of the 1800s by working locally for the abolition of slavery and acquiring voting rights in the 1891 constitution. An iconic figure of the Brazilian feminist movement was Bertha Lutz (1894–). In 1918, she published a seminal article in the newspaper *Revista da Semana* (Weekly Review), and she called on professional and educated women to create an association to fight for their rights. One year later, she represented Brazil at the International Feminine Council, which advocated for equal salaries for women. She was also part of the Brazilian delegation in 1975 attending a conference in Mexico when the United Nations established the International Year of the Woman.

The Brazilian feminist movements have worked on both social and political fronts to gain tangible improvements for the rights of women. For example, female suffrage was approved in 1932 under President Getúlio Vargas (1882–1954). More recently, they were the driving force behind the legislation that approved gender political quotas in 1995 requiring 30 percent of all candidates listed on electoral ballots for women. They also advocated for stricter criminal penalties for domestic violence under the 2006 Maria da Penha Law and for legislation in 2016 to expand maternity and paternity leave nationwide. However, the paradox of the feminist movements in Brazil is that they have been successful with social issues, but their efforts have not translated into a larger number of women elected to public office at the federal level.

The feminist movement in Brazil is certainly not a homogenous group. There are considerable differences among different feminist associations in the country. The initial efforts of the feminist movements in the late 1800s and early 1900s were organized mostly by white middle- and upper-class women, at a time when most of the women were still illiterate. More recently, several feminist organizations in Brazil exclusively representing black women have expressed their differences with other middle-class feminist organizations. For example, black female groups are not necessarily "against men" because they view their male counterparts are part of the potential solution to improve the overall struggle of Afro-Brazilians. They also claim that traditional feminist groups generally do not take into account the unique experience of black women regarding racial discrimination, legal troubles, and sexual exploitation; therefore, they define general feminist movements as white, academic, middle and upper class, and even racist at times. This is an important point of view because almost 50 percent of all Brazilian women are black, and they do not necessarily feel represented by the traditional feminist organizations in Brazil. The urgency of social justice for Afro-Brazilians is slightly different than the rest of the population.

In the last twenty years, Brazil has made tangible social improvements for women by reducing extreme poverty, improving literacy rates, implementing affirmative action policies for higher education, and approving gender quotas in politics. Multiple feminist organizations (with different points of view) continue to work collectively to reduce female unemployment rates, close the gender pay gap, get more women elected to public office, and reduce the alarming recent increase in domestic violence against women in Brazil.

See also: Chapter 2: Vargas, Getúlio (1882–1954). Chapter 3: Women's Rights. Chapter 6: Racism and Discrimination. Chapter 7: Domestic Abuse; Gender and Parenting Roles; Maternity and Paternity Leave; Representation in Government; Suffrage.

Further Reading

Barbara, Vanessa. 2014. "Life as a Brazilian Woman." *New York Times*, April 23. Accessed July 2, 2019. https://www.nytimes.com/2014/04/24/opinion/barbara-life-as-a-brazilian-woman.html

Caldwell, Kia Lilly. 2006. *Negras in Brazil: Re-envisioning Black Women, Citizenship, and the Politics of Identity*. New Brunswick, NJ: Rutgers University Press.

Santana, Bianca. 2015. "On Black Women and Feminism in Brazil." *Huffington Post*, April 6. Accessed July 2, 2019. https://www.huffingtonpost.com/bianca-santana/black-women-and-feminism-_b_6987938.html

Tarlau, Rebecca. 2006. "Experiencing Feminism in Brazil." *Journal of the International Institute* 13, no. 2 (Winter). University of Michigan. https://quod.lib.umich.edu/j/jii/4750978.0013.209/—experiencing-feminism-in-brazil?rgn=main;view=fulltext

Gender and Parenting Roles

As a former Portuguese colony, Brazil has a colonial heritage that imposed a very traditional and male-dominated society. This historical influence created a set of conservative values that defined gender roles at social, public, and household spaces. In general, women were expected to do the cooking, cleaning, and raise children. Men were the financial providers who helped with physical jobs around the house. During the 1960s and 1970s, feminist movements and national plans for modernization in Brazil provided more space for women to be incorporated into the workforce. When women began to obtain more education and economic independence, gender roles began to change significantly. More recently, gender roles in contemporary Brazil are also defined by social class and income levels. Wealthy families may choose to have the father be the provider while the mother can stay at home and raise the children. For middle- and low-income families, however, the economic reality is that both parents usually have to work. In this situation, it is more common for contemporary families to share the responsibilities of raising children. Sometimes, if their income is sufficient, they might even hire a maid to help with the house chores.

The 2010 census data reported by the Instituto Brasileiro de Geografia e Estatística (IBGE) shows that the structure of the family has changed from the traditional composition of a working father and a stay-at-home mother. The demographic data reveals a significant increase in nontraditional family arrangements that include households headed by women, childless families, consensual unions, same-sex marriages, and reconstituted families (where one or both of the parents have children from a previous marriage); moreover, a significant increase was recorded on the number of single-mother families from 19.5 percent in 2002 to 46.4 percent in 2010 (Rocha-Coutinho, 2016, 510–511). Consequently, gender roles had to change to accommodate the needs of new family structures. In addition, divorce and *desquite* (legal separations) have become much more common throughout the country. Part of the explanation for the emergence of a diverse family structure is based on the fact that women have received more education in the last two decades, have entered the workforce in higher numbers, and therefore have also become increasingly financially independent. The challenge for contemporary Brazilian women is to somehow find a balance between their professional responsibilities and their motherhood role at home. For men, it has become more common to be involved in the task of raising children. With that goal in mind, the federal government approved legislation in 2016 providing extended paternity leave from five days to twenty days for fathers to bond with a newborn or a young child.

Brazil has made tangible improvements in the last two decades in the attempt to achieve gender equality. It has been very successful in reducing poverty and illiteracy, especially among women. However, gender, economic, and income inequality still exist. Most high-level professional, political, and administrative positions are still dominated by men. Multiple researchers have claimed that women's salaries are still only 84 percent of men's wages in comparable jobs. The gender pay gap seems discriminatory, and female-rights organizations continue to lobby to pass legislation to achieve economic equality in Brazil.

See also: Chapter 7: Overview; *Desquite* and Divorce; Domestic Violence; Gender and Parenting Roles; Gender Equality; Maternity and Paternity Leave; Raising Children.

Further Reading

Araújo, Clara, and Celi Scalon. 2007. *Gênero, família e trabalho no Brasil*. Rio de Janeiro: Editora Fundação Getúlio Vargas.

Instituto Brasileiro de Geografia e Estatística—Brazilian Institute of Geography and Statistics (IBGE). 2011. *Census 2010*. Accessed May 7, 2019. http://ibge.gov.br

Rocha-Coutinho, Maria Lúcia. 2016. "Gender, Marriage, and Sexuality," in *Brazil*, edited by Antonio Luciano de Andrade Tosta and Eduardo F. Coutinho, 140–155. Santa Barbara, CA: ABC-CLIO.

Gender Equality

Brazil is still a male-dominated society, but the government and multiple feminist organizations have made substantial improvements in the last three decades toward gender equality. Since the late 1980s, women's rights organizations have successfully lobbied for legislation that would mitigate the effect of biased and discriminatory practices against women in education, poverty, politics, the workforce, domestic violence, and social policy. During the 1990s, multiple social and government agencies were created to address gender inequities, including the National Agency of Women's Rights and a national network of police stations dedicated to responding to reports of domestic abuse. However, that was not enough since women were still the largest group of illiterate and poor people in Brazil, significantly underrepresented in government, paid less than men for comparable positions, and lacked sufficient skills to obtain well-paying jobs.

At the start of the twentieth century, some of the social programs implemented during the 1990s were beginning to show positive results. The 2010 census report published by the Instituto Brasileiro de Geografia e Estatística revealed tangible improvements in reducing poverty and illiteracy, especially among women. In school, educational gains were impressive, and Brazilian women are now substantially more educated than men, including university graduate degrees. Consequently, more women were incorporated into the professional workforce in multiple fields at an accelerated rate. In spite of these positive results, the issue of economic inequality is still pervasive in Brazil since women are paid 72 percent of the average salary of men in the same position (Rocha-Coutinho, 2016, 151).

The election of Luiz Inácio Lula da Silva (1965–) as President of Brazil sparked tremendous optimism, especially among the poor, middle-class workers, and women's rights activists. During his two terms in office (2003–2010), he left a legacy of social programs and political reform that benefitted large numbers of Brazilians, especially women. For example, he appointed several women to powerful cabinet ministry positions. One of his most successful social programs was the Bolsa Familia, a conditional cash transfer welfare program for poor families who maintain children in school and make sure they follow prenatal care if they are pregnant. He also signed the Maria da Penha Law specifically designed to combat the endemic problem of domestic violence. Then the election of Lula's protégé, Dilma Rousseff (1947–), as the first female president of Brazil in 2010 reflected that political equity could potentially be achieved. She promised to fight for women's rights and for more female representation in government, business, higher education, and public policy. She definitely inspired more women to run for political office; however, the 2018 national elections were a disappointment because women represent 52 percent of the population but they were only elected to 77 out of 513 seats in Congress, which is only 15 percent.

As Brazil approaches 2020, women have obtained more education and economic independence, but gender inequality and economic wage gaps still exist. Gender roles have also changed significantly since more women try to balance the demands of a professional life with household responsibilities. To help families, the federal government approved in 2016 a substantially expanded program of paternity and maternity leave so both parents can share the challenges of raising a family in contemporary Brazil.

See also: Chapter 3: Lula da Silva, Luiz Inácio (1945–); Rousseff, Dilma (1947–); Women's Rights. Chapter 7: Overview; Feminism; Gender and Parenting Roles; Maternity and Paternity Leave; Representation in Government; Representation in the Workforce.

Further Reading

Gonçalves, Carolina. 2014. "Women's Presence in Brazilian Politics Still Far from Significant." *Agencia Brasil,* August 29. Accessed May 7, 2019. http://agenciabrasil.ebc.com.br/en/politica/noticia/2014-08/womens-presence-brazilian-politics-still-far-significant

Instituto Brasileiro de Geografia e Estatística—Brazilian Institute of Geography and Statistics (IBGE). 2011. *Census 2010.* Accessed May 7, 2019. http://ibge.gov.br

Rocha-Coutinho, Maria Lúcia. 2016. "Gender, Marriage, and Sexuality," in *Brazil,* edited by Antonio Luciano de Andrade Tosta and Eduardo F. Coutinho, 140–155. Santa Barbara, CA: ABC-CLIO.

Wylie, Kristin N. 2018. *Party Institutionalization and Women's Representation in Democratic Brazil.* Cambridge, UK: Cambridge University Press.

LGBTQ Community and Rights

Brazil has more than 300 lesbian, gay, bisexual, transgender, and queer (LGBTQ) organizations that have worked arduously to obtain social equality and the same legal rights as the rest of the population. The University of São Paulo released in 2010 the results of a study carried out in ten capital cities revealing that 10.4 percent of the male population was either gay or bisexual, and 6.3 percent of the female population was lesbian or bisexual. The top five Brazilian cities with the highest number of LGBTQ members were Rio de Janeiro, Fortaleza, Manaus, São Paulo, and Salvador. While the LGBTQ community has made significant social gains, the dark reality is that there is an increasing number of hate crimes perpetrated against its members.

LGBTQ organizations have tried to obtain specific legal protections and social equality for their members. Currently, the 1988 federal constitution has an antidiscrimination law that protects all Brazilians, but nothing specific to protect gays and lesbians. On the positive side, there is no law that specifically stops LGBTQ people from serving in the military. Adoption of children by same-sex couple was approved in 2010. At the beginning of the twentieth century, social approval of the LGBTQ community was more widespread. As a result of much struggle, the Supreme Federal Court approved same-sex civil unions (domestic partnerships) in 2011 throughout the country. Same-sex couples must register their civil union with the state by following the same procedure as opposite-sex couples living together. With civil unions, LGBTQ members registered as a same-sex couple are able to obtain tangible civil and social rights, including prison visitations with a partner, health benefits, income-tax benefits, and pensions from a spouse. Nevertheless, the struggle for the right to marry a person of the same sex remained elusive for decades.

Same-sex marriage was approved in Brazil on May 5, 2013, when the Supreme Federal Court voted 10–0 (with one abstention) to provide same-sex couples with the same legal, social, and financial rights as married couples. This law is most commonly known as *casamento gay.* To follow up, the Brazilian Justice's National Council legalized the

Participants enjoy the annual Pride Parade on Avenida Paulista in São Paulo, Brazil. It is considered the largest LGBTQ parade in the world with about 3 million attendees. Same-sex marriage was approved in Brazil in 2013. (William Rodrigues Dos Santos/Dreamstime.com)

ruling on May 14, 2013, throughout the nation. It also issued a ruling ordering all the civil registers throughout the country to perform same-sex marriages without objections. Civil registers were also ordered to convert any same-sex civil unions into marriages for all couples who requested the legal procedure. Moreover, the Brazilian Senate approved a bill in 2017 to modify the Civil Code by replacing the definition of a family from "a union between a man and a woman" to "a union between two people."

While the LGBTQ community has obtained multiple legal and social rights that attempt to provide a sense of social equity, the country still has a very conservative section of the population that is deeply homophobic. The influential organization Grupo Gay da Bahia (GGB) has been reporting the grim statistics for over a decade. According to GGB reports, one gay, lesbian, or transvestite is brutally murdered every two days, and homophobia is the cause of almost 130 assassinations every year in Brazil. They also reveal that a large number of the homophobic killings are actually committed by police officers. Despite this dark side of Brazilian culture, there is a clear effort to celebrate the accomplishments of gay culture, and the most visible representation is the São Paulo Gay Pride Parade, which is the largest in Brazil. It started in 1999, and its June celebration has grown incrementally ever since in order to bring visibility to the needs for the LBGTQ community.

See also: Chapter 7: Overview; Gender Equality; Maternity and Parental Leave; Raising Children.

> **SAME-SEX MARRIAGE AND RIGHTS**
>
> On May 16, 2013, the National Justice Council approved same-sex marriage as legal throughout Brazil. Two days prior, Joaquim Barbosa, the President of the Supreme Federal Court and the Council of Justice, ordered all the notaries in every state to perform same-sex marriages and to convert existing same-sex legal unions into a marriage, if the couple requested such a motion. Notaries could no longer refuse to perform same-sex civil weddings anywhere in the national territory. The new law provides same-sex couples with the rights of any other marriage, including but not limited to welfare benefits, inheritance tax, health benefits, immigration petitions, joint property, pensions, adoptions, income tax, social security options, hospital and prison visitations, surrogacy, and in-vitro fertilization (IVF) procedures. The law was officially published on May 15, and it went into effect on May 16, 2013.

Further Reading

Grupo Gay da Bahia. https://www.govserv.org/BR/Salvador/136685703140264/Grupo-Gay-da-Bahia

Mott, Luiz R. B. 2004. *Homofobia: Violação dos direitos humanos dos gays, lésbicas, travestis e transexuais no Brasil.* Salvador, Bahia, Brazil: Grupo Gay da Bahia (GGB) and Human Rights Commission.

Maternity and Paternity Leave

During the last ten years, the Brazilian legislature has increased the number of days parents are allowed to take off from work for both maternity and paternity leave in order to take care of a new baby or young child in the household. Their goal is to develop family-friendly policies where children are the ultimate beneficiaries of reforms to the labor code in Brazil.

In 2010, the Brazilian Congress increased maternity leave from the previous four months to six months. Initially, multiple women's rights organizations applauded the new policy because it allows women to retain their health insurance during the paid leave. The extended leave applies to government agencies at all levels (federal, state, and municipal). However, the new policy is required for large firms and optional for small businesses. For companies that expressed their concerns regarding the increased costs of such extended leave, the government provided a stimulus that allows them to deduct the additional cost from the company's income taxes. As part of the same legislative bill, the legislature also extended the compassionate leave benefit from the previous two days to five days. This policy applies to a leave related to the death of a parent, child, sibling, partner, or an employee's dependent. By including the word "partner," this law also applies to same-sex couples. While the new extended maternity leave was certainly helpful to raising a child, several women-based organizations began to see unintended consequences. For example, employers might now reconsider hiring more women because they are likely to take a longer maternity leave, which then becomes an employment trap for women since it reduced the possibility of upward mobility on both society and within a company. Therefore, there was extensive lobbying to have fathers more involved in raising children, which could provide help for women around the house.

The result was that on February 3, 2016, the Brazilian legislature extended paternity leave from the previous five days to twenty days. The new regulation on the strict Brazilian labor laws created further concern from companies regarding the potential loss of productivity based on giving male employees a leave of twenty days. When the legislation was approved, over 18,000 companies were already participating in the maternity extended program, and the government allowed them to apply the same benefit to deduct the additional expense for paternity leave from the company's federal income taxes. In addition, the legislature also provided fathers with an additional three days a year to attend prenatal doctor's appointments with their wives or medical visits with their children up until six years of age. While the policy is a positive step toward gender equality in Brazil, time will tell if fathers actually take the allowed time off from work for paternity leave. The discussion regarding extended maternity and paternity leaves for parents (and the cost for companies) has created heated social debate in Brazil, but the legislature made it clear that the approved social policies were always intended to benefit Brazilian children.

See also: Chapter 7: Overview; Gender and Parenting Roles; Gender Equality; Raising Children.

Further Reading

Barker, Gary, and Mary Robbins. 2014. "The Paternity Leave Stimulus." *Time*, December 22. Accessed July 2, 2019. http://time.com/3642763/paternity-leave-stimulus

International Comparative Legal Guides. 2018. *Brazil: Employment & Labour Law 2018*. Accessed August 2, 2019. https://iclg.com/practice-areas/employment-and-labour-laws-and-regulations/brazil

Raising Children

Children are the center of Brazilian families. Newborn babies receive a lot of attention, and parents usually get help from relatives to take care of them. In an effort to benefit children, Brazilian feminist groups were strong advocates of the current federal law approved on February 3, 2016, that expanded maternity and paternity leave to take care of a baby or young child (six months for the mother and twenty days for the father). The intent of this legislation was to provide the possibility that both parents share the responsibility of raising the children. Sometimes, if the family has the financial means, they hire a maid or a nanny to help with the household chores and taking care of the children.

During childhood, parents teach their kids important values, such as table manners, respect for their elders, religious traditions, the importance of education, and the value of close family ties. Overall, most Brazilian kids seem to enjoy life. They attend school, play sports, and socialize with children living in their neighborhood. They usually do not do any chores around the house. As they get into the teenage years, the influence of a male-dominated society becomes evident; young boys are given a lot more freedom than young girls in terms of going out and dating. Teenage boys are often encouraged to have several relationships before settling down, while teenage girls are encouraged to delay dating, concentrate on their studies, and remain virgins until marriage. Grown children traditionally continue to live at home until they get married since the family sees no reason for them to move out. In comparison to the United States, Brazilian culture does not value independence and individualism as much as family ties and extended-family support.

In modern Brazil, social class and family income influence how children are raised. Wealthy families usually include a father as the financial provider and a stay-at-home mother who can raise the children, often with the help of a nanny. For middle- and low-income families, however, the economic reality is that both parents have to work, and both the father and the mother manage the household chores and the responsibilities of raising the kids. Low-income families used to pull young kids out of school so they could work and contribute to the household. However, the extremely successful anti-poverty Bolsa Família welfare program implemented in 2003 by President Luiz Inácio Lula da Silva (1945–) now provides conditional cash incentives for children to remain in school, which ultimately benefits the entire family.

In contemporary Brazil, the structure of the family has changed from the traditional composition of a working father and a stay-at-home mother. The 2010 census data published by the Instituto Brasileiro de Geografia e Estatística revealed an increase in single-parent households, same-sex marriages, divorced parents, childless couples, and

PADRINHOS, GODPARENTS

Brazilian children are usually raised as part of an extended family that includes continuous contact with parents, uncles, aunts, cousins, and grandparents. As part of the larger family bond, Brazilian networks also include *padrinhos* (godparents). A *madrinha* (godmother) or *padrinho* (godfather) becomes an important part of the close-knit circle that is intended to look out for the godchild. This Catholic religious tradition makes the relationship between the child's parents and godparents even stronger, since they become *compadres* (co-parents). During good times, *padrinhos* socialize with their godchildren and support them in different aspects of their lives. However, *padrinhos* are also supposed to be available for support during difficult times. Consequently, godparents are accepted as part of the child's family.

Sources: Richard, Christopher, and Leslie Jermyn. 2002. *Cultures of the World: Brazil*. New York: Marshall Cavendish.

reconstituted families where each parent might have children from a previous marriage. The diversity of family structures influences parental roles and how children are raised. For example, a household with two working parents often has to hire help with the logistics of feeding the kids and picking them up from school, but the nanny usually cannot help with school homework. Meanwhile, a single mother often has to work two jobs and relies on the child's grandmother and other extended family members to help with the daily tasks of looking after the child, but there is not much time available for mother-child bonding.

See also: Chapter 6: Distribution of Wealth and Income Disparity. Chapter 7: Overview; Dating and Courting; *Desquite* and Divorce; Gender and Parenting Roles; Maternity and Paternity Leave.

Further Reading

Debiaggi, Sylvia Dantas. 2003. "Famílias Brasileiras em um novo contexto cultural," in *Fronteiras cruzadas: Enticidade, gênero, e redes sociais*, edited by Ana Cristina Braga Martes and Soraya Fleischer, 174–197. São Paulo: Paz e Terra.

Illinworth, Sarah. 2016. "The Success and Future of Brazil's Biggest Benefit, Bolsa Familia." *Huffington Post*, November 14. Accessed July 11, 2019. https://www.huffingtonpost.com/sarah-illingworth/the-success-and-future-of_b_12913176.html

Instituto Brasileiro de Geografia e Estatística—Brazilian Institute of Geography and Statistics (IBGE). 2011. *Census 2010*. http://ibge.gov.br

Pimentel Siqueira, Domingos Sávio. 2016. "Family and Etiquette," in *Brazil*, edited by Antonio Luciano de Andrade Tosta and Eduardo F. Coutinho, 187–203. Santa Barbara, CA: ABC-CLIO.

Richard, Christopher, and Leslie Jermyn. 2002. *Cultures of the World: Brazil*. New York: Marshall Cavendish.

Representation in Government

Government and politics in Brazil are dominated by men. The current 2019 legislature has 513 elected members; however, only 77 of them are female. Women are significantly underrepresented in government, and they have struggled to be elected as federal senators, congress deputies, and governors. The paradox of Brazilian feminists—who have a long tradition of activism—is that they have been successful in demanding women's rights, but their political pressure has not translated into tangible elected posts for women.

The goal of electing more female politicians is crucial because they fight for solutions to unique social problems they face. For example, women make up the majority of the poor people in Brazil, and they represent the largest number of the unemployed population. They also face inequalities in the political world. Women make up 51 percent of the electorate, but they hold less than 10 percent of elected seats in Congress.

For decades, women's rights organizations have advocated for more inclusion of women in politics. Eventually, they succeeded in introducing gender quotas in 1995. Electoral law established that 30 percent of all candidates listed on the ballot must be women. Once in office, a small group of congresswomen formed a powerful group called the "lipstick caucus," and they achieved significant legislative victories, including laws against gender discrimination, in favor of extended maternity and paternity leave, and a bill for equal pay to reduce income disparities in Brazil. The problem is that in spite of gender quotas, women are still not being elected in significant numbers. Researchers claim that the main impediment is not the electorate but the structure of the established political parties, which are still controlled by men (Gonçalves, 2014). When it comes to female politicians, these party bosses do not approve enough money for campaigning or television/radio airtime, thus reducing the possible success of female politicians. In addition, political parties do not face any penalties if they fail to fulfill the electoral quota.

In the twentieth century, President Lula da Silva (1945–) actively included more women in government. He appointed several women to powerful cabinet ministry positions, and he mentored Dilma Rousseff (1947–), who succeeded him and became the first female president of Brazil. The other side of politics includes a powerful conservative group who deliberately reduce the role of women in federal and state governments. This is the case of President Temer (1940–). He was Rousseff's vice president and replaced her when she was impeached in 2016. He immediately dismissed her cabinet and appointed new cabinet ministers who were all wealthy white men. Brazil has achieved impressive gains in reducing literacy and extreme poverty; however, it has a long way to go in the journey to integrate more women into the political process.

See also: Chapter 3: Lula da Silva, Luiz Inácio (1945–); Political Parties; Rousseff, Dilma (1947–); Temer, Michel (1940–); Women's Rights. Chapter 7: Gender Equality; Representation in the Workforce; Suffrage.

Further Reading

Gonçalves, Carolina. 2014. "Women's Presence in Brazilian Politics Still Far from Significant." *Agencia Brasil,* August 29. Accessed July 29, 2019. http://agenciabrasil.ebc.com.br/en/politica/noticia/2014-08/womens-presence-brazilian-politics-still-far-significant

Rauen, Alexia. 2017. "Lipstick in Government: Brazil's Inadequate Gender Quota." Council of Hemispheric Affairs, June 3, 2017. Accessed July 29, 2019. http://www.coha.org/lipstick-in-government-brazils-inadequate-gender-quota

Wylie, Kristin N. 2018. *Party Institutionalization and Women's Representation in Democratic Brazil.* Cambridge, UK: Cambridge University Press.

Representation in the Workforce

The 2010 census provided specific information on the Brazilian population as well as labor statistics. The Instituto Brasileiro de Geografia e Estadística (IBGE) stated that the population of Brazil was 196 million people. According to its data, 74.2 percent of

Brazilians are within working age (fifteen to sixty-four years old). From this number, the labor-force participation rate in Brazil was 68.5 percent. That means that 97.9 million people were actively working in Brazil. The IBGE and the International Labor Organization (ILO) both expect the number to increase to 117.1 million people working by the year 2020. Another important statistic is that 17.2 percent of Brazilians only worked part-time. In addition, 12.7 percent of the population was self-employed in running their own business.

The official 2010 census data published by the IBGE, combined with official statistics from the Organization for Economic Co-operation and Development (OECD), provides important demographic information that is crucial for understanding the representation of men and women in the workforce. While 68.5 percent of Brazilians worked, a further breakdown of the numbers reveals that it was 79.7 percent for men and 55.9 percent for women. The male working rate of 79.7 percent is very comparable to other Latin American countries with similar economies, such as Mexico and Chile. However, the labor participation rate for women at 55.9 percent is at least 10 percent higher than the same two countries.

The Brazilian federal government has provided fiscal incentives for companies to incorporate more women into the workforce, especially in nontraditional areas typically dominated by men, including agriculture, industry, mid-level management, and machinery. Such incentives seem to produce encouraging results. For example, the oil conglomerate British Petroleum (which also owns and operates multiple sugarcane mills for the production of ethanol in Brazil) realized that women made up only 7.5 percent of its agricultural, industrial, and maintenance workforce in 2011. Consequently, they decided to implement a training program to provide women with the skills and training necessary to learn how to operate in different jobs and positions related to the ethanol industry. The results of this pilot program from 2012 to 2015 revealed positive improvements. By June 2016, the participation of women in agricultural, industrial, and maintenance jobs had increased from 8 percent to 13 percent.

Brazil has made tangible improvements in the last two decades to achieve gender equality. Brazilian legislation and the expansion of social programs have been very successful in reducing poverty and illiteracy, especially among women. However, economic and income inequality still exist. Multiple researchers have claimed that women's salaries are still only 84 percent of men's wages in comparable jobs, and that wage gap increases even further at higher levels of education. The gender pay gap appears to be a discriminatory practice and a social custom that still expects women to run the household and raise children (Agénor, 2013). This practice reflects gender bias in Brazilian culture. There is still much more work to be done on behalf of women and gender equality.

See also: Chapter 7: Overview; Gender Equality; Gender and Parenting Roles; Raising Children.

Further Reading

Agénor, Pierre-Richard, and Otaviano Canuto. 2013. "Gender Equality and Economic Growth in Brazil." The World Bank—Poverty Reduction and Economic Management

Network, March. https://openknowledge.worldbank.org/bitstream/handle/10986/13174/wps6348.pdf?sequence=1&isAllowed=y

Campos Fonseca, Camila Veneo, Luísa de Azevedo, and Adriana Fontes. 2010. "Brazil Workforce Profile." 2010. Global Perspectives Institute at Boston College, July. Accessed July 29, 2019. https://www.bc.edu/research/agingandwork/archive_pubs/CP23.html

Silva, Joana, Rita Almeida, and Victoria Strokova. 2015. *Sustaining Development and Wage Gains in Brazil: A Skills and Jobs Agenda*. Washington, DC: World Bank Publications.

Suffrage

Universal suffrage (most commonly known simply as suffrage) is mostly defined as the right to vote for all adult citizens without imposing any restrictions on income, race, property ownership, ethnicity, literacy, or gender. Currently in Brazil, voting is mandatory for all Brazilian citizens who are literate and between the ages of eighteen and sixty-nine years old. Any Brazilian who happens to be sixteen or seventeen years old, is over sixty-nine years of age, or is illiterate, may select the option to vote, but it is not mandatory for them.

Achieving universal suffrage, however, was not an easy task to accomplish in Brazil. Men first received the general right to vote in 1891, but this right still restricted the homeless, women, priests, and the military from voting. Congress passed a law providing women with the right to vote in Brazil in 1932, which made Brazil the fourth country in the Western Hemisphere to approve female suffrage after Canada, the United States, and Ecuador. Brazilian president Getúlio Vargas (1882–1954) signed the authorization right away allowing women to vote in the upcoming elections of May 1933 to select the members of the Constituent Assembly of 1934. This was the legislative body assigned with the task of developing the fifth national constitution of Brazil. However, a woman's right to vote took decades of political pressure and activism.

Bertha Lutz (1894–1976) is widely recognized as an iconic figure of the feminist movement in Brazil beginning in the 1920s. She was a tireless advocate for women's social and political rights. (Library of Congress)

Brazil has a history of a powerful feminist movement that was very active since the middle of the 1800s. They actually pushed for the right of women to vote when the 1891 constitution was being drafted, but their efforts failed. The feminist struggle was certainly improved when an attorney named Bertha Lutz created an organization in 1922 called the Brazilian Federation for the Advancement of Women, which then became affiliated with the International Women's Suffrage Alliance. This was a group of Brazilian conservative women who were essentially middle and upper class, and they were interested in the suffrage movement to advance the overall rights of women. Consequently, the political campaign to obtain female suffrage was not really a mass movement in Brazil because most women were still illiterate at that time. Nevertheless, universal suffrage became an accomplishment for nearly all Brazilians.

The current constitution of Brazil dates from 1988, and it finally granted suffrage to the last politically disenfranchised group in Brazil: illiterate people. The 1988 legislature even went a step further by clearly stating in Article 5 of Title II that "men and women have equal rights and duties under the terms of this constitution." This clause indicates a positive step toward comprehensive gender equality in Brazil.

See also: Chapter 2: Vargas, Getúlio (1882–1954); Timeline. Chapter 3: Constitutions; Electoral System; Women's Rights. Chapter 7: Overview; Feminism; Gender Equality; Representation in Government.

Further Reading

Fausto, Boris, and Sergio Fausto. 2014. *A Concise History of Brazil*. Cambridge, UK: Cambridge University Press.

Georgetown University. "Federative Republic of Brazil: 1988 Constitution with 1996 Reforms." Political Database of the Americas. http://pdba.georgetown.edu/Constitutions/Brazil/english96.html

Hahner, June Edith. 1979. "The Beginnings of the Women's Suffrage Movement in Brazil." *Journal of Women in Culture in Society* 5, no.1 (Autumn): 200–204. Accessed May 2, 2019. https://www.journals.uchicago.edu/doi/pdfplus/10.1086/493702

Hahner, June Edith. 1990. *Emancipating the Female Sex: The Struggle for Women's Rights in Brazil, 1850–1940*. Durham, NC: Duke University Press.

Wedding Traditions and Celebrations

Brazilian wedding celebrations reflect cultural traditions, the love for family, and the bond with friends and extended relatives. Most weddings are big events; the notion of a small gathering with only close friends and family is not very common in Brazil. There are multiple traditions that happen before the wedding day. The *noivado* (engagement) follows the marriage proposal, which is usually very practical and still a romantic decision; however, over-the-top, super-creative proposals are not very common. Spectacular engagement rings are also not really a tradition in Brazil; instead, the bride and groom select their wedding bands (*alianças*), and they simply wear them on the right hand until the day of the wedding ceremony. Friends, relatives, and coworkers are often involved in two types of parties before the wedding day. The *festa de despedida* (bachelor/bachelorette parties) often involve a meal and a night of drinking in a merry atmosphere. The bridal parties, however, differ significantly from the ones celebrated in the United States. In Brazil, these events are mostly called *chá de cozinha*, which loosely translates as a "party of kitchen supplies" because the *padrinhos* (godparents) and bridesmaids will often offer a gift to outfit an entire new kitchen for the couple. The rest of the invited guests often pick their gifts from a store registry where the bride and groom have selected their desired items in advance. Weddings tend to be very expensive in Brazil, but the most common practice today is for the couple to pay for the events themselves, sometimes with a little help from close relative and godparents.

On the wedding day, multiple events are celebrated. Most couples marry at a church, where they also sign the official legal marriage license. In regard to clothing and fashion, the tradition is that the bridesmaids do not wear matching dresses, and the godparents wear any type of formal attire they can get; there is no attempt to coordinate the outfits of the entire wedding party. The bride usually wears golden shoes. When it is time to eat, wedding receptions are mostly held at special halls serving buffet-style meals (*bifês*). It is always a happy occasion with music and dancing. Most receptions include at least two unique games to help the bride and groom raise funds for their honeymoon or for the expenses of starting a new life. First, the best man gets the groom's tie and then cuts it into small pieces that are sold for the amounts that people want to contribute. Then one of the bridesmaids gets one of the bride's golden shoes, places it on a tray, and then passes it around for people to insert money in it. These traditions contribute toward the couple's financial future. After a long, festive night of food, music, dancing, games, and laughter, guests receive a special party favor as they leave the reception. They usually get sweets called *bem casados* (translated as "well married"), which are small square cakes beautifully wrapped up and decorated for the trip home; they are symbols of good luck for the future.

See also: Chapter 7: Overview.

Further Reading

Fernandes da Fonseca, Rodrigo, Rafael Mantesso Henriques, and Eder Chiodetto. 2014. *Brazil: A Celebration of Contemporary Brazilian Culture*. London: Phaidon Press.

Puin, Karolina. 2012. "Invited to a Wedding in Brazil." *Brazil Business,* July 6. Accessed July 29, 2019. http://thebrazilbusiness.com/article/invited-to-a-wedding-in-brazil

CHAPTER 8

EDUCATION

OVERVIEW

Brazil has made remarkable progress in raising literacy rates to an enviable 92 percent during the last thirty years; however, the national public school system still needs considerable improvement. The deficiencies in infrastructure, classroom overcrowding, and lack of teacher professional development training have recently driven middle- and upper-class families to enroll their children in private, religious, and international schools. Nevertheless, Brazil has a network of high-caliber public universities, and the national *vestibular* entrance exam sparks fierce competition for the limited number of spots available at these institutions that vastly outperform most private universities in the country and are mostly free for students.

Brazil is one of the most unequal societies in Latin America, and social class disparities are immediately evident in its educational system. Since 2010, the Brazilian education system follows a 9 + 3 pattern: nine years of compulsory primary education and three years of secondary education. This structure applies to all public and private schools. Primary education (*ensino fundamental*) is mandatory for all six- to fourteen-year-old children; it includes six years of elementary schooling and three years of middle school. Secondary education (*ensino médio*) is for fifteen- to eighteen-year-old minors, but it is not compulsory in Brazil. Upon completion, students receive a *certificado de ensino médio*, which is required for university admissions. Public schools represent a stark contrast to private education in Brazil, which offers small class sizes, a more rigorous curriculum, and often a religious foundation. Private schools in Brazil essentially belong to three categories: international schools, religious, and nondenominational. The federal government is keenly aware that it needs to improve the largest public educational system in Latin America. Consequently, the Ministry of Education implemented significant education reforms to the high school programs nationwide in 2016. President Michel Temer (1940–) signed into law a New Education Model targeting education reforms for high school curricula that are deep and significant. Before the program changes, thirteen subjects were required core curriculum. Under the 2016 new model, only mathematics and language (Portuguese) are required subjects, and everything else is optional to be tailored to the student's interests. The persistent problem is that students from private schools graduate high school with significantly higher academic skills to enter university studies than their public school counterparts.

The Brazilian higher education system offers a network of public and private universities ranked the highest in Latin America. However, while the public elementary and secondary school system is quite deficient, the top-ranking universities in Brazil are actually public and almost completely free for Brazilians. Potential students must take the *vestibular* entrance exam to compete for a few positions available at high-caliber public institutions such as the Universidade de São Paulo (USP) and the Universidade Estadual de Campinas (Unicamp). They offer bachelor's (*bacharelado*), master's (*mestrado*), and doctoral (*doutorado*) degrees. An important factor to notice in Brazil is that almost 85 percent of all scientific research is funded by the federal government instead of private industries, and it is mostly assigned to university centers and research facilities. Federal research funds are prioritized for agriculture, industry, health, infrastructure, and defense. However, the need to advance scientific and technical research has recently led to the creation of private centers as an alternative for research and development. As of 2019, there are six of these very successful social organizations:

Brazilian Research and Industrial Innovation Enterprise (EMBRAPII)
Center for Management and Strategic Studies (CGEE)
Institute for Pure and Applied Mathematics (IMPA)
Institute for the Sustainable Development of the Amazon Forest (IDSM)
National Center for Research in Energy and Materials (CNPEM)
National Research and Teaching Network (RNP)

Modern Brazil is still affected by its colonial past, and it is not difficult to see that the most disadvantaged populations are those of African heritage and the people who are racially mixed. These groups are reflected in the lowest economic groups, the ones with significantly less education, and their lack of representation in the professional world. The struggle is how to help such populations to achieve higher education levels that could lead to professional jobs and better income. With that goal in mind, on

---

EDUCATION IN SHIFTS

Brazil has made tremendous improvements in providing access to education in the last twenty years. It has excellent public universities but also a notoriously deficient system of elementary and secondary schools. There are simply too many students and not enough schools. Consequently, most elementary schools run up to three separate daily shifts in which students only attend four hours of instruction per day. When students do not learn enough, it is common to make them repeat the entire grade, which eventually increases dropout rates. As a result, the national educational system actually ranks lower than impoverished countries such as Haiti. The system disproportionately punishes low-income students because middle- and upper-class families can afford to send their children to private schools. A private elementary and secondary education, ironically, prepares a select group of students to benefit from the excellent—but highly selective—public university system.

August 2012, ex-president Dilma Rousseff (1947–) signed into law one of the most ambitious affirmative action programs in the world for university admissions. Officially known as the Law of Social Quotas, it requires all public universities to set aside 50 percent of their available spots to new students who graduated from the underperforming public education system, especially if they are Afro-Brazilians or mixed race (*pardo*). Congress approved this law with overwhelming support, claiming it will democratize higher education while correcting a historical debt with people of African descent. In addition, the Universidade de Zumbi dos Palmares (known simply as Unipalmares) was founded in 2003 in Saõ Paulo with the specific purpose to provide Brazilian black students an opportunity for access to higher education. The institution prepares people of black ancestry to obtain a university education in order to facilitate access to professional careers with better pay so they can begin to earn representation in higher government positions, the legal system, the medical profession, and the business world.

Further Reading

Bartlett, Lesley. 2009. *The Word and the World: The Cultural Politics of Literacy in Brazil.* New York: Hampton Press.

Brazilian National Institute for Educational Studies and Research (INEP). http://portal.inep.gov.br/web/guest/inicio

Carneiro, Julia. 2013. "Brazil's Universities Take Affirmative Action." *BBC News*, August 28. Accessed May 25, 2019. https://www.bbc.com/news/business-23862676

Chiesa Gonçalves, Aline. 2017. *The Influence of the Bolsa Família Program in Education.* Düsseldorf, Germany: Novas Edições Acadêmicas.

Collier, Sabrina. 2017. "Top 10 Universities in Brazil 2018." *QS Top University Rankings*, November 23. Accessed May 29, 2019. https://www.topuniversities.com/university-rankings-articles/brics-rankings/top-10-universities-brazil 2018

FUVEST Vestibular Test for College Admission Official Website. https://www.fuvest.br

Hyuda de Luna Pedrosa, Renato, and Hernan Chaimovich. 2015. "Brazil: UNESCO Science Report towards 2030," in *UNESCO Report,* 210–229. Paris: UNESCO.

Instituto Brasileiro de Geografia e Estatística—Brazilian Institute of Geography and Statistics (IBGE). "Censo 2010." Accessed May 21, 2019. http://ibge.gov.br

Instituto Nacional de Matemática Pura e Aplicada (IMPA). https://impa.br

Ministry of Education and Culture (MEC) Official Website. http://mec.gov.br

Ministry of Science, Technology, Innovation, and Communications. http://www.mctic.gov.br

Rocha, Candyce, and Elisa Diniz. 2017. "Program for Results in Brazil to Support the Implementation of the Upper Secondary Education Reform Benefiting around 2.4 Million Students." The World Bank, December 14. https://www.worldbank.org/en/news/press-release/2017/12/14/brazil-program-for-results-supports-upper-secondary-education-reform

Stanek, Christina. 2013. "The Educational System of Brazil." *IEM Spotlight* 10, no. 1 (March). Accessed May 1, 2019. https://www.pdf-book-search.com/educational/the-educational-system-of-brazil-nafsa-association-of.html

Universidade de Zumbi dos Palmares Official Website. http://www.zumbidospalmares.edu.br

Affirmative Action Policies

On August 2012, ex-president Dilma Rousseff (1947–) signed into law one of the most ambitious affirmative action programs in the world for university admissions. Officially known as the Law of Social Quotas, it requires all public universities to set aside 50 percent of their available spots to new students who graduated from the underperforming public education system, especially if they are Afro-Brazilians or mixed race (*pardo*). Congress approved this law with overwhelming support, claiming it will democratize higher education while correcting a historical debt with people of African descent.

Brazil is still today one of the most unequal societies in Latin America, and the Law of Social Quotas for education is an attempt by the federal government to support racial equality. It is also important to discuss education in a context in which the fifty-nine public federal universities are high-caliber institutions that outperform most private universities in Brazil; in addition, they are funded by the government and free for students. The problem is that slightly over 50 percent of the national population is of African descent, but until five years ago, they only represented less than 5 percent of the student population enrolled in public universities. The students registered at these institutions were mostly white and came from middle and upper social classes who were educated in private elementary and secondary schools. Private schools often include training courses for the competitive *vestibular* university entrance exam, and such students score substantially higher on that test than the ones coming from the deficient public school system. The Minister of Education declared that public universities had four years to implement the 50 percent rule, and the expectation was to raise the number of black and mixed-race students from 8,700 in 2012 to 56,000 by 2016.

The implementation of affirmative action quotas generated spirited controversy on both sides. Supporters claim that the law provides opportunities for underprivileged Brazilians who have traditionally been left out of higher education and consequently out of professional jobs with better pay, which perpetuates the cycle of intergenerational poverty. This social situation has allowed racism and discrimination to continue in Brazil. Opponents argue that the government needs to fix the elementary and secondary education systems instead of forcing unprepared students into university programs. The opposition also claims that there is academic pressure to see these students succeed, which results in graduating students who are not prepared for the professional job market. The result was the implementation of the 2014 law that extends affirmative action quotas for government jobs; by 2016, 20 percent of all federal jobs in public service must be filled by blacks or mixed-race applicants. The government expects to see tangible results by 2020 based on the implementation of affirmative action laws that provide access to higher education, discourage racism, and promote economic equality.

See also: Chapter 2: Overview; Slavery, Abolition, and African Heritage. Chapter 6: Overview; African Ancestry and Influence; Education and Upward Mobility; Racism and Discrimination. Chapter 8: Overview; Public Education: Elementary and Secondary Schooling; Unipalmares, University for Afro-Descendent Students; *Vestibular* Testing for College Admissions.

Further Reading

Carneiro, Julia. 2013. "Brazil's Universities Take Affirmative Action." *BBC News*, August 28. Accessed July 25, 2019. https://www.bbc.com/news/business-23862676

Garcia-Navarro, Lulu. 2016. "For Affirmative Action, Brazil Sets Up Controversial Boards to Determine Race." National Public Radio, September 29. Accessed July 25. https://www.npr.org/sections/parallels/2016/09/29/495665329/for-affirmative-action-brazil-sets-up-controversial-boards-to-determine-race

Romero, Simon. 2012. "Brazil Enacts Affirmative Action Law for Universities." *New York Times*, August 30. Accessed July 25, 2019. https://www.nytimes.com/2012/08/31/world/americas/brazil-enacts-affirmative-action-law-for-universities.html

Ávila, Artur (1979–)

Artur Ávila Cordeiro de Melo was born on June 29, 1979 in Rio de Janeiro, Brazil. He is considered the most famous contemporary mathematician in the country. He won the Fields Medal of Mathematics in 2014, which is often described as the Nobel Prize in this discipline. Ávila was the first candidate from Latin America to ever win this highly competitive award.

Artur Ávila excelled in mathematics at a very early age. He won the gold medal at the International Mathematical Olympiad while attending high school at the Colégio San Agostinho in Rio de Janeiro. He went on to receive his bachelor's degree in mathematics from the Federal University in Rio de Janeiro. In addition, he had received a scholarship for winning the Mathematics Olympiad to attend the Instituto Nacional de Matemática Pura e Aplicada (IMPA) to work on a master's degree. He remained at the same institution for doctoral work at the age of nineteen years old. His dissertation work was focused on the theory of dynamic systems, which was a very contemporary topic when he obtained his doctoral degree in 2001.

Since Artur Ávila has dual nationality (Brazilian and French), he moved to France after finishing his PhD in 2001 to pursue further postdoctoral research. Two years later, he started working as a mathematics researcher at the Centre National de la Recherche Scientifique (CNRS), which is the largest research organization in France. While working at CNRS, Ávila solved the legendary "10 martini problem" in 2005 by using mathematics to explain parts of quantum physics. Then he won the prestigious Salem Prize in 2006 when he was only twenty-seven years old. Ávila's work was so outstanding that he became director of the CNRS French Research Institution in 2008.

Nowadays, Artur Ávila spends his time between Paris and Rio de Janeiro working as a mathematics researcher at both the CNRS and the IMPA—one semester at each institution. This young mathematical genius continues to gather prizes and accolades for his work on contemporary mathematics and applied fields. In 2011, he received the Michael Brin Prize for work on dynamical systems. One year later, the International Association of Mathematical Physics recognized him with the Early Career Award. He received the Fields Medal in 2014 for "profound contributions to dynamic systems theory." Subsequently, he presented the highly coveted Lojasiewicz Lecture at the Jagiellonian University in Krakow, Poland, in 2017. The future certainly seems promising for this contemporary Brazilian researcher and mathematician.

See also: Chapter 8: Overview.

Further Reading

Centre National de la Recherche Scientifique (CNRS). http://www.cnrs.fr

Fajardo, Vanessa. 2014. "Pesquisador brasileiro ganha prêmio equivalente a 'Nobel' de matemática." *G1 Globo News,* December 8. Accessed June 19, 2019. http://g1.globo.com/educacao/noticia/2014/08/pesquisador-brasileiro-ganha-premio-equivalente-nobel-de-matematica.html

Instituto Nacional de Matemática Pura e Aplicada (IMPA). https://impa.br

Lin, Thomas, and Erica Klarreich. 2014. "A Brazilian Wunderkind Who Calms Chaos." *Quanta Magazine,* August 12. Accessed June 18, 2019. https://www.quantamagazine.org/artur-avila-is-first-brazilian-mathematician-to-win-fields-medal-20140812

Talarico, Bruna. 2010. "Genio da matemática carioca." *O dia Online,* January 16. Accessed June 19, 2019. https://web.archive.org/web/20100122050606/http://odia.terra.com.br/portal/rio/html/2010/1/genio_da_matematica_carioca_59005.html

Bolsa Família: Welfare Program with Education Incentives

Toward the end of the twentieth century, Brazil had established multiple social programs aimed at reducing poverty in the country. They were managed by multiple federal, state, and municipal agencies with competing interests. Then, in 2003, the federal executive office under President Luiz Inácio Lula da Silva (1945–) launched a massive comprehensive reform of the social safety net under one single program called Bolsa Família. It galvanized four separate existing social benefits under one federal program managed by a newly created Ministry of Social Development. The overarching goals were to reduce short-term poverty among Brazilian families and to help children prepare for the future. What is unique about Bolsa Família is that it functions as a conditional cash transfer program based on very specific parameters: children have to remain in school and demonstrate 85 percent attendance records, parents must make sure children are vaccinated, children must receive annual medical physical exams funded by a federal insurance program, and pregnant or lactating mothers have to attend regular medical checkups. Families receive roughly $35 U.S. (R$70 reais) a month if they comply with all the requirements.

According to the World Bank, the Brazilian Bolsa Família is by far the largest conditional cash transfer program in the world, and most parameters of evaluation indicate that it is successful in terms of increasing schooling years and reducing poverty. After ten years of being implemented, government surveys indicate that this program provides aid for over 11 million families, or just over 45 million of the most vulnerable people in Brazil. When it comes to education, government reports indicate that over 96 percent of children were compliant with the school attendance requirements (85 percent for children six to fifteen years old and 75 percent for teenagers between sixteen and eighteen years of age), which also implies that children are not leaving school to help the family financially. By investing in children, families increase the chances of breaking the cycle of intergenerational poverty. Another positive indicator is that over 95 percent of children are using health cards for regular medical checkups. Overall, the Bolsa Família program has sparked an unprecedented reduction in extreme poverty in Brazil while only costing the government roughly 0.5 percent of the national gross domestic product. Government reports also show that the poorest families spend most of the money on food, school supplies, and clothing for children. The Ministry of Social Development reported in 2013 that the distribution of Bolsa Família funds is highest in the impoverished northeast region where over 52 percent of all households receive social help to survive. In general, the World Bank has defined the Bolsa Família program as the most successful conditional cash transfer program in the developed world, and it is being studied as a potential model for other developing countries.

See also: Chapter 6: Poverty, Social Conflict, and Protests. Chapter 8: Overview.

Further Reading

Chiesa Gonçalves, Aline. 2017. *The Influence of the Bolsa Família Program in Education*. Düsseldorf, Germany: Novas Edições Acadêmicas.

Rawlings, Laura B., and Gloria Rubio M. 2003. "Evaluating the Impact of Conditional Cash Transfer Programs—Lessons from Latin America." World Bank Policy, August. Accessed June 11, 2019. http://www1.worldbank.org/prem/poverty/ie/dime_papers/195.pdf

Wetzel, Deborah. 2013. "Bolsa Família: Brazil's Quiet Revolution." The World Bank, November 4. Accessed June 11, 2019. http://www.worldbank.org/en/news/opinion/2013/11/04/bolsa-familia-Brazil-quiet-revolution

World Bank. 2007. "Bolsa Família: Changing the Lives of Millions in Brazil." August 22. Accessed June 11, 2019. http://www.worldbank.org/en/news/feature/2007/08/22/bolsa-familia-changing-the-lives-of-millions-in-brazil

Education Reforms of 2016

Brazil has the largest public school system in Latin America. However, education in public high schools traditionally suffers from decaying infrastructure, low teacher salaries, unfocused curriculum expectations, and high dropout rates. Consequently, the federal government, with the coordination of the Ministry of Education, implemented significant education reforms to the high school programs nationwide. President Michel Temer (1944–) signed into law a New Education Model in September 2016. The reforms immediately received both acceptance and criticism.

The Brazilian education reforms for high school curricula are deep and significant. Before the program changes, thirteen subjects were mandatory core curriculum. After the 2016 changes, only mathematics and language (Portuguese) were required subjects, and everything else was optional to be tailored to the student's interests. The flexible curriculum choices now include the addition of technical-vocational education as part of the high school experience. The goal is that students will obtain competence-based knowledge by taking only courses that are related to their interests, which has the potential to reduce chronic school absenteeism and dropout rates. In addition, the option of technical training while in high school will provide students with a tangible skill to obtain a job immediately after completing their secondary education.

Brazil is channeling significantly more funds to implement the education reforms approved in 2016. The Ministry of Education committed almost $365 million U.S. (R$1.5 billion) to fund the transition to the new curriculum. It also provided money to extend the school day from four to five hours a day. In addition, Brazil received $250 million U.S. in operational funding in December 2017 from the World Bank to support the education reforms under the proposed title Program for Results, which is expected to benefit 2.4 million Brazilian high school students. While the expectations are high, there is a lot of optimism that the program will succeed.

Multiple education agencies have already expressed strong criticism of the 2016 education reforms, especially about how they are being implemented. Essentially, politicians made decisions without requesting substantial input from teachers and counselors. In addition, teachers' unions believe that the changes are only cosmetic in nature since they do not really address serious shortcomings in the national education system, including the lack of teacher training, the deplorable state of school infrastructure, overcrowding in the classroom, and declining teacher morale due to low salaries. Despite the criticism, the Ministry of Education believes that the new educational model for high schools will make secondary education more relevant to the students' lives and consequently improve completion rates.

See also: Chapter 6: Education and Upward Mobility; Poverty, Social Conflict, and Protests. Chapter 8: Overview; Public Education: Elementary and Secondary Schooling.

Further Reading

Alves, Lise. 2016. "Brazilian Government Announces New Education Model." *Rio Times*, September 23. Accessed August 1, 2019. https://riotimesonline.com/brazil-news/rio-politics/brazilian-government-announces-new-education-model

Ministry of Education and Culture (MEC) Official Website. http://mec.gov.br

Rocha, Candyce, and Elisa Diniz. 2017. "Program for Results in Brazil to Support the Implementation of the Upper Secondary Education Reform Benefiting around 2.4 Million

Students." The World Bank, December 14. Accessed January 10, 2020. https://www.worldbank.org/en/news/press-release/2017/12/14/brazil-program-for-results-supports-upper-secondary-education-reform

Higher Education and Major Universities

Brazil has some of the highest-ranking universities in Latin America and the BRICS group of countries (Brazil, Russia, India, China, and South Africa). Moreover, several of them are also included in overall international rankings in specific fields. It is important to highlight that some of the highest-performing universities in Brazil are public, which are completely funded by the government and free for students. Consequently, the admission process into such universities is fiercely competitive.

The system of higher education in Brazil is essentially divided into undergraduate and graduate categories. The three types of undergraduate degrees are clustered together under the umbrella term *graduação*. A bachelor's degree (*bacharelado*) allows graduates to seek professional employment is specific areas, such as law, medicine, social

The Universidade de São Paulo (USP) is the largest university in Latin America with more than 95,000 students spread across multiple campuses. In 2018, it was ranked as number two in Brazil and number three in Latin America. Its highest-ranking subjects are law, architecture, and mining engineering. The Museu Paulista at the USP contains a valuable collection of documents relating to the Brazilian Empire era. (Alf Ribeiro/Dreamstime.com)

work, or biology. It takes between three and six years to finish. Future elementary and secondary school teachers typically study three to four years to obtain a licentiate (*licenciatura*) degree. The technology degree (*tecnologia*) takes only two to three years, but it enables graduates to work in a specialized field, such as hotel management or agronomy. Graduate school is divided into two different categories under the umbrella term *pós-graduação*. Students with a bachelor's degree interested in a doctoral program in the future must select a *stricto sensu* postgraduate degree, which follows an academic pathway to obtain a master's degree (*mestrado*) and potentially a doctoral degree (*doutorado*). Both of these programs require a thesis and an oral defense to complete the degree. Another option is for students to enter a *lato sensu* postgraduate program that takes one to two years, and it provides a certificate of completion in a specialized discipline, but the courses are usually not accredited by the Ministry of Education.

University rankings in Latin America, BRICS countries, and international forums consistently rank several Brazilian universities in top-tier levels. The five highest-ranking institutions of higher education in Brazil for 2018 include:

1. Universidade Estadual de Campinas (Unicamp). This public university is ranked as number one in Brazil, number three in Latin America, and also in the top fifty global schools for forestry, dentistry, and agriculture.
2. Universidade de São Paulo (USP) is the largest university in Latin America, with more than 95,000 students spread across multiple campuses. It ranks as number two in Brazil, number three in Latin America, and number thirteen among BRICS countries. Its highest-ranking subjects are law, architecture, and mining engineering.
3. Universidade Federal do Rio de Janeiro (UFRJ). Founded in 1792, it is the oldest among top-ranking universities in Brazil. It is considered number seven in Latin America and number thirty-one among BRICS countries. It also operates a complex network of art museums, hospitals, and research labs.
4. Universidade Estatual Paulista (UNESP). This public state university has eleven campuses within the state of São Paulo. It is considered number ten in Latin America and number thirty-four in BRICS countries. It ranks as number two in Brazil for the highest number of faculty with PhD degrees.
5. Pontificia Universidade Católica de São Paulo (PUC-SP). This private university ranks among the top 300 global universities for linguistics and foreign languages, as well as number forty-two in Latin America.

See also: Chapter 4: BRICS Economic Group. Chapter 8: Overview.

Further Reading

Collier, Sabrina. 2017. "Top 10 Universities in Brazil 2018." *QS Top University Rankings*, November 23. Accessed July 30, 2019. https://www.topuniversities.com/university-rankings-articles/brics-rankings/top-10-universities-brazil-2018

Stanek, Christina. 2013. "The Educational System of Brazil." *IEM Spotlight* 10, no. 1 (March). Accessed July 30, 2019. https://www.pdf-book-search.com/educational/the-educational-system-of-brazil-nafsa-association-of.html

INEP, National Institute for Educational Studies and Research

The Instituto Nacional de Estudos e Pesquisas Educacionais Anísio Teixeira (INEP) is linked to the Brazilian Ministry of Education (MEC). It was founded in 1937, and its main responsibility is to evaluate educational systems and the overall quality of education at all levels (elementary, secondary, and university) in the country. One of its crucial tasks is to assess education by administering national tests and then develop educational statistics at the municipal, state, and federal levels. This data is then used to develop educational policies that determine school funding, government policies, and the accountability of educational standards.

Basic education in Brazil includes twelve years: nine years of primary (elementary and middle school) and three years of secondary (high school) education. To assess the quality of education at those levels, the INEP performs a national school census at municipal, state, and federal levels. As a general guideline, it administers the National Assessment of Alphabetization (ANA), the Exam for the Certification of Proficiency in Portuguese (CELPE-BRAS), and the National Exam of Competences of Youngsters and Adults (ENCCEJA). In addition, they handle the annual test titled National System of Basic Education Assessment (Saeb).

At the university level, the INEP is also in charge of measuring institutional effectiveness and the quality of education. First of all, it must generate an annual higher education student census for accuracy. It evaluates college-level students with the National Exam of Student Performance (ENADE) based on general parameters that all university students must pass regardless of specific majors or careers. To evaluate institutional effectiveness, the INEP performs on site evaluations using the National System of Higher Education Assessment (SINAES). In addition, the INEP must undertake international assessments, such as the Exam for Revalidation of Foreign Medicine Diplomas (REVALIDA) for medical professionals who have a medical degree in another country but want to practice medicine in Brazil. It is also the contact to participate in the coalition Comparative Latin America and Caribe Study (TERCE).

At the very basic level, the data organized and generated by the INEP is extremely useful for parents, students, and institutions. For example, its web-based portal provides transparency by making available data pertaining to the performance of individual schools using the Index of Development of Basic Education (IDEB), which in turn can be used at the municipal level to set educational policy for future funding, priorities, and goals. At the national level, the INEP data could have a significant impact, such as the case when the Brazilian Congress recently approved the New Educational Model of 2016 leading to additional education funding and the transition to an updated curriculum.

See also: Chapter 8: Overview; Higher Education and Major Universities; Public Education: Elementary and Secondary Schooling; *Vestibular* Testing for College Admission.

Further Reading

Alves, Lise. 2016. "Brazilian Government Announces New Education Model." *Rio Times*, September 23. Accessed August 1, 2019. https://riotimesonline.com/brazil-news/rio-politics/brazilian-government-announces-new-education-model

Brazilian Ministry of Education (MEC). http://www.mec.gov.br

Brazilian National Institute for Educational Studies and Research (INEP). http://portal.inep.gov.br/web/guest/inicio

Literacy Rates

According to the UNESCO Institute of Statistics (UIS), the literacy rate for Brazilians who are fifteen years of age and older was 92.6 percent in 2015. This result is higher than the global literacy rate of 86.3 percent. The UIS defines its data as the number of people who know how to read and write. The Instituto Brasileiro de Geografia e Estatística (IBGE) also reported data on literacy rates as part of the 2010 census: 92.2 percent for males and 92.9 for females. These positive numbers are the result of arduous work and government policies implemented since the 1960s.

Brazil has made remarkable progress in improving its literacy rate in the last three decades. The country experienced fast urbanization during the 1970s and 1980s, which coincided with an energized economy. Consequently, the government invested heavily in physical infrastructure and education during the late 1980s and early 1990s. While this data is extremely positive, it also revealed troublesome trends. In 1991, black and mixed-race Brazilians had much higher rates of illiteracy (27 percent) than their white counterparts (11 percent). In addition, the northeast regions of Brazil had a significantly higher rate of illiteracy than the more prosperous and urban southern regions. Such inequitable levels of basic education throughout the country received the attention of politicians with a social agenda.

President Luiz Inácio Lula da Silva (known simply as Lula) served at the executive office from 2003 to 2011, and he got elected on a campaign promising to improve education and literacy in Brazil. Lula argued that the education of young Brazilians was a basic human rights issue, and he launched the program Brazil Alfabetizado (Literate Brazil) with a comprehensive national literacy campaign. It quickly enrolled 1.6 million Brazilians in 2003 and 1.7 million people in 2004. The program proved to be a tremendous success. The IBGE census data for 2010 revealed that illiteracy rates had dropped to 9.6 percent nationwide. More specific data also illustrated that the greater literacy gains were actually in rural and poor regions of the country, while larger cities also demonstrated minor gains. Such data also shows that the literacy disparity that existed among different regions of Brazil was becoming less noticeable. While the public school system is still struggling to improve the education of all Brazilians nowadays, the country has made tremendous gains in literacy rates and overall school attendance.

See also: Chapter 3: Lula da Silva, Luiz Inácio (1945–). Chapter 8: Overview; Bolsa Família: Welfare Program with Education Incentives; Public Education: Elementary and Secondary Schooling.

Further Reading

Bartlett, Lesley. 2009. *The Word and the World: The Cultural Politics of Literacy in Brazil.* New York: Hampton Press.

Brazil Alfabetizado (Literate Brazil) Official Website. http://brasilalfabetizado.fnde.gov.br

Instituto Brasileiro de Geografia e Estatística—Brazilian Institute of Geography and Statistics (IBGE). 2010. "Census 2010." Brasilia. Accessed May 15, 2019. http://ibge.gov.br

Logan, Andrew. 2015. "Increasing Literacy Rates in Brazil." *Borgen Magazine,* July 1. Accessed May 15, 2019. http://www.borgenmagazine.com/increasing-literacy-rates-brazil

UNESCO Institute of Statistics: Literacy Rate in Brazil. http://uis.unesco.org/en/topic/literacy

Private, International, and Religious Schools

Public schools represent a stark contrast to private education in Brazil. While the public school system has increased attendance and literacy rates in the last twenty years, it still suffers from classroom overcrowding and teachers who lack the appropriate class materials and professional development training. In addition, the state and municipal governments cannot keep up with the construction of sufficient schools; consequently, it is quite common for Brazilian schools to run up to three separate shifts with only four hours of instruction per day. This is the social context in which most middle- and upper-class Brazilians choose to enroll their children in private schools. Private education traditionally offers small class sizes, a more rigorous curriculum, and often a religious foundation. Private schools in Brazil essentially belong to three categories: international, religious, and nondenominational.

International schools are usually accredited in another country, and they follow a foreign-approved curriculum. Some of the most popular international schools are linked to the United States, France, Germany, and Great Britain. They offer students a bilingual education system that prepares Brazilian students to continue their education abroad. These schools tend to be located in major metropolitan areas, such as Rio de Janeiro, São Paulo, and Brasília. As a result, they have a diverse student population with children from multiple countries. The Escola Britânica de São Paulo (St. Paul's School), the American School of Brasilia, and the American School of Rio de Janeiro usually have a waiting list due to their high reputation. When it comes to the cost of tuition, international schools are the highest among most private schools, especially if they offer an international baccalaureate diploma.

Religious private schools are extremely popular in Brazil, especially with middle-class Brazilian families. These institutions cost a bit less than the international private schools, but they provide a religious foundation that is highly desirable in Brazil, especially at Catholic and Protestant schools. In addition, most religious schools provide a strong curriculum in foreign languages. They are available not only in large urban centers but also in medium-size cities such as Salvador, Belo Horizonte, and Fortaleza. For example, the Colégio Adventista de Rio de Janeiro is extremely popular.

Nonreligious private schools are an improvement over the underfunded public school system, and they are usually the best value for a private education in Brazil. These schools are accredited in Brazil, and they follow a national curriculum, but it is usually enhanced with foreign languages and more recently a science orientation based on STEM pathways (science, technology, education, and math). Selective private nondenominational schools also prepare students to obtain an international baccalaureate high school diploma. In addition, they prepare students extremely well for the *vestibular* university entrance exam. For example, the Escola Dinamis in Rio de Janeiro has earned a reputation for its advanced curriculum, an integrated digital technology, and a comprehensive sports program.

While the Brazilian public school system still enrolls almost 80 percent of all students, the number of families who select private schools has increased during the 2010s since the booming economy has moved more Brazilians into the middle class.

See also: Chapter 6: Education and Upward Mobility. Chapter 8: Overview; Higher Education and Major Universities.

Further Reading

Edwards, Todd L. 2008. *Brazil: A Global Studies Handbook*. Santa Barbara, CA: ABC-CLIO.

Fujikawa Nes, Cynthia. 2015. "The Brazilian Education System." *Brazilian Business*, August 12. Accessed July 11, 2019. http://thebrazilbusiness.com/article/the-brazilian-educational-system

Public Education: Elementary and Secondary Schooling

The Brazilian constitution of 1988 defines education as a universal right, and it makes the government responsible for the task to protect it and promote it. To keep improving education, the National Education Guidelines Framework Law (LBD) implemented comprehensive reforms in 1996 and 2010 to develop a national curriculum for elementary and secondary schools, establish evaluation rubrics for education at all levels, define parameters for vocational training, codify the number of instructional days, and determine how institutions will be evaluated at municipal, state, and federal levels.

Since 2010, the Brazilian education system follows a 9 + 3 pattern: nine years of compulsory primary education and three years of secondary education. This structure was established by the LBD, and it applies to all public and private schools. Primary

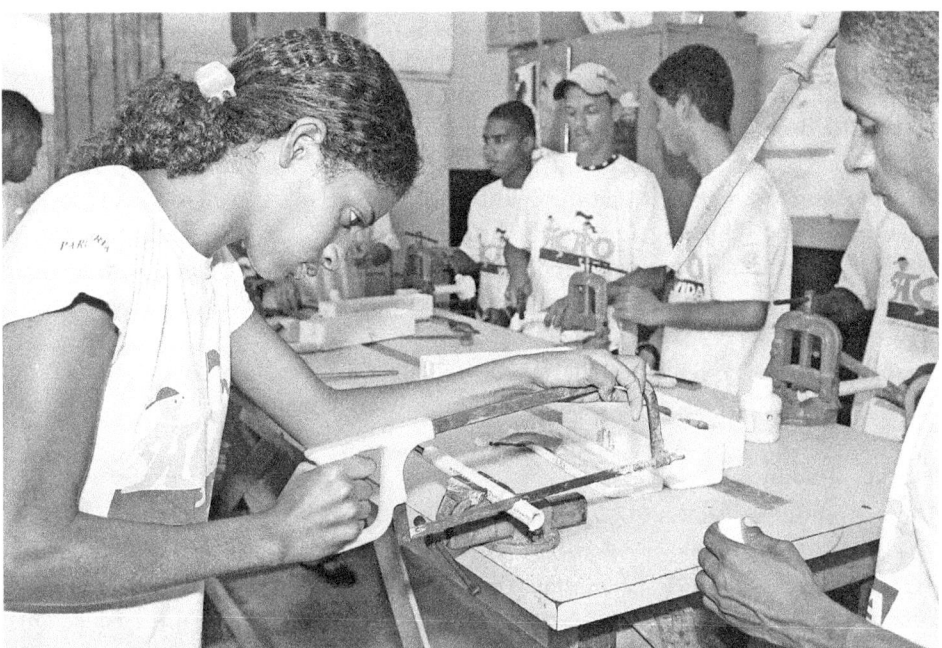

Students who do not attend university often train for a practical trade in order to obtain a job. This young woman is training to become a fitter or plumber in Recife City, Brazil. (Sjors737/Dreamstime.com)

education is called *ensino fundamental* in Brazil; it includes elementary (six years) and middle school (three years) education. It is mandatory for all six- to fourteen-year-old children in Brazil. Federal guidelines require a curriculum that includes Portuguese language, mathematics, science, history, physical education, and geography. Upon completion, students receive a *certificado de ensino fundamental*. Secondary education (*ensino médio*) is for fifteen- to eighteen-year-old minors who might be interested in future university studies. The high school curriculum requires Portuguese, mathematics, geography, history, sociology, biology, chemistry, physical education, and a foreign language (usually English). Upon completion, students receive a *certificado de ensino médio*, which is required for university admissions. Secondary education is not compulsory in Brazil, but the government offers the option of a vocational high school for students who might not attend university but are interested in learning a trade leading to a job right after high school.

Contemporary Brazil faces tremendous challenges to improve its public education system. As the largest public school system in Latin America, it suffers from inadequate infrastructure and insufficient facilities to even house all its students. As a result, classroom overcrowding is almost the norm, and local schools offer education in shifts that usually include only four hours of instruction a day (morning, midday, and evening shifts). In addition, teachers receive low pay, do not have enough professional development opportunities, and lack basic classroom supplies to teach effectively.

Brazil experienced a severe economic recession during the 2010s, which directly affects funding for education. The federal government under President Michel Temer (1940 –) authorized strict austerity measures in 2016 that have further restricted funds for public education and retirement pensions. While the current fiscal budget cuts and social street protests offer a gloomy picture for the future of public education in Brazil, it is important to highlight that the country has made remarkable progress in the last twenty years by achieving a national literacy rate of 92 percent. In addition, national welfare programs with monetary incentives for education (such as Bolsa Família) have contributed to higher enrollment numbers and lower dropout rates nationwide.

See also: Chapter 3: Temer, Michel (1940–). Chapter 8: Overview; Bolsa Família: Welfare Program with Education Incentives; Literacy Rates.

Further Reading

Chiesa Gonçalves, Aline. 2017. *The Influence of the Bolsa Família Program in Education.* Düsseldorf, Germany: Novas Edições Acadêmicas.

Stanek, Christina. 2013. "The Educational System of Brazil." *IEM Spotlight* 10, no. 1 (March). Accessed July 21, 2019. https://www.pdf-book-search.com/educational/the-educational-system-of-brazil-nafsa-association-of.html

Scientific and Technical Research

In the last three decades, Brazil has significantly increased its international ranking in research and development in the fields of science and technology. It has come a long way since President José Sarney (1985–1990) created the Ministry of Science and Technology in 1985. To promote development in these fields, the government created specific research centers: the National Council for Scientific and Technological Development (CNPq), the Funding Authority for Studies and Projects (FINEP), the National Institute of Technology (INT), the Secretariat for Computer and Automation Policy (SPIA), the National Institute of Amazonian Research (INPA), and the National Institute of Space Research (INPE).

Currently, almost 85 percent of scientific research is funded by the federal government, and it takes place mostly at university centers. Federal research funds are prioritized for agriculture, industry, health, infrastructure, and defense. This concentration has yielded tangible results. Innovative agribusiness technology has made Brazil the second-largest producer and exporter of food in the world, only after the United States. Industrial research also delivers specific technological advances to large government-owned industries such as Petrobras. In fact, Petrobras (the government-owned oil company) holds more registered patents than any other Brazilian company. The defense industry has also benefitted from government-funded research since Embraer manufactures both civilian and military aircraft that have made Brazil an economic powerhouse in international markets.

While government funding for scientific and technical research has provided important advantages, it also has an inherent bureaucratic process that restricts innovation. Consequently, a cluster of recent private nonprofit centers emerged as an alternative for research and development. These social organizations have more flexibility to purchase equipment, hire specialized personnel, accept proposals for research, and enter into contracts with private companies. As of 2019, there are six of these very successful social organizations:

National Center for Research in Energy and Materials (CNPEM)
Institute for the Sustainable Development of the Amazon Forest (IDSM)
National Research and Teaching Network (RNP)
Institute for Pure and Applied Mathematics (IMPA)
Center for Management and Strategic Studies (CGEE)
Brazilian Research and Industrial Innovation Enterprise (EMBRAPII)

Brazil experienced an economic boom at the beginning of the twenty-first century, which stimulated the notion to improve scientific research by facilitating investments by private companies. In 2007, the Brazilian Congress approved a new law called the Plan of Action for Science, Technology, and Innovation. It provided tax incentives for individual corporations, created a goal of providing 100,000 university scholarships for doctoral degrees in science and technology fields, as well as the creation of 400 new vocational learning centers throughout the country. The result was that corporations such as Samsung, Motorola, and IBM created or expanded research facilities in Brazil. Furthermore, the federal ministry changed its name to the more inclusive Ministry of Science, Technology, Innovation, and Communications (MCTIC) in 2018 to be more inclusive of all research needs.

FOREIGN LANGUAGE EDUCATION

Most Brazilians receive instruction of a foreign language during their early formative years. The government makes foreign language education mandatory beginning with middle school (*ensino fundamental II*) from grades 6–9, and throughout high school (*ensino médio*) in grades 10–12. English is the foreign language that is taught the most, followed by Spanish. On rare occasions, French is sometimes included in the curriculum of mostly private schools.

During the last twenty years, Brazil has become a leading economic powerhouse in South America, and the need for fluency in foreign languages has increased dramatically. English is the primary foreign language used for international treaties and economic agreements. Consequently, many Brazilians take private courses to learn conversational English. Since Brazil is also a leader in the MERCOSUR economic bloc with Argentina, Paraguay, Uruguay, Bolivia, and Venezuela, the demand for Spanish has increased as well.

Public and private research funding tends to flow based on economic conditions. The global economic crisis from 2008 to 2014 affected Brazil deeply, reducing levels of funding for research and development. However, Brazil technically emerged from its economic depression in 2017, and the federal government is currently facing its own budgetary challenges. Consequently, the level of funding for scientific and technical innovation is pivoting toward private industry.

See also: Chapter 4: Embraer, Empresa Brasileira de Aeronáutica; Petrobras, the National Oil Company. Chapter 8: Overview.

Further Reading

Embraer Aircraft Corporation. https://embraer.com/global/en

Hyuda de Luna Pedrosa, Renato and Hernan Chaimovich. 2015. "Brazil: UNESCO Science Report towards 2030," in *UNESCO Report,* 210–229. Paris: UNESCO.

Ministry of Science, Technology, Innovation, and Communications. http://www.mctic.gov.br

Petrobras Oil Company. http://www.petrobras.com.br/en

Unipalmares, University for Afro-Descendent Students

The Universidade da Cidadania de Zumbi dos Palmares (most commonly known simply as Unipalmares) was founded in 2003 in the humble Luz neighborhood of Saõ Paulo. It was established to provide Brazilian black students an opportunity for access to higher education, but overall it aims to serve underprivileged students in the country. The name of the institution is based on Zumbi de Palmares, a former black warrior and king of Quilombo de Palmares, the largest settlement of runaway slaves in seventeenth-century colonial Brazil. The institution prepares people of black ancestry to obtain a university education in order to facilitate access to professional careers with better pay so they can begin to earn representation in higher government positions, the legal system, the medical profession, and the business world.

Unipalmares offers a comprehensive set of services that include outreach programs, flexible class schedules, and tutoring assistance to help students succeed on their academic pathways. The institution enrolls roughly 1,300 students. It actively recruits students coming from the public school system, and it offers special seminars to improve their skills necessary to score higher in the required *vestibular* entrance exam. Since most of the student population works during the day, the vast majority of the classes offered at Unipalmares are held during the evening and night hours to facilitate attendance. In addition, a crucial component of the curriculum places students in internships directly related to their field of study in order to create opportunities for employment after graduation, especially in business, health care, and finance.

Unipalmares reserves 50 percent of its available spaces specifically for black Afro-Brazilians. That number is potentially an immense pool of students in a country where over 50 percent of the national population claims African ancestry. According to the 2010 census data and the 2016 population estimates, the Brazilian Institute of Geography and Statistics (IBGE) reported that Brazil has a national population of 206 million people, and almost 111 million people are descendants of African slaves. However, racial identification is a complex concept in Brazil because racial mixing has occurred for over 500 years. As a result, the majority of Brazilians do not identify as white or black, but rather a combination somewhere in the middle of a racial continuum, such as *mulatto* (black and white) or *pardo* (mixed race). Unipalmares aims to provide increased access to higher education to disadvantaged students of all backgrounds.

In 2008, Unipalmares signed a joint agreement with historically black colleges and universities (HBCUs) in the United States for an exchange program titled U.S.-Brazil Joint Access Plan to Education. Unipalmares and Xavier University agreed to cooperate in an exchange program that promotes racial equality, fights against discrimination, and increases educational opportunities for Afro-descendent youth.

See also: Chapter 2: Slavery, Abolition, and African Heritage. Chapter 6: African Ancestry and Influence. Chapter 8: Overview; *Vestibular* Testing for College Admission.

Further Reading

FUVEST Vestibular Test for College Admission Official Website. https://www.fuvest.br

Instituto Brasileiro de Geografia e Estatística—Brazilian Institute of Geography and Statistics (IBGE). "Censo 2010." Accessed May 1, 2019. http://ibge.gov.br

Plummer, Robert. 2006. "Black Brazil Seeks a Better Future." *BBC News,* September 25, 2006. Accessed May 1, 2019. http://news.bbc.co.uk/2/hi/americas/5357842.stm

Universidade de Zumbi dos Palmares Official Website. http://www.zumbidospalmares.edu.br

Vestibular Testing for College Admission

The *vestibular* is a rigorous college-entrance exam that Brazilian students take as part of the university admissions process. Since the academic year usually starts in February, the *vestibular* exam is offered between November and January. University-bound students must pick their major before taking the admissions test since their choice determines which test they take. The *vestibular* addresses both broad areas and specific disciplines; consequently, it usually takes several days to complete. Another important fact to consider is that while several private universities are highly regarded in Brazil, competition is even more intense for students seeking admission to one of the federal universities, which are funded by the government, offer high-caliber academics, and are completely free to students.

The *vestibular* is not a national test, but it is the name for an admission test that may take different forms depending on the institution. The most commonly used *vestibular* is administered by the FUVEST (Fundação Universitaria para o Vestibular), which is used by a large number of Brazilian universities. The test is divided into two stages. The first stage includes multiple-choice questions in predetermined disciplines including math, history, biology, physics, foreign language, geography, Portuguese language, Portuguese literature, and Brazilian literature. The exam is corrected electronically. Only the students with the best scores are allowed to proceed to the second stage, which consists of answering questions in writing (usually ten short paragraphs and one longer essay) spread over three days. The writing samples are corrected by a wide range of university professors. Then the last part of the second stage consists of a third day of testing based only on material for a specific discipline (history, psychology, mathematics, etc.). These exams are then graded by a group of academics who ultimately rank all the applicants based on a total score. Depending on the number of university vacancies for each major, only the top-score students are allowed to enroll in their intended major. It is not unusual to have 150 applicants for each vacancy at a prestigious university. Other universities have their own *vestibular* test for admissions with slight variations. However, they all include a combination of multiple-choice and written components.

The *vestibular* process for university student selection has sparked controversies. The most common allegation is that the content of the test favors students from private schools who cover a higher-level curriculum and can afford to take preparatory courses, but it creates a disadvantage to students who struggle to make it through the poor educational system of public schools. The result is that the network of public federal universities now provides a bonus of 15 percent in test scores for students who graduated from public high schools. In addition, the controversial practice of affirmative action currently implemented by the federal government offers racial quotas to students of African and Indian ancestry. Since 2005, all federal universities must abide by a quota to save 50 percent of their vacancies for students of such racial backgrounds and those who came from the public school system. Such racial quotas continue to spark controversy every year, especially at high-caliber universities.

See also: Chapter 8: Overview; Affirmative Action Policies; Higher Education and Major Universities; Unipalmares, University for Afro-Descendent Students.

Further Reading

Alves, Lise. 2015. "University ENEM Entrance Exam in Brazil Attracts Millions." *Rio Times*, October 26. Accessed July 13, 2019. https://riotimesonline.com/brazil-news/rio-politics/university-entrance-exam-in-brazil-attracts-millions

FUVEST Vestibular Test for College Admission Official Website. https://www.fuvest.br

Ministry of Education and Culture (MEC) Official Website. http://mec.gov.br

CHAPTER 9

LANGUAGE

OVERVIEW

Based on population estimates for 2019, the Portuguese language had roughly 261 million speakers worldwide, and 211 million of them are Brazilian. It is the official language of seven countries (Brazil, Portugal, Cape Verde, Guinea-Bissau, Mozambique, Angola, as well as São Tomé and Príncipe). In addition, it is designated as the co-official language of Equatorial Guinea, East Timor, and Macau. Due to its geographical position, Brazilian Portuguese is often compared to Spanish. However, Brazil is linguistically different from its Spanish-speaking neighbors that surround it in South America. Actually, it is a common misconception to think that if someone speaks Spanish, they should be able to speak Portuguese. While they are both romance languages with Latin roots, Portuguese is more complex than Spanish in multiple ways. For example, Portuguese has thirteen vowels (with both open and nasalized sounds), and Spanish has only five. Portuguese also has different verb tenses (including the use of future subjunctive) that are no longer used in Spanish. The result is that Brazilians can usually understand their Spanish-speaking neighbors a lot more than the other way around.

The use of the Portuguese language in Brazil is the result of the European conquest in 1500. However, it was not adopted right away. When the Portuguese started arriving en masse in Brazil during the early 1530s, they were perplexed by the vast number of languages and indigenous groups they found along the Brazilian coastline. It was the Jesuit priests who developed a *língua geral* (common language) made up of the most common features of multiple indigenous languages they encountered. This hybrid language was used for over 150 years as the main form of communication between the Portuguese settlers, religious leaders, and their indigenous labor force. By the late 1700s, the transition had been made to Portuguese, and it was established as the official language in 1807 when King João VI of Portugal was deposed, and he moved his entire court to Rio de Janeiro. Brazil eventually became independent in 1822, and it adopted Portuguese as its official language. At the time, the production of literature in the new country emphasized the description of nature, the concept of nationalism, and the use of colloquial language. In the absence of well-established orthographic conventions, Brazilian and Portuguese writers began to divert in the spelling they used in multiple words, which then affected pronunciation.

The Portuguese language has historically borrowed lexicon from multiple sources, including Latin, Arabic, German, and Italian. In addition, Brazilian Portuguese also borrowed heavily from local African and indigenous languages, especially to name regional flora, fauna, and musical instruments. The influence of Tupi-Guarani was particularly strong. Linguists often describe Portuguese as a language that is both conservative and modern at the same time. For example, it retains the old medieval spelling and pronunciation of the letter "f" in words such as *ferro* (iron) while such archaic spelling has already disappeared in other romance languages like Spanish. On the other hand, Brazilian Portuguese was always very open about borrowing words to enrich its lexicon. In recent times, it continues to adopt large numbers of words from English related to technology and international business.

By the late 1800s, Brazil and Portugal technically shared the same language, but the lack of an orthographic agreement between the two countries led to two different—but related—systems of spelling and pronunciation. They became known as Brazilian Portuguese (BP) and European Portuguese (EP). This process continued for over one hundred years. Today, educated people from both countries can still communicate with one another, but it is also likely that working-class Brazilians and their counterparts from Portugal would have a hard time understanding each other. The differences apply mostly to vocabulary, a few grammatical constructions, and different pronunciation patterns. A common analogy is to compare Portuguese to the use of English in Great Britain and the United States, except that the difference between BP and EP is much greater and markedly more noticeable. To address these concerns, the Academy of Letters in Brazil and its counterpart called the Academy of Sciences in Portugal have been meeting continuously for decades to discuss uses and changes to the Portuguese language. Their purpose, however, is not to develop strict uses of the language that attempt to conserve its structure and purity. Instead, they attempt to bridge the gap between the two main versions of Portuguese by developing guidelines for a universal spelling system.

After multiple failed attempts, Brazil and Portugal finally approved the Portuguese Language Orthographic Agreement in 1990 as their best attempt to reach a universal spelling system. However, implementation of linguistic policy takes time. Brazil ratified the agreement in 2004 and actually implemented it in 2009. Portugal signed it into law in 2008. The new accord was subsequently approved by the other five Portuguese-speaking nations. The overall purpose of the reform was to standardize legal documents, facilitate Internet searches, improve literacy, and promote the language on the global stage. All the signatory countries agreed to a transition period of six years, and the agreement became mandatory on January 1, 2015.

The Novo Acordo Ortográfico da Língua Portuguesa requires specific spelling changes:

- The letters "c" and "p" must be eliminated when they are silent (*optimo* → *otimo*).
- Diaeresis marks (ü) and acute accents will be eliminated from diphthongs (éi, ói).
- The letters "k," "w," and "y" will be added to the Portuguese alphabet for the first time.
- New rules for capitalization and hyphenation are specified.
- A few divergent local spellings will be accepted as legitimate (*anónimo* vs. *anônimo*).

Leaders from the Science Academy of Lisbon and the Brazilian Academy of Letters claim that the new orthographic agreement will eliminate 98 percent of the spelling discrepancies that existed between Brazilian Portuguese and European Portuguese. Time will tell.

People visiting Brazil for tourism or business quickly realize that Brazilians are very expressive with their hands and body language. Nonverbal communication is crucial for daily social interactions. First of all, personal space in Brazil is a lot closer than what Americans consider appropriate. Brazilians are often described as more expressive and affectionate than other European and North American cultures. In addition, Brazilian culture is rather casual, and the concept of time does not seem to have the same urgency for punctuality as it does in other cultures (except in the business world). While Brazilian Portuguese has become a symbol of national pride, the government was aware that it also needed a language policy to address the needs of Brazilians who cannot physically speak.

The deaf population of Brazil is over 3 million strong. On April 24, 2002, the National Congress of Brazil approved a national sign language law on April 24, 2002, that requires the availability of Brazilian Sign Language in educational settings and throughout all federal government services. The law was fully implemented in 2005 under Parliamentary decree 5626, and it is applicable in all states and regions of Brazil. Deaf Brazilians use sign language known as Língua Brasileira de Sinais (or its acronym LIBRAS) as their primary language of communication. The most active organization in Brazil that

---

DAYS OF THE WEEK IN PORTUGUESE

The days of the week follow a unique pattern in Portuguese. Each day does not have an individual name. Instead, they are as follows:

English	Portuguese	Abbreviation
Sunday	Domingo	Dom
Monday	Segunda-feira	2ª
Tuesday	Terça-feira	3ª
Wednesday	Quarta-feira	4ª
Thursday	Quinta-feira	5ª
Friday	Sexta-feira	6ª
Saturday	Sábado	Sab

The general belief is that the first day of the week should be offered to God. Therefore, Sunday is considered God's Day from the Latin root *domini*. After that, the days are simply called *feira* (fair). For example, Tuesday is *terça-feira* (third fair). Saturday (Sábado) makes reference to the Sabbath in Hebrew. In addition, the word *feira* is commonly dropped to simply indicate the number of the day. For example, a college class that meets from Monday to Friday 10–11 a.m. would simply be listed as "2ª a 6ª às 10–11 a.m."

continuously advocates for the education, rights, and integration of the deaf population is the Federação Nacional de Educação e Integração dos Surdos (National Federation of Deaf Education and Integration), or FENESIS.

Language is a crucial component of cultural identity, and Brazilians are certainly aware that Portuguese is a legacy of their colonial heritage. However, they managed to create a version of the language that can be recognized as truly Brazilian based on its cadence and pronunciation. Moreover, as Brazil has gained prominence as an economic powerhouse in South America, its neighboring countries often teach Portuguese as a foreign language because it is viewed as a practical language that could open opportunities in the future.

Further Reading

Azevedo, Milton. 2005. *Portuguese: A Linguistic Introduction.* Cambridge, UK: Cambridge University Press.

Bagno, Marcos. 2004. *Português ou Brasileiro: Um convite à pesquisa.* São Paulo: Parábola.

Barrachini-Haß, Yasmin. 2016. *Indigenous Languages in Brazil. A Country between Monolingualism and Plurilingualism.* Munich, Germany: Grin.

Brazilian Academy of Letters. http://www.academia.org.br

Crocitti, John J., and Monique Vallance (eds.). 2012. *Brazil Today: An Encyclopedia of Life in the Republic* (2 volumes). Santa Barbara, CA: ABC-CLIO.

Instituto Brasileiro de Geografia e Estatística—Brazilian Institute of Geography and Statistics (IBGE). 2010. "Census 2010." Accessed July 3, 2019. http://ibge.gov.br

Lawless, Teresa, and Janie DiCioccio. 2015. "The Portuguese Spelling Reform." *Argos Multilingual,* March 25. Accessed July 3, 2019. http://www.argosmultilingual.com/blog/the-portuguese-spelling-reform

Língua Brasileira de Sinais, LIBRAS/Brazilian Sign Language. http://www.libras.org

Formality Levels

Brazilian culture is rather informal. However, it is also imperative to consider the social context in order to function well in both formal and casual settings. On one extreme of the levels of formality, the Portuguese language uses specific titles to demonstrate respect for specific people of positions. For example, Brazilians express reverence to multiple government officials (judges, federal secretaries, ministers, presidents, governors, and ambassadors) by addressing them with the honorifics Vossa Excelência or Sua Excelência (Your Excellency). University presidents or rectors are usually addressed by the honorific title Vossa Magnificência.

In the business world, formality is also crucial. Business executives tend to wear conservative business attire, especially in corporate-oriented cities such as São Paulo. Most businesspersons use formal titles during initial introductions, but they might move toward using a mid-level honorific of Senhor or Senhora (Mister or Misses) rather soon, and then transition to addressing people on a first-name basis once they are well-acquainted colleagues.

Outside of the corporate world, Brazilians also use the titles Senhor or Senhora to address an older person or a yet-unfamiliar acquaintance. In addition, people apply the title Doutor (Doctor) to make reference to a person with a doctoral degree, but also to address someone that (in their view) is well educated beyond the average level in their respective communities. In rural settings, for example, people with adequate oratory skills and basic knowledge to understand official documents are often called Doutor. In general daily communication, Brazilians use Você (You) to address people familiar to them, including coworkers, someone their own age, younger children, and people perceived to be at their own social and economic level.

Overall, however, Brazilians are rather casual. Most Brazilians have four names: first and middle names, the mother's last name, and the father's last name. Consequently, most people want to use a shortened version of their name. In fact, many Brazilians simply call each other by their first name; it makes them feel closer to one another. It is also rather common to use nicknames. Therefore, populist politicians, celebrities, and famous soccer players are often addressed only by their first name or even a nickname. Few people would recognize the iconic soccer star Pelé by his full name of Edson Arantes do Nascimento. Former presidents Luiz Inácio Lula da Silva and Dilma Vana Rousseff are popularly known simply as Lula and Dilma. Celebrities follow a similar approach. On contemporary television, Xuxa, the iconic blond hostess of a children's show, never uses her given name Maria da Graça Meneghel.

Finally, the concept of time has to be examined within the social context of Brazilian culture. Punctuality is definitely expected in the corporate world. However, Brazilians view time not in traditional hours but rather as a sequence of events. For example, meetings often start late, mostly because an earlier meeting took longer than expected. This version of time also applies to casual settings. A family might have the intention of arriving to a party on time. However, if friends happen to show up at the house unannounced, the family would consider it rude to not socialize for a while, even if it means they would arrive late at the party. Most Brazilians function daily in a social environment that is a blend of formal and informal interactions.

See also: Chapter 9: Overview.

Further Reading

Armour, Nancy. 2014. "Nicknames Reflect Brazilians' Affection for Familiarity." *USA Today*, June 11. Accessed July 22, 2019. http://sports.usatoday.com/2014/06/11/nicknames-reflect-brazilians-affection-for-familiarity

Richard, Christopher, and Leslie Jermyn. 2002. *Cultures of the World: Brazil*. New York: Marshall Cavendish.

Utsumi, Igor. 2014. "Name Prefixes, Titles, and Honorifics in Brazil." *Brazil Business*, May 16. Accessed July 22, 2019. http://thebrazilbusiness.com/article/name-prefixes-titles-and-honorifics-in-brazil

Hand Gestures

Brazilians are very animated in daily communication and social interactions. Depending on the level of formality, greetings often include a possible combination of handshakes, a hug (*abraço*), and multiple kisses (*beijinhos*) on the cheek. In addition, Brazilians often use physical contact in a conversation to be clear or emphasize a point they are trying to make. This approach might include a much closer personal space, touching an arm, clear eye contact, and using a lot of hand gestures to convey an opinion more convincingly.

Nonverbal communication varies from country to country. Several hand gestures used in Brazil have similar meaning in the United States, such as giving the thumbs-up to indicate that everything is fine or to express approval. However, there are multiple Brazilian hand expressions that foreigners might not always interpret appropriately. The following five examples are a good illustration of such gestures.

Delicious! When Brazilians want to express that a meal was delicious, they touch the fleshy part of the earlobe with both the thumb and forefinger while simultaneously wiggling it a few times. They also pout their lips as if to throw an air kiss.

Whatever! Shrugging the shoulders while also shaking both hands back and forth so that the fingertips of both hands brush each other means "It does not really matter" or simply "I do not care."

I've had enough! When Brazilians hold all five fingers together (using both hands) and point them up, they are trying to express either that the place is very crowded or that they have had enough of a situation. Depending on the social context, this gesture could be interpreted as an offensive attitude.

Good luck! The *figa* is the most recognized good luck sign in Brazil. It is used as a hand gesture by placing the thumb between the index and middle fingers and wiggling it a few times. Its purpose is to keep curses away that might cause pain and suffering. The symbol of this hand gesture is often given as a small amulet or good luck charm to keep on a key chain or to be worn with a necklace. People must be given these charms and never purchase one for themselves.

Avoid the OK gesture! The OK gesture used in the United States (forming a circle by putting the thumb and index finger together) has an entirely different meaning in Brazilian culture. In fact, it should be avoided in Brazil as it is interpreted as an extremely obscene gesture that makes reference to the end portion of the human colon, and it is likely to start a fight. It is equivalent to vigorously giving someone the middle finger in the United States.

See also: Chapter 9: Overview. Chapter 10: Overview.

Further Reading

Goffan, Havi. 2011. "The Meaning of Gestures: Body Language in Brazil." Hispanic Marketing, April 12. Accessed June 20, 2019. http://hispanic-marketing.com/the-meaning-of-gestures-body-language-in-brazil

Richard, Christopher, and Leslie Jermyn. 2002. *Cultures of the World: Brazil*. New York: Marshall Cavendish.

Schmiedekampf, Katrin. 2010. "A Quick Guide to Hand Gestures of the World." *Guardian*, December 12. Accessed June 20, 2019. https://www.theguardian.com/science/gallery/2010/dec/12/what-hand-gestures-mean

Indigenous Languages

According to the official 2010 census carried out by the Instituto Brasileiro de Geografia e Estatística (IBGE), Brazil had 185,712,213 inhabitants, which makes it the country with the fifth-largest population in the world (after China, India, the United States, and Indonesia). Since that census, the official IBGE estimated population for 2018 has already increased to 211 million people, and 350,000 of them belong to an indigenous group. While the minority indigenous people make up only 0.2 percent of the national population, they have a rich linguistic diversity. They speak over 170 indigenous languages. There are three indigenous minority groups with sizable populations of over 10,000 people: the Tikuna (settled along the Solimões River in the Amazon Region), the Guarani (found mostly toward the south of the country near Paraguay), and the Yanomami (living on the mountainous region near the border with Venezuela). In addition, there are a few tribes living in small isolated villages with only a few dozen speakers of a unique indigenous language. However, the United Nations Educational, Scientific, and Cultural Organization (UNESCO) has declared most of the 170 indigenous languages of Brazil anywhere from vulnerable to critically endangered due to the small number of speakers who are still alive.

Throughout most of the twentieth century, the Brazilian government policy toward indigenous languages was essentially to encourage assimilation with Portuguese monolingualism. However, multiple indigenous organizations viewed language as a crucial component of cultural identity. Consequently, they continued to lobby at the federal level to obtain control of their local schools in order to teach their own languages and keep them alive. When a new constitution was approved in 1988 (the version still in effect today), Article 231 specifically granted Brazilian Indian groups complete rights over their cultures and languages. This legal definition allowed local indigenous groups to work with their respective states to develop language policies to be implemented into the curriculum of their local schools. The states are responsible for funding the training of indigenous language teachers. By teaching indigenous languages to their children, minority groups could insure the continuation of such languages and cultural traditions. This collaboration became clearly successful in the town of São Gabriel de Cocheira, located in perhaps the most multilingual region of Brazil in the State of Amazonas. The town is the central location for a region that expands almost 70,000 square miles (roughly 112,000 square kilometers). Throughout the area, there are 409 indigenous villages that manage 165 elementary schools following a bilingual curriculum teaching Portuguese and multiple indigenous languages belonging to the Tukano linguistic group. In addition, other indigenous groups have gained enough political influence to declare their native tongues as co-official languages of the municipalities where they live. For example, within the State of Matto Grosso do Sul, the towns of Tacuru and Paranhos both accepted Guarani as a co-official language. In the state of Tocantis, the municipality of Tocantínia accepted Akwê Xerente as co-official language with Portuguese. In Amazonas, the town of São Gabriel de Cocheira approved Tukano, Baniwa, and Nheengatu as co-official languages as well.

While the 1988 constitution provided legal rights that allowed indigenous groups to take control over their language policy, a wider economic problem has recently emerged that has had an impact on regional language education. The IBGE population geographic statistics and estimates for 2016 revealed a dramatic increase in urbanization. Large numbers of indigenous people were simply abandoning their local villages in search of a better life in large cities. Since the policy to rescue the use of indigenous languages was based on teaching them in Indian villages, the government did not have a plan to promote them at large urban settings. As a result, multiple organizations—such as the Brazilian National Indian Foundation (FUNAI) and the Federation of Indian Organizations of Rio Negro (FOIRN)—have argued that this contemporary problem needs to be reexamined in order to obtain funding to teach indigenous languages to minority Indian groups who live in urban settings. The overall concern is that a linguistic shift might already be in process where Portuguese is becoming the dominant language for members of Indian groups, and their respective indigenous languages will become extinct during the twenty-first century.

See also: Chapter 8: Overview. Chapter 9: Overview.

Further Reading

De Oliveira, Gilvan Muller. 2001. "Endangered Languages in Town: The Urbanization of Indigenous Languages in the Brazilian Amazon." *Cultural Survival,* June. Accessed June 5, 2019. https://www.culturalsurvival.org/publications/cultural-survival-quarterly/endangered-languages-town-urbanization-indigenous

Gaspar, Lúcia. 2009. *Indigenous Language in Brazil.* Recife, Brazil: Joaquim Nabuco Foundation.

Instituto Brasileiro de Geografia e Estatística—Brazilian Institute of Geography and Statistics (IBGE). 2010. "Censo 2010." Accessed June 20, 2019. http://ibge.gov.br

Moseley, Christopher. 2010. *Atlas of the World's Languages in Danger.* Paris: UNESCO. Accessed June 5, 2019. http://www.unesco.org/new/en/culture/themes/endangered-languages/atlas-of-languages-in-danger

Rohter, Larry. 2005. "Language Born of Colonialism Thrives Again in Amazon." *New York Times,* August 28. Accessed June 5, 2019. http://www.nytimes.com/2005/08/28/world/americas/language-born-of-colonialism-thrives-again-in-amazon.html

Nicknames

In general, Brazilian culture values informality. When most people call each other by their first name, it makes them feel closer to one another. From that point, it is not a big leap to call a person by a nickname. Therefore, it is not unusual that a populist politician, a movie celebrity, a famous soccer player, or a child in the neighborhood is addressed by either a first name or a nickname.

Many famous people in Brazil are known only by their nicknames, sometimes even more so than their real given names. This approach gives their fans and followers a sense of closeness and friendliness. For example, soccer stars are famous for wearing only their nickname on the official team jerseys. Few people would recognize the iconic soccer star Pelé by his real given name of Edson Arantes do Nascimento. Soccer international star Neymar da Silva Santos Júnior is simply known by his first name: Neymar. In addition, populist politicians use nicknames to appeal to the masses. Former presidents Luiz Inácio Lula da Silva and Dilma Vana Rousseff are popularly known simply as Lula and Dilma. Their constituents (mostly from the Partido dos Trabalhadores, PT Political Party) chant their shortened names at political rallies throughout the country. The same occurs in the field of arts and entertainment. One of the most famous baroque artists of Brazil is mostly recognized by the nickname Alejadinho ("the little cripple," due to his body deformities), and not by his real name Antônio Francisco Lisboa. On contemporary television, Xuxa, the iconic blond hostess of a children's show, never uses her given name Maria da Graça Meneghel.

The birth certificate of most Brazilians follows the convention of including four names: first and middle names, the mother's last name, and then the father's last name. Consequently, most people want to shorten their name. The use of last names is just too formal. In fact, many Brazilians do not really know the last name of their own friends. In the case of nicknames, sometimes it only adds a modifier such as *inho* (small) or *ao* (big). Sometimes, a name is shortened, such as when José becomes simply Zé. Other times, they get a nickname simply because their younger siblings could not pronounce their real name. A nickname may also reflect a place of origin: Mineiro (from Minas Gerais), Baiano (from Bahia), or Carioca (from Rio de Janeiro). Affectionate nicknames sometimes reflect a physical trait of a person, such as Baixinho (Shorty). Overall, the widespread use of first names and nicknames reflects the informal aspects of Brazilian culture.

See also: Chapter 9: Overview. Chapter 15: Overview; *Futebol* (Soccer); Pelé (1940–), Ronaldinho (1980–), and Neymar (1992–).

Further Reading

Armour, Nancy. 2014. "Nicknames Reflect Brazilians' Affection for Familiarity." *USA Today,* June 11. Accessed July 22, 2019. http://sports.usatoday.com/2014/06/11/nicknames-reflect-brazilians-affection-for-familiarity

Féderation Internationale de Football Association. 2010. "Nicknames Reign in Brazil." *FIFA .com* November 12. Accessed July 21, 2019. http://www.fifa.com/news/y=2010/m=11/news=nicknames-reign-brazil-1333656.html

Richard, Christopher, and Leslie Jermyn. 2002. *Cultures of the World: Brazil.* New York: Marshall Cavendish.

Schulz, Nick. 2006. "Why Ronaldinho Has No Last Name." *Slate News,* June 10. Accessed July 22, 2019. http://www.slate.com/articles/news_and_politics/explainer/2006/06/why_ronaldinho_has_no_last_name.html

Sign Language (LIBRAS)

On April 24, 2002, the National Congress of Brazil approved the national sign language law that requires the availability of Brazilian Sign Language in educational settings and throughout all federal government services. The law was fully implemented in 2005 under Parliamentary decree 5626, and it is applicable in all states and regions of Brazil.

Deaf communities in Brazil use sign language nationally known as Língua Brasileira de Sinais, or LIBRAS. In print media, it is also abbreviated as LSB, LGB, or LSCB. National statistics in 2016 revealed that slightly over 3 million Brazilians use LIBRAS as their primary language of communication. The most active organization in Brazil that continuously advocates for the education, rights, and integration of the deaf population is the Federação Nacional de Educação e Integração dos Surdos (National Federation of Deaf Education and Integration), or FENESIS.

Brazilian Sign Language (LIBRAS) has unique features. For example, finger spelling is done with only one hand using a manual alphabet that is very similar to the one used for French Sign Language. Overall, LIBRAS uses forty-four unique and distinct handshapes. In addition, LIBRAS does not have its own writing system. Usually, signs are written in uppercase letters presenting a description of the sign using words in Portuguese. However, the computer program called Signwriting is used in Brazil to transcribe LIBRAS signs into a printed and visual format.

Professor Fernando Capovilla is a nationally known figure who has contributed to the understanding, analysis, teaching, and dissemination of information regarding LIBRAS throughout Brazil. His research in psychology at the University of São Paulo is based on experimental cognitive science, and he has recently focused on the use of computerized sounds and phonemes to help deaf communities with the task of developing reading literacy as well as writing proficiency. In addition, he has authored and participated in the publication and creation of multiple books, encyclopedias, dictionaries, and multimedia instructional videos that directly benefit members of the deaf community and their relatives. His long list of publications and contributions to neuropsychology has advanced the national conversation about the need for continued funding for the use of LIBRAS in education and public services.

See also: Chapter 9: Overview.

Further Reading

Brazilian Sign Language Dictionary Project. http://www.signwriting.org/brazil/brazil00.html

Capovilla, Alessandra G. S., and Fernando Cesar Capovilla. 2007. *Alfabetização fônica computadorizada*, Second Edition. São Paulo, SP: Casa do Psicólogo, CNPq, Capes.

Capovilla, Fernando Cesar, and Walkiria Duarte Raphael (eds.). 2001. *Trilingual Illustrated Encyclopedia Dictionary of Brazilian Sign Language, Volumes 1 and 2*. São Paulo: Edusp Fundação Vitae.

Capovilla, Fernando Cesar, Elizeu C. Macedo, Marcelo Duduchi, Walkiria Duarte Raphael, Silva Charin, and Alessandra G. Capovilla. 1998. "SignoFone: Multimedia System Based on Brazilian Sign Language for Communication both Face to Face and Via Local Networks by the Deaf with Severe Motor Impairments." *Cognitive Science: Theory, Research and Application* 2, no. 3: 161–208.

Ethnologue. "Brazilian Sign Language." http://www.ethnologue.com/17/language/bzs

Língua Brasileira de Sinais, LIBRAS. http://www.libras.org

Müller de Quadros, Ronice et al. (eds.). 2013. *Signed Language Interpreting in Brazil*. Washington, DC: Gallaudet University Press.

SignWriting. http://www.signwriting.org

Spelling Reform

Over the centuries, the Portuguese language developed into two different but related systems: European Portuguese and Brazilian Portuguese. While neighboring Spain and France established language academies in the early 1600s to standardize their respective languages, Portugal's first attempt to establish rules for its written language came in 1911. However, it never consulted Brazil, which was now an independent nation. European Portuguese was influenced by Arabic, Spanish, French, Latin, and multiple Asian languages. Brazilian Portuguese also incorporated elements from indigenous and African languages. Consequently, Brazil and Portugal technically shared the same language, but the lack of an orthographic agreement between the two countries led to two different—but related—systems of spelling and pronunciation. Today, educated people from both countries can still communicate with one another, but it is also likely that working-class Brazilians and their counterparts from Portugal would have a hard time understanding each other.

Brazil and Portugal have tried for over one hundred years to adopt a single standard of spelling that would bridge the gap between the two versions of their language. The first agreement came in 1931, but it was quickly abandoned. Several attempts to delete the written accents during the 1970s and 1980s were also scrapped due to strong negative reactions from education and journalistic groups. Both countries finally approved the Portuguese Language Orthographic Agreement in 1990 as their best attempt to reach a universal spelling system. However, implementation of linguistic policy takes time. Brazil ratified the agreement in 2004 and actually implemented it in 2009. Portugal signed it into law in 2008. The new accord was also approved by the other Portuguese-speaking nations and territories of Angola, Cape Verde, Mozambique, East Timor, Macau, Guinea-Bissau, São Tomé and Príncipe, and East Timor. The overall purpose of the reform was to standardize legal documents, facilitate Internet searches, improve literacy, and promote the language on the global stage. All the signatory countries agreed to a transition period of six years, and the agreement became mandatory on January 1, 2015.

The Novo Acordo Ortográfico da Língua Portuguesa requires specific spelling changes:

- The letters "c" and "p" must be eliminated when they are silent (*optimo* → *otimo*).
- Diaeresis marks (ü) and acute accents will be eliminated from diphthongs (éi, ói).
- The letters "k," "w," and "y" were added to the Portuguese alphabet for the first time.
- New rules for capitalization and hyphenation are specified.
- A few divergent local spellings will be accepted as legitimate (*anónimo* vs. *anônimo*).

Leaders from the Science Academy of Lisbon and the Brazilian Academy of Letters claim that the new orthographic agreement will eliminate 98 percent of the spelling discrepancies that exist between Brazilian Portuguese and European Portuguese. The updated spelling convention will affect over 230 million Portuguese speakers worldwide, 190 million of whom are Brazilian. However, the process of actually implementing the new spelling conventions is already creating complaints and revealing contradictions. For example, the national public school systems in most Portuguese-speaking countries have decided to take a progressive approach since new books have to be created and printed, which implies a hefty price tag. In an ironic twist, the press and the media—who used to be the loudest critics of the new spelling reforms—have adopted the new orthographic system wholeheartedly. Consequently, Portuguese-speaking children read magazines, newspapers, and Internet content that use a different spelling system than the one they are learning in their respective schools. Such contradictions will eventually be resolved, but they are likely to create small headaches for a while.

See also: Chapter 8: Overview; Literacy Rates. Chapter 9: Overview; Indigenous Languages.

Further Reading

Cabral, Thomas. 2010. "Spelling Reform Causes Portuguese Headaches." *Telegraph*, March 1. Accessed August 1, 2019. http://www.telegraph.co.uk/expat/expatnews/7344925/Spelling-reform-causes-Portuguese-headaches.html

Lawless, Teresa, and Janie DiCioccio. 2015. "The Portuguese Spelling Reform." *Argos Multilingual*, March 25. Accessed August 1, 2019. http://www.argosmultilingual.com/blog/the-portuguese-spelling-reform

Valada, Francisco Miguel. 2012. "Portuguese Language Orthographic Agreement of 1990: Inconsistencies and Homographs." *Atiner Conference Paper Series No: LIT2012-0290*, November 15. Athens, Greece: Athens Institute for Education and Research. Accessed August 1, 2019. http://www.academia.edu/9757067/Portuguese_Language_Orthographic_Agreement_of_1990_Inconsistency_and_Homographs

Tupi-Guarani Influence

When the Portuguese arrived at the coastal regions of Brazil in the early 1500s, they found indigenous populations who spoke Tupi (also known as Tupi-Guarani). These early colonists were forced to communicate with the native people by learning their local language. Tupi-Guarani was a language family (instead of an individual language) that incorporated several local languages and dialects. When the Jesuits arrived in Brazil, they created a standardized version of the Tupi-Guarani language based on pieces of the most common languages found in the region. This new language facilitated communication for the Jesuits in order to spread their religious message, but it also helped the Portuguese colonists to talk to local workers. It became known as the *língua geral* (or common language) by the middle of the 1550s. For the next one hundred years, it was the most common language spoken in Brazil, even more than Portuguese.

The use of the Tupi-Guarani language left a tangible imprint on the Portuguese language used in Brazil. Its influence can be seen mostly on vocabulary items. The Portuguese settlers had to use Tupi words to make reference to plants and animals that were present in South America but were not found in European territories. Linguists and researchers have proposed that over 18,000 Tupi-Guarani words were incorporated into Brazilian Portuguese. Tupi words are now routinely used to name flora (banana, *pitanga*, tapioca, *ananás*, *jacoticaba*, *abacaxi*), fauna (jaguar, piranha, *tucano*, *tatu*/armadillo, *sabiá*), and physical places (Curitiba, Ipanema, Sorocaba, and Guarapari). Some of these words have been adopted into other languages as well. However, while the Tupi-Guarani lexicon had a strong influence on Portuguese, it did not really impact its grammatical structure. Multiple linguists have suggested that indigenous languages affected the general pronunciation of Brazilian Portuguese since it has a different accent that differentiates it from other Lusophone (Portuguese-speaking) countries.

Brazilian Portuguese was an open language since its inception; it incorporated new words relatively quickly based on necessity and its unique history. This approach included borrowing words from multiple indigenous and African languages. Currently, Brazilians use Tupi words almost on a daily basis. In addition, Brazil is completely surrounded by Spanish-speaking neighboring countries. As a result, the use of the Tupi-Guarani language nowadays is mostly limited to a few indigenous groups that reside along the new Brazilian-Paraguayan border in South America. They continue to fight for the preservation of their language, including the right to teach it in schools to a new generation of children who face incredible pressure to speak mostly Spanish or Portuguese.

See also: Chapter 9: Overview; Indigenous Languages.

Further Reading

Edwards, Todd L. 2008. *Brazil: A Global Studies Handbook*. Santa Barbara, CA: ABC-CLIO.

Guilherme, Alex, and Édison Hüttner. 2015. "Exploring the New Challenges for Indigenous Education in Brazil: Some Lessons from Ticuna Schools." *International Review of Education: Journal of Lifelong Learning* 61, no. 4 (August): 481–501.

Richard, Christopher, and Leslie Jermyn. 2002. *Cultures of the World: Brazil*. New York: Marshall Cavendish.

CHAPTER 10

ETIQUETTE

OVERVIEW

The stereotype of Brazilian culture is that it is much more relaxed and carefree than other Western societies. The modern reality, however, is much more complex. Lifestyle and cultural traditions vary significantly for people from different social classes, jobs, economic status, and regions of the country. Overall, growing up in a close-knit family provides Brazilian children with a support system that prepares them to face the world outside the home, which is increasingly more violent and dangerous then previous generations. The family unit is where children learn the norms and behaviors expected to carry themselves properly according to Brazilian social etiquette. They learn how to address elders with appropriate respect codified into the Portuguese language, how to follow traditions at the dining table, and how to handle the cultural intricacies of personal space and privacy. As children become teenagers and eventually young adults, they also learn that dressing appropriately for different social situations is important. The beach, a formal dinner, going to church, and attending a Sunday family barbecue all require them to dress accordingly depending on the social event. In addition, social interactions allow them to develop a unique perception of time and punctuality to help them navigate the flexibility that Brazilians apply to this social construct.

Brazilians face multiple obstacles as part of daily life. They are used to the fact that things do not always work as they should, some regulations seem unnecessary, and government bureaucracy is simply too difficult to navigate. Consequently, they have developed a way to deal with these complexities by bending the rules a little bit. This crafty Brazilian way of doing things actually has a name: *jeitinho* (to find a way). It is often nothing more than harmless creativity to get something done. For example, a person can use personal charisma and social skills to get a refund for nonrefundable tickets for a soccer game. Other times, however, Brazilians realize that bureaucracy is a tangled, frustrating mess even for simple transactions dealing with government agencies at all levels. Simple, routine tasks—such as getting a passport or renewing a driver's license—require them to file multiple forms, bring copies of personal documents, stand in long lines, and even visit multiple agencies. This is precisely the social context that encourages the use of intermediaries. The services of *despachantes* (expediters) have a long tradition in Brazil; they help average people to navigate the maze of Brazilian bureaucracy. They use personal contacts, fast-talking rhetoric, and their knowledge of government redundancy. They usually function on a system of a reciprocal exchange of favors. They become experts on bending the rules (not necessarily breaking them) in order to accomplish a positive outcome for a potentially complicated transaction on behalf of a client.

Brazil is an emerging economy, and it is considered one of the top ten economies in the world. Consequently, Brazilians have been thrust into a business environment that is increasingly international. Nevertheless, doing business in Brazil has a few unique characteristics that follow acceptable business etiquette. First of all, while Brazilians tend to be rather flexible with time in social gatherings, they are usually punctual for their business-related obligations, such as formal meetings and job interviews. To insure on-time performance, executives sometimes stress to their employees that an important meeting will start on time by using the expression "*com pontualidade britânica*" (with British punctuality). When it comes to clothing, dressing for the workplace depends on the culture of the company and the position a person has within the organization. Brazil is fairly traditional when it comes to formal business hierarchy, especially in the banking and medical fields. Men usually wear dark-colored suits with a tie, and female executives also use formal suits or dresses with simple accessories. However, there are other major sectors of the modern business world in Brazil (agribusiness, computer applications, textile design, and technology start-ups) that are more casual in their clothing expectations, where men simply wear comfortable slacks and a dress shirt, and women use either slacks or skirts with plain blouses.

On the surface, Brazil appears to be a very liberal and modern society. The 2010 census carried out by the Instituto Brasileiro de Geografia e Estatística (IBGE) shows that literacy rates have reached 92 percent, a tremendous achievement. The data also reflects that women have surpassed men in educational accomplishments, even in graduate degrees. In fact, the Federal Council of Medicine pointed out that for the first time, the majority of doctors in Brazil are women (Tosta and Coutinho 2016, 150). However, Brazil is still a traditional and male-dominated society. The Catholic Church and Brazil's colonial past still have a strong influence on the notion that men are the providers and women are supposed to raise the children and take care of the household. In addition, the country has become increasingly violent in the last two decades. The compounded problem for women is that some of the worst abusers are inside their own homes. Regrettably, machismo is not only alive but actually increasing. Brazilian women suffer incredibly high levels of domestic abuse, and the Human Rights Watch Organization forcefully condemned such chronic violence in 2017. However, the implementation of new federal laws offers hope that Brazil is making improvements by supporting some of its most vulnerable citizens.

Further Reading

Davidson, Nathalie. 2013. "Jeitinho Brasileiro: The Brazilian Way of Doing Things." *Huffington Post,* June 24. Accessed June 28, 2019. https://www.huffingtonpost.com/nathalie-davidson/brazil-protests_b_3490923.html

Fujikawa Nes, Cynthia. 2016. "Dining Culture in Brail." *Brazil Business*, August 13. Accessed June 28, 2019. http://thebrazilbusiness.com/article/dining-culture-in-brazil

Instituto Brasileiro de Geografia e Estatística—Brazilian Institute of Geography and Statistics (IBGE). 2010. "Census 2010." Brasilia. Accessed June 28, 2019. http://ibge.gov.br

Kutesko, Elizabeth, and Joanne B. Eicher. 2018. *Fashioning Brazil: Globalization and the Representation of Brazilian Dress in National Geographic*. London: Bloomsbury Visual Arts.

Lage, Luciana. 2015. "How Brazil's Relationship with Time Affects Personal and Professional Relationships." *Street Smart Brazil*, May 5. Accessed June 28, 2019. https://streetsmartbrazil.com/how-brazils-relationship-with-time-affects-personal-and-professional-relationships

Poelzl, Volker. 2009. *CultureShock! Brazil*. Singapore: Marshall Cavendish.

Tosta, Antonio Luciano de Andrade, and Eduardo F. Coutinho (eds.). 2016. *Brazil*. Santa Barbara, CA: ABC-CLIO.

Uchoa, Pablo. 2016. "Maria da Penha: The Woman Who Changed Brazil's Domestic Violence Laws." *BBC News*, September 22. Accessed June 28, 2019. https://www.bbc.com/news/magazine-37429051

Vincent, Jon S. 2003. *Culture and Customs of Brazil*. Westport, CT: Greenwood Press.

Xinhua News Agency and Luc Changlei. 2015. *BRICS: A Guide to Doing Business in Brazil, Russia, India, China, and South Africa*. Washington, DC: ICP Intercultural Press.

Bargaining

Bargaining for a better deal is a way of life in Brazil. However, there are social norms that allow for that type of shopping strategy while simultaneously being aware of locations where asking for discounts is not acceptable, or is very much frowned upon. There are entire industries in which bargaining is part of the normal and expected process, such as real estate purchases, buying a new or used car, participating in cattle auctions, building a new home, and acquiring farming equipment. Brazilians assume that such industries will actually overcharge customers who agree to pay the initial asking price.

Asking for a lower price is a common practice when shopping in informal and casual businesses. This tradition might work in open markets, small shops (especially in small towns), artsy fairs, carnivals, and small ethnic family stores. These locations usually do not post prices on their products, and customers usually have to ask *Quanto é?* (How much is it?). Sellers are usually not offended when patrons suggest a lower price and then negotiate the final amount. When sellers resist offering a discount, a common strategy is to offer to purchase multiple items and then request a lower collective price. The more people buy, the more they could save. In addition, it always helps to take out the amount of cash being offered as a visual incentive for the seller to accept a mutually agreeable price.

Bargaining is not possible when the business model is based on fixed prices, such as shopping centers, pharmacies, parking lots, hotels, large clothing retailers, restaurants, and supermarkets. While these establishments are unlikely to bargain over a lower price, it is worth asking for something else. For example, a restaurant might be willing to include a free small dessert when a customer books a dinner party for twenty or more people. Since businesses have to pay fees to credit card companies, sometimes stores where the owner is present might be willing to offer a small discount if a patron pays in cash for a large purchase rather than using a credit card. A more recent practice for obtaining discounts in businesses with fixed prices is to join a loyalty program, especially if the purchases take place online at the company's website. This is a relatively modern approach in Brazil. Members of loyalty programs in supermarkets, pharmacies, bookstores, and department stores receive percentage discounts as well as advance seasonal advertisements for Christmas, seasonal clothing, birthdays, and back-to-school specials.

The key to negotiating a better deal is often based on dealing with someone authorized to make the decision, especially if the person in charge is the owner of the business. That is why bargaining in small shops and open markets is likely to result in a slight discount. This cultural strategy also works with self-employed services, including plumbers, caterers, housekeepers, wedding planners, and handypersons. The best way to obtain a potential discount is to simply ask for it.

See also: Chapter 10: Overview; *Jeitinho*, Finding a Way.

Further Reading

DataGroup Americas. 2018. *Electronic Shopping in Brazil*. Amazon Digital Services: Editorial DataGroup Americas.

Garcia, Renata. 2015. "Bargaining in Brazil." *Brazil Business*, April 22. Accessed July 1, 2019. http://thebrazilbusiness.com/article/bargaining-in-brazil

Gouvea, Jose Geraldo. 2015. "How Should I Bargain while Shopping in Brazil?" *Quora*, March 5. Accessed July 1, 2019. https://www.quora.com/How-should-I-bargain-while-shopping-in-Brazil

Clothing and Dressing Appropriately

The large majority of Brazilians follow a dress style that is both casual and comfortable. However, they also dress appropriately for business meetings, the beach, hot weather, and formal dinners. Brazilians in general seem to be more comfortable with their bodies regardless of their physical condition, and this notion affects their fashion choices. Something to keep in mind is that, according to the 2010 census, slightly over 50 percent of Brazilians are under thirty years old. This demographic data influences fashion design toward a more youthful style, even for the middle-aged population.

Dressing for the workplace depends on the culture of the company and the position a person has within the organization. Brazil is fairly traditional when it comes to the formal business hierarchy, especially in fields such as banking, medical, and aircraft manufacturing. Managers and administrators tend to wear formal conservative clothes. Men usually wear dark-colored suits with a tie, and female executives also use formal suits or dresses with simple accessories. However, there are other major sectors of the modern business world in Brazil (agribusiness, computer applications, textile design, and technology start-ups) that are more casual in their clothing expectations. Regional managers in such industries avoid both formal suits and jeans. Instead, men traditionally wear comfortable slacks and a dress shirt, and women wear either slacks or skirts with plain tops.

Television is a major source of entertainment in Brazil, and celebrities in the famous telenovelas (soap operas) and reality shows have a tremendous impact on the fashion industry. Television networks are keenly aware of their social impact, and they even set up specific websites and phone lines dedicated to providing marketing and labeling information related to the clothes featured in their shows.

The fashion industry has grown tremendously in Brazil during the last thirty years, even beyond the typical barely-there bikini. Brazil is one of the leading designers of swimwear in the world; it produces more than 200 million units of swim outfits every year, mostly exported to the United States. The Brazilian flip-flop company Havaianas sold over 200 million pairs of sandals worldwide in 2017. The Brazilian luxury brand Okslen captures a large section of the national market with its metropolitan styles with sports themes. In addition, young Brazilian fashion designers have recently received both national and international acclaim for their contributions to multiple sectors of the fashion industry. Some of the talented contemporary Brazilian designers include Barbara Casasola (textile designs), Sandro Barrios (evening wear), Tufi Duek (designer jeans), and Carlos Miele (sensual yet casual female clothes). Their work will continue to reflect the attitude that Brazilians have toward fashion and society.

See also: Chapter 6: Education and Upward Mobility. Chapter 7: Wedding Traditions and Celebrations. Chapter 10: Formal Business Meetings. Chapter 16: Reality Television Shows; Rede Globo and Other Television Networks.

Further Reading

Baker, Vicky. 2017. "Havaianas: How a Brazilian Took Over the World." *BBC News*, July 16. Accessed July 3, 2019. https://www.bbc.com/news/world-latin-america-40610739

Freeland, Lucy. "10 Brazilian Fashion Designers to Watch." *Culture Trip*, October 5. Accessed July 3, 2019. https://theculturetrip.com/south-america/brazil/articles/top-10-brazilian-fashion-designers-to-watch

Kutesko, Elizabeth, and Joanne B. Eicher. 2018. *Fashioning Brazil: Globalization and the Representation of Brazilian Dress in National Geographic.* London: Bloomsbury Visual Arts.

Novais, Andréa. 2011. "Dress for Success in Brazil." *Brazil Business,* October 2. Accessed July 3, 2019. http://thebrazilbusiness.com/article/dress-for-success-in-brazil

Formal Business Meetings

Business meetings tend to be formal affairs in Brazil. Punctuality is important, especially if the meeting includes representatives from the growing number of foreign companies in the country. During the last three decades, Brazil has increased its economic standing in global trade. The result is that multiple Brazilian corporations (such as the aerospace giant Embraer and the national oil company Petrobras) have partnered with other international firms, and several global manufacturers have made considerable investments in the country. All these corporate mergers and cooperation agreements have infused an international business culture in Brazil. For formal meetings, business attire is rather conservative. Brazilians expect male business managers and administrators to wear formal suits (usually dark colors) with a tie, and female executives to wear suits or dresses with simple, elegant accessories. The distribution of wealth in Brazil is often reflected in the clothing that business executives wear, which makes income disparities even more evident. Business meetings—even formal events—are often held at restaurants rather than at a business office. During the meeting, Brazilians usually do not jump directly into negotiations; they attempt to make a personal connection first by engaging in modest socialization and casual conversation while carefully avoiding discussions on thorny subjects, such as national politics, street protests, and Brazil's relationship with its neighbors Argentina and Venezuela. Building personal relationships is extremely important for Brazilian executives.

While Brazilians tend to be rather flexible with time in social gatherings, they are usually punctual for their business-related obligations, such as formal meetings and job interviews. Nevertheless, companies are aware of potential social situations that can cause time delays for their employees. Consequently, they follow a few strategies to ensure time arrivals for important meetings, such as avoiding early-morning and right-after-lunch meetings, never scheduling back-to-back appointments, and occasionally stressing the time of the meeting followed by the expression "*com pontualidade britânica*" (with British punctuality).

Understanding the style of negotiations that Brazilians use is crucial for a successful business deal. First impressions are extremely important, and hence the need for a professional appearance. The initial casual conversation is only part of Brazilians feeling comfortable with their potential business partners. As a consequence, they place great value on verbal communication, and the eventual written documents are supposed to reflect the content of oral agreements. While discussing the actual content and details of a business arrangement, Brazilians have a different sense of personal space, which is often interpreted as "touchy-feely" by foreigners. Eye contact and a slight touch on the arm are quite common gestures among both men and women. In addition, Brazilians interrupt conversations very often, but they mean no disrespect; instead, it should be viewed as a sign of interest in the negotiations. Final business agreements are usually not made at a single meeting since most Brazilians companies follow a sense of hierarchy, and appropriate business protocol must be followed. Since personal relationships are extremely important in Brazilian culture, most final business decisions are delivered in person rather than by other means of communication, such as e-mail or an impersonal phone call.

See also: Chapter 4: Embraer, Empresa Brasileira de Aeronáutica; Petrobras, the National Oil Company. Chapter 6: Distribution of Wealth and Income Disparity. Chapter 10: Overview; Clothing and Dressing Appropriately; Personal Space and Privacy; Punctuality and Concepts of Time.

Further Reading

LaRock, Hana. 2018. "Business Etiquette in Brazil." *USA Today,* September 7. Accessed May 20, 2019. https://traveltips.usatoday.com/business-etiquette-brazil-16277.html

Vasconcellos, Isabella. 2016. *Doing Business in Brazil: Opportunities and Threats.* Lulu.com. Accessed May 20, 2019. http://www.lulu.com/shop/isabella-vasconcellos/doing-business-in-brazil-opportunities-and-threats/paperback/product-22935780.html

Xinhua News Agency and Luc Changlei. 2015. *BRICS: A Guide to Doing Business in Brazil, Russia, India, China, and South Africa.* Washington, DC: ICP Intercultural Press.

Intermediaries: *Colonels* and *Despachantes*

Brazilian bureaucracy is a tangled, frustrating mess even for simple transactions dealing with government agencies at all levels. Simple routine tasks—such as renewing a driver's license or getting a copy of a birth certificate—require Brazilians to file multiple forms, bring copies of personal documents, stand in long lines, and even visit multiple agencies. More complicated transactions such as expediting a passport application or recording the purchase of a home are even more exasperating for the average person. Given the social context, this is precisely when intermediaries come in handy. The use of services from *despachantes* and regional *colonels* has a long tradition in Brazil; they help average people to navigate the maze of Brazilian bureaucracy.

The word *despachantes* could be translated as "expediters" who help with government transactions by using personal contacts, fast-talking rhetoric, creativity, and their knowledge of government redundancy. They are usually street-smart, well-liked individuals who know lots of people and function on reciprocal exchange of favors. They become experts on bending the rules (not necessarily breaking them) in order to accomplish a positive outcome for a potentially complicated transaction on behalf of a client. In fact, many *despachantes* used to work in government agencies themselves. Many Brazilians simply do not have the time to deal with all the confusing and redundant paperwork required for a simple transaction that often takes all day. The solution is to hire *despachantes* because they offer practical solutions. To get an idea of how wide their services are, the federal legislature approved their request to unionize in 2002; the Federal Council of Document Despachantes has over 30,000 members, which does not include *despachantes* who specialize in processing motor-vehicles forms or immigration-related transactions. Their job allows average Brazilians to focus on their daily lives knowing that someone else can handle the bureaucratic frustrations for them.

Another type of intermediary that is still somewhat influential in rural Brazil are the *colonels*. They do not have a military title. Instead, they are prominent members of isolated poor communities who exercise a strong political influence among the local citizens. For political candidates, the value of a *colonel* relies on delivering a substantial number of votes on election day. Usually, local people vote for whomever the *colonel* supports because they expect to get help in the future from the elected candidate when the *colonel* intervenes on their behalf. These regional legendary *colonels* thrived in the interior poor hinterlands that used to be geographically isolated. He could get help for average citizens because he was involved in getting people appointed to key government positions. While rural *colonels* still have an impact in modern Brazil, their influence has been limited by progress, urbanization, infrastructure, and technology. Local people can now receive help from federal government programs that bypass the need for local authorities. Nevertheless, the few surviving *colonels* still live mostly in the isolated and poor northeast regions of the country, and they are extremely well respected in their local communities.

See also: Chapter 10: Overview; Bargaining; *Jeitinho*, Finding a Way.

Further Reading

Federal Council of Document Despachantes Official Website (Portuguese). https://www.cfdd.org.br

Fernández Campbell, Alexia. 2016. "A Day in the Life of Brazil's Insane Bureaucracy." *Atlantic*, August 4. Accessed June 4, 2019. https://www.theatlantic.com/international/archive/2016/08/brazil-bureaucracy-despachantes/494426

Hoge, Warren. 1983. "Rural 'Colonels' of Brazil: Their Power Never Dies." *New York Times*, January 25. Accessed June 4, 2019. https://www.nytimes.com/1983/01/25/world/rural-colonels-of-brazil-their-power-never-dies.html

Vincent, Jon S. 2003. *Culture and Customs of Brazil*. Westport, CT: Greenwood Press.

Jeitinho, Finding a Way

Brazilians face multiple obstacles as part of daily life. They are used to the fact that things do not always work correctly, some rules and regulations seem unnecessary, and government bureaucracy is too difficult to navigate. Consequently, they have developed a way to deal with these complexities by bending the rules a little bit. This crafty Brazilian way of doing things actually has a name: *jeitinho*. The closely related expression *dar un jeito* means "to find a way" to overcome a given problem. It is not necessarily considered a bribe because it does not involve an exchange of money. It simply means that there is a way of doing things when life gets too complicated with bureaucracy and unnecessary procedures. It is the way to improvise to deal with everyday complications, regardless of the rules that might be in place. It implies that a person can use relationships and resources, as well as family connections, street smarts, and creativity to adapt and overcome a difficult situation.

The use of *jeitinho* can sometimes be nothing more than harmless creativity. For example, a person can use personal charisma and social skills to get a refund for non-refundable tickets for a soccer game, or to convince a family member who works at a medical office to set up an appointment without having to wait three weeks like everyone else. This is where having a large network of friends and family comes in handy.

Bureaucracy permeates almost every aspect of Brazilian life. Simple government transactions (such as registering the birth of a child, expediting a passport, or getting a driver's license) have become overwhelmingly complex. It often requires a burdensome exercise to fill out multiple forms, stand in long lines, and visit several agencies for the simplest of tasks. The complexity of municipal, state, and federal laws makes simple procedures rather arbitrary, especially for businesses trying to obtain permits and licenses. Consequently, the use of facilitators called *despachantes* (expediters), who are in a position to help navigate the maze of filling out documents, comply with rules, and satisfy requirements for government agencies, has become popular. These *despachantes* work for a fee, and they rely heavily on their business contacts in government agencies to facilitate a successful transaction on behalf of a client.

The *jeitinho brasileiro* can certainly be abused and even lead to insidious consequences. The most evident problem is that *jeitinho* leads to nepotism at the workplace because it is not unusual for Brazilians to recommend relatives for a job, even if they are not the most qualified candidates. Similarly, elected politicians are notorious for appointing family members and friends to government positions. The problem becomes more complex (and perhaps illegal) when businesses try to "find a way" to circumvent government regulations or obtain a lucrative government contract. Their use of *jeitinho* can easily turn into bribes, which encourages corruption. In the last ten years, Brazil has exposed multiple cases of large-scale corruption that have resulted in prison terms for federal senators, high-level bureaucrats, and even former president Lula da Silva (1945–). While moderate versions of *jeitinho* occur all over the world, it is evident that it affects individual people, businesses, government agencies at all levels, and even politics in Brazil.

See also: Chapter 3: Corruption and Political Scandals; Lula da Silva, Luiz Inácio (1945 –). Chapter 10: Overview; Intermediaries: *Colonels* and *Despachantes*.

Further Reading

Davidson, Nathalie. 2013. "Jeitinho Brasileiro: The Brazilian Way of Doing Things." *Huffington Post,* June 24. Accessed July 14, 2019. https://www.huffingtonpost.com/nathalie-davidson/brazil-protests_b_3490923.html

Fujikawa Nes, Cynthia. 2016. "The Brazilian Way of Doing Things." *Brazil Business,* August 22. Accessed July 14, 2019. http://thebrazilbusiness.com/article/the-brazilian-way-of-doing-things

Vincent, Jon S. 2003. *Culture and Customs of Brazil.* Westport, CT: Greenwood Press.

Machismo

Brazilian culture sometimes reflects inherent contradictions. On the surface, it appears to be very liberal and contemporary. However, beyond the physical beauty displayed at the beaches of Rio de Janeiro and the evidence of modern-day conveniences of technology and electronics, Brazil is still a traditional and male-dominated society. Multiple cultural anthropologists and sociologists offer explanations for these traits based on the national colonial heritage and the pervasive influence of the Catholic Church. Both institutions promoted the notion that men were the providers who offered material stability for families; women were supposed to raise the children and take care of the household without questioning the husband. These values are still present in contemporary Brazil. In addition, the country has become increasingly violent in the last two decades. The compounded problem for women is that some of the worst abusers are inside their own homes. Regrettably, machismo is not only alive but actually increasing in Brazil.

The consequences of uncontrolled machismo are alarming, especially because women are the victims of incredibly high levels of domestic abuse. In fact, Brazil has the seventh-highest rate of violence against women in the world; a woman is assaulted every fifteen seconds, and one is murdered every two hours. Since 1985, over 92,000 Brazilian women have been killed by a husband, partner, or family member (Hargreaves, 2015). Such rampant violence against women in Brazil was forcefully condemned by the Human Rights Watch Organization in 2017.

In spite of the well-documented increase in domestic abuse cases in Brazil, there is hope that things are beginning to change. The federal government is aware of this epidemic social problem. Consequently, on September 22, 2006, President Lula da Silva (1945–) signed legislation approving the Maria da Penha Law for Violence against Women to punish perpetrators of domestic abuse. In addition, President Rousseff (1947–) signed another law in March 2013 that changed the federal penal code to include "femicide," which was defined as crimes that involve domestic violence, discrimination, or contempt for women that result in their death. These laws also included funding for training multiple police forces on how to handle reports of domestic abuse, how to create legal documentary evidence, as well as the creation of safe houses where women can seek refuge with their children in cases where they are running away from domestic abuse. The goal is to address preventable cases of extreme family violence. Moreover, the court system has also been instructed to treat such crimes more seriously to protect the lives of women and children in a violent household. While these laws and resources are being applied, the government has also mounted an extensive public awareness campaign on television, radio, posters, and social media to promote the notion that violence is not normal in Brazilian modern society.

See also: Chapter 3: Women's Rights; Lula da Silva, Luiz Inácio (1945–); Rousseff, Dilma (1947–). Chapter 5: Catholicism. Chapter 6: Maria da Penha Law for Violence against

Women Sidebar. Chapter 7: Gender and Parenting Roles; Raising Children. Chapter 10: Overview.

Further Reading

Armand de Bonneval, Philippe. 2016. "Brazil's Stubborn Machismo." Council on Hemispheric Affairs, October 25. Accessed July 22, 2019. http://www.coha.org/brazils-stubborn-machismo

Darlington, Shasta. 2018. "Domestic Abuse Shown Blow by Blow Shocks Brazil." *New York Times*, August 7. Accessed July 22, 2019. https://www.nytimes.com/2018/08/07/world/americas/domestic-abuse-shown-blow-by-blow-shocks-brazil.html

Hargeaves, Melanie. 2015. "Brazil's 'Machismo': A Licence for Abuse." *New Internationalist*, May 13. Accessed July 22, 2019. https://newint.org/features/web-exclusive/2015/05/13/brazil-domestic-violence

Uchoa, Pablo. 2016. "Maria da Penha: The Woman Who Changed Brazil's Domestic Violence Laws." *BBC News*, September 22. Accessed July 22, 2019. https://www.bbc.com/news/magazine-37429051

Personal Space and Privacy

The Brazilian concepts of personal space and privacy are very similar to those of other Latin American cultures but significantly different than social customs in the United States. In general, people in Brazil have a tendency to stand closer to each other in all forms of social interactions, including personal, social, public, family, and work environments. These customs contribute toward the Brazilian identity that is founded on family ties, cooperation, and social involvement, and not based on claims of self-made individual achievement.

Family relationships are extremely important in Brazil. Children grow up in homes where they view relatives supporting each other by constant displays of affection that include words of encouragement, strong handshakes, hugs, and kisses. Consequently, they develop a perception of personal space as being rather close and somewhat intimate, even for casual interactions. The concept of family is even expanded to the *parentela*, or extended family relationships that create a support network that includes uncles, aunts, grandparents, cousins, and godparents. In time, Brazilians carry the same type of social conventions into the public arena. For example, when it comes to face-to-face conversations, it is common for Brazilians to stand or sit very close to each other, keep constant eye contact, tap each other on the shoulder, and even extend an occasional touch on the arm.

The notions of privacy and personal space are on full display when Brazilians deal with public transportation on a daily basis. The crowded metro and city buses of São Paulo—with a population of over 20 million people—offer an appropriate venue to analyze the Brazilian level of comfort with personal space. First of all, people riding the

A crowded beach in Rio de Janeiro. Brazilian culture encourages social interaction and personal relationships. As a result, the concept of personal space is much closer than the typical distance in other cultures. At the beach, Brazilians are likely to set up their umbrellas very close to neighboring beachgoers, even if there is plenty of room available. (Luizsouzarj/Dreamstime.com)

metro are shoved into extremely crowded cars that would test the boundaries of privacy anywhere, and yet they socialize by talking and interacting with other fellow passengers while also being vigilant for any potential outbursts of crime or violence. Even in these crowded conditions, the respect for family members is visible when young people give up their seats for handicapped and elderly riders. In addition, during certain peak hours of the day, the metro system sometimes designates special cars reserved only for mothers with children. Moreover, the concept of "family lines" extends to other crowded venues, such as government offices, airports, and supermarkets in order to give families priority in public spaces.

Foreigners arriving in Brazil to do business often describe the local culture as being more "touchy-feely." They also notice that Brazilians do not usually apologize for walking too close to a person or standing right next to them. They are not being rude; it is just that Brazilians have a closer sense of personal space, and they do not think it is a social faux pas. However, they will say "excuse me" if they actually bump into another person, even accidentally. The Brazilian notion of personal space also reflects how much they value social connections. For example, if they go to the beach early enough to find only a handful of beachgoers, they will set up right next to them rather than occupying an isolated spot.

See also: Chapter 6: Overview; *Parentela*; Urban Crime. Chapter 10: Overview; Formal Business Meetings.

Further Reading

Erickson, Amanda. 2017. "What 'Personal Space' Looks Like around the World." *Washington Post*, April 24. Accessed June 12, 2019. https://www.washingtonpost.com/news/worldviews/wp/2017/04/24/how-close-is-too-close-depends-on-where-you-live/?noredirect=on&utm_term=.f86676c1dcd2

Fadel, Leila, and Lulu Garcia-Navarro. 2013. "How Different Cultures Handle Personal Space." National Public Radio (NPR), May 5. Accessed June 12, 2019. https://www.npr.org/sections/codeswitch/2013/05/05/181126380/how-different-cultures-handle-personal-space

Poelzl, Volker. 2009. *CultureShock! Brazil*. Singapore: Marshall Cavendish.

Punctuality and Concepts of Time

Brazilians have a perception of time that is slightly different than other cultures. This does not mean, however, that they are consistently and chronically late to every event or appointment. When Brazilians are asked about their tolerance for time flexibility, possible explanations for lateness often begin with the expression "Well, it depends." Punctuality in Brazil really does depend on the social situation, such as a job interview, a casual social gathering, an official business meeting, or a music concert. As part of the daily routine, especially in metropolitan areas, being slightly delayed is generally accepted as a fact of life because factors beyond a person's control (such as traffic, weather conditions, and last-minute family situations) change previously scheduled plans. Consequently, Brazilians constantly try to control time to fit their own needs instead of the other way around.

Brazilians do arrive on time for certain formal events. All business-related obligations are expected to start on time because they reflect professionalism. This includes job interviews, formal meetings, and scheduled business arrangements at a restaurant. When business owners and managers want to emphasize that they expect employees to be on time for a meeting, they are likely to use the expression *"com pontualidade britânica"* (with British punctuality). In addition, the arrival of international companies to Brazil, as well as the partnerships created by local Brazilian companies with foreign firms, has started to change business culture within individual companies. However, businesses also adapt to the needs of the people by implementing certain practices to reduce the possibility of late events; this includes avoiding back-to-back meetings, bypassing early-morning conferences, and avoiding job interviews scheduled at a quarter hour (such as 10:15) because they simply confuse Brazilians.

Social events in Brazil require a more casual approach. A gathering with friends is more likely to start about thirty minutes later than the suggested time because other prior events caused a delay: a soccer match went into overtime, a friend dropped by unexpectedly, or a doctor's appointment started later than scheduled. In certain social situations, it is actually impolite to arrive on time. For example, if a party at a friend's house is announced at 7 p.m., people should arrive roughly thirty minutes late simply because the host might not actually be ready to receive guests at the scheduled time. For other social events, it is important to be aware of how time and social customs flow in Brazil. For example, music concerts start notoriously late, usually about an hour. However, movies always start at the posted time, and movie theaters usually do not show as many trailers for future movies as they do in other countries; therefore, moviegoers should definitely arrive earlier than the scheduled time. Finally, it is important to realize that regional attitudes in regard to punctuality vary throughout Brazil. In general terms, the north and northeast regions of the country are more tolerant of time delays than their southern counterparts, and São Paulo has developed a reputation for business punctuality and efficiency.

See also: Chapter 10: Overview; Formal Business Meetings.

Further Reading

Lage, Luciana. 2015. "How Brazil's Relationship with Time Affects Personal and Professional Relationships." *Street Smart Brazil*, May 5. Accessed May 12, 2019. https://streetsmartbrazil.com/how-brazils-relationship-with-time-affects-personal-and-professional-relationships

Novais, Andréa. 2013. "Can Brazilians Be on Time?" *Brazil Business,* August 22. Accessed May 12, 2019. http://thebrazilbusiness.com/article/can-brazilians-be-on-time

Vincent, Jon S. 2003. *Culture and Customs of Brazil*. Santa Barbara, CA: ABC-CLIO.

Table Manners

Brazilian culture shares a set of customs that show respect. When it comes to dining etiquette, Brazilians use table manners that are applicable at both restaurants and family homes. In some cases, their traditions are comparable to table manners in the Western world; occasionally, however, Brazil has unique eating practices that stand out from other countries.

Brazilians follow multiple Western-style table manners similar to the United States, Europe, and Latin America. For example, they tend to keep their hands visible at all times (not under the table), and elbows are not placed on top of the table. Brazilians also avoid chewing and talking with their mouth open; it is considered impolite, and it makes most other people uncomfortable. In addition, they avoid certain actions at the dining table: burping loudly, blowing one's nose, coughing repeatedly, and using a toothpick. Sometimes, those behaviors are unavoidable, but they should be done away from the table. One addition to manner rules in contemporary Brazilian homes is to prohibit the use of video games and mobile phones at the dining table. When it is time to start eating, Brazilians often say *"Bom apetite."*

The use of utensils differs slightly in Brazil from that of the United States. Brazilians follow a "Continental style" used in Europe and Latin America but not in the United States. This means that Brazilians use the left hand for the fork and the right hand for the knife. However, they do not switch hands while they eat; after cutting something, the fork remains on the left hand. A rather unique feature is that Brazilians use a knife and fork to eat just about everything, including pizza, French fries, and fruit. Brazilian children are usually taught that eating food with their bare hands is not very hygienic. However, the arrival of more casual food in the last twenty years has forced Brazilians to adapt their table manners. For example, they certainly enjoy eating hamburgers, and chicken wings, but they always hold them with a napkin to avoid getting their hands dirty. When the meal is finished, Brazilians place their fork and knife on top of the plate in a parallel position to indicate that they are done eating.

Finally, there are a few table customs to keep in mind at restaurants. First, it is important to arrive on time for a reservation. Then, when multiple sets of utensils are set at the table, Brazilians start from the outside and work their way in as the wait staff brings different courses. At restaurants, it is considered rude to snap fingers at the wait staff to get their attention; establishing eye contact is enough. At the end of the meal, the tradition is that the person who invited the other is the one who pays, but it is always polite to offer to pick up the check. A 10 percent tip is enough for good service and sometimes 15 percent for an exceptional experience.

See also: Chapter 10: Overview; Formal Business Meetings; Punctuality and Concepts of Time. Chapter 14: Overview, *Cafezinho*, a Small Shot of Coffee; Mealtimes.

Further Reading

Bilyeu, Mary. 2016. "Bom Apetite: A Taste of Brazil." *Blade,* August 2. Accessed June 13, 2019. http://www.toledoblade.com/Food/2016/08/02/Bom-apetite-A-taste-of-Brazil.html

Fujikawa Nes, Cynthia. 2016. "Dining Culture in Brail." *Brazil Business,* August 13. Accessed June 13, 2019. http://thebrazilbusiness.com/article/dining-culture-in-brazil

Roberts, Yaya. 2009. *The Brazilian Table.* Layton, UT: Gibbs Smith.

CHAPTER 11

LITERATURE AND DRAMA

OVERVIEW

Brazilian literature was heavily influenced by the artistic trends in Portugal. In addition, specific events in Brazilian history coincided with multiple literary movements in Europe. At first, most colonial literature (1500–1822) was produced to send reports to Europe or to teach Catholicism to new indigenous converts. After independence in 1822, Brazilians searched for authentic ways to define themselves, including in literature. The nineteenth century includes a prolific production of literary material that aims to describe the Brazilian social and cultural experience. In 1922, the Modern Art Week held in São Paulo was a seminal event that unified artists, literati, and musicians to develop a new way of expression that was truly Brazilian. The novelists, poets, and playwrights that emerged from this period produced some of the most memorable literature in Brazil. Then, in 1944, a new challenge emerged: a call to create a Brazilian literary canon, a list of works that best reflected Brazilian culture and society. The result was a list of twenty-two books: eleven novels, three poem collections, one essay, and seven nonfiction stories (on history, economics, and sociology). While the national literary canon is certainly controversial, it has endured as a practical guide for Brazilian students and book lovers. As the beginning of the twenty-first century, the use of digital media has made it possible for contemporary writers to publish their work and disseminate it faster and more efficiently than ever before.

COLONIAL LITERATURE (1500–1822)

Religious, Historical, and Baroque Styles

Literary critics often question the genesis of Brazilian literature. During the colonial period, it was essentially written by Portuguese people who were in Brazil at that time. For example, poetry and plays written by Jesuit priests had a specific didactic purpose to indoctrinate the indigenous population, at least until 1759 when they were expelled from Brazil. The famous *Carta a El Rei D. Manuel* (Letter to the King D. Manuel)—written by Pero Voz de Caminha (1450–1500)—is often also considered a possible beginning for Brazilian literature, but it was a report to the king. It narrates the events when the Portuguese colonizers first met the indigenous people. Then Frei Vicente do Salvador (1564–1636) wrote the first comprehensive history of Brazil in 1627, but it was published two centuries later in 1889. Most critics agree that Gregório de

Matos (1623–1696) is the first native-born writer to produce original literature that reflected Brazilian life. His baroque-style poems were erotic, satirical, and even religious. A collection of his best poems titled *Poesias completas 1882–1943* was published in 1969, and it earned him a solid position in the Brazilian literary canon.

Neoclassicism

During the 1700s, the Portuguese discovered gold and diamonds in the interior state of Minas Gerais. The newly found wealth sparked regional interest in painting, architecture, and literature. Writers from this period copied European authors and, oddly, produced literature describing pastoral landscapes with happy shepherds, even when the local reality was based on slavery and forced labor. As a reaction to such literary topics, Tomás Antônio Gonzaga (1744–1810) wrote *Cartas Chilenas* as satirical poems with a scathing political critique of regional politicians. They circulated in a clandestine form during the 1780s, but they were actually published as a collection in 1863.

POSTINDEPENDENCE LITERATURE (1822–1950S)

Romanticism

Brazil became independent in 1822. The event coincided with the style of romanticism prevalent in Europe. In Brazil, novelists, poets, and playwrights exhibited a profound sense of nationalism throughout the 1800s. The literary movement "Indianism" became popular as Brazilians attempted to define who they were. One of the most romantic novels published in 1865 was the iconic *Iracema* written by José de Alencar (1829–1977). It reflected the blend of races and cultures in Brazil; the novel remains extremely popular today, and it is the oldest novel included in the national literary canon.

Realism

By the 1850s, Brazilian writers worked hard to change the overtly romantic style of novels and poetry into a more realistic view of Brazilian society. The most prominent author of this period was Joaquim Maria Machado de Assis (1839–1908). He reproduced some of the most recognized novels in Brazilian literature: *Memórias postumas de Brás Cubas* (1881) and *Dom Casmurro* (1900). In fact, he is the only writer to have two novels included in the national literary canon.

Modernism

The origins of the modernism style in Brazil can be pinpointed to the Semana de Arte Moderno in 1922. The goal was to inspire new ways of expression in music, art, and literature that were truly Brazilian. Quite a few seminal writers emerged from this group. For example, Mário de Andrade (1893–1945)—one of the Modern Art Week organizers—published the highly acclaimed novel *Macunaíma* in 1928 by using local and colloquial language to explore the topic of ethnic mixture in Brazil. In addition,

Jorge Amado (1912–2001) released his best-known novel, *Gabriela, cravo e canela* (Gabriela, Clove and Cinnamon) in 1958. He is recognized for a simple writing style that made literature available to the masses. He also used average people as characters in his novels, such as peasants, prostitutes, and street children.

During the late 1950s (postmodernism period), two writers published outstanding works that elevated the status of Brazilian literature worldwide. João Guimaráes Rosa published *Grande sertão: Veredas* (The Devil to Pay in the Backlands) in 1956 that narrated the living conditions of *sertanejos* and the extremely harsh living conditions in the semiarid rural environment. Moreover, his use of archaic expressions, new words, and colloquial language made his work truly innovative. For many Brazilians, he is considered the best national writer of all time. One of his contemporaries, Clarise Lispector, is perhaps one of the most recognized female writers in Brazil, but she does not have a book in the national canon. Her highly publicized work titled *Laços de família* (Family Ties) was published in 1960. She tells multiple stories from a female (not feminist) point of view where all the main characters are women—a revolutionary concept at the time.

MILITARY DICTATORSHIP (1964–1985) AND CENSORSHIP

A series of five generals ruled Brazil during a twenty-year military dictatorship. They established the Departamento de Censura e Diversões Públicas (DCDP) to officially censure censor the media, academia, music, the arts, and all public gatherings. Nothing was published or released without prior consent from the DCDP. Despite the risk, courageous writers—such as Rubem Fonseca and Roberto Drummond—defied the regime and published work that was labeled protest literature, subversive prose, and marginal poetry. They told stories of urban violence, sadistic torture, unexplained disappearances, and brutal assassinations.

RETURN TO DEMOCRACY AND CONTEMPORARY WRITERS

Brazil returned to democratic rule in 1985. At first, testimonials of returning writers in exile dominated the literary scene. Then a new energy emerged with the release of new innovative novels, poetry renewal, and most of all a resurgence of theater. At the beginning of the 2000s, a new generation of young writers became extremely active in the literary scene, and they are likely to define the future of Brazilian literature. They have a strong digital presence in social networks, which is something not available to previous authors. They are more cosmopolitan. Their work is translated into multiple languages faster than ever before—a process that gives them more exposure to international markets. In addition, new awards for national literature have been established in Brazil to recognize the work of new talent as it emerges. Examples of award-wining Brazilian contemporary authors include the talented novelist Carol Bensimon (1980–), the popular poet Adrian Lisboa (1970–), as well as the brilliant playwrights Jô Bilac (1984 –) and Renata Mizrahi (1979–). Their literary contributions are likely to influence the way Brazilians see the world (and themselves) as it continues to evolve.

Further Reading

Brazilian Academy of Letters/Academia Brasileira de Letras. www.academia.org.br/

Gama, Rinaldo. 1994. "Biblioteca Nacional." *Veja* 27, no. 47 (November 23): 108–112. Accessed June 18, 2019. http://bussolaliteraria.blogspot.com/2010_01_24_archive.html

Goldberg, Isaac. 2009. *Brazilian Literature*. New York: Knopf.

Semana de Arte Moderna/Modern Art Week. http://semana-arte-moderna.info

Universidade Federal de Santa Catarina. *Literatura Brasileira*. Accessed June 18, 2019. http://www.literaturabrasileira.ufsc.br

Vincent, Jon S. 2003. *Culture and Customs of Brazil*. Westport, CT: Greenwood Press.

Amado, Jorge (1912–2001)

Jorge Leal Amado de Faria (1912–2001) was born on August 10, 1912, in a rural setting near the town of Itabuna, within the state of Bahia, Brazil. He was a Brazilian writer whose work remains extremely popular even today. Literary critics place him in the modernist movement of writers who were influenced by the literary foundations created during the Modern Art Week held in São Paulo in 1922. Jorge Amado wrote over thirty books that have been translated to over forty-five languages worldwide, many of which have been adapted to cinema and television soap operas.

Growing up in rural Bahia, Jorge Amado was exposed to the needs and struggles of people working in agriculture settings in extreme poverty and isolated from the rest of the country. During his teenage years, his family moved to Salvador, the capital of Bahia state, where he attended high school. He also graduated from law school, but he never practiced that profession. In regard to his family, he married Matilde Garcia Rosa when he was twenty years old, and they had only one daughter, named Lila. His second marriage was to writer Zélia Gattai, with whom he had a son, João Jorge, and a daughter, Paloma.

Jorge Amado was a prolific writer whose career started at a very young age. He was only fourteen years old when he began writing for regional magazines. In fact, he published his first novel, *O país do Carnaval* (The Country of Carnival), in 1931 when he was only eighteen years old. His experience with rural and poor populations influenced both his literary work and his political activism. As a writer, his books resonated with the general population because his protagonists were often average people, such as street children, peasants, prostitutes, fishermen, and black caretakers. He was a strong critic of racism in Brazil, and he confronted traditional Brazilian values that used pejorative language to describe people of mixed racial heritage. From a political point of view, he was an ardent communist, denouncing social injustice in Brazil—especially against the Afro-Brazilian population—which made him a target of the dictatorship of Getúlio Vargas (1930–1945). Consequently, he was arrested in 1935, and he had to witness piles of his books being burned in public. Due to his militant communist views, he was forced into exile in Argentina and Uruguay from 1941 to 1942 and then again to France and Czechoslovakia from 1949 to 1954.

When Jorge Amado returned to Brazil in 1954, he abandoned all aspects of his political work, and he started on a renewed path of creative writing. In 1958, he published his most recognized masterpiece, *Gabriela, cravo e canela* (Gabriela, Clove and Cinnamon). It is the most recent novel included in the Brazilian literary canon. This folk novel was extremely popular in Brazil and abroad; it was the beginning of a string of novels based on female protagonists including *Dona Flor and Her Two Husbands* (1966) and *Tereza Batista: Home from the Wars* (1972).

Jorge Amado defined himself as a storyteller rather than a novelist. He left a strong imprint on Brazilian literature that made him one of the most recognizable writers in the nation's history. His writing style was accessible to the masses, and his characters were relatable to average people in Brazil. He used common language, which might be the reason why so many of his novels have been turned into films, theatrical plays, and extremely popular television soap operas. Jorge Amado was elected to the Brazilian Academy of Letters in 1961, a position he held until he died on August 6, 2001.

See also: Chapter 2: Vargas, Getúlio (1882–1954). Chapter 11: Overview; Literary Canon; Literary Censorship by the Military; Modernism in Brazil.

Further Reading

Dias Carneiro, Julia. 2012. "Jorge Amado: Brazil Celebrates Its Master Story-Teller." *BBC Journal,* August 10. Accessed June 6, 2019. http://www.bbc.com/news/world-latin-america-19160439

Fundação Casa de Jorge Amado/Jorge Amado Foundation. http://www.jorgeamado.org.br

Globo Teatro. 2012. "Bis! Clássicos de Jorge Amado adaptados para cinema, TV e teatro (in Portuguese)." Rede Globo, August 10. Accessed June 6, 2019. http://redeglobo.globo.com/globoteatro/bis/noticia/2013/09/jorge-amado-classicos-adaptados-para-cinema-televisao-e-teatro.html

Ministry of Culture. *Ministério da Cultura*. http://www.cultura.gov.br

Semana de Arte Moderna/Modern Art Week. http://semana-arte-moderna.info

Young, Richard, and Odile Cisneros. 2001. *Historical Dictionary of Latin American Literature and Theater.* Lanham, MD: Scarecrow Press.

Bandeira, Manuel (1886–1968)

Manuel Carneiro de Soussa Bandeira Filho (1886–1968) was born on April 19, 1886, in the city of Recife in the state of Pernambuco in the northeast region of Brazil. He was a poet, translator, literary critic, and university professor. Considered one of the canonical poets that define the literary genre in Brazil, he lived in Rio de Janeiro for most of his childhood. In 1903, his family moved to São Paulo, and he enrolled in the Polytechnic School in order to study architecture. However, one year later, he discovered that he had contracted tuberculosis, and his family moved back to Rio de Janeiro for its tropical climate. Subsequently, he went to Switzerland to receive treatment for a few years. After an arduous recovery, he returned to Brazil in 1917.

Manuel Bandeira published his first poetry book titled *Cinza das horas* (Ash from the Hours) in 1907. It had an overall sadness throughout the book that reflected hurt feelings, melancholy, and resentment. He used heavy symbolism and metaphors to explore topics of grief and disappointment. Two years later, he released his second book of poems, *Carnaval* (Carnival), which also had melancholic and sentimental themes but a more optimistic point of view. Bandeira now offered hints of modernism by focusing on national icons based on his native land and childhood memories. When the famous Semana de Arte Moderna (Modern Art Week) was held in São Paulo in 1922, Bandeira was already an accomplished poet. He participated in the event of literary discussions, but he remained mostly marginal to the entire modernist movement. During that week, he presented his poem titled "The Toads," which offered a strong criticism of the Parnassian style of poetry with a French influence based on formal language and exact meter but without much feeling or inspiration. The setting was appropriate since the modernist event in São Paulo aimed to create a new artistic direction for Brazil to break away from European influence. In addition, Bandeira published his most recognized poetry book, *Libertinism*, in 1930 when the popularity of modernism was already declining. He kept his own style while simultaneously adopting features of other emerging literary movements. Bandeira went on to write more than twenty books of poetry and prose. His book *Poesías completas* (Complete Poems by Manuel Bandeira) was selected to be part of the national literary canon.

At a later stage of his life, Manuel Bandeira became a professor of Latin American literature at the prestigious Colégio Pedro II in Rio de Janeiro. During this time, he translated numerous classical books of world literature into Portuguese, and he also published anthologies of Brazilian literature. In recognition of his contributions to national literature and culture, he was inducted into the Academia Brasileira de Letras in 1940. He was eighty-two years old when he died on October 18, 1968, in Rio de Janeiro. Despite having been diagnosed with tuberculosis at an early age, he lived a long life that left an indelible imprint on Brazilian poetry.

See also: Chapter 11: Overview; Literary Canon; Modernism in Brazil.

Further Reading

Bishop, Elizabeth, and Emanuel Brasil (eds.). 1997. *An Anthology of Twentieth-Century Brazilian Poetry*. Middletown, CT: Wesleyan University Press.

Gama, Rinaldo. 1994. "Biblioteca Nacional." *Veja* 27, no. 47 (November 23): 108–112. Accessed June 12, 2019. http://bussolaliteraria.blogspot.com/2010_01_24_archive.html

Semana de Arte Moderna/Modern Art Week. http://semana-arte-moderna.info

Slater, Candace (translator). 1989. *This Earth, That Sky: Poems by Manuel Bandeira*. Berkeley: University of California Press.

Contemporary Writers

Contemporary Brazilian writers have generated a new vibrant energy with new literary work they started to publish in the early twenty-first century. Modern literature incorporates more voices previously segregated, such as the stories written by women, people of color, immigrants, and members of the LGTBQ community. Their work is translated from Portuguese into multiple languages much faster than ever before. These new novelists, poets, and playwrights promote their work in digital format, and they have an active presence in social networks. They are more concerned with connecting with their readers than they are with belonging to a specific literary style or school. In addition, there are now more Brazilian literary awards that recognize the emergence of new talent and promote their work both domestically and abroad.

A wave of new Brazilian novelists has recently released extremely innovative stories. Carol Bensimon (1982–) was identified by the literary *Granta Magazine* in 2012 as one of their outstanding Young Brazilian Novelists. Her 2013 novel *Todos nós adorávamos caubóis* (We All Loved Cowboys) was extremely popular, and literary critics mentioned that it was likely to define the future of Brazilian literature. João Almino (1950–) became established as an award-wining literary figure when he published his famous *Brasília Quintet*—a series of five novels released within the space of a decade from 2003 to 2013. His most recent novel, *Enigmas da primavera* (Enigmas of Spring), published in 2015, received the Jabuti Award (Second Place) for Best International Novel in 2017. His reputation was further enhanced when he became one of the forty members elected to the prestigious Brazilian Academy of Letters.

Poetry continues to be popular in Brazil. Adriana Lisboa (1970–) is a prominent poet who has been defined as one of the most important Latin American writers under forty years old. While she also writes novels and essays, her poems have created an impetus for the genre. Her book *Parte da paisagem* (Part of the Landscape), published in 2014,

---

FESTA LITERÁRIA INTERNACIONAL DE PARATY

The Festa Literária Internacional de Paraty (FLIP) started in 2003 as an annual literary festival. It is held in the historic coastal city of Paraty in the state of Rio de Janeiro. The event is focused on literature, but it also includes musical concerts, films, dance performances, poetry sessions, cultural lectures, and writing workshops. Every July (or August if there is a World Cup), the festival honors a Brazilian writer with the purpose of preserving and promoting the Portuguese language. In 2018, the honoree was Hilda Hilst (1930–2004) to recognize her prolific work as a poet, novelist, and playwright. The program also disseminates the work of emerging talent, such as writers Leïla Slimani and André Aciman.

Sources: Festa Literária Internacional de Paraty Official Webpage. http://www.flip.org.br
Watson, Elizabeth. 2012. "Ten Years of FLIP Party." *Publishing Trends*, July 19. Accessed June 29, 2019. http://www.publishingtrends.com/2012/07/ten-years-flip-paraty

provokes the reader to consider simultaneous contradictions between lights and shadows, fertile and arid landscapes, as well as stagnation and progress. She has also received multiple international awards for her children's books.

The popularity of Brazilian theater has increased tremendously in the last twenty years thanks to a new generation of brilliant playwrights, producers, as well as technical advances in the field. In addition, the work of Brazilian dramatists is now recognized abroad with much more frequency. Renata Mizrahi (1979–) is an actress, director, and playwright who won the impressive Zilka Salaberry Award in 2012 for her young-literature play *Joaquim e as estrelas* (Joaquim and the Stars). Then her 2015 play *Galápagos* was selected to be presented at the Segal Theater in New York as part of a series titled "Contemporary Theater from Brazil" in November 2015. Her colleague Jô Bilac (1984–) was also included in the Segal project with his drama titled *Fluxorama*. Their acclaimed work sparked interest in other artistic institutions to commission translations of Brazilian theater into English.

The new generation of Brazilian writers has infused optimism into the national literary scene. They represent a diversity of voices with new ideas and topics. Their contributions are likely to shape the way Brazilians see the world and also the manner in which they see themselves.

See also: Chapter 11: Overview.

Further Reading

Adriana Lisboa Official Website. Accessed July 10, 2019. https://www.adrianalisboa.com

Carol Bensimon Official Website. Accessed July 10, 2019. http://www.carolbensimon.com

Feith, Roberto, and Marcelo Ferroni. 2012. "The Best Young Brazilian Novelists." *Granta: The Magazine of New Writing*. Granta.com, November 12. Accessed July 11, 2019. https://www.granta.com/foreword-the-best-of-young-brazilian-novelists

Mendez de Oliveira, Angela Francisca. n.d. "Século XXI: A presença de jovens escritores no sistema literário do Grande Do Sul (XXI Century: The Presence of Young Writers in the Literary System of Grande do Sul State)." *Monografias.com* Accessed July 11, 2019. http://br.monografias.com/trabalhos3/presenca-jovens-escritores-sistema-literario/presenca-jovens-escritores-sistema-literario2.shtml

Universidade Federal de Santa Catarina. *Literatura Brasileira*. Accessed July 11, 2019. http://www.literaturabrasileira.ufsc.br

Da Cunha, Euclides (1866–1909)

Euclides Rodrigues Pimenta da Cunha (1866–1909) left an indelible print on Brazilian literature. He had three professions that influenced his view of Brazilian life. He worked in the military as a civil engineer. He then made the transition to a journalist as a war correspondent. Finally, he settled as a writer who had firsthand experience with multiple controversial aspects of Brazilian society. He was a contemporary of Joaquim

Maria Machado de Assis. In fact, literary critics often pair them together because both writers defied clear definitions and boundaries of literary conventions.

Euclides da Cunha was born in Rio de Janeiro on January 20, 1866. During his early adulthood years, military discipline played an important role in his life. He was accepted to the Escola Militar da Paria Vermelha when he was twenty years old, but he was expelled in 1888 for insubordination due to his role in a protest regarding the visit of the Brazilian War Minister. Three years later, he enrolled in the Escola de Guerra (Brazilian War School), but he left the military in 1896 to pursue work in civil engineering and eventually transition into journalism. While working for the newspaper *O Estado de São Paulo* as a correspondent, he traveled with the Army during the Campanha de Canudos to squash a rebellious group of peasants in the backlands of Bahia state who were following the teachings of a rural miracle worker called Antônio Conselheiro. As a result, Euclides da Cunha was exposed to the brutal repression by the military of the rural population in the inhospitable interior territory. The Army killed most of the 30,000 inhabitants. His experiences with military expeditions and his contact with the less fortunate populations of Brazil shaped his point of view dramatically.

Euclides da Cunha wrote very few but significant literary works. He published three novels: *Õs sertões* (Rebellion in the Backlands), *Contrastes e confrontos* (Contrasts and Confrontations), and *Peru vs. Bolivia*. The newspaper *O Estado de S. Paulo* published posthumously two series of articles that the author had written during the Canudos War: *Canudos, diário de una expedição* (1939) and *Canudos e inéditos* (1967). His masterpiece, however, is *Õs sertões*, published in 1902. Without hesitation, most literary critics agree that this novel definitely earned its place in the Brazilian literary canon. It is a traditional historical narrative placed in a military setting. It is also a sociological and anthropological study that decries the social injustices that took place in the barren backlands of the country in the state of Bahia. The novel also offers a critical analysis of Brazil at the beginning of the 1900s as a deeply divided nation among three types of populations: the sophisticated urban centers, the developed coastal communities, and the poor and uneducated backlands (*sertão*). Euclides da Cunha writes a detailed attack on the government that highlights their funding priorities that neglect rural populations while politicians are willing to invest heavily in the speculation of potential industrial centers. The end of *Õs sertões* offers strong suggestions on how to incorporate the indigenous populations (as well as the *caboclos* of mixed Indian and European backgrounds) into Brazilian society.

The end of Euclides da Cunha's life was also related to the military since he was killed on August 15, 1909, by an Army lieutenant who was his wife's lover. Today, his literary work is celebrated in Brazil every year in the middle of August during the popular Semana Euclideana (Euclides da Cunha's Week).

See also: Chapter 1: The *Sertão* and Devastating Droughts. Chapter 5: Messianism and Miracle Workers. Chapter 11: Overview; Machado de Assis, Joaquim Maria (1839–1908).

Further Reading

Goldberg, Isaac. 2009. "Euclides da Cunha," in *Brazilian Literature*, 210–221. New York: Knopf.

Johnson, Randal (ed.). 1992. *Tropical Paths: Essays on Modern Brazilian Literature*. Abingdon, UK: Taylor & Francis Group.

Levine, Robert M. 1995. *Vale of Tears: Revisiting the Canudos Massacre in Northeastern Brazil, 1893–1897*. Oakland: University of California Press.

De Andrade, Oswald (1890–1954)

José Oswald de Souza Andrade (1890–1954) was born on January 11, 1890, in the city of São Paulo, where he spent the majority of his life. From an intellectual point of view, he was one of the founding members of the Semana de Arte Moderna (Modern Art Week) held in São Paulo from February 11 to February 18, 1922. He belonged to the famous Group of Five who provided the intellectual and theoretical foundation for the Modern Art Week including painter Anita Malfatti, journalist Paulo Menotti del Picchia, poet Mário de Andrade, and painter Tarsila do Amaral. This seminal event effectively defined a new artistic direction for Brazil to break away from European influence and create a new movement that focused on local native cultures, Brazilian colloquial language, and folklore legends. Oswald de Andrade came from a wealthy family, and he firmly believed that the new modernist movement would spark a significant social reform in Brazil. Consequently, he used his money to finance the work of multiple modernist artists, including painters, writers, and playwrights.

Oswald de Andrade produced significant literary pieces toward the end of the modernist movement. He had a strong nationalist point of view, and he was a political activist who advocated radical social reforms to benefit the less fortunate people of Brazil. He published his novel *Manifesto antropófago* (Cannibal Manifesto) in 1928 as an open and honest critique of the social rhetoric that was prevalent in Brazil at the time. He claimed that Brazil already had a long history of borrowing a lot of traditions and traits from other cultures (which he labeled as Cannibalism), and that such an approach could actually be used to develop a unique Brazilian style to challenge the influence of European literary and artistic movements. His other significant novel was *Serafim Ponte Grande*, published in 1933 in what literary critics define as the postmodernism period. His work certainly defied traditional European rhetorical styles by challenging Brazilian established cultural norms and using innovative colloquial language (as opposed to "proper" Portuguese). He remained a consistent writer in Brazilian literary circles until the 1950s. His other works include a collection of poems titled *Pau-brasil* in 1925, and several novels: *Meu testamento* in 1944, *A Arcádia e a inconfidência* in 1945, *A crise da filosofia messiânica* in 1950, *Um aspecto antropofágico da cultura Brasileira: O homem cordial* in 1950, and *A marcha das utopias* in 1953. Oswald de Andrade died in his native city of São Paulo on October 22, 1954.

See also: Chapter 11: Overview; Modernism in Brazil. Chapter 12: Modern Art Week, São Paulo 1922.

Further Reading

Bishop, Elizabeth, and Emanuel Brasil (eds.). 1997. *An Anthology of Twentieth-Century Brazilian Poetry*. Middletown, CT: Wesleyan University Press.

Jauregui, Carlos A. 2008. *Canibalia, canibalismo, calibanismo, antropofagia cultural y consumo en América Latina* (in Spanish). Madrid: Vervuert ETC: Ensayos de Teoría Cultural.

Jauregui, Carlos A. 2012. "Antropofagia," in *Dictionary of Latin American Cultural Studies* edited by Robert McKee Irwin and Mónica Szurmurk, 22–28. Gainesville: University Press of Florida.

Johnson, Randal (ed.). 1992. *Tropical Paths: Essays on Modern Brazilian Literature*. Abingdon, UK: Taylor & Francis Group.

Semana de Arte Moderna/Modern Art Week. http://semana-arte-moderna.info

Young, Richard, and Odile Cisneros. 2001. *Historical Dictionary of Latin American Literature and Theater*. Lanham, MD: Scarecrow Press.

Guimarães Rosa, João (1908–1967)

João Guimarães Rosa (1908–1967) was born on June 27, 1908, in the town of Cordisburgo within the state of Minas Gerais, Brazil. During his childhood, he attended elementary and secondary school in Belo Horizonte and São João del Rei. He then went to the Faculdade de Medicina da Universidade Federal de Minas Gerais. Subsequently in 1932, he served as a volunteer doctor in Minas Gerais. One year later, he worked for the military, and he was sent to Barbacena (in Minas Gerais) to serve as the doctor for the 9th Infantry Battalion, which provided crucial experience for his future career in diplomacy. His first diplomatic post was in Hamburg, Germany, as assistant consul; this is where he met his wife, with whom he had two daughters. He worked as a diplomat in multiple countries. In the field of literature, he was a novelist and short story writer.

Guimarães Rosa published only one novel, but it certainly established him as part of the national literary canon. His masterpiece novel titled *Grande sertão: Veredas* (The Devil to Pay in the Backlands) was released in 1956. It became immediately popular with average readers and literary critics. Literature experts, however, have struggled to classify him within a specific literary period or school of thought. Guimarães Rosa presented a unique writing style and innovative use of language that was considered extremely groundbreaking at the time it was published. It provided general natural descriptions of the Brasilian *sertão* as semiarid backlands where people experienced extremely difficult living conditions. The novel also incorporated the use of common vocabulary, archaic phrases, and neologisms used in rural regions, even if they did not conform to the expectations of "high" literature in Brazilian society. International literary surveys consider *Grande sertão: Veredas* one of the best one hundred books of all time in world literature. However, Rosa's inventive prose and the use of regional expressions are difficult to translate, and his work has not been widely available in other languages.

While Guimarães Rosa is considered one of the greatest Brazilian novelists of all time, he also wrote several books of short stories, including *Magma* (1936), *Corpo de baile* (1956), and *Tutaméia* (1967). Most of his stories portray the harsh living conditions of rural populations, especially the plight of *sertanejos* (people from the *sertão*) in the northeast region of the country. Two of Rosa's short story books are widely available in English under the following titles: *Saragana* (1946) and *Primeiras estórias* (translated as *Third Bank of the River and Other Stories*, 1962). Both of these books offer detailed descriptions of the semiarid landscape in the interior regions of Brazil.

See also: Chapter 1: The *Sertão* and Devastating Droughts. Chapter 11: Overview; Literary Canon; Modernism in Brazil.

Further Reading

Bokklubben. 2002. "The Library of World Literature: The Best 100 Books of All Time." Oslo, Norway: Bokklubben. *Bokklubben.com* Accessed June 10, 2019. https://www.bokklubben.no/SamboWeb/side.do?dokId=65500

Gama, Rinaldo. 1994. "Biblioteca Nacional." *Veja* 27, no. 47 (November 23): 108–112. Accessed June 10, 2019. http://bussolaliteraria.blogspot.com/2010_01_24_archive.html

Guimarães Rosa, João. 2006. *Grande sertão: Veredas (The Devil to Pay in the Backlands)*. Rio de Janeiro: Editora Nova Fronteira.

Vincent, Jon S. 2003. *Culture and Customs of Brazil*. Westport, CT: Greenwood Press.

Lima Barreto, Alfonso (1881–1922)

Alfonso Henriques de Lima Barreto was born on May 13, 1881, in Rio de Janeiro, where he lived most of his life. He practiced two related professions simultaneously during his adult life: novelist and journalist. He is widely recognized simply by his two last names, Lima Barreto. Literary critics place him under the premodernism period that lasted from 1895 until 1922; this is an era without specific predominant styles that clearly define writers. Lima Barreto's work, however, was highly critical of Brazilian society by using ironic humor and satirical rhetoric. He was a dark-skinned *mulatto* who grew up poor and had a keen understanding of the prejudices that existed in carioca (from Rio de Janeiro) society against people of mixed racial background.

Lima Barreto had a rough childhood. His mother died when he was very young. As a result, he was sent to a boarding school, where he demonstrated a definite aptitude for education. He then enrolled at the prestigious Liceu Popular Niteroiense after a benefactor paid for his tuition. In 1985, he entered the Colégio Pedro II to continue his studies. Then he attended the Escola Politécnica do Rio de Janeiro, but he never finished his higher education because he started working to support his younger brothers.

Lima Barreto started writing as a journalist in 1902, and he published a series of articles in 1905 that brought him fame and recognition. While still working at a newspaper, he published his first novel in 1909 titled *Recordações do escrivão Isaías Caminha*. This novel provided an extremely strong and honest satirical view of Brazilian high society, especially in Rio de Janeiro. He certainly gained notoriety in social and literary circles. His masterpiece, however, came six years later with his novel *O triste fim de Policarpo Quaresma* (The Sad End of Policarpo Quaresma) in 1915. It was published a few chapters at a time in *feuilleton* format, which is a supplement published in a newspaper. Given its overwhelming success, it was released later in 1915 in book form. The protagonist in this story was a staunch patriot who wanted to improve his country. However, he soon realizes that Brazilians love foreign cultures more than Brazilian traditions, and his goal is to change their mediocre minds. In his quest to do so, the nationalist character provides a scathing criticism of the social structure and the main political institutions in Brazil. He highlights the indifference, arrogance, and hypocrisy that exist among Brazilians when it comes to the less fortunate populations in the country. The quixotic main character then offers specific guidelines on how to undertake three types of much-needed reforms: agricultural, cultural, and military. At the end of the story, Policarpo is, ironically, killed for committing high treason against the country. This novel is still relevant today, and contemporary Brazilians often cite it as one of the top ten novels ever included in the national literary canon.

Lima Barreto wrote other well-known novels, including *Numa e a ninfa* (1915), *Vida e morte de M. J. Gonzaga de Sá* (1919), *Cemitério dos vivos* (1920), *Histórias e sonhos* (1920), and *Clara dos Anjos* (posthumously in 1924). He remained a prolific writer until the end of his life. However, since the early 1900s, he suffered from acute depression that resulted in severe alcoholism and multiple psychiatric breakdowns. He suffered a massive heart attack and died on November 1, 1922, when he was only forty-one years old.

See also: Chapter 11: Overview; Literary Canon; Modernism in Brazil.

Further Reading

Angiolillo, Francesca. 2016. "Ten Works of Fiction to Better Understand Brazil: A Country in Crisis and Its Vital Literature." *Literary Hub*. Lithub.com May 18, 2016. Accessed July 8, 2019. https://lithub.com/10-works-of-fiction-to-better-understand-brazil

Barbosa, Francisco de Assis. 2002. *A vida de Lima Barreto* (in Portuguese). Rio de Janeiro: José Olympio Editora.

Goldberg, Isaac. 2009. *Brazilian Literature*. New York: Knopf.

Johnson, Randal (ed.). 1992. *Tropical Paths: Essays on Modern Brazilian Literature*. Abingdon, UK: Taylor & Francis Group.

Literary Canon

Harold Bloom published his controversial book *The Western Canon* in 1994. His ambitious goal was to select the most important literary books ever published in the

Table 11.1: TOP 20 BRAZILIAN BOOKS THAT BEST REPRESENT NATIONAL CULTURE

Title	Genre	Author	Year	# of Votes
Os sertões	Essay	Euclides da Cunha	1902	15
Casa-grande & senzala	Sociology	Gilberto Freyre	1933	14
Grande sertão	Novel	João Guimarães Rosa	1956	13
Macunaíma	Novel	Mário de Andrade	1928	11
Dom Casmurro	Novel	Machado de Assis, Joaquim	1900	8
Raízes do Brasil	Sociology	Sérgio Buarque de Holanda	1936	8
Memórias póstumas de Brás Cubas	Novel	Joaquim Machado de Assis	1881	7
Vidas secas	Novel	Graciliano Ramos	1938	6
Um estadista do império	Biography	Joaquim Nabuco	1897	6
Formação da literatura Brasileira	Literary Criticism	Antonio Candido	1975	5
O tempo e o vento—Trilogy	Novel	Érico Veríssimo	1949–1962	5
Fogo morto	Novel	José Lins do Rego	1943	5
Formação econômica do Brasil	Economics	Celso Furtado	1960	5
Poesias completas 1882–1943	Poetry	Gregório de Matos	1969	5
Os donos do poder, First Edition	History	Raymundo Faoro	1958	4
Triste fim de Policarpo Quaresma	Novel	Lima Barreto	1915	4
Formação do Brasil contemporâneo	History, Economics	Caio Prado Júnior	1942	4
Os donos do poder, Second Edition	History	Raymundo Faoro	1975	4
Iracema	Novel	Jose de Alencar	1865	4
Gabriela, cravo e canela	Novel	Jorge Amado	1959	4
Poesias completas 1930–1970	Poetry	Carlos Drummond	1987	4
Poesias completas 1917–1966	Poetry	Manuel Bandeira	1966	4

Western world. He handpicked 26 authors that reflect the best of Western literature plus another 824 writers who make up the second group of outstanding authors. Two Brazilian poets made that exclusive list: Carlos Drummond de Andrade and Fernando Pessoa. In the same year, the editors at the prestigious political/cultural news magazine *Veja* from São Paulo decided to gather fifteen intellectuals and literati to create a Brazilian literary canon made up of twenty books that best represent the national culture. They came up with a list of twenty-two works that include eleven novels, three collections of poetry, one essay, and seven nonfiction books (on history, sociology, and economics). They are listed in Table 11.1 in order of how many votes they each received.

The creation of an exclusive list of this nature immediately raises questions, and a few observations are quickly apparent. For example, the *Veja* report does not explain how the judges were appointed to this task or the criteria they used to select the books. A quick glance also reveals that there is not a single woman author on that list. In addition, it is clear that the definition of literature varies from country to country since economic and sociological treatises would not usually qualify in that category outside of Brazil. Overall, the national canon seems to value novels and poetry but not theater since none of the playwrights were included on the list. In general, the majority of the books selected reveal the national preoccupation of Brazilians with attempting to define who they are as a nation. Finally, book lists are by definition ephemeral. The last of the literary books (novels and poetry) in the canon was published in the 1960s, which indicates that all the creative talent of contemporary Brazilian writers was not taken into account.

See also: Chapter 11: Overview; Amado, Jorge (1912–2001); Bandeira, Manuel (1886–1968); Da Cunha, Euclides (1866–1909); De Andrade, Oswald (1890–1954); Guimarães Rosa, João (1908–1967); Lima Barreto, Alfonso (1881–1922); Machado de Assis, Joaquim Maria (1839–1908); Modern Theater and Playwrights.

Further Reading

Bloom, Harold. 1994. *The Western Canon: The Books and School of the Ages*. London: Penguin.

Gama, Rinaldo. 1994. "Biblioteca Nacional." *Veja* 27, no. 47 (November 23): 108–112. Accessed May 28, 2019. http://bussolaliteraria.blogspot.com/2010_01_24_archive.html

Goldberg, Isaac. 2009. *Brazilian Literature*. New York: Knopf.

Haberly, David T. 1983. *Three Sad Races: Racial Identity and National Consciousness in Brazilian Literature*. New York: Cambridge University Press.

Rector, Monica (ed.). 2005. *Dictionary of Literary Biography: Brazilian Writers, v. 370*. Detroit, MI: Thompson Gale.

Universidade Federal de Santa Catarina. *Literatura Brasileira*. Accessed May 28, 2019. http://www.literaturabrasileira.ufsc.br

Vincent, Jon S. 2003. *Culture and Customs of Brazil*. Westport, CT: Greenwood Press.

Literary Censorship by the Military

A repressive military dictatorship ruled Brazil for over twenty years (1964 to 1985). However, this authoritarian regime was different than the other military governments that proliferated in South America during the 1970s. It was ruled by five successive generals and without a central dominating figure such as Fidel Castro in Cuba or Augusto

Pinochet in Chile. All the five Brazilian rulers received the official title of President of Brazil. In sequential order, they were: Humberto de Alencar Castelo Branco (1964–1967), Artur da Costa e Silva (1967–1969), Emílio Garrastazu Médici (1969–1974), Ernesto Geisel (1974–1979), and João Figueiredo (1979–1985). They ruled using the existing constitution, but they issued Institutional Acts (decrees) that concentrated most of the power in the hands of the executive leader—all in the name of national security. During this period, the military suppressed its own population in order to further its economic agenda, social reforms, and political control. Unjustified arrests, torture, exile, and murder became commonplace. In addition, all public gatherings and political activities were forbidden.

In order to maintain complete control over all aspects of Brazilian society and repress any potential protests, the authoritarian regime applied heavy censorship of the media, literature, academia, and the arts. The government immediately removed university presidents and placed military administrators in those jobs; scientists were expelled from academic and research positions; and prominent writers, playwrights, and musicians were arrested, tortured, or forced into exile. Then the military hired an immense number of censors to target all aspects of public life and entertainment that might transmit messages of subversion and resistance. The government's strategies were carried out by two main organizations. The National Information System (SIN) had the task of detecting public opinions critical of the government or promoting democratic ideals, and then labeling them as subversive, communist, or terrorist. The consequences for those involved were arrest, torture, disappearance, exile, or even murder. The Departamento de Censura e Diversões Públicas (DCDP) was particularly pernicious in the repression of public expression in any format. They focused on books, magazines, theater, cinema, radio, and television. Nothing could be published or released in Brazil without prior approval of the DCDP censors. In addition, Institutional Acts 1–5 specifically targeted intense censorship of artists and the imprisonment of writers and journalists. Given the sociopolitical context of the military dictatorship, it is not surprising that Brazil produced a unique style of literature in the 1970s and 1980s that is often identified with multiple names, such as protest literature, subversive prose, marginal poetry, resistance narrative, and testimonial stories.

In spite of all the dangers of publishing literature of resistance under military censorship, multiple writers excelled in their efforts during the 1970s and 1980s. Their work was a reaction to political repression. Rubem Fonseca published a book of short stories that highlighted urban violence with the ironic title *Feliz ano novo* (Happy New Year) in 1973; it was immediately placed on the national censored-book list. Well-established writers such as Roberto Drummond published *A morte de D. J in Paris* (The Death of D. J in Paris) in 1975, and it was defined as a crucial narrative of political resistance dealing with totalitarian governments. During the late 1970s, the voice of female writers finally began to emerge. *O conto da mulher brasileira* (Stories of Brazilian Women), released in 1978, was the first anthology ever published to include all female writers, just as the political system began to offer concessions to transition back to a democracy. The government proposed an *abertura* (political opening) in the same year, and democracy returned in 1985. During the 1980s, large numbers of political exiles returned to Brazil, and their testimonial literature became extremely popular as it covered topics of urban violence, civil rights, political power, and freedom. Alfredo Sirkis published his novel *Os carbonários* (The Carbonari) in 1980 with the gut-wrenching testimony of a political exile; it quickly became a best seller. Once democracy and constitutional rights were reestablished in Brazil, a new generation of writers explored other forms of expression that provided a voice for other marginalized groups in society, including immigrants, gays, feminists, and Afro-Brazilian artists.

See also: Chapter 2: Operation Condor and Military Rule. Chapter 11: Overview.

Further Reading

Bettine de Almeida, Marco Antonio et al. 2013. "Leisure in Brazil: The Transformations during the Military Period (1964–1984)." *Revista brasileira de educacão física e esporte* 27, no. 1 (January/March): 101–115. Accessed June 15, 2019. http://www.scielo.br/pdf/rbefe/v27n1/v27n1a11.pdf

Ginway, Elizabeth. 1999. "Literature under the Dictatorship," in *The Brazil Reader: History, Culture, and Politics*, edited by Robert M. Levine and John J. Crocitti, 248–257. Durham, NC: Duke University Press.

Goldberg, Isaac. 2009. *Brazilian Literature*. New York: Knopf.

Reimão, Sandra L. 2010. *Livros e censura na ditadura militar brasileira/Books and Censorship during the Brazilian Military Dictatorship*. Fundação de Amparo à Pesquisa do Estado de São Paulo (FAPESP). www.fapesp.br December 31, 2010. Accessed June 15, 2019. http://www.bv.fapesp.br/pt/auxilios/38871/livros-e-censura-na-ditadura-militar-brasileira

Machado de Assis, Joaquim Maria (1839–1908)

Joaquim Maria Machado de Assis (1839–1908) is often considered the greatest writer in Brazilian literature. He is most commonly known simply as Machado de Assis. He was a prolific writer who excelled in multiple genres, including as a poet, novelist, short story author, and playwright. He was born in Rio de Janeiro on June 21, 1839, at a time when the city was the capital of the Brazilian Empire. He was the son of a *mulatto* house painter. His mother died when he was only ten years old, and he was raised by his stepmother, who was also of a mixed racial background. Machado married Carolina Augusta Xavier de Novais in 1869, but they did not have any children.

Machado attended public school, and he was not a particularly good student. However, he was extremely eager to learn, and he taught himself English, German, and French. While he was not formally trained in literature, he was an avid reader who devoured all the literary classics in multiple languages. His interest in letters led him to work as a proofreader at a newspaper and an editor at a magazine. Eventually, he pursued a job as a government bureaucrat in order to have a consistent paycheck. Then he started writing during his free time, especially essays and poetry following the romanticism style common in Brazil at the time.

Machado de Assis wrote a large collection of plays, poetry, essays, and novels, but he is mostly remembered for two masterpieces that are part of the national literary canon. The highly acclaimed novel *Memórias póstumas de Brás Cubas* (often translated as the *Epitaph of a Small Winner*) was published in 1881, and it is considered his greatest achievement. While Romantic authors of the time were writing works based on emotions, feelings, and the Brazilian indigenous past to define national identity, Machado broke away from those literary conventions. His book *Memórias póstumas* offers a style that is essentially pessimistic, with a protagonist who provides a rather cynical and disillusioned view of society.

The Brazilian monarchy was overthrown in 1889, but Machado remained a strong supporter of Dom Pedro II. He was not kind to the new leaders of the Republican government of Brazil, and he became extremely critical of the new emerging Brazilian society. It was in this context that he published the novel *Dom Casmurro* in 1900. While fellow writers were publishing pastoral descriptions of the countryside with nostalgic views of rural populations, his style was unapologetically urban, somewhat indifferent, and cynical. Machado never traveled outside Brazil, and he never ventured too far from Rio de Janeiro. Consequently, his novels were very cosmopolitan. He also exposed the contradictions and hypocrisy of Brazilian society. Despite his pessimistic style, his work was also skillfully infused with wit and humor. By the end of the 1800s, Machado had earned his reputation as a writer. In fact, he was one of the founding members of the Brazilian Academy of Letters, and he served as its first president from 1897 until his death on September 29, 1908.

Literary critics usually struggle to classify Machado de Assis within a specific literary period or style. He fits somewhat within the boundaries of romanticism, realism, and premodernism. His sophisticated style, however, broke away from neatly defined literary traditions, and he achieved popularity with both readers and critics. To honor his memory and his contributions to national literature, the Brazilian Academy of Letters created the Prêmio Machado de Assis in 1941. The annual award is considered the most prestigious literary recognition presented to a Brazilian writer. He influenced generations of future writers, and he contributed to the definition of a Brazilian cultural identity.

See also: Chapter 11: Overview; Da Cunha, Euclides (1866–1909); Modernism in Brazil; Theater Playwrights.

Further Reading

Chalhoub, Sidney. 2003. *Machado de Assis, historiador*. São Paulo: Companhia das Letras.

Goldberg, Isaac. 2009. *Brazilian Literature*. New York: Knopf.

Johnson, Randal (ed.). 1992. *Tropical Paths: Essays on Modern Brazilian Literature*. Abingdon, UK: Taylor & Francis Group.

McNeil, Rhett (translator). 2014. *Joaquim Maria Machado de Assis: Stories*. Champaign, IL: Dalkey Archive Press.

Reginald, Daniel G. 2012. *Machado de Assis: Multiracial Identity and the Brazilian Novelist*. University Park: Penn State Press.

Modern Theater and Playwrights

There is a long tradition of theatrical performances in Brazil. During the colonial period (1500–1822), the Portuguese used *autos* (brief religious plays) to convert the indigenous populations to Catholicism. After independence in 1822, the playwright Luis Carlos Martins Pena (1815–1848) wrote over thirty works of drama that can truly be considered as the origin of Brazilian theater. His plays were strongly critical of social institutions, including the Catholic Church, politicians, and even marriage. By the end of the 1800s, Brazilian theater was still designed mostly for small audiences made up of elite members of society.

During the 1900s, Brazilian literature produced a large number of successful playwrights, as well as numerous theatrical production groups. Oswald de Andrade (1890–1954) released two separate plays in 1937: *O rei da vela* (The Candle King) and *A morta* (The Dead Woman), which ridicule the decadent lifestyle of the elites in Brazil. Then two crucial plays changed Brazilian theatrical history due to their innovation and complexity. First, Nelson Rodrigues published *Vestido de noiva* (The Wedding Dress) in 1943, which revolutionized Brazilian theater by introducing a structure that takes place at three levels: hallucinations, memories, and reality. Alfredo Dias Gomes released his play *O pagador de promessas* in 1960, which became an instant success with the masses. It offers a critical analysis of clashes between rural and urban populations during the 1960s. The popular play was adapted to television and cinema.

Contemporary Brazilian theater became widespread in the 1990s thanks to an entire new generation of prolific playwrights. Two of the most recognized modern dramatists are Miguel Falabella and Nelson Rodrigues. Falabella published his highly successful play *A partilha* (The Inheritance) in 1990 and initially staged it in a small university theater. He is a new type of dramatist who is also an actor, producer, and director while also functioning in multiple mediums of entertainment: theater, television, and cinema. Since then, *A partilha* has toured all over Brazil (and abroad) in much larger venues. His plays are written for a middle-class audience who can appreciate meaningful plots with a social message, not just a simple comedy for quick laughs. Another notable modern playwright is Nelson Rodrigues, who died in 1980. Most of his plays—including *The Wedding Gown*, *The Woman without Sin*, and *The Kiss of the Asphalt*—force the audience to analyze themselves through themes of prejudice, jealousy, guilt, and deception. In general terms, his work explores the hypocrisy that exists in Brazilian middle-class societies.

At the beginning of the twenty-first century, Brazilian playwrights are finally being discovered abroad. Their work is being translated into other languages, which allows their stories to reach wider audiences. For example, in November 2015, the Martin E. Segal Theater in New York exhibited four new plays written by Brazilian dramatists and translated to English. They included: *The Meal* by Newton Moreno, *Galápagos* by Renata Mizrahi, *The Front Door* by Julia Spadaccini, and *Fluxorama* by Jô Bilac. The Segal Theater also organized in November 2017 multiple panel discussions titled "Female Voices from Brazil with Ana Maria Gonçalves, Cidinha da Silva, and Marcia Zanelatto." The work of these three talented contemporary female playwrights was extremely well received and attended. Female voices in Brazilian literature are now a strong contribution that has not historically been included or appreciated.

See also: Chapter 11: Overview; Contemporary Writers; De Andrade, Oswald (1890–1954); Literary Canon; Postindependence Literature.

Further Reading

Brooke, Elizabeth Heilman. 1994. "The One-Man Whirlwind of Brazilian Theater." *New York Times,* August 27. Accessed June 15, 2019. https://www.nytimes.com/1994/08/27/theater/the-one-man-whirlwind-of-brazilian-theater.html

George, David. 1992. *The Modern Brazilian Stage.* Austin: University of Texas Press.

James, Tia (director). 2017. "Female Voices from Brazil with Ana Maria Gonçalves, Cidinha da Silva, and Marcia Zanelatto." The Martin E. Segal Theater Center, New York City. TheSegalCenter.org, November 6. Accessed June 15, 2019. http://thesegalcenter.org/event/female-voices-from-brazil

Rother, Larry. 2000. "Reawakening the Giant of Brazilian Theater." *New York Times,* December 17, 2000. Accessed June 15, 2019. http://www.nytimes.com/2000/12/17/theater/theater-reawakening-the-giant-of-brazilian-theater.html

Young, Richard, and Odile Cisneros. 2001. *Historical Dictionary of Latin American Literature and Theater.* Lanham, MD: Scarecrow Press.

Modernism in Brazil

Literary and artistic movements usually arrive at a country following a gradual process. That is the way the modernism aesthetic styles (including surrealism, cubism, and dadaism) arrived throughout Spanish-speaking Latin America. Brazil, however, was different. The case of Brazil was unusual because the start of the modernism movement can actually be pinpointed to a specific place and date. The Semana de Arte Moderna (Modern Art Week) took place in São Paulo from February 11 to February 18, 1922. The year was not accidental since it marked exactly one hundred years from the date of Brazilian independence. The modernist goal was essentially to inspire a movement seeking new ways of expression in the arts that were truly Brazilian. It had three interrelated sections: literature, music, and art. However, Brazilian modernism ended up influencing not only literature but also studio arts (painting, sculpture, design) and performing arts (music, theater, dance, and cinema).

The famous Group of Five provided the theoretical foundation of the modernist movement in Brazil that rejected European influence and had the goal to create a literary and artistic movement where native folklore and local icons developed national pride. This group included painter Anita Malfatti, journalist Paulo Menotti del Picchia, poet Mário de Andrade, painter Tarsila do Amaral, and the multifaceted Oswald de Andrade. They aimed to achieve greater social reform that defined the way Brazilians thought about themselves. Other well-known Brazilian artists and intellectuals who also contributed to the organization of the Semana de Arte Moderno included writer

Graça Aranha, illustrator Emiliano Augusto Cavalcanti, and music composer Heitor Villa-Lobos. They all agreed that it was crucial to break artistic and literary paradigms in order to create something unique to Brazilian culture.

In terms of literature, the Brazilian modernist style created novels, theater, and poetry that focused on native themes and the use of folklore traditions. Local writers abandoned the traditional notions of literary values imported from Portugal. Instead, they incorporated the use of regional colloquial speech rather than always relying on appropriate and formal language as a means of expression. By the 1930s, a large number of amateur writers had been influenced by the innovative writing style. However, the movement started to diverge into two main groups: those who sought radical social reform with nationalistic rhetoric (such as writer Oswald de Andrade), and those who were more concerned with literature and art but did not necessarily advocate political confrontations (such as poet Manuel Bandeira). The poetry book that defined Bandeira as a modernist writer was titled *Libertinism*. Published in 1930, it included simple and accessible language, irony and melancholy. It also created a transition to other styles that extended into the 1950s.

The year 1945 marked the end of modernism in Brazil. From a historical point of view, it was the end of World War II, and it also closed the chapter on the dictatorial regime of Getúlio Vargas in Brazil. In the same year, Mário de Andrade (one of the intellectual founders of Brazilian modernism) died. In fact, a new literary group called the Generation of 1945 emerged as a postmodernist collection of writers that included João Guimarães Rosa. His most famous novel, *Gabriela, cravo e canela* (Gabriela, Clove and Cinnamon), published in 1958, is part of the national literary canon, and his innovative use of language had a profound impact on Brazilian literature.

See also: Chapter 11: Overview; De Andrade, Oswald (1890–1954); Bandeira, Manuel (1886–1968); Guimarães Rosa, João (1908–1967).

Further Reading

Goldberg, Isaac. 2009. *Brazilian Literature*. New York: Knopf.

Rector, Monica (ed.). 2005. *Brazilian Writers (Dictionary of Literary Biography, v. 370)*. Detroit, MI: Thompson Gale.

Semana de Arte Moderna/Modern Art Week. http://semana-arte-moderna.info

Skidmore, Thomas E. 2010. *Brazil: Five Centuries of Change*. Oxford, UK: Oxford University Press.

Young, Richard, and Odile Cisneros. 2001. *Historical Dictionary of Latin American Literature and Theater*. Lanham, MD: Scarecrow Press.

Postindependence Literature

Brazil became independent from Portugal in 1822. Then it became the Brazilian Empire, a period that lasted until 1888. As a new nation, it struggled to create a unique national culture, and literature was an important tool to disseminate such vision. Intellectuals did not want to appeal to their European past since they had just obtained independence from Portugal. The notion of highlighting its African background was not an appealing option in a society in which slavery was still thriving. Therefore, Brazil embraced its indigenous population as the image for a new nationalist expression. While novelists and poets were influenced by European romanticism, Brazilian writers glorified nativism (by describing exotic tropical landscapes) and Indianism (by promoting the notion of "noble savages").

In the field of poetry, Antônio Gonçalves Dias (1823–1864) is one of the most renowned Indianism writers in Brazil. His 1843 poem titled "Canção do Exílio" ("Song of Exile") offers a nostalgic view of the countryside that immediately became popular nationwide. By the 1870s, the abolitionist movement became stronger in Brazil, and Antônio Castro Alves published a critical collection of antislavery poetry titled *Os escravos* (The Slaves) in 1883.

During the 1880s, Joaquim Machado de Assis (1839–1908), José de Alencar (1829–1877), and Aluízio Azevedo (1857–1913) were the most prominent novelists in Brazil. Machado de Assis published *Memórias póstumas de Brás Cubas* (Epitaph of a Small Winner) in 1881; it was a scathing social criticism of his native city Rio de Janeiro. Due to several best-selling novels, Machado de Assis is quite possibly the most recognized writer in Brazilian literature. In the same decade, a progressive Indianist social agenda was evident in José de Alencar's poetry book *Iracema*, released in 1886. The story portrays the union of a Portuguese soldier with an Indian woman and their biracial son. The concept of miscegenation is intended to symbolize the mixed-race origin of Brazil. This novel earned a spot on the national literary canon, and it was later adapted into a soap opera. During the same period, Aluízio Azevedo published multiple novels denouncing the social policies that kept laws of slavery in place while the rest of Latin America had already abolished the institution. One of his novels, *O mulato* (The Mulatto, 1881), deals with how thoroughly the concepts of race and prejudice were ingrained in the heavily stratified social system of the period.

Brazilian theater was popular during the Portuguese colonial period, but it was mostly limited to religious plays with pedagogical purposes. Original Brazilian drama was developed after independence largely by the playwright Luis Carlos Martins Pena (1815–1848). He wrote over thirty works of drama mostly in the comedy genre but with a heavy satirical twist. His plays attracted large numbers of people to regional theaters because his work reflected the culture, language, and customs of the lower classes of Brazil. His critical dramas were in fact direct criticism of social institutions, including the Catholic Church, politicians, and even marriage.

By the end of the 1800s, Brazilian literature included prolific poets, and playwrights; it had also matured to reflect national cultural and social values. Brazil was the last country in the Americas to abolish slavery in 1888. It eventually expelled its emperors and replaced them with a new republic that offered a democratic system of government. In addition, intellectuals and literati founded the Brazilian Academy of Letters in 1896, with Machado de Assis elected as its first president. It was established in Rio de Janeiro, and its purpose was to celebrate Brazilian literature and to promote it in society.

See also: Chapter 2: Overview; Brazilian Empire: Pedro I (1798–1834) and Pedro II (1825–1891); Slavery, Abolition, and African Heritage. Chapter 11: Overview; Machado de Assis, Joaquim Maria (1839–1908); Modern Theater and Playwrights.

Further Reading

Brazilian Academy of Letters/Academia Brasileira de Letras. www.academia.org.br/

Goldberg, Isaac. 2009. *Brazilian Literature*. New York: Knopf.

McNeil, Rhett (translator). 2014. *Joaquim Maria Machado de Assis: Stories*. Champaign, IL: Dalkey Archive Press.

Rector, Monica (ed.). 2005. *Brazilian Writers (Dictionary of Literary Biography, v. 370)*. Detroit, MI: Thompson Gale.

Skidmore, Thomas E. 2010. *Brazil: Five Centuries of Change*. Oxford, UK: Oxford University Press.

Young, Richard, and Odile Cisneros. 2001. *Historical Dictionary of Latin American Literature and Theater*. Lanham, MD: Scarecrow Press.

CHAPTER 12

ART AND ARCHITECTURE

OVERVIEW

Brazilians are very creative, and their talent is reflected in colorful art, detailed crafts, and striking architecture, all of which have been influenced by historical events. The term "Indian art" has been used to describe the early creations of indigenous groups before the European conquest of Brazil. For example, the Marajoara cultures have produced painted pottery for centuries that is still valued today. During the colonial period (1500–1822), miscegenation (the mixing of Indians, Africans, and Europeans) was also represented in the art that emerged during those centuries, especially under the influence of Catholic and African religions. It was during the 1700s that the artistic style called Barroco Mineiro emerged as a local artistic expression that was uniquely Brazilian, especially in the town of Ouro Preto. Then the arrival of the French Artistic Mission in 1816 officially changed the way art was taught and produced in the country by establishing an Academy of Fine Arts. The neoclassical style favored by this movement had a profound impact on both art and architecture. During the twentieth century, the Week of Modern Art Festival in 1922 officially solidified the modernism movement in Brazil. It was a radical call to abandon European traditions and develop new forms of artistic expression that reflected Brazilian themes but also included an intrinsic agenda to institute social change. An overall theme in Brazilian art is the continuous search for a national identity.

COLONIAL PERIOD (1500–1822)

Baroque Style and Religious Influence

The Portuguese arrived on the Brazilian coast in 1500. During the initial stages of the colonial period, the Portuguese founded the cities of São Paulo, Rio de Janeiro, Recife, and Salvador. They essentially used the European architectural style they knew to build homes, forts, churches, as well as civic and government buildings. Most of the oldest Brazilian colonial towns included churches and cathedrals that were filled with sacred art. Then the Portuguese discovered gold (in 1696) and diamonds (in 1725) in the interior state of Minas Gerais. The town of Ouro Preto became the epicenter of the Brazilian gold rush that sent over 800 tons of gold to Portugal. However, considerable wealth remained in the region, which sparked a renewed interest in religious art and architecture in the towns of Diamantina, Mariana, and Congonhas. The most important architect and sculptor of the period was Antônio Francisco Lisboa (1738–1814)—better known as *Aleijadinho*—who designed and built multiple churches in Minas Gerais. He often worked with Manoel Costa de Ataíde (1762–1830), who was one of the most renowned painters of the time. They both adapted a baroque style that encouraged opulent ornamentation, detailed carvings, as well as architecture with curved walls and round bell towers. Most of the fresco paintings were based on religious biblical themes. Their unique style became known as Barroco Mineiro, and it influenced the work of their followers until the end of the eighteenth century.

Neoclassicism

The Portuguese royal court invited the French Artistic Mission in 1816 with the specific purpose to change artistic expression in Brazil from a religious orientation and workshop apprenticeship to a more sophisticated level of artistry. They created the Academy of Fine Arts, and it revolutionized the way painting, sculpture, design, and architecture were taught and implemented. They infused the neoclassical style that was prevalent in Europe at the time, which encouraged simple and elegant designs, straight lines, roman arches, classical columns, and the absence of excessive ornamentation. Examples of such influence include the Municipal Theater of São Paulo and the Manaus Teatro Amazonas. This type of construction remained popular for large government projects until the end of the 1800s.

POSTINDEPENDENCE PERIOD

Romanticism

Brazil became independent in 1822. The event coincided with the style of romanticism prevalent in Europe. In Brazil, artists and literary figures developed a profound sense of nationalism that lasted throughout the 1800s. The "Indianism" movement became popular as Brazilians attempted to define who they were. Painters followed a "realism" style focused on Brazilian landscapes and portraits of average farmers and workers.

Modernism

The origins of the modernism style in Brazil can be pinpointed to the Semana de Arte Moderna in 1922. The goal was to inspire new ways of expression that were truly Brazilian in music, art, architecture, and literature. One of the most renowned modernist painters was Cândido Portini (1903–1962). He was a prolific artist who produced over 5,000 works, but he became mostly known for his large muralist-style paintings. Since the 1950s, architecture became an important field that reflected Brazil's goal to become an industrialized nation, and large architectural projects became tangible symbols of progress. Some of the most prominent architects of the period include Oscar Niemeyer (1907–2012) and Lúcio Costa (1902–1998). They both worked on one of the largest architectural projects ever undertaken in the Americas: the design of a brand-new capital city called Brasília in the interior region of the country.

The National Congress building in Brazil. Located in the capital city of Brasília, the National Congress houses both the Federal Senate and the Chamber of Deputies. Architect Oscar Niemeyer finished the building in 1960 using a modernist style. (Pixattitude/Dreamstime.com)

Niemeyer designed most of the official government buildings, including the Brazilian Congress, the Supreme Court, the Presidential Palace, the Cathedral of Brasília, and all the federal ministries. Costa was the urban planner who designed the entire city as well as the residential homes and neighborhoods called *superquadras* (superblocks). The entire city was built in only four years, and it was inaugurated in 1960. It was the largest experiment in modernist architecture, and it continues to impress people even today.

Contemporary Art

Brazil continues to produce artists who have gained exposure in both national and international markets. The Museu de Arte Moderna (MAM) in São Paulo provides a forum to showcase emerging and innovative Brazilian talent. The work of painter Lygia Clark and sculptor Hélio Oiticica is regularly presented in prominent art exhibitions. Sandra Cinto (1968–) is an internationally renowned Brazilian artist who works with painting, sculpture, and performance installations. Her recent work explores the concept of water when she paints pouring rain and turbulent oceans, or when she uses actual water in performance installations in elegant patterns that engage viewers. Her work is displayed in galleries and public spaces that include Madrid, New York, São Paulo, Tokyo, and Seattle. While erudite art is showcased in galleries and museums, popular arts and crafts are sold in public markets and outside churches. They certainly have a valuable place in Brazilian society because they are inexpensive, and they are used by people as they go about their daily lives. Religious ex-votos figurines, animal wood carvings, and *candoblé* charm bracelets are extremely popular, and they continue to be produced the same way they were created hundreds of years ago. They reflect traditions and cultural knowledge. The talent of contemporary artisans, painters, sculptors, and architects is reflected in their work as they present it to the world, and it reflects their Brazilian heritage.

Further Reading

Andreoli, Elisabetta. 2005. *Brazil's Modern Architecture*. New York: Phaidon.

Barnitz, Jacqueline, and Patrick Frank. 2015. *Twentieth-Century Art of Latin America*. Austin: University of Texas Press.

El-Dahdah, Farès. 2005. *Lúcio Costa: Brasilia's Superquadra*. Munich, Germany: Prestel.

Escola de Belas Artes, Universidade Federal do Rio de Janeiro. http://www.eba.ufrj.br

Mann, Graciela, and Hans Mann. 2014. *The Twelve Prophets of Aleijadinho*. Austin: University of Texas Press.

Meurs, Paul et al. (ed.). 2009. *Brazil Contemporary: Architecture, Art, and Visual Culture and Design*. Rotterdam, Netherlands: Nai010.

Museu Casa de Portinari. https://www.museucasadeportinari.org.br

Museu de Arte Moderna (MAM) de São Paulo. http://mam.org.br

Segawa, Hugo. 2010. *Architecture of Brazil*. São Paulo: Edusp.

Semana de Arte Moderna/Modern Art Week. http://semana-arte-moderna.info

Vincent, Jon S. 2003. *Culture and Customs of Brazil*. Westport, CT: Greenwood Press.

Aleijadinho (1730 or 1738–1814)

Antônio Francisco Lisboa is mostly known by his Portuguese nickname Aleijadinho, which means "little cripple." He is the most important artist from the eighteenth-century Brazilian baroque period of arts and architecture. Documentation about his birth offers two separate dates (1730 and 1738), both of which are cited in multiple sources. He was born in the town of Villa Rica in the state of Minas Gerais; the town changed its name later to Ouro Preto (Black Gold). His parents were Manuel Francisco da Costa Lisboa (a Portuguese carpenter who migrated to Brazil) and his African slave, Isabel. His father arrived in Brazil a few years after gold was discovered in 1696 in Minas Gerais. The gold rush generated a renewed interest to invest in cultural events and religious architecture in the region. It was in this historical environment that his father's skills were quickly recognized and in high demand; consequently, he was quickly elevated to work as an architect on multiple projects.

Antônio Francisco Lisboa started working for his father as a simple laborer on a church he designed in Ouro Preto: the Church of Nossa Signora del Monte Carmelo. Antônio learned his craft of building, designing, and sculpting without formal education, but he was trained by his father while working on multiple projects. He developed an identity of his own, and he was hired as a sculptor for religious sites throughout Minas Gerais using mostly stone and wood. He was not even thirty years old when he was hired as an architect to design the Chapel of the Third Order of Saint Francis of Assisi in Ouro Preto, which he completed in 1776. The unique features of round bell towers, a richly-decorated interior, and an intricate façade established his reputation as an architect in the Brazilian baroque style. This building eventually earned the designation of a UNESCO World Heritage Site. Antônio Lisboa went on to become a prolific sculptor and architect. Most of his works were completed in the state of Minas Gerais in the towns of São João del Rei, Congonhas do Campo, Sabará, and Ouro Preto. He continued to work arduously even when he contracted leprosy in the late 1770s, a debilitating disease that progressively left him disabled and with atrophied extremities. He retreated from public life, but continued to work as a sculptor mostly in seclusion at night by having a chisel and hammer tied to his stubby hands. This is the period when he was given the nickname Aleijadinho (Little Cripple).

Antônio Francisco Lisboa reached his greatest accomplishment with the Church of Bom Jesus de Matosinhos in Congonhas. He did not design or build the rococo-style church itself; it had been envisioned and funded by a wealthy businessman named Feliciano Mendes. Aleijadinho was commissioned as a sculptor to carry out two separate but related projects. First, between 1796 and 1799, he created sixty-six life-size sculptures out of cedar wood representing all the Stations of the Cross in the Catholic religion. They illustrate scenes beginning with the Last Supper and ending with the Crucifixion of Christ. In addition, between 1800 and 1805, Aleijadinho sculpted another set of twelve stunning and imposing soapstone figures representing the twelve apostles. The *Twelve Prophets* sculptures were placed outdoors on a monumental courtyard and a stairway positioned in front of the church. The interior of the church also includes other baroque features such as an intricate altar, detailed ceiling paintings, and smaller sculptures completed by other artists.

Antônio Francisco Lisboa lived a productive life. In spite of his debilitating disease, he lived to be seventy-six years old. He left an undeniable baroque imprint on the colonial towns of Minas Gerais. He died on November 18, 1814. His remains are buried in the Church of Nossa Senhora da Conceição de Antônio Dias in his beloved town of Ouro Preto, Minas Gerais. The church eventually closed for religious services, and it now houses the Museum of Aleijadinho to honor his work and his memory. It went through a massive renovation, and it reopened in 2007 to include and preserve unique pieces that highlight his artistic legacy.

See also: Chapter 1: World Heritage Sites in the UNESCO. Chapter 2: Gold Rush and Minas Gerais. Chapter 12: Overview; Baroque Art and Architecture in Minas Gerais; Ouro Preto.

Further Reading

Bretas Ferreira, Rodrigo José. 2002. *Antônio Francisco Lisboa*. Belo Horizonte, Brazil: Editora Itatiaia.

Brum Lemos, Maria Alzira. 2009. *Aleijadinho: Homem barroco, artista brasileiro*. Rio de Janeiro: Editora Garamond.

Mann, Graciela, and Hans Mann. 2014. *The Twelve Prophets of Aleijadinho*. Austin: University of Texas Press.

Whistler, Catherine. 2001. *Opulence and Devotion: Brazilian Baroque Art*. Oxford, UK: Ashmolean Museum.

Baroque Art and Architecture in Minas Gerais

Slave hunters (*bandeirantes*) discovered gold in the state of Minas Gerais in 1696. Soon after in 1725, there was another mineral discovery in the region: diamonds. These two findings unleashed an unprecedented demographic, cultural, and economic transformation of the interior region of Brazil. First, the speculative nature of a gold rush sparked a massive movement of people from the north areas of Brazil to the southern and interior states such as Minas Gerais. The economic influence of the sugar industry in the north shifted to the southern interior area because plantation owners relocated to towns throughout Minas Gerais, and they brought their money and slaves with them. The town of Ouro Preto became the epicenter of the gold rush, and it quickly attracted fortune seekers, intellectuals, and artists from different regions of Brazil, neighboring countries, and even Europe. In addition, the newfound wealth generated interest in funding creative ventures including a wave of artistic production mainly with a religious approach to sculpture, painting, and the construction of churches.

Since Brazil was a Portuguese colony during the 1700s, the resurgence of an artistic movement in Minas Gerais was heavily influenced by the baroque model that was still popular in Europe. It encouraged opulent ornamentation, architecture with curved walls, extremely detailed carvings of wood and stone, and painted ceilings depicting religious themes. For the first half of the eighteenth century, the Jesuit orders led the architectural and artistic movement with the construction of colonial churches in towns in Minas Gerais, including Ouro Preto, Diamantina, São João del Rei, Mariana, Sabará, and Congonhas. When the Jesuits were expelled from Brazil in 1759, most of the funding for such projects relied on affluent private donors and patrons of the arts.

The two most significant figures of the baroque period in Brazil are architect and sculptor Aleijadinho (1730 or 1738—1814) and painter Manoel da Costa Ataíde (1762–1830). Their work provided a strong foundation for an artistic movement that developed into a unique regional style known as Barroco Mineiro (from Minas Gerais) that lasted throughout most of the eighteenth century. Antônio Francisco Lisboa, known simply as Aleijadinho (Little Cripple), was a prolific architect and master carver who transformed the appearance of multiple towns throughout Minas Gerais. As an architect, he designed and built multiple churches, including the Chapel of the Third Order of St. Francis of Assisi in Ouro Preto, which also includes detailed stone carvings on the façade. His masterpiece, however, is *The Twelve Prophets at Congonhas*, which is based on his carving and sculpting skills. He created imposing soapstone figures of the twelve apostles placed outdoors, arranged throughout the front courtyard of the church Sanctuary of Bom Jesus de Matosinhos in the town of Congonhas. He performed this remarkable task between 1800 and 1805 when he was already suffering from leprosy and had lost control of his deformed extremities. He reportedly carved the statues by having a hammer and chisel strapped to his stubby hands. Since most of the baroque art of the period is located in churches, the most valuable baroque paintings are also found in church ceilings and retablo boards behind the altar. Manoel da Costa Ataíde was better known as Mestre Ataíde, and he had a strong influence on the painting style of the Brazilian baroque period. He received multiple commissions to paint church ceilings throughout Minas Gerais. He used a lot of bright colors (especially multiple shades of blue) to bring light into otherwise dark churches and chapels. His most recognized work is the striking fresco titled *The Glorification of the Virgin* on the main nave ceiling of the Chapel of the Third Order of St. Francis of Assisi in Ouro Preto, which was designed and built by Aleijadinho. Mestre Ataíde was a strong influence on the artistic development of Minas Gerais, and he trained a large number of students and craftsmen in the unique blend of Barroco Mineiro and rococo styles during his commissioned projects. The artistic resurgence in Minas Gerais during the 1700s expanded to other baroque fields including the poetry of Gregório de Matos and Basílio da Gama, as well as the music of composers Pedro da Fonseca and Francisco de Vacas.

The unique architecture and artistic styles of a region are often a reflection of its history. The state of Minas Gerais developed very differently than the rest of Brazil during the 1700s. The discovery of gold and diamonds forced a transformation of this interior region into a powerful economic and artistic epicenter of colonial Brazil. Besides speculative gold adventurers, it also attracted artists, intelligentsia, architects, religious leaders, and investors. The result was that Minas Gerais was not simply another mineral-rich colonial site that was plundered and then abandoned in complete destruction. Instead, the wealth generated by the gold rush was used to fund local cultural and religious works that left a tangible presence in the form of architecture, painting, and sculpture in small towns throughout the state. The colonial legacy of the Barroco Mineiro style is recognized worldwide. In fact, the entire towns of Ouro Preto and Diamantina were designated as World Heritage Sites by the United Nations Educational, Scientific, and Cultural Organization (UNESCO). Today, they still attract large numbers of visitors who can enjoy the display of colonial architecture and art sprinkled throughout Minas Gerais.

See also: Chapter 1: World Heritage Sites in the UNESCO. Chapter 2: Overview; *Bandeirantes*; Gold Rush and Minas Gerais; Timeline. Chapter 12: Overview; Aleijadinho (1730 or 1738–1814).

Further Reading

Bury, John. 1991. *Arquitetura e arte do Brasil colonial*. São Paulo: Editora Nobel.

Brum Lemos, Maria Alzira. 2009. *Aleijadinho: Homem barroco, artista Brasileiro*. Rio de Janeiro: Editora Garamond.

Mann, Graciela, and Hans Mann. 2014. *The Twelve Prophets of Aleijadinho*. Austin: University of Texas Press.

Newman, Robert. 2012. *Baroque and Rococo Art and Architecture*. Upper Saddle River, NJ: Pearson.

Segawa, Hugo. 2010. *Architecture of Brazil*. São Paulo: Edusp.

UNESCO World Heritage Sites. http://whc.unesco.org

Whistler, Catherine. 2001. *Opulence and Devotion: Brazilian Baroque Art*. Oxford, UK: Ashmolean Museum.

Cinto, Sandra (1968–)

Sandra Cinto is a contemporary Brazilian artist who works in multiple formats, including pen drawings, paintings, sculptures, and performance installations. She was born in 1968 in Santo André, a municipality located in the greater metropolitan region of São Paulo. She was formally trained in the arts at the Facultades Integradas Teresa D'Ávila in Santo André where she finished her university degree in 1990. Her unique art has been influenced by the European romanticism movement and Japanese prints done in the unique ukiyo-e style. Some of her small-scale works include prints that highlight drawings of fine lines with silver ink against dark blue backgrounds. She has also ventured into alabaster sculptures that allow her to play with translucent light.

Cinto, however, has become most recently noted for her room-size installations that highlight the use of water as a central theme. She found a connection to that natural element while in residence at the Aomori Contemporary Art Center in Aomori, Japan. Sometimes, she creates extra-large canvases to paint pouring rain, rolling waves, and turbulent oceans—all of which express fluidity and movement. Other times, she uses actual water (tinted with dark ink) in performance installations by allowing it to flow over simple and elegant patterns that engage the viewers.

Sandra Cinto lives and works in São Paulo, where she regularly showcases her work in local galleries and solo exhibits. Toward the end of the twentieth century, she ventured into international institutions and museums, which promoted her work as a contemporary Brazilian artist. Some of the most important recent exhibitions include:

- 2018. Tanya Bonakdar Gallery. Frieze New York.
- 2018. Casa Triângulo Collection. At ARCO Madrid.
- 2017. Graphicstudio at University of Southern Florida at the INK Miami Beach Gallery.
- 2016. *Chance and Necessity Series* at the West Gallery, curated by Noel Smith at the University of Southern Florida Contemporary Art Museum (CAM) in Tampa.
- 2015. Museu Dançante Collection. Museu de Arte Moderna de São Paulo (MAM).

> **ADRIANA VAREJÃO (1964–),**
> **A TWENTY-FIRST-CENTURY ARTIST**
>
> Adriana Varejão is an accomplished artist from Rio de Janeiro who works with paintings, photography, and sculpture. She vividly explores themes that include Brazil's colonial past, national identity, and controversial views on race. Her oil paintings and photographs reside in multiple permanent collections of modern art, including the Guggenheim Museum in New York and the Tate Museum in London. Her sculptures portray Brazil's brutal colonial history with simultaneous themes of sensuality and violence. Her recent collection of oil-painting portraits titled *Polvo* (2017) illustrates the wide range of racial diversity of Brazil.
>
> **Sources:** Adriana Varejao Official Website. http://www.adrianavarejao.net
> Brooks, Katherine. 2017. "Stunning Self-Portraits Make You Think Twice about Racial Identity in South America." *Huffington Post,* December 6. Accessed June 4, 2019. https://www.huffingtonpost.com/2014/04/25/adriana-varejao_n_5208101.html

- 2014. Centro Atlántico de Arte Moderno (CAAM), Madrid, Spain.
- 2010. Imitaçao de Água Collection, curated by Jacopo Crivelli Visconti. Instituto Tomie Ohtake, São Paulo.

By the beginning of the twenty-first century, Sandra Cinto had attracted the attention of an international audience. As a result, she received multiple commissions to design performance pieces to be installed in public spaces, including:

- 2012–2014. *Encounter of the Waters.* Commissioned by the Seattle Art Museum at the Olympic Art Pavilion.
- 2012–2013. *One Day, after the Rain.* Commissioned by the Phillips Collection in Washington, D.C.
- 2013. *A Casa das Fontes* (*A House of Fountains*). Commissioned by the Casa do Sertanista in São Paulo.

Sandra Cinto continues to express her worldview by using her contemporary art that is well received by both Brazilian and international art lovers.

See also: Chapter 12: Overview.

Further Reading

Bennett, Lennie. 2016. "New Exhibits by Brazilian Artists Capture a Nation's Tension." *Tampa Bay Times,* January 20. Accessed May 23, 2019. http://www.tampabay.com/things-to-do/visualarts/review-new-exhibits-by-brazilian-artists-capture-a-nations-tension/2262011

Institute for Research in Art. 2016. "Histórias/Histories: Contemporary Art from Brazil." University of South Florida, Contemporary Art Museum (CAM), March 15. Accessed May 23, 2019. http://www.usfcam.usf.edu/CAM/exhibitions/2016_1_Brazil_Histories/Historias.html

Museu de Arte Moderna (MAM) de São Paulo. http://mam.org.br

Costa, Lúcio (1902–1998): Brasília's Urban Planner

Lúcio Marçal Ferreira Ribeiro Lima Costa was a talented Brazilian architect and urban planner. Both of his parents were Brazilian (Joaquim Ribeiro da Costa and Alina Ferreira da Costa), but he was born in Toulon, France, on February 27, 1902. During his early life, he was educated at the Royal Grammar School in Newcastle upon Tyne, England, and then at the Collège National in Montreux, Switzerland. His family then moved to Rio de Janeiro, where he studied architecture at the Escola Nacional de Belas Artes and graduated in 1924.

Lúcio Costa was a prolific architect. He quickly adopted a modernist style that incorporated the use of reinforced concrete, glass, and steel. The goal was to design mostly rectangular buildings using straight lines with an air of simplicity. This style was evident in Costa's building for the Ministry of Education and Health (1937–1943), which is considered the first modernist building in Latin America. He worked with another famous Brazilian architect: Oscar Niemeyer. They also collaborated on the design of the Brazilian Pavilion at the 1939 World's Fair in New York. For the following decade, Costa worked at the National Institute of Historic and Artistic Patrimony restoring colonial buildings throughout Brazil.

Lúcio Costa's greatest accomplishment was the design for the brand-new national capital city named Brasília. President Juscelino Kubitschek called for an international competition to develop a new capital city from scratch in 1956. It was part of his campaign motto and promise "fifty years of progress in five." Costa won the competition and received the commission for this gigantic project. The new city was symbolic for Brazil because it reflected the hopes and aspirations of the country on a path of economic growth. His *Plano Piloto* (*Pilot Plan*) was the proposal for a city with an overall shape of an irregular cross. The urban planning design has been compared to an airplane, a dragonfly, or even a stretched bow and arrow. The plan, in general terms, divided the new city into two equally important parts: the Monumental Axis and the Residential Axis. The Monumental Axis runs east to west, and it displays a sense of grandeur with government buildings that house most ministries and all three branches of government. The Residential Axis runs from north to south, and it includes all the commercial and residential buildings.

A dream team of three talented individuals accomplished the monumental task of creating a new capital city for Brazil: Lúcio Costa focused on urban planning and the design of residential neighborhoods, Oscar Niemeyer (1907–2012) designed most of the government buildings, and Roberto Burle Marx coordinated all the parks and landscaping projects. Costa's design of ninety-six residential *superquadras* (superblocks) blended luxury and moderate-price housing units using six-story buildings connected to civic infrastructure that included hospitals, commerce, schools, parks, and churches. Another twelve *superquadras* were limited to three-story buildings. The purpose of the residential units' design was to create self-sufficient communities with a peaceful residential buzz that contrasted with the imposing architecture of federal government buildings.

The entire city of Brasília was designed, built, and landscaped in only four years (1956–1960). It was inaugurated in 1960, and its modernist style still feels contemporary today. Lúcio Costa and his unique designs left a legacy of urban planning for future generations. Due to its unique architecture, the UNESCO included Brasília as a World Heritage Site in 1987, a designation that brings visitors to discover this architectural gem in the interior of Brazil.

See also: Chapter 1: Brasília and the Federal District; World Heritage Sites in the UNESCO. Chapter 2: Kubitschek de Oliveira, Juscelino (1902–1976). Chapter 11: Modernism in Brazil. Chapter 12: Overview; Niemeyer, Oscar (1907–2012).

Further Reading
Andreoli, Elisabetta. 2005. *Brazil's Modern Architecture*. New York: Phaidon.
El-Dahdah, Farès. 2005. *Lúcio Costa: Brasilia's Superquadra*. Munich, Germany: Prestel.
Hess, Alan, and Alan Weintraub. 2009. *Oscar Niemeyer Buildings*. New York: Rizzoli.
Lara, Fernando Luiz. 2008. *The Rise of Popular Modernist Architecture in Brazil*. Gainesville: University Press of Florida.
UNESCO World Heritage Site List: Brasilia. https://www.worldheritagesite.org/list/Brasilia

French Artistic Mission

The French Artistic Mission (Missão Artística Francesa) was a group of architects and artists who arrived in Brazil in March 1816. They were invited by the royal court of Portugal, which was residing in Rio de Janeiro after Napoleon Bonaparte took control of Lisbon in 1808 and sent King João VI into exile. At this time, Rio de Janeiro was the capital city of the United Kingdom of Portugal, Brazil, and the Algarves. It was the first time a European empire was effectively managed from a site located in one of its colonies. The Portuguese king wanted to transform the way the arts were previously taught in Brazil—mainly from a religious orientation—and bring workshop apprenticeships to a more sophisticated level of artistic expression. Consequently, he invited the French Artistic Mission, led by Joachim Lebreton, to establish an arts and crafts school in Rio de Janeiro. The initial French Mission had seven members, whose occupations illustrate the importance of the trades considered relevant at that time: three sculptors (Zéphirin Ferrez, Marc Ferrez, and Auguste Marie Taunay), two painters

(Jean-Baptiste Debret and Nicolas Antoine Taunay), one architect (Grandjean de Montigny), and one master engraver (Charles-Simon Pradier).

The French Artistic Mission accomplished its goal by establishing the Escola Real de Ciências, Artes, e Ofícios (the Royal School of Sciences, Arts, and Crafts) in 1816. The school introduced radical changes to how art was produced, and it also established new pedagogical systems to train artists, architects, and artisans. The new approaches had a tremendous influence on the development of Brazilian artistic expression. More than seventy years after its foundation, it changed its name to the Escola Nacional de Belas Artes (National School of Fine Arts) on November 8, 1890. It was extremely popular, and quickly grew to robust enrollment. As a result, it joined the University of Rio de Janeiro, and it became an important school within the current Federal University of Rio de Janeiro. Some of the most prominent contemporary Brazilian architects, urban planners, painters, and sculptors graduated from the *Escola Nacional de Belas Artes* including: urban planner Lúcio Costa (1902–1998), architect Oscar Niemeyer (1907–2012), painter Candido Portinari (1903–1962), and sculptor Rubens Gerchman (1942–2008). These graduates left their imprint on Brazilian artistic, architectural, and cultural world.

See also: Chapter 2: Overview. Chapter 12: Overview; Niemeyer, Oscar (1907–2012); Popular Arts and Crafts.

Further Reading

Escola de Belas Artes, Universidade Federal do Rio de Janeiro. http://www.eba.ufrj.br

Fundação Oscar Niemeyer Official Website. http://www.niemeyer.org.br

Jorge, Marcelo. 2012. "History of Brazilian 19th Century Art." Art Renewal Center, August 7. Accessed June 11, 2019. https://www.artrenewal.org/Article/Title/history-of-brazilian-19th-century-art

Lemos, Carlos, Jose Roberto, and Teixeira Leite (eds.). 1983. *The Art of Brazil*. New York: HarperCollins.

Long, Ciara. 2016. "Rio's Museum of Fine Arts Celebrates French Artistic Influence." *Rio Times,* December 16. Accessed June 11, 2019. http://riotimesonline.com/brazil-news/rio-entertainment/rios-museum-of-fine-arts-celebrates-french-artistic-influence

Mendes da Rocha, Paulo (1928–)

Paulo Mendes da Rocha is an influential contemporary Brazilian architect. He was born in Vitória in the state of Espírito Santo. He graduated in 1954 from the Universidade Presbiteriana Mackenzie College of Architecture located in São Paulo. He quickly established a private practice, and he finished his first massive project soon after in 1957: the Athletic Club of São Paulo. Other commissions followed, including the Guaimbê Residential Building in 1964 and the Serra Dorada Stadium in Goiânia. Mendes developed a unique style that became known as Paulist Brutalist. This approach used steel and reinforced-concrete components that were prefabricated and mass-produced off the building site. This style became aesthetically controversial, but it made buildings cheaper and faster to design and produce.

Mendes da Rocha continued to transform the look of São Paulo during the following three decades (1980s–2000s) with new construction and revitalization projects. He designed and built a string of civil buildings that left an imprint on the regional cultural world: the Saint Peter Chapel (1987), the Brazilian Sculpture Museum (1988), the Pinacoteca do Estado (1993), the FIESP Cultural Center (1997), and the Patriarch Plaza (2002). His work became recognized globally, which led him to multiple international projects: the Boulevard des Sports Complex for the Olympic Games in Paris, France (2008); the general master plan for the Vigo University in Galicia, Spain (2007); and the Museu dos Coches and the Quelas House in Lisbon, Portugal (2015).

Mendes da Rocha has earned multiple domestic and international awards that reflect the caliber of his work in the field of architecture. In 2000, he received the Mies van der Rohe Latin American Architecture Prize. Then in 2006, Mendes received the Pritzker Prize, which is the highest international architectural honor possible in the profession. It is often dubbed the Architecture Nobel Prize. It is awarded annually to a living architect whose work demonstrates unique talent, vision, and commitment with significant contributions to humanity and the environment. In addition, he was awarded the Praemium Imperiale Arts Prize from the Japan Art Association in 2016. After that, the Royal Institute of British Architects awarded Mendes the Royal Gold Medal for Architecture in 2017. Due to his prolific work and unique style, Paulo Mendes da Rocha became one of the two most recognized architects in Brazil (together with Oscar Niemeyer who designed most of the buildings for the capital city of Brasília). Even with all the international recognition, Mendes da Rocha's style remains committed to the concept of architectural simplicity in design and construction, an approach that has led to the visual transformation of his beloved São Paulo.

See also: Chapter 12: Overview; Niemeyer, Oscar (1907–2012).

Further Reading

Ada Edita Global Architecture. 2016. *Residential Masterpieces 23: Paulo Mendes da Rocha.* Tokyo: Ada Edita Global Architecture.

"Paulo Mendes da Rocha Pritzker Prize." 2006. *Architecture Week*. April 12. Accessed July 1, 2019. http://www.architectureweek.com/2006/0412/news_1-2.html

Pisani, Daniel, and Francesco Dal Co. 2015. *Paulo Mendes da Rocha: Complete Works.* New York: Rizzoli.

Pritzker Architectural Prize Official Website. https://www.pritzkerprize.com/laureates/2006

Modern Art Week, São Paulo, 1922

The Semana de Arte Moderna (Modern Art Week) was an arts festival that took place from February 10 to February 18, 1922, at the Municipal Theater in São Paulo

Brazil. The year 1922 was symbolic because it marked the one hundredth anniversary of Brazilian independence. The main goal was to challenge aesthetic traditions that were based on European models. The purpose was also to create a complete cultural disruption of the established patterns in art, literature, and social sciences. This single week affected most forms of expression in Brazilian cultural circles, including literature, painting, poetry, sculpture, architecture, music, and theater. This week is often viewed as the official beginning of the modernist movement in Brazil. The festival served as a gathering to coordinate a call to action to create artistic forms that were truly Brazilian.

The Semana de Arte Moderna included academic lectures, musical concerts, poetry readings, painting exhibitions, literary discussions, and sculpture displays by prominent Brazilian figures. In literature, modernist poet Mário de Andrade (1893–1945) and novelist Oswaldo de Andrade (1890–1954) both rejected the traditional Portuguese literary values. Instead, they experimented with indigenous folklore legends, and they incorporated colloquial language that actually reflected the speech patterns of rural Brazilians. In addition, they proposed not just to change the literary conventions, but to use such reforms to initiate social change in Brazil via political activism. Literature and the arts moved toward expressing regionalist themes, especially in the semiarid northeast region of Brazil with its harsh living conditions. Some of the most important regionalist novels in Brazilian literature emerged from this period, including the masterpiece *Vidas secas* (Barren Lives) by Graciliano Ramos (1892–1953) in 1938. In addition, sociologist Gilberto Freyre (1900–1987) wrote a monumental analysis of Brazilian culture in his 1933 sociological treatise *Casa ganda e sensala* (Masters and Slaves) that forced Brazilians to think about themselves on a different light.

Brazilian painters and architects were also influenced by the modernist movement. Painters adopted a nativist and regional approach to art. Tarsila do Amaral (1886–1973) was one of the main proponents of change by switching to painting landscapes and people from rural settings. In the field of architecture, Lúcio Costa (1902–1998) and Oscar Niemeyer (1907–2012) created a unique Brazilian style that used reinforced concrete, glass, and steel to create elegant buildings using basic shapes and straight lines. They eventually worked together on the largest architecture and urban planning project ever attempted in Brazil: the creation of a brand-new capital city in the interior of the country. They managed to design, construct, and landscape the entirely new city of Brasília in only four years.

Modernism created a comprehensive transformation of Brazilian cultural life. The artistic movement lasted until 1945, and its demise coincided with three major events: the death of one of modernism's intellectual founders, Mário de Andrade; the end of World War II; and the fall of the Getúlio Vargas dictatorship (1937–1945).

See also: Chapter 11: Overview; De Andrade, Oswald (1890–1954); Literary Canon; Modernism in Brazil. Chapter 12: Overview; Costa, Lúcio (1902–1998): Brasilia's Urban Planner; Niemeyer, Oscar (1907–2012).

Further Reading

Andreoli, Elisabetta. 2005. *Brazil's Modern Architecture*. New York: Phaidon.

Bishop, Elizabeth, and Emanuel Brasil (eds.). 1997. *An Anthology of Twentieth-Century Brazilian Poetry*. Middletown, CT: Wesleyan University Press.

Goldberg, Isaac. 2009. *Brazilian Literature*. New York: Knopf.

Hess, Alan, and Alan Weintraub. 2009. *Oscar Niemeyer Buildings*. New York: Rizzoli.

Lara, Fernando Luiz. 2008. *The Rise of Popular Modernist Architecture in Brazil*. Gainesville: University Press of Florida.

Semana de Arte Moderna/Modern Art Week. http://semana-arte-moderna.info

Vincent, Jon S. 2003. *Culture and Customs of Brazil*. Westport, CT: Greenwood Press.

Niemeyer, Oscar (1907–2012)

Oscar Ribeiro de Almeida Niemeyer Soares Filho (1907–2012) is perhaps the most recognized architect in Brazil. He was born and died in his beloved Rio de Janeiro. He attended the Escola Nacional de Belas Artes at the Federal University of Rio de Janeiro. Niemeyer was one of the leaders of modern architecture; he often used reinforced concrete to enhance the beauty of commercial and residential buildings with form, light, and color.

Niemeyer was noticed immediately for his first major commission, called the Pampulha Architectural Complex in Belo Horizonte in 1940. He designed multiple residential units, a casino, restaurants, a golf club, a yacht club, and the famous Saint Francis of Assisi church—all around an artificial lake. During the 1950s, he built several skyscrapers, including the Museum of Modern Art in Caracas and several buildings in Brazil: the Edifício Sede do Banco Mineiro, the Edifício Montreal, and the Edifício Triângulo.

His greatest accomplishment was the completion of the city of Brasília, which is still the current national capital of Brazil. President Juscelino Kubitschek (1902–1976) recruited Niemeyer to build an entirely new capital city from scratch in 1956. Niemeyer put together a team of three people to accomplish this monumental task: Lúcio Costa (1902–1998) focused on urban planning, Niemeyer designed most of the government and city buildings, and Roberto Burle Marx (1904–1994) coordinated all the parks and landscaping projects. Brasília was designed to house all three branches of government, all the federal ministries, all the international embassies, as well as a sizable civilian population. Niemeyer designed all the residential, commercial, and government buildings, including the Cathedral of Brasília, the National Congress, the Ministries Esplanade, the Presidential Palace (Palácio da Alvorada), and many others. The entire city was designed, built, and landscaped in only four years. It was part of President Kubitschek's motto "fifty years of progress in five." It was inaugurated in 1960, and its modernist style of architecture still feels contemporary today.

Niemeyer received multiple awards both in Brazil and at international forums for recognition of his work. Multiple projects outside of Brazil exposed his architectural style on a global stage: the plan for the University of Haifa in Israel (1964), the University of Technology-Houari Boumediene in Algeria (1974), and the Headquarters for the French Communist Party in Paris (1981). Some of the most prestigious awards he received include: the Golden Lion of Venice (1963), the Honor Member of the Academy of Arts USSR (1983), the Pritzker Architectural Prize (1988), the Gold Medal from the Colegio de Arquitectos de Barcelona (1990), the Royal Gold Medal from the Royal Institute of British Architects (1998), and the ALBA Award of Venezuela (2008).

Niemeyer lived a long and productive life. He remained socially and professionally active even toward the end of his life. He designed the Serpentine Gallery Summer Pavilion in Hyde Park, London, in 2003. On a personal level, he remarried in 2006 when he was ninety-nine years old. Then he collaborated with the design and opening of the Oscar Niemeyer International Cultural Center in Asturias, Spain, in 2011. He died soon after on December 5, 2012, when he was 104 years old.

See also: Chapter 1: Brasília and the Federal District; World Heritage Sites at the UNESCO. Chapter 2: Kubitschek de Oliveira, Juscelino (1902–1976). Chapter 12: Overview.

Further Reading

Fundacão Oscar Niemeyer Official Website. http://www.niemeyer.org.br

Hess, Alan, and Alan Weintraub. 2009. *Oscar Niemeyer Buildings.* New York: Rizzoli.

Phillippou, Styliane. 2008. *Oscar Niemeyer: Curves of Irreverence.* New Haven, CT: Yale University Press.

Pritzker Architectural Prize Official Website. https://www.pritzkerprize.com/laureates/1988-niemeyer

Ouro Preto

Ouro Preto is a small city located in the state of Minas Gerais with a strong colonial heritage and a unique independent spirit. As a former mining town, it was the epicenter of the Brazilian gold rush that proliferated in the Serra do Espinhaço Mountains during the 1700s. It was founded in 1698, but it was actually named Vila Rica when it was officially recognized as a city in 1711. Later, it changed to its current name Ouro Preto (Black Gold).

During the 1700s, the gold rush in Ouro Preto exported over 800 tons of gold to Portugal, but it also generated large fortunes in the region, which generated local investments that sparked a renewal of art and architecture, mostly on religious buildings. The most famous sculptor and architect of the time was Antonio Francisco Lisboa (1738–1814), nicknamed Aleijadinho (Little Cripple), who followed a baroque style that displayed intricate ornamentation and architecture with curved walls. At the same time, Manoel da Costa Ataíde (1762–1830) was an influential painter of the period that became uniquely known as Barroco Mineiro. His most recognized work is the striking fresco titled *The Glorification of the Virgin* on the main nave ceiling of the Chapel of the Third Order of St. Francis of Assisi in Ouro Preto, a church that was both designed and built by Aleijadinho.

Ouro Preto was also the site of the Inconfidência Mineira, the very first regional (but defeated) attempt to obtain independence from Portugal in 1789. The local hero Joaquim Jose da Silva Xavier (1746–1792), nicknamed Tiradentes, was executed in a brutal public display in order to discourage any future attempts at rebellion against colonial rule. Over time, Tiradentes became a martyr, and the entire nation now celebrates the official holiday of Tiradentes on April 21. Today, the Museum of Inconfidência is housed within a baroque-style colonial building located right in the center of the Historic Town of Ouro Preto.

The UNESCO recognized the Historic Town of Ouro Preto in Minas Gerais as a World Heritage Site in 1980 based on its extremely well-preserved baroque architecture and its artistic legacy. In modern times, Ouro Preto attracts large numbers of visitors seeking to learn about its colonial past, view priceless jewels at the Mineralogy Museum, and admire a striking group of churches that contain the largest collection of baroque-style architecture and art in Brazil.

See also: Chapter 1: World Heritage Sites in the UNESCO. Chapter 2: Overview; Gold Rush and Minas Gerais; Tiradentes (1746–1792) and the Inconfidência Mineira. Chapter 12: Overview; Aleijadinho (1730 or 1738–1814); Baroque Art and Architecture in Minas Gerais.

Further Reading

Barnitz, Jacqueline, and Patrick Frank. 2015. *Twentieth-Century Art of Latin America.* Austin: University of Texas Press.

Fausto, Boris, and Sergio Fausto. 2014. *A Concise History of Brazil,* Second Edition. Cambridge, UK: Cambridge University Press.

Matias, Herculano Gomes. 2001. *Autos de devassa da Inconfidência Mineira: Conplementação documental.* Ouro Preto, Minas Gerais, Brazil: Museo da Inconfidência.

Museu da Inconfidência in Ouro Preto, Brazil. http://www.museudainconfidencia.gov.br/pt_BR

Ouro Preto Official Website. http://www.ouropreto.com.br

Whistler, Catherine. 2001. *Opulence and Devotion: Brazilian Baroque Art.* Oxford, UK: Ashmolean Museum.

Popular Arts and Crafts

Popular art has existed in Brazil for centuries, even before the arrival of the Portuguese in 1500. Most of the traditional folk art is not found in galleries and museums of established art but rather at *feiras* (outdoor markets) and makeshift stands located on sidewalks and outside churches. Popular art is not usually influenced by art movements or periods (such as modernism, neoclassical, etc.); instead, it has been produced the same way for centuries. In addition, popular crafts are often based in deep-rooted traditions, and they are accessible to the masses due to their low cost.

Popular religious art emerged in Brazil during the colonial period (1500–1820), and it reflects two strong influences from its European and African past. While religious themes are included in established art found in churches and erudite museums, the vast majority of the Brazilian population views popular religious artifacts as something tangible they can use and touch on a daily basis. One example of relatively inexpensive Catholic popular art is the pious use of *ex votos*. These are small figurines made of clay or metal that Catholic followers offer their favorite saint for having received a favor or a positive response to a prayer. Such miniature figurines are about 2 inches (5 centimeters) in size and are often in the shape of a leg or an arm to represent a body part that is now healing. *Ex votos* could also be small paintings either on a canvas or metal surface that highlight the role of a saint in the healing process of a Catholic follower. The African influence is evident in the good luck charms that craftspeople produce as symbolic figurines in the Candomblé religion that represent their *orixás* (African gods). These charms are produced from multiple metals from inexpensive tin to intricate silver designs. A collection of these figurines is often worn as part of a necklace or a bracelet called *balangandã* with the intention to ward off evil spirits.

The use of wood is very practical for Brazilian arts and crafts. Original indigenous art was mostly utilitarian in the form of bowls and boxes, but it also included animal figurines and carvings. Today, wood carvings are an irresistible art form that most foreigners cannot avoid purchasing throughout Brazil. They include detailed religious figurines, intricate flower bouquets, and—for some reason—lots of lions. In addition, wood is also used to create wood-carved illustrations on the cover of literary booklets with multiple themes collectively called *literatura de cordel* (string literature). The name comes from the fact that these booklets of poetry and fantastic stories are displayed hanging from a string at the places where they are sold, especially in the northeastern regions of Brazil.

See also: Chapter 5: Candomblé and Macumba; Catholicism; *Orixás*, African Gods. Chapter 12: Overview.

Further Reading

Barnitz, Jacqueline, and Patrick Frank. 2015. *Twentieth-Century Art of Latin America*. Austin: University of Texas Press.

Richard, Christopher, and Leslie Jermyn. 2002. *Cultures of the World: Brazil*. New York: Marshall Cavendish.

Vincent, Jon S. 2003. *Culture and Customs of Brazil*. Westport, CT: Greenwood Press.

Portinari, Cândido (1903–1962)

Cândido Portinari was an influential Brazilian painter. He was born on December 29, 1903, in a coffee plantation near Brodowski, a municipality in the state of São Paulo. Both of his parents were Italian immigrants. As a young adult, he moved to Rio de Janeiro to attend university at the Escola Nacional de Belas Artes. Portinari worked in multiple formats of painting, including small prints, canvas paintings, murals, and frescoes. The predominant colors in a large majority of his works were different shades of red and blue.

Portinari traveled to Paris for lengthy periods of time between 1928 and 1933; this was a period when he learned a lot about art but did not actually paint much. However, he was extremely prolific during the next two decades, creating a unique modernist style that effectively captured the hardships and struggles of average Brazilian peasants and workers. He depicted the life of poor families from the semiarid northeastern region of Brazil but with an air of dignity. One of his famous paintings titled *The Mestizo* shows a working-class character who is certainly demoralized but still strong and proud. Portinari created hundreds of paintings that illustrated the harsh living conditions of average Brazilian workers but with a noble spirit that still reflected confidence in themselves.

Portinari produced more than five thousand paintings and drawings, but he became internationally known based on his murals. Six of these masterpieces were actually created for the United States. In 1941, he painted four murals for the Library of Congress in Washington, D.C.; they are a reflection of the social struggles experienced by Hispanic Americans. The murals are titled *Discovery of the Land, Entry into the Forest, Teaching of the Indians,* and *Discovery of Gold.* Then in 1956, he donated two extremely large murals titled *War* and *Peace* to the United Nations Headquarters building in New York. They are intended to illustrate a contrast between happiness and violence. They essentially represent a political criticism against social injustices experienced by average people around the world.

Cândido Portinari was extremely active in producing modern art. He was a monumental influence in Brazilian artistic and cultural circles. Ironically, exposure to so much paint actually killed him. His doctors diagnosed that he was essentially poisoned for the last ten years of his life by being exposed to so much lead included in the paints he used. He died on February 6, 1962. He left an artistic legacy based on the notion that art can raise awareness about social problems and the struggles of large numbers of vulnerable and disadvantaged populations. The Museu Casa de Portinari was established in Brodowski, São Paulo, to preserve his work for future generations.

See also: Chapter 12: Overview.

Further Reading

Alisson, Elton. 2012. "Portinari's War and Peace Are Shown for the First Time in São Paulo." FAPESP News Agency, March 7. Accessed May 6, 2019. http://agencia.fapesp.br/portinaris-war-and-peace-are-shown-for-the-first-time-in-sao-paulo/15258/

Barnitz, Jacqueline, and Patrick Frank. 2015. *Twentieth-Century Art of Latin America*. Austin: University of Texas Press.

Hoge, Warren. 1983. "Brazil Gathers Archive on Its Painter Portinari." *New York Times,* May 30, 1983. Accessed May 6, 2019. https://www.nytimes.com/1983/05/30/arts/brazil-gathers-archive-on-its-painter-portinari.html

Museu Casa de Portinari. https://www.museucasadeportinari.org.br

CHAPTER 13

MUSIC AND DANCE

OVERVIEW

Music and dance are crucial components of social gatherings in Brazil, including carnivals, family events, youth parties, religious celebrations, and romantic dates. In addition, Brazil has a long legacy of talented musicians who have actively participated in creating, adapting, and developing musical genres that in turn influence future generations of music aficionados both in Brazil and around the world.

Most foreigners are familiar with the Brazilian musical genres of samba and bossa nova. The famous song "Garota de Ipanema" ("The Girl from Ipanema") created in 1962 often evokes melancholic images of a tropical beach paradise in Rio de Janeiro. This soothing bossa nova song is the second most recorded song in the world, only after "Yesterday" by the Beatles. The song was a collaboration of music composer Antônio Carlos Jobim (1927–1994) and poet Vinicius de Morales (1913–1980). Their inspiration was a local carioca girl named Heloísa Eneida Menezes Paes Pinto, who is now mostly known by her married name Helô Pineiro. They were struck by her beauty when she walked in front of the Veloso Bar where the team was socializing. The image of a young and tall Brazilian girl with tanned skin and long wavy hair who moved gracefully was captured by the two artists by using a captivating jazz-style bossa nova rhythm. The English version of the song recorded by Astrud Gilberto then spread the musical genre worldwide by the middle of the 1960s. However, the most iconic images of Brazilian music are often associated with Carnival celebrations and the intoxicating rhythms of samba music and dance. The Carnival festivities last six days beginning with Friday before Ash Wednesday (fifty-one days prior to Easter) and continue until Ash Wednesday at noon (forty-five days before Easter). In large cities such as Rio de Janeiro and São Paulo, Carnival parades include intoxicating samba music, colorful costumes, captivating dance choreographies, and allegorical cars. These large parade competitions full of pageantry are led by samba schools, and they are usually watched on television or by purchasing tickets at the large Sambódromo. However, the majority of Brazilians actually take part in the celebrations by joining *blocos de rua*, which take place in almost every neighborhood in large cities and small towns where local musical groups meander through the streets with a live band and the public joins them to celebrate together. The heart of Carnival is the energetic samba music and accelerating dance style that are deeply rooted in African religious traditions practiced during the slave trade period (1500s to 1888). The samba de roda (dance circle) was the foundation for the performance style at the northern state of Bahia during the 1600s–1700s. The dance and rhythms became the pillars to develop the current samba carioca in Rio de Janeiro. The most recognizable samba sound is provided by the *bateria* (band based on drums), which dictates the contagious rhythm for the dancers. Today, there are samba variations throughout the country, but the contemporary musical style was created in urban Rio de Janeiro early in the twentieth century. Samba is so crucial to Brazilian identity that it has its own national holiday on December 2 to celebrate its historical roots and dance traditions.

Brazilians also enjoy other musical genres that are extremely popular in Brazil but are often relatively unknown outside of the country, including classical music, *música sertaneja*, *música popular brasileira*, and *tropicália*. Heitor Villa-Lobos (1887–1959) is still considered one of the national masters of classical music. He was a prolific Brazilian composer who wrote over 2,000 musical works in multiple genres, including chamber music, orchestra compositions, instrumental masterpieces, and vocal pieces. He is also well known in Brazil for a wide range of patriotic works that he created during the 1930s to highlight respect and veneration of national symbols, such as the flag, motto, and national anthem during the dictatorship of Getúlio Vargas (1930–1945). In addition, during the decade of the 1960s, there was a creative wave of innovation that developed multiple regional music styles. *Música sertaneja* (Brazilian country music) is by far one of the most popular regional genres nowadays, and it has achieved nationwide appeal thanks to radio programming and television exposure with contemporary artists such as Sérgio Reis, Michel Teló, and Maria Cecília. Another unique musical genre that has increased its following over several decades since the 1960s is the *música popular Brasileira* (MPB); most of its classic songs were composed during the late 1970s and early 1980s based on acoustic roots and socially conscious lyrics. Today, the MPB style is very common in people's homes since multiple radio stations dedicate their entire programming to this genre. Some of the most influential contemporary MPB artists include Chico Buarque, Maris Gadú, Ivan Lins, and the musical group Os Novos Baianos. *Música popular brasileira* continues to thrive in Brazil, garnering international recognition. It is so popular that it became an official category of the Latin Grammy Awards in the United States in the year 2000. Brazil experienced a brutal military dictatorship from 1964 to 1985, and its repressive tactics sparked a counterculture artistic movement known as Tropicália. In practical terms, it blended traditional African instruments with the popularity of rock and roll and the use of electric guitar sounds that were popular in foreign countries. *Tropicalistas* used songs to express strong criticism of the military coup d'état in 1964 and the repressive steps the government had implemented in terms of censorship, torture, and unexplained disappearances. From a musical perspective, the *tropicália* artistic movement provided a platform to blur the lines between traditional and innovative styles. For example, *tropicalistas* mixed bossa nova with psychedelic sounds from the Beatles, samba with rock and roll, as well as boleros with tropical sounds. At a social level, it sparked a common acceptance of long hair, a casual approach to sex, and a new wave of fashion that was considered "indecent" by traditional people in Brazilian society. It also promoted a contrarian view of politics. Consequently, it became a target for the military dictatorship that was still in power in Brazil, and its musicians were often incarcerated or tortured. Overall, the *tropicália* movement had a strong influence on future generations of musicians, theater actors, film directors, and poets.

Finally, Brazilians also enjoy pop music and multiple genres of regional music that continue to delight people with unique sounds and instruments. The rhythms and artists of *axé*, *choró*, and funk carioca genres constitute a smaller piece of the musical diversity, but they continue to be commercially profitable and generally popular. In addition, pop music continues to generate talented artists with large numbers of fans. Singer Roberto Carlos (1941–) is known as the King of Latin American music, dominating the pop genre for almost four decades. As a result, most Brazilians know the lyrics of his romantic ballads. On the younger side, the attractive and talented Anitta (1993–) is considered a contemporary pop superstar who continues to release music that topped the Brazilian and Latin American musical charts in 2018. The future of Brazilian music seems bright with the emergence of more artists who will contribute to the richness of Brazil's musical heritage.

Further Reading

Antunes, Anderson. 2013. "Could Brazil's Latest Music Sensation Anitta Be a Global Superstar in the Making?" *Forbes,* August 30. Accessed July 6, 2019. https://www.forbes.com/sites/andersonantunes/2013/08/30/could-brazils-latest-music-sensation-anitta-be-a-global-superstar-in-the-making/#c3c9672432aa

Brill, Mark. 2017. *Music of Latin America and the Caribbean.* Abingdon-on-Thames, UK: Routledge.

Castro, Ruy (trans. by Kyla Salisbury). 2000. *Bossa Nova: The Story of the Brazilian Music That Seduced the World.* Chicago: A Capella Books.

Dávila, Jerry. 2013. *Dictatorship in South America.* Hoboken, NJ: Wiley.

Dunn, Christopher. 2001. *Brutality Garden: Tropicália and the Emergence of a Brazilian Counterculture.* Chapel Hill: University of North Carolina Press.

Fryer, Peter. 2000. *Rhythms of Resistance: African Musical Heritage in Brazil.* London: Pluto Press.

Henry, Clarence Bernard. 2008. *Let's Make Some Noise: Axé and the African Roots of Popular Brazilian Music.* Jackson: University Press of Mississippi.

Hentschke, Jens R. (ed.). 2006. *Vargas and Brazil: New Perspectives.* New York: Palgrave Macmillan.

McGowan, Chris, and Ricardo Pessanha. 1998. *The Brazilian Sound: Samba, Bossa Nova, and the Popular Music of Brazil.* Philadelphia: Temple University Press.

Maria, Vasco. 2005. *História da música no Brasil.* Rio de Janeiro: Nova Fronteira.

Murphy, John P. 2006. *Music in Brazil: Experiencing Music, Expressing Culture.* Oxford, UK: Oxford University Press.

Ribeiro, Darcy, and Gregory Rabassa. 2000. *The Brazilian People: The Formation and Meaning of Brazil.* Gainesville: University Press of Florida.

Talmon-Chvaicer, Maya. 2008. *The Hidden History of Capoeira: A Collision of Cultures in the Brazilian Battle Dance*. Austin: University of Texas Press.

Tupinambá de Ulhôa, Martha, Cláudia Azevedo, and Felipe Trotta (eds.). 2014. *Made in Brazil: Studies in Popular Music*. Abingdon-on-Thames, UK: Routledge.

Veloso, Caetano. 2003. *Tropical Truth: A Story of Music and Revolution in Brazil*. Cambridge, MA: Da Capo Press.

Vincent, Jon S. 2003. *Culture and Customs of Brazil*. Westport, CT: Greenwood Press.

Bossa Nova

The smooth sound of bossa nova is perhaps one of the most recognized genres of Brazilian music. It was developed in the 1950s in the southern part of Rio de Janeiro, and it became popular among young Brazilians. In addition, it attained international attention during the 1960s. The Portuguese term "bossa nova" can be best translated as "new trend," and this new musical genre provided a creative blend of rhythmic samba with the listening pleasure of jazz instruments and soulful lyrics. The first documented use of the term "bossa nova" can be traced to 1957 when a journalist named Moysés Fuks introduced a group at a live concert by saying "Today, we have Sylvia Telles and a Bossa Nova group" (Afonso, 2010).

The unique bossa nova sound is created with acoustic guitars, piano, electric organ, acoustic bass, and drums. The use of a classical guitar is crucial, and musicians play it with their fingers and not a pick. The masterful skills of guitarist João Gilberto (1931–2019) set a high standard for bossa nova as played simply with a guitar and vocals. When other instruments are included, the acoustic guitar still guides the basic rhythm of the composition. The percussion component often sounds similar to the style used in the Cuban mambo musical genre. When it comes to vocals, most bossa nova singers adapted a unique nasal and softer sound that was typical of the northeast region of Brazil, and lyrics commonly tell tales of homesickness, women, love, and betrayal.

The most recognized bossa nova song worldwide is titled "Garota de Ipanema" ("The Girl from Ipanema"). The hit song was created as a fusion of bossa nova and jazz styles; Antônio Carlos Jobim (1927–1994) composed the music, and Vinicius de Morales (1913–1980) wrote the lyrics in Portuguese. The original version was recorded by musicians Stan Getz and João Gilberto in 1962. One year later, Norman Gimbel wrote the lyrics in English, and Astrud Gilberto sang it in English for the first time. Once available to English-speaking audiences, the song provided global recognition to the emerging musical style of Brazilian bossa nova that would eventually captivate the world. As a result, Antônio Carlos Jobim and João Gilberto are widely considered as the musical co-creators of a truly unique Brazilian sound.

See also: Chapter 13: Overview; "Girl from Ipanema" Song; Jobim, Antônio Carlos (1927–1994); Samba Music and Dance.

Further Reading

Afonso, Carlos Alberto. 2010. "Moysés Fuks na Calçada da Fama de Ipanema." *Blog da Toca*, February 20. Accessed May 13, 2019. http://blogdatocadovinicius.blogspot.com/2010/02/0025-moyses-fuks-na-calcada.html

Antônio Carlos Jobim Institute. http://www.jobim.org/acervodigital/ -

Castro, Ruy (trans. by Kyla Salisbury). 2000. *Bossa Nova: The Story of the Brazilian Music That Seduced the World*. Chicago: A Capella Books.

McGowan, Chris, and Ricardo Pessanha. 2008. *The Brazilian Sound: Samba, Bossa Nova, and Popular Music of Brazil*. Philadelphia: Temple University Press.

Murphy, John P. 2006. *Music in Brazil*. Oxford, UK: Oxford University Press.

Carnival

Carnival is definitely the largest and most popular holiday in Brazil. The iconic celebrations in Rio de Janeiro have become emblematic of Brazilian culture and recognized worldwide. The festivities last six days beginning with Friday before Ash Wednesday (51 days prior to Easter) and continue until Ash Wednesday at noon (45 days before Easter). The word *"carnival"* comes from *carnelevare*, which means "to remove meat," making reference to the tradition practiced by large groups of Catholics and Christians to avoid eating meat during certain days of Lent.

Carnival is synonymous with elaborate parades that include intoxicating samba music, colorful costumes, captivating dance choreographies, and allegorical cars with elaborate decorations. However, there are considerable differences in how Brazilians enjoy carnivals throughout the country. Rio de Janeiro and São Paulo hold large parade competitions full of pageantry led by samba schools that are meant to be watched by the public either on television or by purchasing tickets at the Sambódromo. These samba schools gather all year long to create an original song, design unique costumes, practice with the band for optimal performance, and perfect elaborate dance routines. They will be judged in all those categories. The São Paulo Carnival parade is held on Friday and Saturday night, and the one in Rio takes place on Sunday and Monday night. These commercial productions attract large numbers of observers; the Rio Carnival routinely draws more than 5 million people. The Globo television network purchased the rights to air both the Rio and São Paulo carnivals live in 1990, and they dominate television programming for a few days nationwide.

While carnivals in Rio and São Paulo capture the international attention, the large majority of Brazilians actually take part in the celebrations by joining *blocos de rua*, which take place in almost every neighborhood both in large cities and small towns. In southern cities such as Rio de Janeiro, individual celebrations take place in the neighborhoods of Ipanema, Copacabana, Leblon, and downtown. In the northern cities of Recife, Salvador, Olinda, and Porto Seguro, multiple organized groups meander through the streets with a live band, and the public joins them to celebrate together. These *blocos*

> ### *CHORO* INSTRUMENTAL MUSIC
>
> *Choro* is a purely instrumental music genre. The term *"choro"* literally means "to cry," which does not reflect its festive and joyous beat. Instead, the word *choro* makes reference to the unique weeping sound created by clarinets and flutes. Choro Brazilian rhythms evoke images of samba and bossa nova styles by incorporating a classical guitar, clarinet, saxophone, mandolin, trumpet, and percussion instruments in improvisation sessions by talented musicians with outstanding technical skills without using vocals. The *choro* genre developed in Rio de Janeiro during the 1920s, and it became increasingly popular during the 1940s. It also experienced a renewed interest in the 1970s. Records released by Jacob do Mandolin and Conjunto Época de Ouro continue to be played on the radio today.
>
> **Sources:** Choro Music Reference and Songbooks. https://www.choromusic.com

encourage participation in singing and dancing rather than purchasing tickets to watch events from afar. In the northern regions, the influence of Afro-Brazilian culture is reflected in the musical styles that include not only samba, but also *axé* and a fusion of samba-reggae. These neighborhood celebrations incorporate multiple musical bands, and they do not have competitions; instead, the focus is on entertaining the participating public. Another unique twist on the way Carnival is celebrated takes place in the state of Minas Gerais, where the *blocos carnavalescos* are mostly organized by university student groups. In the colonial towns of Diamantina, Mariana, and Ouro Preto, college students roam the streets with live bands composed mostly of drums and brass instruments, and they invite people to join them in the festivities. Regardless of location, Brazilian carnival celebrations are always joyous occasions.

See also: Chapter 6: African Ancestry and Influence. Chapter 13: Overview; Samba Music and Dance. Chapter 16: Rede Globo and Other Television Networks.

Further Reading

McGowan, Chris, and Ricardo Pessanha. 2008. *The Brazilian Sound: Samba, Bossa Nova, and Popular Music of Brazil.* Philadelphia: Temple University Press.

Teissl, Helmut. 2000. *Carnival in Rio.* New York: Abbeville.

Vianna, Hermano (trans. by John C. Chasteen). 1999. *The Mystery of Samba: Popular Music and National Identity in Brazil.* Chapel Hill: University of North Carolina Press.

"Girl from Ipanema" Song

The Brazilian song titled "Garota de Ipanema" ("The Girl from Ipanema") was a worldwide success when it was first released in 1964. Ipanema is an upscale bohemian beach neighborhood in southern Rio de Janeiro. The hit song, based on a bossa nova and jazz style, was a collaboration of two friends: composer Antônio Carlos Jobim wrote the music, and poet Vinicius de Morales wrote the lyrics in Portuguese. The first and original version was recorded by singers Stan Getz and João Gilberto under the record label Verve. The song became extremely popular, winning the Grammy award for record of the year in 1965. It is considered the second most recorded pop song in global music history, only after "Yesterday" by the Beatles. Norman Gimbel wrote the lyrics in English in 1963, and Astrud Gilberto recorded the English version. "Garota de Ipanema" provided global recognition to the emerging musical style of Brazilian bossa nova during the 1960s.

The writers of the song were inspired when they saw a girl walking by the Veloso Bar, where they were socializing in late 1962. Her name was Heloísa Eneida Menezes Paes Pinto (nowadays most commonly known by her married name Helô Pinheiro); she was a seventeen-year-old girl who lived in the Ipanema neighborhood. According to the authors, she personified an iconic image of a carioca girl (from Rio de Janeiro) with tanned skin, tall slender body, long wavy hair, youthful appearance, and graceful moves as she walked around the seaside neighborhood. As the popularity of the song increased, people were curious about who this girl was, and she became a recognized celebrity.

While the song was written over fifty years ago, it remains a crucial part of the Brazilian musical identity. In addition, it is the song that most foreigners identify with Brazil. The national legacy of the song was evident during the recent 2016 Summer Olympics held in Rio de Janeiro. Helô Pinheiro participated as one of the torchbearers for the games. One of Antônio Jobim's grandsons, Daniel, performed the song during the opening ceremony. In addition, the two mascots for the 2016 Olympics and Paralympics Games were called Vinicius and Tom to honor the two authors of the song. Evidently, the legacy of "Garota de Ipanema" is certainly still alive in Rio de Janeiro.

See also: Chapter 13: Overview; Bossa Nova; Jobim, Antônio Carlos (1927–1994).

Further Reading

Kim, Eun Kyung. 2016. "Brazilian Beauty! Meet the Woman Who Inspired 'Girl from Ipanema.'" *Today,* August 8. Accessed July 11, 2019. https://www.today.com/news/brazilian-beauty-meet-woman-who-inspired-girl-ipanema-t101592

McGowan, Chris, and Ricardo Pessanha. 2008. *The Brazilian Sound: Samba, Bossa Nova, and Popular Music of Brazil*. Philadelphia: Temple University Press.

Jobim, Antônio Carlos (1927–1994)

Antônio Carlos Brasileiro de Almeida Jobim was an innovative Brazilian musician who worked in multiple areas of the industry as a singer, songwriter, piano player, composer, and arranger. Commonly known as Tom Jobim, he is recognized as the main creator of the Brazilian bossa nova style that captivated the world in the 1960s. His songs have been recorded and performed by musicians internationally.

Antônio Jobim was born on January 25, 1927, in Rio de Janeiro, where he grew up in a semi-affluent neighborhood. His parents, Jorge de Oliveira Jobim and Nilza Brasileiro de Almeida, divorced when he was still an infant, and his mother later married Celso da Drota Pessoa, who actively supported young Antônio's musical interests, buying him his first piano. Jobim spent his youth working as a musician in bars and nightclubs around Rio de Janeiro. By the 1940s, he started writing songs about love, sad relationships, and Brazilian folk traditions.

In 1956, Antônio Jobim worked with poet Vinicius de Moraes (1913–1980) to write the music for a play titled *Orfeu da Conceição*. They did not know it at the time, but their collaboration would have a worldwide impact. The theater production was an acclaimed hit in Brazil, and it was subsequently adapted as the film *Orfeu negro* in 1959. Their friendship later produced one of the most famous Brazilian songs ever recorded, "Garota de Ipanema" ("The Girl from Ipanema"), in 1962. This song made the bossa nova style extremely popular in Brazil. Two years later, Jobim ventured into another crucial collaboration with three talented musicians: Stan Getz (an American jazz saxophone player), João Gilberto (a prolific Brazilian singer in Portuguese), and Astrud Gilberto (a Brazilian singer who also recorded in English). They released two albums that introduced Jobim's bossa nova style to English-speaking audiences during the 1960s. The songs "Corcovado" and "Girl from Ipanema" became an international success and established Antônio Jobim as a renowned musician and composer for the next three decades. His jazz compositions and songs were recorded by gifted performers including Frank Sinatra, Ella Fitzgerald, Oscar Peterson, and Herbie Hancock.

Antônio Jobim experienced health complications in 1994. He had an operation to remove a bladder tumor, but suffered two cardiac arrests. He died on December 2, 1994, at a hospital in New York City. His family transported his body back to Rio de Janeiro, where he was buried. Jobim left a powerful legacy in the music world, and he is considered one of the best jazz composers of the twentieth century.

See also: Chapter 13: Overview; Bossa Nova; "Girl from Ipanema" Song.

Further Reading

Cabral, Sérgio. 2008. *Antônio Carlos Jobim—Uma biografia*. São Paulo: Lazuli Editora Nacional.

Castro, Rudy. 2000. *Bossa Nova: The Story of the Brazilian Music That Seduced the World*. Chicago: A Capella Books.

Murphy, John P. 2006. *Music in Brazil*. Oxford, UK: Oxford University Press.

Música Popular Brasileira (MPB)

Música popular brasileira (MPB) is a style that emerged in the late 1960s, producing non-electric music and combining other regional styles that included *baião*, samba, and samba-*canção*. Its influence has created high-caliber musicians who continue to entertain the masses even after five decades. MPB came after the bossa nova style that was popular in Brazil during the 1950s and early 1960s. Initially, MPB was mostly instrumental in nature with heavy reliance on acoustic guitar sounds. The goal was to create a unique Brazilian style based on traditional music throughout the country. It became a blend of regional trends with the addition of jazz and rock styles. During the 1970s, it was so popular with students and intellectual populations that it became known as university music. The use of large festivals throughout the country headlining important MPB musicians sparked a nationwide popularity. Then, during the early 1980s, MPB musicians became social advocates who used their music to speak out against the abuses of the military dictatorship (1964–1985) in Brazil. Subsequently, their lyrics went further by addressing topics of social injustice such as poverty, the unequal distribution of land, and an inadequate educational system. Most of the MBP classic songs were composed during the late 1970s and early 1980s based on acoustic roots and socially conscious lyrics. Today, the MPB style is very common in people's homes since multiple radio stations play entire collections of the genre. Some of the most popular contemporary MPB artists include Adriana Calcanhotto, Chico Buarque, Maris Gadú, Ivan Lins, and the musical group Os Novos Baianos.

Música popular brasileira continues to thrive in Brazil, and it has gained international recognition. It is so popular that it became an official category of the Latin Grammy Awards in the United States in the year 2000. Since MPB blends several styles of regional music, the award is given to an album that contains a minimum of 51 percent of new material, either vocal or instrumental. The recipients could be a solo artist, duos, or a musical group. The first artist to receive the Latin Grammy Award for Best MBP Album was Caetano Veloso in 2000 for his album titled *Livro*. The winner in 2016 was the gifted Elza Soares with her album *Mulher do fim do mundo*. The award for Best MPB in 2017 was special because it was the collaboration of three outstanding, well-established musicians (Edu Lobo, Romero Lubambo, and Mauro Senise) with their album titled *Dos navegantes*. The genre of *música popular brasileira* continues to grow with talented and prolific musicians who make Brazilians happy with their music.

See also: Chapter 13: Overview; Bossa Nova; Regional Music and Dance; Samba Music and Dance. Chapter 16: Overview.

Further Reading

Dunn, Christopher. 2001. *Tropicália and the Emergence of a Brazilian Counterculture*. Chapel Hill: University of North Carolina Press.

Latin Grammy Awards. https://www.latingrammy.com/en

McGowan, Chris, and Ricardo Pessanha. 1998. *The Brazilian Sound: Samba, Bossa Nova, and the Popular Music of Brazil*. Philadelphia: Temple University Press.

Slater, Russ. 2010. "What Is Brazilian MPB Music?" *Sounds and Colours*. SoundsAndColours.com. April 19. Accessed May 2, 2019. https://soundsandcolours.com/articles/brazil/mpb-brazilian-popular-music-116

Música Sertaneja

Música sertaneja is Brazilian country music. It is extremely popular but relatively unknown outside of the country. The name "sertanejo" is based on the term *sertão*, which references the interior rural regions away from the large urban coastal cities and more specifically the semiarid northeast region of the country. The popular genre of *música sertaneja* was created in the interior rural lands of Minas Gerais, Goiás, Matto Grosso do Sul, São Paulo, and Paraná during the 1920s. The *sertanejo* musical style continues to be adapted and revitalized, which has contributed to its growing commercial success. In fact, for the last thirty years, it is one of the most played genres in radio programming nationwide. To recognize the importance of *música sertaneja*, the Latin Grammy Awards created a specific category and award for this musical style.

Música sertaneja has demonstrated its enduring power lasting roughly one hundred years by entertaining audiences mostly in the countryside of southeastern and center-western Brazil. The genre has evolved through four distinct periods that are discernible by the adaptation of new instruments, the themes of its lyrics, and its fusion with other rhythms and musical styles. The first period started in the late 1920s when Cornélio Pires first wrote songs and released records evoking the beauty of daily life in the countryside in contrast with a hectic urban lifestyle. His songs provided inspiration for a new wave of *sertanejo* artists. The second period lasted from the 1940s until the late 1960s, and it reflects an experimentation with other instruments (violin, trumpet, and accordion), other musical genres (mariachi, samba, ranchera, and polka), as well as lyrical topics (more about love and less about the country landscape). Band duos (Sulino e Marrueiro, Palmeira and Bía) became extremely popular. The third period started in the 1970s; it was an extremely prolific era for *música sertaneja*, and it essentially defined what Brazilian country music is nowadays. The incorporation of the electric guitar changed the sound and appeal of the genre. Singer Sérgio Reis (1940–) emerged as an iconic figure who achieved substantial commercial success, and pushed the music from being performed in small rodeos to much larger venues and audiences. During the 1980s, the musical style achieved much wider market penetration when it was promoted on FM radio and television programming nationwide. The success of multiple duo bands (such as João Paulo & Daniel, Leandro e Leonardo, and Gilberto e Gilman), however, led to a feeling of commercial exploitation. Consequently, talented young musicians launched the fourth *sertanejo* period during the early 2000s by crafting a slightly different style called *sertanejo universitário*. They abandoned the traditional acoustic guitars and accordions in favor of a heavier use of electric guitars. In addition, they infused funk and samba rhythms while still maintaining a clearly identifiable *sertanejo* sound. The lyrics became less about the melancholy of the countryside and more about love, betrayal, sex, and drinking. The style appealed to younger masses, especially the college student crowd.

Modern *música sertaneja* remains one of the most played musical genres on Brazilian radio stations. Contemporary *sertanejo* artists (including Paula Fernandes, Michel

A traditional musical trio, typical of the semiarid northeastern music of Brazil, is always present in the famous Festas Juninas (June Festivals). The colorful festivities are mostly celebrated in farming communities toward the end of the rainy season. (Jaboticaba Fotos /Dreamstime.com)

Teló, and Maria Cecília) have become extremely successful in the Brazilian mainstream musical world.

See also: Chapter 13: Overview.

Further Reading

Dent, Alexander. 2009. *River of Tears: Country Music, Memory, and Modernity in Brazil*. Durham, NC: Duke University Press.

McGowan, Chris, and Ricardo Pessanha. 2008. *The Brazilian Sound: Samba, Bossa Nova, and Popular Music of Brazil*. Philadelphia: Temple University Press.

Murphy, John P. 2006. *Music in Brazil*. Oxford, UK: Oxford University Press.

Musical Instruments

Brazilian music is much more diverse than simply carnival and samba. The miscegenation of European, African, and indigenous backgrounds that has occurred in Brazil over centuries has influenced the development of a truly unique set of Brazilian sounds and rhythms. These three groups developed their own musical traditions, and the instruments they introduced continue to be used in Brazil. Some of them have been incorporated into new musical traditions, but others have been adapted to reflect regional sounds. Overall, the availability of musical instruments from different cultures has contributed to the unique modern Brazilian sounds of samba, *choro*, *axé*, *música sertaneja*, capoeira, *carimbó*, *lambada*, *arrocha*, and pop music.

Brazil has a rich musical heritage, and it includes several instruments that are not well known outside of the country. For example, the composition of samba music includes a large array of instruments, especially in the percussion category. The *atabaque* drums have Arab origin, and they are played with both hands. They have metal rings at the top and bottom, as well as ropes in between used to adapt the pitch. They are crucial to samba and *axé* music to provide rhythms with fast tempo. They are also considered sacred instruments in Candomblé religious celebrations. The *repinique* is a

Bateria is the musical component of the Samba School at Rio de Janeiro. The *chocalho* is a local instrument adapted from the tambourine and converted into a rectangular frame with jingles attached. Musicians shake it to produce the sound that accompanies the drum band for samba music. (Zts/Dreamstime.com)

double-headed drum with skins on both sides, and it is usually carried on the shoulder. It was specifically developed for Carnival by samba schools, and it is played with a hand on one side and a drumstick on the other. Two instruments with African origin are the *afoxé* and the *xequerê*. The former is a round gourd, and the latter is another gourd but with a long bottle shape. Both instruments are wrapped with a net that has threaded beads, and musicians shake it to make a rattling sound. The Portuguese brought tambourines to Brazil, and they were adapted to take different local forms. Nowadays, the *pandeiro* is emblematic of the Carnival at Rio de Janeiro. It took the structure of the tambourine and adapted a head that can be tuned to produce either high or low notes to provide unique sounds. The *chocalho* is also a representation of Brazilian ingenuity, taking a round tambourine and morphing it into a long and rectangular frame with jingles attached to both sides. Samba musicians shake it to accompany the rhythm of the *bateria* samba drum band. When it comes to the traditional Brazilian capoeira, the use of a *berimbau* musical bow is crucial. This single-string instrument sets the rhythm of capoeira dance for the choreographic-style martial art. All these unique instruments have enriched multiple genres that provide unique characteristics to Brazilian music.

See also: Chapter 13: Overview; Carnival; *Choro* Instrumental Music Sidebar; Samba Music and Dance.

Further Reading

Assis, Gilson de. 2016. *Brazilian Conga: Atabaque*. Van Nuys, CA: Alfred Music.

Henry, Clarence Bernard. 2008. *Let's Make Some Noise: Axé and the African Roots of Popular Brazilian Music*. Jackson: University Press of Mississippi.

Tupinambá de Ulhôa, Martha, Cláudia Azevedo, and Felipe Trotta (eds.). 2014. *Made in Brazil: Studies in Popular Music*. Abingdon-on-Thames, UK: Routledge.

Uribe, Ed. 1994. *The Essence of Brazilian Percussion & Drum Set*. Van Nuys, CA: Alfred Music.

Regional Music and Dance

Brazil has an incredible musical diversity. While the world has been captivated by the sounds and dance rhythms of samba and bossa nova, the reality is that Brazilians listen to a wide range of musical styles, including multiple genres of regional music that reach large audiences via radio programming on a daily basis. Examples of such unique regional sounds include *axé, carimbó, música sertaneja*, and funk carioca.

Axé music emerged during the 1980s in the state of Bahia. It is a mix of multiple Afro-Latino styles (*merengue, forró*, reggae, and *maracatu*) but with a distinct Brazilian rhythm relying heavily on percussion instruments. Modern *axé* artists (such as Claudia Leitte and Ivete Sangalo) are extremely successful with their spicy lyrics and sensual dance moves.

Carimbó music was created in eastern Amazonia during the late 1950s, and it quickly became a popular style. Its sound was transformed during the early 1970s with the incorporation of electric guitars and synthesizers. It also evolved as a fusion with samba and reggae rhythms. The eventual result was the creation of *lambada* music in the state of Bahia; it reached international success in 1986 with songs such as "Chorando se foi" and a sensual dance style.

Música sertaneja is Brazilian country music, and it has been extremely popular since the 1920s. The name "sertanejo" is based on the term *sertão*, which references the interior rural regions of Brazil and more specifically the semiarid northeast region of the country. During the 1980s, the musical style achieved much wider market penetration when it was promoted on FM radio and television programming nationwide. Modern *música sertaneja* is one of the most played musical genres on the radio nowadays.

Contemporary *sertanejo* artists (including Paula Fernandes and Maria Cecília) have become commercially successful in the Brazilian mainstream musical world.

Funk carioca was first created during the 1970s in the poor hillside *favelas* of Rio de Janeiro. Despite the name, it does not resemble the typical U.S. funk style. Instead, it is closer to the Miami Bass dance sound. During the late 1980s and early 1990s, funk carioca artists used lyrics to denounce the poor living conditions and the police harassment that poor black Brazilian populations experienced as part of a daily struggle. Despite a reputation for vulgar language and its alleged links to drug use, funk carioca increased in popularity during the 2000s in urban nightclubs that catered to middle- and upper-class Brazilian youth.

All these regional musical and dance genres continue to enrich the lives of millions of Brazilians on a daily basis. The contemporary national musical scene also includes other rhythms, such as Brazilian pop, heavy metal, folk-rock, *choro, forró,* hip-hop, gospel, rap, gaucho, and samba-reggae.

See also: Chapter 13: Overview; *Música Sertaneja*.

Further Reading

Brill, Mark. 2017. *Music of Latin America and the Caribbean.* Abingdon-on-Thames, UK: Routledge.

Maria, Vasco. 2005. *História da música no Brasil.* Rio de Janeiro: Nova Fronteira.

McGowan, Chris, and Ricardo Pessenha. 1998. "Carimbó, Lambada, and the North," in *The Brazilian Sound: Samba, Bossa Nova, and the Popular Music of Brazil.* Philadelphia: Temple University Press, 154–157.

Murphy, John P. 2006. *Music in Brazil: Experiencing Music, Expressing Culture.* New York: Oxford University Press.

Samba Music and Dance

Brazilian samba is both an energetic musical genre and an attractive dance style. It is rooted in African religious traditions practiced during the slave trade period (1500s to 1888). The *samba de roda* (dance circle) was the foundation for the performance style in the northern state of Bahia during the 1600s–1700s. The dance and rhythms became the pillars to develop the captivating samba carioca in Rio de Janeiro. Nowadays, there are samba variations throughout the country, but the current musical style was created in urban Rio de Janeiro early in the twentieth century. Samba is so crucial to Brazilian identity that it has its own national holiday on December 2 to celebrate its historical roots and dance traditions. The most recognizable sound is provided by the *bateria* (samba band based on drums), which dictates the contagious rhythm for the dancers. Other instruments used in samba are tambourines, rattles, cowbells, and cymbals. In northern Brazil, samba bands also use trumpets, flutes, and clarinets to accompany the percussion instruments.

The song "Pele Telefone" was released in 1917, and it is considered the first true samba song ever recorded. It was registered by Ernesto dos Santos, also known by the artistic name Danga. The song was very successful, and it helped to make the samba genre and its accompanying dance style extremely popular. At that time, middle- and upper-class Brazilians were not fond of samba due to its Afro-Brazilian origins. However, the use of radio expanded in urban areas during the 1920s, and early samba composers—such as Ary Barroso, Elton Medeiros, Ciro Monteiro, and Ismael Silva—produced outstanding songs that quickly captivated audiences across racial, social, and economic boundaries. Then Brazilian president Getúlio Vargas (1883–1954) actively supported samba music during the 1930s and 1940s, which increased its national exposure; it also became popular internationally with performances by Carmen Miranda.

Samba has become synonymous with Carnival. While there are astonishing carnivals in Salvador, Recife, Porto Seguro, Vitória, and São Paulo, the most iconic celebration takes place at the Sambódromo in Rio de Janeiro. This cultural tradition is centered on the samba schools (large dance clubs) that compete every year for the best presentation. Samba schools are neighborhood organizations, and they prepare for months to develop an original musical samba score for the year. Each samba school collaborates with custom designers, painters, sculptors, and musicians to create a unique song, carnival float, and dance choreography while also engaging local residents in the creative process.

Samba has been transformed from a cultural tradition that was reluctantly tolerated in the late 1800s to becoming an emblematic symbol of Brazilian national identity in the twentieth century. In fact, the *samba de roda* (dance circle) was declared a symbol of Heritage for Humanity by the UNESCO organization in 2005. Contemporary Brazilian artists continue to experiment with samba by creating fusion arrangements with reggae, rock, rap, and hip-hop.

See also: Chapter 2: Vargas, Getúlio (1883–1954). Chapter 13: Overview; Carnival; Musical Instruments.

Further Reading

Hertzman, Marc A. 2013. *Making Samba: A New History of Race and Music in Brazil*. Durham, NC: Duke University Press.

McGowan, Chris, and Ricardo Pessanha. 2008. *The Brazilian Sound: Samba, Bossa Nova, and Popular Music of Brazil*. Philadelphia: Temple University Press.

Vianna, Hermano. 2000. *The Mystery of Samba: Popular Music and National Identity*. Chapel Hill: University of North Carolina Press.

Tropicália

Tropicália (also known as *tropicalismo*) was a counterculture artistic movement that emerged in Brazil during the 1960s. One of its main tenets was the concept of *antrofagia*, which promulgated the fusion of different styles and influences. In practical terms, it blended traditional African instruments with the popularity of rock and roll and the use of electric guitar sounds that were popular in foreign countries. While *tropicália* is most commonly associated with music, it also influenced artistic expression in the fields of poetry, theater, film, and television. In fact, the intellectual leaders of this approach came from multiple disciplines, including singer-songwriters Gilberto Gil and Caetano Veloso, lyricist José Carlos Capinan, arranger Rogério Duprat, singer Nara Leão, and poet Rogélio Duarte.

The musical album *Tropicália: Ou panis et circencis* defined the cultural movement with its release in 1968. The collaboration of multiple fields elevated the lyrics from a simple countermovement to the level of poetry with clear expression of ideas. Musicians mixed traditional styles with new rhythms, and the lyrics were extremely critical of the existing social conditions of the country. *Tropicalistas* used songs to express strong criticism of the military coup d'état in 1964 and the repressive steps the government had implemented in terms of censorship, torture, and unexplained disappearances.

The *tropicália* artistic movement provided a platform to blur the lines between traditional and innovative styles. Much to the dismay of conservative musicians who complained about the preservation of music quality, *tropicalistas* mixed bossa nova with psychedelic sounds from the Beatles, samba with rock and roll, as well as boleros with tropical sounds. In other cultural forums, this artistic movement also encouraged the fusion of high culture with mass culture, as well as classical art with traditional arts and crafts. The movement had a strong influence on multiple aspects of society that included the adoption of the hippie counterculture popular in the United States, the widespread acceptance of long hair, a casual approach to sex, and a new wave of fashion that was considered "indecent" by traditional people in Brazilian society.

The *tropicália* movement was widely criticized for being immoral and for promoting an antiestablishment view of politics. Consequently, it became a target for the military dictatorship that was still in power in Brazil. The two main leaders—Gilberto Gil and Caetano Veloso—were arrested in February 1969 due to the antiauthoritarian content expressed in their music. They were released from prison after a few months once they agreed to apply for exile in the United Kingdom. They were able to return to Brazil in 1972. Other *tropicália* leaders were savagely tortured or forced into "special psychiatric care" to make them understand the error of their ways.

The *tropicália* movement had a strong influence on future generations of musicians, theater actors, film directors, and poets. In 1993, Caetano Veloso and Giberto Gil released another album, *Tropicália 2*, to commemorate twenty-five years since the release of their first album that marked the beginning of a cultural transformation on Brazil. Then, almost forty-five years later, in 2012, filmmaker Marcelo Machado directed the documentary *Tropicália* to illustrate the artists' struggle to challenge the traditional music and cultural norms prevalent in Brazil during the late 1960s. It was a nostalgic view of a cultural movement that managed to thrive even under the censorship of a brutal military dictatorship.

See also: Chapter 2: Overview; Operation Condor and Military Rule; Timeline. Chapter 10: Overview.

Further Reading

Dunn, Christopher. 2001. *Brutality Garden: Tropicália and the Emergence of a Brazilian Counterculture*. Chapel Hill: University of North Carolina Press.

McGowan, Chris, and Ricardo Pessanha. 2008. *The Brazilian Sound: Samba, Bossa Nova, and Popular Music of Brazil*. Philadelphia: Temple University Press.

Murphy, John P. 2006. *Music in Brazil*. Oxford, UK: Oxford University Press.

Veloso, Caetano. 2003. *Tropical Truth: A Story of Music and Revolution in Brazil*. Cambridge, MA: Da Capo Press.

Villa-Lobos, Heitor (1887–1959)

Heitor Villa-Lobos was a prolific Brazilian music composer, born in Rio de Janeiro on March 5, 1887. He did not receive formal training; in fact, he taught himself how to play the clarinet, guitar, and cello. In general, he was influenced by European classical music and exposed to Brazilian folk music. He wrote over two 2,000 musical works in multiple genres, including chamber music, orchestra compositions, instrumental masterpieces, and vocal pieces. He is well known in Brazil for a wide range of patriotic works that he created during the 1930s to highlight respect and veneration of national symbols, such as the flag, motto, and national anthem during the dictatorship of Getúlio Vargas (1930–1945).

During the early 1900s, Villa-Lobos played with multiple improvised street bands to make a living. He also played at theater orchestras and as a cellist for the opera in Rio de Janeiro. These experiences provided a musical foundation and a sense of urgency to start a career as a serious music composer. He released a series of orchestra and chamber music concerts from 1913 to 1921 that were well received in Brazil. His works reflected his European influence blended with indigenous folklore traditions. During the 1920s, Villa-Lobos continued to make musical contributions during the seminal Modern Art Week held in São Paulo in 1922 and with a series of guitar concerts commissioned by the legendary Spanish guitarist Andrés Segovia.

In 1932, Villa-Lobos accepted the government position as the director of the Superintendência de Educação Musical e Artística (SEMA) under the Vargas regime. At this federal post, Villa-Lobos composed patriotic music that was often used as propaganda to promote the authoritarian government. For example, he created the *Guia Prático* as an eleven-volume collection of patriotic songs for a national school curriculum, a large compilation of songs for civic occasions, and government propaganda to promote Brazilian pride.

When the Vargas dictatorship fell in 1945, Villa-Lobos emerged with a damaged reputation in professional musical circles. Nevertheless, he received commissions to create concertos for classical guitar (for Andrés Segovia in 1956), harp (for Nicanor Zabaleta in 1953), as well as piano, harmonica, and cello. He also composed musical scores for the film industry commissioned by MGM films and United Artist Records during the late 1950s.

Heitor Villa-Lobos left a musical legacy that makes Brazilians proud. He died on November 17, 1959, in Rio de Janeiro. His funeral was the last major national civic event held in Rio before the capital city was relocated to Brasília a few months later in 1960.

See also: Chapter 2: Vargas, Getúlio (1883–1954). Chapter 12: Modern Art Week, São Paulo, 1922. Chapter 13: Overview.

Further Reading

Murphy, John P. 2006. *Music in Brazil*. Oxford, UK: Oxford University Press.

Negwer, Manuel. 2009. *Villa-Lobos e o florescimento da música brasileira*. São Paulo: Martins Fontes.

Tarasti, Eero. 1995. *Heitor Villa-Lobos: The Life and Works*. Jefferson, NC: McFarland.

Williams, Daryle. 2001. *Culture Wars in Brazil: The First Vargas Regime, 1930–1945*. Durham, NC: Duke University Press.

CHAPTER 14

FOOD

OVERVIEW

Three ethnic and racial groups have made significant historical contributions to what is now contemporary Brazil: the Portuguese colonizers, the existing indigenous groups, and imported African slaves. In the process of miscegenation, these three groups mixed at extraordinary rates in Brazil. Each one of them also had its own culinary traditions, which had to be adapted to the new land in the context of available ingredients and exposure to other cooking methods. The Portuguese brought coffee, sugarcane, salted cod, and beans. The African slaves introduced bananas and *dendê* oil from the palm tree. Amerindians cultivated the cassava plant, used to make manioc flour, which is still a main ingredient in the contemporary Brazilian diet. The fusion of these ingredients and cooking customs created the beginning of a new Brazilian cuisine based on regional dishes.

Contemporary Brazilian cuisine is actually a collection of regional dishes that reflect local traditions and styles of cooking. For example, *carne de sol* (sun-dried meat) is a traditional way of preparing beef in the northeastern semiarid region of Brazil known as the *sertão*. The *sertanejos* cut fresh beef into thin slices, salt it slightly, and place it outdoors to dry for two or three days. Since the *sertão* region usually has dry heat, the wind allows the salted meat to dry quickly on the exterior while keeping it tender on the inside. The meat can be preserved for weeks without refrigeration. Besides meat dishes, multiple regional sweets (*brigadeiro, beijinho, goiabada,* and *campota*) provide the perfect way to end a meal. If there is such a thing as a national dish and drink, it would be *feijoada* and *caipirinha*. The word *feijão* means "beans" in Portuguese. *Feijoada* is a hearty stew with black beans, different cuts of pork or beef cooked together in a clay pot at very low heat. It is served with white rice, other meats (usually different sausages such as *morcela* and *chouriço*), and collard greens. The final taste is not spicy, but rather salty and smoky, which is provided mainly by the natural flavors of the pork and beans. *Caipirinha* is often cited as Brazil's national drink. It is an alcoholic cocktail prepared with sugar, lime, and *cachaça*, which is a hard liquor distilled from sugarcane. *Cachaça* is by far the most consumed distilled alcoholic beverage in Brazil and largely produced in the state of Minas Gerais. Bartenders create the cocktail *caipirinha* by muddling the lime and sugar together and then adding the liquor at the end. It is usually served on the rocks over ice cubes. Actually, Minas Gerais also produces many products (coffee, condensed milk, artisan cheeses, *cachaça,* and *dolce de leite*) that are used in multiple dishes and recipes throughout Brazil. Its regional cuisine is well known;

consequently, Minas Gerais is frequently selected to represent Brazil at international gastronomy exhibitions and competitions.

Contemporary Brazilian cuisine is being discovered abroad with modern chefs who have elevated local dishes and provided recognition of Brazilian gastronomy at international levels. For example, master chefs Rodrigo Oliveira, Roberta Sudbrack, Yara Roberts, and Felipe Rameh all own and operate successful restaurants that have earned recognition and multiple culinary awards in Brazil. They range from Michelin-star elegant establishments located in posh areas of Rio de Janeiro to family-style affordable restaurants available in modest suburbs of São Paulo. In addition, chefs have successfully exposed Americans to *churrascaria* (Brazilian barbecue and steak houses) to allow customers in the United States to enjoy the style of cooking by following the traditional method of roasting meats over an open fire. For example, chef Evandro Caregnato is the culinary director for the famous *churrascaria* chain of restaurants called Texas de Brazil, and his cookbooks provide a wealth of recipes for grilling savory meats. Another chain that eventually came to the United States is Fogo do Chão, which also operates *churrascaria* restaurants in Mexico and Brazil.

While Brazilian cuisine is receiving international recognition and master chefs in exclusive restaurants provide upscale eating experiences for foodies, another stark reality is that Brazil still struggles with significant problems of poverty, hunger, and malnutrition. The existing income inequalities mean that poor people still suffer from basic food insecurities. However, the government has implemented and funded national programs during the last two decades that have lifted people out of poverty and drastically reduced hunger. In 2003, President Luiz Inácio Lula da Silva (1945–) implemented the Fome Zero program (Zero Hunger Strategy) with the explicit purpose of reducing extreme poverty and hunger nationwide. The results are impressive, and now Brazil is a model for other developing nations on effective strategies to combat hunger.

Meals are social events, and Brazilians love to share food with family and friends. During the twentieth century, large waves of immigrants from Italy, Japan, and the Middle East enriched the culinary options for Brazilians by adding pasta, pizza, sushi, tempura, tabbouleh, and sweet desserts. One thing most Brazilians agree on is that a *cafezinho* (a small shot of strong coffee) is a great way to end a meal.

Further Reading

Brazilian Coffee Exporters Council (Ce Café) Official Website. http://www.cecafe.com.br/en

Caragnato, Evandro. 2016. *Churrasco: Grilling the Brazilian Way.* Layton, UT: Gibbs Smith.

Castanho, Thiago, and Luciana Bianchi. 2014. *Brazilian Food.* Richmond Hill, Ontario, Canada: Firefly Books.

Da Silva, José Graziano, Mauro Eduardo del Grossi, and Caio Galvão de França (eds.). 2011. *The Fome Zero (Zero Hunger) Program: The Brazilian Experience.* Brasília: Food and Agriculture Organization of the United Nations.

Elias, Rodrigo. 2008. "Feijoada: A Short History of an Edible Institution," in *Flavors from Brazil,* edited by the Minister of External Relations from Brazil, 35–41. Brasíilia: Ministry of External Relations.

Ministry of Social Development and Fight against Hunger (MDS) Official Website. http://www.mds.gov.br

Roberts, Yara. 2009. *The Brazilian Table*. Layton, UT: Gibbs Smith.

Tosta, Antonio Luciano de Andrade, and Eduardo F. Coutinho (eds.). 2016. *Brazil*. Santa Barbara, CA: ABC-CLIO.

Tudisco, Ana Luiza. 2016. *10 Receitas típicas de Minas Gerais*. São Paulo: Editora 101 Seleções.

Weimann, Erwin. 2006. *Cachaça: A bebida brasileira*. São Paulo: Editora Terceiro Nome.

Cafezinho, A Small Shot of Strong Coffee

Brazilians love coffee, and a *cafezinho* is ubiquitous as part of daily life. The word is the diminutive in Portuguese meaning "little coffee." It is served in a very small cup similar to the one used for an espresso. Coffee (Brazilian style) is a rather potent brew usually served with lots of sugar to counter the strength of the flavor. A *cafezinho* is considered the national nonalcoholic drink, and it has become a crucial part of any social gathering with friends, family, or business acquaintances. When business meetings take place, it is quite common to begin with a *cafezinho* and friendly conversation before discussing the purpose or agenda items for the meeting. When coffee is consumed at home, it is usually served after all the relatives have finished eating the main meal. Fortunately, Brazil can supply all the coffee it needs for its daily cultural ritual.

Brazil is both the largest coffee producer and exporter in the world. In 2018, the total amount of coffee global exports was a combined $30.6 billion U.S. Brazil generates more than 30 percent of international coffee production, and it represents almost 10 percent of the total Brazilian export commodities. As of 2019, the United States was the largest market for Brazilian coffee exports, followed by the European Union and Japan. The Brazilian Coffee Exporters Council (Ce Cafe) projects that coffee exports will continue to rise while also supplying enough Arabica beans for its national hot drink.

Brazilians visit *cafezinho* stand-up bars regularly for a quick shot of strong coffee, and these establishments are usually sprinkled throughout neighborhoods in every city in the country. They sell mainly coffee but also other popular drinks and juices, which means that Brazilians usually linger at cafés for a long time to socialize and relax. As a coffee-producing nation, it was expected to attract the attention of giant coffee corporations, such as Starbucks, which operates over one hundred stores in Rio de Janeiro and São Paulo alone. This company caters to the local tastes by crafting a special lineup of espresso drinks using a unique brand called Brazilian Blend for drinks such as Espresso Mocha, and Espresso Doce de Leite (Flandreau, 2016). The company's arrival in Brazil has been both embraced and vilified. The modern crowds made up mostly of young people seem to enjoy the ambiance provided by the company cafés with drinks based on *cafezinho* traditions but with a contemporary twist. However, lots of Brazilians claim that corporate versions of their national drink cannot be mass produced, and they are happier supporting their small and local *cafezinho* bars. There is enough coffee for everyone.

See also: Chapter 4: Overview; Coffee Exports; Trading Partners. Chapter 14: Overview.

Further Reading

Bateman, Michael. 1999. *Café Brazil*. Chicago: Contemporary Books.

Brazilian Coffee Exporters Council (Ce Café) Official Website. http://www.cecafe.com.br/en

King, Winfield Conwell. 2017. *Brazil's Coffee Industry*. Bel Air, CA: Forgotten Books.

Workman, Daniel. 2018. "Coffee Exports by Country." *World's Top Exports,* May 29. Accessed May 1, 2019. http://www.worldstopexports.com/coffee-exports-country

Caipirinha, a National Cocktail

Caipirinha is often cited as Brazil's national drink. It is an alcoholic cocktail prepared with sugar, lime, and *cachaça*, which is a hard liquor distilled from sugarcane. *Cachaça* is by far the most consumed distilled alcoholic beverage in Brazil; sometimes, it goes by the name *caninha*. The alcohol is extracted by the fermentation of fresh sugarcane juice, which is then distilled. Bartenders throughout Brazil create the cocktail *caipirinha* by muddling (mashing the two ingredients into a mix by using a muddler or a wooden spoon) the lime and sugar together and then adding the liquor at the end. It is finally served on the rocks over ice cubes. Brazilians can enjoy it served as an individual drink, or it can be prepared in a large jar to be shared by multiple people served into single glasses.

The origin of the cocktail cannot be definitely attributed to a single person or location. First of all, the word *caipirinha* is the diminutive form of the Portuguese word *caipira*; it references a woman from the countryside, mostly interpreted as a woman from the south-central regions of Brazil. The word carries a connotation similar to the word "hillbilly" in the United States. Searching for the history of the drink, the Brazilian Institute of Cachaça (IBRAC) explains that it likely originated with a popular recipe for the common cold that includes garlic, honey, lemon, and distilled spirits. Along the way, someone removed the honey and the garlic because they were strong flavors; then someone else added sugar to moderate the strong acidic lime flavor. Brazilian historians often give credit to the sugarcane industry in agricultural sections in the interior of the state of São Paulo for adding the sugarcane liquor *cachaça* needed to make the actual cocktail of *caipirinha*.

During the last twenty years, the *cachaça* liquor (used to make *caipirinha*) has gained international recognition due to the fact that Brazil has produced more refined brands of the alcoholic beverage. The liquor has been widely available throughout the country for decades, but it only recently became recognized abroad, mostly due to the availability of premium export labels, such as Beija, Ypioca, Yaguara, and Magnifica. The Brazilian government went as far as protecting the production of *cachaça* by declaring it a national beverage by publishing a federal decree that makes its production an exclusive process based on Brazilian sugarcane. The government also declared September 13 as National Cachaça Day. As of 2018, the countries that import the highest amounts of *cachaça* liquor are Germany, the United States, and Portugal. According to the 2010 census, Brazil now includes over 40,000 small producers of the liquor. The states that produce the most *cachaça* are São Paulo, Pernambuco, Ceará, and Minas Gerais (Bruha 2015). On the global stage, the International Bartenders Association (IBA) designated *caipirinha* as one of its official cocktails. Its recipe is posted as follows:

- 5 cl (centiliter) of *cachaça*
- ½ fresh lime (4 wedges)
- 2 tablespoons of sugar
- Place lime and sugar in an old-fashioned glass and muddle. Fill glass with ice and *cachaça*. To make a variation of this drink called the Caipiroska, use vodka instead of *cachaça*.

See also: Chapter 14: Overview; Minas Gerais Gastronomy.

Further Reading

Bruha, Patrick. 2015. "Cachaça Industry in Brazil." *Brazil Business*, February 6. Accessed July 6, 2019. http://thebrazilbusiness.com/article/cachaca-industry-in-brazil

International Bartenders Association (IBA). 2018. "Cocktails: Caipirinha." *IBA Official Cocktails*. https://iba-world.com/cocktails/caipirinha

Weimann, Erwin. 2006. *Cachaça: A bebida brasileira*. São Paulo: Editora Terceiro Nome.

Carne de Sol, Dried Salted Meat

Carne de sol, which literally means "sun meat," is a traditional way of preparing beef in the northeastern semiarid region of Brazil known as the *sertão*. It is mostly made from beef, but *sertanejos* (people who live in the isolated, poor *sertão* region) sometimes use goat's meat as well. The process involves cutting fresh beef into thin slices of meat. Then it is lightly salted without any other spices and placed outdoors to dry for approximately two to three days. The name "sun meat" is misleading because the pieces of meat are actually hung in a covered area with cross ventilation and bug screens (not directly facing the sun) to avoid flies and other insects but still taking advantage of the strong winds that blow most of the year in the area. Since the *sertão* region usually experiences devastating droughts and extremely dry heat, the wind allows the salted meat to dry quickly on the exterior while keeping it tender inside. The meat is completely cured after a few days, and it can be preserved for weeks without spoiling; it does not need to be refrigerated.

The technique of drying *carne de sol* was developed to solve a common problem of preserving meat in the hot weather of the northeast region at a time when there was no refrigeration available. However, this technique was certainly not new. Previous civilizations throughout history have used similar ways of preparation by applying salt in order to dehydrate meat for preservation. The Portuguese brought the practice with them to Brazil since they had used it for centuries to prepare their salted *bacalhau* (codfish). When people of the northeast of Brazil saw this technique, they just adapted it to their available source of protein based on beef and occasionally goat meat.

The process of drying salted meat has other names. In parts of Brazil, it is also called *jabá*. In other countries of South America, this type of meat was called *ch'arki* in the Quechua language of the former Inca Empire. The Inca made *ch'arki* from llama meat in the territories that are now Bolivia, Peru, and Ecuador. The United States used the pronunciation of *ch'arki* to create the anglicized version of the word "jerky." In addition, the *saladeros* in Argentina and Uruguay used the same technique of drying meat to process their livestock, but they took it one step further to create a lucrative export industry without using refrigeration during the Spanish colonial period (1500s to 1800s).

Brazilians prepare *carne de sol* in a variety of ways, such as adding entire pieces to meat and vegetable stews, shredded and sautéed as a snack, fried and served as a hamburger with two buns, baked in the oven with white cream, or grilled directly on the fire. While this traditional dish of dried meat represents the northeastern region, it is actually served all over Brazil. Multiple contemporary Brazilian chefs (such as Thiago Castanho and Yara Roberts) include *carne de sol* (or *carne seca*) as part of the delicious national Brazilian dish called *feijoada* (black-bean stew) and other meals in their recipe books so people discover how Brazilians like to enjoy and share meals.

See also: Chapter 1: Overview; The *Sertão* and Devastating Droughts. Chapter 14: Overview; Contemporary Brazilian Chefs; *Feijoada*, Brazil's National Dish.

Further Reading

Castanho, Thiago, and Luciana Bianchi. 2014. *Brazilian Food*. Richmond Hill, Ontario, Canada: Firefly Books.

Elias, Rodrigo. 2008. "Feijoada: A Short History of an Edible Institution," in *Flavors from Brazil*, edited by the Minister of External Relations from Brazil, 35–41. Brasília: Ministry of External Relations.

Roberts, Yara. 2009. *The Brazilian Table*. Layton, UT: Gibbs Smith.

Churrasco, Brazilian Barbecue

Churrasco is the Brazilian version of a barbecue based on grilled meat. A *churrascaria* is essentially a steak house, but it also serves lots of other meats and cuts, including lamb, sausage, pork ribs, pork loin, and chicken. This type of meal is especially famous in the gaucho region of southern Brazil. The process of preparation consists of a rustic style of placing the meat cuts on long skewers (about two feet long); then they are placed on top of a large coal barbecue pit to be roasted. The Brazilian-style barbecues usually do not have a grill since the skewers are placed directly on top of the red-hot embers. Most meat cuts generate natural flavor based on the method of cooking, and they are only lightly seasoned with salt and no other spices. It is definitely heaven for meat lovers.

Churrascarias are extremely popular in Brazil. Some of these restaurants have a *rodízio* system where servers bring the long skewers to the dining area and slice pieces of meat directly onto the customer's plate. The sizzle of the meat and the pleasant aromas are irresistible. This service is also sometimes called *espeto corrido*, which means that clients pay one fixed price and can eat as much meat as they want. The servers and customers engage in a system that tells each other what the expectations are. Every table has a two-color card (or disk) with two options: the green color tells the server to keep the meats coming, and the red side indicates the waiters should stop the parade of meats. While the meat is the main ingredient at *churrascarias*, they also provide other dishes to complement the meal. For example, there is usually a buffet-style arrangement with a salad bar, soups, and other hot dishes that might include the famous black-bean stew *feijoada*. If customers are still hungry, they can linger at the table for conversation by enjoying desserts usually also available at the buffet.

The Brazilian-style barbecue called *churrasco* started in southern Brazil. However, it quickly became popular in neighboring countries that include Argentina, Uruguay, Paraguay, Chile, and Colombia, where it is most often called *"asado"* in Spanish. In the United States, restaurants following the *churrascaria* tradition have also recently become popular. For example, chef Evandro Caregnato is the culinary director for the famous *churrascaria* chain of restaurants called Texas de Brazil that have successfully exposed Americans to the Brazilian-style barbecue. His cookbooks provide multiple recipes for grilling savory meats. Another chain that eventually came to the United States is Fogo do Chão, which provides a more upscale style of *churrascaria*, but still following the traditional method of roasting meats over an open fire. They operate almost fifty restaurants distributed in Brazil, the United States, and Mexico. These restaurant chains provide evidence that the world is discovering the delicious flavors of Brazilian cooking.

See also: Chapter 14: Overview; Contemporary Brazilian Chefs; *Feijoada*, Brazil's National Dish.

Further Reading

Caragnato, Evandro. 2016. *Churrasco: Grilling the Brazilian Way*. Layton, UT: Gibbs Smith.

Fujikawa Nes, Cynthia. 2016. "Dining Culture in Brazil." *Brazil Business*, August 13. Accessed July 7, 2019. http://thebrazilbusiness.com/article/dining-culture-in-brazil

Roberts, Yara. 2009. *The Brazilian Table*. Layton, UT: Gibbs Smith.

Contemporary Brazilian Chefs

In the last ten years, a group of innovative Brazilian chefs with international experience have opened successful restaurants and published recipe books that reflect their culinary traditions, unique ingredients, and flavorful dishes. As a result, the status of Brazilian gastronomy has been elevated at home and more recognized abroad. Three contemporary Brazilian chefs are making an indelible mark on the international culinary world.

Roberta Sudbrack opened a restaurant in 2005 that bears her name in Rio de Janeiro. Her exclusive and classy restaurant quickly earned a Michelin star, and it now ranks as number three in Brazil, fifteen in Latin America, and among the one hundred best restaurants in the world. The self-taught chef uses simple local ingredients to create elegant-looking dishes. Customers can choose either a three- or five-course meal, which includes at least one appetizer, the main course, and dessert. Her high-cuisine menu includes traditional Brazilian dishes with a contemporary approach, such as *carne seca* (sun-dried meat) with fermented broth, boneless ribs on top of a fava-bean purée, lobster with mushroom broth, slow-roasted duck, and a wide range of simple but delicate desserts (chocolate mousse, cheeses, guava jelly, and *dolce de leite* pastries).

Chef Rodrigo Oliveira opened his family-style restaurant Mocotó in a modest northern suburb of São Paulo in 2001. Mocotó is a dish made from cow's feet, stewed beans, and vegetables. This famous chef uses simple ingredients to create savory dishes that reflect the traditions of the northeastern semiarid backlands of Brazil (often called the *sertão*) but with an innovative twist. His menu includes delicacies such as *joelho de porco* (braised pork leg) served with couscous, *favada* (a bean dish with sausage, bacon, and jerked beef), and *linguiça con cebola roxa e cachaça* (spicy pork sausage with red onion flambée with *cachaça* liquor), plus a large array of desserts, coffees, and liquors. Oliveira quickly earned multiple awards in Brazil, including Chef of the Year. His restaurant also earned the Good and Affordable Restaurant Award granted by São Paulo's *Veja* magazine, and it was listed among the Top 50 Best Latin American Restaurants in 2017. His unpretentious restaurant approach was so successful that now he owns and manages four similar restaurants around São Paulo.

Yara Castro Roberts is a Brazilian chef who was formally trained in culinary arts in Boston, Cambridge (England), and Paris. She spent years promoting the richness of Brazilian cuisine by teaching classes at universities, culinary centers, and television programs. Her book *The Brazilian Table*, published in 2009, includes one hundred recipes that highlight regional traditional dishes from the states of Amazonas, Minas Gerais, Bahia, and Cerrado. The book was a finalist for both the Gourmet International Cookbook Award and the Julia Child First Book Award. Chef Roberts returned to Parity, Brazil, to run the famous Academy of Cooking and Other Pleasures, where she offers cooking classes for foodies and aspiring chefs and demonstrates how Brazilian regional cultures are reflected in its delicious food.

See also: Chapter 10: Overview; Minas Gerais Gastronomy.

Further Reading

Academy of Cooking and Other Pleasures Official Website. http://chefbrasil.com

Castanho, Thiago, and Luciana Bianchi. 2014. *Brazilian Food*. Richmond Hill, Ontario, Canada: Firefly Books.

Roberts, Yara. 2009. *The Brazilian Table*. Layton, UT: Gibbs Smith.

Sims, Shannon. 2015. "Why Hot Brazilian Chef Rodrigo Oliveira Is Serving Uncool Food." *Ozy News*, May 16. Accessed July 5, 2019. https://www.ozy.com/rising-stars/why-hot-brazilian-chef-rodrigo-oliveira-is-serving-uncool-food/40915

Feijoada, Brazil's National Dish

Feijoada can be prepared with multiple regional variations, but it is considered the national dish of Brazil. The word *feijão* means "beans" in Portuguese. This delicious meal is prepared as a hearty stew with black beans as the main ingredient boiling together with different cuts of pork, but sometimes beef (loin and tongue) as well. This dish cannot he hurried; traditionally, it is cooked in a large clay pot at very low heat. Most people enjoy it served with white fluffy rice, other meats (usually different sausages such as *morcela* and *chouriço*), collard greens, *farofa* (toasted pieces of manioc flour), and a few orange slices. While some spices (garlic, coriander, bay leaves, and pepper) are added during the cooking process, the final taste is provided by the main ingredients of pork and beans; it is not necessarily spicy but rather a bit salty and smoky.

The origin of *feijoada* has at least two versions. First of all, there is no dispute that the Portuguese introduced beans to Brazil; they also forcibly brought slaves. The most common version is that African slaves used to cook beans mixed with leftover pieces of pork (pig's feet, tail, eyeballs, ears, and others), which the master did not use. After slavery was abolished in 1888, the dish was adopted by all the racial and social classes in Brazil. More recently, however, several sociologists and anthropologists have challenged that version, and they have offered a slightly different account of how the dish originated based on the agricultural history of the cultivation of beans. They claim that both rich and poor people ate beans, and they became a staple food during the Portuguese colonial period, especially because the crop was relatively easy to grow and maintain. The difference, however, was that the upper classes ate them with meat and vegetables while the poor (including African slaves) ate beans mostly with manioc flour (Elias 2008, 40).

Regional preferences determine how (and sometimes when) *feijoada* can be enjoyed. The first difference is based on the type of beans. The regions of Minas Gerais and Rio de Janeiro normally use black beans, but the states of Bahia and Goiás usually prepare *feijoada* using either red or brown beans. This variation changes the overall appearance of the dish, even if the rest of the ingredients are the same. In addition, in the northeast regions, it is common to add vegetables, such as okra, cabbage, and carrots. Families and friends usually enjoy *feijoada* on the weekends without being in a hurry since they often have second servings. Restaurants make the dish available on specific

Feijoada is considered the national dish of Brazil. It is a hearty stew with black beans and different cuts of pork, and sometimes beef. It is then served with white rice, collard greens, and orange slices. (iStockPhoto)

days (usually at midday); Rio de Janeiro typically offers it on Fridays and São Paulo on Wednesdays. To accommodate modern dietary preferences, *feijoada* is now also available with premium meat cuts (pork loin or beef brisket) or even as a vegetarian version. Either way, Brazilians usually linger for hours enjoying their serving of *feijoada* as part of a social event or a gathering with extended family.

See also: Chapter 6: African Ancestry and Influence; Chapter 14: Overview; Minas Gerais Gastronomy.

Further Reading

Castanho, Thiago, and Luciana Bianchi. 2014. *Brazilian Food*. Richmond Hill, Ontario, Canada: Firefly Books.

Elias, Rodrigo. 2008. "Feijoada: A Short History of an Edible Institution," in *Flavors from Brazil,* edited by the Minister of External Relations from Brazil, 35–41. Brasília: Ministry of External Relations.

Fajans, Jane. 2012. *Brazilian Food; Race, Class, and Identity in Regional Cuisines.* Oxford, UK: Berg.

Moreinos Schwartz, Leticia. 2012. *The Brazilian Kitchen: 100 Creative Recipes for the Home Cook.* London: Kyle Books.

Mealtimes and Eating Habits

Brazilian mealtimes and eating habits are a little bit different than common traditions in the United States. For example, breakfast is usually from 7 to 10 a.m., but it is a rather simple meal during the week consisting of strong coffee, milk, and toasted bread with jam. Sometimes, the toasted bread includes ham and cheese, especially if the next meal is not planned until much later. Since Brazil produces so much tropical fruit, there is usually a portion of it to round out the breakfast meal. When Brazilians eat breakfast on the go, they frequently stop at casual and modest bakeries (*padarias*) and cafés that seem to be everywhere; the most popular morning combination is coffee with a toasted French roll.

Lunch is the main meal of the day, and it is normally served from 1 to 3 p.m. Brazilians usually leave their offices, factories, and other workplaces in mass numbers to enjoy a sit-down lunch without being too much in a hurry. This substantial meal usually includes rice and beans, vegetables, and a small portion of meat. It is also a time to socialize with friends and colleagues. They frequent *lanchonetes* (snack bars) that offer reasonably priced meals in a simple ambiance of metal foldable tables and portable chairs. Most Brazilian businesses provide at least one hour for lunch; therefore, Brazilians would never consider the option of eating lunch at their desk or workstation. Business lunches are expected to be even longer social affairs.

Dinner is served rather late (compared to U.S. mealtimes) from 8 to 10 p.m. Overall, it is a meal slightly lighter than lunch. This is usually a family meal for catching up with the activities of all the household members. During the week at home, dinner often consists of a simple sandwich, coffee with milk, a salad, or leftovers from a previous lunch. During the weekend, restaurants are certainly busy since those are the nights when families often go out to dinner.

An interesting concept available in Brazil is a specific type of restaurant that offers the option to buy a "buffet by the kilo" during lunch or dinner. Customers simply serve themselves whatever they want on a plate, walk to the weight station, and pay based on how much it all weighs. Drinks are usually ordered separately. These types of buffets are traditionally a good value, and they offer tasty regional hot food, but customers know that they cannot expect premium meat cuts or high-quality organic vegetables.

Brazilians have a few eating habits that may surprise visitors from the United States. First of all, rice is by far the preferred carbohydrate for main meals, as opposed to bread or potatoes in the United States. An interesting observation is that Brazilians would never eat food or consume drinks as they are walking, driving, or riding public transportation. In Brazil, that is simply considered disrespectful to other people. Another interesting trait of Brazilian table manners is the use of utensils for almost everything, including pizza, pieces of boned chicken, and fruit. When Brazilians must hold something with their hands (like a hamburger), they will wrap it with a napkin. However, the arrival of American fast food restaurants is beginning to change that part of eating etiquette in Brazil, much to the regret of older adults.

See also: Chapter 10: Table Manners. Chapter 14: Overview.

Further Reading

Fujikawa, Cynthia Nes. 2016. "Dining Culture in Brazil." *Brazil Business*, August 13. Accessed June 20, 2019. http://thebrazilbusiness.com/article/dining-culture-in-brazil

Roberts, Yara. 2009. *The Brazilian Table*. Layton, UT: Gibbs Smith.

Teixeira, Elisa Duarte. 2016. "Food," in *Brazil*, edited by Antonio Luciano de Andrade Tosta and Eduardo F. Coutinho, 286–307. Santa Barbara, CA: ABC-CLIO.

Minas Gerais Gastronomy

The interior state of Minas Gerais is well recognized within Brazil for its unique gastronomy. Most of its traditional cooking methods were developed during the gold rush period (1690s to late 1700s) when large numbers of both Brazilians and foreigners migrated to the region in search of quick fortunes. They all brought their own culinary traditions, which were adapted to the local farmhouse-style of cooking in Minas Gerais. In addition, the state has been a major producer of coffee and milk since the colonial period (1500 to early 1800s). The combination of recipes, available ingredients, and cooking style created the fusion that is now called *comida Mineira*. In addition, the state actually established factories that produce iconic foods used in recipes throughout Brazil, such as the alcoholic beverage *cachaça* to make the national drink *caipirinha*, the unique *pão de queijo* (cheese rolls), and the famous artisan *queijo de Minas* (cheese from Minas), which was officially recognized as a national cultural heritage in 2008. Consequently, the state of Minas Gerais is often selected to represent Brazilian food at international competitions or exhibitions.

An excellent way of trying multiple regional dishes is to visit a buffet-style restaurant called *buteco* available throughout the state. These establishments usually include more than twenty traditional country foods beautifully displayed in clay pots and cast-iron skillets. Most of the dishes are prepared with local meats, vegetables, fruit, and cheeses. In fact, Belo Horizonte (the state capital) organizes the largest food festival in Brazil around this concept; the Comida di Buteco bar and food festival is held during April and May as a major tourist event that attracts over 400,000 people.

Feijão tropeiro is a bean dish from the colonial period that expeditioners used to prepare for a long journey. The name translates roughly as "cattleman's beans." It is a mixture of manioc flour, meat (usually bacon or sausage), boiled eggs, beans, and collard greens. It provides a balance of carbohydrates, protein, and vegetables. Almost every family in Minas Gerais has its own version of this traditional recipe.

Frango ao molho pardo (chicken with brown gravy sauce) consists of chicken cooked in a gravy sauce made from its own blood. When the chicken is killed by cutting its neck, the blood is poured into a pan that contains a bit of vinegar to avoid coagulation. The blood is then cooked with onion, tomatoes, garlic, salt, and pepper, which becomes a brownish thick gravy sauce. Chicken is cooked in a separate skillet and then added to the blood sauce at low fire for at least two hours for the flavors to penetrate the meat. The final product is served over white rice and a small side salad.

Doce de leite (*dulce de leche* in Spanish) is a decadent dessert typical of Minas Gerais. It is prepared by mixing condensed milk and sugar until it turns a light brown color with a thick consistency. It can be eaten by itself, but it is often included in other desserts, such as stuffed inside pastries, mixed with ice cream, spread on top of cheese, or served over fresh fruit. Since Minas Gerais has a large milk industry, multiple local factories produce *doce de leite* for commercial purposes. In fact, the 2016 National Competition of Lactose Products awarded three of the top ten prizes for the best *doce de leite* in Brazil to three brands produced in Minas Gerais: Viçosa, Dom Coimbra, and Boreal.

See also: Chapter 2: Gold Rush and Minas Gerais. Chapter 14: Overview; Regional Sweets.

Further Reading

Acevedo, Gezaine. 2016. "12 Comidas típicas para provar em Minas Gerais." *Mineiros na Estrada*, October 26. Accessed June 14, 2019. http://www.mineirosnaestrada.com.br/comidas-tipicas-minas-gerais

Roberts, Yara. 2009. *The Brazilian Table*. Layton, UT: Gibbs Smith.

Tudisco, Ana Luiza. 2016. *10 Receitas típicas de Minas Gerais*. São Paulo: Editora 101 Seleções.

Regional Sweets

Brazil is a country of continental proportions. As a result, regional differences are common based on a diverse heritage of African, Amerindian, European, and recent immigrant influences. All these groups brought with them their own culinary traditions, which were then adapted to local influences and available ingredients. As a result, Brazilian cuisine is actually a collection of regional dishes. Overall, the country produces a wide variety of tropical fruits often used in desserts, such as papaya, banana, mango, guava, açaí, coconut, passion fruit, pineapple, *cupuaçu*, and multiple citric options. In addition, Brazil also produces a variety of nuts, regional cheeses, and creams that make excellent ingredients for desserts.

For the purpose of discussing regional gastronomy, most Brazilian cookbooks separate the country into five distinct regions: north, northeast, midwest, southwest, and south. Each region has unique ingredients available and often a recognizable way of cooking that evokes memories of specific aromas and tastes. Brazilian food includes a wealth of sweet treats based on regional specialties that are usually available throughout the year, occasionally based on seasonal fruits, or sometimes only prepared for a specific holiday. In general, desserts tend to be extremely sweet, at least compared to American palates. However, Brazilians usually enjoy them with a strong cup of coffee, which balances the sweet flavor of the desserts. The most common regional desserts are described below.

The north region is famous for its tropical fruit, which is widely used to prepare mouth-watering ice cream and several types of pudding. The *pudim de tapioca* is extremely rich and delicious; it is prepared by adding caramelized tapioca to a pudding. Tapioca is also a crucial ingredient for *beijus*, which are made with a unique tapioca flour to make thin crepes that are then filled with coconut and cream.

Bolo de rolo is a favorite dessert that originated in the northeast region. It has the spongy consistency of a cake but cut into very thin sheets that are topped with guava preserves, thick marmalade, and sometimes sweet cream. Then the entire sheet is rolled into a log. It is served by cutting into slices that reveal the layers of all the interior ingredients.

The midwest region also produces lots of tropical fruits and milk. It is not, then, surprising that many of the local desserts include both ingredients. The tasty *pastelim* are local small tarts with cream custard that has been caramelized. They are extremely sweet, but they can be enjoyed in small bite-size portions. In addition, the region also shines with the famous *furrundum*, which is a typical dessert from the Pantanal area. It combines the flavor of shredded green papaya, brown sugar, ginger, and sometimes cinnamon.

The most famous dessert from the southeast region is called *Romeu e Julieta*, just like the protagonists in Shakespeare's play. It is made by combining *goiabada* (guava fruit marmalade) and cheese (white or *catupiry*); both of these ingredients are made in Minas Gerais. It is simply served as a layer of *goiabada* on top of a layer of cheese. It is simple but delicious. Other widely available desserts are *brigadeiro* (chocolate truffle balls), *Maria-mole* (a soft-but-messy marshmallow), and *pé-de-moleque* (peanut brittle with brown sugar).

See also: Chapter 14: Overview.

Further Reading

Farah, Fernando. 2014. *Brazilian Food and Cooking.* Northampton, MA: Hermes House Press.

Pomela, Marina. 2015. "Typical Brazilian Sweets and Desserts." *Brazil Business*, April 8. Accessed July 10, 2019. http://thebrazilbusiness.com/article/typical-brazilian-sweets-and-desserts

Teixeira, Elisa Duarte. 2016. "Food," in *Brazil*, edited by Antonio Luciano de Andrade Tosta and Eduardo F. Coutinho, 286–307. Santa Barbara, CA: ABC-CLIO.

Zero Hunger Strategy in Brazil

Brazil is a country with significant social and income inequalities where the wealthy live lavishly and the poor struggle with basic food insecurities, which affects their health, school performance, and income potential. However, during the last twenty years, Brazil has implemented multiple government programs that have successfully lifted people out of poverty and drastically reduced hunger. In 2003, President Luiz Inácio Lula da Silva (1945–) implemented the Fome Zero program (Zero Hunger Strategy) with the explicit purpose to reduce extreme poverty and combat hunger in Brazil. Then he created a federal-level cabinet position called the Minister of Social Development and Fight against Hunger (MDS) in 2004 precisely to provide disadvantaged people with access to basic food staples. Consequently, Fome Zero is not a single program but rather a comprehensive government strategy that brings together over thirty government programs into a cohesive plan to facilitate proper nutrition, support small family-owned farms, distribute crucial vitamins and supplements, create cisterns to provide clean water in drought regions, serve well-balanced meals at schools, and train people with skills that can generate income.

Brazil has been combating hunger with a multipronged approach that combines cash incentives for poor families to keep children in school, offering subsidies to small-farm owners, coordinating a complex national system of food storage and distribution centers, and feeding children in schools with nutritious meals. After almost twenty years of feeding hungry people, the statistics are certainly impressive. Between 2000 and 2006, malnutrition for children under two years old was slashed from 12.7 percent to 3.5 percent. In addition, the government programs reduced infant mortality rates by 47 percent. The northeast region (by far the poorest area of the country) also reported a dramatic reduction of malnutrition from 1996 to 2005 among both children and adults from 17.9 to 6.6 percent (World Food Programme, 2010).

The success of the Zero Hunger Strategy in Brazil has become a model for developing nations, and it has received international acclaim. As a result, multiple global agencies are discovering that Brazil's approach to fighting hunger depends on a strategic coordination of a network of government programs that depend on each other for their collective success. For example, the World Food Programme (WFP) reported in 2005 that 80 percent of the Bolsa Família funding went to poor families where it improved education outcomes and food consumption while reducing child labor exploitation (WFP, 2005). However, the food to feed families covered under the Bolsa Família program comes mostly from small family-owned farms, which get federal subsidies to sell their crops to the government under the Programa Nacional de Fortalecimento da Agricultura Familiar (PRONAF). Congress even provides risk management insurance to protect farmers. Moreover, the government also created a federal Food Acquisition Program (PAA) to purchase food, operate warehouses, and distribute food to schools, municipalities, and state agencies. Then in 2009, the government passed a new law requiring that at least 30 percent of the food purchased by the federal government for school meals programs come from small family farms. As of 2014, there were more than 130,000 small farmers participating in the national plan (Kimmett, 2014). Then another government agency, the National Program of School Nutrition (PNAE), was put in charge of the gigantic task of providing meals to public schools nationwide to ensure that all children get at least one free nutritious meal per day. All the purchases of meat and produce are managed at the local level, which supports regional farmers and local jobs. The cooperation among all these government agencies has contributed to the drastic reduction of hunger in Brazil.

See also: Chapter 2: Lula da Silva, Luiz Inácio (1945–). Chapter 8: Bolsa Família: Welfare Program with Education Incentives. Chapter 14: Overview.

Further Reading

Da Silva, José Graziano, Mauro Eduardo del Grossi, and Caio Galvão de França (eds.). 2011. *The Fome Zero (Zero Hunger) Program: The Brazilian Experience*. Brasília: Food and Agriculture Organization of the United Nations.

Kimmett, Colleen. 2014. "How Brazil Cracked the Local Food Distribution Puzzle." *Farm to Cafeteria*, June 18. Accessed July 15, 2019. http://www.farmtocafeteriacanada.ca/2014/05/lessons-from-brazil-2

Ministry of Social Development and Fight against Hunger (MDS) Official Website. http://www.mds.gov.br

CHAPTER 15

LEISURE AND SPORTS

OVERVIEW

Brazilians are passionate sports fans, and soccer (*futebol*) is by far the most popular sport in Brazil. However, basketball, Brazilian jiu-jitsu, volleyball, and Formula One auto racing are all very popular as well. This South American country has produced high-caliber athletes who have earned coveted awards. Some of these sports figures—including Pelé (soccer), Oscar Schmidt (basketball), Hortência Marcari (basketball), Royce Gracie (jiu-jitsu), Ayrton Senna (car racing), and Neymar (soccer)—have reached iconic status in their relative sports, both domestically and internationally. Their legend status inspires immense national pride in Brazilians.

Brazil recently hosted multiple international sports competitions. It staged the 2014 Soccer FIFA World Cup for thirty-two teams in twelve different venues sprinkled throughout the country. While Germany was the champion in 2014, Brazil still has the record as the only country that has won such global competition five times (in 1958, 1962, 1970, 1994, and 2002). Then two years later, Rio de Janeiro hosted the 2016 Summer Olympics; this was the first time the Olympics had ever been held in South America. This time, Brazil coordinated competitions for 11,237 athletes in 306 different events clustered under thirty-eight sports. Soccer was the only sport that had its matches played in five different cities by using the new or updated stadiums prepared for the previous FIFA World Cup. For the 2016 Summer Olympics, the United States was the first-place winner with 121 medals, while Brazil finished in thirteenth place with 19 medals. One month later in September, Brazil also hosted the 2016 Paralympic Games, which engage athletes with disabilities in multiple sports competitions. This time, 4,342 male and female athletes representing 159 nations competed in 158 events clustered under twenty-two sports. A record 2.15 million tickets were sold for these international competition events. China earned first place with 239 medals, and Brazil came in eighth place with 72 medals.

All these international competitions focused the spotlight on Brazil, and the government was desperate to show that it was a modern and prosperous country capable of successfully hosting such events. As a result, multiple cities experienced an incredible boom of infrastructure projects to accommodate the international competitions. Brazilians were excited and bursting with national pride. However, massive demonstrations became common when Brazilians realized that the government was providing billions of dollars to subsidize the international competitions while simultaneously announcing budget cuts for education and health care. In addition, street protests decried the destruction of entire poor neighborhoods to make way for infrastructure projects related to sporting events, often leaving hundreds of families scattered without compensation to relocate.

In addition to sports, Brazilians use public spaces for leisure and entertainment. With 4,655 miles of coastline (7,491 kilometers) along the Atlantic Ocean, beaches are hubs for active sports, leisurely pastimes, romantic getaways, and family time. Brazilian beaches are likely to include live music, dancing, and large numbers of vendors selling cold drinks, hot food, hats, clothing, and inflatable toys for the kids. While multiple social anthropologists have claimed that the beach is the ultimate social equalizer, a quick visit nowadays quickly reveals that people actually congregate in distinct groups, such as family areas, teenage kids with loud music, people practicing capoeira, sections of expensive restaurants, and individuals who bring large coolers with their own drinks and food. Regardless of people's social and economic status, Brazilian beaches are shared public spaces for fun, exercise, and entertainment.

Finally, the last two decades have had an economic impact on Brazilians. This is a country that is still vastly divided between extremely wealthy individuals and millions of people who can barely afford the basic necessities of life. Nevertheless, millions of Brazilians have also been lifted out of extreme poverty, and more people have moved into the middle class. As a result, socioeconomic status determines possibilities for families regarding leisure and vacation options. Middle-class urban families often take weekend trips to the beach or to a mountain retreat to get away from the stress of a fast-paced lifestyle. People from the interior and rural regions tend to travel to large cities to enjoy sporting events, shopping, family educational museums, and general attractions that include aquariums, nightlife, and artistic venues. In addition, the introduction of budget airlines (including GOL and Azul) has made travel more accessible throughout Brazil and abroad.

The ultimate source of entertainment for Brazilians might just be in their living rooms. Sports channels are extremely popular, especially on the weekends. Brazilians watch soccer religiously, including international matches in leagues where famous Brazilian players are competing. In addition, reality television shows have become a staple of midday television, including *Big Brother Brazil* (BBB), *The Voice Brazil*, and *A facenda* (The Farm). However, nothing tops the famous telenovelas (soap operas). Rede Globo's telenovelas titled *O sétimo guardião* (The Seventh Guardian) and *Espelho da vida* (Mirror of Life) were extremely popular in 2019. Contemporary Brazilian telenovelas usually only last a few months, and they have a strong social impact because they introduce new fashion trends, adopt popular street language, address current social concerns, and contribute overall to Brazilian culture. Finally, most Brazilians dream of becoming millionaires, and the Mega Sena lottery keeps that hope alive. Even Brazilians who do not play the lottery throughout the year are likely to participate in the Mega da Virada. This is a special lottery drawing held on New Year's Eve on December 31 and televised live to a wide audience. The jackpot is enormous, and it gets people involved in the end-of-the-year festivities.

Further Reading

Ayrton Senna Legacy. http://www.ayrton-senna-dasilva.com

Goldblatt, David. 2014. *Futebol Nation: The Story of Brazil through Soccer*. New York: Nation Books.

McKenna, Erin Flynn. 2016. "Leisure and Sports," in *Brazil*, edited by Antonio Luciano de Andrade Tosta and Eduardo F. Coutinho, 308–324. Santa Barbara: ABC-CLIO.

Mega Sena Brazilian Lottery Official Website. http://www.megasena.com/en

Oscar Schmidt Official Website. http://www.oscarschmidt.com.br

Paralympic Games Rio de Janeiro 2016 Official Website. https://www.paralympic.org/rio-2016

Pelé Official Website. https://pele10.com

Puin, Karolina. 2012. "What Brazilians Watch on TV." *Brazil Business,* June 9. Accessed on May 11, 2019. http://thebrazilbusiness.com/article/what-brazilians-watch-on-tv

Rede Globo Official Website. http://www.globo.com

Röhrig Assuncão, Matthias. 2005. *Capoeira: The History of an Afro-Brazilian Martial Art*. New York: Routledge.

Vincent, Jon S. 2003. *Culture and Customs of Brazil*. Westport, CT: Greenwood Press.

Walder, Marc. 2008. *Essential Brazilian Jiu-Jitsu: An Illustrated Guide to the Fighting Art*. Champaign, IL: Human Kinetics.

Zimbalist, Andrew. 2017. *Rio 2016: Olympic Myths, Hard Realities*. Washington, DC: Brookings Institution Press.

Basketball

Augusto Shaw introduced the game of basketball to Brazil in 1896. Within twenty years, Brazilians were already excited about the game played by local teams. Today, basketball is extremely popular in Brazil. Both national basketball teams (male and female) are regulated by the Confederação Brasileira de Basketball (CBB), which in turn has been an active member of the International Federation of Basketball (FIBA). Both national teams have impressive statistics since they both compete in three world events: the Olympic Games, the FIBA World Cup, and the Pan American Games. The female team has qualified for the Olympic Games seven times, and won a silver medal in 1996 and bronze in 2000. They really shine at the FIBA Women's World Cup, where they earned a gold medal in 1994 and bronze in 1971. The men's national team is the only team in the world (together with the United States) that has qualified for every single Basketball World Cup competition since 1950. At this level, they have earned four gold medals, two silver medals, and another four bronze medals. The men's team has played at the Olympic Games fifteen times, and they have earned bronze medals in 1948, 1960, and 1964.

Brazilian basketball has two legendary figures: Oscar Schmidt (1958–) and Hortência Marcari (1959–). Schmidt played professionally in Brazil with multiple teams (Sírio, Bandeirantes, Flamingo, and Barueri) as well as teams in Italy and Spain. In addition, Schmidt holds the record of the Olympic Summer Games basketball all-time leading scorer with 1,093 points. Given his prolific career, he earned the nickname Mano Santa (Holy Hand) in Brazil. One of the highlights of his career was to participate as a guest in the opening ceremonies of the 2016 Olympics in Rio de Janeiro. Hortência Marcari is by far the most renowned Brazilian female basketball player. Her talent got her a spot on the Brazilian national team when she was only fourteen years old. Then she played professionally with teams in Malaysia, Bulgaria, Singapore, and Peru. She earned a silver medal with the Brazilian team at the 1996 Olympics in Atlanta. She was also part of the national team that earned three medals at the Pan American Games (gold in 1991, silver in 1987, and bronze in 1983). She is known in Brazil as "the queen." She was proud to be one the torchbearers at the 2016 Summer Olympics in Brazil.

Brazilians enjoy watching basketball games especially when Brazilian players play in international leagues. For example, the National Basketball Association (NBA) in the United States had nine Brazilian players for the 2016–2017 season playing for teams such as the Chicago Bulls, the Los Angeles Lakers, and the Golden State Warriors.

See also: Chapter 15: Overview. Chapter 16: Sports Icons.

Further Reading

Confederação Brasileira de Basketball Official Website. http://www.cbb.com.br

National Basketball Association, NBA. 2016. "NBA Rosters Feature Record 113 International Players from 41 Countries and Territories." *NBA Communications*. October 15. Accessed June 20, 2019. http://pr.nba.com/nba-rosters-international-players-2016-17

Oscar Schmidt Official Website. http://www.oscarschmidt.com.br

Beach and Sand

Brazil has 4,655 miles (7,491 kilometers) of coastline, and the beach is an important aspect of Brazilian culture. Most foreigners who have never been to Brazil are often familiar with Copacabana and Ipanema, which are perhaps the most famous beaches in Rio de Janeiro. Brazilian anthropologists and sociologists often claim that beaches are truly democratic public spaces where everyone can mingle. In addition, Brazilians in general seem to be more comfortable with their bodies regardless of their physical condition, which has an impact on their fashion choices. In fact, the country is well known for its revealing beachwear: most men wear very short swim trunks, and women often wear the world-famous string bikinis. However, it is important to keep in mind that according to the 2010 census, over 50 percent of Brazilians are under thirty years old. Consequently, fashion design leans toward a youthful style, even for the middle-age population.

Since the large majority of Brazilians live along the coast, beaches have different types of activities throughout the day. Large numbers of people come out for exercise early in the morning. Most beaches have a paved path for running, walking, bicycling, and riding either skateboards or rollerblades. When the temperatures start to rise, people engage in more water-based activities, such as swimming, surfing, kayaking, and paddleboarding. Sand sports range from formal beach volleyball matches to simply kicking a soccer ball. In fact, Brazil has produced multiple successful male and female beach volleyball athletes who have earned gold, silver, and bronze medals in the Olympics. As the sun goes down, different crowds come to the beach, including romantic couples and young people frequenting beach bars and music venues. The weekends are always extremely popular for families. Overall, people like to relax on the sand, but beaches traditionally also include music, dancing, and lots of vendors selling cold drinks, food, hats, and inflatable toys for the kids.

While it is true that large numbers of people congregate on Brazilian beaches, the notion that they are truly democratic spaces where everyone mingles without social or class distinctions no longer applies. In reality, people create spaces for their own groups. Families tend to congregate near areas with swings and bathrooms facilities, and teenagers create their own spaces where they can dance and listen to music. Serious surfers prefer a specific section of a beach that seems to intimidate beginner or recreational surfers. In addition, there are sections with restaurants and bars that cater to a more affluent clientele, which reveals a marked social and economic contrast with lower-income people, who bring their own coolers with food and drinks and frequently leave trash behind. Regardless of people's social status, Brazilian beaches are shared public spaces for fun, exercise, and entertainment.

See also: Chapter 10: Clothing and Dressing Appropriately. Chapter 15: Overview.

Further Reading

Instituto Brasileiro de Geografia e Estatística—Brazilian Institute of Geography and Statistics (IBGE). 2011. "Census 2010." Brasilia. Accessed July 7, 2019. http://ibge.gov.br

McKenna, Erin Flynn. 2016. "Leisure and Sports," in *Brazil*, edited by Antonio Luciano de Andrade Tosta and Eduardo F. Coutinho, 308–324. Santa Barbara: ABC-CLIO.

Richard, Christopher, and Leslie Jermyn. 2002. *Cultures of the World: Brazil*. New York: Marshall Cavendish.

Brazilian Jiu-Jitsu

Jiu-jitsu has Japanese origins, but it evolved into a distinct Brazilian martial art. The general premise of Brazilian jiu-jitsu (BJJ) is that the advantage of a taller, stronger, and more powerful opponent can be minimized by bringing such a fighter to the ground where chokeholds and joint locks can debilitate and subdue the opponent. Comparatively speaking, BJJ fighters spend more time on the ground than other martial arts that have a foundation based on defense and attack moves from a standing position. Consequently, many observers describe it as a combination of wrestling and martial arts.

The first martial arts school offering a combination of judo and jiu-jitsu in Brazil was established in 1909 by Geo Omori. Other practitioners followed, including Mitsuyo Maeda, Gastão Gracie, and Carlos Gracie. However, Hélio Gracie (1913–2009) is often considered the father of Brazilian jiu-jitsu. He is an iconic figure because he changed Japanese-style martial arts and adapted it to be used by anybody in real-fighting situations regardless of their physical build. The new style called Gracie jiu-jitsu became well known on the global stage during the 1990s due to the accomplishments of other martial arts fighters in the family (Royce Gracie and Rickson Gracie). Now, the sport is widely popular in Brazil.

Brazilian jiu-jitsu uses multiple grappling and ground-fighting techniques to defeat and subdue opponents. For example, the "side control" technique allows a fighter to pin the opponent to the ground by placing his body on top of the opponent's torso to limit his movement. In addition, during the "full-mount" strategy, the BJJ practitioner sits on top of the other fighter's chest by using his body weight and hips to minimize the opponent's movement. Moreover, chokes and strangling capabilities are quite common in BJJ. An air choke restrains the windpipe to limit the opponent's breathing. The "blood choke" consists of grabbing an opponent from behind and placing the bicep around the front of the neck while simultaneously placing pressure on the carotid arteries, which typically makes opponents lose consciousness in about five seconds.

Contemporary Brazilian jiu-jitsu has produced exceptional fighters. For example, Rorion is one of Hélio Gracie's sons, and one of the founding members of the Ultimate Fighting Championship (UFC) as a forum where athletes from different martial arts backgrounds could fight one another. When his brother Royce Gracie won the first UFC in 1993, BJJ gained popularity and legitimacy in the mixed martial arts (MMA) world that blends elements of Thai kickboxing, Brazilian jiu-jitsu, boxing, karate, and wrestling. As a result, modern Brazilian-style jiu-jitsu is an extremely popular sport worldwide.

See also: Chapter 15: Overview. Chapter 16: Sports Icons.

Further Reading

Gracie, Renzo, and Royler Gracie. 2001. *Brazilian Jiu-Jitsu: Theory and Technique.* Chicago: Invisible Cities Press.

Pedreira, Roberto. 2016. "Top 30 Myths and Misconceptions about Brazilian Jiu-Jitsu." *Global Training Report,* May 29. Accessed June 11, 2019. http://www.global-training-report.com/myths.htm

Royce Gracie Official Website. http://www.roycegracie.tv

Walder, Marc. 2008. *Essential Brazilian Jiu-Jitsu: An Illustrated Guide to the Fighting Art.* Champaign, IL: Human Kinetics.

Capoeira

Capoeira is a unique Brazilian martial art with a fusion of fights, music, dance, and acrobatic movements. Most historians agree that capoeira emerged as a truly Brazilian form of expression used by African slaves during the 1600s. There is no consensus, however, regarding its original purpose as either a type of diversion or a form of fighting training for slaves. *Capoeiristas* usually gather around a *roda* (circle) with two participants fighting in the middle while they play instruments, clap, and sing. When slavery was abolished in Brazil in 1888, the practice of capoeira by Afro-Brazilians was viewed as a social threat, and it was officially prohibited nationwide. Consequently, it became an underground tradition. For decades, *capoeiristas* camouflaged their activities by making their moves more acrobatic, which is why it appears to be a dance nowadays.

As a martial art, capoeira has a fast-paced style, and it focuses on using the lower body to kick, sweep, and take down opponents who might be bigger or using weapons. Fighters stay in constant motion, especially by swinging their bodies back and forth to avoid being a target. They also use fake punches to create an opportunity for a decisive attack, such as swing high kicks, powerful knee hits, and leg sweeps. The element that gives capoeira a sense of choreography is based on creating opportunities for attack and recovering quickly when losing balance.

There are two Brazilians who are crucial figures in the establishment of capoeira as it is recognized in modern times. Manuel dos Reis Machado (known as Mestre Bimba) created the Capoeira Regional style in 1932 to emphasize the martial art component that was beginning to disappear. Since capoeira was still prohibited, he called it Luta Regional Baiana (Regional Fight from Salvador, Bahia). His school earned a reputation for rigorous training. The other influential person was Vicente Ferreira Pastinha (known as Mestre Pastinha); he created the Capoeira Angola style in 1937. He was also from Salvador, Bahia, and he focused on the African roots of the martial art while purifying the sport from other influences. Both styles incorporate music in their fighting circles. Due to their valuable contributions, capoeira was legalized in 1940. In 1953, Mestre Bimba gave a demonstration for President Getúlio Vargas, which was extremely well received, and it began to change the perception of capoeira as a dangerous tradition practiced by Afro-Brazilians.

Today, Brazil considers capoeira a crucial element of its culture; it was designated in 2014 as part of its "intangible cultural patrimony." Capoeira has certainly grown in international recognition, and it is now quite common to see capoeira street performances and exhibitions throughout Brazil. Even a new style called Capoeira Contemporânea has emerged that seems to be more choreographed and acrobatic in nature.

See also: Chapter 15: Overview.

Further Reading

McKenna, Erin Flynn. 2016. "Martial Arts: Capoeira," in *Brazil,* edited by Antonio Luciano de Andrade Tosta and Eduardo F. Coutinho, 309–311. Santa Barbara, CA: ABC-CLIO.

Röhrig Assuncão, Matthias. 2005. *Capoeira: The History of an Afro-Brazilian Martial Art*. New York: Routledge.

Talmon-Chvaicer, Maya. 2008. *The Hidden History of Capoeira: A Collision of Cultures in the Brazilian Battle Dance*. Austin: University of Texas Press.

Family Outings and Vacations

Brazil is a country with tremendous cultural and geographic diversity. In addition, its culture openly embraces families and children in most social interactions. Differences among urban, suburban, and rural areas determine the leisure options available for families. For example, in crowded Rio de Janeiro, families enjoy Leblon Beach for its calm waters and sections reserved for children. In addition, living in large cities (such as São Paulo, Recife, and Rio de Janeiro) causes stress, and families often take weekend trips to nearby locations where they can reconnect with nature by hiking, camping, and enjoying local festivals. São Paulo residents often find refuge in nearby Ubatuba (only 2.5 hours by car) to enjoy the beach, surfing, and visiting the giant sea turtles conservation sanctuary. Brazilians who live in rural locations do the opposite by making trips to the beach or large cities where they can shop, visit museums, watch plays, attend sporting events, and explore other cultural activities not available in remote locations. For example, the São Paulo Aquarium is the largest in South America, and soccer fans can watch a live *futebol* match at the iconic Maracanã Stadium in Rio de Janeiro.

Socioeconomic status is an important factor that determines some of the possibilities for families regarding leisure and vacation options. For example, there are regional activities that do not cost money, such as going to the beach, having a picnic at a park, or attending a free open-air concert. Other family activities are low cost, such as going to the movies, visiting children's museums, an aquarium, or a bird park. Increasingly, however, families are taking vacations that require transportation to more distant destinations.

For the last twenty years, Brazil has developed a robust national tourism industry. For middle-class families, taking vacations has become a more viable option based on three factors: credit has become more available, more people own cars, and discount airlines (such as GOL and Azul) have introduced lower airfares nationwide and abroad. The top destinations for families within Brazil are São Paulo, Rio de Janeiro, Iguaçu Falls, Salvador de Bahia, Minas Gerais, and the Amazon region. In addition, middle- and upper-class families have increasingly vacationed in international destinations in the last ten years. South American locations are increasingly popular, including Machu Pichu and Lima in Peru, as well as Patagonia and Buenos Aires in Argentina. Longer trips to Spain, Portugal, France, and the United States are costlier, but the number of Brazilians traveling to such destinations is also on the rise.

The Brazilian travel industry attracted over 11 million foreign visitors in 2018. However, the Brazilian Tourist Board (Embratur) and the Ministry of Tourism are keenly aware that the domestic market is much more significant. For example, the 2018 report published by the Fundação Instituto de Pesquisas Econômicas (FIPE) reveals that 51 million Brazilians made more trips than did foreign tourists, and they spent five times more money than their international counterparts. This data suggests that the demand for family vacations increased as more Brazilians reached middle-class income levels during the last decade.

See also: Chapter 4: Tourism. Chapter 15: Overview; Beach and Sand.

Further Reading

Brazilian Tourism Board Official Website. http://www.embratur.gov.br

Eisenhammer, Stephen. 2012. "Domestic Tourism Rises with Middle Class." *Rio Times*. February 14. Accessed July 9, 2019. https://riotimesonline.com/brazil-news/rio-business/domestic-tourism-rises-with-middle-class

Nelson, Belem. 2018. "Brazil's Tourism Sector Growing in First Half of 2018." *Rio Times*, August 16. Accessed July 19, 2019. https://riotimesonline.com/brazil-news/rio-business/brazils-tourism-sector-surging-in-first-half-of-2018

Palhares, Guilherme Lohmann. 2012. *Tourism in Brazil: Environment, Management, and Segments*. Abingdon-on-Thames, UK: Routledge.

Futebol (Soccer)

Futebol (soccer) is the king of all sports in Brazil. The national team is officially governed by the Confederação Brasileira de Futebol. This South American country continues to produce legendary players who have elevated the level of *futebol* worldwide, including Pelé, Tostao, Ronaldinho, Ronaldo, Kaká, and Neymar. However, the most legendary soccer player in Brazil (and perhaps the world) is Edson Arantes do Nascimento (1940–), known simply as Pelé. In fact, both the International Federation of Football History and Statistics (IFFHS) and the International Olympic Committee voted Pelé in 1999 as the Best World Athlete of the twentieth century. He is the only player in the world to have won three FIFA World Cup titles (1958, 1962, and 1970) with his national team. His charismatic personality paired with his agile style of playing brought international attention and pride to Brazil. Such players are a source of tremendous pride for Brazilians, and a few of them become extremely wealthy and famous celebrities due to their playing abilities and lucrative endorsement deals. As a result, most Brazilians feel familiar enough with them to call them only by their first name or even their childhood nickname. On any given Sunday, most of the country actually comes to a stop during a televised soccer match. Brazilian fans are known for being fanatical and passionate when watching a live game at a stadium. At home, they also enthusiastically cheer their favorite team in front of the television.

Modern-day soccer was created in England during the 1860s. The origin of *futebol* in Brazil goes back to 1894 when Charles Miller introduced the sport in São Paulo, but it quickly spread throughout the country. He was born in Brazil, but he learned the sport while he studied in England. At the beginning of the twentieth century, *futebol* in Brazil was essentially practiced by wealthy white players. However, the popularity of the sport spread beyond expectations, especially because it required very little equipment. Consequently, the masses were able to play *futebol* in any open space (parks, streets, beaches, and empty lots) using a ball. The rules were universal and easy to understand. As a result, talent, speed, and personal agility (instead of wealth and personal connections) became indicators of outstanding soccer players. In only a couple of decades, *futebol* had been claimed by the lower social classes of Brazil.

While the national team receives international attention, Brazilians usually follow their local teams with fervor and enthusiasm at both the state and national levels, which provides opportunities to support their favorite teams throughout the year. The state-level leagues usually play from January through April, and the national-level competitions take place from May until early December. Regional rivalries are common, especially among the four teams in Rio de Janeiro (Flamengo, Botofago, Fluminense, and Vasco da Gama), but the most intense match is played between Flamengo and Fluminense. This annual epic game is frequently called the "Fla-Flu" match, and it is played at the legendary Maracanã Stadium, which can hold 78,838 people using its current configuration. At a very basic level, Brazilian children grow up playing *futebol* in multiple teams, leagues, schools, clubs, and simple pickup games on the street. A large

Brazil's national soccer team celebrates its victory over Germany in the 2002 World Cup final played in Yokohama, Japan. With five World Cup awards, Brazil still holds the record as the country with the most World Cup titles in history. (FIFA)

> ## MARACANÃ SOCCER STADIUM
>
> Soccer (*futebol*) is the king of sports in Brazil, and the Maracanã Stadium in Rio de Janeiro is the largest national venue. Since 1966, the official name has been Estádio Jornalista Mário Filho, named after a journalist who advocated vigorously for its construction. The Maracanã Stadium is the host for four local teams: Fluminense, Botafogo, Flamengo, and Vasco da Gama. Owned by the state of Rio de Janeiro, it was inaugurated in 1950 to host the FIFA World Cup. The first match was between Brazil and Uruguay, and it accommodated 199,854 soccer fans. When the FIFA World Cup returned to Brazil in 2014, the stadium went through extensive renovations; the architects removed the terraces for standing fans, and its current capacity was reduced to 78,838 seats. The venue has also been used for popular music concerts, massive religious services, and the 2016 Olympics.

majority of Brazilian boys dream of playing professionally and eventually represent their country at international competitions.

Brazilian soccer statistics are impressive. It is the only country in the world to qualify and play in every single FIFA World Cup since its inception in 1930. In addition, Brazil holds the record as the only country to win such an international competition five times, in 1958, 1962, 1970, 1994, and 2002. It is also the only country in South America to have hosted the FIFA World Cup twice, in 1950 and 2014. In addition, Brazil has established a successful female *futebol* national team; their first competition on the global stage was in 1986 against the United States. They have won seven championships at the regional Copa América Femenina, in 1991, 1995, 1998, 2003, 2010, 2014, and 2018. They also obtained first place at the Pan American Games in 2007. They have participated in the Female Soccer World Cup eight times, but they have not been able to earn the top title. The Brazilian female national team came in fourth place at the 2016 Olympic Games in Rio de Janeiro.

Brazil does an incredible job of training and nurturing talented *futebol* players. However, professional top-level teams in the national league do not pay as much as foreign clubs. Consequently, the large majority of the best Brazilian players are recruited to play in foreign leagues, especially with lucrative contracts on European teams. For example, Neymar made recent history with a five-year contract for €150 million Euros (US$171.1 million) when he transferred from the famous Barcelona team to the Paris Saint-Germain club in 2017. The result is that Brazilian audiences also closely follow games and scores in European leagues in order to stay informed about Brazilian players and their performance in such international leagues.

See also: Chapter 2: Timeline. Chapter 15: Overview; Maracanã Soccer Stadium Sidebar; Pelé (1940–), Ronaldinho (1980–), and Neymar (1992–). Chapter 16: Sports Icons.

Further Reading
Bellos, Alex. 2014. *Futebol: The Brazilian Way of Life*. New York: Bloomsbury USA.

Buckley Jr., James. 2007. *Pelé*. New York: DK.

Goldblatt, David. 2014. *Futebol Nation: The Story of Brazil through Soccer*. New York: Nation Books.

Master, James, Vasco Cotovio, and Tom McGowan. 2017. "Neymar Signs 5-Year Deal with Paris Saint-Germain." CNN, August 4. Accessed July 11, 2019. https://edition.cnn.com /2017/08/03/football/neymar-barcelona-psg-transfer/index.html

McKenna, Erin Flynn. 2016. "Modern Sports," in *Brazil*, edited by Antonio Luciano de Andrade Tosta and Eduardo F. Coutinho, 312–320. Santa Barbara: ABC-CLIO.

Milleret, Margo. 2003. "Social Customs," in *Culture and Customs of Brazil*, edited by Jon S. Vincent, 81–94. Westport, CT: Greenwood Press.

Puin, Karolina. 2012. "What Brazilians Watch on TV." *Brazil Business*. June 9. Accessed July 11, 2019. http://thebrazilbusiness.com/article/what-brazilians-watch-on-tv

Mega Sena, Brazilian Lottery

Mega Sena is the biggest lottery game in Brazil, and the winning numbers are drawn twice a week on Wednesday and Saturday. In a country where Brazilians are suspicious of the government, they actually trust Mega Sena because it is managed by the highly respected Caixa Econômica Federal Bank.

Mega Sena is relatively easy to play. Players simply select six numbers between 01 and 60. Then on Wednesday or Saturday, the numbers are drawn on live television. The winning numbers are always two digits. However, the unique feature about how the numbers are picked is based on the fact that the Brazilian lottery uses two separate machines; each one of them draws a single digit number, and combined, they come up with one of the winning numbers. For example, the first machine draws a number between 0 and 5, and the second machine draws a number between 0 and 9. Together, they create combinations such as 05, 24, or 56. This unique twist on the process makes Mega Sena more dramatic and suspenseful than other generic lotteries. Lucky winners have three possible ways to win based on how many of the six winning numbers they matched:

- The third prize has to match four of the winning numbers; it is called the *quadra*.
- The second prize matches five of the winning numbers; it is called the *quina*.
- The first prize must match all six numbers to get the highest jackpot called *sena*.

The most basic way of playing is to buy a ticket and select only six numbers from the possible choices between 01 and 60; this option costs R$3.50, which is almost $1 U.S. However, if players want to increase their chances, they can select up to fifteen numbers. This option certainly increases the possibility of hitting the jackpot, but the cost goes up significantly with each additional number a player selects. The cost for selecting 15 numbers is R$15,517 ($4,146 U.S.).

The amount of the jackpots depends on the number of total ticket sales. The top prize gets 35 percent of the amount sold. The second and third prizes each get 19 percent of the total accumulated pool. The other 27 percent is held in the Mega Sena fund, and 22 percent of it is added to the total jackpot every fifth game. Mega Sena winners must claim their prize within ninety days of the drawing date. If the prize is lower than R$800 ($214 U.S.), they can cash it out at any lottery-selling location. Larger amounts must be claimed from the federal bank. Many Brazilians who do not play the lottery throughout the year are still likely to participate in the Mega da Virada. This is a special lottery drawing held on New Year's Eve on December 31. The jackpot is enormous, and it gets people involved in the end-of-the-year festivities.

See also: Chapter 15: Overview.

Further Reading
Mega Sena Brazilian Lottery Official Website. http://www.megasena.com/en

Motor Sports: Formula 1 and Grand Prix

The Grande Prêmio do Brasil (Brazilian Grand Prix) is a Formula One (F1) championship car race that has a long tradition in both South America and the world. This is the highest rank of single-seater auto racing sanctioned by the Fédération Internationale de l'Automobile (FIA). Brazil has had two main venues for Grand Prix races: the current Autódromo José Carlos Pace, which is a circuit located in the Interlagos suburban neighborhood near São Paulo and the Jacarepaguá motorsport circuit in Rio de Janeiro. The Brazilian Grand Prix competitions have been scheduled in the Formula One calendar continuously since 1972, and such races are traditionally held in either October or November. The circuit in Rio de Janeiro has scheduled the F1 championship three times, in 1978, 1981, and 1989. The rest of the time, the Formula One races have been held at the Interlagos motorsport circuit in São Paulo at different periods from 1972 to 1977, 1979 to 1980, and ever since 1990.

The Interlagos circuit opened in 1940, and it certainly offers race car drivers a challenge. First of all, it is not the typical oval circuit, and it is unusually designed to run counterclockwise, which is the opposite of most race circuits around the world. The entire track consists of fifteen turns, and it measures 2.677 miles (4.309 kilometers). At this circuit, it is not unusual for cars to reach speeds topping 205 miles per hour (330 km/h). Michael Schumacher holds the record as the race car driver with the most wins (four) at the Brazilian Grand Prix. The record for the fastest lap was set by Valtteri Bottas at 1:08.322 minutes in 2017.

Brazil has produced multiple Formula One race car drivers of high caliber. So far, five Brazilians have won the Brazilian Grand Prix championship: Emerson Fittipaldi (1973 and 1974), José Carlos Pace (1975), Nelson Piquet (1983 and 1986), Ayrton Senna (1991 and 1993), and Felipe Massa (2006 and 2008). The only existing Formula One circuit in Brazil (Interlagos) was renamed as the Autódromo José Carlos Pace to honor the outstanding Brazilian race car driver. Another highly accomplished Brazilian car racer was Ayrton Senna da Silva (1960–1994). He won three championships (1988, 1990, and 1991) in the Formula One circuit for the McLaren Team. He died when he was thirty-four years old in an accident at the 1994 San Marino Grand Prix. The government of Brazil declared three days of national mourning for Brazilians to remember their national sports icon.

The 2018 Brazilian Grand Prix was recently held in November. The sport has become extremely popular to watch on television, and Brazilians always root for their local race car drivers. In recent negotiations, Fernando Haddad (mayor of São Paulo) agreed with the FIA president to make the requested necessary upgrades and thus extend the contract to keep the Brazilian Grand Prix in the Formula One calendar until 2022.

See also: Chapter 15: Overview.

Further Reading

Autódromo José Carlos Pace (Interlagos) Official Website. http://www.autodromodeinterlagos.com.br/wp1

Brazilian Grand Prix Official Website. https://www.gpbrasil.com.br

Formula 1 Official Website. https://www.formula1.com

Olympic Games, Rio de Janeiro 2016

Rio de Janeiro hosted the 2016 Summer Olympics from August 5 to 21; it was the first time that any city in South America had ever held the Olympic Games. The Jogos Olímpicos de Verão de 2016 included 11,237 athletes competing in 306 events clustered under thirty-eight sports. Most of the competitions were held in different venues in

---

ZIKA VIRUS AND THE 2016 OLYMPICS

Brazil reported continued transmission of the Zika virus via mosquitos in 2015. However, a person infected with the virus can also transmit it via unprotected sex. This virus can cause babies to be born with usually small heads (microcephaly) and other brain malformations. Rio de Janeiro was scheduled to host two large global events in 2016: the Summer Olympics and the Paralympic Games. Therefore, the potential dangers created great concern among large numbers of athletes and spectators planning to gather in Rio de Janeiro. Consequently, the World Health Organization (WHO) and the Centers for Disease Control (CDC) provided specific advice, including the following: (a) pregnant women—or those planning to be pregnant—should not travel to Brazil; (b) everyone should use insect repellent on exposed skin; and (c) all travelers should either use a condom or avoid sex altogether.

Table 15.1: TOP FIVE METALS TABLE FOR 2016 SUMMER OLYMPICS IN RIO DE JANEIRO

RANK	COUNTRY	GOLD	SILVER	BRONZE	TOTAL
1	United States	46	37	38	121
2	Great Britain	27	23	17	67
3	China	26	18	26	70
4	Russia	19	17	19	55
5	Germany	17	10	15	42
13	**Brazil (host)**	7	6	6	19

Rio de Janeiro, but most of the *futebol* (soccer) events were also held in São Paulo, Salvador, Brasília, Manaus, and Belo Horizonte. The opening ceremony was held at the famous Maracanã Stadium in Rio. Under the motto *Um mundo novo* (A New World), the International Olympic Committee allowed ten refugees to compete for the first time on the Refugee Olympic Team using the Olympic flag.

Preparations and management related to the 2016 Rio Olympic Games sparked serious controversies and scandals. First, Brazilians protested the immense cost of $4.6 billion U.S. for the Olympics because the government was willing to fund the operational expense while simultaneously claiming it had to cut the federal budget for education, health care, and retirement pensions. Second, the existing political dysfunction resulted in the suspension of President Dilma Rousseff (1947–) for 180 days, and Acting President Michel Temer (1940–) presided over the Olympic ceremonies. Third, the emergence of the Zika virus coincided with the Olympics, creating fear and uncertainty among potential athletes. Fourth, Brazil scheduled the windsurfing and sailing competitions at Guanabara Bay, which is notorious for its high levels of pollution. Multiple athletes refused to participate in fear for their health. Finally, corruption became apparent when multiple arrests were made for money laundering, violations of currency laws, and running a criminal organization. The people who ended up in prison for crimes related to the Olympic Games include Carlos Nuzman (president of the Brazilian Olympic Committee), Sergio Cabral (ex-governor of Rio de Janeiro State), and Leonardo Gryner (former head of the Brazilian Olympic Committee). While no athletes got sick due to pollution or the Zika virus, the political chaos and street protests continue in Brazil.

At the end of the 2016 Olympics, the United States dominated first place with the most medals; Brazil earned the thirteenth place. Table 15.1 shows the top five ranks with cumulative medal count.

See also: Chapter 3: Corruption and Political Scandals; Rousseff, Dilma (1947–); Temer, Michel (1940–). Chapter 6: Poverty, Social Conflict, and Protests. Chapter 16: Overview; Zika Virus and the 2016 Olympics Sidebar.

Further Reading

BBC News. 2017. "Rio Olympic Head Carlos Nuzman Charged with Corruption." *BBC News*. October 19. Accessed July 11, 2019. https://www.bbc.com/news/world-latin-america-41678338

Zimbalist, Andrew. 2017. *Rio 2016: Olympic Myths, Hard Realities*. Washington, DC: Brookings Institution Press.

Paralympic Games 2016

Rio de Janeiro held the fifteenth Summer Paralympic Games from September 7 to 18, 2016. This global event is governed by the International Paralympic Committee (IPC), and its purpose is to engage athletes with disabilities in competitions held in multiple sports. In 2016, a total of 4,342 athletes participated in the games, representing 159 nations in a total of 528 events clustered around twenty-two sports. The division by gender was 2,657 male and 1,671 female athletes. The president of the IPC expressed during the opening ceremony that these courageous athletes were likely to change people's perceptions based on apparent limitations to a world of possibilities and opportunities.

The 2016 Paralympic Games offered important highlights. For example, two new sports were added to the games, including canoeing and para-triathlon. It was the first time a Latin American city ever hosted this international competition. Over 2.15 million tickets were sold, surpassing Beijing 2008 as the second-most-attended games in the history of such events. The entire Russian group of participants was banned based on the results of doping tests. An unfortunate event was that for the first time, an athlete died during competition; the cyclist was Bahman Golbarnezhad, representing Iran.

All the paralympic events were held at four cluster locations distributed throughout Rio de Janeiro. President Michel Temer (1940–) officially opened the Paralympic Games at the iconic Maracanã Stadium on September 7, 2016; the closing ceremony on September 18 was also held there. In the same Maracanã Cluster, the Sambadrome Marquês de Sapucaí was the site for archery competitions, and the Estádio Olímpico João Havelange was used for all the athletic events. The Deodoro Cluster included three locations: the National Equestrian Center and the National Shooting Center for those two sports and the Deodoro Stadium for football. The Copacabana Cluster used the Flamengo Park, Marina da Glória, and the Lagoa Rodrigo da Freitas for cycling, sailing, and rowing respectively. The Barra Cluster included multiple arenas and centers that held competitions on judo, wheelchair fencing, boccia, goalball, swimming, wheelchair tennis, track cycling, and wheelchair basketball. The Barra cluster also included the Athlete's Village for their accommodations.

The president of the Brazilian Paralympic Committee, Andrew Parsons, declared the 2016 Summer Paralympic Games a tremendous success, even though Brazil came in eighth place in terms of medals earned. The countries that dominated the top five positions for medals are listed in Table 15.2.

Table 15.2: TOP FIVE METALS TABLE FOR 2016 SUMMER PARALYMPICS

COUNTRY	GOLD	SILVER	BRONZE	TOTAL
1. China	107	81	51	239
2. Great Britain	64	39	44	147
3. Ukraine	41	37	39	117
4. United States	40	44	31	115
5. Australia	22	30	29	81
8. Brazil	14	29	29	72

See also: Chapter 15 Overview; Olympic Games Rio de Janeiro 2016.

Further Reading

International Paralympic Committee. 2016. "Games On! Brazil Welcomes the Paralympics." *Rio 2016 Paralympic Games*. September 7. Accessed July 19, 2019. https://www.paralympic.org/news/games-brazil-welcomes-paralympics

Paralympic Games Rio de Janeiro 2016 Official Website. https://www.paralympic.org/rio-2016

Pelé (1940–), Ronaldinho (1980–), and Neymar (1992–)

Brazilians are passionate about *futebol* (soccer). While there is a long list of high-caliber soccer players who have emerged out of Brazil, three of them have provided their national fan base with indelible memories during several decades: Pelé, Ronaldinho, and more recently Neymar. It is worth noting that Brazilian culture values informality. Therefore, most famous Brazilian soccer players are known only by their nicknames, sometimes even more so than their real given names. This approach gives their fans and followers a sense of closeness and friendliness with the players. As a result, Brazilian soccer stars are notorious for wearing only their nickname on the official team jerseys. In fact, very few people would recognize either Pelé or Neymar by their full given names.

Edson Arantes do Nascimento (known simply as Pelé) is the most legendary soccer player ever. In fact, both the International Federation of Football History and Statistics (IFFHS) and the International Olympic Committee voted Pelé in 1999 as the Best World Athlete of the twentieth century. That is how powerful his athletic legacy is. He started playing professionally with the team Santos when he was only fifteen years old, and he made the national team (*seleção*) right away. He is also the only player in the world to have won three FIFA World Cup titles (1958, 1962, and 1970) with his national team. His charismatic personality paired with his agile style of playing brought international attention and pride to Brazil.

Ronaldo de Assis Moreira is more commonly known by two nicknames: Ronaldinho and Ronaldinho Gaúcho. At a professional level, he quickly developed a reputation as an agile midfielder who also specialized in accurate free kicks. He started playing for the Grêmio team (1998–2000) in Brazil before he moved to Europe at age twenty to start playing for multiple European clubs that included the Paris Saint-Germain (2001–2003), Barcelona (2003–2008), and the AC Milan (2008–2011). He also proudly returned to Brazil to play for the national team in multiple international competitions, including two FIFA World Cups and the 2008 Summer Olympics. His awards include the highly coveted FIFA World Player of the Year in 2004. Ronaldinho certainly made valuable contributions to the sport and his country.

Neymar da Silva Santos Júnior (or simply Neymar) is one of the most famous contemporary Brazilian *futebol* stars. Similar to Pelé, Neymar emerged as a professional player at seventeen years old playing for the club Santos in 2009. He quickly earned the South American Footballer of the Year Award in 2011 and 2012. He then played for the Barcelona team from 2013 to 2017. Subsequently, he announced his lucrative transfer in 2017 to the Paris Saint-Germain team with a five-year contract worth €150 million Euros ($171.161 million U.S). His recent participation at the 2018 World Cup in Russia continues to show the world that Brazil produces extremely talented soccer players.

Futebol, also known as soccer, is the king of sports in Brazil, and Edson Arantes do Nascimento, better known as Pelé, is its most iconic star. (Library of Congress)

See also: Chapter 9: Nicknames. Chapter 15: Overview; *Futebol* (Soccer).

Further Reading

Bellos, Alex. 2014. *Futebol: The Brazilian Way of Life*. New York: Bloomsbury USA.

Beting, Mario, and Simon Saito Navarro (trans.). 2014. *Me llamo Neymar: Conversación entre padre e hijo*. Madrid: Ediciones B.

Buckley, James, Jr. 2007. *Pelé*. New York: DK.

Goldblatt, David. 2014. *Futebol Nation: The Story of Brazil through Soccer*. New York: Nation Books.

Nichols, Elizabeth Gackstetter, and Timothy R. Robins. 2015. *Pop Culture in Latin America and the Caribbean*. Santa Barbara, CA: ABC-CLIO.

Torres, John Albert. 2014. *Soccer Star Ronaldinho*. New York: Speeding Star.

Soccer FIFA World Cup 2014

Brazilians are extreme *futebol* (soccer) fans. Every four years, the Fédération Internationale de Football Association (FIFA) organizes the Soccer World Cup, which is the largest soccer competition worldwide. Brazil was the proud host of the 20th World Cup from June 12 to July 13, 2014. This was the second time that Brazil staged the international event; the previous time was in 1950. The opening ceremony was held at the Arena do São Paulo Stadium, and the closing ceremony was at the Maracanã Stadium in Rio de Janeiro. Overall, FIFA provided $576 million U.S. toward the prize money and operational expenses to be split among participating nations; the wining team (Germany) took home $35 million U.S.

Statistics are important in professional soccer, and FIFA keeps meticulous records related to international competitions. The 2014 World Cup in Brazil included thirty-two teams from five different confederations playing sixty-four games in twelve different venues. Each team had twenty-three players, including three required goalkeepers. Overall, 3,429,873 tickets were sold to watch the soccer matches.

The 2014 World Cup in Brazil included a few innovations and adaptations for the games. It was the first time that FIFA allowed goal-line technology, which included fourteen cameras directed to the two goals (seven each) to make definite goal determinations. In addition, FIFA authorized the use of vanishing foam to mark the exact place for a free kick and the line for the ten-yard line for a defending wall. In addition, since some of the matches were played in high temperatures that exceeded 90° F (32° C), the referees could authorize cooling periods after playing thirty minutes of each half game.

After multiple grueling elimination games, Germany won the final match against Argentina (1–0), which provided the European nation with its fourth World Cup title. Brazil lost to Germany (7–0) in a disappointing semifinals match, which resulted in Brazil's overall fourth place. Table 15.3 summarizes the final ranking positions.

While most Brazilians love soccer, they were not necessarily happy about the cost of $14 billion U.S. for the 2014 World Cup covered by the federal government. Controversy and protests were common as infrastructure projects were implemented before the event. For example, massive street demonstrations decried the massive use of so much public money while the federal government simultaneously proposed budget cuts to education and health care. In addition, the homes belonging to thousands of families at the Favela do Metrô were destroyed to make way for an access road, and

Table 15.3: 2014 FIFA WORLD CUP RESULTS

Rank	Country
Winner—First Place	Germany
Runner Up—Second Place	Argentina
Third Place	Netherlands
Fourth Place	Brazil

the people were scattered without much compensation. On opening day, Brazilian president Dilma Rousseff (1947–) did not give any speeches due to the heavy opposition and loud demonstrations against the government. Overall, Brazilians enjoy the fact that the country still holds the record of having won five World Cup titles (1958, 1962, 1970, 1994, and 2002); no other country on the planet has accomplished such an athletic feat.

See also: Chapter 15 Overview; *Futebol* (Soccer).

Further Reading

Fédération Internationale de Football Association (FIFA) Official Website. https://www.fifa.com

FIFA World Cup Brazil 2014 Official Website. https://www.fifa.com/worldcup/archive/brazil2014/index.html

Phillips, Tom. 2011. "Rio World Cup Demolitions Leave Favela Families Trapped in Ghost Town." *Guardian*, April 26. Accessed July 12, 2019. https://www.theguardian.com/world/2011/apr/26/favela-ghost-town-rio-world-cup

Telenovelas

Brazilian telenovelas are an extremely popular form of daily entertainment. They usually broadcast from Monday through Saturday at prime time from 8:30 to 10 p.m., and they reach the majority of the Brazilian population. When the genre started during the 1950s, it was common to create historical pieces based on famous literary works. During the 1970s and 1980s, however, the giant TV Globo network started recruiting actors and writers from film and theater productions, which elevated the level of telenovelas to viable commercial programming. They quickly acquired large audiences. As opposed to open-ended soap operas popular in the United States (such as *General Hospital*), Brazilian telenovelas have a finite number of episodes that traditionally last only a few months. Today, telenovelas dominate evening programming, and they attract a wide audience of men, women, young adults, and older populations because they spark discussion on contemporary social topics that include alcoholism, street violence, divorce, regional celebrations, homosexuality, political scandals, corruption, drug

Table 15.4: TOP-FIVE MOST POPULAR TELENOVELAS IN BRAZIL

Ranking	Title	Year
1	*Roque Santeiro*	1985–1986
2	*Tieta*	1989–1990
3	*O Salvador da pátria*	1989
4	*Renascer*	1993
5	*Rainha da sucata*	1990

Table 15.5: TOP-FIVE MOST EXPORTED BRAZILIAN TELENOVELAS

Ranking	Title	Year	# Countries
1	*Avenida Brasil*	2012	106
2	*Da cor do pecado*	2004	100
3	*Terra nostra*	1999–2000	95
4	*O Clone*	2001–2002	91
5	*Caminho das Índias*	2009	90

addiction, and average daily struggles. The top broadcasters for telenovelas are TV Globo, TV Record, Sistema Brasileiro de Televisão (SBT), and TV Bandeirantes. TV Globo is currently by far the largest television network in Brazil and a major producer of high-quality telenovelas. Based on data published by the Brazilian Institute of Public Opinion and Statistics (IBOPE), the top five most popular Brazilian telenovelas ever are shown in Table 15.4.

The level of acting, writing, and production has made Brazilian telenovelas extremely popular and financially successful. In fact, their work has been recognized with four International Emmy Awards for Best Telenovela since the inception of the award in 2008. In addition, they are exported to a large number of countries, which reflects how well Brazilian telenovelas are perceived abroad. Table 15.5 shows the top five most exported telenovelas.

Since 2010, Brazil has experienced an increase of young people watching television programming on their mobile phones. However, IBOPE statistics also reveal a recent decline in the audience that watches telenovelas, especially among young people who seem to prefer new reality shows and American light comedy programming. Nevertheless, Rede Globo telenovelas titled *O sétimo guardião* (The Seventh Guardian) and *Espelho da vida* (Mirror of Life) were extremely popular in 2019. Contemporary Brazilian telenovelas have a strong social impact because they introduce new fashion trends, adopt popular street language, address current social concerns, incorporate contemporary music, and contribute overall to Brazilian culture.

See also: Chapter 15 Overview. Chapter 16: Overview; Rede Globo and Other Television Networks.

Further Reading

Bruha, Patrick. 2015. "Most Popular Brazilian Telenovelas." *Brazil Business*, March 27. Accessed July 8, 2019. http://thebrazilbusiness.com/article/most-popular-brazilian-telenovelas

Puin, Karolina. 2012. "What Brazilians Watch on TV." *Brazil Business,* June 9. Accessed July 8, 2019. http://thebrazilbusiness.com/article/what-brazilians-watch-on-tv

Rede TV Globo Official Website. http://www.globo.com

Vincent, Jon S. 2003. *Culture and Customs of Brazil*. Westport, CT: Greenwood Press.

CHAPTER 16

MEDIA AND POPULAR CULTURE

OVERVIEW

Brazilians are very creative and talented; they also have a wide array of fun activities available. For example, television is an extremely popular form of entertainment, especially the famous telenovelas (soap operas) and musical variety shows. Brazil also has a rich musical history that is a crucial feature of national culture. Moreover, sports icons have earned a prominent place in national pride, especially in soccer and Brazilian jiu-jitsu. In addition, a new wave of Brazilian filmmakers (such as Fernando Meirelles and Walter Salles Jr.) has recently portrayed national social concerns artfully, earning them multiple awards and international recognition. In the twenty-first century, however, the expansion of the Internet, social networks, and mobile phones has changed how Brazilians communicate with one another, watch entertainment, stay informed, and listen to music.

Printed, Broadcasting, and Digital Media

Brazilians have a variety of information and entertainment choices available to them. Newspapers are not only thriving but actually growing in circulation in Brazil, which is unusual because recent global trends reflect a tendency for printed newspapers to go into bankruptcy. The top five Brazilian newspapers with the largest circulation in 2017 include *Folha de S. Paulo, O Globo, Super Noticia, Estado de S. Paulo,* and *Extra*. Meanwhile, television is the most popular national form of entertainment, especially reality shows, telenovelas, and musical variety weekend shows. Rede Globo is by far the largest broadcasting network in Brazil, and it reaches over 96 percent of all Brazilians with its wide array of programs based on trustworthy news, sports, and soap operas.

Digital media has grown tremendously in Brazil during the last ten years, mostly due to Internet growth, mobile phone availability, and the expansion of social networks. According to international statistics reports, Brazil reached 123.21 million Internet users in 2018, which makes it the fourth largest in the world after China, India, and the United States. Recent statistics also reveal that, from 2014 to 2018, almost 80 percent of Internet users in Brazil use social media. As of 2016, Facebook had the most extensive penetration rate (63 percent) of Internet users in the country. WhatsApp was in second place at 53 percent, and 40 percent of Brazilian Internet users followed

Instagram. These applications have reported that the most common topics that dominated the conversation for Brazilians using social media were family, soccer, and soap operas.

Cinema

Contemporary Brazilian cinema deals mostly with social national issues following a very realistic and raw approach that has elevated the stature of several Brazilian directors to international fame. Fernando Meirelles (1955–) is a prolific filmmaker who was noticed in 2004 when he released his masterpiece *Cidade de Deus* (City of God). It vividly portrays the poverty and violence that is commonplace in the now-famous favela (slum) in Rio de Janeiro. The film garnered multiple domestic and international film awards. Another important modern Brazilian filmmaker is Walter Salles Jr. (1956–). He emerged as a popular director in the late 1990s. His first commercial success was *Central do Brasil* (Central Station) in 1998. This deeply emotional film illustrates the reality of poor children and the harsh living conditions in the northeast region of Brazil. Then in 2004, Salles released his most celebrated film, *Diarios de motocicleta* (The Motorcycle Diaries), based on the life of the legendary figure Ernesto Che Guevara during his early years. It was a box office success, and it established his reputation in the film industry. Today, multiple regional film festivals actively promote up-and-coming filmmakers while simultaneously exposing Brazilians to a plethora of foreign films.

Popular Culture

Brazilians are extremely social, and personal relationships are highly regarded. Music, sports, and television shows create a space for lively discussion and social interaction. Contemporary popular culture is influenced by national icons in several fields, and it continues to evolve with new generations. For example, the musical traditions of samba, bossa nova, *tropicalía*, and *musica popular brasileira* (MPB) are identified as uniquely Brazilian. The famous song "Garota de Ipanema" ("The Girl from Ipanema") evokes emotions based on a sultry bossa nova jazz style that have made it the second-most-recorded song in the world. All this rich musical and dance heritage provided the background for contemporary artists, such as the current pop star Anitta. The 1980s television icon Xuxa entertained both children and adults while setting up the foundation for the recent boom in reality television shows that keep Brazilians engaged nowadays, including *Big Brother Brazil* (BBB), *The Voice Brazil*, and *A facenda* (The Farm). Television also allows Brazilians to watch sports religiously. The soccer legend Pelé (1940–) is the most decorated *futebol* player in the world. In fact, the International Olympic Committee selected him as the best athlete of the twentieth century. For most Brazilians, he is an inspiration and an incredible source of national pride. He set the stage for future Brazilian players to be recognized at global stadiums, including contemporary players such as Ronaldinho (1980–), Neymar (1992–), and Coutinho (1992–). The current generation of Brazilians is already reshaping their social environment, especially as they become more politically active and engage in political and environmental activism. Their unique talents, opportunities, and challenges will continue to shape Brazilian culture.

Further Reading

Directory of Online Brazil Newspapers. http://www.onlinenewspapers.com/brazil.htm

Heise, Tatiana Signorelli. 2012. *Remaking Brazil: Contested National Identities in Contemporary Brazilian Cinema*. Cardiff: University of Wales Press.

Holmes, Ryan. 2013. "The Future of Social Media? Forget about the U.S., Look to Brazil." *Forbes*, September 12. Accessed June 28, 2019. http://www.forbes.com/sites/ciocentral/2013/09/12/the-future-of-social-media-forget-about-the-u-s-look-to-brazil/#280efe6a3c9a

Kittleson, Roger. 2014. *The Country of Football: Soccer and the Making of Modern Brazil*. Berkeley: University of California Press.

Kwon, Oliver, and Steve Solot. 2015. *Brazilian Cinema Today: Essays by Critics and Experts from across Brazil*. Rio de Janeiro: Latin American Training Center.

Pomela, Marina. 2015. "Top 10 Printed Newspapers in Brazil." *Brazil Business*, April 13. Accessed June 28, 2019. http://thebrazilbusiness.com/article/top-10-printed-newspaper-in-brazil

Puin, Karolina. 2012. "What Brazilians Watch on TV." *Brazil Business*, June 9. Accessed June 28, 2019. http://thebrazilbusiness.com/article/what-brazilians-watch-on-tv

Rede Globo Official Website. http://www.globo.com

Statista. "Penetration of Leading Social Networks in Brazil as of 4th Quarter 2017." *Statista: The Statistics Portal*, Statista.com. Accessed June 28, 2019. https://www.statista.com/statistics/284424/brazil-social-network-penetration

Vincent, Jon S. 2003. *Culture and Customs of Brazil*. Westport, CT: Greenwood Press.

Cinema and Film Festivals

Brazilians saw their first movie in 1896. Then foreign films dominated the national market during the silent period up until the late 1920s. With the arrival of sound, the Brazilian film industry introduced the genre *chanchada* (light comedy) during the 1930s and 1940s. Carmen Miranda became the stereotypical Brazilian figure in a format that combined musical numbers with carnival themes and comedy performances. By the early 1950s, the company Vera Cruz attempted to compete with foreign films by creating serious films and moving away from the vulgar movies associated with the *chanchada* genre. Brazilian filmmakers were searching for forms of expression that represented the "real" Brazil instead of the stereotypical beaches and palm trees. The result was the creation of Cinema Novo, or "New Cinema," developed in the 1960s.

Brazilian filmmakers working under the Cinema Novo created films that highlighted the reality of national social and political problems, such as urban violence, hunger, poverty, and economic exploitation. Directors worked independently, had low budgets, used nonprofessional actors, shot scenes on location, used handheld cameras, and set up their own distribution plans. One of the greatest filmmakers from this period was Glauber Rocha (1939–1981). His masterpiece was *Deus e o diablo na terra do sol* (Black God, White Devil) released in 1964. It tells of the harsh living conditions of the barren *sertão* landscape in the northeast. He also combines the melancholic cadence of peasant speech patterns while infusing folk indigenous music on the background.

In an artistic irony, Cinema Novo coincided historically with a brutally oppressive military dictatorship in Brazil (1964–1985). Given the political conditions, it was a tremendous accomplishment that director Joaquim Pedro de Andrade (1932–1988) adapted the novel *Macunaíma* to the big screen in 1969, a film that was highly acclaimed by both audiences and critics. Strangely enough, the military government actually became involved in film production, financing, and distribution to boost its national image. However, to denounce the authoritarian rule, filmmakers used tools to overcome censorship reviewers, including idiomatic expressions, regional language with ambiguous meaning, complex metaphors, and irony. Somehow, the 1970s and early 1980s represented a low point in Brazilian cinema as most of the production switched to a *porno chanchada* genre based on erotic comedy.

Contemporary Brazilian film gained respectability again in the late 1990s and early 2000s with a new generation of prolific filmmakers. In 1998, *Central do Brasil* (Central Station), directed by Walter Salles (1956–), was highly praised at both domestic and international film festivals; it earned the Golden Globe Award for Best Foreign Film. Then in 2004, Fernando Meirelles (1955–) released *Cidade de Deus* (City of God) depicting gut-wrenching violence in Rio de Janeiro's favela (slum). It was a box-office hit with multiple international awards.

Cinema is extremely popular in Brazil today. Multiple film festivals offer Brazilians ample opportunities to view local, regional, and international films. The most well-established annual events include the Festival de Brasília do Cinema Brasileiro, the São Paulo Mostra International Film Festival, the Recife Audiovisual Festival, the Anima Mundi Animation Festival, and the Festival do Rio.

See also: Chapter 16: Overview; Meirelles, Fernando (1955–); Salles, Walter Jr. (1956–).

Further Reading

Heise, Tatiana Signorelli. 2012. *Remaking Brazil: Contested National Identities in Contemporary Brazilian Cinema*. Cardiff, Wales: University of Wales Press.

Kwon, Oliver, and Steve Solot. 2015. *Brazilian Cinema Today: Essays by Critics and Experts from across Brazil*. Rio de Janeiro: Latin American Training Center.

Nagib, Lucia. 2003. *The New Brazilian Cinema*. London: I.B. Taurus in Association with Centre for Brazilian Studies, University of Oxford.

Ramos, Fernão, and Luis F. Miranda. 2000. *Enciclopédia do cinema brasileiro*. São Paulo: Editora Senac.

São Paulo International Film Festival. http://www.mostra.org

Cultural Icons

Some of the most recognizable cultural icons that represent Brazil include places, events, and people. Three of the most recognized locations in the country are the Statue of Christ the Redeemer, Iguazu Falls, and the Amazon Rainforest. The Christ statue sits atop the Corcovado Mountain in Rio de Janeiro. Measuring 98 feet (30 meters) in height, it is by far the most visited location in Brazil. In the southern region, the Iguazu Falls are formed by the waters of the Iguazu River at the border with Argentina. The complex set of falls in both countries makes it the largest waterfall system on the planet. Meanwhile, the Amazon Basin in the northern region is the largest tropical rain forest in the world; it covers an area of 2.7 million square miles (7 million square kilometers) shared by nine countries. Brazil has more than 60 percent of the most diverse biological region of flora and fauna in the world.

The most iconic celebration in Brazil is Carnival, held in Rio de Janeiro. It is one of the largest annual festivals in the world. While it is based on a religious calendar, it evokes Brazilian images of samba music, exotic dancers, colorful costumes, elaborate parades, and never-ending parties. The event takes place forty-six days before Lent. The Carnival in Rio is the most famous, but other similar events are held in the cities of Recife, Porto Seguro, and Salvador. This period is definitely high season for tourism, providing evidence that cultural events are profitable.

Three Brazilians have reached iconic status in sports, the environment, and music. The soccer legend Pelé (1940–) remains by far the most popular *futebol* player in Brazil. He holds the world record as the only soccer player to ever win three separate World Cup titles. In Rio de Janeiro, Antônio Carlos Jobim (1927–1994) became famous when he composed the song "Garota de Ipanema" ("The Girl from Ipanema") in 1964 with a unique bossa nova jazz style. It

An aerial view of the Statue of Christ the Redeemer in Rio de Janeiro. The massive, iconic monument highlights the importance of Catholicism in Brazil. (Joseph Luoman/iStockphoto.com)

became the most-recorded song in Brazil's rich musical history. Two decades later, Chico Mendes (1944–1988) was an environmental activist who was killed in 1988 for demanding the rights of rubber trappers and advocating the sustainable management of crops in the Amazon. A new generation of talented Brazilians continues to stand out for their contributions to modern national culture in fields that include the arts, science, music, sports, politics, and the environment.

See also: Chapter 1: Mendes, Chico (1944–1988). Chapter 13: Carnival; "Girl from Ipanema" Song; Jobim, Antônio Carlos (1927–1994). Chapter 15: *Futebol*; Pelé (1940–), Ronaldinho (1980–), and Neymar (1992–). Chapter 16: Overview.

Further Reading

Greenberg, Arnold, and Harriet Greenberg. 2007. *Rio & the Best of Brazil Alive!* Edison, NJ: Hunter.

Kittleson, Roger. 2014. *The Country of Football: Soccer and the Making of Modern Brazil.* Berkeley: University of California Press.

McGowan, Chris, and Ricardo Pessanha. 1998. *The Brazilian Sound: Samba, Bossa Nova, and the Popular Music of Brazil.* Philadelphia: Temple University Press.

Tosta, Antonio Luciano de Andrade, and Eduardo F. Coutinho (eds.). 2016. *Brazil.* Santa Barbara, CA: ABC-CLIO.

Folia de Reis, Three Wise Men Celebration

From December 24 until January 6, a large number of Brazilians engage daily in a colorful and musical event called Folia de Reis. The Catholic tradition is often translated as Celebration of the Three Wise Men in English or Locura de Reyes in Spanish. While the tradition has almost disappeared from the urban areas, it is a folklore event quite common in the interior and rural regions of the country. It was introduced by the Portuguese colonizers during the 1700s. It is intended to recreate the journey that the Three Wise Men made to Bethlehem to meet the newborn baby Jesus and back to their respective homeland.

The Folia is a group of people that embark on a mini-parade going from house to house in a neighborhood while singing, dancing, and collecting donations for upcoming festivities. They begin on December 24 (the announcement of the birth of baby Jesus) and continue until January 5 in order to prepare for a large festival that takes place on January 6. The Folia includes volunteers who play crucial roles: the Three Wise Men (Melchior, Gaspar, and Balthasar), an ambassador who coordinates the entire event with the neighborhood, the flag carrier (*alférez*), two or three clowns for fun entertainment, a choir, and the group of musicians. Each Folia has a unique flag that people use to express their devotion by pinning religious icons, monetary donations, flowers, photographs, and thank-you cards. Everything attached to it will be part of the larger celebration on January 6. The musical ensembles use traditional instruments that include flutes, a metal triangle, tambourines, violas, and a drum. The choir sings mostly Christmas religious songs based on the celebration of the birth of Jesus Christ.

The Folia de Reis is also a popular social event throughout the country. The most famous Folia events take place in towns such as Rubim (state of Minas Gerais), Salvador (state of Bahía), Quirinópolis (state of Goiás), Sorocaba (state of São Paulo), and Rio das Flores (state of Rio de Janeiro). The two-week celebration usually includes art exhibits, nativity scenes, cultural events, and lots of stands with food, candy, drinks, and games. The carnival-like ambience is also supported by religious services to commemorate these special dates for Catholics in Brazil. The highlight of the popular tradition is a large celebration on January 6 (Epiphany) funded largely with all the donations collected throughout the previous Folia de Reis festivities.

See also: Chapter 16: Overview.

Further Reading

Figueiredo, Karoline. "Folia de Reis." Info Escola: Navegando e Aprendendo. InfoEscola.com Accessed May 25, 2019. https://www.infoescola.com/datas-comemorativas/folia-de-reis

Folia de Reis. *Sua Portal de Pesquisas Temáticas e Educacionais.* SuaPesquisa.com. Accessed on May 25, 2019. https://www.suapesquisa.com/musicacultura/folia_reis.htm

Tremura, Welson. 2010. *Brazilian Folia de Reis: With an Open Heart: A Spiritual Journey through Song.* Saarbrücken, Germany: VDM Verlag Dr. Muller Omniscriptum.

Major Newspapers

Brazil got a late start in establishing newspapers compared to the rest of the Western Hemisphere. Part of the explanation is that the printing press was not allowed in Brazil until 1808 when King João was forced to move his entire court to Rio de Janeiro after Napoleon had conquered Portugal. While multiple countries in North and South America had been printing newspapers for almost a century, Brazil published its first four newspapers during the 1800s, all of which are still being published today.

It is worth noting that the *Diario de Pernambuco* is the oldest newspaper with a continuous daily circulation in Latin America and also the oldest continuously printed newspaper in Portuguese. Throughout the 1900s, printed newspapers played a crucial role in society informing people about political, social, sports, and cultural topics.

At the start of the twenty-first century, the expansion of the Internet threatened the existence of newspapers in printed format worldwide. In several countries, multiple daily papers have gone bankrupt when the sales declined dramatically. Brazil, however, seems to be a unique case where newspaper circulation actually continues to increase. The Circulation Verification Institute (IVC) in Brazil reviews one hundred titles and publishes an annual report with the exact number of circulation copies. The

Table 16.1: THE OLDEST NEWSPAPERS IN BRAZIL

Name / Title	Year Established	City / Location	Status
Diario de Pernambuco	1825	Recife	Still published.
Jornal do Commercio	1827	Rio de Janeiro	Still published.
Estado de São Paulo	1875	São Paulo	Still published.
Jornal do Brasil	1891	Rio de Janeiro	Still Published.

Table 16.2: NEWSPAPERS WITH THE LARGEST CIRCULATION IN BRAZIL IN 2017

Name / Title	City / Location
Folha de S. Paulo	São Paulo
O Globo	Rio de Janeiro
Super Noticia	Minas Gerais
Estado de S. Paulo	São Paulo
Extra	Rio de Janeiro

results for the top five newspapers (with the largest print and digital circulation numbers combined) in 2017 are listed in Table 16.2.

One of the main explanations for the increase in subscriptions is that well-established newspapers began to offer paid digital subscriptions that keep their readers informed all day long by providing digital content via their phones or computers. Recent surveys reveal that most Brazilians still trust the news from newspapers (digital or print) a lot more than from other online digital platforms such as Google, Facebook, or Twitter. Consequently, in contrast to other countries, Brazilian journalistic research institutes are projecting that newspaper subscriptions will continue to modestly increase until 2020, along with their respective advertisement accounts.

In addition to the major newspapers, Brazilians have a plethora of local and regional daily papers at their disposal. They also read specialized papers on sports, religion, financial news, and celebrity gossip. Many of these dailies are free and widely available at bus and train stations. While the printing press was late to arrive in Brazil, it will continue to have a lasting and powerful presence in society.

See also: Chapter 16: Overview; Social Media and Internet Use.

Further Reading

Bonilla, Laura. 2012. "Newspapers Alive and Kicking in Brazil." *News.com.au*, August 2. Accessed May 22, 2019. http://www.news.com.au/world/breaking-news/newspapers-alive-and-kicking-in-brazil/news-story/dea36922af14ba7ebc06c8a835cff46c

Circulation Verification Institute, Brazil. https://ivcbrasil.org.br/#/home

Clark, Andrew. 2009. "Brazilian Newspapers Celebrate a Rise in Circulation." *Guardian,* October 11. Accessed May 22, 2019. https://www.theguardian.com/media/2009/oct/12/brazil-newspapers-circulation

"Directory of Brazil Online Newspapers." http://www.onlinenewspapers.com/brazil.htm

Pomela, Marina. 2015. "Top 10 Printed Newspapers in Brazil." *Brazil Business,* April 13. Accessed May 22, 2019. http://thebrazilbusiness.com/article/top-10-printed-newspaper-in-brazil

Statista. "Average Paid Circulation of Selected Newspapers in Brazil in December 2018." *Statista: The Statistics Portal,* Statista.com. Accessed May 22, 2019. http://www.statista.com/statistics/261629/leading-newspapers-in-brazil-by-circulation

Meirelles, Fernando (1955–)

Fernando Ferreira Meirelles is a Brazilian filmmaker who functions as a producer, director, and screenwriter. He was born on November 9, 1955, in the metropolis of São Paulo. He works well in both film and television media platforms. His background might originally appear to be a series of disconnected interests, but they are in reality the reason why he became successful as a filmmaker. He attended the University of São Paulo in the early 1980s to study architecture and urban planning. He was an average student. For his graduation thesis, he proposed a video project instead of the traditional architectural plans developed by most students. His culminating film project was barely approved, but he managed to graduate with grades that were acceptable. His interest in film was already obvious. Then he soon shifted his attention to advertisement. After working in the field for a few years, he and a few friends founded O2 Films in 1990. Over the next decade, it became one of the largest commercial advertisement companies in Brazil, where Meirelles produced numerous video projects. He married Ciça Meirelles, with whom he has two children: Carolina and Quico.

Meirelles's film masterpiece was the adaptation of Paulo Lin's book *Cidade de Deus* (City of God) for the big screen in 2004. It is an action film that illustrates the grim poverty, violence, and oppression in the now-famous favela (slum) in Rio de Janeiro. The film was extremely well received in Brazil and international markets. It received multiple nominations at the Cannes Film Festival: Best Cinematography, Best Film Editing, Best Adapted Screenplay, and Best Director. Meirelles was also nominated for an Academy Award as Best Director. What followed was work in Hollywood as director of the films *Blindness* in 2008 and *360* in 2011. Then Meirelles turned his attention to television, where he produced *A verdade de cada um* (To Each His Own) for the National Geographic Channel in 2013 and *Felizes para sempre?* (Happily Ever After?) for Rede Globo in 2015. Due to his status in the entertainment industry in Brazil, he was selected as one of the creative directors to organize the opening ceremony of the 2016 Summer Olympics in Rio de Janeiro. This prolific filmmaker is likely to still surprise world audiences in the future.

See also: Chapter 15: Olympic Games, Rio de Janeiro 2016. Chapter 16: Overview; Cinema and Film Festivals; Rede Globo and Other Television Networks.

Further Reading

Kwon, Oliver, and Steve Solot. 2015. *Brazilian Cinema Today: Essays by Critics and Experts from across Brazil*. Rio de Janeiro: Latin American Training Center.

Tosta, Antonio Luciano de Andrade. 2013. "Fictional and Everyday Violence: the Brazilian Audience as an Interpretive Community of Brazilian Cinema." *Canadian Journal of Latin American and Caribbean Studies* 38, no. 1 (May): 17–34. Accessed July 13, 2019. http://connection.ebscohost.com/c/essays/100973072/fictional-everyday-violence-brazilian-audience-as-interpretive-community-brazilian-cinema

Turan, Kenneth. 2016. "Why Was Edgy Director Fernando Meirelles Chosen to Direct Rio's Opening Ceremony? A Revealing Film Review." *Los Angeles Times,* August 5. Accessed July 13, 2019. http://www.latimes.com/entertainment/movies/la-et-mn-city-of-god-20160805-snap-story.html

Reality Television Shows

The genre of reality television shows became popular toward the end of the 1990s worldwide. Shows in the United States such as *The Amazing Race, Survivor,* and *American Idol* captured the attention of large audiences, and they became franchises to be replicated in other countries. The first reality show in Portuguese was *Big Brother Brazil* (BBB) broadcasted by Rede Globo in 2002. The host, Pedro Bial, is a respected journalist who has hosted all seventeen seasons since the beginning. The concept of a group of strangers living together without outside contact while all their movements were being recorded quickly captivated audiences. The result was a proliferation of TV reality shows that were transmitted during prime time (6 p.m. to midnight), and they even competed for airtime with the beloved Brazilian telenovelas. According to the Internet Movie Database (IMDb) and the Instituto Brasileiro de Opinião Pública e Estatística (IBOPE), which is the leader in public media research in Latin America, the five most popular reality television shows in Brazil in 2017–2018 are:

1. *Ultimate Beast Master* (since 2017). The new show follows a similar format to *American Ninja Warrior* in the United States where participants compete to overcome a series of challenging physical obstacles for a substantial cash prize.
2. *The Voice Brazil* (since 2014). Amateur singers compete to be selected and trained by one of four celebrity musical coaches to obtain a cash prize and a potentially lucrative recording contract.
3. *Big Brother Brazil* (since 2002). Participants are recorded living together in a house without privacy and trying to avoid getting kicked out every week based on tasks assigned.
4. *A facenda*/The Farm (since 2009). A group of former celebrities live and work together in a farm for twelve weeks, unless they get ejected in any given week.

5. *Pedro pelo mundo*/The Wonderer (since 2016). Television journalist Pedro Andrade is recorded going to off-the-beaten-path destinations while covering travel adventures, exotic food, and cultural topics.

Advertisers pay careful attention to the ratings generated by reality TV shows. In addition to prime-time television, each season of these shows sets new records on comments posted in social media accounts, including Facebook, Twitter, and Instagram. As the show increases in popularity, so does the price of advertising commercials. Moreover, given the continuing increase in Internet use and the availability of mobile phones in Brazil, advertising firms are likely to also increase the number of commercials targeting audiences of reality television shows.

See also: Chapter 16: Overview; Rede Globo and Other Television Networks; Social Media and Internet Use.

Further Reading

Holmes, Ryan. 2013. "The Future of Social Media? Forget about the U.S., Look to Brazil." *Forbes*, September 12. Accessed on June 22, 2019. http://www.forbes.com/sites/ciocentral/2013/09/12/the-future-of-social-media-forget-about-the-u-s-look-to-brazil/#280efe6a3c9a

Internet Movie Database. http://www.imdb.com

Internet Movie Database. "Most Popular Reality-TV Titles with Country of Origin, Brazil." IMDb.com. Accessed June 22, 2019. http://www.imdb.com/search/title?countries=br&genres=reality_tv&sort=moviemeter,asc

Phillips, Dominic. 2012. "Brazil's Spicy Reality TV War Gets More Revealing." *Bloomberg News*, January 12. Accessed June 22, 2019. https://www.bloomberg.com/view/articles/2012-01-12/brazil-s-spicy-reality-tv-war-gets-more-revealing-dom-phillips

Puin, Karolina. 2012. "What Brazilians Watch on TV." *Brazil Business*. June 9. Accessed on June 22, 2019. http://thebrazilbusiness.com/article/what-brazilians-watch-on-tv

ZIGT Media. "The Power of Reality TV Shows in Brazil." *ZIGT Media*. Zigtmedia.com. January 9. Accessed June 22, 2019. https://zigt.com/power-reality-tv-shows-brazil

Rede Globo and Other Television Networks

Rede Globo (known simply as Globo) is the largest commercial television network in Brazil. The free-to-air network was created on January 1, 1965, by Roberto Marinho, and his family is still the main owner. Globo actually managed to grow during the military dictatorship (1964–1985) by working together with the authoritarian government to create light entertainment, promote national pride, and control the political discourse nationwide. Throughout the 1970s and 1980s, Globo expanded tremendously due to its popular programming and investment in technology. Today, in terms of annual revenue generated worldwide, Globo is the second-largest network in the world, after

ABC in the United States. The main headquarters are located in Rio de Janeiro. From this location, Rede Globo coordinates the programming of its 122 affiliate stations throughout Brazil, Globo Portugal, as well as its Globe TV International. In the United States, cable channels such as DirectTV, Dish Network, Spectrum, and Charter carry the channel Globo TV International as part of their programming.

For a large number of Brazilians, television provides the main source of entertainment. According to the Instituto Brasileiro de Opinião Pública e Estatística (IBOPE)—the leader on public media research in Latin America—average Brazilians spend at least five hours a day watching TV. Rede Globo reaches 99.6 percent of Brazilians, delivering daily content to over 184 million viewers. Globo is well known for its programming of intriguing telenovelas, major sporting events, reliable news, and general entertainment.

Globo has been a leader in developing special programming catering to the needs of the Brazilian market. In the 1970s, it established itself as the world leader in telenovelas (soap operas) that are now the main source of entertainment in Brazil. Globo hired large numbers of writers, actors, and directors to develop telenovelas that were truly unique and not simply a copy of foreign soap operas. The result was that the network became the leading exporter of telenovelas. Recent popular telenovelas include *Avenida Brasil* (2012), *Novo mundo* (2017), and *Deus salve o rei* (God Save the King) (2018). In another example of leadership, Globo introduced the first reality show to the national audience; *Big Brother Brazil* (BBB) became an instant hit in 2002, and it led to a proliferation of such shows in multiple networks in Brazil.

Within Brazil, Rede Globo competes with other television networks including (in order of popularity) Rede Record, Sistema Brasileiro de Televisão (SBT), Rede Bandeirantes (Band), TVCultura, and RedeTV. In addition, it competes with the cable channel NET and multiple satellite channels that include ESPN Brasil, Cine Brazil TV, Animal Planet, HBO Brazil, and a vast array of foreign satellite channels in several languages. Overall, competition generates positive results for television viewers since their choices in different genres continue to expand.

See also: Chapter 15: Overview; Telenovelas. Chapter 16: Overview; Reality Television Shows.

Further Reading

Early Television Museum. "The History of Television in Brazil." Early Television Museum. http://www.earlytelevision.org/brazil_tv_history.html

Phillips, Dominic. 2012. "Brazil's Spicy Reality TV War Gets More Revealing." *Bloomberg News,* January 12. Accessed May 18, 2019. https://www.bloomberg.com/view/articles/2012-01-12/brazil-s-spicy-reality-tv-war-gets-more-revealing-dom-phillips

Porto, Mauro P. 2013. *Media Power and Democratization in Brazil: TV Globo and the Dilemmas of Political Accountability.* Routledge: New York.

Puin, Karolina. 2012. "What Brazilians Watch on TV." *Brazil Business,* June 9. Accessed May 18, 2019. http://thebrazilbusiness.com/article/what-brazilians-watch-on-tv

Rede Globo Official Website. http://www.globo.com

Salles, Walter, Jr. (1956–)

Walter Moreira Salles Jr. is a prolific Brazilian filmmaker, producer, and director. He was born on April 12, 1956, in Rio de Janeiro and trained in Los Angeles at the School of Cinematic Arts at the University of Southern California. He has made more than twenty films to date, and forged a professional career that has placed him among the best filmmakers in the world. On a personal level, he married Maria Klabin, with whom he had one son named Vicente Salles.

Salles established his reputation as a filmmaker in Brazil during the 1990s. His first movie, *Terra estrangeira* (Foreign Land), in 1995 was well received but a minor success commercially. However, his next film in 1998, *Central do Brasil* (Central Station), was not only a hit in Brazil, but it did tremendously well internationally with two Academy Award nominations and a Golden Globe Award for Best Foreign Language Film. No other Brazilian had ever achieved that honor before, especially with a movie that depicts the harsh conditions of poor children in Brazil. It also received the Golden Bear Award at the Berlin International Film Festival. However, Salles did not slow down after achieving notoriety on the global stage. His 2001 film *Abril despedaçado* (Behind the Sun) also received international acclaim and was nominated for another Golden Globe Award.

In 2004, Salles worked on non-Portuguese films for the first time. His most celebrated work so far is *Diarios de motocicleta* (The Motorcycle Diaries), based on the early years of the legendary Ernesto Che Guevara. As a director, he worked with actor Gael García Bernal to release this film in Spanish that became a monetary success in both Latin American and European markets. Continuing his work in Spanish, he coproduced *Hermanas* (Sisters) in Argentina, released in 2005; it was highly acclaimed by regional film critics. Then Salles accepted the challenge to direct his first film in English; *On the Road* was released in 2012. He worked with producer Francis Ford Coppola to bring to the screen an adaptation of Jack Kerouac's original novel *On the Road*. The film was nominated for a Palme d'Or Award at the Cannes Film Festival. Given the prolific nature of this talented Brazilian director and filmmaker, it is likely that his best work still lies ahead.

See also: Chapter 16: Overview; Cinema and Film Festivals.

Further Reading

Bozzola, Lucia. "Walter Salles Jr. Biography, Filmography, and Awards." AllMovie.com. Accessed April 25, 2019. https://www.allmovie.com/artist/walter-salles-jr-p109635

Heise, Tatiana Signorelli. 2012. *Remaking Brazil: Contested National Identities in Contemporary Brazilian Cinema*. Cardiff: University of Wales Press.

Kwon, Oliver, and Steve Solot. 2015. *Brazilian Cinema Today: Essays by Critics and Experts from across Brazil*. Rio de Janeiro: Latin American Training Center.

Nagib, Lucia. 2003. *The New Brazilian Cinema*. London: I. B. Taurus in Association with Centre for Brazilian Studies, University of Oxford.

Social Media and Internet Use

The Brazilian government has actively promoted the expansion of Internet access throughout the country in partnership with the private sector, even to remote rural and isolated locations. In a country of roughly 210 million people, the middle class has grown at the beginning of the twenty-first century, and over 50 percent of the population now has access to the Internet. According to 2017 international statistics reports, Brazil had 119.7 million Internet users, which makes it the fourth largest in the world after China, India, and the United States. The numbers in 2018 reached 123.21 million.

Recent statistics from 2014 to 2018 reveal that almost 80 percent of Internet users in Brazil use social media. At the end of 2016, Facebook had the most extensive penetration rate, with 63 percent of Internet consumers using it. WhatsApp was in second place at 53 percent, and 40 percent of Brazilian Internet users followed Instagram. It is worth noting that the topics that dominated the conversation on social media were family, soccer, and soap operas.

From a marketing perspective, Brazilians seem to have positive attitudes about purchasing items online. Major companies (such as Coca-Cola, L'Oreal, Nike, and Adidas) have increased their advertising campaigns dramatically on social networks. However, most of the advertising budget in Brazil (over 60 percent) is still mostly allocated to prime-time shows on television.

The expansion of the Internet has threatened the existence of printed newspapers worldwide. Brazil, however, seems to go against the current because newspaper circulation actually continues to increase. Part of the strategy was that well-established newspapers offered paid digital subscriptions via their phones or computers. Recent surveys reveal that most Brazilians still trust the news from newspapers (digital or print) a lot more than from other online digital platforms such as Google, Facebook, or Twitter.

ANITTA (1993–), A CONTEMPORARY POP ARTIST

Larissa de Macedo Machado is better known by her artistic name Anitta. She is a contemporary Brazilian singer, actress, dancer, and television host. Her musical style blends international pop with reggae, bossa nova, and R&B. Anitta certainly understands the power of digital media. She was discovered in 2010 with a YouTube video showing her signing talent. In 2012, the success of her song "Meiga e Abusada" (Sweet and Pushy) led to a recording contract with Warner Music Brazil. In 2017, she released her first English song "Will I See You" as part of her album *CheckMate*, which reveals her international aspirations. In 2018, she won the iHeart Music Award in the Social Star Category.

Sources: Antunes, Anderson. 2013. "Could Brazil's Latest Music Sensation Anitta Be a Global Superstar in the Making?" *Forbes*, August 30. Accessed June 19, 2019. https://www.forbes.com/sites/andersonantunes/2013/08/30/could-brazils-latest-music-sensation-anitta-be-a-global-superstar-in-the-making/#c3c9672432aa

The use of the Internet and social media platforms is predicted to grow in Brazil. Two recent major global events—the 2014 Soccer World Cup and the 2016 Summer Olympics—brought international attention to Brazil, and advertising budgets for them were increased exponentially on social media. In addition, the large majority of Internet users in Brazil are still under twenty-five years of age, and the use of social networks has already affected social patterns. For example, transportation apps, such as Uber and Cabify, are so popular in Brazil that they have disrupted the traditional cab networks. Therefore, the National Congress of Brazil was forced to pass national legislation in March 2018 in order to regulate the business practices of such companies.

See also: Chapter 16: Overview; Major Newspapers.

Further Reading

Alves, Lise. 2018. "Brazilian Congress Approves Rules for Transportation Apps." *Rio Times,* March 1. Accessed May 3, 2019. http://riotimesonline.com/brazil-news/rio-business/brazilian-congress-approves-rules-for-transportation-apps

Bonilla, Laura. 2012. "Newspapers Alive and Kicking in Brazil." *News.com.au.* August 2. Accessed May 3, 2019. http://www.news.com.au/world/breaking-news/newspapers-alive-and-kicking-in-brazil/news-story/dea36922af14ba7ebc06c8a835cff46c

Holmes, Ryan. 2013. "The Future of Social Media? Forget about the U.S., Look to Brazil." *Forbes,* September 12. Accessed May 3, 2019. http://www.forbes.com/sites/ciocentral/2013/09/12/the-future-of-social-media-forget-about-the-u-s-look-to-brazil/#280efe6a3c9a

Statista. "Number of Internet Users in Brazil from 2017 to 2023." *Statista: The Statistics Portal*, Statista.com. Accessed May 3, 2019. https://www.statista.com/statistics/255208/number-of-internet-users-in-brazil

Statista. "Penetration of Leading Social Networks in Brazil as of 4th Quarter 2017." *Statista: The Statistics Portal*, Statista.com. Accessed May 3, 2019. https://www.statista.com/statistics/284424/brazil-social-network-penetration

Sports Icons

Brazilians love to practice and watch sports. While *futebol* (soccer) is the king of sports, basketball, jiu-jitsu, volleyball, and motorsports (Formula One) are also widely popular. There is a long list of athletes who have received multiple awards in Brazil, but a few of them have reached iconic status in their relative sports, both domestically and internationally. The top four most popular athletes are:

Pelé (Soccer)

Edson Arantes do Nascimento (1940–), simply known as Pelé, is the most legendary *futebol* (soccer) player ever. In fact, both the International Federation of Football History and Statistics (IFFHS) and the International Olympic Committee voted Pelé in

1999 as the Best World Athlete of the twentieth century. He started playing professionally with the team Santos when he was only fifteen, and he made the national team right away. He is also the only player in the world to have won three FIFA World Cup titles (1958, 1962, and 1970) with his national team. His charismatic personality paired with his agile style of playing *futebol* brought international attention and pride to Brazil.

Oscar Schmidt (Basketball)

Oscar Schmidt Bezerra (1958–) is a retired Brazilian basketball athlete of international stature. He played professionally in Brazil with multiple teams (Sírio, Bandeirantes, Flamengo, and Barueri) as well as teams in Italy and Spain. In addition, Schmidt holds the record of the Olympic Summer Games basketball all-time leading scorer with 1,093 points. He also earned the record for the most points at any Olympic games (338 points scored at the Seoul Olympics in 1988). Given his prolific career, he earned the nickname Mano Santa (Holy Hand) in Brazil. One of the highlights of his career was to participate as a guest in the opening ceremonies of the 2016 Olympics in Rio de Janeiro.

Hélio Gracie (Brazilian Jiu-Jitsu)

Hélio Gracie (1913–2009) is considered the father of Brazilian jiu-jitsu. He is an iconic figure in Brazil because he adapted the martial art of Japanese jiu-jitsu to be used by anybody in real-fighting situations regardless of their physical build. The new style called Gracie jiu-jitsu became well known on the global stage during the 1990s due to the accomplishments of other martial arts fighters in the family (Royce Gracie and Rickson Gracie). Now, the sport is widely popular in Brazil.

Ayrton Senna (Formula One)

Ayrton Senna da Silva (1960–1994) was an accomplished Brazilian race car driver often lauded as one of the best drivers worldwide. Brazilian motorsports are widely watched in television, and Senna had a large fan base. He won three championships (1988, 1990, and 1991) in the Formula One circuit for the McLaren Team. He died when he was only thirty-four years old in an accident at the San Marino Grand Prix race in 1994. The government of Brazil declared three days of national mourning for Brazilians to remember their national sports icon.

These four sport legends have touched the lives of millions of Brazilians who dream of becoming famous athletes or who simply feel immense national pride based on their sports idols.

See also: Chapter 15 Overview; Brazilian Jiu-Jitsu; *Futebol*; Motor Sports: Formula 1 and Grand Prix; Olympic Games Rio de Janeiro 2016; Pelé (1940–), Ronaldinho (1980–) and Neymar (1992–). Chapter 16: Overview.

Further Reading

Ayrton Senna Legacy. http://www.ayrton-senna-dasilva.com

Kittleson, Roger. 2014. *The Country of Football: Soccer and the Making of Modern Brazil.* Berkeley: University of California Press.

Oscar Schmidt Official Website. http://www.oscarschmidt.com.br

Pedreira, Roberto. 2016. "Top 30 Myths and Misconceptions about Brazilian Jiu-Jitsu." *Global Training Report,* May 29. Accessed May 11, 2019. http://www.global-training-report.com/myths.htm

Pelé Official Website. https://pele10.com

Xuxa (1963–)

Maria da Graça Meneghel was born on March 27, 1963, in Santa Rosa, in the state of Rio Grande do Sul. Commonly known as Xuxa, she is a model, actress, pop singer, television presenter, and a savvy businesswoman. She became a celebrity in Brazil in the 1980s with her television program *Xou da Xuxa* (Xuxa's Show) on TV Globo, the largest network in Brazil. The attractive blonde delivered a daily high-energy show that included dancing, singing, and games in a party atmosphere to entertain children. She earned the nickname Rainha dos Baixinhos (Queen of the Little Ones), as she called all the children. *Xou da Xuxa* was a tremendous success, with 2,000 shows broadcast from 1986 to 1992. Her image also inspired collections of toys, dolls, and a clothing line.

The premise of her show launched Xuxa into international television markets. A Spanish version, *El Show de Xuxa*, was released in Argentina in 1992, and it soon became a continental sensation throughout Latin America for three seasons. The show aired on a daily basis in sixteen different countries. Then a similar show was launched in Spain titled *Xuxa Park* with limited success. After working on multiple music and television projects for a few years, Xuxa reappeared on RecordTV in 2015 as a judge on *Dancing Brasil*, a reality show similar to the popular *Dancing with the Stars* in the United States.

Xuxa has had a prolific and profitable music career. The songs from the *Xou da Xuxa* show earned eight platinum records and sold more than 2 million copies. Considering that she sang children songs, her tremendous accomplishments include: 915 recorded songs, 28 LPs, 400 gold records, two Latin Grammy Awards, and collectively sales of over 45 million copies. She has also managed her money well; numerous publications have named her the richest artist in Brazil.

At a social level, Xuxa has used her fame and image to bring attention to important issues in Brazil, especially those affecting children. For example, she earned a presidential medal of honor in 1989 for her active involvement in a children's campaign to completely eradicate polio in the country. Through her Xuxa Meneghel Foundation, she embarked on a long campaign titled Uso Responsável da Internet (Responsible Use of the Internet) in 2008 to educate young people on the potential dangers of social media. Starting in 2013, Xuxa also lent her image and resources through her foundation to work with agencies in Argentina and Paraguay to combat sexual exploitation of children and teenagers across international borders. There is no doubt that Xuxa is a popular cultural icon in Brazil who continues to revel in her title as the Rainha dos Baixinhos.

See also: Chapter 16: Overview; Rede Globo and Other Television Networks; Reality Television Shows; Social Media and Internet Use.

Further Reading

Duncan, Amy. 1991. "Meet Brazil's Queen of Kid TV." *Christian Science Monitor,* January 22. Accessed June 1, 2019. https://www.csmonitor.com/1991/0122/pxuxa.html

Nichols, Elizabeth Gackstetter, and Timothy R. Robins. 2015. *Pop Culture in Latin America and the Caribbean.* Santa Barbara, CA: ABC-CLIO.

"Xuxa Meneghel Trajetória." *TV Globo,* Globo.com. Accessed June 1, 2019. http://memoriaglobo.globo.com/perfis/talentos/xuxa-meneghel/trajetoria.htm

APPENDIX A

A DAY IN THE LIFE

Note: The following four stories are fictional, but they are based on the realities of daily life in different regions of Brazil.

A DAY IN THE LIFE OF A UNIVERSITY STUDENT

Isabella Oliveira is a student at the Universidade Federal de São Paulo, where she studies economics. She was admitted based on her high score on the *vestibular* entrance exam. At this institution, the government covers most of the expenses for students, but the admission process is extremely competitive.

Isabella wakes up at 7:30 a.m., and she eats a light breakfast consisting of coffee and toast with jam. While eating, she checks her mobile phone for messages and postings from her friends on social media. She responds quickly to a few messages before getting ready for school. She packs her books, supplies, and a snack. She then walks to the metro stop of the North-South line. São Paulo has over 20 million inhabitants, and the traffic is always heavy. Therefore, Isabella must plan on at least forty minutes to get to the university.

Her first class (Principles of Macroeconomics) begins at 9:30 a.m. This class takes place in a large lecture hall with almost one hundred students since it is an introductory course required for all economics majors. The professor lectures without taking any questions to cover all the material from the textbook. The class ends at 11:30 a.m., and Isabella has an opportunity to socialize briefly with her classmates and eat a light snack she brought from home.

Isabella's second class (International Trade) begins at 12 p.m. This class only has about twenty-five students because it is a specialized course reserved for students focused on the economic intricacies of international trade, such as exports and imports. The professor makes the course more interactive by encouraging student questions and participation. The instructor also discusses specific guidelines for a group research project where students must work in collaboration to develop a project together. All the details of the assignment are posted on the class portal webpage accessible to all registered students. The class ends at 1:30 p.m.

Isabella had previously made plans to meet two of her friends at the university cafeteria after class. They meet at 2 p.m. to eat a light meal consisting mostly of sandwiches and drinks while catching up on the latest topics of the day and making plans to attend a live concert the following week. She then goes to the library to study for about an hour.

After a long day at the university, Isabella goes home at 5 p.m., and the metro is already extremely crowded. When she gets home, she goes to her room to relax, check her e-mail, reply to messages, and listen to music for a while. Isabella's parents arrive from their jobs at 8:30 p.m. Then they all eat dinner together at 9:30 p.m. It is a simple meal consisting of a salad and reheated leftovers from the day before. While eating, they share what is going on in their lives.

A DAY IN THE LIFE OF AN OFFICE WORKER

Gabriel Silva is a twenty-nine-year-old office manager who works for a real estate company in Rio de Janeiro. The company specializes in commercial real estate for businesses that need office space in high-rise buildings in Rio. Gabriel migrated to the city from the town of Diamantina in Minas Gerais in order to find better employment opportunities, and he now lives with a roommate. He was promoted to his current office position after working at the company for five years doing different jobs.

Gabriel wakes up early at 5 a.m. to exercise before going to work. He likes to run early in the morning. Then he showers quickly, and he usually goes out of the house in a hurry. On the way to the bus stop, he eats at one of the modest bakeries (*padarias*) near his house to get a coffee and a toasted French roll with jam.

Gabriel's work at the office begins at 9 a.m. Today, the agenda shows a meeting with potential international investors at 10 a.m. Consequently, he prepares informational materials, checks the digital equipment, and directs other office staff to prepare the conference room. He also coordinates the mandatory *cafezinho* (espresso, or little coffee) service, which is usually served in business settings to facilitate a friendly conversation before actually discussing the purpose or agenda items for the meeting. The meeting lasts two hours, and the office staff has to clean up, follow up on editing the business minutes, record financial commitments made during the meeting, and prepare a list of contacts for future communications.

Gabriel and two friends leave the office for lunch at 1:30 p.m. Since they have an hour, they go to a reasonably priced *lanchonete* (snack bar) near their building. It is a casual location with foldable chairs and tables. Their substantial meal includes rice, beans, vegetables, and a small portion of meat. It is also a time to socialize with friends and colleagues. They return to the office by 2:30 p.m. Gabriel checks the inventory for necessary office supplies, and he fills out a purchase order to be sent to their supplier. Then two real estate agents give Gabriel a copy of two finalized real estate sale contracts that have to be reviewed by an attorney as soon as possible. Therefore, he contacts a courier service to come and pick them up right away. Finally, he closes the office at 6 p.m.

On his way home, Gabriel stops at a small neighborhood market to buy fruit and milk, and he gets home by 7:30 p.m. He checks his mobile phone for personal e-mails, and he calls his parents. His roommate arrives at 8:30 p.m., and they have a light dinner together at 9:30 p.m. Gabriel shares with him that he would like to take a vacation to visit his parents in Minas Gerais. However, he is waiting for the bonus *décimo terceiro salário* (thirteenth salary), which will be paid in December. Brazilian labor law requires companies to provide an extra monthly salary payment to all registered employees who worked the entire year. This is a concept that does not exist in the United States, but it is legally mandatory in Brazil. Gabriel goes to bed at 11:30 p.m., and he gets ready for another hectic day.

A DAY IN THE LIFE OF A HOUSEWIFE

Ana Souza is a housewife in the city of Fortaleza in the northeastern part of the country. The family moved here three years ago in search of better economic opportunities in a large city by the beach that thrives on tourism, fishing, and manufacturing. Her husband works two entry-level jobs to provide for the family. They have two children: a seven-year-old boy and an eleven-year-old girl. Ana starts her day bright and early by 6:45 a.m. when she wakes up to get breakfast ready for everyone. The house is somewhat chaotic in the morning when kids shuffle to get ready for school and her husband leaves for work in a hurry. She leaves the house by 7:30 a.m. to walk the children to school; they start classes at 8 a.m.

Ana has a busy schedule. On her way back home, she stops at the local market to buy food for the next two days. When she gets home, she sets a load on the washing machine. She then decides to cook *feijoada* for tonight. It is a lot of work, but it is her family's favorite dish. It is a hearty stew with black beans and different cuts of pork or beef cooked together on a clay pot at very low heat. While it cooks for a few hours, she makes the beds, washes the dishes from breakfast, and picks up around the house.

She leaves the house at 12:30 p.m. to pick up the children from school at 1 p.m. While Fortaleza appears to be a picture-perfect tropical beach location that displays wealth on the surface, another reality lies beneath: the tourism industry functions on extremely low wages in order to be profitable. The economic reality of most local Brazilians is that they face high living costs, and they have to enroll their children in low-performing and crowded schools that function on two shifts a day with extremely reduced hours. Ana walks home with her children for thirty minutes.

They will be home only for a few hours. First, both children eat a light snack. Then, while they do their homework, Ana takes the clothes out of the washer to hang them outside; she then prepares rice to serve with the *feijoada* tonight. Children watch television for a while before getting ready for their after-school activities. By 4 p.m., they walk together to the neighborhood sports complex, where her son practices soccer and her daughter takes dancing lessons. They return home by 7 p.m., and the fight begins when the sweaty children question whether they really need to take a shower. She eats dinner with her children at 8 p.m., but her husband is still not home due to his second job at a factory. The children brush their teeth, and they go to bed at roughly 9:30 p.m. Ana still has to clean up after dinner. While she is doing the dishes, her husband arrives at 10:30 p.m. Shen then warms up a dish for him, and they chat about what happened during the day. They go to bed at 11:30 p.m. completely exhausted. They must rest for a similar day tomorrow.

A DAY IN THE LIFE OF AN AGRICULTURAL WORKING FAMILY

Pedro Santos is an agricultural worker in the Amazon Basin area in the northern part of Brazil. He moved his entire family here from the northeastern *sertão* region because the recurring severe droughts over there did not allow him to make a living anymore out of his own plot of land. He now works for a large export corporation that owns extensive sections of land for agriculture and cattle. The family lives in a cramped, poorly constructed home, but they dream of owning their own piece of land someday. Pedro's routine starts early at 4 a.m. He prepares breakfast for himself and his wife consisting of strong coffee, toast, and some fruit. His wife, Júlia, wakes up shortly after about 4:30 a.m. to prepare his meals for the long working day under the hot punishing sun. She warms food she cooked the day before, and she prepares two plastic containers. One of them has black beans and chunks of beef, and the other one contains rice, vegetables, and *carne de sol* (salted dried meat). He also needs a large container of water for the entire day. Then he washes his face, takes his hat, and walks out of the house about 5 a.m. to catch the company truck that picks up workers in his neighborhood. He prepares mentally for a twelve-hour workday.

At home, it is 7 a.m., and Júlia gets the children ready for school. They eat breakfast, brush their teeth, prepare their backpacks, and get their lunch sack for the day. They all leave about 7:30 a.m., and they stop at the neighbor's house to pick up another three children. Júlia takes them all to school, and the other children's mom will pick them all up after school so Júlia can go to work. She drops off all the children right before school begins at 8 a.m. In this agricultural region, they only have class for four hours and thirty minutes for lunch. Júlia then rushes to make it to work by 8:30 a.m. She only works a part-time shift of six hours at an export packing company that sends soybeans to China, which is now Brazil's number one trading partner. She must stand all day while she works, and she complains about leg pains, but the company does not offer medical benefits to part-time or seasonal workers. Therefore, she quietly puts up with it.

Meanwhile, Pedro works in the fields under the relentless sun. During his thirty-minute lunch break, he talks to his tired coworkers. They all suffer from multiple body pains, but that is the nature of a peasant life. They talk about how they wish a better life for their children. They all have similar aspirations of obtaining a piece of land through the ever-elusive agrarian reform promised by the federal government. Then Pedro and his friends get back to work; they have another six hours left.

Júlia picks up the children at the neighbor's house at 4 p.m. They go home to do homework while she cooks dinner and picks up around the house. Pedro gets home extremely tired by 8 p.m., and they all eat dinner together. They talk about their activities during the day, even if they are repetitive. Finally, they go to bed about 10 p.m., as they get ready for another day.

APPENDIX B

GLOSSARY OF KEY TERMS

Açai: Fruit from northern Brazil, rich in minerals, vitamins, and antioxidants.

***Alagados*:** Slums in the state of Bahia, similar to the word *favelas* in Rio de Janeiro.

***Aldeias*:** Villages.

ANA: Agência Nacional de Águas—National Water Agency of Brazil.

ANP: National Agency of Petroleum, Natural Gas, and Biofuels.

Antropofagia: Artistic wave that emphasized national pride rooted in the Brazilian indigenous traditions while rejecting the European colonial past.

Arquivo: Files and records.

***Autos*:** Brief religious plays.

Baiana: Woman from the state of Bahia.

Bairro: District or neighborhood within a city or a town.

Banco de dados: Database; a collection of data.

***Bandeirantes*:** Slave hunters who explored the interior of Brazil from São Paulo during the colonial period.

Blocos: Neighborhood dancing groups popular during Carnival.

BM&F BOVESPA: Stock Exchange of São Paulo.

BN: Biblioteca Nacional—National Library.

Bolsa Família: Conditional cash transfer program for low-income families that requires school attendance and vaccinations for minor children.

Bossa nova: Brazilian musical genre from 1950 to 1960s blending jazz and samba rhythms.

BRICS: International alliance of emerging economies that includes Brazil, Russia, India, China, and South Africa.

Caboclo: Person with indigenous and white ancestry.

Cachaça: Brazil's national alcoholic drink used in traditional cocktails such as *caipirinha*.

Cafezinho: A small, strong shot of coffee.

Cafuso: Person of indigenous and African heritage.

Caipira: Country people usually identified as hardworking but with little education.

Caipirinha: Brazil's national cocktail made with sugarcane, ice, lime, and mostly *cachaça* liquor.

Candomblé: Religion based on African rituals based on Yoruba and Bantu traditions.

Capoeira: Afro-Brazilian martial arts accompanied by music, dance, and choreography.

Cariocas: People from Rio de Janeiro.

Carne de sol: Thin slices of beef salted and dried out in the sun.

Cavaquinho: Small instrument with four strings often used in samba music.

CBS: Confederação Brasileira de Futebol—Brazilian Soccer Confederation.

Chafarizes: Public fountains.

Chanchada: Musical light comedy.

Churrasco: Brazilian barbeque prepared on a pit and sold at a *churrascaria*.

Colegas: Acquaintances.

Comércio eletrônico: E-commerce.

Comida a/por kilo: Buffet-style restaurants that charge food by the weight (kilo).

Concretismo: Artistic movement of the 1950s and 1960s based on the use of geometric shapes and abstract images.

Copacabana: One of the most popular beaches in Rio de Janeiro.

Colonel: In non-military terms, a person in rural regions who provides favors in exchange for political loyalty.

Cortiço: Multifamily dwelling units with communal bathrooms and little privacy for low-income populations.

Cristo Redentor: Iconic statue of Christ the Redeemer at the top of Corcovado Mountain in Rio de Janeiro.

Degregados: Criminals who were expelled from Portugal.

Democracia racial: Outdated sociological term used to describe race relations in Brazil with the basic premise that the country does not have racial discrimination because everyone essentially gets along with one another.

Dendê: Palm oil with an orange-like color used in cooking.

Despachantes: Intermediaries who facilitate complex bureaucratic transactions.

Desquite: Legal separation but not quite a legal divorce.

Electrobras: The national electrical company; one of the major utility companies providing electricity nationwide and to neighboring countries.

Embraer: Airplane manufacturer of midrange airplanes and military aircraft.

Embratur: Brazilian Institute of Tourism.

Empregada doméstica: A maid who cooks and cleans the homes of middle- and upper-income households.

Fantasias: Costumes for Carnival celebrations.

Favela: Slums or shantytowns in urban areas usually with unsanitary conditions and few public services.

Fazendeiro: Farmer who owns a large farming estate.

Feijoada: Brazil's national dish usually prepared as a stew with black beans, salted beef, and pork sausages cooked in a clay pot and served with white rice and collard greens.

Feitorias: Trading posts.

Folha de São Paulo: The largest newspaper in Brazil, published in both Portuguese and English, with wide coverage of sports, politics, business, entertainment, and culture.

Folia de Reis: Three Wise Men celebration held in January.

FUNAI: Fundação Nacional do Índio—National Indigenous Foundation, which promotes and protects the rights of indigenous population in Brazil.

Futebol: Soccer, by far the most popular sport in Brazil.

Guaraná: Fruit originated from the Amazon region with a high content of caffeine; it is also a popular soft drink in Brazil.

IBAMA: Instituto Brasileiro do Meio Ambiente e Dos Recursos Naturais Renováveis—Brazilian Institute for the Environment and Renewable Resources.

IBGE: Instituto Brasileiro de Geografia e Estadística—Brazilian Institute of Geography and Statistics; it also publishes the national census.

Inconfidência Mineira: Unsuccessful regional independence attempt in 1789 to separate from Portugal during colonial rule.

Índio: Indian or indigenous.

INEP: National Institute for Educational Studies and Research.

INPA: Instituto Nacional de Pesquisas da Amazônia—Brazilian National Institute of Amazonian Research.

Ipanema: Beach in Rio de Janeiro popularized by the bossa nova song "The Girl from Ipanema."

Itamaraty: Brazilian Ministry of Foreign Relations.

JBS SA: Brazilian company and the largest producer of meat in global markets.

Jeito/jeitinho: An ability to improvise in order to solve difficult tasks.

Jogo bonito: The Brazilian style for playing soccer (beautiful game).

Lanchonete: Small establishments to grab a quick meal, such as sandwiches, shakes, and juices.

Lei Alfonso Arinos: Law that established racism as an official crime in 1951.

Lei Áurea: The Golden Law that abolished slavery in 1888 when it was signed by Isabel Princess Regent of Brazil, which made Brazil the last country in the Western Hemisphere to abolish the practice.

Lei de Cotas: Law of Social Quotas, providing affirmative action policies for university admission and civil government jobs for disadvantaged groups in Brazil.

Lei de Migração 2017: New immigration law approved in 2017 that provides immigrants with the same legal rights and obligations as native-born citizens and regulates their entry and stay in Brazil.

Lei Maria da Penha: Law enacted in 2006 to protect women from domestic violence.

Macumba: African religion popular in Brazil.

Maloca: A longhouse in the Amazon region typically used as a communal dwelling.

Mameluco: Person of white and indigenous heritage.

Maracanã: Iconic soccer stadium in Rio de Janeiro built in 1950 and then upgraded for the 2014 World Cup.

Maracujá: Passion fruit.

Marajás: Overpaid public employees.

MEC: Brazilian Ministry of Education.

Mega-Sena: National Brazilian lottery.

Mercosul/Mercosur: Economic alliance among South American nations including Brazil, Argentina, Uruguay, and Paraguay.

Movimento dos Trabalhadores Sem Terra (MST): Landless Rural Workers' Movement with over 1.5 million members seeking land reform for poor farmers.

Mulatto: Person of black and white ancestry.

Música sertaneja: Brazilian country music, one of the most popular contemporary musical genres on the radio.

Navegador: Internet browser.

Negro retinto: A black person with very dark complexion.

Nossa Senhora Aparecida: Our Lady of Aparecida, widely venerated by Brazilian Catholics and often regarded as Brazil's patron saint.

Operação Lava Jato: Undercover operation "Car Wash" that exposed unprecedented levels of corruption and money laundering in 2015 between high-level politicians and government corporations.

Orixás: African Gods in Afro-Brazilian religions.

Padaria: Bakery that usually also sells juices, milk, and candy.

Padrinhos: Godparents.

Panelinha: A small group of people with shared ideas who offer support for its members.

Pão de Açúcar: The iconic Sugar Loaf Mountain, one of the most photographed locations in Rio de Janeiro.

Pão de queijo: Cheese roll with chewy filling and made with either wheat or tapioca flour; typical snack from the interior state of Minas Gerais.

PARADASP: Pride Organization for the LGBTQ community.

Pardo: Literally "brown" and a general term used to address people with mixed heritage, an official category in the national census.

Parentela: Network of nuclear and extended family members.

Patrão: Person who commands privilege based on wealth.

Paulistas: People from São Paulo.

Petrobras: National Oil Corporation.

Praça: Town square.

Quilombos: Communities for runaway slaves.

Radionovelas: Radio soap operas.

Real: Brazilian currency with the sign R$.

Redes Sociais: Social networks.

Salgados: Small savory snacks sold at bakeries and *lanchonetes;* usually made with dough and filling and prepared either baked or deep-fried; also called *salgadinho.*

Samba: One of the most recognized Afro-Brazilian rhythms based on a popular dance style and percussion instruments.

Samba-reggae: Musical genre linked to Carnival based on a fusion of samba, reggae, and other tropical rhythms.

Santos: Statues based on Catholic saints.

Sertanejos: People who live in the *sertão* region.

Sertão: Semiarid backlands in the inhospitable northern region of Brazil covering parts of the states of Pernambuco, Bahia, Alagoas, Ceará, Rio Grande do Norte, and Piauí.

SUS: Sistema Único de Saúde, Brazilian public health system funded by the government.

Telenovelas: Television soap operas, one of the most popular forms of entertainment.

Terreiro: Open space in Umbanda religion used for ceremonies and worshipping, roughly equivalent to a churchyard.

Tropicalismo: Artistic movement popular in the 1960s based on a fusion of Brazilian and foreign approaches.

TSE: Tribunal Superior Eleitoral—Superior Electoral Court.

Tupi-Guarani: The largest indigenous language group in Brazil.

Umbanda: Brazilian urban religion based on African and indigenous traditions with spiritualist beliefs.

Unipalmares: University for Afro-Brazilian students.

Vestibular: Entrance exam for university admission.

APPENDIX C

FACTS AND FIGURES

Table 1: GEOGRAPHY

Location	Located in central and northeastern South America, Brazil is the continent's largest country. It is bordered to the north by Colombia, Venezuela, Guyana, Suriname, and French Guiana; to the west by Peru and Bolivia; and to the south by Paraguay, Argentina, and Uruguay. The country also has a long eastern coastline on the Atlantic Ocean.
Time Zone	1 hour ahead of U.S. Eastern Standard
Land Borders	9,129 miles
Coastline	4,655 miles
Capital	Brasília
Area	3,286,500 square miles
Climate	In the Amazon basin's tropical rain forest, the climate is hot and wet. In the central and southern uplands' savannah grasslands, the climate is temperate, with warm summers and mild winters. Temperatures in Rio de Janeiro range from 63° F to 85° F.
Land Use	28.56% arable land; 2.32% permanent crops; 10.47% cropland; 23.45% permanent meadows and pastures; 58.93% forest land. (2016)
Arable Land	28.6% (2016)
Arable Land Per Capita	0.37 hectares per person (2015)

Table 2: POPULATION

Population	207,353,000 (estimate) (2017)
World Population Rank	5th (2017)
Population Density	24.8 people per square kilometer (2017)
Population Distribution	86.6% urban (2018)
Age Distribution	
0–14:	22.33%
15–24	16.36%
25–54	43.86%
55–64	9.12%
65+:	8.33% (2017)
Median Age	32.0 years (estimate) (2017)
Population Growth Rate	0.7% per year (estimate) (2018)
Net Migration Rate	−0.1 (estimate) (2018)
Languages	Portuguese
Religious Groups	Christian (% not available)

Table 3: HEALTH

Average Life Expectancy	74.3 years (2018)
Average Life Expectancy, Male	70.7 years (2018)
Average Life Expectancy, Female	78.0 years (2018)
Crude Birth Rate	13.9 per 1,000 people (2018)
Crude Death Rate	6.7 per 1,000 people (2018)
Maternal Mortality	44 per 100,000 live births (2015)
Infant Mortality	13 per 1,000 live births (2017)
Doctors	1.9 per 1,000 people (2016)

Table 4: ENVIRONMENT

CO_2 Emissions	2.6 metric tons per capita (2014)
Alternative and Nuclear Energy	12.5% of total energy use (2014)
Threatened Species	990 (2017)
Protected Areas	2,485,099 square miles (2016)
Total Renewable H_2O Resources per Year	41,316 cubic meters, per person, per year (2017)

Table 5: ENERGY AND NATURAL RESOURCES

Electric Power Generation	578,900,000,000 kilowatt hours per year (estimate) (2016)
Electric Power Consumption	460,800,000,000 kilowatt hours per year (estimate) (2016)
Nuclear Power Plants	1 (2018)
Crude Oil Production	2,622,000 barrels per day (2017)
Crude Oil Consumption	3,087,000 barrels per day (2017)
Natural Gas Production	23,960,000,000 cubic meters per year (estimate) (2017)
Natural Gas Consumption	34,350,000,000 cubic meters per year (estimate) (2017)
Natural Resources	Bauxite, gold, iron ore, manganese, nickel, phosphates, platinum, tin, rare earth elements, uranium, petroleum, hydropower, timber

Table 6: NATIONAL FINANCES

Currency	Real
Total Government Revenues	$819,000,000,000 (estimate) (2017)
Total Government Expenditures	$845,700,000,000 (estimate) (2017)
Budget Deficit	−1.3% (estimate) (2017)
GDP Contribution by Sector	Agriculture: 6.2%; Industry: 21%; Services: 72.8% (2017)
External Debt	$554,500,000,000 (estimate) (2017)
Economic Aid Extended	$0 (2011)
Economic Aid Received	$674,630,000 (2017)

Table 7: INDUSTRY AND LABOR

Gross Domestic Product (GDP)—official exchange rate	$1,868,630,000,000 (estimate) (2018)
GDP per Capita	$9,344 (estimate) (2019)
GDP—Purchasing Power Parity (PPP)	$3,240,319,000,000 (estimate) (2017)
GDP (PPP) per Capita	$15,603 (estimate) (2017)
Industry Products	Textiles, footwear, passenger and commercial vehicles, synthetic rubber, electricity, steel, machinery, cement.
Agriculture Products	Coffee, oranges, soybeans, sugarcane, maize, rice, cocoa, cassava, cattle, milk.
Unemployment	11.5% (2016)
Labor Profile	Agriculture: 10%; Industry: 39.8%; Services: 50.2% (2016)

Table 8: TRADE

Imported Goods	Minerals, machinery and appliances, chemicals, petroleum, plastic and rubber products, coal, metals, foodstuffs, clocks and watches, photographic equipment.
Total Value of Imports	$153,200,000,000 (estimate) (2017)
Exported Goods	Foods and beverages, mineral products, machinery and transportation equipment, fruits and vegetables, coffee, tobacco, textiles, leather footwear.
Total Value of Exports	$217,200,000,000 (estimate) (2017)
Import Partners	China 18.1%, U.S. 16.7%, Argentina 6.3%, Germany 6.1% (2017)
Export Partners	China 21.8%, U.S. 12.5%, Argentina 8.1%, Netherlands 4.3% (2017)
Current Account Balance	$-9,762,000,000 (estimate) (2017)
Weights and Measures	The metric system is in use.

Table 9: EDUCATION

School System	Primary education begins at the age of seven in Brazil. After eight years, students continue to three years of secondary education. Students may also choose to enroll in vocational education, for programs lasting between three and five years, rather than academic secondary school.
Mandatory Education	8 years, from ages 7 to 15
Average Years Spent in School for Current Students	15 (estimate) (2015)
Average Years Spent in School for Current Students, Male	15 (estimate) (2015)
Average Years Spent in School for Current Students, Female	16 (estimate) (2015)
Primary School-age Children Enrolled in Primary School	16,299,166 (2016)
Primary School-age Males Enrolled in Primary School	8,487,784 (2016)
Primary School-age Females Enrolled in Primary School	8,188,141 (2016)
Secondary School-age Children Enrolled in Secondary School	23,501,784 (2016)

Secondary School-age Males Enrolled in Secondary School	11,692,167 (2016)
Secondary School-age Females Enrolled in Secondary School	11,809,617 (2016)
Students Per Teacher, Primary School	21.5 (2016)
Students Per Teacher, Secondary School	16.5 (2016)
Enrollment in Tertiary Education	8,285,475 (2016)
Enrollment in Tertiary Education, Male	3,557,882 (2016)
Enrollment in Tertiary Education, Female	4,727,593 (2016)
Literacy	93% (2016)

Table 10: MILITARY

Defense Spending (% of GDP)	1% (2017)
Total Active Armed Forces	730,000 (2017)
Annual Military Expenditures	$23,676,000,000 (2016)
Military Service	Military service is by conscription, with terms lasting 12 months. (2016)

Table 11: TRANSPORTATION

Airports	4,093 (2013)
Paved Roads	13.0% (2016)
Registered Vehicles	91,600,729 (2015)
Railroads	29,850 miles (2017)
Ports	Major: 20 (including Santos, Rio de Janeiro, Paranagua, ItajaI, Rio Grande, Salvador).

Table 12: COMMUNICATIONS

Facebook Users	139,000,000 (estimate) (2017)
Internet Users	122,841,218 (2016)
Internet Users (% of Population)	61.0% (2016)
Land-based Telephones in Use	41,842,233 (2016)
Mobile Telephone Subscribers	244,067,356 (2016)

Table 13: BRAZIL'S POLITICAL SYSTEM

Official Name	República Federativa do Brasil—Federative Republic of Brazil
Local Name	Brasil
Government	Federal Republic
Head of State	Jair Messias Bolsonaro (January 2019–)
Head of Government	Jair Messias Bolsonaro (January 2019–)
Current Constitution	Approved in 1988
Legislature	The Congresso Nacional (National Congress) is a bicameral body that includes the Senado Federal (Federal Senate) and the Câmara dos Deputados (Chamber of Deputies).
Major Political Parties	The Social Liberal Party (PSL), the Workers' Party (PT), the Brazilian Social Democracy Party (PSDB), the Progressive Party (PP), the Brazilian Democratic Movement Party (PMDB), the Democrats (DEM), the Green Party (PV), and the Christian Social Party (PSC).

Sources: Brazil's Federal Government, http://brasil.gov.br; Brazil's National Congress, https://www.congressonacional.leg.br; CIA World Factbook, http://www.cia.gov; Instituto Brasileiro de Geografia e Estatística (IBGE) 2018 Population Estimates, https://ibge.gov.br; World Bank http://www.worldbank.com;

Table 14: PRESIDENTS OF BRAZIL IN CHRONOLOGICAL ORDER

Presidents	Years in Office
Manoel Deodoro da Fonseca	1889–1891
Floriano Vieira Peixoto	1891–1894
Prudente José de Morais e Barros	1894–1898
Manoel Ferraz de Campos Salles	1898–1902
Francisco de Paula Rodrigues Alves	1902–1906
Afonso Augusto Moreira Penna	1906–1909
Nilo Procópio Peçanha	1909–1910
Hermes Rodrigues da Fonseca	1910–1914
Wenceslau Braz Pereira Gomes	1914–1918
Francisco de Paula Rodrigues Alves	He was elected again but died before taking office.
Delfim Moreira da Costa Riveiro	1918–1919
Epitácio Lindolfo da Silva Pessoa	1919–1922
Artur da Silva Bernardes	1922–1926
Washington Luís Pereira de Sousa	1926–1930
Júlio Prestes de Albuquerque	He was elected, but the government was overthrown in 1930 before he could take office.

General João de Deus Menna Barreto, General Augusto Taso Fragoso, and Admiral José Isaías de Noronha	They seized power by military force and declared a joint government that lasted a week from October 24, 1930, to November 1, 1930, when power was handed over to Getúlio Vargas.
Getúlio Dornelles Vargas	1930–1945
José Linhares	1945–1946
Eurico Gaspar Dutra	1946–1951
Getúlio Dornelles Vargas	1951–1954
José Fernandes Campos Café Filho	1954–1955
Carlos Coimbra da Luz	1955
Nereu de Oliveira Ramos	1955–1956
Juscelino Kubitschek de Oliveira	1956–1961
Jânio da Silva Quadros	1961
Pascoal Ranieri Mazzilli	1961
João Belchior Marques Goulart	1961–1964
Pascoal Ranieri Mazzilli	1964
Humberto de Alencas Castelo Branco	1964–1967
Arthur da Costa e Silva	1967–1969
Aurélio de Lira Tavares, Augusto Hamann Rademaker Grünewald, and Márcio de Souza e Melo	Costa da Silva was removed from office after suffering from a cerebral thrombosis illness. These three officers took over the government as a military junta from August 31, 1969, until October 30, 1969, when Emílio Médici was sworn in as the next president.
Emílio Garrastazu Médici	1969–1974
Ernesto Geisel	1974–1979
João Baptista de Oliveira Figueiredo	1979–1985
Tancredo de Almeida Neves	He was elected but died before taking office.
José Sarney	1985–1990
Fernando Alfonso Collor de Mello	1990–1992
Itamar Augusto Cautiero Franco	1992–1995
Fernando Henrique Cardoso	1995–2003
Luiz Inácio Lula da Silva	2003–2011
Dilma Vana Rousseff	2011–2016
Michel Miguel Elias Temer Lulia	2016–2018
Jair Messias Bolsonaro	2019–

Sources: Biblioteca Presidencia da República (Brazil's Presidential Library), http://www.biblioteca.presidencia.gov.br; Pesquisa Escolar, https://pesquisaescolar.site/presidentes-do-brasil

Table 15: TOP 20 BRAZILIAN CITIES BY POPULATION (JULY 2018)

Rank	City	State	Population
1	São Paulo	São Paulo	12,176,866
2	Rio de Janeiro	Rio de Janeiro	6,688,927
3	Brasília	Distrito Federal	2,974,703
4	Salvador	Bahia	2,857,329
5	Fortaleza	Ceará	2,643,247
6	Belo Horizonte	Minas Gerais	2,501,576
7	Manaus	Amazonas	2,145,444
8	Curitiba	Paraná	1,917,185
9	Recife	Pernambuco	1,637,834
10	Goiânia	São Paulo	1,495,705
11	Belem	Pará	1,485,732
12	Porto Alegre	Rio Grande do Sul	1,479,101
13	Guarulhos	São Paulo	1,365,899
14	Campinas	São Paulo	1,194,094
15	São Luis	Maranhão	1,094,667
16	São Gonçalo	Rio de Janeiro	1,077,687
17	Maceió	Alagoas	1,012, 382
18	Duque de Caxias	Rio de Janeiro	914,383
19	Natal	Rio Grande do Norte	877,640
20	Teresina	Piauí	861,442

Source: Instituto Brasileiro de Geografia e Estatística (IBGE), Population Estimates on July 1, 2018, https://ibge.gov.br

APPENDIX D

HOLIDAYS

Brazil has nine national official holidays. In addition, it celebrates a wide range of festivities that highlight its unique history, religious heritage, ethnic backgrounds, nature's cycles, and cultural traditions. Holidays can be approved by a legislative process at three levels: national (*nacionais*), state (*estaduais*), and municipal (*municipais*). Sometimes, individual cities and towns also celebrate regional or religious holidays, and they offer employees time off from work. In the national Portuguese language, a public holiday is called *feriado público*. If any holidays happen to fall on a Sunday, then Brazilians get Monday off from work. The following chart lists all the official holidays celebrated at a national level in 2019.

Date	Holiday Name (English)	Holiday Name (Portuguese)	Holiday Type and Description
January 1	New Year's Day	Confraternização Universal/Ano Novo	On December 31, Brazilians celebrate the end of a year by counting down the last ten seconds until midnight. January 1 commemorates the beginning of the New Year, and it denotes the end of the previous December holiday season. January 1 also marks the first day of the Gregorian calendar.
April 9	Easter	Páscoa	Brazil has one of the largest Catholic populations in the world, and the Evangelical Christian movement is growing fast. Both groups celebrate Semana Santa (Easter Week). Brazilians attend religious festivities and give people chocolate Easter eggs. However, the tradition of Easter egg hunting is not practiced in Brazil.
April 21	Day of Tiradentes	Dia de Tiradentes	Joaquim José da Silva Xavier, known as Tiradentes, was a martyr of the Inconfidência Mineira, a regional rebellion protesting excessive taxes

			and fighting for independence from the Portuguese Crown. This holiday marks the anniversary of his violent punishment and death ordered by the Portuguese rulers in 1792.
May 1	Labor Day / May Day	Dia do Trabalhador/Dia do Trabalho	It is a celebration of workers. It highlights both the struggles and successes of labor movements in Brazil. It also focuses on the achievements of workers' benefits.
September 7	Independence Day	Proclamação de Independência do Brasil	It commemorates September 7, 1822, as the day when Brazil officially declared independence from the United Kingdom of Portugal, Brazil, and the Algarves.
October 12	Our Lady of Aparecida	Nossa Senhora Aparecida/Dia das Crianças	Nossa Senhora Aparecida (Virgin Mary) is the official patron saint of Brazil. The same day celebrates Children's Day (Dia das Crianças) by having carnivals and school events for children.
November 2	All Souls' Day/ Day of the Dead	Dia de Finados	As part of Brazil's religious heritage, this holiday remembers the departed in a solemn way. Many Brazilians attend a requiem mass. They also visit cemeteries and decorate graves with candles and flowers, especially chrysanthemums.
November 15	Republic Day	Proclamação da República	It celebrates the official end of the Brazilian Empire and the subsequent event proclaiming Brazil as a Republic on November 15, 1889.
December 25	Christmas Day	Natal	Many Brazilians attend a Midnight Mass on Christmas Eve, December 24. It is called Missa do Galo, and it celebrates the birth of Jesus Christ. Catholic and Christian churches, as well as many homes, display nativity scenes (*precepios*) that replicate bible stories related to this event.

There are a few more considerations to take into account when discussing holidays in Brazil. Based on the national constitution, labor law provides workers with twenty-two paid vacation days. In addition, election days are considered national holidays, and they are held every two years. To follow the electoral process, Brazilians get the first

Sunday of October off from work in order to participate in the compulsory voting process. If a second round of votes is necessary, then people also get the last Sunday of October to vote again. The list below highlights the additional holidays celebrated in 2019.

Date	Day of the Week	Holiday Name (English)	Holiday Type
January 1	Tuesday	New Year's Day	National Holiday
March 1	Friday	Carnival Friday	Observance
March 2	Saturday	Carnival Saturday	Observance
March 3	Sunday	Carnival Sunday	Observance
March 4	Monday	Carnival Monday	Optional Holiday
March 5	Tuesday	Carnival Tuesday	Optional Holiday
March 6	Wednesday	End of Carnival (until 2 p.m.)	Optional Holiday
March 20	Wednesday	March Equinox	Seasonal Holiday
April 19	Friday	Good Friday	National Holiday
April 21	Sunday	Easter Sunday	Observance
April 21	Sunday	Day of Tiradentes	National Holiday
May 1	Wednesday	Labor Day	National Holiday
May 12	Sunday	Mother's Day	Observance
June 12	Wednesday	Valentine's Day	Observance
June 20	Thursday	Corpus Christi	Observance
June 21	Friday	June Solstice	Season
August 11	Sunday	Father's Day	Observance
September 7	Saturday	Independence Day	National Holiday
September 23	Monday	September Equinox	Season
October 12	Saturday	Our Lady of Aparecida/Children's Day	National Holiday
October 15	Tuesday	Day of the Teacher	Observance
October 28	Monday	Public Service Holiday	Optional Holiday
November 1	Friday	All Saints Day	Observance
November 2	Saturday	All Souls' Day	National Holiday
November 15	Friday	Republic Proclamation Day	National Holiday
November 20	Wednesday	Black Consciousness Day (official state holiday in Alagoas, Amapá, Amazonas, Mato Grosso, and Rio de Janeiro)	Observance
December 22	Sunday	December Solstice	Season
December 24	Tuesday	Christmas Eve (after 2 p.m.)	Optional Holiday
December 25	Wednesday	Christmas Day	National Holiday
December 31	Tuesday	New Year's Eve (after 2 p.m.)	Optional Holiday

In addition to paid holidays, all registered employees of companies in Brazil also qualify for an annual Christmas bonus salary check. In Portuguese, it is known as the *décimo terceiro salário* (or thirteenth salary) because it is equivalent to an additional monthly check. Companies issue these bonus checks at the beginning of December, which helps the local economy. Employees who worked with a registered company the entire year are entitled to a full check, but part-time workers get only a prorated check.

Further Reading

Richard, Christopher, and Leslie Jermyn. 2002. *Cultures of the World: Brazil*. New York: Marshall Cavendish Publishers.

SELECTED BIBLIOGRAPHY

OFFICIAL GOVERNMENT WEBSITES

Brasilia Federal Government—Governo do Distrito Federal. http://www.brasilia.df.gov.br

Brazilian Academy of Letters. Academia Brasileira de Letras. http://www.academia.org.br/

Brazilian Coffee Exporters Council (Ce Café). http://www.cecafe.com.br/en

Brazilian Electricity Regulatory Agency (ANEEL). http://www2.aneel.gov.br

Brazilian Government Official Portal. http://brasil.gov.br

Brazilian Institute for the Environment and Renewable Resources. Instituto Brasileiro do Meio Ambiente e Dos Recursos Naturais Renováveis (IBAMA). http://www.ibama.gov.br

Brazilian Ministry of Culture. Ministério da Cultura. http://www.cultura.gov.br

Brazilian Ministry of Development and Foreign Trade (MDIC). http://www.mdic.gov.br

Brazilian Ministry of Mines and Energy (MME). http://www.mme.gov.br

Brazilian Ministry of Science, Technology, Innovation, and Communications. http://www.mctic.gov.br

Brazilian Ministry of the Environment. Ministério do Meio Ambiente (MMA). http://mma.gov.br

Brazilian Ministry of Tourism. http://www.turismo.gov.br

Brazilian National Bank for Economic and Social Development (BNDES). https://www.bndes.gov.br/wps/portal/site/home

Brazilian National Institute of Amazonian Research—Instituto Nacional de Pesquisas da Amazônia (INPA). http://portal.inpa.gov.br

Embraer (Empresa Brasileira de Aeronáutica). https://embraer.com/br/pt

Embratur Brazilian Institute of Tourism. http://www.embratur.gov.br

Instituto Brasileiro de Geografia e Estatística (IBGE). 2011. *Censo demográfico de 2010: Resultados do universo*. Rio de Janeiro: IBGE. http://ibge.gov.br

Instituto de Matemática Pura e Aplicada (IMPA). https://impa.br

Itaipu Dam for Hydroelectric Power. https://www.itaipu.gov.br/en

National Agency of Petroleum, Natural Gas, and Biofuels (ANP). http://www.anp.gov.br

National Indian Foundation—Fundação Nacional do Índio (FUNAI) Official Website in Brazil. http://www.funai.gov.br

National Water Agency of Brazil. Agência Nacional de Águas (ANA). http://www3.ana.gov.br

Natural Resource Governance Institute. https://resourcegovernance.org/our-work/country/brazil

Petrobras National Oil Company. http://www.petrobras.com.br/pt

Save the Amazon Rainforest. https://www.amazon-rainforest.org

Superior Electoral Court (TSE) Official Government Website. http://english.tse.jus.br

United Nations Official Website. http://www.un.org

GENERAL REFERENCES

Crocitti, John J., and Monique Vallance (eds.). 2012. *Brazil Today: An Encyclopedia of Life in the Republic* (2 volumes). Santa Barbara, CA: ABC-CLIO.

Del Priore, Mary, and Renato Pinto Venâncio. 2001. *O livro de ouro da história do Brasil*. Rio de Janeiro: Ediouro.

Edwards, Todd L. 2008. *Brazil: A Global Studies Handbook*. Santa Barbara, CA: ABC-CLIO.

Fausto, Boris, and Sergio Fausto. 2014. *A Concise History of Brazil*. Cambridge, UK: Cambridge University Press.

Instituto Brasileiro de Geografia e Estatística (IBGE). 2016. "Estimativas da População Residente no Brasil e Unidades da Federação com Data de Referência em 1 de Julho de 2016." Instituto Brasileiro de Geografia e Estatística—Brazilian Institute of Geography and Statistics (IBGE). Accessed July 11, 2019. http://ibge.gov.br

Meade, Teresa A. 2010. *A Brief History of Brazil*. New York: Checkmark Books.

Richard, Christopher, and Leslie Jermyn. 2002. *Cultures of the World: Brazil*. New York: Marshall Cavendish.

Sachs, Ignacy, Jorge Wilheim, and Paulo Sérgio Pinheiro. 2009. *Brazil: A Century of Change*. Chapel Hill: University of North Carolina Press.

Skidmore, Thomas E. 2010. *Brazil: Five Centuries of Change*. New York: Oxford University Press.

Tosta, Antonio Luciano de Andrade, and Eduardo F. Coutinho (eds.). 2016. *Brazil*. Santa Barbara, CA: ABC-CLIO.

Vincent, Jon S. 2003. *Culture and Customs of Brazil*. Westport, CT: Greenwood Press.

CHAPTER 1: GEOGRAPHY

Abell, Sam, and Torben Ulrik Nissen. 2010. *Amazonia*. Eugene, OR: Jordan Schnitzer, Museum of Art.

Angelini, Alessandro. 2011. *Favela: Four Decades of Living on the Edge of Rio de Janeiro*. New York: Oxford University Press.

Arons, Nicholas G. 2004. *Waiting for Rain: The Politics and Poetry of Drought in Northeast Brazil*. Tucson: University of Arizona Press.

Bortman, Marci. 2003. *Environmental Encyclopedia*. Detroit, MI: Gale.

Decker, Thomas. 2016. *Brasilia: Life beyond Utopia*. New Haven, CT: Yale University Press.

Penn, James R. 2001. *Rivers of the World: A Social, Geographical, and Environmental Sourcebook*. Santa Barbara, CA: ABC-CLIO.

Petrobras National Oil Company Official Website. http://www.petrobras.com.br/pt

Philander, George S. 2012. *Encyclopedia of Global Warming and Climate Change*, Second Edition. Princeton, NJ: Princeton University Press.

Revkin, Andrew. 2004. *The Burning Season: The Murder of Chico Mendes and the Fight for the Amazon Rain Forest*. Washington, DC: Island Press.

CHAPTER 2: HISTORY

Applebaum, Nancy P., Anne Macpherson, and Karin A. Rosemblatt (eds.). 2003. *Race and Nation in Modern Latin America*. Chapel Hill: University of North Carolina Press.

Araujo, Ana Lucia. 2015. *African Heritage and Memories in Brazil and the South Atlantic World*. Amherst, NY: Cambria Press.

Barman, Roderick J. 1998. *Brazil: The Forging of a Nation, 1798–1852*. Redwood City, CA: Stanford University Press.

Barman, Roderick J. 2002. *Princess Isabel of Brazil: Gender and Power in the Nineteenth Century*. Wilmington, DE: Wilmington Scholarly Resources.

Beattie, Peter M. 2001. *The Tribute of Blood: Army, Honor, Race, and Nation in Brazil, 1864–1945*. Durham, NC: Duke University Press.

Carvalho Franco, Francisco de Assis. 1989. *Dicionário de bandeirantes e sertanistas do Brasil*. São Paulo, Brasil: Editora da Universidade de São Paolo.

Dávila, Jerry. 2013. *Dictatorship in South America*. Hoboken, NJ: Wiley.

Foundation Getúlio Vargas Official Website. http://portal.fgv.br/en

Hentschke, Jens R. (ed.). 2006. *Vargas and Brazil: New Perspectives*. New York: Palgrave Macmillan.

Hooker, Terry D. 2008. *The Paraguayan War*. Nottingham, UK: Foundry Books.

Klein, Herbert S., and Francisco Vidal Luna. 2009. *Slavery in Brazil*. Cambridge, UK: Cambridge University Press.

Longo, James McMurtry. 2008. *Isabel Orleans-Bragança: The Brazilian Princess Who Freed the Slaves*. Jefferson, NC: McFarland.

McSherry, J. Patrice. 2005. *Predatory States: Operation Condor and Covert War in Latin America*. Lanham, MD: Rowman & Littlefield.

Meade, Teresa A. 2010. "Bandeirantes," in *A Brief History of Brazil*, 21–23. New York: Checkmark Books.

Ribeiro, Darcy, and Gregory Rabassa. 2000. *The Brazilian People: The Formation and Meaning of Brazil*. Gainesville: University Press of Florida.

Silva, Benedita da, Medea Benjamin, and Maisa Mendonça. 1997. *Benedita da Silva: An Afro-Brazilian Woman's Story of Politics and Love*. Oakland, CA: Institute for Food and Development Policy.

Skidmore, Thomas. 2003. *Uma história do Brasil*, Fourth Edition. São Paolo: Paz e Terra.

CHAPTER 3: GOVERNMENT AND POLITICS

Ames, Barry. 2002. *The Deadlock of Democracy in Brazil*. Ann Arbor: University of Michigan Press.

Amorim, Celso, and Michael Marsden (trans.). 2017. *Acting Globally: Memoirs of Brazil's Assertive Foreign Policy*. Lanham, MD: Rowman & Littlefield.

Caetano, André J., and Joseph E. Potter. 2004. "Politics and Female Sterilization in Northern Brazil." *Population and Development Review* 30, no. 1 (March): 79–108.

Castro, Celso, Vitor Izecksohn, and Hendrik Kraay. 2004. *Nova história militar brasileira*. Rio de Janeiro: Fundaçaõ Getulio Vargas.

Edwards, Todd L. 2008. "Politics and Government," in *Brazil: A Global Studies Handbook*, 137–195. Santa Barbara, CA: ABC-CLIO.

Gardini, G. (ed.). 2016. *Foreign Policy Responses to the Rise of Brazil: Balancing Power in Emerging States*. New York: Palgrave Macmillan.

Gómez Bruera, Hernán F. 2013. *Lula, the Workers' Party, and the Governability Dilemma in Brazil*. Florence, KY: Routledge.

Human Rights Watch—Brazil. https://www.hrw.org/americas/brazil

Hunter, Wendy. 2010. *The Transformation of the Workers' Party in Brazil, 1989–2009*. Cambridge, UK: Cambridge University Press, 2010

Kingstone, Peter R., and Timothy J. Power (eds.). 2000. *Democratic Brazil: Actors, Institutions, and Processes*. Pittsburg, PA: University of Pittsburgh Press.

MERCOSUR Mercado Común del Sur Official Website. http://www.mercosur.int

Power, Timothy, and Matthew Taylor (eds.). 2011. *Corruption and Democracy in Brazil: The Struggle for Accountability*. Notre Dame, IN: University of Notre Dame Press.

CHAPTER 4: ECONOMY

Alston, Lee J. et al. 2016. *Brazil in Transition: Beliefs, Leadership, and Institutional Change*. Princeton, NJ: Princeton University Press.

Baer, Werner. 2013. *The Brazilian Economy: Growth and Development*. Denver, CO: Lynne Rienner.

Brazilian Ministry of Development and Foreign Trade (MDIC) Official Website. http://www.mdic.gov.br

BRICS Official Website. http://www.infobrics.org

Chun, Kwang. 2013. *The BRICS Superpower Challenge: Foreign and Security Policy Analysis*. Burlington, VT: Ashgate.

King, Winfield Conwell. 2017. *Brazil's Coffee Industry*. London: Forgotten Books.

Koifman, Fábio. 2002. *Presidentes do Brasil: De Deodoro a FHC*. Rio de Janeiro: Editora Rio.

Kumar, Anjali. 2005. *Assessing Financial Access in Brazil*. Washington, DC: World Bank.

Margheritis, Ana (ed.). 2003. *Latin American Democracies in the New Global Economy*. Boulder, CO: Lynne Rienner.

Martin, Phillip. 2006. *Managing Labor Migration in the Twenty-First Century.* New Haven, CT: Yale University Press.

Mercosur Official Website. http://www.mercosur.int

Penglase, R. Ben. 2014. *Living with Insecurity in a Brazilian Favela: Urban Violence and Daily Life.* New Brunswick, NJ: Rutgers University Press.

Reid, Michael. 2012. *Brazil: The Troubled Rise of a Global Power.* New Haven, CT: Yale University Press.

Rivera, Salvador. 2014. *Latin American Unification: A History of Political and Economic Integration Efforts.* Jefferson, NC: McFarland.

Vidal Luna, Francisco. 2014. *The Economic and Social History of Brazil since 1889.* Cambridge, UK: Cambridge University Press.

Workman, Daniel. 2019. "Brazil's Top 15 Trading Partners." *World's Top Exports,* January 26. Accessed June 11, 2019. http://www.worldstopexports.com/brazils-top-import-partners

World Trade Organization (WTO) Official Website. https://www.wto.org

Ximenes, Ângela. 2016. *Eduardo da Rocha Azevedo: A Bovespa e a BM&F.* São Paulo: Contexto.

CHAPTER 5: RELIGION AND THOUGHT

Alberto, Paulina L. 2011. *Terms of Inclusion: Black Intellectuals in Twentieth-Century Brazil.* Chapel Hill: University of North Carolina Press.

Bragdon, Emma. 2004. *Kardec's Spiritism: A Home for Healing and Spiritual Evolution.* Lakeland, FL: Lightening Up Press.

Bramley, Serge. 1994. *Macumba.* San Francisco, CA: City Lights Books.

Capone, Stefania. 2010. *Searching for Africa in Brazil: Power and Tradition in Candomblé.* Durham, NC: Duke University Press.

Chacon, Vamireh. 1990. *Deus é Brasileiro: O imaginário do mesianismo político no Brasil.* Rio de Janeiro: Civilização Brasileira.

Darder, Antonia. 2017. *Reinventing Paulo Freire: A Pedagogy of Love.* New York: Routledge.

Freire Institute of Critical Pedagogy. http://www.freire.org/paulo-freire

Freston, Paul. 2008. *Evangelical Christianity and Democracy in the Global South.* New York: Oxford University Press.

Isfahani-Hammond, Alexandra. 2005. *White Negritude: Race, Writing, and Brazilian Cultural Identity.* London: Palgrave Macmillan.

Matory, J. Lorand. 2005. *Black Atlantic Religion: Tradition, Transnationalism, and Matriarchy in the Afro-Brazilian Candomble.* Princeton, NJ: Princeton University Press.

Mayo, Peter. 2008. *Liberating Praxis: Paulo Freire's Legacy for Radical Education and Politics.* Westport, CT: Praeger.

McLaren, Peter. 2000. *Che Guevara, Paulo Freire, and the Pedagogy of Revolution.* Lanham, MD: Rowman & Littlefield.

Schmidt, Bettina E. 2016. *Contemporary Religions in Brazil.* Oxford, UK: Oxford University Press.

CHAPTER 6: SOCIAL CLASS AND ETHNICITY

Alexander, Robert J. 2003. *A History of Organized Labor in Brazil*. Santa Barbara, CA: Praeger.

Araujo, Ana Lucia. 2015. *African Heritage and Memories of Slavery in Brazil*. Amherst, NY: Cambria Press.

Barbara, Vanessa. 2015. "In Denial over Racism in Brazil." *New York Times*. March 23. Accessed July 21, 2019. https://www.nytimes.com/2015/03/24/opinion/vanessa-barbara-in-denial-over-racism-in-brazil.html

Bohn, Simone. 2016. "Social Classes and Ethnicity," in *Brazil*, edited by Antonio Luciano de Andrade Tosta and Eduardo F. Coutinho, 120–140. Santa Barbara, CA: ABC-CLIO.

Chiesa Gonçalves, Aline. 2017. *The Influence of the Bolsa Família Program in Education*. Düsseldorf, Germany: Novas Edições Acadêmicas.

Freyre, Gilberto. 1987. *The Masters and Slaves: A Study in the Development of Brazilian Civilization*. Translated by Samuel Putnam. Berkeley: University of California Press.

Fundação Nacional do Índio (FUNAI). http://www.funai.gov.br

Landless Peasant Movement, Movimento Sem Terra (MST) Official Website. http://mstbrazil.org

Meszaros, George. 2013. *Social Movements, Law, and the Politics of Land Reform: Lessons from Brazil*. London: Routledge.

Ondetti, Gabriel A. 2008. *Land, Protest, and Politics: The Landless Movement and the Struggle for Agrarian Reform in Brazil*. University Park: Pennsylvania State University Press.

Sansone, Livio. 2003. *Blackness without Ethnicity: Constructing Race in Brazil*. New York: Palgrave Macmillan.

Simões, Soraya Silveira. 2012. *Favelas Cariocas*. Rio de Janeiro: Editora Garamond.

Twine, France Winddance. 1998. *Racism in a Racial Democracy: The Maintenance of White Supremacy in Brazil*. New Brunswick, NJ: Rutgers University Press.

Wolford, Wendy. 2010. *This Land Is Ours Now: Social Mobilization and the Meanings of Land in Brazil*. Durham, NC: Duke University Press.

CHAPTER 7: GENDER, MARRIAGE, AND SEXUALITY

Coutinho, Rodrigo R. 2016. "Abortion and Family Planning," in *Brazil*, edited by Antonio Luciano de Andrade Tosta and Eduardo F. Coutinho, 334–335. Santa Barbara, CA: ABC-CLIO.

Daniel, Herbert. 1993. *Sexuality, Politics, and AIDS in Brazil: In Another World?* Milton Park, Abington, UK: Taylor and Francis.

Green, James N. 2001. *Beyond Carnival: Male Homosexuality in Twentieth Century Brazil*. Chicago: University of Chicago Press.

Parker, Richard G. 2009. *Bodies, Pleasures, and Passions: Sexual Culture in Contemporary Brazil*. Nashville, TN: Vanderbilt University Press.

Thayer, Millie. 2010. *Making Transnational Feminism: Rural Women, NGO Activists, and Northern Donors in Brazil*. New York: Routledge.

Wylie, Kristin N. 2018. *Party Institutionalization and Women's Representation in Democratic Brazil*. Cambridge, UK: Cambridge University Press.

CHAPTER 8: EDUCATION

Bartlett, Lesley. 2009. *The Word and the World: The Cultural Politics of Literacy in Brazil*. New York: Hampton Press.

Brazilian Ministry of Education (MEC). http://www.mec.gov.br

Brazilian National Institute for Educational Studies and Research (INEP). http://portal.inep.gov.br

Chiesa Gonçalves, Aline. 2017. *The Influence of the Bolsa Família Program in Education*. Düsseldorf, Germany: Novas Edições Acadêmicas.

FUVEST Vestibular Test for College Admission Official Website. https://www.fuvest.br

Heyck, Denis. 2010. *Schools in the Forest: How Grassroots Education Brought Political Empowerment to the Brazilian Amazon*. Boulder, CO: Kumarian Press.

Instituto Nacional de Matemática Pura e Aplicada (IMPA). https://impa.br

Ministry of Education and Culture (MEC) Official Website. http://mec.gov.br

Ministry of Science, Technology, Innovation, and Communications. http://www.mctic.gov.br

UNESCO Institute of Statistics: Literacy Rate in Brazil. http://uis.unesco.org/en/topic/literacy

Universidade de Zumbi dos Palmares Official Website. http://www.zumbidospalmares.edu.br

CHAPTER 9: LANGUAGE

Barrachini-Haß, Yasmin. 2016. *Indigenous Languages in Brazil. A Country between Monolingualism and Plurilingualism*. Munich, Germany: Grin.

Brazilian Academy of Letters. http://www.academia.org.br

Brazilian Sign Language Dictionary Project. http://www.signwriting.org/brazil/brazil00.html

Capovilla, Fernando Cesar and Walkiria Duarte Raphael (eds.). 2001. *Trilingual Illustrated Encyclopedia Dictionary of Brazilian Sign Language, Volumes 1 and 2*. São Paulo: Edusp Fundação Vitae.

Gaspar, Lúcia. 2009. *Indigenous Languages in Brazil*. Recife, Brazil: Joaquim Nabuco Foundation.

Lawless, Teresa, and Janie DiCioccio. 2015. "The Portuguese Spelling Reform." *Argos Multilingual*, March 25. Accessed July 13, 2019. http://www.argosmultilingual.com/blog/the-portuguese-spelling-reform

Língua Brasileira de Sinais, LIBRAS/Brazilian Sign Language. http://www.libras.org

Perini, Mário. 2002. *Modern Portuguese: A Reference Grammar*. New Haven, CT: Yale University Press.

CHAPTER 10: ETIQUETTE

Aloian, Molly. 2012. *Cultural Traditions in Brazil*. New York: Crabtree.

Darlington, Shasta. 2018. "Domestic Abuse Shown Blow by Blow Shocks Brazil." *New York Times*. August 7. Accessed July 22, 2019. https://www.nytimes.com/2018/08/07/world/americas/domestic-abuse-shown-blow-by-blow-shocks-brazil.html

De Holanda, Sérgio Buarque. 2005. *Raízes do Brasil*, Twenty-Sixth Edition. São Paulo: Cia de Letras.

Federal Council of Document Despachantes Official Website (Portuguese). https://www.cfdd.org.br

Fernández Campbell, Alexia. 2016. "A Day in the Life of Brazil's Insane Bureaucracy." *Atlantic*, August 4. Accessed June 23, 2019. https://www.theatlantic.com/international/archive/2016/08/brazil-bureaucracy-despachantes/494426

Kutesko, Elizabeth, and Joanne B. Eicher. 2018. *Fashioning Brazil: Globalization and the Representation of Brazilian Dress in National Geographic*. London: Bloomsbury Visual Arts.

LaRock, Hana. 2018. "Business Etiquette in Brazil." *USA Today*, September 7. Accessed May 29, 2019. https://traveltips.usatoday.com/business-etiquette-brazil-16277.html

Poelzl, Volker. 2009. *CultureShock! Brazil*. Singapore: Marshall Cavendish.

Roberts, Yaya. 2009. *The Brazilian Table*. Layton, UT: Gibbs Smith.

Uchoa, Pablo. 2016 "Maria da Penha: The Woman Who Changed Brazil's Domestic Violence Laws." *BBC News*, September 22. Accessed July 9, 2019. https://www.bbc.com/news/magazine-37429051

Xinhua News Agency and Luc Changlei. 2015. *BRICS: A Guide to Doing Business in Brazil, Russia, India, China, and South Africa*. Washington, DC: ICP Intercultural Press.

CHAPTER 11: LITERATURE AND DRAMA

Angiolillo, Francesca. 2016. "Ten Works of Fiction to Better Understand Brazil: A Country in Crisis and its Vital Literature." *Literary Hub*, Lithub.com, May 18. Accessed July 18, 2019. https://lithub.com/10-works-of-fiction-to-better-understand-brazil

Barbosa, Francisco de Assis. 2002. *A vida de Lima Barreto*. Rio de Janeiro: José Olympio Editora.

Ferreira Pinto, Cristina. 2004. *Gender, Discourse, and Desire in Twentieth-Century Brazilian Women's Literature*. West Lafayette, IN: Purdue University Press.

Fundação Casa de Jorge Amado/Jorge Amado Foundation. http://www.jorgeamado.org.br

Gama, Rinaldo. 1994. "Biblioteca Nacional." *Veja* 27, no. 47 (November 23): 108–112. Accessed July 14, 2019. http://bussolaliteraria.blogspot.com/2010_01_24_archive.html

George, David. 1992. *The Modern Brazilian Stage*. Austin: University of Texas Press.

Ginway, Elizabeth. 1999. "Literature under the Dictatorship," in *Brazil Reader: History, Culture, and Politics* edited by Robert M. Levine and John J. Crocitti, 248–257. Durham, NC: Duke University Press.

Goldberg, Isaac. 2009. *Brazilian Literature*. New York: Knopf.

Haberly, David T. 1983. *Three Sad Races: Racial Identity and National Consciousness in Brazilian Literature*. New York: Cambridge University Press.

Jauregui, Carlos A. 2012. "Antropofagia," in *Dictionary of Latin American Cultural Studies*, edited by Robert McKee Irwin and Mónica Szurmurk, 22–28. Gainesville: The University Press of Florida.

Johnson, Randal (ed.). 1992. *Tropical Paths: Essays on Modern Brazilian Literature*. Abingdon, UK: Taylor & Francis.

Rector, Monica (ed.). 2005. *Brazilian Writers (Dictionary of Literary Biography, v. 370)*. Detroit: MI: Thompson Gale.

Reginald, Daniel G. 2012. *Machado de Assis: Multiracial Identity and the Brazilian Novelist*. University Park: Penn State Press.

Semana de Arte Moderna/Modern Art Week. http://semana-arte-moderna.info

Young, Richard, and Odile Cisneros. 2001. *Historical Dictionary of Latin American Literature and Theater*. Lanham, MD: Scarecrow Press.

CHAPTER 12: ARTS AND ARCHITECTURE

Ada Edita Global Architecture. 2016. *Residential Masterpieces 23: Paulo Mendes da Rocha*. Tokyo: Ada Edita Global Architecture.

Andreoli, Elisabetta. 2005. *Brazil's Modern Architecture*. New York: Phaidon.

Bretas Ferreira, Rodrigo José. 2002. *Antônio Francisco Lisboa*. Editora Itatiaia: Belo Horizonte, Brazil.

Brum Lemos, Maria Alzira. 2009. *Aleijadinho: Homem barroco, artista brasileiro*. Rio de Janeiro: Editora Garamond.

Bury, John. 1991. *Arquitectura e arte do Brasil colonial*. São Paulo: Editora Nobel.

El-Dahdah, Farès. 2005. *Lúcio Costa: Brasilia's Superquadra*. Munich, Germany: Prestel.

Hess, Alan, and Alan Weintraub. 2009. *Oscar Niemeyer Buildings*. New York: Rizzoli.

Lemos, Carlos, Jose Roberto, and Teixeira Leite (eds.). 1983. *The Art of Brazil*. New York: Harper Collins.

Mann, Graciela, and Hans Mann. 2014. *The Twelve Prophets of Aleijadinho*. Austin: University of Texas Press.

Meurs, Paul et al. (ed.). 2009. *Brazil Contemporary: Architecture, Art, and Visual Culture and Design*. Rotterdam, Netherlands: Nai010.

Museu de Arte Moderna (MAM) de São Paulo. http://mam.org.br

Omari-Tunkara, Mikelle. 2005. *Manipulating the Sacred: Yorubá Art, Ritual, and Resistance in Brazilian Candomblé*. Detroit: MI: Wayne State University Press.

Pisani, Daniel, and Francesco Dal Co. 2015. *Paulo Mendes da Rocha: Complete Works*. New York: Rizzoli.

Segawa, Hugo. 2010. *Architecture of Brazil*. São Paulo: Edusp.

UNESCO World Heritage Sites. http://whc.unesco.org

CHAPTER 13: MUSIC AND DANCE

Dunn, Christopher. 2001. *Tropicália and the Emergence of a Brazilian Counterculture*. Chapel Hill: University of North Carolina Press.

Fryer, Peter. 2000. *Rhythms of Resistance: African Musical Heritage in Brazil*. London: Pluto Press.

Henry, Clarence Bernard. 2008. *Let's Make Some Noise: Axé and the African Roots of Popular Brazilian Music*. Jackson: University Press of Mississippi.

McGowan, Chris, and Ricardo Pessanha. 2008. *The Brazilian Sound: Samba, Bossa Nova, and Popular Music of Brazil*. Philadelphia: Temple University Press.

Murphy, John P. 2006. *Music in Brazil*. Oxford, UK: Oxford University Press.

Talmon-Chvaicer, Maya. 2008. *The Hidden History of Capoeira: A Collision of Cultures in the Brazilian Battle Dance*. Austin: University of Texas Press.

Veloso, Caetano. 2003. *Tropical Truth: A Story of Music and Revolution in Brazil*. Cambridge, MA: Da Capo Press.

CHAPTER 14: FOOD

Academy of Cooking and Other Pleasures Official Website. http://chefbrasil.com

Bateman, Michael. 1999. *Café Brazil*. Chicago: Contemporary Books.

Caragnato, Evandro. 2016. *Churrasco: Grilling the Brazilian Way*. Layton, UT: Gibbs Smith.

Castanho, Thiago, and Luciana Bianchi. 2014. *Brazilian Food*. Richmond Hill, Ontario, Canada: Firefly Books.

Fajans, Jane. 2012. *Brazilian Food: Race, Class, and Identity in Regional Cuisines*. Oxford, UK: Berg.

Farah, Fernando. 2012. *The Food and Cooking of Brazil: Traditions, Ingredients, Tastes, Techniques, and 65 Classic Recipes*. Wigston, Leicester, UK: Lorenz Books.

Farah, Fernando. 2014. *Brazilian Food and Cooking*. Northampton, MA: Hermes House Press.

Ministry of Social Development and Fight Against Hunger (MDS) Official Website. http://www.mds.gov.br

Moreinos Schwartz, Leticia. 2012. *The Brazilian Kitchen: 100 Creative Recipes for the Home Cook*. London: Kyle Books.

Roberts, Yara. 2009. *The Brazilian Table*. Layton, UT: Gibbs Smith.

Tudisco, Ana Luiza. 2016. *10 Receitas típicas de Minas Gerais*. São Paulo: Editora 101 Seleções.

Weimann, Erwin. 2006. *Cachaça: A bebida brasileira*. São Paulo: Editora Terceiro Nome.

CHAPTER 15: LEISURE AND SPORTS

Bellos, Alex. 2014. *Futebol: The Brazilian Way of Life*. New York: Bloomsbury USA.

Brazilian Grand Prix Official Website. https://www.gpbrasil.com.br

Bruha, Patrick. 2015. "Most Popular Brazilian Telenovelas." *Brazil Business*, March 27. Accessed July 8, 2019. http://thebrazilbusiness.com/article/most-popular-brazilian-telenovelas

Buckley Jr., James. 2007. *Pelé*. New York: DK.

Confederação Brasileira de Basketball Official Website. http://www.cbb.com.br

FIFA World Cup Brazil 2014 Official Website. https://www.fifa.com/worldcup/archive/brazil2014/index.html

Formula 1 Official Website. https://www.formula1.com

Gracie, Renzo, and Royler Gracie. 2001. *Brazilian Jiu-Jitsu: Theory and Technique.* Chicago: Invisible Cities Press.

Kittleson, Roger. 2014. *The Country of Football: Soccer and the Making of Modern Brazil.* Berkeley: University of California Press.

Lesser, Jeffrey, and Kitron Uriel. 2016. "The Social Geography of Zika in Brazil." *NACLA Report on the Americas* 48, no. 2 (Summer): 123.

Mega Sena Brazilian Lottery Official Website. http://www.megasena.com/en

Oscar Schmidt Official Website. http://www.oscarschmidt.com.br

Palhares, Guilherme Lohmann. 2012. *Tourism in Brazil: Environment, Management, and Segments.* Abingdon-on-Thames, UK: Routledge.

Pelé Official Website. https://pele10.com

Puin, Karolina. 2012. "What Brazilians Watch on TV." *Brazil Business,* June 9. Accessed May 21, 2019. http://thebrazilbusiness.com/article/what-brazilians-watch-on-tv

Rede TV Globo Official Website. http://www.globo.com

Royce Gracie Official Website. http://www.roycegracie.tv

Talmon-Chvaicer, Maya. 2008. *The Hidden History of Capoeira: A Collision of Cultures in the Brazilian Battle Dance.* Austin: University of Texas Press.

Zimbalist, Andrew. 2017. *Rio 2016: Olympic Myths, Hard Realities.* Washington, DC: Brookings Institution Press.

CHAPTER 16: MEDIA AND POPULAR CULTURE

Clark, Andrew. 2009. "Brazilian Newspapers Celebrate a Rise in Circulation." *Guardian,* October 11. Accessed May 12, 2019. https://www.theguardian.com/media/2009/oct/12/brazil-newspapers-circulation

Directory of Brazil Online Newspapers. http://www.onlinenewspapers.com/brazil.htm

Holmes, Ryan. 2013. "The Future of Social Media? Forget about the U.S., Look to Brazil." *Forbes,* September 12. Accessed June 22, 2019. http://www.forbes.com/sites/ciocentral/2013/09/12/the-future-of-social-media-forget-about-the-u-s-look-to-brazil/#280efe6a3c9a

Kwon, Oliver, and Steve Solot. 2015. *Brazilian Cinema Today: Essays by Critics and Experts from across Brazil.* Rio de Janeiro: Latin American Training Center.

Nichols, Elizabeth Gackstetter, and Timothy R. Robins. 2015. *Pop Culture in Latin America and the Caribbean.* Santa Barbara, CA: ABC-CLIO.

Porto, Mauro P. 2013. *Media Power and Democratization in Brazil: TV Globo and the Dilemmas of Political Accountability.* Routledge: New York.

São Paulo International Film Festival. http://www.mostra.org

Index

abertura, 59
Abortion Laws, 173, 174–175
Affirmative Action Policies, 153, 157–158, 197, 198–199
African Ancestry and Influence, 127, 154–156; art, 267; capoeira, 327; carnival, 287, 292; education, 197; food, 305; literature, 265; musical instruments, 297; *orixas*, 145; popular arts and crafts, 284; samba music, 300–301
Agência Nacional de Águas (ANA), 28
Agrarian Reform, 103–104
AIDS, 176
Aleijadinho, 268, 270–272, 282
Álvares Cabral, Pedro, 3, 31, 37, 47–48, 52
Alves da Silva, Darcy, 25
Amado, Jorge, 247–248
Amazon Basin and Rainforest, 3, 5, 6–9, 10, 18, 347; tourism, 328
Amazon River, 1–2, 6, 10
Anitta, a Contemporary Pop Artist, 356
Annual Christmas Bonus Salary, 120
Arts and Architecture, 267–286; *Aleijadinho* (1738–1814), 270–272; Baroque Art and Architecture in Minas Gerais, 272–274; Cinto, Sandra (1968–), 274–276; Costa, Lúcio (1902–1998): Brasilia's Urban Planner, 276–277; French Artistic Mission, 277–278; Mendes da Rocha, Paulo (1928–), 278–279; Modern Art Week, São Paolo 1922, 279–281; Niemeyer, Oscar (1907–2012), 281–282; Ouro Preto, 282–283; Popular Arts and Crafts, 283–284; Portinari, Cândido (1903–1962), 285–286
Austerity Measures of 2016, 104–105
Automobile Industry, 106–107, 120
Ávila, Artur (1979–), 199–200

Bandeira, Manuel, 248–249, 264
Bandeirantes, 37, 48–49, 54, 272; gold rush, 54
Bargaining, 231–232
Baroque Art and Architecture in Minas Gerais, 267, 272–274; Ouro Preto, 29, 38, 270, 272, 282–283
Barros, José de Morais, 40
Basketball, 321, 323–324
Beach and Sand, 324–325
Bolsa Família: Welfare Program with Education Incentives, 35, 153, 156–157, 166, 183, 188, 200–201
Bolsonaro, Jair, 36, 55, 101, 103, 159, 161–162, 173
Bonaparte, Napoleon, 39, 50, 277
Bossa Nova, 290–291
Bovespa stock exchange, 125
Bragança dynasty, 38
Brasil Sem Miséria, 153, 156, 166
Brasília and the Federal District, 2, 4, 9–10, 22, 29, 34, 58, 69; architecture, 268, 281; Costa, Lucio, 9, 276–277; Kubitschek de Oliveira, Juscelino, 9, 34, 39, 58–59; Niemeyer, Oscar, 58, 281–282, 268, 276, 278, 280
Brazilian Academy of Letters, 250, 261
Brazilian Empire: Pedro I and Pedro II, 32, 39, 49–51, 65, 108

Brazilian Institute of Geography and Statistics (IBGE), 114, 131, 152, 156, 159–160, 163, 178, 188, 190, 206, 221, 230
Brazilian Jiu-Jitsu, 321, 325–326, 343
Brazilian National Indian Foundation, 222
brazilwood, 31
BRICS Economic Group, 82, 100, 107–108, 118, 128, 165, 203

cachaça liquor, 305–306, 309
Cafezinho, a Small Shot of Strong Coffee, 306, 307–308, 362
Caipirinha, a National Cocktail, 305, 308–309
Candomblé and Macumba, 131–132, 134–135, 145–146, 155; arts and crafts, 270; music, 298
Canudos Massacre, 40
Capoeira, 327–328
Captaincy Colonial System, 31, 51–54, 103
Cardoso, Fernando Enrique, 35, 42, 108–109, 120
Carne de Sol, Dried Salted Meat, 305, 309–310, 364
Carnival, 155, 387, 291–292, 301, 347
Casa Grande & Senzala, 41, 133, 140, 280
Catholicism, 135–137, 146, 150, 177, 262, 284; divorce, 177; holidays, 348–349; Jesuit missionaries, 131, 135, 227; popular arts and crafts, 284; theater, 262, 265
cattle ranching, 5, 7, 11, 24, 100
census 2010, 176, 191
Central do Brasil film, 344, 346, 355
Cerveró, Nestor, 77
Children as Healers and Miracle Workers, 147
choro instrumental music, 292
Christianity, 131
Christmas Bonus Salary, 120
Churrasco, 306, 310–311
Cícero, Romão Batista, 142
Cidade de Deus film, 344, 346
Cinema and Film Festivals, 344, 345–346
Cinto, Sandra, 274–276
Climate, 10–11
Clothing and Dressing Appropriately, 230, 232–233
coffee, 5, 38; Brazilian Coffee Exporters Council, 111, 307; *cafezinho*, 110, 306; exports, 109–111

Coffee Exports, 5, 100, 109–111
Collor de Mello, Fernando, 35, 42
Constitutions, 67, 69, 73–76; Constitution of 1888, 35, 81, 84
Contemporary Brazilian Chefs, 312–313
Contemporary Writers, 250–251
Corruption and Political Scandals, 16, 72, 76–79; Cerveró, Nestor, 77; Lula da Silva, Luiz Inácio, 76, 87; Operation Car Wash, 72, 77, 99, 125, 167; Rousseff, Dilma, 78–79, 99; Temer, Michel, 94
Costa, Lúcio, 9, 268, 276–277, 278, 280
Crivella, Marcello, 133, 147, 150
Cultural Icons, 347–348

Da Cunha, Euclides, 251–253
Dating and Courting, 176–177
Days of the week, 217
De Andrade, Oswald, 253–254, 263, 280
de Matos, Gregório, 244–245
de Souza Chauí, Marilena, 133, 137–138
Deforestation, 2, 7, 11–13, 14, 24
Democratic Movement Party (PMDB), 94, 99
derrama tax collection, 65
despachantes, 229, 235–236
desquite, 177
Desquite and Divorce, 172, 177–178, 182
dictatorships, 59–60
Distribution of Wealth and Income Disparity, 156–157
divorce, 177, 188
Domestic Violence, 178–179
Don Casmurro, 243

Earth Summit, Rio 2012, 13–14
Economy, 100–130; Agrarian Reform, 103–104; Austerity Measures of 2016, 104–105; Automobile Industry, 106–107; BRICS Economic Group, 107–108; Cardoso, Fernando Enrique (1931–), 108–109; Coffee Exports, 109–111; Embraer, Empresa Brasileira de Aeronáutica, 111–112; Energy Industry: Electricity, Oil, Ethanol, and Renewable Sources, 112–114; *Favelas*, Slums, 114–115; Foreign Investment, 115–116; Labor Migration, 117–118; Major Exports, 118–119; Manufacturing, 119–121; Mercosul/Mercosur, 121–122; Mineral

Wealth, 122–123; Petrobras, the National Oil Company, 123–125; Stock Exchanges: Bovespa, BM&F, and B3, 125–126; Tourism, 126–127; Trading Partners, 128–129; World Trade Organization (WTO), 129–130
Education, 195–214; Affirmative Action Policies, 198–199; Ávila, Artur (1979–), 199–200; Bolsa Família: Welfare Program with Education Incentives, 200–201; Education Reforms of 2016, 201–203; Higher Education and Major Universities, 203–204; INEP, National Institute for Educational Studies and Research, 205–206; Literacy Rates, 206–207; Private, International, and Religious Schools, 207–208; Public Education: Elementary and Secondary Schooling, 208–210; Scientific and Technical Research, 210–212; Unipalmares, University for Afro-descendent Students, 212–213; Vestibular Testing for College Admission, 213–214
Education Reforms of 2016, 201–203
Education in Shifts, 196
Education and Upper Mobility, 157–158
Electoral System, 79–81
Embraer, Empresa Brasileira de Aeronáutica, 111 112, 120
Energy Industry: Electricity, Oil, Ethanol, and Renewable Sources, 5, 25, 112–114; Petrobras, the National Oil Company, 25–26
Environment, 14–15
Estado Novo, 34, 37, 41
Etiquette, 229–243; Bargaining, 231–232; Clothing and Dressing Appropriately, 232–233; Formal Business Meetings, 234–235; Intermediaries: *Colonels* and *Despachantes*, 235–236; *Jeitinho*, Finding a Way, 236–237; Machismo, 238–239; Personal Space and Privacy, 239–241; Punctuality and Concepts of Time, 241–242; Table Manners, 242–243
Exporting Natural Resources, 26

Facts and Figures, 373–380
Family Outings and Vacations, 328–329
Favelas, Mocambos, and *Alagados* (Slums), 158–160, 168
Favelas, Slums, 10, 22, 114–115

Feijoada, Brazil's National Dish, 154, 310, 313–315, 363
Feminism, 180–181
Festa Literária Internacional de Paraty, FLIP, 250
Folia de Reis, Three Wise Men Celebration, 348–349
Food, 305–320; *Cafezinho*, a Small Shot of Strong Coffee, 307–308; *Caipirinha*, a National Cocktail, 308–309; *Carne de Sol*, Dried Salted Meat, 309–310; *Churrasco*, 310–311; Contemporary Brazilian Chefs, 312–313; *Feijoada*, Brazil's National Dish, 313–315; Mealtimes and Eating Habits, 315–316; Minas Gerais Gastronomy, 316–317; Regional Sweets, 317–319; Zero Hunger Strategy in Brazil, 319–320
Foreign Aid, 82
Foreign Investment, 16, 26, 115–116
Foreign Language Education, 211
Foreign Policy, 81–83
Formal Business Meetings, 234–235, 240
Formality Levels, 218–219
Fortaleza, 22, 159, 184, 208
Freedom of the Womb Law, 46, 56, 64
Freire, Paulo, 133, 138–139; Pedagogy of the Oppressed, 133
French Artistic Mission, 268, 277–278
Freyre, Gilberto, 133, 139–140, 168, 280; Casa Grande & Sensala, 140
Futebol (Soccer), 154, 321, 328, 329–332, 337–340, 343, 347

Gender and Parenting Roles, 181–182
Gender Equality, 182–184
Gender, Marriage, and Sexuality, 172–194; Abortion Laws, 174–175; Dating and Courting, 176–177; *Desquite* and Divorce, 177–178; Domestic Violence, 178–179; Feminism, 180–181; Gender and Parenting Roles, 181–182; Gender Equality, 182–184; LGTBQ Community and Rights, 184–186; Maternity and Paternity Leave, 186–187; Raising Children, 187–189; Representation in Government, 189–190; Representation in the Workforce, 190–192; Suffrage, 192–193; Weddings Celebrations and Traditions, 193–194

Geography, 1–30; Amazon Basin and Rainforest, 6–9; Brasília and the Federal District, 9–10; Climate, 10–11; Deforestation, 11–13; Earth Summit, Rio 2012, 13–14; Environment, 14–15; Infrastructure: Roads, Airports, Ports, and Railways, 16–17; Interoceanic Highway, 17–18; Islands and Archipelagos, 18–19; Itaipú Hydroelectric Power Plant, 20–21; Main Cities and Urban Regions, 21–23; Major Rivers, 23–24; Mendes, Chico (1944–1988), 24–25; Off Shore Oil and Natural Gas, 25–27; *Sertão* and Devastating Droughts, 27–28; World Heritage Sites in the UNESCO, 28–30

"Girl from Ipanema" Song, 41, 287, 290, 292–293, 344, 347

Gold Rush and Minas Gerais, 5, 38, 54–56, 245, 267, 272; architecture, 272; art, 267, 270; literature, 245

Golden Law of Abolition—Lei Áurea, 57

Goulart, João, 34

Government and Politics, 69–99; Constitutions, 73–76; Corruption and Political Scandals, 76–79; Electoral System, 79–81; Foreign Policy, 81–83; Human Rights, 83–84; Law Enforcement, 84–86; Lula da Silva, Luiz Inácio (1945–), 86–87; Political Parties, 87–90; Political Patronage, 90–91; Rousseff, Dilma (1947–), 91–93; Temer, Michel (1940–), 93–95; United Nations and Brazil, 95–96; Women's Rights, 96–98; Workers' Party (PT) in Power, 98–99

Gracie, Hélio, 326, 358

Guimarães Rosa, João, 254–255, 264

Hand Gestures, 220–221

Higher Education and Major Universities, 203–204

History, 31–68; Álvares Cabral, Pedro (1467 or 1468–1520), 47–48; *Bandeirantes*, 48–49; Brazilian Empire: Pedro I (1798–1834) and Pedro II (1825–1891), 49–51; Captaincy Colonial System, 51–54; Gold Rush and Minas Gerais, 54–56; Isabel, Princess Regent of Brazil (1846–1921), 56–57; Kubitschek de Oliveira, Juscelino (1902–1976), 58–59; Operation Condor and Military Rule, 59–61; Paraguayan War, 61–62; Silva, Benedita Da (1942–), 62–63; Slavery, Abolition, and African Heritage, 63–65; Tiradentes (1746–1792) and the Inconfidência Mineira, 65–66; Vargas, Getúlio (1883–1954), 66–68

Holidays, 381–384

Human Rights, 83–84; UNICEF, 83; United Nations, 83

independence, 39, 49–51, 61, 67; Incofidência Mineira, 65; literature, 244, 264

Indigenous Languages, 221–222; Guaraní, 20

Indigenous Populations, 15, 18–19, 24, 31, 160–161; art, 267; *bandeirantes*, 49; food, 305; musical instruments, 297; slavery, 63

INEP, National Institute for Educational Studies and Research, 205–206

Infrastructure: Roads, Airports, Ports, and Railways, 12, 16–17

Intermediaries: *Colonels* and *Despachantes*, 229, 235–236

Interoceanic Highway, 15, 17–18, 128

Iracema, 246, 265

Isabel, Princess Regent of Brazil, 40, 51, 56–57, 64

Islands and Archipelagos, 18–19

Itaipú Hydroelectric Power Plant, 5, 20–21, 23

Jeitinho, Finding a Way, 229, 236–237

Jesuit missionaries, 131, 135, 227

Jobim, Antônio Carlos, 41, 287, 290, 293–294

Kardec, Allan, 132, 148

King João III of Portugal, 31

Kubitschek de Oliveira, Juscelino, 9, 34, 39, 58–59, 276, 281

Labor Migration, 5, 117–118

land reform, 42; Goulart, João, 59

Landless Rural Workers Movement (MST), 101, 103, 153, 162–163

Language, 215–228; Formality Levels, 218–219; Hand Gestures, 220–221; Indigenous Languages, 221–222; Nicknames, 222–223; Sign Language (LIBRAS), 224–225; Spelling Reform, 225–226; Tupi-Guarani Influence, 227–228

Law Enforcement, 84–86
law of social quotas, 198
Leisure and Sports, 321–342; Basketball, 323–324; Beach and Sand, 324–325; Brazilian jiu-jitsu, 325–326; Capoeira, 327–328; Family Outings and Vacations, 328–329; *Futebol* (Soccer), 329–332; *Mega-Sena*, Brazilian Lottery, 332–333; Motor Sports: Formula 1 and Grand Prix, 333–334; Olympic Games, Rio de Janeiro 2016, 334–336; Paralympic Games 2016, 336–337; Pelé (1940–), Ronaldinho (1980–), and Neymar (1992–), 337–339; Soccer FIFA World Cup 2014, 339–340; Telenovelas and TV Programming, 340–342
Lemman, Jorge Paulo, 116
LGTBQ Community and Rights, 173, 184–186
Liberation Theology, 141–142
Lima Barreto, Alfonso, 255–256
Literacy Rates, 206–207
Literary Canon, 244, 249, 256–258
Literary Censorship by the Military, 258–260
Literature and Drama, 244–266; Amado, Jorge (1912–2001), 247–248; Bandeira, Manuel (1886–1968), 248–249; Contemporary Writers, 250–251; Da Cunha, Euclides (1866–1909), 251–253; De Andrade, Oswald (1890–1954), 253–254; Guimarães Rosa, João (1908–1967), 254–255; Lima Barreto, Alfonso (1881–1922), 255–256; Literary Canon, 256–258; Literary Censorship by the Military, 258–260; Machado de Assis, Joaquim Maria (1839–1908), 260–261; Modern Theater and Playwrights, 262–263; Modernism in Brazil, 263–264; Postindependence Literature, 264–266
Lula da Silva, Luiz Inácio, 35, 43, 86–87, 92, 120, 125, 138, 157, 162, 167, 170, 183, 188, 190, 200, 206, 219, 306, 319; Bolsa Família, 35; Rousseff, Dilma, 92; scandals, 76, 87
Lutz, Bertha, 180; suffrage, 192
Luzia Woman, 47

Macedo, Edir, 131, 149–150
Machado de Assis, Joaquim Maria, 40, 260–261, 265
Machismo, 238–239
Macumaíma, 346

Main Cities and Urban Regions, 2, 21–23, 101
Major Exports, 5, 25–26, 118–119
Major Newspapers, 343, 349–351
Major Rivers, 1, 4–6, 19–20, 23–24
Manufacturing, 101, 119–121
Maracanã Soccer Stadium, 331
Marcari, Hortência, 323–324
Maria da Penha Law for Violence against Women, 170, 174, 176, 238
Marquis of Pombal, 38
Maternity and Paternity Leave, 186–187
Mealtimes and Eating Habits, 315–316
Media and Popular Culture, 343–360; Cinema and Film Festivals, 345–346; Cultural Icons, 347–348; *Folia de Reis,* Three Wise Men Celebration, 348–349; Major Newspapers, 349–351; Meirelles, Fernando (1955–), 351–352; Reality Television Shows, 352–353; *Rede Globo* and other Television Networks, 353–354; Salles, Walter, Jr. (1956–), 355; Social Media and Internet Use, 356–357; Sports Icons, 357–359; Xuxa (1963–), 259–360
Mega-Sena Lottery, 332–333
Meirelles, Fernando, 343, 351–352; *Cidade de Deus* film, 344, 34
Memórius pustumus de Brás Cubas, 243, 264
Mendes da Rocha, Paulo, 278–279
Mendes, Chico, an Environmental Activist, 24–25, 42, 348
Mercosul/Mercosur, 45, 82, 112, 118, 121–122, 127–129
Messianism and Miracle Workers, 142–143, 252
military dictatorship, 34
Minas Gerais, 54, 101, 127; food, 313; gastronomy, 305, 312–313, 316–317; Inconfidência Mineira, 66; nicknames, 223; Ouro Preto, 282; Rousseff, Dilma, 91; tourism, 328
Mineral Wealth, 101, 122–123
miracle workers, 142
Mixed Ethnicities: *Caboclo, Cafuso, Mameluco,* and *Mulatto,* 152, 163–164
Modern Art Week, São Paolo 1922, 40, 245, 265, 279–281; Amado, Jorge, 247; de Andrade, Oswald, 253; literature, 244
Modern Immigration, 164–165

Modern Theater and Playwrights, 262–263
Modernism in Brazil, 244, 247, 253, 263–264; architecture, 268; literature, 244
Moraes, Vinicius, 41
Motor Sports: Formula 1 and Grand Prix, 321, 333–334
Music and Dance, 287–304; Bossa Nova, 290–291; *Carnival*, 291–292; "Girl from Ipanema" Song, 292–293; Jobim, Antônio Carlos (1927–1994), 293–294; *Música Popular Brasileira* (MPB), 294–295; *Música Sertaneja*, 296–297; Musical Instruments, 297–299; Regional Music and Dance, 299–300; Samba Music and Dance, 300–301; *Tropicália*, 301–303; Villa-Lobos, Heitor (1887–1959), 303–304
Música Popular Brasileira (MPB), 288, 294–295, 344
Música Sertaneja, 296–297, 299
Musical Instruments, 297–299

National Conference of Brazilian Bishops, 135
Neves, Tancredo, 35
Nicknames, 222–223
Niemeyer, Oscar, 4, 9, 58, 268, 276, 278, 280, 281–282
Nossa Senhora Aparecida, Brazil's Patron Saint, 143–145

Off Shore Oil and Natural Gas, 25–27
Olympic Games, Rio de Janeiro 2016, 5, 72, 105, 115, 127, 167, 321, 334–336, 357; "Girl from Ipanema song," 293; Temer, Michel, 105
Operation Car Wash, 72, 77, 99, 125, 167; Rousseff, Dilma, 78–79, 99
Operation Condor and Military Rule, 34, 59–61; censorship, 258–259; literature, 246; *tropicália*, 302; United States, 60
Orixás, African Gods, 132, 134, 145–146, 155, 284
Ouro Preto, 29, 38, 55, 267, 270, 272, 282–283

Padrinhos, Godparents, 188
Palácio da Alvorada, 9
Palheta, Francisco de Melo, 109
Palmares, 38; Universidade de Zumbi dos Palmares, 197

Paraguayan War, 32, 40, 61–62
Paralympic Games 2016, 336–337
Parentela, 165–166
Partido dos Trabalhadores (PT), 35, 63, 71, 76, 153; de Souza Chaui, Marilena, 138; Lula da Silva, Luiz Inácio, 86, 98; Pedagogy of the Oppressed, 139; Rousseff, Dilma, 98
Pedro I, 33, 38–39, 50, 66, 73
Pedro II, 50, 56, 66, 261
Pelé, 154, 223, 329, 337, 344, 347, 357
Pelé, Ronaldinho, and Neymar, 154, 223, 330–331, 337–339
Personal Space and Privacy, 239–241
Petrobras, the National Oil Company, 16, 25–26, 68, 92, 123–125; Cerveró, Nestor, 77; scandals, 77; Vargas, Getúlio, 68
Plan Real, 35
Political Parties, 87–90
Political Patronage, 90–91
Popular Arts and Crafts, 283–284
Portinari, Cândido, 285–286
Postindependence Literature, 264–266
Poverty, Social Conflict, and Protests, 22, 152, 166–168, 198, 339
Private, International, and Religious Schools, 195, 207–208
Protestant Religions, 146–148
protests, 22, 35, 156–157, 166–168, 334, 340
Public Education: Elementary and Secondary Schooling, 208–210
Punctuality and Concepts of Time, 230, 234, 241–242

Quilombos and Land Rights for Descendants of Runaway Slaves, 65

racial democracy, 139, 152, 176
Racism and Discrimination, 152, 168–169
Raising Children, 187–189
Reality Television Shows, 344, 352–353
Rede Globo and other Television Networks, 291, 322, 341, 351, 352, 353–354, 359
Regional Music and Dance, 299–300
Regional Sweets, 317–319; Minas Gerais, 312
Religion and Thought, 131–151; Candomblé and Macumba, 134–135; Catholicism, 135–137; de Souza Chauí, Marilena

(1941–), 137–138; Freire, Paulo (1921–1997), 138–139; Freyre, Gilberto (1900–1987), 139–140; Liberation Theology, 141–142; Messianism and Miracle Workers, 142–143; Nossa Senhora Aparecida, Brazil's Patron Saint, 143–145; *Orixás*, African Gods. 145–146; Protestant Religions, 146–148; Spiritism, 148–149; Universal Church of the Kingdom of God, 149–151
Representation in Government, 189–190
Representation in the Workforce, 190–192
Rio de Janeiro, 21, 38; capital city, 32; carnival, 301; samba, 288; tourism, 328
Rousseff, Dilma, 16, 35, 43, 60, 71, 82, 91–93, 101, 138, 157, 161, 172, 179, 183, 190, 197, 219, 238, 340; alias, 60; austerity measures, 104; Lula da Silva, Luiz Inácio, 92; scandals, 76; women's rights, 97
royal fifth, 54–55

Salles, Walter, Jr., 343, 355; *Central do Brasil* film, 344, 346, 355
Salvador de Bahia, 22, 29, 31, 38; capital city, 3; carnival, 301; tourism, 328
Samba Music and Dance, 287, 296, 298, 300–301
same-sex marriage, 184, 186
São Paulo, 21–22, 184, 239; carnival, 287, 291, 301; Semana de Arte Moderna, 263
Schmidt, Oscar, 323–324, 358
Scientific and Technical Research, 210–212
Senna da Silva, Ayrton, 334, 358
Sertão and Devastating Droughts, 1, 3, 10, 15, 27–28, 364; *carne de sol*, 309; cinema, 28, 346; food, 305, 312; literature, 27, 252; *música sertaneja*, 296, 299
Sign Language (LIBRAS), 217, 224–225
Silva, Benedita Da, 62–63
slavery, 3, 22, 51, 54, 63–65, 117; Freedom of the Womb Law, 40; Golden Law (Lei Áurea), 32; imports, 32; trade, 39
Slavery, Abolition, and African Heritage, 3, 32, 51, 54, 63–65, 117
Soccer FIFA World Cup 2014, 5, 44, 72, 114, 127, 167, 321, 339–340, 357
Social Classes and Ethnicity, 152–171; African Ancestry and Influence, 154–156; Distribution of Wealth and Income Disparity, 156–157; Education and Upper Mobility, 157–158; *Favelas, Mocambos*, and *Alagados* (Slums), 158–160; Indigenous Populations, 160–161; Landless Rural Workers Movement (MST), 162–163; Mixed Ethnicities: *Caboclo, Cafuso, Mameluco*, and *Mulatto*, 163–164; Modern Immigration, 164–165; *Parentela*, 165–166; Poverty, Social Conflict, and Protests, 166–168; Racism and Discrimination, 168–169; Urban Crime, 169–171
Social Media and Internet Use, 343, 353, 356–357, 359
Spelling Reform, 225–226
Spiritism, 148–149
Sports Icons, 357–359
Stock Exchanges: Bovespa, BM&F, and B3, 125–126
Suffrage, 192–193; Lutz, Bertha, 192
sugar, 31, 100; production, 32
Superior Electoral Court, 71, 80, 87

Table Manners, 242–243
Telenovelas and TV Programming, 322, 340–342, 343
Temer, Michel, 15, 36, 44, 93–95, 101, 103, 105, 114, 159, 162, 165, 167, 170, 173, 190, 195, 202, 210; scandals, 94
terreiros, 134
Tiradentes and the Inconfidência Mineira, 38, 65–66, 283
Tourism, 126–127
Trading Partners, 18, 100,107, 128–129
Trans-Amazonian Highway, 42
Treaty of Madrid, 49
Treaty of Tordesillas, 37, 48, 51
Tropicália, 288–289, 301–303
Tupi oil field, 77
Tupi-Guarani Influence, 216, 227–228

Unipalmares, University for Afro-descendent Students, 212–213
United Kingdom of Brazil, Portugal and Algarves, 52
United Nations and Brazil, 83, 95–96, 101, 115, 165; UNICEF, 83

Universal Church of the Kingdom of God, 131, 147, 149–151
Urban Crime, 169–171

Varejão, Adriana, 275
Vargas, Getúlio, 33–34, 40, 66–68, 74, 123, 303; constitutions, 74; music, 288; Petrobras, 123, 164, 180, 280
Vestibular Testing for College Admission, 198, 212, 213–214
Villa-Lobos, Heitor, 288, 303–304

War of the Triple Alliance, 61
Weddings Celebrations and Traditions, 193–194

Women's Rights, 96–98; Rousseff, Dilma, 97
Workers' Party (PT) in Power, 98–99, 138; Partido dos Trabalhadores (PT), 35, 63, 71, 76, 153
World Heritage Sites in the UNESCO, 5, 9, 22, 28–30, 127, 221, 271–272, 277, 283, 301
World Trade Organization (WTO), 106, 119, 129–130

Xuxa, 219, 259–360

Zero Hunger Strategy in Brazil, 306, 319–320
Zika Virus during the 2016 Olympics, 334

About the Author

Javier A. Galván, PhD, is a professor of history and Spanish at Santa Ana College. His other books include *Culture and Customs of Puerto Rico* (2009), *Culture and Customs of Bolivia* (2011), *Latin American Dictators of the 20th Century* (2012), and *They Do What? A Cultural Encyclopedia of Extraordinary and Exotic Customs from around the World* (2014).

www.ingramcontent.com/pod-product-compliance
Lightning Source LLC
Chambersburg PA
CBHW060505300426
44112CB00017B/2550